A Variorum Edition of Tennyson's
Idylls of the King

JOHN PFORDRESHER

Columbia University Press
New York & London   1973

Library of Congress Cataloging in Publication Data
Tennyson, Alfred Tennyson, Baron, 1809-1892.
  A variorum edition of Tennyson's Idylls of the King.

  I. Pfordresher, John, ed.   II. Title.
PR5558.A1   1973   821'.8   73-4852
ISBN 0-231-03691-4

'Thou read the book, my pretty Vivien!
O ay, it is but twenty pages long,
But every page having an ample marge,
And every marge enclosing in the midst
A square of text that looks a little blot,
The text no larger than the limbs of fleas;
And every square of text an awful charm,
Writ in a language that has long since gone by...
And every margin scribbled, crost, and crammed
With comment, densest condensation, hard
To mind and eye...
                    "Merlin and Vivien," 11.665-677.

This one's for Jin.

Acknowledgements

To the Graduate School of the University of Minnesota

and the Arthur J. Schmitt Foundation of Chicago, who

provided matching grants to help finance research for

this project; and to the Central University Research

Fund of the University of New Hampshire which paid to

have it retyped.

To Gerhard Joseph, advisor and friend, who counseled

from afar, rewrote my writing, and kept after me to

keep it accurate for those who might care.

To countless library personnel on two continents, whose

quiet, dusty work makes scholarship possible, and es-

pecially to Lola Szladits of the Berg Collection, June

Moll of the University of Texas Library, A. Halcrow at

the Trinity College (Cambridge, England) Library, and

Jean Preston of the Huntington Library who worked with

ACKNOWLEDGEMENTS

me by letter, and without whose particular help I could never have gotten anywhere.

To Pat Gibbons and Ken Atchity, friends, who were called upon, unexpectedly, to do research and rose to the occasion.

To Ellen Thurston and Denise Holt who (God help them) typed it all.

To Karen, for endless help, of all kinds.

And particularly, to the present Lord Tennyson and Sir Charles Tennyson, whose cooperation and help made the way clear to a complete edition.

Contents

CONTENTS

How To Use This Book

1. The Text.

The text of the poem is that of the Eversley Edition. This is the final version which Tennyson left us, and is the version approved by the family. Close students of the successive changes Tennyson worked on his _Idylls_ recognise that it is the most perfect form of the poem.

2. The Variants.

This edition attempts to record every significant variant from every extant manuscript, printer's proof, and published edition from the poet's first drafts of the "Morte d'Arthur" (done c. 1833) to the publication of the Eversley Edition in 1908. This is what it offers:

a. Every verbal variant from every known manuscript.

b. Every verbal and punctuation variant from every known printer's proof and from all published editions of the poem.

c. Further, it reproduces early prose and verse drafts in their entirety.

What this edition does not offer:

a. Punctuation variants in manuscripts. This, because Tennyson was very casual about punctuation before the first proof state and to reproduce manuscript punctuation variants would be to reproduce virtually every line from every manuscript.

b. With a few exceptions, this edition does not record spelling variants, primarily because the project is already sufficiently large. Some spelling variants of particular interest (i.e. proper names and archaic terms) have been included at the editor's discretion.

3. How to Read the Variants.

a. Insofar as is possible, variants are listed line by line.

b. Under each line number variants run in chronological order. When a variant enters the printed stage this edition follows it until it is finally "corrected," i.e. put in its final form. The first instance of the correct version is noted as the last entry for a line, and employs the abbreviation (c) for "corrected."

c. Variant entries record not the entire line, but only the variant portion of a line, plus the words and punctuation just before and after a variant. Triple dots appear if the variant begins after the beginning of a line or ends before the end of the line, or both. Thus triple dots before an entry indicate that part of the line preceding the variant has been omitted; triple dots after an entry indicate that part of a line after the entry has been omitted. As a result, a reader can spot the "difference" between the variant and the final version more quickly than if the entire line were reproduced.

d. Many of the variants consist of emendations by the poet. When Tennyson has corrected a word or phrase, the original version is given on one line, the corrected version is printed above.

e. Tennyson's cancellations (generally in the form of a line through a word or a punctuation mark) are indicated by slashes.

f. This edition carefully indicates when a

proof sheet has been corrected in manuscript.

1. Punctuation corrections.

When Tennyson has corrected an element of punctuation, the earlier, printed punctuation is repro-duced first, his manuscript correction second. Then, to alert the reader to the fact that the correction is in manuscript, the right hand portion of the variant entry will either contain a parenthetical notation provided by the editor of what has been changed, or there will be a reproduction of the printer's correction symbols which Tennyson himself jotted down on the margin of his proof copy. These symbols consist either of a simple repro-duction of the punctuation correction which has been made in the text, or that correction plus a slash mark. This edition, whenever possible, indicates whether manu-script corrections were made in ink or pencil by the ab-breviations (I) and (P).

Some examples. The symbol (, I) means that in the text Tennyson has altered punctuation to a comma in ink manuscript, and that he made no marginal notation of the change. Symbols such as , (I) or ,/ (I) indicate that Tennyson himself marked the correction on the mar-gin of his proof sheet, and that the correction was in ink manuscript.

When there are several indentical punctuation marks in a proof variant the notation will indicate which one has been altered. So, for instance, the notation (1st, I) means that the first comma in the variant entry was not printed, but rather was added in ink manuscript by the author.

2. Verbal corrections.

When Tennyson has altered words on a proof sheet the correction is reproduced above the printed version, and a notation in the right hand column indicates that the correction is in manuscript by the abbreviation (MS) and, when possible, also indicates if the correction is in ink or pencil. Thus (I MS) means that the correction is in ink manuscript.

g. Because manuscripts are frequently fragmentary, this edition does not record the absence of lines from continuous passages in manuscript form. But once a poem has entered the proof stage the absence of any line is recorded, and is indicated by the symbol (omitted).

h. The symbol (Par.) indicates paragraph indentation. It is used in the reproduction both of prose

xiii

drafts and of verse variants to ensure that readers are certain where such indentation occurs. When the printed version of a poem omits proper paragraph indentation the abbreviation (No par. indent.) appears.

i. Tennyson's handwriting is sometimes difficult to decipher. When the editor has made a guess as to the words on a page, the conjectural reading is followed by a question mark and is placed in parentheses. If the editor has found some words impossible to decipher, this is indicated by a parenthetical notation which records the number of unreadable words: (2?)

j. Since the editor employs parentheses to indicate his own intrusion into Tennyson's writing, in the variants all of Tennyson's parentheses have been converted to brackets.

3. How to Read the Citations.

In the extreme right hand column the reader will encounter one or two element citations.

a. For manuscript variants, citations record first the library which owns the manuscript; second, some form of notation whereby the particular manuscript could be located in the library. When a collection is numbered, this second element is usually the library's own number, or a condensation thereof. When the library has not numbered an item the editor has arbitrarily assigned it a number. A full list of library and manuscript abbreviations, in alphabetical order, follows this explanation.

b. Proof sheet entries also appear, for the most part, in two parts, the first part indicating the library, the second part a number for the proof itself. Proof sheet abbreviations are included in the list of libraries which follows this explanation.

c. Published editions are indicated by an abbreviation of the date of publication; i.e. 73 indicates the Library Edition of 1873. A full list of relevant editions and their abbreviations follows the list of libraries, with the entries printed in chronological order.

Alphabetical Key To Library Abbreviation Symbols

(Note: Individual items are grouped according to the
repositories which hold them. For each item the reference number assigned it by the repository appears first,
followed by a reference code developed for this list.
The code, here in parentheses, contains two bits of information. The first is a letter which indicates the repository, e.g. A for Ashley Library. Second comes an abbreviated version of the reference number for the individual item. When repositories do not number their
holdings this list assigns an arbitrary number.)

(A)

Ashley Library, British Museum

    2101   (A-2101)   Proof of "The Last Tourna-
                                   ment."

LIBRARY ABBREVIATION SYMBOLS

2104	(A-2104)	Proof of The Holy Grail, Etc. This volume once had portions of manuscript bound in. These have now been removed and are kept in the manuscript room of the British Museum. Here they are designated Ashley Scraps (A-S)
2109	(A-2109)	Proof of "Gareth and Lynette."
2111	(A-2111)	Leaflet version of the "Epilogue."
4521	(A-4521)	Manuscript of a portion of "The Coming of Arthur."

(B)

Berg Collection, New York Public Library

(Note: The Collection is without reference numbers.)

| B-I | Manuscript of "The Coming of Arthur." |
| B-II | Proof of "Gareth and |

	Lynette."
B-III	Manuscript of "The Last Tournament."
B-IV	Manuscript of "Gareth and Lynette."
B-V	Manuscript of the "Song of the Battleaxe" from "The Coming of Arthur."
B-VI	Proof of "The Holy Grail."
B-VII	Proof of the explanatory paragraph for Gareth and Lynette, Etc.
B-VIII	Proof copy of The Holy Grail, Etc.

(Bd)

Bodleian Library, Oxford

MS Eng. B.3 (Bd-3)	Manuscript of "Gareth and Lynette."

(BM)

British Museum Library

c.59.a.25 (BM-1) (BM-I)	Trial book Enid and Nimuë:

xix

<u>The</u> <u>True</u> <u>and</u> <u>the</u> <u>False</u>
(1857) containing proofs
for "The Marriage of Ge-
raint," "Geraint and Enid,"
and "Merlin and Vivien."

c.133.a.7.　(BM-2)　　Proofs for "Lancelot and
Elaine" and "Guinevere."

c.59.i.2.　(BM-3)　　Four page leaflet edition
of the "Dedication."

(F)

Forster Library, Victoria and Albert Museum Library

F.48.C.40　(F)　　Proofs for "The Marriage of
Geraint" and "Geraint and
Enid" (two, designated
F-ENI and F-EN2), "Merlin
and Vivien" (two, desig-
nated F-I and F-II),
"Lancelot and Elaine," and
"Guinevere."

LIBRARY ABBREVIATION SYMBOLS

(H)

Harvard University Library

EC 85/ T2586/869 hag (H-HGP) Proof of "The Holy

Grail."

Houghton Library, Harvard University

(Note: This collection holds both notebooks -- under the number MS Eng. 952. 54m-203 -- and loose sheets
of paper under the number MS Eng. 952.1 54m-204. Separate items within these categories have individual numbers, which are given below.)

MS Eng. 952. 54m-203:

16	(H-16)	Notes on Arthurian legends.
21	(H-21)	Copy of "Morte d'Arthur" in the hand of James Spedding.
26	(H-26)	Note on Arthur; early sketch for "Merlin and Vi-vien."
30	(H-30)	Manuscript for "Merlin and Vivien."
31	(H-31)	Manuscript for "Merlin and Vivien" and "Guinevere."
32	(H-32)	Manuscript for "Gareth and Lynette," "Balin and Balan,"

		and "Epilogue."
33	(H-33)	Manuscript for "Merlin and Vivien."
34	(H-34)	Manuscript for "Merlin and Vivien."
35	(H-35)	Manuscript for "The Marriage of Geraint" and "Geraint and Enid."
36	(H-36)	Manuscript for "Guinevere."
37	(H-37)	Manuscript for "Balin and Balan" and "Merlin and Vivien."
38	(H-38)	Manuscript for "The Holy Grail."
39	(H-39)	Manuscript for "The Coming of Arthur," "Merlin and Vivien," and "The Passing of Arthur."
40	(H-40)	Manuscript for "The Last Tournament" and "Gareth and Lynette."
47	(H-47)	Manuscript for "Balin and Balan."

MS Eng. 952.1 54m-204:

29	(H-29a)	Manuscript for "The Coming of Arthur."
71	(H-71a)	Manuscript for "The Marriage of Geraint" and "Geraint and Enid."
73	(H-73a)	Manuscript of "Guinevere."
95	(H-95a)	Manuscript of "Dedication."
96	(H-96a)	Manuscript of "Dedication."
97	(H-97a)	Manuscript of a rejected fragment in another hand.
114	(H-114a)	Manuscript of "Merlin and Vivien."
152	(H-152a)	Manuscript of "Merlin and Vivien."
153	(H-153a)	Manuscript of "Merlin and Vivien."
159	(H-159a)	Manuscript of "Morte d'Arthur" in another hand.
MS Eng. 952.8		Manuscript draft of the title page for the 1859 edi-

tion of <u>Idylls</u> <u>of</u> <u>the</u> <u>King</u>.

(HM)

Huntington Museum and Art Gallery, San Marino, California

HM-1323	(HM-1323)	Manuscript of portions of "The Holy Grail," "The Last Tournament," and "Balin and Balan."
HM-1324	(HM-1324)	Manuscript of the song from "Pelleas and Ettarre."
HM-1326	(HM-1326)	Manuscript of "Merlin and Vivien."
HM-19494	(HM-19494)	Manuscript, in another hand, with authorial corrections, of the song from "Pelleas and Ettarre."

(Hth)

Fitzwilliam Museum, Cambridge

Heath Commonplace Book (Hth) Manuscript copy of
"Morte d'Arthur."

(L)

The Tennyson Research Centre, City Library, Lincoln

(Note: The Collection is without catalogue numbers.)

xxiv

LIBRARY ABBREVIATION SYMBOLS

> (L-I) and (L-II) Two proof states for "Mer-
> lin and Vivien."
>
> (L-EN1), (L-EN2), and (L-EN3) Three proof
> states for "The Marriage of
> Geraint" and "Geraint and
> Enid."
>
> (L-L2) Proof for "Lancelot and Elaine."
>
> (L-HGI) and (L-HGII) Two proof states for
> The Holy Grail, Etc.
>
> (L-B1) and (L-B2) Two proof states for
> "Balin and Balan."
>
> (L-HG3) Proof for "The Holy Grail" as
> (H-HGP).

(Lo)

Harvard University Library, Amy Lowell Collection

> Lowell 1827.12 (Lo-1) Manuscript of "Merlin and
> Vivien," and a portion of
> "Geraint and Enid."

(PM)

Pierpont Morgan Library, New York City

> (PM)   Short manuscript portion of

"The Coming of Arthur."

(S)

Sterling Library, The University of London

SLC.1.925   (S-925)   Proof of The Holy Grail, Etc.

SLC.1.929   (S-929)   Proof of "Gareth and Lyn-

ette."

(T)

Miriam Lutcher Stark Library, The University of Texas

Wp T 258
872 ga/v.1   (T-GP2)   The second proof state for

"Gareth and Lynette."

Ten.Works 9/B (T-GP3)   Third proof state for

"Gareth and Lynette."

Ten.Works 10/B (T-C73)   The (72) edition of Gareth

and Lynette, Etc. with manu-

script corrections for (73).

Ten.Works 16   (T-LTP)   Proof for "The Last Tourna-

ment."

Ten.Works 11, 15 (T-S)   Fragmentary drafts, in manu-

script, for "The Coming of

Arthur," "Balin and Balan,"

		"The Passing of Arthur," and "Gareth and Lynette."
Ten.Works 13	(T-C)	Manuscript of "The Coming of Arthur."
Ten.Works 6/B	(T-E)	Manuscript of "The Marriage of Geraint," and "Geraint and Enid" in the hand of Emily S. Tennyson, with manuscript corrections by Alfred Tennyson.
T.Works 14/13	(T-P)	Manuscript of "Pelleas and Ettarre."

(Tn)

Trinity College Library, Cambridge

0:15:17	(Tn-17)	Two manuscript drafts for the "Morte d'Arthur."
0:15:28	(Tn-28)	Short sketch for "Lancelot and Elaine."
0:15:29	(Tn-29)	Manuscript of "The Holy Grail."
0:15:30	(Tn-30)	Manuscript of "The Marriage of Geraint" and

LIBRARY ABBREVIATION SYMBOLS

"Geraint and Enid."

0:15:31　(Tn-31)　Manuscript of "Balin and

Balan."

0:15:39　(Tn-39)　Manuscripts of "Guinevere"

and "Lancelot and Elaine."

(V)

The University of Virginia Library, Alderman Library

(V)　　　　Manuscript of "Lancelot and

Elaine."

(W)

Widener Library, Harvard University

(W-S)　　　　Manuscript passage from

"The Passing of Arthur."

(W-Pf)　　　　Manuscript passages from

"Gareth and Lynette" bound

into a set of proofs for

the 1873 Library Edition.

(Y)

Yale University Library

(Y-I)　　　　Manuscript of "Merlin and

	Vivien."
(Y-II)	Manuscript of "The Marriage of Geraint."
(Y-III)	Manuscript of "Geraint and Enid" and "Merlin and Vivien."
(Y-IV)	Manuscript of the song from "Guinevere."
(Y-V)	Manuscript of the "Dedication" in another hand.
(Y-VI)	Proof of the "Dedication."
(Y-VII)	Proof of "Merlin and Vivien."

B. Published Editions of the Idylls of the King
(Note: Only those editions are listed which play a significant part in the evolution of the text. The title page descriptions come from actual copies studied in the British Museum Library. An Abbreviated reference symbol, enclosed in parentheses, precedes each entry.)

(BM-I)   Enid and Nimuë:/ The True and the False./ By/ Alfred Tennyson, D.C.L.,/ Poet Laureate./ London: Edward Moxon, Dover Street./ 1857.

PRINTED EDITIONS

(F)   The/ True and the False./ Four Idylls of
           the King./ By Alfred Tennyson,/ P.L.;
           D.C.L./ London:/ Edward Moxon & Co.,
           Dover Street./ 1859.

(59)   Idylls of the King./ By/ Alfred Tennyson,
           D.C.L.,/ Poet Laureate./ 'Flos Regum Ar-
           thurus.'/ Joseph of Exeter./ London:/
           Edward Moxon & Co., Dover Street./ 1859.

(62)   Idylls of the King./ By/ Alfred Tennyson,
           D.C.L.,/ Poet Laureate./ 'Flos Regum Ar-
           thurus.'/ Joseph of Exeter./ A New Edi-
           tion./ London:/ Edward Moxon & Co., Dover
           Street./ 1862.

(67)   Idylls of the King./ By/ Alfred Tennyson,
           D.C.L.,/ Poet Laureate./ 'Flos Regum Ar-
           thurus.'/ Joseph of Exeter./ A New Edi-
           tion./ [Dev.] / London:/ Edward Moxon &
           Co., Dover Street./ 1867.

(69)   The Holy Grail/ and Other Poems/ By Al-
           fred Tennyson, D.C.L./ Poet Laureate/
           "Flos Regum Arthurus."/ Joseph of Exeter/
           [Dev.] / Strahan and Co., Publishers/ 56
           Ludgate Hill, London/ 1870

     xxx

(69)   Idylls of the King/ By Alfred Tennyson,

D.C.L./ Poet Laureate/ "Flos Regum Ar-

thurus."/ Joseph of Exeter/ [Dev.] /

Strahan & Co., Publishers/ 56 Ludgate

Hill, London/ 1869/ All rights reserved.

(70)   (Miniature Edition of the Works.)

The Works of/ Alfred Tennyson,/ Poet

Laureate./ [Dev.] /[Number and title of

the volume] [Dev.] / Strahan and Co. Pub-

lishers,/ Ludgate Hill, London./ 1870.

(The Idylls occupy Volumes IV, V and VI

of the Miniature Edition.)

(72)   Gareth and Lynette/ Etc./ By Alfred Ten-

nyson, D.C.L./ Poet Laureate/ Strahan and

Co./ 56 Ludgate Hill, London/ 1872/ (All

rights reserved.)

(73)   (Library Edition)

The Works of/ Alfred Tennyson/ Poet Lau-

reate/ Vol. V. Idylls of the King/ "Flos

Regum Arthurus."/ Joseph of Exeter./

Strahan & Co./ 56 Ludgate Hill, London/

1873

(The Idylls occupy Volumes V and VI of

the Library Edition.)

(74)   (Cabinet Edition)

The Works of/ Alfred Tennyson./ [Title of

Volume]/ Henry S. King & Co./ 65, Corn-

hill, & 12, Paternoster Row, London./

1874.

(The Idylls occupy Volumes V, VI and VII

of the Cabinet Edition.)

(75)   (Author's Edition)

The Poetical Works of/ Alfred Tennyson./

[Volume number] / Henry S. King & Co., Lon-

don./ 1874.

(The Idylls occupy Volume II of the Au-

thor's Edition.)

(78)   (The Crown Edition)

The Works/ of/Alfred Tennyson/ Poet

Laureate/[Dev.] / London/ C. Kegan Paul

& Co.,/ Paternoster Square/ (Successors

to the Publishing Department of Henry S.

King & Co.)/ 1878.

(84-1)   (Collected Edition)

The Works/ of/ Alfred Tennyson/ Poet Lau-

reate/ London/ Macmillan and Co./ 1884.

PRINTED EDITIONS

(84-2)   (New Collected Edition)

             The Works of/ Alfred/ Lord Tennyson/ Poet

             Laureate/[Volume number]/ London/ Macmil-

             lan and Co./ 1884

             (The Idylls occupy Volume III of this edi-

             tion. In later printings Tiresias and

             Other Poems occupy Volume X.)

(85)   Tiresias/ and Other Poems/ By Alfred Ten-

             nyson/ D.C.L. P.L./ London/ Macmillan and

             Co./ 1885

(86)   (The New Miniature Edition)

             The/ Poetical Works/ of/ Alfred/ Lord

             Tennyson/ D.C.L. P.L./ [Number and title

             of volume]/ London/ Macmillan and Co./

             And New York/ 1886

             (The Idylls occupy Volumes VII, VIII and

             IX of the New Miniature Edition.)

(88)   (The New Library Edition)

             (Note: Each volume of this edition has

             a separate title page.)

             Idylls of the King/ By/ Alfred/ Lord Ten-

             nyson/ D.C.L. P.L./ London, Macmillan and

             Co./ and New York/ 1888

PRINTED EDITIONS

(92)   (Complete Edition)

Idylls of the King/ By/ Alfred/ Lord

Tennyson/ Poet Laureate/ London/ Macmil-

lan and Co./ 1892

(94)   (Complete One Volume Edition)

The Works of/ Alfred/ Lord Tennyson/ Poet

Laureate/ London/ Macmillan and Co./ And

New York/ 1894

(96)   (The People's Edition)

The/ Poetical Works/ of/ Alfred Lord Ten-

nyson/ [Title of separate volume] / London/

Macmillan and Co., Ltd./ New York: Mac-

millan and Co./ 1896 (The Idylls occupy

Volumes XII through XVII of this edition.)

(99)   (Edition Deluxe)

The works of/ Alfred/ Lord Tennyson/ Poet

Laureate/ [Volume number] / London/ Macmil-

lan and Co., Limited/ 1899/ All rights re-

served

Introduction

Alfred Tennyson took a remarkable amount of time to
write his _Idylls of the King_. He spent nearly thirty
years mulling over ideas for the project, and the actual
publication took even longer--thirty-five years. Considering such a time span one begins at once to wonder
what technical problems must have troubled the poet.
Could he readily fit new additions into older poems and
continue to maintain a consistency of style and tone?
As the poem grew, did he have to suppress passages?

Questions such as these inevitably lead to investigation, and it is not very surprising that studies of the
growth and development of the Idylls began appearing
only three years after Tennyson's death. But the work of
these early researchers, while fascinating, was necessa-
rily incomplete. Too much of the material di-

1

rectly related to the poem was in the hands of people
who either were not scholars, or who were hostile to the
ambitions of scholars. A proper study of the poem's
development required all of the manuscripts, all of the
printer's proofs, and all of the published editions
which the poet supervised through the press, and, for a
very long time, both manuscripts and proofs were in the
hands of Tennyson's family and friends, unknown to the
world of scholarship.

Consider, first, the collection which remained under the control of the Tennyson family, after the poet's
death. It was by far the largest library of Tennyson
papers, comprising a large quantity of notebooks filled
with early drafts and sketches, fair copies of many of
the poems, evidently prepared for the typesetters, and
numerous proof copies, some fragmentary, many complete,
most with manuscript corrections. During his lifetime
Tennyson had expressed a repugnance for literary researchers and the custom of prowling through a poet's
manuscripts.

> He 'gave the people his best,' and he
> usually wished that his best should re-
> main without variorum readings, 'the
> chips of the workshop,' as he called
> them. The love of bibliomaniacs for

>   the first editions filled him with hor-
>   ror, for the first editions are obvious-
>   ly in many cases the worst editions...[1]

Sensitive to these feelings, Tennyson's son and "offi-

cial" biographer, Hallam Tennyson, determined to keep

the family collection from public scrutiny. But he was

also preparing his Memoir, and soon succumbed to the

temptation which takes hold of every researcher to tell

all he knows. In the end, Hallam "quoted from many

manuscripts never meant for the public eye, many of

which I have burnt."[2] This curiously ambivalent prac-

tice, of showing a little and then destroying the rest,

indicates the twin poles Hallam Tennyson sought to steer

between--not telling all, but, at the same time, not

destroying all.

Years later, Hallam gave a careful selection of

manuscripts to Tennyson's own college, Trinity, at Cam-

bridge. But he attached a proviso to the bequest. No

one was to copy from the manuscripts in any way; they

were to remain as exhibits only. He also gave a single

manuscript, "Gareth and Lynette," to the Bodleian Li-

brary at Oxford with the same restriction. It was only

in 1969 that the Tennyson family finally lifted this

interdict, and opened these manuscripts to serious

3

scholarship for the first time. In 1956 a second portion of the family collection went to the Houghton Library at Harvard University. This group of early manuscript drafts is by far the most important in the world
for the study of the Idylls of the King. The collections at Trinity College and the Bodleian Library hold
only late, fair drafts of the Idylls. The Houghton collection contains the earliest sketches and drafts, and
consequently is essential to any attempt to reconstruct
the embryonic state of the poem. Finally, in 1964 the
present Lord Tennyson loaned the last portion of the
family library to the Tennyson Research Centre in the
city of Lincoln, England. As a result the Centre now
possesses the world's largest collection of Idylls proof
states, as well as letters and Tennyson's own books.
The collections at Harvard and Lincoln were both open
to full scrutiny from their inception.

Tennyson did not keep all of his manuscripts. He
was indifferent to these fragments of his creative work
and freely gave them away to those who asked for them.[3]
Consequently, even during his lifetime many manuscripts
and proof states passed into the libraries of his close
associates. These materials were, of course, not open

4

to study but were rather precious mementoes. And when
Tennyson's friends died their libraries were auctioned
and sold, eventually making their way primarily to
wealthy American collectors. A perfect example of this
progression is the library of Frederick Locker-Lampson.
A close friend of Tennyson, he often helped the Laureate
prepare his poems for the press. To reward his devotion
Tennyson gave him both proof states and manuscripts.
When Locker-Lampson died significant portions of his
Rowfant Library were purchased at auction (1904-1905) by
the book dealer Thomas J. Wise. Wise in turn sold individual items to American collectors such as John Henry
Wrenn. In this way the materials stayed in private collections until their second generation of owners died.
Only then were the collections finally purchased by libraries and made available for proper study, the Wrenn
collection, for instance, going to the University of
Texas.

But though most of the materials relevant to a
study of the _Idylls_ _of_ _the_ _King_ were kept from the public gaze, persistent scholars began, right after the
poet's death, to write studies of his epic. The first
sustained study, and until our time one of the finest,

5

was the work of an American professor, Richard Jones.

His The Growth of the Idylls of the King[4] is based on a

careful collation of two volumes of proof states, one

in the British Museum and one in the library of the

South Kensington Museum, now known as the Victoria and

Albert Museum. The available materials permitted only

a brief account of the very latest variants (i.e., those

which persisted into proof states) for the four first

published poems of the cycle. This was not much, but

for seventy-five years his work has remained the only

careful Idylls collation.

The next serious student of Tennyson's Idylls was,

among other things, a forger. And therein lies one of

the most remarkable tales in modern bibliography.[5]

Thomas J. Wise was a clever man who saw early in his

life that the book trade was developing in new and re-

markable ways, and he determined to profit from the

change. He was, essentially, a book dealer who acquired

rare editions and manuscripts and sold them at a profit.

His market was the growing number of moneyed Americans

who wanted to build fine libraries, but who were far

more interested in the works of writers they knew, writ-

ers of the nineteenth century, than in the books and

manuscripts of earlier times, which had previously been the main concentration of the rare book market. Wise acted the role of the gentleman scholar who dabbles in selling as a sideline. His main preoccupation seemed to be bibliography, and he is in fact responsible for many of the fullest bibliographies yet prepared for nineteenth-century authors.

But for some inexplicable reason Wise became a forger. To help his scheme, history provided him with a curious loophole. Many of the best nineteenth-century authors had indulged in limited and sometimes private printings of their works. This was certainly true of Tennyson, who had limited editions prepared as he worked on his Idylls. It was easy for Wise, forty to sixty years after the fact, to forge "rare trial issues" he could sell to ignorant, wealthy collectors.

And the knavish way in which he did it, his complete affrontery, is astounding. Wise was known and respected as a bibliographic authority. He used this position to build an entire history of references to his Idylls forgeries. This began in 1895, when he and a crony, H. Buxton Foreman, published their two-volume Literary Anecdotes of the Nineteenth Century.[6] This collection con-

tained an article by Foreman which was evidently "de-
signed to authenticate four spurious Tennyson pamphlets,"[7] three of which were directly related to the
Idylls. The article also contains, however, a valuable
outline of the true history of the poem. Such is the
maddening nature of Wise's work: it is at once indis-
pensible and yet filled with carefully conceived lies.

In 1901 he carried his project a step further.
Luther D. Livingston was at work on a Tennyson bibliography to be published as a part of a sale by Dodd,
Mead, and Company. The grateful Livingston records that
he had been "much favored and much aided in preparing
the description of this set by having the privilege of
consulting the proof sheets of a part of [Wise's] bibliography."[8] Wise pulled the same trick again in 1905.
J. C. Thomson was at work on another Tennyson list and
records in his preface that

> My grateful acknowledgements are due,
> in the first place, to Mr. T.J. Wise,
> who placed at my disposal full biblio-
> graphic descriptions of seventeen of
> the 'trial issues,' including several
> unknown to me.[9]

In both cases Wise was carefully deluding these researchers, palming off information on his forgeries as valua-

ble discoveries only recently made.

Finally, in 1908, Wise published his own two-volume
bibliography, by far the best bibliographic study of Tennyson extant. And it contains, scattered through the citations, a careful list of Wise forgeries described with
all the scientific punctilio Wise lavished on actual editions. It was only in the nineteen-thirties, using
chemical tests for paper age and close typographic investigation, that two young bibliographers, Carter and
Pollard, found Wise out, and published their discoveries
in An Enquiry into the Nature of Certain Nineteenth Century Pamphlets.[10] Employing their study and consulting
further investigation conducted since then, the Tennyson student can weed the true from the false and pro-
fitably use the Wise Bibliography. It is, perforce, the
bibliographic basis for this edition.

In 1936 Tennyson's grandson, Sir Charles Tennyson,
published a study of the Idylls manuscripts he was later
to sell to Harvard University. His article, titled
"Some MSS of the Idylls of the King...,"[11] has remained one of the central studies of the development
of the poem. Sir Charles deals with the Idylls in the
chronological order of their publication. He describes

all of the manuscripts in the collection, frequently inserting long quotations from subsequently altered or rejected passages. He reconstructs Tennyson's methods of composition, and makes fruitful conjectures on some of the most vexatious problems of Idylls history, always basing his theories on all the available facts. Since its first publication, this article has been one of the chief sources for information on Tennyson manuscripts, as witnessed by the remarkable frequency with which it turns up in the footnotes of Tennyson students down to our own day.

Finally, in 1969, the first attempt at a scholarly edition of Tennyson appeared, edited by Christopher Ricks.[12] But the dimensions of his undertaking were so large that, in the editor's own words, he "had to make some drastic decisions, and one of them was not to give MS variants for the Idylls."[13] What he did do was to collate all the published editions for verbal variants only, and then to rely on secondary sources, such as Sir Charles Tennyson's article, for supplementary information. Consequently, the Ricks edition contains only a small number of verbal variants, some inaccurately noted, and no punctuation variants. Until now, there has not been a proper and complete study of the development of this major poem.

That is precisely the purpose of this volume. The manuscripts long held by family and friends have found their way into public repositories. The careful efforts of Wise and his colleagues to perpetuate a set of forgeries have been thwarted. And for the first time a full variorium edition of the _Idylls_ can become a reality.

What does this volume contain? First, it contains every _verbal_ variant from both manuscript and printer's proof. In cases in which there is substantial variation, whole blocks of poetry are reproduced. In every case, scrupulous care has been maintained to reprint Tennyson's language and punctuation exactly as he set it down.

Second, this edition records every punctuation variant, beginning with the first printed version. Tennyson never concerned himself with punctuation when he was writing out his poetry. Many times he would write on for lines without a single punctuation mark, frequently even neglecting to capitalize the first word of a sentence. He was a wealthy and successful poet by the

time he actually began the _Idylls_, and his publishers
were evidently happy to cater to his preference. He
sent them manuscript copies of his poems and they would
send him back proof sheets on which he would make innumerable additions and alterations, most of them in punctuation. Evidently he preferred to create his punctuation when he could see how a poem looked in print. It
is for this reason, I suspect, that we have so many
proof states for some poems. To give an extreme example:
Tennyson had five different versions of "Merlin and Vivien" set up before the first edition. Years later,
when preparing "Gareth and Lynette," he reduced the number of printed states, but heavily punctuated two different copies of an early proof, evidently intending to
get the punctuation "right" on the first try. Even then
he required yet two more proof states before the actual
first edition was set up. The present edition records
all of the manuscript corrections which Tennyson made on
the proof sheets.

All of these variants, both words and punctuation,
from both manuscript and printer's proof, have been ar-
ranged line by line, and in chronological succession.
They provide the careful reader with as full a picture

of the growth of this great poem as the existing source materials will permit. But this mass of variants by itself is distant and, potentially, confusing. What are all these source documents, cryptically indicated by numbers and abbreviations? Where are they kept and what do they look like? And, beyond that, how does this mass of materials fit together? What was the actual "growth" of the Idylls of the King? The next few pages will attempt to set forth the bare facts of the situation--to tell what source materials still do exist, and what they contain.

II.

We are going to be examining what still remains of Tennyson's working drafts--the scraps of manuscript and the proof sheets which formed the basis of his daily labor. How did he work? What was his method of composition? What can we expect to find in his manuscripts, and what will we miss?

Tennyson was a poet who began to ply his pen only after a great deal of work was finished in his head; he was not a man given to scratch pads and doodling. His work was, for him, intensely serious, and he evolved a method of creation which was extremely efficient. He

always initiated a new work with a period of brooding

which, for his longer works, could last for months. In

his later years he described the purpose of this habit

to a friend.

> 'I can always write,' he said, 'when
> I see my subject, though sometimes
> I spend three quarters of a year with-
> out putting pen to paper.'[14]

Such a practice, of course, rules out false starts and

half-formed conceptions appearing in manuscript. Since

the work of shaping the outline of the whole was done

within the mind, it is lost to posterity. We possess

few remains of the tantalizing blind alleys which Ten-

nyson tried and found impossible. In general we see

only the evolution of the final plan of the poem; al-

ternate plans are lost.

Only when he had roughed out the entire pattern of

the poem, when he could "see" it, would Tennyson begin

the work of versification. This too was done mentally,

either during certain hours which he formally set aside

for work, or during his long rambles about the downs of

the Isle of Wight. He would begin, his son tells us,

with a "single phrase" which he would "roll about" in

his head, over and over, elaborating it into poetry.[15]

As he worked he muttered the lines aloud, testing their

sound and feel; his poetry was always "verbal."[16] At

this stage the verse was in a fluid state. As a friend

of his tells us,

> He might say aloud and almost as it
> were to himself, some passage he had
> just made, but seldom twice in the
> same words, and unless written down at
> once, the first and original form of
> it was lost or 'improved.'[17]

It is at this point in his creative process that Ten-

nyson would begin jotting down his lines. The overall

plan was established and he was creating poetry to fit

that plan. As it came to him he would write it down,

even if, as was often the case, he had only two or three

lines ready. It seems evident from the confusion of his

notebooks that he did not work through his poems from

the first line to the last, creating them in sequence.

Rather, he would work on whatever passage or scene

seemed "ready" for composition. The end result of this

method is the jumbled state of the earliest drafts which

have survived. These are usually scattered across the

pages without order or pattern and frequently appear in

a scrawl which clearly mirrors its writer's hurry.

15

INTRODUCTION

As he continued to work Tennyson would commence
molding these random scraps together into a continuous
narrative, altering phrases, lines, sometimes entire
blocks of lines. Though the overall patterns persist,
minor characters and incidental scenes appear and dis-
solve as the final poem begins to emerge. Sir Lamorack falls into shadow; elsewhere, Sir Bors appears.
The final text is, in fact, the product of relentless
and persistent craft. Though Tennyson may have la-
bored hours shaping a line, he is merciless with his
creations, and again and again he will write and re-
write, cut or expand. For some poems we have draft
after draft, each filled with new revisions, some of
which seem to us as perhaps inordinately picayune,
but which to Tennyson were, in fact, of equal impor-
tance to the cancellation of an entire passage. When
Tennyson began working on his second set of four Idylls
he turned to a new compositional procedure. The process
of slowly molding scraps of poetry in his head was evidently enormously taxing, and consequently he began to
write out prose drafts of his poems before the actual
versification.

INTRODUCTION

Most of the manuscripts, both prose and verse, which have survived are on a variety of pale blue paper which Tennyson liked. He purchased this paper unbound and worked on it in quires, often ripping out pages if he was dissatisfied. As the work progressed from fragmentary scraps to continuous narrative, he would begin writing on only the right hand page, reserving the left for the inevitable alterations and additions. In this manner he was sometimes able (e.g. in the Trinity "Enid"--Tn-30) to assemble pages from various drafts into a fair copy. When the poem was finished his wife would frequently sew the pages into small "notebooks" and hand cover them with marbled boards and orange-red spines.

Following the final manuscript draft would come the spate of proof sheets, over which Tennyson worked with great care. He had an intense awareness of his audience, and throughout his life was exact in supervising the publication of his works. Again and again we find him altering the most subtle point of punctuation, to get the pace of a line "just right." This scrupulosity, this endless, nagging concern for his poems drove Tennyson to tinker with them even after they were finally placed

17

under the public gaze. In successive editions, words,
whole lines are altered, and sometimes entirely new passages join the older poem. The final state of the Idylls
did not, in fact, appear until after the poet's death,
for he instructed his son Hallam to insert a line into
the "Epilogue" to the Idylls, and this was not finally
done until 1899. Consequently, the full story of the
building of the Idylls includes manuscripts which range
from prose narratives and short first drafts to the final, "fair" copies, a large number of proof states, and
the many editions of his works which appeared during
Tennyson's lifetime.

III.

Alfred Tennyson was always a poet. From the days
of his boyhood he trained himself solely for this role.
Though for a long while it entailed great sacrifice, he
evidently refused ever to seek any kind of formal em-
ployment, preferring to live on the slender income left
him by his father and to work at his craft. He was
never, even in his later years, a "literary man." He
did no reviewing or essay writing--he never dabbled in

the novel. The entire pattern of his life was fashioned for a single function: to write poetry.

Evidently from the days of his youth Tennyson had resolved on creating a "major poem," and from an equally early period he settled upon the Arthurian legends as a subject which had not yet been exhausted. Hallam Tennyson reprints in his biography three different sketches for an Arthur poem, all dating from the 1830's. One is a short prose draft, one a set of jottings which create an allegorical framework (presumably for a large work), one an outline for a five-act play. And there were evidently further attempts, now lost. In 1859, when Tennyson was finally polishing his first four Idylls for the press, he wrote his friend the Duke of Argyll that,

> Many years ago I did write 'Lancelot's Quest of the Grail' in as good verse as I ever wrote, no, I did not write, I made it in my head, and it has now altogether slipt out of memory.[18]

The significance of these sketches and early, mentally composed poems is that the Arthurian legends represented for Tennyson, from the early days of his creative life, the monumental project which, in the future, it was his destiny to complete.

19

INTRODUCTION

The poem as we now have it germinated during the intense emotional crisis which struck Tennyson on hearing the death of his friend Arthur Hallam in 1833. Tennyson felt a serious personal loss. As the long sequence of lyrics In Memoriam: A.H.H. demostrates, in Hallam's death Tennyson discovered the reality of death itself. The poems begun in this period are filled not only with laments for the departed Hallam, but with morose brooding over man's mortality.[19] And it is in the midst of these sorrows and fears that the first draft of "Morte d'Arthur" appears, written out in a notebook between In Memoriam lyrics and sketches for "The Two Voices," once titled "Thoughts of a Suicide."[20] This first draft appears in a Trinity College Manuscript (Tn-17) and is clearly headlined First Draft. The manuscript also contains a second draft of the poem, this time with the lines numbered. Sir Charles Tennyson is sure these drafts were done during the year 1833.[21] Tennyson was evidently finished with the poem by 1834, when "he told Tennant he was busily copying out his 'Morte d'Arthur'..."[22]

The poem was not published until the now-famous two-volume edition of Tennyson poems which appeared in

20

1842. But this does not mean that it rested on the shelf during the interval between its drafting and its first publication. Tennyson was habitually reading his poems to his friends; and Edward FitzGerald, the translator of Omar Khayyam, tells of hearing Tennyson read the "Morte" in 1835.[23] In addition, Tennyson permitted close friends to copy from his manuscript. Several such copies still exist. One is in The Heath Commonplace Book (Fitzwilliam Museum, Cambridge), a manuscript collection of poems copied out by a friend of Tennyson. At the Houghton Library, Harvard, there are two more copies of the poem, one probably in the hand of James Spedding (H-21).

While the poem was popular with his friends, Tennyson was not at all sure of its public reception. He intended it to be a test of public reaction to his long meditated Arthurian epic. Tennyson hoped a short poem would be readily accessible. "I thought that a small vessel, built on fine lines, is likely to float further down the stream of Time than a big raft."[24] Regardless of the merit of the poem itself, Tennyson's fears were probably justified. "In 1842," as Kathleen Tillotson has written, "Arthurian story was still strange to the ordinary reader, and even felt to be unacceptable as a subject for poetry."[25] To prepare the public, Tennyson cushioned his Arthurian tale with a framing poem called "The Epic" which describes a drowsy Christmas Eve party at which the poet Everard Hall is persuaded to read his Arthurian poem, one of "some twelve books"[26] which he had burnt, dissatisfied "that nothing new was said, or else/Something so said 'twas nothing...."[27]

The experiment, even with the cushion, was a failure. The 1842 collection as a whole drew praise, but the "Morte d'Arthur" was criticized, particularly by John Sterling who felt that "The miraculous legend of 'Excalibur' does not come very near to us, and as reproduced by any modern writer must be a mere ingenious exercise of fancy."[28] Though he often affected indifference, Tennyson was deeply hurt by critical remarks, and in this case he himself confessed that Sterling's strictures "finally decided him to postpone this project, making him feel his powers were not adequate to the task."[29] With this melancholy, though perhaps accurate self-assessment, Tennyson let his Arthurian project lapse for fifteen years. It was twenty-seven years until the "Morte d'Arthur" would be integrated into a new and growing epic whole.

But while Tennyson busied himself with other work it is clear that the Idylls were never far from his mind. In 1843, the year after Sterling's review, he was already fashioning the first lines of "Merlin and Vivien" (228-231) while on a trip to Ireland.[30] In subsequent years he made other trips, with his purpose even more evident. In 1848 he visited Bude, Tintagel (Mark's Castle), and Land's End at the tip of Cornwall, legendary land of Lancelot.[31] Sir Charles Tennyson tells us that on his return home he began work on a Merlin poem, but was interrupted.[32] In August of 1853 Tennyson traveled to Glastonbury,[33] the ruined abbey which legend says Joseph of Arimathea founded when he reached England. Readers of the Idylls will recognize at once that these are all places which the poem mentions or describes. Though he may not have admitted it at the time, Tennyson was doing research.

When Tennyson began writing again, he began in earnest, though the exact date of his new start is subject to debate. Sir Charles Tennyson says that a rough draft for this new Arthurian poem, now called "Merlin and Vivien," was finished by January of 1856.[34] Hallam

INTRODUCTION

Tennyson tells us the poem was begun February 1856 and complete (at least in its first form) by March 31st.[35] There still exist a remarkable number of manuscripts and proof states for this poem. We have no less than five different manuscripts representing the early stages of composition, probably written out in the early months of 1856. Two of these manuscripts are single sheets of paper. (H-152) covers lines 237-261, and (Y-III), actually a torn shred of paper, includes lines 916-918, with a fragmentary jotting from "Enid" on the reverse. Then there are three small notebooks which contain more extensive sketches and drafts--(H-30) and (H-31) are both bound, and both have been severly mutilated. (H-30) covers lines 315-353, c. 691ff., 805-826. (H-31), which also includes drafts for "Guinevere," covers lines 811-843. (H-153a), 16 pages of paper sewn together, contains extensive drafts, in somewhat scrambled order, covering 267-458, 553-630, 666-683, 838-862.

All of these manuscripts represent Tennyson's first steps in composition. All of them, save (Y-III), remained in the family collection until the 1950's. There are also two fair drafts of the whole poem still extant. The first, presented to Frederick Locker and auctioned

24

in 1924,[36] is now in the Huntington Museum, (HM-1326).

This draft precedes the second fair copy, now in the

Harvard Library as Lowell 1827.12.[37]   Tennyson gave this

manuscript to Mrs. Julia Cameron, the pioneer photogra-

pher and his neighbor on the Isle of Wight. She sent to

him asking for the manuscript of "Guinevere," the Victo-

rian favorite from the first volume of the Idylls. Evi-

dently Emily Tennyson was slightly piqued at this, and

Alfred sent Mrs. Cameron the draft for "Merlin and Vi-

vien".[38]   It, like the Huntington, is complete, and it

is evidently one of the last copies made before the

first printed proof.

"Merlin and Vivien" was not, in its early stages,

known by that title. In fact, the wily seductress of

Arthur's wizard is called, on all the manuscript drafts

and in the early proof states, Nimuë. And that name was

the first title given the poem.

There are five different states of printer's proofs

for "Nimuë"--"Vivien," the first four employing the name

"Nimuë." The first of these is in the British Museum

"trial book" Enid and Nimuë: The True and the False,

designated here as (BM-1). The second is one of two

proof states bound in the Forster library volume, The

25

INTRODUCTION

True and the False. It can be distinguished from the later Forster proof by the name of the villainess, and by its length, 97 pages. The third proof state is represented by three different copies, two in the Tennyson Research Centre in Lincoln, (designated L-MI), one in the Yale Library (Y-VIII), which is fragmentary. The fourth state, in two copies, can also be found at the Tennyson Centre, and is here called (L-M2). In the fifth state the name is finally altered to "Vivien." The sole known copy of this state is the second proof for "Merlin and Vivien" in the Forster collection. It is 101 pages in length. Finally, there is the actual first edition state, which appeared in 1859. A quick glance will show the vital role these successive proof stages played in the development of the poem's punctuation, as well as in the final polishing of certain phrases and lines. Tennyson was not finished with "Merlin and Vivien" after the 1859 publication. He was to return to it again in the years 1872-1874, to alter a number of passages, and add 140 new lines. I will describe the manuscripts relating to these changes in my account of the 1873 and 1874 editions.

Having finished a draft of "Merlin and Vivien"

26

INTRODUCTION

Tennyson turned at once to another tale which he called, initially, "Enid," but which modern readers know as two distinct idylls, "The Marriage of Geraint," and "Geraint and Enid." In 1870 the poem was retitled "Geraint and Enid " and in 1873 Tennyson split it in half, numbering the parts I and II. Only in 1886 was the first half called "The Marriage of Geraint." For convenience I will presently deal with it as Tennyson first did, as a single entity titled "Enid."

Emily Tennyson's diary mentions from time to time the progress her husband was making on this, his second idyll. He began it on 16 April, 1856.[39] On June 1st he was working on the Song "Come in."[40] June 16th he wrote his wife that Enid was "a little harder to manage than Merlin."[41] By July 27 he had finished the scene describing Geraint asking for Enid's hand[42] and on August 1st the tournament was done.[43] By October 17 he was far enough along to read aloud from "Enid" to his friends, but on November 11 he was still "working at Enid."[44] Only on May 6, 1857 could he finally write his wife from London telling her that the final proof sheets had been sent to press.[45]

27

INTRODUCTION

In the existing manuscripts one can see the struggle which consumed Tennyson over these long months.
"Enid" is a long poem even by Victorian standards. And
it was all composed, bit by bit, in the poet's head, and
the scraps jotted down as they came. The notebook (H-35)
is filled, from cover to cover, with such jottings,
scattered in random order, written right side up, up
side down, sideways. (H-71a) is just slightly more or-
ganized.[46] These two manuscripts show us Tennyson la-
boring over every line. And he faces even more prodigious difficulties when it comes time to join these
scraps, along with the "Enid" drafts from (Lo-1) and from
manuscripts now lost into a single, continuous whole.
We can see these difficulties in the Trinity manuscript
(Tn-30). By this point Tennyson is pulling things together, but the struggle involved is manifest in the
large number of alterations and revisions which crowd
the pages of the Trinity copy. And his labors extend
even into the poem's numerous proof states. The first
state exists in two copies, one in the Forster _True and
False_ volume, (F-ENI), the other at the Tennyson Centre
(L-ENI). The student can readily spot them by the
early textual variant in line 74 of "The Marriage of

Geraint," "the column of his knotted throat." The se-

cond "Enid" proof state is in the British Museum trial

book Enid and Nimuë (BM-1). The third and fourth states

are both in the Tennyson Research Centre and are here

called (L-EN2),(L-EN3). The final proof state, again in

the Forster volume, is called (F-EN2).

Once Tennyson had finished the first manuscript

drafts for both "Nimuë" and "Enid," he had them set up

in type and bound together into a "trial book," a job his

printer had finished by May 6, 1857.[47] As we have al-

ready said, this book contains the first "Nimuë" state

and the second "Enid" state. Tennyson titled it Enid

and Nimuë: The True and the False. Evidently he was

seriously considering publishing only these first two

poems. And as Hallam Tennyson tells us,

> Several friends urged the immediate pub-
> lication of the newly-written Idylls, a-
> mong them Jowett, who says...'Anyone
> who cares about you is deeply annoyed
> that you are deterred by critics from
> writing or publishing...'[48]

But Tennyson decided against publishing the pair. F.T.

Palgrave tells the story.

> These two Idylls it was A.T.'s origi-
> nal intention to publish by themselves.
> Six copies were struck off, but owing
> to a remark upon Nimuë which reached

> him, he at once recalled the copies
> out: ...From this change of purpose &
> delay given (sic) the idea of pub-
> lishing the four as 'Idylls of the King':
> a felicitous accident for English litera-
> ture![49]

So Tennyson withdrew his "trial book." But he did not

turn from his Arthurian epic. Instead, he recommenced

writing idylls.

The third, in fact, was already begun by July 9,

1857, when he presented his wife with lines 575-577 of

what was to be the poem "Guinevere."[50] By January 8,

1858 he had written the parting of Arthur and Guine-

vere.[51] February 1st, Guinevere's final speech, March

5th the song "Too late," and on March 15th, a finished

fair copy.[52] This was faster work than "Enid" had been,

and in later life Tennyson confidently told a friend he

had written the poem in "a fortnight."[53]

The most fascinating "Guinevere" manuscript is

(H-31), a set of sketches for lines 238-253. They tell

of the first, magical days of the reign of Arthur, and

depict a kingdom of marvels, filled with fairies. These

early drafts are narrated in the first person. In later

drafts Tennyson put the tale into the mouth of the lit-

tle novice, thus altering it into a fable recounted of

the distant past. (H-36) is, however, the most impor-

tant of the "Guinevere" manuscripts. As Sir Charles

Tennyson describes it,

> A characteristic of this fragmentary
> rough draft is the number of rough notes,
> often mere indicators of the rhythm and
> wording of the final text, which are
> jotted down, here and there, apparently
> just to fix an idea which had come into
> the poet's mind.[54]

As the manuscript goes on there appear longer continu-

ous passages. The whole covers lines 127-209, 398-682.

(Yale-IV) contains a manuscript copy of the song "Too

late," and (H-73a), a single sheet, includes lines

365-394. The Trinity manuscript (Tn-39) is a fair draft

of the whole poem and leads directly to the first proof

state. This can be found in a small volume in the Bri-

tish Museum catalogued as C.133.a.7 (Here, BM-2). A

second state is in the Forster _True_ _and_ _False_ volume.

Guinevere was finished and copied in March, 1858.

By mid-June Emily writes, "He told me his plan for 'The

Maid of Astolat.'"[55] We hear little else about the new

poem until February 4, 1859, when Tennyson was "finished

writing down all but a little of 'The Maid of Astolat.'"[56]

This poem--which we now know as "Lancelot and Elaine"--

retained "The Maid of Astolat" title through two proof

31

states, then becoming "Elaine." Only in 1870 was the
title finally altered to the present "Lancelot and
Elaine."

Little seems to have survived from the creation of
this long poem. The Houghton Library has a single sheet
(H-114a) covering lines 1346-1352. There exists only
one other early manuscript, but that an important one.
Once in the library of Templeton Croaker, it is now in
the collection of the University of Virginia. Consist-
ing of thirty leaves, this manuscript contains about
725 lines, written, as in the early drafts of the three
preceding idylls, in scraps and short blocks of verse.
It is in the Trinity College manuscript (Tn-39) that
these blocks come together. This, while a continuous
draft, can hardly be called final. There are many variants, and sometimes, as in the case of Lancelot's final
soliloquy, the poet is still roughing out the shape and
length of the poem itself. Three proof states survive.
The first two are both titled "The Maid of Astolat,"
though in the second state this is crossed out and re-
placed (in manuscript) with the new title "Elaine." The
first state is found in the small (BM-2) book which also
contains a proof of "Guinevere." The Tennyson Research

32

Centre holds portions of another copy of this state.

The Centre also possesses the sole copy of the second

state, called here (L-L2). Finally, there is a third

proof state in the Forster volume.

It is time now to talk at greater length about that

peculiar book which contains the last proof states of

all four Idylls as well as the first state of "Enid" and

the second of "Nimuë." All are bound together and head-

ed with a title page which was later rejected. Evident-

ly Forster obtained both a complete version of a very

late "trial book," created just before the first edition,

and some earlier proofs as well, and had them all bound

together. This would then be, in part, a second "trial

book," and it is considered such by most bibliographers.

It bears the title The/ True and the False./ Four Idylls

of the King. The University of Virginia possesses an-

other copy of this title page, altered by Tennyson into

the final form which was used for the first printing.

Why did he change The True and The False to Idylls of

the King? Wise suggests that the 1859 publication of a

novel by Lena Eden, False and True, forced the altera-

tion.[57] Whatever the reason, the title page was reset,

and yet another set of plates prepared, but this time

33

for actual publication.

In March 1859 Tennyson went to London to work on

the final proofs, and in May the last proofs of "Elaine"

were complete.[58] Forty thousand copies were ordered for

the first printing and, in the first week of sales,

10,000 copies were sold.[59] The volume was in the end

both financially and poetically very successful.

But with success came the burden of pressure. The

first four idylls were not at all a closed entity.

Their episodic nature left them open to addition. Fur-

ther, by this date the initial criticisms of "Morte

d'Arthur" were part of a distant past, and any ardent

Tennyson reader would have wished that poem to be inte-

grated somehow into a larger whole.

On 24 September 1859 the Duke of Argyll wrote Ten-

nyson,

> ...Macaulay...was in great hopes that you
> would pursue the subject [of King Arthur],
> and particularly mentioned the Legend of
> the "Sangreal" as also the latter days
> and death of Lancelot.[60]

But Tennyson was not ready and replied on October 3 that

> As to Macaulay's suggestion of the San-
> greal, I doubt whether such a subject
> could be handled in these days, without
> incurring a charge of irreverence...
> The old writers believed in the Sangreal.[61]

34

So, for the moment, the _Idylls_ gave way to other con-
cerns.

On 14 December 1861 Albert, the Prince Consort,
died. Tennyson began, almost immediately,[62] to compose
a dedication to Albert, who once had personally indicated pleasure in the _Idylls_.[63] By January 9, 1862,
Tennyson's publishers had the poem set in type.[64]
Special copies were printed up and circulated free to
those who already possessed a copy of the _Idylls_. Tennyson sent some copies to the princess Alice; she replied on January 19, that the Queen felt the poem's
lines "had soothed her aching, bleeding heart."[65] There
are three manuscript copies of this dedication still extant. (H-96a) is clearly a first draft, with (H-95a)
coming as a second draft, embodying the corrections of
the first. There is also a peculiar copy made in another hand (Y-V), which evidently transcribed from
(H-96a) before it was corrected. The Yale Library also has the only known printer's proof for the Dedication (Y-VI) with manuscript corrections in Tennyson's
hand. The British Museum has a copy of the free leaflet, under the press mark C.59.i.2. In 1862 a fourth
edition of the _Idylls_ appeared, with a few minor cor-

rections. This edition included, for the first time,

the Dedication.

In the meantime the Holy Grail project continued

to trouble Tennyson. In January 1862, Emily Tennyson

writes that

> A.T. talks of writing an Idyll on the
> Quest of the Sangraal but fears han-
> dling the subject lest it become ir-
> reverent.[66]

The external pressures to expand the Idylls continued

as well. On February 23 of the same year Argyll wrote

that the Princess Royal

> is very anxious that you should make
> the Morte d'Arthur an ending of the
> Idylls--adding only something to con-
> nect it to Guinevere.[67]

It seems evident that Tennyson wanted to go on, but

could not find the way.

The dam finally broke in March of 1868. Emily

writes, "A.T. now worked regularly...writing 'The Holy

Grail.'"[68] In April yew trees rich with pollen in-

spired both lines 13-16 of "The Holy Grail" and lyric

XXXIV of In Memoriam.[69] By the 9th and 11th of Sep-

tember Tennyson was reading bits of the new poem aloud.[70]

September 14 Emily writes that Alfred is "...almost

finished with the 'San Gral' in about a week (he had

the subject clearly for some time). It came like a
breath of inspiration."[71] This at first sounds self-
contradictory, since there are so many references to
earlier composition. Evidently Tennyson must have been
considering the poem as a whole for some time and
creating only scraps until the momentous week in September when it all came like an "inspiration." The
Houghton notebook (H-38) bears this out. It consists
of a rough draft of the entire poem in prose, the first
instance of Tennyson's following this practice in the
creation of a particular idyll. The prose draft occa-
sionally slips into sections of verse, and these could
be the bits and pieces he had created incidentally before setting down the prose version. Following the
prose comes a verse draft, written out with relative
confidence. This is probably the work book for that
week of inspiration. Huntington (HM-1323) contains a
few further drafts for "The Holy Grail," drafts of
passages which were still being developed after (H-38).
On October 22 Emily tells us that Tennyson "finished
copying out his 'Holy Grail' for the press."[71] She is
probably referring to what is now Trinity notebook
(Tn-29), which contains a complete draft of the poem in

37

a form very close to the first proof state. In November the poem was sent to the printer.[72]

This brings us to a peculiar problem. Tennyson went on, immediately after composing "The Holy Grail," to write three further idylls. All four were set up in proof at the same time and appear, grouped together, in four different proof states. It is easy to arrange these in order. But, in addition, there are two proofs for "The Holy Grail" alone. In both of these proofs the page numbers are printed between parentheses at the center of the page top. The problem is to determine the order of succession.

We begin with the four states of proof for the entire volume, The Holy Grail, Etc. The first of these is in the Ashley Library at the British Museum (A-2104). This volume, originally owned by Frederick Locker-Lampson, was purchased at his death by T. J. Wise. It bears no title page. Of the four idylls therein, three have titles differing from the final version. "The Coming of Arthur" is called "The Birth of Arthur," "Pelleas and Ettarre" is "Sir Pelleas," and "The Passing of Arthur" is "The Death of Arthur." There are manuscript corrections. The second state of proof is in the John Sterling Li-

INTRODUCTION

brary at the University of London (S-925). This volume

contains the four <u>Grail</u> idylls plus copies of the 1859

idylls, all bound together to form a trial version. The

last two proof states are both represented in the col-

lection of the Tennyson Research Centre, Lincoln. There

is one copy of (L-HGI) with the last idyll ending on page

156. The Berg Collection also has a copy of this state

(B-VIII), with manuscript corrections. Lincoln holds

two copies of (L-HG2), with the last idyll ending on

page 158. Both of the last two states employ the now-

standard titles for the poems. This sequence of four

states is readily established. The difficulty arises

when one tries to explain where the two special "Holy

Grail" proofs belong. The following is my conjecture.

Tennyson first had the four poems set up in the

volume (A-2104) He made a few corrections in this ver-

sion (only eight in the case of "The Holy Grail"), and

a second copy was set up and pulled, (S-925). Mean-

while, for the sake of ease, Tennyson had his printers

make up some sheets from the Ashley version for further

correction and emendation. The corrections from both

(A-2104) and this new set of proofs (Berg VI) were em-

bodied in a second "Holy Grail" proof (H-HGP). Mean-

while, following the Ashley/Sterling tradition only,
another version of all four idylls was set up (L-HGI)
and (B-VIII). Then Tennyson combined the corrections
from the (L-HGI) (B-VIII) state and the (H-HGP) state
into yet another proof state, (L-HG2). This became
the source of the first edition.

        A-2104   B-VI

        S-925

        L-HGI/B-VIII   H-HGP

              L-HG2

               '69

This explanation is complex, and not terribly satisfy-
ing. But it seems at least possible, given the existing confusion of the data.

   We have dealt with the proof states for all the
idylls included in The Holy Grail, Etc. But we must
return now to a brief description of the creation of the
three poems which accompanied the title idyll. These
poems--"The Coming of Arthur," "Pelleas and Ettarre,"
and "The Passing of Arthur"--were all written within a
short period of time. The earliest drafts have all
been mutilated mercilessly, and probably for commercial
motives. It was the custom in the late nineteenth cen-

tury for a book dealer to increase the value of an item

by binding with it manuscript fragments which had an

"associational value." A rich collector would be more

tempted to purchase a first edition of the Idylls if

some manuscript scraps were bound in with the book.

Evidently the first drafts for "The Passing of Arthur"

were in the possession of Frederick Locker-Lampson,

whose Rowfant Library was auctioned in 1904-1905.

Thomas J. Wise bought much of this collection, and a

few years later he sold John Henry Wrenn, a wealthy

Chicago collector, a copy of The Holy Grail, Etc. vol-

ume with numerous scraps of manuscript bound in.[73] Wise

himself retained the proof copy (A-2104) we have already

discussed and had more scraps bound therein. It seems

reasonable to assume that Wise possessed sketches of

these three poems, cut up the manuscripts, and evenly

distributed the fragments between his copy and Wrenn's.

We find further support for this conjecture in the fact

that Wise possessed a fair draft of lines 20-71 of the

"Coming" while he sold Wrenn the rest of the manuscript

covering lines 74-423.[74] It is difficult to guess how

much was lost as Wise plied his lucrative scissors.

Certainly, we will never know in what manner these

41

drafts were placed within the notebooks, nor how many

draft passages have been destroyed. It is only now, in

the present edition, that the remaining portions have

been brought back together.

Once finished with the story of "The Holy Grail"

Tennyson turned to the problem of rendering the very

earliest days of Arthur's reign. By February 13, 1869

he was reading portions of "the birth and marriage of

Arthur" to his wife.[75] Before the end of February he

had read her "all" of the poem, though on May 7 he had

just finished "'Leodogran's dream,'"[76] the vision which

finally persuades Guinevere's father to give her to

Arthur in marriage. Probably he had finished the bulk

of the poem in February but continued to add to it in

later months. We possess early drafts of the poem in

the Ashley and Texas (Wrenn) scraps. Next, there is an

early full draft of the poem which exists partly in the

Ashley collection (A-4521), partly in the Wrenn collec-

tion at Texas (T-C). Finally, there is a late draft in

the Berg collection (B-I). This came to New York via the

A.H. Japp collection and the library of Jerome Kern.[77]

These manuscripts give an account of the writing of the

poem as it appeared in 1869. But Tennyson was not yet

finished. In the 1873 Library Edition he added lines

66, 94-133, 459-469, 475-502. I will discuss these ad-

ditions in relation to that volume.

On May 19th of 1869 Tennyson was already reading

drafts for a new poem, "Sir Pelleas," to his wife.[78]

This tale had been on his mind for some time. On 28

June 1859 he had read Malory's "Sir Pelleas and Et-

tarre" to Mrs. Cameron and Emily Tennyson "with a view

to a new poem."[79] Now, in the spring of 1869, he car-

ried out his plan. As with "The Coming of Arthur,"

there are rough drafts, some in prose, extant in the

Ashley and Texas scraps. Texas also has a continuous

draft of the poem (T-P). Lines 387-403 were added in

the 1873 edition.

There seems to be no reliable means for dating

the composition of "The Passing of Arthur," though it

is safe to say that the work was done in the spring of

1869. Of course, much of the idyll was finished de-

cades earlier, as the "Morte d'Arthur." Tennyson now

surrounded this poem with new material, fitting it into

the overall pattern of his epic. Some early sketches

for this framing material still exist. (H-37), (H-39),

and a scrap of paper included in the proof state (B-VIII)

all contain drafts for Sir Bedivere's speech c. line 51.

(H-37) also has further sketches. The Ashley and Texas

scraps offer some drafts, and a sheet bound into a copy

of The Holy Grail, Etc. in the Widener collection holds

a draft of lines 144-154. These are all preparatory

manuscripts. There is no known fair copy. As it was

published in 1869, "The Passing of Arthur" lacked

lines 6-28, added in the 1873 edition.

On November 1, 1869, Emily Tennyson reports that

"we were very busy about the new volume of poems, 'The

Holy Grail.'"[80] It was around this time, then, that

the four trial books already described were set up and

corrected. On November 25, Emily continues, "A.T. went

with Mr. Locker to look after his proofs in London..."[81]

Forty thousand copies of the book were printed up at

once, and, as Hallam Tennyson tells us, "in consequence

of the large sale, my father made more in this year than

in any other, the profit realizing over 10,000 pounds."[82]

The title page of this volume, The Holy Grail, Etc., is

dated 1870, but the book was actually published in Decem-

ber to take advantage of the Christmas trade. Conse-

quently, it is referred to in the present edition as

(69). At the same time, Tennyson's publishers released

44

an edition of the Idylls of the King which included

not only The Holy Grail, Etc. poems, but the first four

idylls as well. This text is subsequent to The Holy

Grail, Etc. embodying certain corrections not in The

Holy Grail, Etc. (In this variorum edition the 1869

Idylls of the King is designated (69)). Both these vol-

umes refer, for the first time, to the tales framed by

"The Coming" and "The Passing" as "The Round Table."

In 1870 Strahan issued an edition of Tennyson's complete

works in small volumes, called the Miniature Edition.

It contains all the idylls written to that date and is

significant in that there are a number of changes in the

titles of the poems. "Enid" becomes "Geraint and Enid,"

"Vivien," "Merlin and Vivien," and "Elaine," "Lancelot

and Elaine." There are few textual alterations.

Tennyson was now past the hurdle posed by the San

Graal tale, and he evidently regarded the Holy Grail

volume as only a step towards his final end. In Novem-

ber of 1870 Emily records the fact that Tennyson has al-

ready written parts of a new poem, "The Last Tourna-

ment."[83] This project, like the Pelleas tale, had been

in Tennyson's mind for some time. As far back as May

24, 1859 he had read that portion of Malory "where Sir

45

Lancelot behaves so courteously to Sir Palamedes, and

where Arthur goes to see La Belle Isoude (with a view

to a poem on Tristram and Isolt)."[84] On July 17, 1866

he composed lines 12-15 of this idyll,[85] though the real

work did not begin until November of 1870. May 21, 1871,

Emily writes, "He read me his 'Tristram' the plan of

which he had been for some weeks discussing with me."[86]

and by the end of May the poem was sent to the printer.[87]

It is difficult to tell which printer this is, because

"The Last Tournament" first appeared in The Contempo-

rary Review for December, 1871. There are at least

three proof states for this publication, all represented

in the Texas collection. But there were also two proof

states set up before the first book edition. October

23, 1871 Emily again talks of proof, saying, "We ar-

ranged 'The Last Tournament' for the press."[88] It seems

probable Tennyson at first had the book proofs set up,

and only later decided to let the poem first appear in

the periodical.

In (H-40) there is a brief prose draft for the o-

pening of "The Last Tournament." No other prose exists

for this poem. Huntington Museum manuscript (HM-1323)

has a draft of the lines describing the tournament day

46

INTRODUCTION

(lines 151-187) and the Berg collection has a complete

draft (B-III) from the collection of Sir James Knowles,

auctioned in 1928.[89] Tennyson had given the manuscript

to Mrs. Knowles, whose husband edited the Contemporary

Review.[90] Two proof states precede the first edition.

The first state is represented by two copies, (A-2101)

in the Ashley library of the British Museum, and a Berg

Collection copy (B-III), acquired from the library of

Sir James Knowles in 1928. There is a copy of the se-

cond state in the University of Texas Library, from the

collection of Frederick Locker-Lampson.[91]

As he readied "The Last Tournament" for the printers

Tennyson was already at work on yet another idyll, again

a project he had long considered. On February 18, 1861

he had read the tale of Sir Gareth in Malory, doubtless

considering it for his epic.[92] Emily tells us that on

October 19, 1869 Tennyson "gave me his beginning of

'Beaumains' (Sir Gareth) to read, written (as was said

jokingly) to 'describe a pattern of youth for his

boys.'"[93] Evidently the poet set this project aside in

favor of "The Last Tournament." Only when that poem is

in print do we again hear of Gareth. November 20, 1871--

INTRODUCTION

"A.T. read the beginning of his new poem of 'Sir Gareth' which he had just written down."[94] It is a long poem, and Tennyson worked at it for sometime.[95] But by July 9th of 1872 he records the manuscript sent to the printers, though he feared that the manuscript was so "ill written" that it would confuse his typesetters.[96] He worked over the proofs during September and by the 24th was able to return them to the printers,[97] his task finished.

There are a large number of "Gareth" manuscripts in existence. Tennyson began his work for the poem with prose drafts. (H-40) has a long draft for the opening to the tale, part of which was later rejected. The Texas collection includes two pieces of paper with prose sketches, and the Butcher's Book, (H-32), has a sequence of prose passages. This manuscript represents the bridge between prose and verse for the poem, and is one of the most fascinating of the Tennyson manuscripts. Unlike the orderly translation of "The Holy Grail" from prose to verse, "Gareth" was evidently done in a confusion of bits and pieces, leaving bursts of prose and poetry scattered in random order over the many pages of this manuscript. It seems that Tennyson simply grabbed

48

the book at odd times as he worked, only later trou-

bling to bring everything together. The Widener Col-

lection possesses an unusual volume which may directly

relate to (H-32). This book, clearly created for a

wealthy collector, contains "Gareth" proof sheets for

the 1873 Library Edition and numerous drafts for the

poem in manuscript. These drafts have been cut from

some earlier source and pasted onto pages by the bind-

ers. At least one student of Tennyson manuscripts

thinks that these Widener scraps come from (H-32).[98]

The first continuous draft of the poem can be found in

(B-IV) (lines 1-125), while the Bodleian Library copy

contains a complete text, on pages the same size as the

Butcher's Book. This, in all probability, is the "ill

written" manuscript Tennyson sent to his publisher.

There are three proof states for "Gareth." The

first, in which the heroine's name is spelled "Lineth,"

exists in two copies, (A-2109) in the British Museum,

and (S-929) in the University of London Library. Both

contain numerous authorial corrections. There are also

two copies of the second state, one in the Berg Collec-

tion (B-II), one at the University of Texas. The Texas

collection holds as well a unique copy of the third

proof state (T-GP3), this embodying many of the corrections made on the Texas copy of the second state. (T-GP3) in turn holds even further authorial manuscript corrections, these appearing printed in the first edition.

In December 1872 "The Last Tournament" and "Gareth and Lynette" were published together as Gareth and Lynette, Etc. That edition contained an explanatory paragraph which, in its proof state, indicated that these two poems concluded the Idylls. This was corrected before the book was published, but it indicates the possibility that Tennyson may not have been completely sure of the final shape of the poem, even at this late date. The proof for this paragraph is now in the Berg collection.

But, Gareth and Lynette, Etc. was not to be the end, for Tennyson had long since begun work on still further additions to his poem. As "The Last Tournament" went to press Tennyson was already "Busy about Strahan's Library Edition..." (October 23, 1871).[99] This was to be, like the Miniature Edition of 1870, a multi-volume collection of Tennyson's works to date. Tennyson seized on the event to further develop his Idylls. This would be the

first edition to contain all of the poems he had finished (including the Gareth poems), and so he decided
that it would also be a good moment to take a second
look at the poem as a whole. Consequently, he began
work in 1871 and continued emending the text into 1873.
Tennyson made hundreds of minor alterations, expanded
four earlier poems, and wrote an "Epilogue."

To "Merlin and Vivien" he added lines 187-192.
(H-39) has the manuscript draft for these lines. It also contains a draft for some of the additions to "The
Coming of Arthur" (lines 59-115). This poem received
the most additions, including lines 94-133, 459-469,
475-502. The Pierpont Morgan Library contains a draft
for lines 459-467 bound in a copy of The Holy Grail,
Etc. (H-29a), a single sheet of paper not in Tennyson's
hand, contains a copy of lines 94-134. And the Berg
Collection possesses a draft of "The Song of the Battleaxe" (lines 475-502), probably written out November 6, 1872.[100] At the same time[101] Tennyson decided
to add a song to "Pelleas and Ettare" (lines 387-403),
and there survive two manuscripts, both in the Huntington Museum (Hm-1324 , Hm-19494), the second in another
hand, with manuscript corrections by Tennyson. Finally,

he added lines 6-28 to "The Passing of Arthur."

To conclude the Idylls volumes of the Library Edition, Tennyson decided to write an "Epilogue" addressed to Queen Victoria. This was already finished and "copied out" by Emily Tennyson on December 25, 1872.[102] Drafts for the "Epilogue" can be found in (H-32), the Butcher's Book which contains so many "Gareth and Lynette" sketches. Tennyson's publishers set up an early printing of the poem in eight pages for presentation and had fifty copies printed. The Ashley Library has one, (A-2111). Tennyson sent his "Epilogue" to the Queen and she acknowledged the poem on February 26, 1873.[103] The Library Edition volumes V and VI, which contain the Idylls, were published in 1873.

In 1874 two more editions of Tennyson's collected works appeared--the Cabinet Edition in ten volumes and the Author's Edition in six.[104] Both contained a new text for "Merlin and Vivien," which included, for the first time, lines 6-146. Several manuscripts for this addition have survived. (H-33) has sketches, some of which were afterwards abandoned. This manuscript also contains passages from "Balin and Balan" and illustrates Sir Charles Tennyson's contention that the "Vivien" al-

52

terations and "Balin", published so much later, were in fact products of the same creative period.[105] (H-37), in the midst of further "Balin" sketches, has one page with a draft for lines 128-144 of "Merlin and Vivien." There are also two fairly complete drafts of the addition, both headed "The Beginning of Vivien" in the author's hand. The earlier, (H-34), has many alterations, while the Yale Library (Y-I) copy, purchased in 1949 from the library of Col. Prinsep, is quite fair and clearly is close to the first printing.

Further editions appeared through the next ten years, but gave no indication that Tennyson was at work on any further Idylls. Doubtless most readers considered the set complete. Then, in November of 1885,[106] Tennyson published a collection of his later work called Tiresias, and Other Poems which included "Balin and Balan" subtitled in that edition, "An introduction to 'Merlin and Vivien.'" All the evidence seems to indicate that, in fact, this idyll was composed early in the 1870s, probably after "Gareth and Lynette" and was contemporaneous to the additions being made for "Merlin and Vivien."[107]

INTRODUCTION

There are a number of quite early manuscripts relating to this idyll. (H-37) contains fragments of prose sketches as well as verse. (H-33) has very early drafts for passages around lines 246 and 455. (H-32) has a large number of drafts, chiefly in the form of discrete blocks of poetry, covering lines 9-81, 150-192, 306-329, 386-391. (H-47) contains only two pages of drafts for lines 430-457. The next creative stage is represented by the Huntington Library's (HM-1323), a full draft of the poem, but with many alterations. (Tn-31) is clearly a manuscript copy made up for the printer. It is a ruled notebook with manuscript on various pieces of paper glued in. Evidently the poet cut up a number of his fair drafts and glued them into this notebook for his typesetters.

There is one puzzle surrounding "Balin and Balan." Sir James Knowles, a close friend of the poet, gave Tennyson's son Hallam what he called a "prose sketch" for "Balin and Balan." Hallam printed it in both his Mem-oir of his father and in the annotated Eversley Edition of Tennyson's works. Since Knowles has said that Tennyson dictated the draft to him, we do not expect to find it in the Tennyson manuscripts. But, what we do find

54

are short prose drafts other than the Knowles copy,
and many verse fragments which appear to precede any
prose draft. Sir Charles Tennyson concludes that these
jottings "seem...to represent Tennyson's first thoughts
...and to have been written before the composition of
the prose sketch dictated to Knowles."[108] This sketch
then becomes little more than a curiosity which played
no organic part in the composition of the poem. On
these grounds I have omitted it from this edition.

"Balin and Balan" was readily integrated with the
rest of the Idylls of the King in the 1886 New Miniature Edition. Tennyson's life was now essentially complete. He worked on his last poems, helped his son and
biographer prepare an annotated edition of his works,
and reminisced. But in 1891 he instructed his son to
insert one more line into the Epilogue to the Idylls
(1.38), describing Arthur as "Ideal manhood closed in
real man." This was first published in the Edition Deluxe of 1899. In 1908 the Eversley Edition, with Tennyson's notes, was published, and the long period of
the growth of the Idylls finally came to an end.

NOTES

(Hallam Tennyson's Memoir of his father is a primary
source for any study of Tennyson's life. His first
draft, privately published in a limited edition of
four volumes, titled Materials for a Life of A.T. Collected for My Children appeared without notation of
publisher or date of publication. In these notes it
is referred to as Mat. The published biography, Alfred
Lord Tennyson, A Memoir (London, 1897) is designated
Mem.)

1. Mem., I, 118.

2. Ibid., pp. xv-xvi.

3. Mat., II, 220.

4. Philadelphia, 1895.

5. For further information on Wise and his work, see:
Wilfred Partington, Forging Ahead, The True Story of the
Upward Progress of Thomas James Wise (New York, 1939);
Fannie E. Ratchford, ed. Letters of Thomas J. Wise to
John Henry Wrenn (New York, 1944); William B. Todd, ed.
Thomas J. Wise Centenary Studies (Austin, 1959).

6. W. Robertson Nicoll and Thomas J. Wise, eds. Literary Anecdotes of the Ninteenth Century, (London, 1898),
II, 219-272.

7. Ratchford, p. 59.

8. Todd, p. 113.

9. J. C. Thomson, Bibliography of the Writings of Alfred Tennyson (Wimbledon, 1905), p. iii.

10. New York, 1934.

11. Cornhill, CLIII (1936), 534-557; reprinted in
Charles Tennyson, Six Tennyson Essays (London, 1954),
pp. 153-187.

12. Christopher Ricks, ed. The Poems of Tennyson
(London, 1969).

NOTES

13. Letter to the author dated 17 February 69.

14. James Knowles, "Aspects of Tennyson Ⅱ (A Personal Reminiscence)," The Ninteenth Century, XXXIII (January 1893), 168.

15. Mem., I, 268.

16. Ibid., p. 378.

17. Knowles, p. 168.

18. Mem., I, 457.

19. "the essential Tennyson is a morbid and unhappy mystic...afraid of death, and sex, and God." Harold Nicolson, Tennyson, Aspects of His Life, Character, and Poetry (London, 1925), pp. 27-28.

20. Mem., I, 109.

21 Charles Tennyson, Alfred Tennyson (London, 1949), p. 146.

22. Mem., I, 138.

23. Ibid., p. 153.

24. Hallam, Lord Tennyson, ed. Idylls of the King (London, 1908), p. 436.

25. Kathleen Tillotson, "Tennyson's Serial Poem," Mid-Victorian Studies (London, 1965), p. 82.

26. l. 28.

27. ll. 30-31.

28. (John Sterling), "Poems by Alfred Tennyson," The Quarterly Review, LXX, CXL (September 1842), 401.

29. Charles Tennyson, Alfred Tennyson, p. 297.

30. Mem., I. p. 218.

57

NOTES

31. Ibid, pp. 274-275.

32. Charles Tennyson, ed. The Idylls of the King and The Princess (London, 1956), p. 17.

33. Mem., I, 376-377.

34. Charles Tennyson, Alfred Tennyson, p. 299.

35. Mem., I, 414; Mat., II, 161.

36. American Book Prices Current, (1925-1926), p. 849.

37. Auctioned February 17, 1913 from the library of Matthew C. Borden for $3,200. American Book Prices Current, (1912-1913), p. 860.

38. Mat., II, 220.

39. Ibid., I, 161.

40. Ibid., p. 164.

41. Ibid., p. 165.

42. Ibid., p. 167.

43. Ibid., p. 168.

44. Ibid., p. 173.

45. Ibid., p. 180.

46. Charles Tennyson, Six Tennyson Essays, (London, 1954), p. 154, says they are contemporaneous.

47. Mat., II, 180.

48. Mem., I, 425-426.

49. From a manuscript note written in Enid and Nimuë. Tennyson gave the volume to Palgrave, who in turn donated it to the British Museum Library.

50. Mem., I, 419.

NOTES

51. <u>Mat</u>., II, 193.

52. <u>Ibid</u>., p. 195.

53. <u>Mem</u>., II, 202.

54. Charles Tennyson, <u>Six Tennyson Essays</u>, p. 158.

55. <u>Mat</u>., II, 200.

56. <u>Ibid</u>., p. 213.

57. Thomas J. Wise, <u>A Bibliography of the Writings of Alfred, Lord Tennyson</u> (London, 1908), I, 153.

58. <u>Mem</u>., I, 437.

59. <u>Ibid</u>., p. 444.

60. <u>Mat</u>., II, 236.

61. <u>Mem</u>., I, 457.

62. Hallam Lord Tennyson, <u>Tennyson and His Friends</u> (London, 1911), p. 208.

63. <u>Mem</u>., I, 455.

64. Charles Tennyson, <u>Alfred Tennyson</u>, p. 335.

65. <u>Mem</u>., I, 479-480.

66. <u>Mat</u>., II, 342.

67. Ricks, p. 1465.

68. <u>Mat</u>., II, 79.

69. <u>Mem</u>., II, 53.

70. <u>Mat</u>., III, 88.

71. <u>Ibid</u>., p. 90.

72. <u>Mem</u>., II, 59.

NOTES

73. See Fannie E. Ratchford, _An_ _Exhibition_ _of_ _Manu-_
scripts...Alfred _Lord_ _Tennyson_ (Austin, 1942), p. 10.

74. _Ibid._, p. 14.

75. _Mem._, II, 63.

76. _Ibid._, p. 65.

77. _American_ _Book_ _Prices_ _Current_, (1928-1929), p. 763.

78. _Mat._, III, 107.

79. _Ibid._, II, 220.

80. _Mem._, II, 83.

81. _Mat._, III, 134.

82. _Ibid._, p. 138.

83. _Mem._, II, 100.

84. _Mat._, II, 218.

85. _Mem._, II, 39.

86. _Ibid._, p. 104.

87. Charles Tennyson, _Alfred_ _Tennyson_, p. 394.

88. _Mat._, III, 177.

89. _Book_ _Prices_ _Current_, XLII, (1927-1928), p. 944.

90. _Mat._, III, 179.

91. Fannie E. Ratchford, _Certain_ _Ninteenth_ _Century_
Forgers (Austin, 1946), p. 46.

92. _Mem._, I, 471.

93. _Mat._, III, 133.

94. _Ibid._, p. 178.

NOTES

95. Charles Tennyson says a full year in his _Alfred Tennyson_, p. 397.

96. _Mem._, II, 113.

97. _Ibid._, p. 116.

98. Joan E. Hartman, "The Manuscripts of Gareth and Lynette," _Harvard Library Bulletin_, XIII, 2 (Spring 1959), 241.

99. _Mat._, III, 177. There is debate on the title. Wise insists on saying _Imperial_ Library Edition. (See Wise, II, 30.) Edgar F. Shannon disagrees in "The Proofs of _Gareth and Lynette_ in the Widener Collection," _The Papers of the Bibliographical Society of America_, 41, 4 (1947), 323. Wise often worked from publisher's lists. I found a list of Henry S. King bound into the British Museum copy of Henry Elsdale's _Studies of the Idylls of the King_ (press mark 11824 bb 12) which does use the word Imperial. But I avoid it in my text, since it was not used by the family.

100. _Mem._, II, 117.

101. _Mat._, III, 198.

102. _Mem._, II, 119.

103. Wise, I, 224.

104. _Ibid._, II, 33-37.

105. See his _Six Tennyson Essays_, passim.

106. Wise, I, 271.

107. Charles Tennyson, _The Idylls_, p. 19.

108. Charles Tennyson, _Six Tennyson Essays_, p. 170.

BIBLIOGRAPHY FOR THE INTRODUCTION

Anon. Description of an Important Collection of Holograph Manuscript Poems by Lord Tennyson...London, 1914.

Anon. Illustrated Catalogue of Rare Tennyson Items... On Sale by Henry Southern & Co. London, 1902.

Baum, Paull Franklin. "Alfred Lord Tennyson," The Victorian Poets ed. Fredrick E. Faverty. Cambridge Mass., 1956.

Carter, John, Graham Pollard. An Enquiry Into the Nature of Certain Ninteenth Century Pamphlets. London, 1934.

Hartman, Joan E. "The Manuscripts of Tennyson's Gareth and Lynette," Harvard Library Bulletin, XIII, 2 (Spring 1959) 239-264.

Jones, Richard. The Growth of the Idylls of the King. Philadelphia, 1895.

Knowles, James. "Aspects of Tennyson II (A Personal Reminiscence)," The Nineteenth Century, CXCI (January 1893), 164-188.

(Livingston, Luther D.) Bibliography of the First Editions in Book Form of the Works of Alfred, Lord Tennyson...New York, 1901.

Marshall, George O. A Tennyson Handbook. New York, 1963.

Nicoll, W. Robertson, Thomas J. Wise, eds. Literary Anecdotes of the Nineteenth Century. 2 vols. London, 1892.

Nicolson, Harold. Tennyson, Aspects of His Life, Character, and Poetry. London, 1925.

Partington, Wilfred. Forging Ahead. New York, 1939.

Ratchford, Fannie F. An Exhibition of Manuscripts...Alfred Lord Tennyson 1809-1892. Austin, 1942.

--------------------Certain Nineteenth Century Forgeries. Austin, 1946.

BIBLIOGRAPHY FOR THE INTRODUCTION

------------------Letters of Thomas J. Wise to John Henry Wrenn. New York, 1944.

------------------A Review of Reviews. Austin (?) 1949(?).

Ricks, Christopher, ed. The Poems of Tennyson. London, 1969.

------------------Tennyson's Methods of Composition. London, 1966.

Shannon, Edgar F. "Literary Manuscripts of Alfred Tennyson in the Harvard College Library," Harvard Library Bulletin, X, 2 (Spring 1956), 254-274.

------------------"Lord Tennyson," The Victorian Newsletter, 12 (Autumn 1957), 26-27.

------------------"The Proofs of Gareth and Lynette in the Widener Collection," The Papers of the Bibliographic Society of America, 41, 4 (1947), 321-340.

(Sterling, John) "Poems by Alfred Tennyson 1842," The Quarterly Review, LXX, CXL (September 1842), 385-416.

Tennyson, Charles. Alfred Tennyson. London, 1949.

------------------ed. The Idylls of the King and the Princess. London, 1956.

------------------Six Tennyson Essays. London, 1954.

Tennyson, Hallam Lord. Alfred Lord Tennyson, A Memoir. 2 vols. London, 1897.

------------------Materials for a Life of A.T. Collected for My Children. 4 vols. (No place or date.)

------------------ed. Tennyson and His Friends. London, 1911.

BIBLIOGRAPHY FOR THE INTRODUCTION

Thomson, J. C. Bibliography of the Writings of Alfred, Lord Tennyson. Wimbledon, 1905.

Tillotson, Kathleen. "Tennyson's Serial Poem," Mid-Victorian Studies. London, 1965. 80-109.

Todd, William B. ed. Thomas J. Wise Centenary Studies. Austin, 1959.

University of Virginia. The Tennyson Collection Presented... In Honor of Edgar Finley Shannon, Jr. Charlottesville, 1961.

Usher Gallery, Lincoln. Tennyson Collection. Lincoln, 1963.

Wise, Thomas J. The Ashley Library, A Catalogue. 10 vols. London, 1925.

-------------------A Bibliography of the Writings of Alfred, Lord Tennyson. 2 vols. London, 1908.

-------------------A Catalogue of the Library of the Late John Henry Wrenn. 5 vols. Austin, 1920.

SOME EARLY NOTES ON ARTHURIAN LEGEND

(From H-16)

(Following draft of In Memorian lyric "Fair ship, that
from the Italian shore")

    - and there he found ye braunche of an holy herbe
                 that was ye

signe of the Sancgraill & he kne found such tokens but
               he were a good
lyver - M. d'A. 4. B. c.s.

Morgause

    King Lot's wife of Orkney. Arthur's sister.

Her sons

    Gawayn
    Gaheyrs
    Agramaynes
    Gareth

    Son by Arthur
    Modred
    Morgan le fay. [Arths sister]
    wife to King Uriens. Sir Wwayne [her son]
    Sir Aceólon her paramour
    [She steals Arths scabbard as he sleeps & throws it
                 into the lake]

Dame Igraine. Arths mother. wife of the Duke of Tinta-
               gil.
[a mighty duke in Cornewaile]
Sir Ector. King Arth: fostr father. Sir Kay. foster
               broth.
Guenevere. [the king's daughter of Camyliarde]
[Lodegreans] with Gui - Arth. received the table round
               & C.
knights from Lod. the tab. round when complete CL
               knights

    Pellinore
    Sons
    Percyval of Walys

SOME EARLY NOTES ON ARTHURIAN LEGEND

Lamorak (d o)
by the cowherd's wife
Sir Tor.

Nineve [one of the damoysels of ye lake] who de-
                        ceived Merlyn.

King Ban - Elayne
Launcelot

(From Houghton 26)
    King Arthur

As in ye day of blast & driving rain
When the oak roars, & half the lake is white
And the cairn'd mountain is a shadow.   H-26
(See "Merlin and Vivian", 634-636.)

A DISCARDED IDYLLS PASSAGE

(written in another hand)
(From H-97a)

    Not without reason have we raised the land
And drawn a force together, worthy men,
That think with us. If ancient prophecies
[As human providence forecalculates
The possible] & dim presentments
That racing with a people's blood foretell
And fashion sequent change - if these hold firm -
The time is come wherein this state of things
Should fail or alter. Better it should fail,
Than not to alter. Who that sees the court
At full spring - tide of profligacy, who
That looks upon the land, the husbandmen
Withdrawn from wholesome tillage of the soil
To gaze on pomps and shows - The whole long year
Almost one holiday - so week by week
Much treasure lavisht & the people drained -
Who last, that contemplates our greatest grief
The table round, two hundred knights, maintained
At public charge - who by their vows are bound
To deeds of honour, yet at license ride
And pillage, wringing half the little left
From worthier men - who sees all this can doubt
But that the time is here? Up then & do.
For since the older sort with Arthur keep
We younger bloods, that make & suit the time
Must turn it where the choice of judgment leads.

TITLE PAGES

(Manuscript title page for the 1859 edition.   Harvard
MS Eng. 952.8.)

Idyls of the King / By Alfred Tennyson,   DCL / Poet
Laureate / ~~P.L. D.C.L./ God has not made, since Adam
wed// The man more perfect than Arthur/ But a ab
Arthur~~ /'Flos Regum Arthurus / Joseph of Exeter / London / E. Moxon & Co / 1859

(A proof of the Title page for the 1872 edition of <u>Ga-
reth</u> <u>and</u> <u>Lynette, Etc.</u>, in Berg VIII.)

Of these two Idylls, Gareth follows   T.'s I MS
The coming of Arthur & The Last   T.'s I MS
          immediately   T.'s I MS
Tournament precedes Guinevere   T.'s I MS

~~With these two poems the Author concludes the~~ Printed,
~~Idylls of the King./~~   w. I cancellation.
~~Gareth follows THE COMING OF ARTHUR/ and THE~~ Printed,
~~LAST TOURNAMENT precedes GUINEVERE./~~   w. I cancellation.
          concluding   T.'s I MS
The ~~forthcoming~~ volumes of the Library Edition Printed,
will contain the whole series in its proper   w. I
shape and order.   cancellation.

68

Variants

Dedication

These to His Memory--since he held them dear,
Perchance as finding there unconsciously
Some image of himself--I dedicate,
I dedicate, I consecrate with tears--
These Idylls.

       And indeed He seems to me   5

---

1   M   -
 ...His m̸emory, since...dear /̸,   -/,/ (I)   Y-VI
1 (C)   BM-3

2 Perhaps at   there
 As finding i̸n̸ t̸h̸e̸m̸ a̸l̸l̸ unconsciously   H-96a
2 As finding in them all unconsciously   Y-V

3 ...dedicate /̸,   (, I)   Y-VI
3 (C)   BM-3

5 These Idylls. And in truth he seems to me H-96a
5 (Omitted)   Y-V
5   i̸n̸ t̸r̸u̸t̸h̸ stet   I MS
 (Par.) And i̸n̸d̸e̸e̸d̸ He...   Y-VI

DEDICATION

Scarce other than my king's ideal knight,
'Who reverenced his conscience as his king;
Whose glory was, redressing human wrong;
Who spake no slander, no, nor listened to it;
Who loved one only and who clave to her--'   10
Her--over all whose realms to their last isle,

---

6   seem'd   mine own
  ~~For /2/7/ he the pure ideal Knight~~   H-96a
6 Scarce other than mine own ideal Knight   H-96a;H-95a
6 For seem'd not he mine own ideal knight,   Y-V
6   my   I MS
  Scarce other than ~~mine~~ own ideal knight,   Y-VI
6 Scarce other than my own ideal knight,   BM-3
6 (C)   84

7 ...his ~~own~~ conscience...   H-96a
7 'Who...   (' I)   Y-VI
7 (C)   BM-3

8   se glory was
  Who ~~moved abroad~~ redressing human wrong,   H-96a
8 Who moved abroad redressing...   Y-V
8   glory was,
  Whose ~~ranged abroad~~ redressing human wrong,   H-95a

10   h
  ...who cleaved to ~~H~~er -   H-96a
10 ...who cleaved to Her -   Y-V
10 ...her -'   (' I)   Y-VI
10 (C)   BM-3

13 The shadow of ~~whose~~ his life moved like
                        eclipse   H-96a
13 ...loss moved like...   Y-V
13 ...loss moved like eclipse,   Y-VI
13 (C)   67

14 Dimming
  Darkening the world? we...   H-96a
14   That maiden-manly soul
  Darkening the world. ~~We have lost him; he is~~
                     ~~gone;~~   H-95a

72

DEDICATION

Commingled with the gloom of imminent war,
The shadow of His loss drew like eclipse,
Darkening the world. We have lost him: he is gone:
We know him now: all narrow jealousies   15
Are silent; and we see him as he moved,
How modest, kindly, all-accomplished, wise,
With what sublime repression of himself,
And in what limits, and how tenderly;
Not swaying to this faction or to that;   20
Not making his high place the lawless perch
Of winged ambitions, nor a vantage-ground

Alt. after 14
    Before we took him at his height, is gone: H-95a

15   Those ~~our~~ narrow jealousies
   We know him now: ~~we see him as he moved~~   H-96a
15 ...now: our narrow...   Y-V
15 ...now: Those narrow jealousies   H-95a

16 Are silenced, & we see him, as he moved   H-96a
16 Are silenced, & we...   Y-V;H-95a

Alt, after 16
    ~~Along a limited line, how tenderly~~
    ~~Within his limits, & how tenderly~~   H-96a

17-18 (Omitted)   Y-V

17 How modest, bounteous, all-accomplisht, wise   H-95a
17   -
   ...kingly, all accomplish~~t~~, wise,   -/'d/(I)   Y-VI
17 (C)   BM-3

19 Within what limits, & how tenderly -   H-96a;Y-V
19 And in   I MS
   ~~Within~~ what limits...   Y-VI
19 (C)   BM-3

21 ...the lowest perch   H-96a

73

DEDICATION

For pleasure; but through all this tract of years
Wearing the white flower of a blameless life,
Before a thousand peering littlenesses,   25
In that fierce light which beats upon a throne,
And blackens every blot: for where is he,
Who dares foreshadow for an only son
A lovelier life, a more unstained, than his?
✓ Or how should England dreaming of <u>his</u> sons   30
Hope more for these than some inheritance
_____

23 For pleasure̸, but...   H-96a
23 For pleasures, but...   Y-V

24-25 B̸e̸f̸o̸r̸e̸ ̸a̸ ̸t̸h̸o̸u̸s̸a̸n̸d̸ ̸s̸t̸a̸r̸i̸n̸g̸/̸l̸i̸t̸t̸l̸e̸n̸e̸s̸s̸e̸s̸/̸
      Wearing the white flower of h̸i̸s̸ a blameless
                          life,   H-96a

24 ...flower of his blameless...   Y-V

25 ...thousand staring littlenesses   Y-V

Draft 27 ff
    And blackens every blot: for what man lives,
                     was cd wish
    What father, [hoping for] an only son
    A lovelier wife, [a more unstained,] than his?
    Ev'n in a dream
    Or how sd
    A̸n̸d̸ ̸w̸h̸a̸t̸ can England, dreaming of <u>his</u> sons,   H-96a
Draft 27 ff
    ...blot: for what man l̸i̸v̸e̸s̸ breathes
    C̸a̸n̸ ̸w̸i̸s̸h̸ ̸f̸o̸r̸ ̸a̸ ̸d̸e̸a̸r̸ ̸s̸o̸n̸/̸ ̸a̸ ̸l̸o̸v̸l̸i̸e̸r̸ ̸w̸i̸f̸e̸/̸
    S̸h̸a̸d̸o̸w̸i̸n̸g̸ ̸i̸n̸ ̸f̸a̸n̸c̸y̸ ̸f̸o̸r̸ ̸h̸i̸s̸ ̸o̸n̸l̸y̸ ̸s̸o̸n̸
    A̸ ̸l̸o̸v̸l̸i̸e̸r̸ ̸w̸i̸f̸e̸/̸/̸a̸ ̸m̸o̸r̸e̸ ̸u̸n̸s̸t̸a̸i̸n̸e̸d̸/̸ ̸t̸h̸a̸n̸ ̸h̸i̸s̸?̸   H-95a
Draft 27 ff
                         for where is he
    And blackens every blot: for what man breathes
    Who dares foreshadow
    S̸h̸a̸d̸o̸w̸i̸n̸g̸ ̸i̸n̸ ̸f̸a̸n̸c̸y̸ for an only son
    A lovlier life, a more unstain'd, than his?   H-95a

27 ...blot: for what man lives,   Y-V

                        74

DEDICATION

Of such a life, a heart, a mind as thine,
Thou noble Father of her Kings to be,
Laborious for her people and her poor--
Voice in the rich dawn of an ampler day--   35
Far-sighted summoner of War and Waste
To fruitful strifes and rivalries of peace--
Sweet nature gilded by the gracious gleam
Of letters, dear to Science, dear to Art,

---

28 What father, who could wish for an only son,   Y-V

31   s   I MS
   ...for the $\not{r}$e than...   s/ (I)   Y-VI
31 (C)   BM-3

33 Thou noble
   Ø $\not{s}\not{i}\not{l}\not{e}\not{n}\not{t}$ father...   H-96a
33 Thou silent father...   Y-V

34 ...poor -   -/ (I)   Y-VI
34 (C)   BM-3

Alt. after 34 Modest, affectionate, as wise as
                              fair,   H-96a
Alt, after 34 Modest, affectionate, as wise as
                              true,   Y-V

35-37 (Omitted)   Y-V

35 ...day -   -/ (I)   Y-VI
35 (C)   BM-3

36 Thou bright-faced
   $\not{F}\not{a}\not{r}$ $\not{s}\not{i}\not{g}\not{h}\not{t}\not{e}\not{d}$ summoner of war & waste   H-95a

37   fruitful
   To $\not{g}\not{o}\not{o}\not{d}\not{l}\not{i}\not{e}\not{r}$ strifes, ...   H-95a

38 Sweet nature
   $\not{W}\not{i}\not{s}\not{e}\not{l}$ $\not{m}\not{o}\not{d}\not{e}\not{s}\not{t}$, gilded by the gracious gleam   H-96a

DEDICATION

Dear to thy land and ours, a Prince indeed,   40
Beyond all titles, and a household name,
Hereafter, through all times, Albert the Good.

    Break not, O woman's-heart, but still endure;
Break not, for thou art Royal, but endure,

Draft 40 ff
       ~~thy~~ thine own
    Dear to ~~his~~ ~~land~~ & ours, a Prince indeed,
    Beyond all titles,modest, tender, wise
           sacred
    Worthy the ~~great~~ ~~old~~ ~~name~~ of gentleman
    Break O   sacred   still endure
    ~~O~~ ~~break~~ not, woman's heart, but ~~bear~~ ~~it~~ ~~out~~,   H-96a

Alt. after 40 Loving the sacred name of gentle-
                 man   Y-V

41-42 (Omitted)   Y-V

41 ...titles, and...   (, I)   Y-VI
41 (C)   BM-3

43 ...heart, but bear it out,   Y-V
43 ...woman's-heart, ...   -/ (I)   Y-VI
43 (C)   BM-3

DEDICATION

Remembering all the beauty of that star   45
Which shone so close beside Thee that ye made
One light together, but has past and leaves
The Crown a lonely splendour.

                          May all love,
His love, unseen but felt, o'ershadow Thee,
The love of all Thy sons encompass Thee,   50
The love of all Thy daughters cherish Thee,
The love of all Thy people comfort Thee,
Till God's love set Thee at his side again!

---

46 ...Thee, that...   Y-VI
46 (C)   BM-3

47 ...past & left   Y-V
47   l̸e̸a̸v̸e̸s̸/stet   I MS
   ...past and l̸e̸f̸t̸   Y-VI
47 ...past and left   BM-3
47 (C)   67

49 (Omitted)   H-96a;Y-V

53 Till God's love call Thee to his side again!   H-96a
53 ...again.!   ! (I)   Y-VI
53 (C)   BM-3

The Coming of Arthur

Leodogran, the King of Cameliard,
Had one fair daughter, and none other child;
And she was fairest of all flesh on earth,
Guinevere, and in her his one delight.

    For many a petty king ere Arthur came   5
Ruled in this isle, and ever waging war
Each upon other, wasted all the land;
And still from time to time the heathen host
Swarmed overseas, and harried what was left.
And so there grew great tracts of wilderness,   10
Wherein the beast was ever more and more,
But man was less and less, till Arthur came.
For first Aurelius lived and fought and died,
And after him King Uther fought and died,

---

1 Leodogrance, the...of Cameliarde,	A-4521
4 Guinevere and...	A-2104
4 (C)	S-925
5 ...King i̶n̶ ere...	B-I
9 ...left;	A-2104
9 (C)	L-HGI
12 ...came:	A-2104
12 (C)	L-HGI

THE COMING OF ARTHUR

But either failed to make the kingdom one.   15
And after these King Arthur for a space,
And through the puissance of his Table Round,
Drew all their petty princedoms under him,
Their king and head, and made a realm, and reigned.

    And thus the land of Cameliard was waste,   **20**
Thick with wet woods, and many a beast therein,
And none or few to scare or chase the beast;

---

15 ...one: A-2104
15 (C)   L-HGI

19   2   1
   ...head; & reign'd, & made a realm.   B-I

20 And thus
   ~~For~~ ~~all~~ his land of Cameliarde was waste   A-4521
20 ...waste   A-2104
20 (C)   L-HGI

21 And thick with woods...   A-4521;B-I
21 And thick with woods, and...   A-2104
21 Thick   wet   PMS
   ~~And~~ ~~thick~~ with woods, and...   B-VIII
21   T   wet   PMS
   ~~And~~ thick with woods, and...   L-HGI
21 (C)   L-HGII

22 And few there were to scare or chase the
                              beast--   A-4521

23 So that ~~the~~ ~~boar~~ & ~~bear~~, wild-dog & wolf,
                              & boar & bear   A-4521

25 ...the king: A-2104
25 ...the king.   L-HGI
25 (C)   73

29 & the children housed   A-4521

80

So that wild dog, and wolf and boar and bear
Came night and day, and rooted in the fields,
And wallowed in the gardens of the King.   25
And ever and anon the wolf would steal
The children and devour, but now and then,
Her own brood lost or dead, lent her fierce teat
To human sucklings; and the children, housed
In her foul den, there at their meat would growl,   30
And mock their foster-mother on four feet,
Till, straightened, they grew up to wolf-like men,
Worse than the wolves. And King Leodogran
Groaned for the Roman legions here again,
And Caesar's eagle: then his brother king,   35
Urien, assailed him: last a heathen horde,

---

30 To human sucklings; ⍽ ⍽⍽⍽ ⍽⍽⍽⍽⍽ would growl,   A-4521

31 In her foul den, & at their meat   A-4521

33 ...wolves: and...   A-2104
33 (C)   L-HGI

35 ...king   A-2104
35 (C)   L-HGI

sketch 36 ff Horrors! & last a horde of heathen brake
             In on the land, so that he was amazed
             Not knowing whither he should turn for
                        aid -
             Worse than the wolves: & then his brother
                        King,
             Urience, made war upon him: last a horde
             Of heathen vext him so that all amazed
             He knew not whither he sd turn for aid.
             (Par.) But Arthur the great king was newly
                        crown'd,
             To whom he sent 'Arise, & help us thou,
                                                A-4521

36 ⍽⍽⍽⍽⍽⍽⍽ ⍽⍽⍽⍽ ⍽⍽⍽ ⍽⍽⍽⍽ ⍽⍽⍽⍽ /⍽⍽⍽⍽ ⍽ ⍽⍽⍽⍽⍽   B-I
36 Rience   last
   Urien assail'd him: ⍽⍽⍽⍽ a heathen horde,   B-I
36 Rience, assail'd...   A-2104
36 (C)   73

Reddening the sun with smoke and earth with blood,
And on the spike that split the mother's heart
Spitting the child, brake on him, till, amazed,
He knew not whither he should turn for aid.   40

    But--for he heard of Arthur newly crowned,
Though not without an uproar made by those
Who cried, 'He is not Uther's son'--the King
Sent to him, saying, 'Arise, and help us thou!
For here between the man and beast we die.'   45

38	spike	
	...the p̸o̸i̸n̸t̸ that...	B-I
39	till	
	...him, ⱥ ⱥl̸l̸ amazed	B-I
39	...him, till amazed	A-2104
39	(C)	L-HGI
41	...crown'd	A-2104
41	(C)	S-925
42	n uproar	
	...without a t̸u̸m̸u̸l̸t̸ made...	B-I
43	...cried, 'he is...the king	A-2104
43	...the king	S-925
43	(C)	73
44	...him saying...	A-2104
44	(C)	L-HGI
47	But heard at once, ...	A-4521
51	...among the knights,	A-4521
52	many	
	And m̸o̸s̸t̸ of these...	B-I
54	...many tho'...	A-2104
54	(C)	L-HGI
55	...Arthur looking...past	A-2104
55	(C)	L-HGI

And Arthur yet had done no deed of arms,
But heard the call, and came: and Guinevere
Stood by the castle walls to watch him pass;
But since he neither wore on helm or shield
The golden symbol of his kinglihood,   50
But rode a simple knight among his knights,
And many of these in richer arms than he,
She saw him not, or marked not, if she saw,
One among many, though his face was bare.
But Arthur, looking downward as he past,   55
Felt the light of her eyes into his life
Smite on the sudden, yet rode on, and pitched
His tents beside the forest. Then he drave
The heathen; after, slew the beast, and felled

---

56   life
    ...into his ~~heart~~   A-4521

57   yet
    .. sudden, ~~but~~ rode   A-4521

58 (Par.) And Arthur heard & coming quickly, drove T-S
58 ...forest: & he drove   A-4521
58 ...the forest: and he...   A-2104
58 ...the forest. And he...   L-HGI
58 (C)   73

sketch c. 59   from where out
            A stalwart savage all in armour strode
                Chieftain of the horde
            Strode mocking Art thou come to eat me lad
            Said Arthur Thou has eaten up the land
            And thou too, raw, Sir Stripling, will I
                    eat
            But thee the worms, said Arthur, & with
                    might
            Smote him & after deadly contest, slew
            Him falling on the host, they fled: he
                    drave
            The heathen, & he kill'd the beast & fell'd
            The forest, letting in the Sun, &
                    made   H-39

The forest, letting in the sun, and made   60
Broad pathways for the hunter and the knight
And so returned.

      For while he lingered there,
A doubt that ever smouldered in the hearts
Of those great Lords and Barons of his realm
Flashed forth and into war: for most of these,   65
Colleaguing with a score of petty kings,
Made head against him, crying, 'Who is he
That he should rule us? who hath proven him
King Uther's son? for lo! we look at him,

---

59 Scatter'd the heathen slew the beasts & fell'd   T
59 The heathen, & he slew the beasts, & fell'd   A-4521
59 ...the heathen, & he slew...   B-I
59 The heathen, and he slew...   A-2104
59 The heathen, after, slew...   73
59 (C)   84

60 The forest, & let in...   T-S;A-4521;B-I
60 The forest, and let in...   A-2104
60 (C)   73

61 ...knight,   A-2104
61 ...knight;   L-HGI
61 (C)   73

62 ...he linger'd here   A-4521

65 Brake out, & into war; for...   A-4521
65 ...these   A-2104
65 (C)   73

66 (omitted)   A-2104
66 (C)   73

67 ...him crying 'who is he   A-2104
67 (C)   L-HGI

69 son? for when lo! we...   A-4521
69 ...him   A-2104
69 ...him,   ,/(I)   L-HGI
69 ...him   L-HGII
69 (C)   69

And find nor face nor bearing, limbs nor voice,   70
Are like to those of Uther whom we knew.
This is the son of Gorloïs, not the King;
This is the son of Anton, not the King.'

And Arthur, passing thence to battle, felt
Travail, and throes and agonies of the life,   75
Desiring to be joined with Guinevere;
And thinking as he rode, 'Her father said
That there between the man and beast they die.
Shall I not lift her from this land of beasts

---

70 ...face, nor...   A-2104
70 (C)   L-HGI

71 Are t̶h̶o̶u̶ like...   A-4521

72 ...the king.   A-2104
72 ...the king;   L-HGI
72 (C)   73

73 ...the king.'   A-2104
73 (C)   73

74   And   battle
   (Par.) So Arthur passing thence to front the
                        felt
                        war,   T-C

75 Passionate throes & agonies of the heart   T-C
75 ...of the h̶e̶a̶r̶t̶ life   B-I
75 ...the life   A-2104
75 (C)   S-925

76 Desiring to be joined with
   But lost in musings upon Guinevere   T-C

77 Thought as he rode - her father - said he not,   T-C
77 ...rode 'her father...   A-2104
77 (C)   S-925

78 ...beast we die?   T-C

79 ...not take her...   T-C

THE COMING OF ARTHUR

Up to my throne, and side by side with me?   80
What happiness to reign a lonely king,
Vext--O ye stars that shudder over me,
O earth that soundest hollow under me,
Vext with waste dreams? for saving I be joined
To her that is the fairest under heaven,   85
I seem as nothing in the mighty world,
And cannot will my will, nor work my work
Wholly, nor make myself in mine own realm
Victor and lord. But were I joined with her,
Then might we live together as one life,   90
And reigning with one will in everything
Have power on this dark land to lighten it, ✓
And power on this dead world to make it live.'

    Thereafter--as he speaks who tells the tale--

---

80 And set her on my throne, & side by side?   T-C

82-84 Vext with waste dreams? for saving I be
        join'd   T-C

83 ...earth, that...   A-2104
83 (C)   L-HGI

85 ...fairest of all flesh   T-C

88   the race of
   Wholly, nor prove a victor among man   T-C

89 Victor,   but if we two became as one,   T-C
89 ...lord; but...   A-2104
89 (C)   L-HGI

90   as   life
  ...together t̸o̸/one o̸n̸d̸   T-C

91 ...reigning as one...   T-C

92-93   land
   Have power on this dead w̸o̸r̸l̸d̸ to make it
             live
             c̸h̸a̸n̸g̸e̸   T-C

When Arthur reached a field-of-battle bright   95
With pitched pavilions of his foe, the   world
Was all so clear about him, that he saw
The smallest rock far on the faintest hill,
And even in high day the morning star.
So when the King had set his banner broad,   100
At once from either side, with trumpet-blast,
And shouts, and clarions shrilling unto blood,
The long-lanced battle let their horses run.
And now the Barons and the kings prevailed,
And now the King, as here and there that war   105
Went swaying; but the Powers who walk the world
Made lightnings and great thunders over him,
And dazed all eyes, till Arthur by main might,
And mightier of his hands with every blow,
And leading all his knighthood threw the kings   110

94-133 (Omitted)   T-C;B-I
94-133 (Omitted)   A-2104
94-133 (Added)   73

104 ...prevail'd   73
104 (C)   75

106 Went swaying; but the Lady of the Lake,   H-29a

alt after 106 Who walks the waters in the times of
                   storm,   H-29a

108 by main might   H-39

sketch 109 ff A̶n̶d̶ m̶i̶g̶h̶t̶i̶e̶r̶ o̶f̶ h̶i̶s̶ h̶a̶n̶d̶s̶ w̶i̶t̶h̶/e̶v̶e̶r̶y̶ w̶i̶s̶h̶
                W̶i̶t̶h̶ I̶I̶/?I̶ y̶e̶ k̶n̶o̶w̶ t̶h̶e̶ K̶i̶n̶g̶ a̶t̶ e̶v̶e̶r̶y̶
                          b̶l̶o̶w̶   H-29a

109 And mightier of his hands with every blow (T.'s hand)
                                                        H-29a
109 With 'ha, Sirs, and I King' at every stroke   H-39

110   thru the Kings
     And leading all his knighthood, t̶h̶r̶e̶w̶ t̶h̶e̶ K̶i̶n̶g̶s̶
              o̶v̶e̶r̶t̶h̶r̶o̶w̶   H-29a

THE COMING OF ARTHUR

Carados, Urien, Cradlemont of Wales,
Claudias, and Clariance of Northumberland,
The King Brandagoras of Latangor,
With Anguisant of Erin, Morganore,
And Lot of Orkney. Then, before a voice   115
As dreadful as the shout of one who sees
To one who sins, and deems himself alone
And all the world asleep, they swerved and brake
Flying, and Arthur called to stay the brands
That hacked among the flyers, 'Ho! they yield!'   120
So like a painted battle the war stood
Silenced, the living quiet as the dead,
And in the heart of Arthur joy was lord.
He laughed upon his warrior whom he loved

sketch 110 ff The foremost of his Knighthood thru the
                      Kings
                Carados, Urien, Cradlemont of Wales
                Ulfius & Braslias & Bedivere
                Smote down the rebel lords & men of arms
                And Arthur smote not his own lords, but
                      s̸t̸i̸l̸l̸ made still
                Made for the Kings, & by main might cast
                      down
                And Then King Clariance of Northumberland
                The King Brandagoras of Latangor,
                And Anguisant of Ireland, Morganore
                And Lot of Orkeney.   H-39

117   deems
    ...sins, & d̸r̸e̸a̸m̸s̸ himself...   H-29a

118 ...asleep, their battle brake   H-29a

120 ff That flash'd & hack'd among the flyers. 'Hold'
          Ho, there! We fight to conquer not to kill
          And make our ways to set the land at one
          That all may smite the heathen. Ho! They
                      yield!   H-29a

124 ...upon that warrior...   H-29a

Alt after 126 Glory to thee true knight,' & he replied
          They doubt thee King who will but wan-
                      tonness

88

And honoured most. 'Thou dost not doubt me King,   125
So well thine arm hath wrought for me today.'
'Sir and my liege,' he cried, 'the fire of God
Descends upon thee in the battle-field:
I know thee for my King!' Whereat the two,
For each had warded either in the fight,   130
Sware on the field of death a deathless love.
And Arthur said, 'Man's word is God in man:
Let chance what will, I trust thee to the death.'

    Then quickly from the foughten field he sent
Ulfius, and Brastias, and Bedivere,   135
His new-made knights, to King Leodogran,
Saying, 'If I in aught have served thee well,
Give me thy daughter Guinevere to wife.'

Alt after 126 (continued)
    ~~For thou art he that ever wills the highest~~
       Glory to thee, true Lord! the fire of
          God   H-29a

129 Thine is an arm of flesh: where at the two,   H-29a

130   either
   ...warded ~~other~~ in...   H-29a

134 (Par.) And Arthur from the field of battle
             sent   T-C; B-I
134 (Par.) And Arthur from the field of battle
             sent   A-2104
134 Then quickly from the foughten field he sent
    ~~Then quickly from the battlefield he sent~~   H-29a
134 (C)   73

135 ...Brastias and...   A-2104
135 (C)   S-925

136 ...King Leodogrance,   T-C
136 ...knights to...Leodogran   A-2104
136 (C)   L-HGI

137 Saying 'if I in...   A-2104
137 (C)   S-925

Whom when he heard, Leodogran in heart
Debating--'How should I that am a king,   140
However much he holp me at my need,
Give my one daughter saving to a king,
And a king's son?'--lifted his voice, and called
A hoary man, his chamberlain, to whom
He trusted all things, and of him required   145
His counsel: 'Knowest thou aught of Arthur's birth?'

Then spake the hoary chamberlain and said,
'Sir King, there be but two old men that know:
And each is twice as old as I; and one
Is Merlin, the wise man that ever served   150
King Uther through his magic art; and one

---

139 ...heard Leodogrance in...   T-C

140   ing
     Debat*ed* how...   T-C
140 Debating - how...   A-2104
140 (C)   L-HGI

141 ...me in my...   T-C

143   lifted his voice &
     And thereupon he call'd   T-C
143 ...son - lifted...   A-2104
143 ...son' - lifted...   L-HGI
143 (C)   73

144 His chamberlain, a hoary man, to whom   T-C

146 ...counsel 'knowest...birth'?   A-2104
146 ...birth'?   S-925
146 (C)   70

147-148 (Par.) O King he said there be *two* *and* *each*
                    but two that know,   T-C
147 ...said   A-2104
147 (C)   S-925

148 'Sir king...   A-2104
148 (C)   73

Is Merlin's master (so they call him) Bleys,
Who taught him magic; but the scholar ran
Before the master, and so far, that Bleys
Laid magic by, and sat him down, and wrote   155
All things and whatsoever Merlin did
In one great annal-book, where after-years
Will learn the secret of our Arthur's birth.'

    To whom the King Leodogran replied,
'O friend, had I been holpen half as well   160
By this King Arthur as by thee today,
Then beast and man had had their share of me:
But summon here before us yet once more

---

149   each is
      Is thrice as...   T-C

152 ...him] Bleyse   T-C
152 ...Bleys   A-2104
152 (C)   S-925

153 ...,but the taught forwent   T-C

154 The teacher & so far that Bleyse surceased   T-C

155 Laid magic by
        weaker
    H̸i̸s̸ v̸i̸r̸t̸u̸t̸i̸e̸s̸, & sat d̸o̸w̸n̸ & wrote   T-C

156 All things whatever Merlin said or did   T-C

157 ...great b̸o̸o̸k̸ annal - book where...   T-C
157 ...where after years   A-2104
157 (C)   L-HGI

158 Will find the secret...   T-C

159 (Par.) Then spake the King Leodogran & said   T-C
159 ...replied   A-2104
159 (C)   S-925

163 But go & call before us whom he sent   T-C
163 ...us o̸n̸c̸e̸ a̸g̸a̸i̸n̸ yet...   B-I

Ulfius, and Brastias, and Bedivere.'

    Then, when they came before him, the King said,   165
'I have seen the cuckoo chased by lesser fowl,
And reason in the chase: but wherefore now
Do these your lords stir up the heat of war,
Some calling Arthur born of Gorloïs,
Others of Anton? Tell me, ye yourselves,   170
Hold ye this Arthur for King Uther's son?'

    And Ulfius and Brastias answered, 'Ay.'
Then Bedivere, the first of all his knights
Knighted by Arthur at his crowning, spake-
For bold in heart and act and word was he,   175
Whenever slander breathed against the King-

---

164 ...Brastias and Bedivere.	A-2104
164 ...Bedivere.	L-HGI
164 (C)	69
165 (Par.) These, when...King ask'd	T-C
165 ...him, the king ask'd	A-2104
165 ...him, the king said,	S-925
165 ..., the king said,	L-HGI
165 (C)	73

166-168 *W̸h̸e̸r̸e̸f̸o̸r̸e̸ t̸h̸e̸s̸e̸ l̸o̸r̸d̸s̸ s̸t̸i̸r̸r̸'d̸ u̸p̸ t̸h̸e̸ h̸e̸a̸t̸*
                         o̸f̸ w̸a̸r̸   B-I

166 ...fowl	A-2104
166 (C)	S-925
168 Wherefore these lords stirr'd up...	T-C
168 ...war	A-2104
168 (C)	L-HGI
170 ...of Anton. Tell...	A-2104
170 (C)	L-HGI
172 (Par.) Then Ulfius...	T-C
172 ...answer'd 'Ay'	A-2104
172 ...answer'd 'Ay.'	S-925
172 (C)	L-HGI

'Sir, there be many rumours on this head:
For there be those who hate him in their hearts,
Call him baseborn, and since his ways are sweet,
And theirs are bestial, hold him less than man: 180
And there be those who deem him more than man,
And dream he dropt from heaven: but my belief
In all this matter--so ye care to learn--
Sir, for ye know that in King Uther's time
The prince and warrior Gorlois, he that held   185
Tintagil castle by the Cornish sea,
Was wedded with a winsome wife, Ygerne:

---

173 But Bedivere,...	T-C
173 Then	
B̷u̷t̷ Bedivere...	B-I
173 ...Bedivere the...	A-2104
173 (C)	S-925

174 After his crowning made by Arthur, said -	T-C
174 ...crowning, s̷a̷i̷d̷ &̷ spake -	B-I

175 For bold was he in heart, & act & word	T-C
175 For bold w̷a̷s̷ h̷e̷ in...	B-I

176 ...the king -	A-2104
176 (C)	73

177 Sir	
(Par.) For, there...	T-C

179-180 Call him base-born & hold him less than man	T-C

183 ...matter - if ye care to know -	T-C

185 ...he who held	T-C

186 Tintagel castle...	T-C
186 Tintagel castle...	A-2104
186 (C)	L-HGI

187 ...wife Ygraine	T-C
187 ...wife, Igerne:	B-I
187 ...wife, Igerne:	A-2104
187 (C)	S-925

And daughters had she borne him,--one whereof,
Lot's wife, the Queen of Orkney, Bellicent,
Hath ever like a loyal sister cleaved   190
To Arthur,--but a son she had not borne.
And Uther cast upon her eyes of love:
But she, a stainless wife to Gorloïs,
So loathed the bright dishonour of his love,
That Gorloïs and King Uther went to war: 195
And overthrown was Gorloïs and slain.
Then Uther in his wrath and heat besieged
Ygerne within Tintagil, where her men,
Seeing the mighty swarm about their walls,
Left her and fled, and Uther entered in,   200
And there was none to call to but himself.

---

188 ...one thereof   T-C
188 ...whereof   A-2104
188 (C)   70

190 Hath
    W̶h̶ø̶ ever...   T-C

193 And she...   T-C
193 ...she a...   A-2104
193 (C)   L-HGI

194 So
    B̶u̶t̶ loathed...   T-C
194 ...love   A-2104
194 (C)   L-HGI

195 at
    Th̶e̶n̶ Gorlois...   T-C

197 And Uther...   T-C

198 Ygraine within Tintagel & her...   T-C
198 ...Tintagel...   A-2104
198 (C)   L-HGI

199   ir
    ...mighty host about the K̶i̶n̶g̶ walls   T-C
199   swarm
    ...mighty h̶o̶s̶t̶ about...   B-I

So, compassed by the power of the King,
Enforced she was to wed him in her tears,
And with a shameful swiftness: afterward,
Not many moons, King Uther died himself,   205
Moaning and wailing for an heir to rule
After him, lest the realm should go to wrack.
And that same night,the night of the new year,
By reason of the bitterness and grief
That vext his mother, all before his time   210
Was Arthur born, and all as soon as born
Delivered at a secret postern-gate
To Merlin, to be holden far apart
Until hi hour should come; because the lords
Of that fierce day were as the lords of this,   215
Wild beasts, and surely would have torn the child

---

202 So compass'd...the king   A-2104
202 ...the king,   S-925
202 (C)   73

203 ...him all in tears,   T-C

204 ...swiftness: after this   T-C
204 ...swiftness; after which,   B-I
204 ...swiftness; after which,   A-2104
204 ...swiftness: after which,   L-HGI
204   afterward   (I MS - another hand)
    ...swiftness: ~~after which,~~   B-VIII
204 (C)   L-HGII

205 ...himself   A-2104
205 (C)   L-HGI

206 ...heir to rule   A-2104
206 (C)   L-HGI

208-209 And that same night by reason of the grief   T-C

208   the night of the new year   (Not T.'s hand)
    ...night, ~~by reason of the grief~~   B-I
208 ...year   A-2104
208 (C)   S-925

211 Arthur was born, & ...   T-C

Piecemeal among them, had they known; for each
But sought to rule for his own self and hand,
And many hated Uther for the sake
Of Gorloïs. Wherefore Merlin took the child,   220
And gave him to Sir Anton, an old knight
And ancient friend of Uther; and his wife
Nursed the young prince, and reared him with her own;
And no man knew. And ever since the lords
Have foughten like wild beasts among themselves,   225
So that the realm has gone to wrack: but now,

---

217 A̶m̶o̶n̶g̶ t̶h̶e̶m̶ Piecemeal among...   T-C

220 Of Gorlois: then did Merlin take the child   T-C
220   Wherefore   took
    Of Gorlois. T̶h̶e̶n̶ d̶i̶d̶ Merlin t̶a̶k̶e̶ the child,   B-I
220 ...Gorlois: wherefore...   A-2104
220 (C)   L-HGI

221 ...to Sir Hector, an...   T-C

223 Suckled the prince...   T-C
223 ...own -   A-2104
223 (C)   S-925

224 ...knew: but ever...   T-C
224 ...knew: and...   A-2104
224 (C)   L-HGI

225 ...themselves   A-2104
225 (C)   S-925

226 ...realm hath gone to wrack; & now,   T-C

227 ...[for the hour...   T-C

229 Proclaiming 'here...king'   A-2104
229 Proclaiming 'Here...king,'   S-925
229 Proclaiming, 'Here...king,'   L-HGI
229 (C)   69

230 ...cried 'Away...   A-2104
230 ...cried, 'Away...   L-HGI
230 (C)   69

This year, when Merlin (for his hour had come)
Brought Arthur forth, and set him in the hall,
Proclaiming, "Here is Uther's heir, your king,"
A hundred voices cried, "Away with him!   230
No king of ours! a son of Gorloïs he,
Or else the child of Anton, and no king,
Or else baseborn." Yet Merlin through his craft,
And while the people clamoured for a king,
Had Arthur crowned; but after, the great lords   235
Banded, and so brake out in open war.'

Then while the King debated with himself
If Arthur were the child of shamefulness,
Or born the son of Gorloïs, after death,
Or Uther's son, and born before his time,   240

---

231 ...Gorlois, he: A-2104
231 ...Gorlois he: S-925
231 (C)   L-HGI

232 Or else of child of Hector & ...   T-C
232 ...Anton and...   A-2104
232 (C)   L-HGI

233 ..., thro his power,   T-C
233 ...baseborn.' Yet...craft   A-2104
233 ...baseborn.' Yet...craft,   (, P)   S-925
233 ...baseborn.' Yet...   L-HGI
233 (C)   69

234 (Omitted T-C; B-I;A-2104)
234 While all the people clamour'd for their King, (PMS)
                                                   S-925
234 (C)   L-HGI

235 ...crown'd: & after...   T-C
235 ...great Lords   A-2104
235 (C)   L-HGI

237 ...debated in himself,   T-C
237 ...the king...   A-2104
237 (C)   73

239 ...born, the...   A-2104
239 (C)   L-HGI

Or whether there were truth in anything
Said by these three, there came to Cameliard,
With Gawain and young Modred, her two sons,
Lot's wife, the Queen of Orkney, Bellicent;
Whom as he could, not as he would, the King   245

---

242 ...to Cameliarde   T-C
242 ...Cameliard   A-2104
242 (C)   S-925

243 With Modred & with Gawain, her...   T-C
243 With Modred & young Gawain, her...   B-I
243 With Modred and young Gawain, her...   A-2104
243 (C)   L-HGI

245 Whom, as he might Leodogran entertain'd.   T-C
245 ...the king   A-2104
245 (C)   73

246 And while they sat at meat he ask'd the Queen   T-C
246 Feasted, & ask'd her, as...   B-I
246 F̶e̶a̶s̶t̶e̶d̶/ a̶n̶d̶ a̶s̶k̶'̶d̶ h̶e̶r̶, as they sat at meat A-2104
    Made feast for, saying   PMS
246 Feasted, and ask'd her, as they sat at meat,   S-925
246 (C)   L-HGI

Sketch   Whence come ye? & she said from Arthur's
after 246   court,
              And he hath vanquish'd all his enemies
              And these & all men hail t̶h̶e̶m̶ him for
                              their king.   T-C
Sketch
after 246   W̶h̶e̶n̶c̶e̶ c̶a̶m̶e̶ y̶e̶? & s̶h̶e̶ s̶a̶i̶d̶ f̶r̶o̶m̶ A̶r̶t̶h̶u̶r̶'̶s̶
                          c̶o̶u̶r̶t̶l̶y̶
            W̶h̶a̶t̶ s̶a̶w̶ y̶e̶ t̶h̶e̶r̶e̶? T̶h̶e̶ b̶r̶a̶n̶d̶ E̶x̶c̶a̶l̶i̶b̶u̶r̶   B-I
Sketch
after 246   Ye came from Arthur's court? think ye this
                          king--
            Brave are his knights, how few soever they be
            Hath body enow to beat his foeman down?
            She said I saw   B-I

Made feast for, saying, as they sat at meat,

  'A doubtful throne is ice on summer seas.
Ye come from Arthur's court. Victor his men
Report him! Yea, but ye--think ye this king-
So many those that hate him, and so strong,   250
So few his knights, however brave they be-

247-251 'A doubtful throne is ice on summer seas
                                (Added in PMS)
      (Par.) Ye come from Arthur's court: think
                      ye this king-
      So few a̸r̸e̸ his knights, how brave soe'er they
                 be-   A-2104
247-251 (247 omitted)
      (Par.) Ye come from Arthur's court: think ye
                   this king -
      Few are his knights, how brave soe'er they
                 be-   S-925
247-251 (Par.) 'Ye come from Arthur's court: a
                    doubtful throne
      Is ice on summer seas - think ye this king-
      Few are his knights, how brave soe'er they
                 be-   L-HGI
247-251 'A doubtful throne is ice on summer seas-
                            (I MS another)
      (Par.) /Ye come from Arthur's court: a̸
                 d̸o̸u̸b̸t̸f̸u̸l̸ t̸h̸r̸o̸n̸e̸ :/   (I)
      I̸s̸ i̸c̸e̸ o̸n̸ s̸u̸m̸m̸e̸r̸ s̸e̸a̸s̸ ̸ think ye this king-
      S̸o̸ f̸e̸w̸   Stet   I MS
      Few are his knights, how brave soe'er they be-
                       B-VIII
247-251 ...seas-
      Ye come from Arthur's court: think ye this
                    king-
      So f   however
      F̸ew are his knights, h̸o̸w̸ brave s̸o̸e̸'̸e̸r̸ they I MS
                 be-   L-HGII
247-251   ...seas-
      Ye come from Arthur's court: think ye this
                    king-
      So few his knights, however brave they be-   69
247-251 (C)   73

Hath body enow to hold his foemen down?'

'O King,' she cried, 'and I will tell thee: few,
Few, but all brave, all of one mind with him;
For I was near him when the savage yells   255
Of Uther's peerage died, and Arthur sat
Crowned on the daïs, and his warriors cried,
"Be thou the king, and we will work thy will
Who love thee." Then the King in low deep tones,
And simple words of great authority,   260

---

252 ...to beat his...   B-I
252 ...enow to beat his foeman down?   A-2104
252 ...enow to beat his foeman down?'   S-925
252 ...to beat his...   69
252 (C)   73

253 (Par.) 'O king' she cried 'and...   A-2104
253 (Par.) 'O king,' she cried, 'and...   S-925
253 (Par.) 'O king,'...   L-HGI
253 (C)   73

254 ...him-   A-2104
254 (C)   S-925

257 ...cried   A-2104
257 (C)   S-925

258 Be...king and...will,   A-2104
258 ...king and...will,   S-925
258 (C)   L-HGI

259 Who love thee' then the king in low sweet
                        tones   A-2104
259 Who love thee" Then the king in low sweet
                        tones,   S-925
259   low deep   I MS
   ...the king in deep 𝑙𝑜𝑤 𝑡𝑜𝑛𝑒𝑠   L-HGI
259 ...the king in...   L-HGII
259 (C)   73

Bound them by so strait vows to his own self,
That when they rose, knighted from kneeling, some
Were pale as at the passing of a ghost,
Some flushed, and others dazed, as one who wakes
Half-blinded at the coming of a light.   265

   'But when he spake and cheered his Table Round
With large, divine, and comfortable words,
Beyond my tongue to tell thee--I beheld

---

262 That as they...   B-I
262 That as they...   A-2104
262   when   I MS
   That a̸s̸ they...   L-HGI
262 (C)   L-HGII

(263-269 underwent numerous changes which, for the sake
of clarity, are grouped in blocks.)

Sketch C. 263-268
    Yet I when next he spake & bad think
    Bold of the boldest with all gentleness,
    Pure of the purest with all warmth of love-
    'Be ye my Table Round & work my will
    And change the fashion of the world' I saw   T-S

Sketch C. 263-268
    Were pale as at the passing of a ghost,
    One red as fire: & what his knighthood sware
    I heard not; but one told me, that the King
    Had bound his knights to walk the ways of life
    Bold as the boldest among men, & yet
    Pure as the purest among women--vows
    Scarce to be kept by men: yet when he spake
    'Be ye my table round & work my will
    And change the fashion of the world' I saw   A-S
          (Variants for C. 263-268 cont. on next page)

From eye to eye through all their Order flash

Sketch C. 263-268

        Then Arthur spake 'Be ye my Table Round when
                ye fight
        Be boldest of the boldest in your wars, when ye
                speak,
        Be truest of the Truest in your words, when ye
                love,
        Be purest of the purest in your loves,
        And walk the ways of our fair father Xt
        And change the world.'
                And while he spoke I saw   A-S
263-268 Were red as chidden boys, & others pale,
        Some trembled & one wept; but when he spake,
        ~~Call'd them his Table Round/ the flower of men~~
        ~~To serve as model for the world to be/~~
        ~~And/told them those high vows might well be~~
                ~~kept~~
        ~~So that they loved him utterly~~-I beheld   B-I
263-268 'Be ye my Table Round & work my will
        My vows are not too high & hard to keep
        So that ye love me utterly'   B-I

First Printed Version

263-268 Were red as chidden boys, and others pale,
        Some trembled and one wept; but when he
                spake,
        'Be ye my Table Round and work my will
        My vows are not too high and hard to keep
        So that ye love me utterly' I beheld   A-2104
263-268 Were red as chidden boys, and others pale,
        Some trembled and one wept; but when he
                spake,
        "Be ye my Table Round and work my will:
        My vows are not too high and hard to keep
        So that ye love me utterly," I beheld   S-925

A momentary likeness of the King: 270

---

263 (C save) ...ghost.
264-268 (Omitted)
Alt. line after 263 ~~But when he spake thereafter I~~
                    ~~beheld~~
Subsequent alt. lines at page bottom in I MS
        Yet I-when first he spake "be ye my Knights!
        Bold of the boldest with all gentleness
        Pure of the purest with all warmth of love
        And change the fashions of the world."   I
                      saw   L-HGI
Alt. lines after 263
        Then spake the King "be ye my Table Round!
        Be boldest of the boldest when ye fight,
        Be truest of the truest when ye speak
        Be purest of the purest when ye love
        And change the world" and while he spake I saw
                        (I MS-another hand)
                                   B-VIII

264-268 Some flush'd & others dazed as men who wake
        Half blinded by a sudden-coming light.
        But when he spake & cheer'd his Table Round
        With large divine & comfortable words
        Beyond my tongue to tell thee-I beheld
                        (I MS-another hand)
                                   B-VIII
263 (C)   L-HGII
264-268 added w. following variants
264 ...dazed as...   L-HGII
265 Half blinded by a sudden-coming light. L-HGII
266 (Par.) But...   L-HGII
267 With large divine and comfortable words L-HGII

264-266 (C)   69

267 (C)   86

269 ...their order...   A-2104
269 (C)   L-HGI

270 ...the king: A-2104
270 (C)   73

And ere it left their faces, through the cross
And those around it and the Crucified,
Down from the casement over Arthur, smote
Flame-colour, vert and azure, in three rays,
One falling upon each of three fair queens,   275
Who stood in silence near his throne, the friends
Of Arthur, gazing on him, tall, with bright
Sweet faces, who will help him at his need.

    'And there I saw mage Merlin, whose vast wit
And hundred winters are but as the hands   280
Of loyal vassals toiling for their liege.

    'And near him stood the Lady of the Lake,
Who knows a subtler magic than his own--

---

272 ...the crucified,	A-2104
272 C	P MS
...the crucified,	L-HGI
272 (C)	L-HGII
274 Flame colour, ...rays	A-2104
274 ...rays	S-925
274 (C)	69
275 One each	
~~Each~~ falling upon ~~one~~ of...	B-I
278 ...his need~~/~~ ~~in his ways~~	B-I
278 ...need	A-2104
278 (C)	S-925
279-281 (Omitted)	A-2104
279-281 (C)	S-925
282 (No par.) And near...of the lake	A-2104
282 ...of the lake	S-925
282 (C)	L-HGI
284 ...wonderful,	A-2104
284 (C)	S-925

sketch 285 ~~Who/gave the King his brand Excalibur~~
        ~~To fight the heathen~~   B-I

Clothed in white samite, mystic, wonderful.
She gave the King his huge cross-hilted sword,   285
Whereby to drive the heathen out: a mist
Of incense curled about her, and her face
Wellnigh was hidden in the minster gloom;
But there was heard among the holy hymns
A voice as of the waters, for she dwells   290
Down in a deep; calm, whatsoever storms
May shake the world, and when the surface rolls,
Hath power to walk the waters like our Lord.

---

285 She
     A̶n̶d̶ gave...   B-I
285 And gave the king his huge cross hilted sword A-2104
285 She gave the king his huge cross-hilted sword S-925
285 ...the king his...   L-HGI
285 (C)   73

286   out
     ...the heathen f̶r̶o̶m̶ h̶i̶s̶ r̶e̶a̶l̶m̶-her face   B-I
286   - a cloud   I MS
     Of incense curl'd about her, &   I MS
     Whereby to drive the heathen out - her face   A-2104
286 ...out: her face   L-HGI
286 (C)   L-HGII

287 (Omitted) (B-I;A-2104;L-HGI)
287 (Added, I MS)   B-VIII
287 ...her, and...   ,/ (I)   L-HGII
287 (C)   69

288 Well nigh...gloom,   A-2104
288 ...gloom,   L-HGI
288 (C)   L-HGII

291 ...deep, calm whatsoever...   A-2104
291 ...deep, calm, whatsoever...   S-925
291 ...deep, calm...   69
291 (C)   86

(After 291, ll. 279-281 were printed in A-2104. This
was C. in S-925.)

'There likewise I beheld Excalibur
Before him at his crowning borne, the sword   295
That rose from out the bosom of the lake,
And Arthur rowed across and took it--rich
With jewels, elfin Urim, on the hilt,
Bewildering heart and eye--the blade so bright
That men are blinded by it--on one side,   300
Graven in the oldest tongue of all this world,
"Take me," but turn the blade and ye shall see,

---

294 (Par.) There...   A-2104
294 (C)   S-925

298 ...Urim; on...   A-2104
298 (C)   S-925

300 ...side   A-2104
300 (C)   S-925

301 ...world   A-2104
301 (C)   S-925

302 ...and you shall...   B-I
302 ...me," but...and you shall see,   ,/,/ (I)   A-2104
302 ...and you shall...   S-925
302 (C)   73

303 ...yourself,   (, I)   A-2104
303 (C)   S-925

304 ...away!" and sad...   (! I)   A-2104
304 (C)   L-HGI

305 ...him,   ,/ (I)   A-2104
305 (C)   S-925

306 "Take...   "/ (I)   A-2104
306 (C)   S-925

307 ...far-off;" so...   (; and" I)   A-2104
307 ...far-off"; so...   S-925
307 (C)   L-HGI

And written in the speech ye speak yourself, ✓
"Cast me away!" And sad was Arthur's face
Taking it, but old Merlin counselled him,   305
"Take thou and strike! the time to cast away
Is yet far-off." So this great brand the king
Took, and by this will beat his foemen down.'

    Thereat Leodogran rejoiced, but thought
To sift his doubtings to the last, and asked,   310
Fixing full eyes of question on her face,
'The swallow and the swift are near akin,
But thou art closer to this noble prince,
Being his own dear sister;' and she said,
'Daughter of Gorloïs and Ygerne am I;'   315

---

308 Took, and...		,/ (I)	A-2104
308 (C)			S-925
310		&	
...this matter to the last, he ask'd			T-C
310 ...ask'd,		(, I)	A-2104
310 (C)			S-925
311 ...face,		(, I)	A-2104
311 (C)			S-925
Alt. after 311 Art thou not Arthur's sister & she			
said			T-C
Alt. after 311 A̶r̶t̶ t̶h̶o̶u̶ n̶o̶t̶ A̶r̶t̶h̶u̶r̶'s̶ s̶i̶s̶t̶e̶r̶ & she			
said			B-I
312 ...akin,		(, I)	A-2104
312 (C)			S-925
313 ...prince,		(, I)	A-2104
313 (C)			S-925
314 ...sister,' and she said			A-2104
314 (C)			L-HGI
315 ...& Igraine am...			T-C
315 ...and Igerne am...			B-I
315 ...and Igerne am I'			A-2104
315 (C)			L-HGI

'And therefore Arthur's sister?' asked the King.
She answered, 'These be secret things,' and signed
To those two sons to pass, and let them be.
And Gawain went, and breaking into song
Sprang out, and followed by his flying hair   320
Ran like a colt, and leapt at all he saw:

---

316 ...sister said the King   T-C
316 ...sister' said the King   B-I
316 ...sister' said the King: A-2104
316 ...sister,' said the King.   L-HGI
316 ...sister,' ask ' d...   69
316 (C)   75

317 T̸ø ẃh̸øm̸ She...things' & waved   T-C
317 ...answer'd' these be secret things,' and...   A-2104
317 (C)   L-HGI

318 A signal to her sons to leave the hall   T-C
318 ...pass and...   A-2104
318 (C)   86

319 And Gawain rose & whistling as he rose   T-C

321 ...leapt at everything   T-C

322 ...his ear̸s beside...   T-C

323 ..half-heard what made him afterwards   T-C
323   the same that
    ...heard; ẃh̸át̸ m̸ád̸é h̸ím̸ afterward   B-I
323 ...half heard...   A-2104
323 (C)   84

324 ...throne, & l̸øs̸é h̸ís̸ h̸ striking lose his life   T-C
324   uck   found   doom
    Str̸ík̸é for the throne & striking f̸ín̸d̸ his d̸és̸át̸h̸ B-I
324 ...throne and...   A-2104
324 (C)   L-HGI

But Modred laid his ear beside the doors,
And there half-heard; the same that afterward
Struck for the throne, and striking found his doom.

And then the Queen made answer, 'What know I?   325
For dark my mother was in eyes and hair,
And dark in hair and eyes am I; and dark
Was Gorloïs, yea and dark was Uther too,
Wellnigh to blackness; but this King is fair
Beyond the race of Britons and of men.   330
Moreover, always in my mind I hear
A cry from out the dawning of my life,
A mother weeping,and I hear her say,

---

325   And
    (Par.) Then Bellicent made...   T-C
325 ...answer 'what...   A-2104
325 (C)   L-HGI

328 ...too   A-2104
328 (C)   L-HGI

329 ...blackness, but this king...   A-2104
329 ...this king is...   L-HGI
329 (C)   73

draft 331-335
   ~~I hear it/in my mind but far away~~
   ~~A voice from out the dawning of my life/~~
   ~~My mother weeping/ & I hear her say~~
   ~~'No brother hast thou/ O my pretty maid/~~
              ~~thee~~
   ~~To guard in the rough ways of the world/'~~   T-C

331 Moreover always...   A-2104
331 (C)   73

332 ...life,   (, I)   A-2104
332 (C)   S-925

333 ...say   A-2104
333 (C)   L-HGI

"O that ye had some brother, pretty one,
To guard thee on the rough ways of the world."'   335
'Ay,' said the King, 'and hear ye such a cry?
But when did Arthur chance upon thee first?'

  'O King!' she cried, 'and I will tell thee true:
He found me first when yet a little maid:
Beaten I had been for a little fault   340
Whereof I was not guilty; and out I ran
And flung myself down on a bank of heath,
And hated this fair world and all therein,
And wept, and wished that I were dead; and he--
I know not whether of himself he came,   345
Or brought by Merlin, who, they say, can walk
Unseen at pleasure--he was at my side,
And spake sweet words, and comforted my heart,

---

334 Thou hast no brother, O my pretty one,		T-C;B-I
334 "Thou hast no brother O my pretty one (" I)		A-2104
334 "O that ye had some brother, pretty one,		
	(I MS, another)	
"T̸h̸o̸u̸ h̸a̸s̸ n̸o̸ b̸r̸o̸t̸h̸e̸r̸ O̸ m̸y̸ p̸r̸e̸t̸t̸y̸ o̸n̸e̸/		B-VIII
334 (C)		L-HGII
335 ...thee in the rough...		T-C;B-I
335 ...world."	(" I)	A-2104
335 (C)		S-295
336 (Par.) 'Ay' said the King 'and...cry? (? I)		A-2104
336 (Par.) 'Ay' said the King' and...		S-925
336 (C)		L-HGII
338 (Par.) 'O king! she cried' and...		A-2104
338 (Par.) 'O King! she...		L-HGI
338 (C)		73
339 ...maid -		A-2104
339 (C)		L-HGI
341 ...guilty, & out I went		T-C
342 ...myself upon a bank...		T-C
346-347 Or brought by Merlin, who can walk unseen -		T-C

And dried my tears, being a child with me.
And many a time he came, and evermore   350
As I grew greater grew with me; and sad
At times he seemed, and sad with him was I,
Stern too at times, and then I loved him not,
But sweet again, and then I loved him well.
And now of late I see him less and less,   355
But those first days had golden hours for me,
For then I surely thought he would be king.

'But let me tell thee now another tale:
For Bleys, our Merlin's master, as they say,
Died but of late, and sent his cry to me,   360
To hear him speak before he left his life.
Shrunk like a fairy changeling lay the mage;

---

347 Unseen, at...   A-2104
347 (C)   L-HGI

348 He spake...   T-C

351 ...greater with me grew: & sad   T-C

355 ...less,   (I)   A-2104
355 (C)   S-925

356 But these first hours were golden hours to me   T-C
356   days had   for
    ...first ~~hours~~ ~~were~~ golden hours ~~to~~ me,   B-I

357 And then...   T-C

358 (Par.) But...   A-2104
358 (C)   L-HGI

360 ...me,   (, I)   A-2104
360 (C)   S-295

361 To ~~speak~~ hear...   T-C

362 ...mage: (: I)   A-2104
362 ...mage   S-925
362 ...mage,   L-HGI
362 (C)   73

And when I entered told me that himself
And Merlin ever served about the King,
Uther, before he died; and on the night   365
When Uther in Tintagil past away
Moaning and wailing for an heir, the two
Left the still King, and passing forth to breathe,
Then from the castle gateway by the chasm
Descending through the dismal night--a night   370
In which the bounds of heaven and earth were lost--
Beheld, so high upon the dreary deeps
It seemed in heaven, a ship, the shape thereof
A dragon winged, and all from stem to stern
Bright with a shining people on the decks,   375
And gone as soon as seen. And then the two
Dropt to the cove, and watched the great sea fall,
Wave after wave, each mightier than the last,

---

363 So when I went he told...   T-C
363 Só whéń I ćámé hé told...   B-I

364 ...the king,   A-2104
364 (C)   73

365 ...died, and...   A-2104
365 (C)   73

Alt. before 366 That he & Merlin on that night of
                          storm   A-S

366 ...Tintagel...   A-2104
366 (C)   L-HGI

368 ...still king...   A-2104
368 (C)   73

Alt. after 369   Dropt from the castle to the cove,
                     & saw
                     Far off a light at sea such as the moon
                     Crost by a cloud may cast upon the wave A-S

370   dismal
    ...thro' the dreary night...   T-C

371 ...bounds of earth & heaven were...   B-I

112

Till last, a ninth one, gathering half the deep
And full of voices, slowly rose and plunged   380
Roaring, and all the wave was in a flame:
And down the wave and in the flame was borne
A naked babe, and rode to Merlin's feet,

---

sketch c. 372   No
                The wind, no moon, & sea & sky were one
                So black the night: & all at once the two
                Hung as in heaven high on the dreary deep
                Beheld a ship in shape the dragon wing'd,
                        & all
                Bright with a shining people on the
                        decks   A-S

sketch c. 372   high-hung upon the dreary deeps
                        passing
                And flying as it were in heaven - the shape
                A dragon wing'd, a ship from stem to
                        stern   A-S

373 ...in heaven - a ship...   A-2104
373 (C)   L-HGI

376 ...seen: and...   A-2104
376 (C)   L-HGI

377 ...watch'd the waters fall   T-C
377 ...cove and...fall,   (,I)   A-2104
377 ...cove and...   S-925
377 (C)   69

378 ...wave, each...   (,I)   A-2104
378 (C)   S-925

379 ...one gathering...   A-2104
379 (C)   L-HGI

380 Drew in, & full of voices, rose & plunged   T-C

383   babe
     A naked child & laid at Merlin's feet: T-C
383 ...babe and...   A-2104
383 (C)   L-HGI

Who stoopt and caught the babe, and cried "The King!
Here is an heir for Uther!" And the fringe   385
Of that great breaker, sweeping up the strand,
Lashed at the wizard as he spake the word,
And all at once all round him rose in fire,
So that the child and he were clothed in fire.
And presently thereafter followed calm,   390
Free sky and stars: "And this same child," he said,
"Is he who reigns; nor could I part in peace
Till this were told." And saying this the seer

---

384 And Merlin caught...   T-C
384 ...cried 'The...   A-2104
384 (C)   L-HGI

385 ...heir of Uther!'...   T-C
385 ...Uther!' and...   A-2104
385 (C)   L-HGI

386 ...breaker, sweeping...strand,   (,, I)   A-2104
386 (C)   S-925

387 ...word,   (, I)   A-2104
387 (C)   S-925

388 ...once about him...   A-S; B-I
388 ...once about him...fire,   (, I)   A-2104
388 ...once about him...   S-925
388   all around him   (I MS another)
    ...once a̶b̶o̶u̶t̶ h̶i̶m̶ rose...   B-VIII
388 (C)   L-HGII

391 Free sky & stars: a̶l̶l̶ t̶h̶i̶s̶ h̶e̶ & this same child'
                       he said   A-C
391 ...stars: 'and...child' he said,   A-2104
391 (C)   L-HGI

392 ...I pass in peace   A-S
392   part
    ...I p̶a̶s̶s̶ in...   B-I
392 'Is...   A-2104
392 (C)   L-HGI

114

Went through the strait and dreadful pass of death,
Not ever to be questioned any more   395
Save on the further side; but when I met
Merlin, and asked him if these things were truth--
The shining dragon and the naked child
Descending in the glory of the seas--
He laughed as is his wont, and answered me   400
In riddling triplets of old time, and said:

'"Rain, rain, and sun! a rainbow in the sky!
A young man will be wiser by and by;

Alt. for 393 ff.   Till this were told:' ~~small wont~~
                          ~~der not the less/~~
                    ~~If in the/strait and dreadful pass of death~~
                    ~~He wandey'd in his wit/ before he died./~~
                                                                A-S

393 Then ~~suddenl~~ all at once the seer   A-S
393 ...told.' And...   A-2104
393 (C)   L-HGI

394 Went
    ~~Past~~ thro'...   A-S
394 ...the straight and...death,   (, I)   A-2104
394 ...the straight and...   S-925
394 (C)   L-HGI

395 Groaning, nor ever to be question'd ~~any~~ more   A-S

397 ~~Old~~ Merlin, ~~& repeated all he said~~ & ask'd him if
            these things were truth,   A-S

401 ...triplets of the past & said   A-S
401 ...said;   (; I)   A-2104
401 ...said   S-925
401 (C)   L-HGI

402 (Par.) "Rain...   A-2104
402 (C)   L-HGII

403 ...by: A-2104
403 (C)   L-HGI

An old man's wit may wander ere he die.
 Rain, rain, and sun! a rainbow on the lea!   405
And truth is this to me, and that to thee;
And truth or clothed or naked let it be.
 Rain, sun, and rain! and the free blossom blows:
Sun, rain, and sun! and where is he who knows?
From the great deep to the great deep he goes."   410

 'So Merlin riddling angered me; but thou
Fear not to give this King thine only child,
Guinevere: so great bards of him will sing
Hereafter; and dark sayings from of old
Ranging and ringing through the minds of men,   415
And echoed by old folk beside their fires
For comfort after their wage-work is done,
Speak of the King; and Merlin in our time

---

404 A wise man's wit may wander ere he die   A-S

407 ...naked let her be.   A-S

408   free
    ...& the ~~heath~~-blossom blows   A-S

411 ...riddling, made me wroth: but thou   A-S
411 (Par.) So...   A-2104
411 (Par.) "So...   L-HGI
411 (C)   L-HGII

412 ...this king...child   A-2104
412 ...this king...   L-HGI
412 (C)   73

Alt. after 412 ~~Seeing that there be mighty prophecies~~
          ~~Of Arthur some in truth this riddler's own/~~
          ~~That he shall pass away but shall not~~
                    ~~die~~   A-S

414 Such prophecies, & down from ancient time   T-C
414 ...from ~~old~~ of old   B-I
414 Hereafter, and...   ,/ (I)   A-2104
414 (C)   L-HGI

415 Ranging, and...   A-2104
415 (C)   L-HGI

116

Hath spoken also, not in jest, and sworn
Though men may wound him that he will not die,   420
But pass, again to come; and then or now
Utterly smite the heathen underfoot,
Till these and all men hail him for their king.'

     She spake and King Leodogran rejoiced,
But musing 'Shall I answer yea or nay?'   425
Doubted, and drowsed, nodded and slept, and saw,
Dreaming, a slope of land that ever grew,
Field after field, up to a height, the peak
Haze-hidden, and thereon a phantom king,

---

418 ...king - wh Merlin in our days   T-C
418 ...the king...   A-2104
418 (C)   73

419-420 Has echoed saying that he will not die-   T-C

422 Utterly beat the heathen...   T-C

423 ...him as their...   T-C

Sketch 424 ff (Par.) She spake/ & King Leodogran
                       rejoiced
      But musing 'shall I answer yea or nay?'
      Linger 'd & doubted/ but at length he sent
      Olfins & Bastias & Bedivere
      Back to King Arthur/ answering yea/ & he
      Bad Lancelot to go forth/& bring the Queen:
      To whom so brought by Doubtic the high saint/
      Head of the Church in Britain then/ the King
      Was married/ founding on his marriage both/
      And binding by retail vows to his own self/
      The glorious order of his Table/Round
      True men/ to serve as model for the world/
      And be the fair beginning of a time/   B-I
424 ...and king Leodogran...   A-2104
424 (C)   69

425 ...musing 'shall...nay'   A-2104
425 (C)   L-HGI

429 ...king,   , (I)   A-2104
429 (C)   S-925

Now looming, and now lost; and on the slope   430
The sword rose, the hind fell, the herd was driven,
Fire glimpsed; and all the land from roof and rick,
In drifts of smoke before a rolling wind,
Streamed to the peak, and mingled with the haze
And made it thicker; while the phantom king   435
Sent out at times a voice; and here or there

---

431 L̷i̷g̷h̷t̷e̷n̷/d̷ t̷h̷e̷ s̷w̷o̷r̷d̷/ f̷i̷r̷e̷ f̷l̷a̷s̷h̷/d̷/ t̷h̷e̷ s̷h̷e̷p̷h̷e̷r̷d̷
                              l̷a̷y̷   B-I

432 M̷u̷r̷d̷e̷r̷/d̷; & all   B-I
432 And from the roofs in fire up the long hill   T-S
432 ...rick   A-2104
432 (C)   L-HGI

433 Gray drifts of smoke before a creeping breeze   T-S
433   rolling
     ...before a c̷r̷e̷e̷p̷i̷n̷g̷ wind   B-I
433 ...wind   A-2104
433 (C)   L-HGI

435 ...thicker; & the phantom...   T-S

436 Sent forth at times a voice; but those below   T-S

437   toward
     ...pointed t̷o̷ the voice...   B-I

438 ...burnt crying 'no...ours,   ,(I)   A-2104
438 ...burnt crying 'no...   S-925
438 (C)   L-HGI

Alt. for 439 This is a son of Gorlois not the King;   T-S

439 ...Uther, and...ours';   ,(I)   A-2104
439 ...ours';   S-925
439 (C)   70

440 Then with...   T-S

118

Stood one who pointed toward the voice, the rest
Slew on and burnt, crying, 'No king of ours,
No son of Uther, and no king of ours;'
Till with a wink his dream was changed, the haze   440
Descended, and the solid earth became
As nothing, but the King stood out in heaven,
Crowned. And Leodogran awoke, and sent
Ulfius, and Brastias and Bedivere,
Back to the court of Arthur answering yea.   445

    Then Arthur charged his warrior whom he loved

---

441 ...solid fields became   T-S

442   Arthur
    A phantom, & King stood in Heaven   T-S
442 ...nothing, & the King...   B-I
442 As nothing and the king...   A-2104
442 As nothing, and the king...   S-925
442 (C)   73

443 Crown'd; and...   A-2104
443 (C)   L-HGI

444 ...Bedivere   A-2104
444 (C)   L-HGI

Sketch for 446 ff So
        T̷h̷e̷n̷ Arthur bad Sir Lancelot, whom
           he loved
    And honour'd most, ride forth & bring the
           Queen.
    Then stood beside the gateway watching him
    And Lancelot past away among the flowers
    For it was latter April - & return'd
    Among the flowers, in May, with Guinevere
        (I MS on A-2104 after text)

446 Then Arthur bad Sir Lancelot bring the Queen: B-I
446 (No indent.) Then Arthur bad Sir Lancelot bring
          the Queen: A-2104

And honoured most, Sir Lancelot, to ride forth
And bring the Queen;-and watched him from the gates:
And Lancelot past away among the flowers,
(For then was latter April) and returned   450
Among the flowers, in May, with Guinevere.
To whom arrived, by Dubric the high saint,
Chief of the church in Britain, and before
The stateliest of her altar-shrines, the King
That morn was married, while in stainless white, 455
The fair beginners of a nobler time,
And glorying in their vows and him, his knights
Stood round him, and rejoicing in his joy.
Far shone the fields of May through open door,
The sacred altar blossomed white with May,   460
The Sun of May descended on their King,

447-451 (Omitted A-2104; L-HGI)
447-451 (Added in I MS by another hand on B-VIII
   correctly save for following variant)

449 ...the flowers 𝑠𝑜 𝑓𝑜𝑟 𝑡ℎ𝑒𝑛   B-VIII

447-451 (printed in L-HGII with following variants.)

447   u   u/(I)
  ...honor'd   L-HGII
447 (C)   69

448 ...Queen,;-and...   ,/-/(I) L-HGII
448 (C)   69

450 [For...April/] and return'𝘦d /,/(I) L-HGII
450 (C)   69

452 ...saint   A-2104
452 (C)   L-HGI

454 ...the king   A-2104
454 (C)   73

455 ...in maiden white,   B-I;A-2104
455 (C)   L-HGI

They gazed on all earth's beauty in their Queen,
Rolled incense, and there past along the hymns
A voice as of the waters, while the two
Sware at the shrine of Christ a deathless love: 465
And Arthur said, 'Behold, thy doom is mine.
Let chance what will, I love thee to the death!'
To whom the Queen replied with drooping eyes,
'King and my lord, I love thee to the death!'
And holy Dubric spread his hands and spake,   470
'Reign ye, and live and love, and make the world
Other, and may thy Queen be one with thee,
And all this Order of thy Table Round
Fulfil the boundless purpose of their king!'

---

457 ...him, the knights	B-I;A-2104
457 his	I MS
...him, ŧh́é knights	L-HGII
457 (C)	69

458 ...him and...	A-2104
458 ...him, and... ,/ (I)	L-HGII
458 (C)	69

459-469 (Omitted from A-2104 until 73)
(MS variants 459-469)

463 ...there passed among the hymns	PM
466 said	
And Arthur śṕáḱé, 'man's word is God in man.	PM
467 I love thee, & I trust thee, to the death.'"	PM
459-469 added, C	73

470 ...spake	A-2104
470 (C)	L-HGI

473 this Order	
And all ŧh́é Ḱńíǵh́ŧh́óód́ of...	B-I

474 boundless	
...the ḿíǵh́ŧý purpose...	B-I
474 ...king.'	A-2104
474 (C)	73

So Dubric said; but when they left the shrine   475
Great Lords from Rome before the portal stood,
In scornful stillness gazing as they past;
Then while they paced a city all on fire
With sun and cloth of gold, the trumpets blew,
And Arthur's knighthood sang before the King:-   480

'Blow trumpet, for the world is white with May;
Blow trumpet, the long night hath rolled away!
Blow through the living world--"Let the King reign."

'Shall Rome or Heathen rule in Arthur's realm?
Flash brand and lance, fall battleaxe upon helm,   485
Fall battleaxe, and flash brand! Let the King reign.

'Strike for the King and live! his knights have
                        heard

475-513 (Omitted A-2104)
503-513 (Added L-HGI)
475-502 (Added 73)
(Variants for all lines follow below in numerical order
                        of lines.)
c. 475 So (I ?) when they left the shrine the trumpets
                        blew,   B-V

480 And all his knighthood sang before the King.   B-V

485   ,! & lance
    ...brand & p̸i̸e̸r̸c̸e̸ s̸p̸e̸a̸r̸! fall.   B-V

492 Fall battleaxe & flash brand!...   B-V

Alternate stanza after 493
                              strong
    (Par.) Strike battleaxe, & s̸m̸i̸t̸e̸ brand on shield
                        & crest?
                        loves
    The King is he that ever w̸i̸l̸l̸s̸ the best.
                        strong
    Strike battleaxe, & s̸m̸i̸t̸e̸ brand! Let the
                        King reign!   B-V

THE COMING OF ARTHUR

That God hath told the King a secret word.
Fall battleaxe, and flash brand! Let the King reign.

  'Blow trumpet! he will lift us from the dust.   490
Blow trumpet! live the strength and die the lust!
Clang battleaxe, and clash brand! Let the King reign.

  'Strike for the King and die! and if thou diest,
The King is King, and ever wills the highest.
Clang battleaxe, and clash brand! Let the King
                    reign.   495

  'Blow, for our Sun is mighty in his May!
Blow, for our Sun is mightier day by day!
Clang battleaxe, and clash brand! Let the King reign.

  'The King will follow Christ, and we the King
In whom high God hath breathed a secret thing.   500
Fall battleaxe, and flash brand! Let the King reign.'

  So sang the knighthood, moving to their hall.
There at the banquet those great Lords from Rome,
The slowly-fading mistress of the world,

---

494 ...die! for tho' thou...   B-V

495 The King is he that ever...   B-V

501 Clang battleaxe, & clash brand!...   B-V

502   the knighthood
                they slowly   to
 (Par.) So sang the Knighthood moving toward their
                hall
503 There at the marriage feast &   B-V
503 (Par.) Then at the marriage feast came in from
                     Rome   L-HGI
503 (Par.) Then at the marriage feast came in from
                    Rome,   69
503 (C)   73

504 (Omitted still from L-HGI)
504 (Added P)   L-HGII
504 (C)   69

Strode in, and claimed their tribute as of yore.   505
But Arthur spake, 'Behold, for these have sworn
To wage my wars, and worship me their King;
The old order changeth, yielding place to new;
And we that fight for our fair father Christ,
Seeing that ye be grown too weak and old   510
To drive the heathen from your Roman wall,

---

505 Great lords, demanding tribute as of yore.   L-HGI
505   who claim'd the   P MS
    Great lords, d̸ḗm̸ā̸n̸d̸ī̸n̸g̸ tribute as of yore. L-HGII
505 Great lords, who claim'd the tribute as of yore. 69
505 (C)   73

507 To fight my wars, and worship me their king;   L-HGI
507 (C)   73

508 (Omitted)   L-HGI
508 (included in P MS)   L-HGII
508 (C)   69

509 (Omitted)   L-HGI
509   And
    (Complete in P MS with this var.) B̸ū̸t̸ we...   L-HGII
509 (C)   69

510 And seeing ye are grown to old and weak   L-HGI
510   be   too
    And seeing ye ā̸r̸ḗ grown t̸ō̸ ō̸l̸d̸ ā̸n̸d̸ weak   B-VIII
510   S   that
    Ā̸n̸d̸ s̸eeing ye be grown too weak and old   L-HGII
510 (C)   69

THE COMING OF ARTHUR

No tribute will we pay:' so those great lords
Drew back in wrath, and Arthur strove with Rome.

    And Arthur and his knighthood for a space
Were all one will, and through that strength the
                    King   515
Drew in the petty princedoms under him,
Fought, and in twelve great battles overcame
The heathen hordes, and made a realm and reigned.

------

511 And cannot drive the heathen from your wall,   L-HGI
511   To   the Roman   I MS
    ~~And~~ ~~cannot~~ drive the heathen from ~~your~~ wall, B-VIII
511   your
    ...from ~~the~~ Roman...   L-HGII
511 (C)   69

515 Were all   will
    ~~Made~~ ~~but~~ one ~~mind~~ & thro' his knights the King B-I
515 Were all one will and thro' his knights the
                    King   A-2104
515 ...the king   L-HGI
515 (C)   73

516   in
    Drew ~~all~~ the...   B-I

Rejected Passage
    They doubt thee King who will but wantonness
                   and lawless outrage
    The Kings who ruled in Camelot of old time were
                   paramount   H-39

Gareth and Lynette

(Prose draft for lines 1 to 725)
(From H-40)

Lots wife Bellicent, the Queen of Orkney sat in her
castle on the˙ sea & she was lost in thought: for there
had come to her ~~a~~ ~~twelvemonth~~ ~~before~~ a noise that Queen
Guinevere was false with Lancelot: & thereupon the
Queen who had been long haunted by a passion for Sir
Lamorack had yielded herself to him & thus dishonoured
her house.

(Par.) But now she said to herself Lo if Guinevere have
not sinned & this rumour is untrue I shall be the first
woman who have broken the fair order of the Table Round
& made a knight forego his vows & so my name shall go
down thro' the world for ever: but if Guinevere have
sinned the sin will be hers & my shame covered by her

shame.

(Par.) And there came in to her Gareth her son & he said

O mother for here my life is spilt & lost among rocks &

stones that never heard the sound of a trumpet blowing

the knights together in the lists but let me have thy

leave to go to the halls of Arthur & be made knight by

Arthur as my brethren Modred & Gawain are.

(Par.) And she answered Yea my son Gareth so that thou

wilt swear a vow to me to do my will when thou comest to

Arthur. And Gawain sware a vow that he would do her

will. Then the Queen spake & said I have heard for this

long time that Queen Guinevere is false to the King & my

heart is troubled thereby & my life darkened for I love

him.

but thou shalt go & be made knight & seek into this

scandel & dwell among them & bring me word whether there

be truth therein

(Par.) Then said Gareth O mother shall I ask the Knights

of the Table Round whether the King is dishonoured by

his wife Grieved am I that I have taken such a vow.

(Par.) And the Queen said thou hast taken it & shalt a-

bide by it but think not to ask this of the Knights for

they hold together by their vows & are sworn to speak no

slander & from them wilt thou learn nothing but thou
shalt mingle with the thralls of the house & with those
that hand the dish across the bar for these are they
that know the things of a house & delight in the evils
thereof & from them shalt thou learn & bring back the
truth of this matter to me thy mother: for it were
shame that Arthur should be shamed by his own Queen not
knowing, moreover this sin will pass thro all the Table
Round & ruin the King's purpose, if t̷h̷e̷ it be not known
& put an end to.

(Par.) And Gareth said An evil vow have I sworn. Are
not Modred & Gawain (1 ?) than I?

(Par.) And the Queen answer'd Modred & Gawain were liars
from their youth upward but thou hast ever spoken the
truth

(Par.) So Gareth took two of the house & sware them to
silence & disguised himself & came before the King.

(Par.) And the King was holding the feast of Pentecost
at King-Kerldon in Wales.

(Par.) And the sides of the hills were green, & the
earth quickened with flowers & the birds warbled in the
bush for it was the feast of Pentecost.

(Par.) Then came Gareth into hall & he was clad like a

tiller of the s̸o̸i̸l̸ field but his raiment was without

soil & he moved heavily as tho' he were faint & about to

fall & he leaned his hands on the shoulders of those

twain with whom he came & the twain were richly (beseen?)

like those in the court of a King & his hands were the

largest & fairest that ever men saw.

(Par.) And the day was one of driving showers: & as

they drew near to Camelot, sometimes the city gleam'd

out at top while the rest of it was hidden, sometimes

only the middle of it was seen, sometimes only the great

gate of Arthur at the bottom & sometimes it disappeared

altogether. And the two that were with Gareth were a-

mazed & said to him Lo now my lord let us go no further

for we have heard that this is a city of enchanters &

was built by Fairy Kings & Queens

(Par.) And the other said There is no such city: it is

a vision.

(Par.) But Gareth brought them to the great gate: &

there was no gate like it under heaven: for the deeds

of Arthur were sculptured there in strange types & old &

new was mingled together so that it made a man dizzy to

look at it.

(Par.) And the two that were with Gareth stared so long

at the figures on the gateway that it seemed to them

that the tails of the dragons & other strange shapes on

the gate began to move & to twine & to curl.

(Par.) And they caught hold of Gareth saying to him O my

Lord 'The gate is alive.

(Par.) And Gareth lookd also so long that the figures

seemed to him also to move.

(Par.) And there came a blast of music from the town &

the three started back

(Par.) And while they were thus amazed Old Merlin came

out from under the gate. & he saw them staring & askd

Who be ye? my sons?

(Par.) And Gareth answer'd O master we be tillers of the

soil & come to see the state of the King: but these men

are feared to go into the city for they have heard it

was built by enchantment & by fairy Kings & Queens. &

now they have been frighted with this music nor care to

go in

(Par.) And Merlin I will speak the truth as thou hast

spoken it to me: for truly O son this city was built by

a fairy king & many fairy Queens & they came from out

the cleft of a mountain toward the sunrise: & they

built it to the sound of their harps & as thou sayst it

131

is enchanted & nothing in it is what it seems, saving the

King & many hold the city is real & the King is unreal:

& like thou of him for if thou pass under this gateway

thou wilt become subject to this enchantment & the King

will swear thee to vows which it is a shame that a man

should not swear & which yet no man can keep: but if ye

be afeard to swear pass not beneath the gateway but a-

bide here among the cattle of the field: for the city

is built to music, & therefore not built at all, & there-

fore built for ever.

(Par.) And Gareth was angry & answer'd Old Master, hast

thou no reverence for thine own white beard which is

wellnigh as long as thou art tall that thou mockest

strangers - Why mockest thou me & my men who have been

fairspoken to thee?

(Par.) And Merlin answer'd Have ye never heard the rid-

dling of the bards? I mock thee because thou mockest me

& all that look at thee. Thou art not what thou seemest

but I know thee & who thou art, & thou goest up to mock

the Great King.

(Par.) And Gareth was abashed & said to his men Here

sits a white lie like a little ghost on the threshold of

our enterprise. But let my good mother - heaven bless

her - bear the blame.

(Par.) And he & his men past up into the city & they had never seen stranger or statelier palaces & they came to the doors of the great Hall & Arthur was speaking to his knights & rendering thanks for such service as they had done him in subduing the heathen: & Gareth saw in the eyes of each of them loyalty & clear honour sparkling like the morning star in heaven, & high promise, & the light of victory, And glory t̸o̸ b̸e̸ gain'd & glory yet to be gaind.

(Par.) Then went Gareth & lived & ate among the grooms; & he heard them talk of the love that was between Lancelot & the King & at times they talked in such fashion that he brake out into whistling & into singing; so that the thralls marvelled at him & at last reverenced him; & he was the best among them at putting the bar & stone;& if there ever chanced to be a tourney he was ever at the barrier & his eyes kindled.

(Par.) But after a while he tired of their company & on a morning when the great King paced before the Hall alone, he came upon him & said

(Par.) I am Gareth thy nephew & I bound myself by a foolish vow to one whom I loved that I would live among thy

133

thralls for a season; but now am I come to thee for those other two boons which thou hast promised. Make me thy knight in secret & give me the first adventure that comes to thy court that I may spring like flame out of ashes.

(Par.) And Gareth gave the King secret signs whereby he should know that he was Gareth - & the King granted him what he would, nor revealed his name

(Par.) Then there came a maiden into hall: & she was of high lineage, & her eye was sharp as a falcon's when he sees his prey beneath him, & her colour clear as a rose, & her nose tilted up at the tip & she spake to the King

(Par.) O King, for thou hast driven the heathen - but there be thieves & bandits enow left to ruin a realm & everyone that has a tower is King for a league round, nor canst thou be verily & indeed King till these be driven as thou hast driven the heathen.

Why sit ye there? were I thou I would not rest till the whole land were as free from accursed bloodshed as the altar cloth from the blessed wine which it is a sin to spill

(Par.) Comfort thyself said Arthur I rest not nor my knights & so they keep their vows but for a year the

134

whole realm will be safe as the centre of this hall.

(Par.) Lo now she answer'd Is it not foul wrong - my sister whom even the heathen spared when they spoilt the land - she left in great heritage - & rich she is & comely - yea & comlier than I myself - & there ever waits a knight nor lets her stir abroad but vows that he will wed her perforce save that one of thine own knights overthrow him.

(Par.) Then cried out Sir Gareth. O King thy promise. I can overthrow twenty such: for thou knowest I have been thy Kitchen knave, & so am I full of thy meats & drinks & strong as a lion.

(Par.) Well spoken kitchenboy said Sir Kay. Thou wilt lose nothing for the asking.

(Par.) But the damsel Linette cried out upon the King Fie on thee: I asked thee for a knight & thou hast given me a Kitchen knave. & right so past quickly out of the hall.

(Par.) And there were men of Sir Gareth in the city & they brought him his armour & he mounted his horse & rode swiftly down the street & past thro' the gate & found the damsel i̶n̶ hardby the tourney-field: & she was inflamed with wrath as she looked at the field, saying could not

the King have lent me one of the knights that fight in

this field rather than a kitchen-knave?

(Prose draft for lines 37 to 57)
(From H-40)

(Par.) And Gareth knelt by his mother & she blest him

laying hand on head & he ask'd her.

(Par.) Sweet Mother know ye the parable of the Golden

Goose And she said Thou art a Goose to mind me of so

foolish a parable.

(Par.) And he Foolish enow, sweet Mother for it is the

Eagle that lays the golden egg. here is my parable.

There was a youth & he was poor but lusty. & he knew

that the Eagle had laid a golden egg high up on a - call

it a palmtree. & it seemd to him that he would be rich

& happy if he could climb the tree & get the egg from

the nest. & as he was about to climb one that loved him

laid hold on him & prayd him by his love, not to climb

lest he should break his neck; & many times the youth wd

have climbd save for the love between them but he still

longed for the egg day & night, & so sweet mother, he

brake not his neck but he brake his heart

136

GARETH AND LYNETTE

(Prose draft for lines 376 to 410)
(From H-40)

(Par.) Now as the king ceased speaking & Gareth stood

yet among the crowd there came in a messenger from King

Mark of Cornwall & he held in his hand a cloth of gold,

& spake to him that Mark was on his way to Arthur, for

he had heard that the King had made Tristram his kins-

man knight of his Table, & that he was of the greater

state, being a King, & therefore trusted that Arthur

would all the more give him this honour, & to show his

reverence to Arthur he sent him this cloth of gold.

(Par.) And Arthur said 'Take it & cast it on the hearth

Shall the shield of Mark stand among those? For in the

middle of the side of the g̸r̸e̸a̸t̸ Hall there rose over the

hearth a̸ m̸i̸g̸h̸t̸y̸ p̸i̸l̸e̸ a great arch & over that a mighty

pile of stone work: & as many knights as made the Table,

so many shields were there & the name & every knight was

written thereon, in the stone, & on some of these the

arms were only carven, & some were carven & blazoned, &

some were blank. for this was the custom of Arthur.

When a knight had achieved one deed of prowess his arms

were carven, & when he had achieved twain, they were bla-

zoned & those that had achieved one had their shields

137

blank: & Gareth saw that the shield of Gawain was bla-

zoned

& that of Modred was blank, & there was a vast oak-log

smouldering on the hearth, so that the King said Cast it

on the log.

(Prose draft for lines 433 to 442)
(From Texas)

And Gareth came before Arthur & said

(Par.) O King deem ye not that I must fain be faint &

weary when ye behold me hauling my feet along thy hall &

leaning on the shoulders of these twain? wherefore I

pray thee, grant me a boon for to grant it will be

neither against thyself nor thy realm nor thy Table

Round, & the boon I beg thee to grant is this that I may

live & eat among thy thralls & those that hand the dish

across the bar, for as long as I will

(Par.) And Arthur said Thou seemest the goodliest boy I

ever look'd on, yet grant I thy request: hast thou

ought else to ask for this request of thine is below

thee, & my heart warms toward thee. And Gawain: yea,

King, there be two other boons which I would fain have

thee grant me & they are neither against thyself nor thy

138

Table Round: but I ask them not now, but when the time

comes.

(Par.) And the king said If these be not against me nor

my state nor my Round Table & provided they be nobler in

their nature than eating & drinking they are granted to

thee.

(Prose draft of lines 650 to 718.)
(From H-32)

Now there two entries into the great hall, one, whereun-

to a man cd walk only, & there was also, a side-entry,

huge & lofty whereunto a man cd. And Gareth past to the

side entry: & there stood a great & goodly charger giv-

en by the King, & there likewise were those twain who

had come with Gareth one whereof held a helmet & a

shield & one the horse; & Gareth when he came without

threw off a rough dress that veil'd him from head to

foot, & shone forth all in complete armour; & there was

a tumult in the street. he

        & mounted horse

took shield & put on helm, & all the thralls ran into

the street & when they saw their fellow whom they loved,

everyone threw up his cap & rejoiced in him & the King &

cried out God bless the King & all his fair fellowship

& the people mingled with the cry of the thralls &

Gareth rode down between the shouters & so past down by

the gate

(Par.) But Sir Kay stood by the door & was wroth with

the

                       my kitchen K sent on a quest

thralls & the people & Gareth; & said of a surety that

old wound on the head wh the king got in Badon battle

hath broken out again - this is madness Thralls to your

work! why - now let the good sun roll backward let there

be dawn in west & Eve in East. The boy was tame enow

when I had him in keeping. Now will I after my kitchen

knave & see whether he know me for the better man. Out

of the smoke hath he come & into the mire shall he go, &

thence into the smoke again

(Par.) But Lancelot said Told I thee not there was a

mystery. Abide: the lad is great lusty & knowing of

sword & lance & thou art past thy force; & moreover thou

goest against the King's will & that did never he whom

ye rail at.

(Par.) But Sir Kay armed & rode down the street & the

people gazed him at silence.

GARETH AND LYNETTE

(Prose draft for lines 797 to 833.)
(From H-32)

& so set him upright on his feet whereon he said I owe

thee my life & ask for what reward I may give thee wh

is in my power

(Par.) And Gareth I will no reward have. I have my

deed for the deeds sake & in uttermost obedience to the

King but an thou wilt give this gentle damsel & myself

harbourage for this night, then were I well-rewarded.

(Par.) And the damsel said Weenest thou that I have joy

of thee for this deed thou hast done it hath but mishap-

pened thee for these were all craven thieves. fie how

ye smell after your exercise of the tallowgrease! but

if my Lord the Baron will yield me harbourage then I

grateful

(Par.) So when they came to his Castle wh was hard at

hand, the Baron made them t̶h̶e̶ great cheer & goodly; &

there was set a peacock in his pride before the damsel &

the Lord sat Gareth before the damsel but she arose &

cried fie fie Sir Baron ye are uncourteous to set a kit-

chen boy beside me. I went this morning to King Arthur

141

GARETH AND LYNETTE

(Prose draft for lines 852 to 865)
(From H-32)

(Par.) Friend whether thou beest kitchen knave or no

thou art a strong man & a goodly & I owe thee my life &

therefore bethink thee as to this quest; for here be

four of the mightiest knights living, tho' they be but

the scum of Uther's time. & three in their fantastic

fashion call themselves the Day, the morning star, the

noonday sun & the evening star, & the fourth calls him-

self the night, & sometimes Death for he hath a skeleton

painted on his harness & his helmet is fashion'd like a

skull, whereby he have men know that even if any sd over-

throw the three he will be at last slain by himself &

pass into dismal night. Wherefore I beseech thee be-

think thyself whether thou will not return with the lady

Linette that she may choose another champion for by my

faith if thou pass on I count thee but as lost, & all

this I say for thy b̸e̸n̸e̸f̸i̸t̸ avail & because thou hast

saved my life.

(Par.) And Gareth said whether I be kitchen knave or not

T̸h̸e̸ will be shown hereafter: but the King has (given?)

me this quest & I follow it to the death

142

GARETH AND LYNETTE

(Preliminary versification of preceding prose, cor-
responding to lines 852 to 865)
(From H-32)

Friend, whether thou be kitchenpage or no
Yet strong thou art & goodly therewithal,
And thou hast saved my life; & therefore now
Bethink thee; thou wilt have to joust with four
Mighty & there be four; & three thereof have named
       themselves
In their fantastic pride the Day,
The morning
The fourth who fain wd wed
   shall I
Friend, let me speak to thee one friendly word, to
      thee?
For, whether thou be kitchenpage or not,
Or whether it be the damsel's fantasy
 ask   or strong
I know not: but thou strikest ~~Knightly~~ strokes
Or whether she be mad or the good King
For strong thou art, & goodly therewithal
And thou has saved my life; & therefore now (?)
       mighty
Think, for for here be ~~some~~ ~~strong~~ men
To joust with, sons of one of Uther's knights
(Three undeciphered lines.)

Morning star & noon-Sun, & Evening-Star
Such is their folly, & he, the fool of all, These be
     strong fools & (4 ?)
    ever himself
The fourth who arms in black & calls himself
      the night
~~The night~~ And names himself, & sometimes Death
And wears his helmet fashiond like a skull
And hath a skeleton painted on his arms
     who (1 ?)
And means thereby that one who (1 ?) the three
Slain by himself shall pass to dreamless night
And all these four be mighty men ~~to~~ ~~fight~~ but fools.
Sir (1 ?) if thou wilt (look?) again
~~Thy~~ ~~pardon~~ With this thy damsel into Arthur's hall
And let her take Sir Lancelot for her quest
Now, if I wrong thee, whether knight or knave

143

GARETH AND LYNETTE

(One undecipherable line)
Full pardon but I
Said Gareth   I will follow out the Quest
Despite of Day & Night & Death & Hell

(Prose draft for lines 1163 to 1181.)
(From H-32)

And lifting up the torch she show'd him on the cavern-

walls painted figures of Day & night & Death & evil cus-

tom pursuing the soul drest like a bride - the work of

the hermit who had lived there - & to whom the four wd

confess themselves, & while he lived they (rechaind?)

themselves & fear'd the King, & now they care not for

the King but fear the cave - & from these walls these

unfurnished fools --said I not they were fools have

suckd their allegory.

(Prose draft for lines 1248 to 1350.)
(From H-32)

(Par.) So when they had eaten the baken venison & drank

as much as they wd of the red wine of Southland, Gareth

disarmed himself & lay down & slept. Then the damsel

Lynette said to Lancelot. 'Wilt thou do me a grace? I

sware to the black knight that I wd bring thee to fight

him. Wilt thou fight him in the lieu of Sir Gareth? Nay

fair damsel, for therein wd be too much discourtesy but

an he overthrow Sir Gareth then shall he not scape me.

'Yet she said, an thou refuse me this

(so that my sister's heart may be comforted & I may
                     not

(

(thou wilt yield me another grace.' Willingly fair

(seem foresworn at first sight

(

(damsel, so that I may' Thou shalt let Gareth have

thine armour, & he shall take thine. Willingly said

Lancelot so that Gareth agree thereto.

(Par.) And when Gareth had awaked he was mighty again as

any lion, & he sware that an he had Lancelots harness on

him he wd have tenfold might from the touch thereof, &

tenfold might from the thought that he wd never disgrace

the shadow of Lancelot in the arms of Lancelot.

(Par.) And so it was done: & Gareth said ~~shall/we/not~~

~~fall~~ let us go on the instant. Fair Sir said the damsel

it yet wanteth 6 hours to the sunrise. Care not for

that we will be there to fall on him when it dawneth.

(Par.) Then they rode thence & when they gained the

space before the castle, they ware of a huge black pa-

vilion under the stars, & the harp of Arthur beckend

over it, & a great black horn hung by the side of the

pavilion. And Gareth was so fresh & eager that ere

Lancelot or the damsel cd stay him he blew it. & in

the black night horribly brayed the horn. & light

flashd in a tower & past away; & Gareth once more

winded the great horn & there were many lights but when

he had blown it thrice, the castle doors were flung open

& there came out two & two men bearing torches till all

was as light as day.

(Par.) Then the great black pavilion opend & yielded up

Night on a huge black horse, & he was ghastly to gaze

upon, & he rode like a (base-witt'd?) Death & the scull

grinn'd over him

(Par.) And when he saw Gareth he cried out Art thou her

Lancelot & he said I am all that thou wilt find for him

(Prose draft for lines 1298 to 1310.)
(From H-32)

(Par.) Wd God had made us tongueless. all the day I

rode & reviled thee: & now have I got Sir L. to give

thee his shield & horse & let thee fight in his stead; &

now I repent me yet again, for thou hast gaind thee

glory enough in overthrowing those three knights but be-

fore this last thou wilt surely go down: for he is the

mightiest living: & he will slay thee, for ~~his squire~~

he hath spared not man nor woman nor babe; & some say

he hath eaten childs flesh - a monster. And I know not

his face, but it is too horrible be looked upon & never

have I seen it, nor heard him speak but ever his squire

spoke for him, & the squire was sore sick when I left,

& like to die

GARETH AND LYNETTE

The last tall son of Lot and Bellicent,
And tallest, Gareth, in a showerful spring
Stared at the spate. A slender-shafted Pine
Lost footing, fell, and so was whirled away.
'How he went down,' said Gareth, 'as a false knight   5
Or evil king before my lance if lance
Were mine to use--O senseless cataract,
Bearing all down in thy precipitancy--
And yet thou art but swollen with cold snows
And mine is living blood; thou dost His will,   10
The Maker's, and not knowest, and I that know,
Have strength and wit, in my good mother's hall
Linger with vacillating obedience,

---

1 The   tall
  Gareth, fifth son of Lot & Bellicent   H-40
1 (Par.) The fifth tall...   B-IV

2 And youngest, Gareth in a showerful spring   H-40

3 Sat staring at the m̸o̸u̸n̸t̸a̸i̸n̸ spate. A t̸e̸n̸ slender
                              shafted pine   H-40

4 ...fell, and...   ,/ (I)   A-2109
4 (C)   B-II

5   knight
  ...false K̸i̸n̸g̸   B-IV

9 ...snows,   A-2109
9 (C)   73

12 W̸i̸t̸h̸ Have...   H-40
12 ...mother's hall̸s̸   (I)   A-2109
12 (C)   B-II

Alt. after 13
   Rather a tame submission, c̸a̸g̸e̸d̸ & p̸r̸i̸c̸k̸y̸d̸ to her
                              will   H-40
Alt. after 13
   Rather a tame submission to her will,   B-IV

149

Prisoned, and kept and coaxed and whistled to--
Since the good mother holds me still a child!　　　　15
Good mother is bad mother unto me!
A worse were better; yet no worse would I.
Heaven yield her for it, but in me put force
To weary her ears with one continuous prayer,
Until she let me fly discaged to sweep　　　　　20
In ever-highering eagle-circles up
To the great Sun of Glory, and thence swoop
Down upon all things base, and dash them dead,
A knight of Arthur, working out his will,
To cleanse the world. Why, Gawain, when he came　　25

Alt. after 14
　　And pamper'd on my perch with delicacies -　　H-40;
　　　　　　　　　　　　　　　　　　　　　　　B-IV

15 ...a child -　　　　　　　　　　　　　　　A-2109
15 (C)　　　　　　　　　　　　　　　　　　　73

17 The worse the better - ~~better still the~~ yet no
　　　　　　　　　　　　　　worse for me -　　H-40

18　　　　　　　　　　　but in me put force
　　Heaven bless her for it & ~~send me quickly hence~~　H-40
18　　　yield
　　Heaven ~~bless~~ her...　　　　　　　　　B-IV

20 ...let me ~~hence~~ fly...　　　　　　　　H-40

21 In ever-widening eagle-circles up　　　H-40;B-IV
21　　　　highering　　　　　　　　　　　(P corr.)
　　In ever-~~widening~~ eagle-circles up　　Bd-3

22 ...glory & from thence　　　　　　　　H-40
22 Toward the high Sun...　　　　　　　　B-IV

23 Swoop down on all...　　　　　　　　　H-40

24　　　　　　　　　working out his ends
　　A knight of Arthur, ~~why when Gawain came~~　H-40

150

GARETH AND LYNETTE

With Modred hither in the summertime,
Asked me to tilt with him, the proven knight.
Modred for want of worthier was the judge.
Then I so shook him in the saddle, he said,
"Thou hast half prevailed against me," said so--he-- 30
Though Modred biting his thin lips was mute,
For he is alway sullen: what care I?'

   And Gareth went, and hovering round her chair
Asked, 'Mother, though ye count me still the child,
Sweet mother, do ye love the child?' She laughed,   35
'Thou art but a wild-goose to question it.'
'Then, mother, an ye love the child,' he said,

---

26 Thither with Modred in...   H-40
26 ...in the summertide,   B-IV

27 ...him, & said, he said   H-40

29 ...said   A-2109
29 (C)   T-GP3

30 T hast prevaild against him said so - yea   H-40

31 ...his dry lips...   H-40

32 ...care I. ?'   (? I)   A-2109
32 (C)   B-II

34-35 Ask'd Mother, dost thou love thy child' she
                          said   H-40
34-35   tho' ye count me still the child
      Ask'd Mother, d̸ǿs̸t̸ t̸h̸ǿu̸ l̸ǿv̸é t̸h̸y̸ c̸h̸i̸l̸d̸ s̸h̸é
                     s̸a̸i̸d̸   B-IV

35 ...the child'? She...   A-2109
35 (C)   T-GP3

37 Then mother if ye love me Gareth said   H-40;B-IV

151

'Being a goose and rather tame than wild,
Hear the child's story.' 'Yea, my well-beloved,
An 'twere but of the goose and golden eggs.'   40

    And Gareth answered her with kindling eyes,
'Nay, nay, good mother, but this egg of mine
Was finer gold than any goose can lay;
For this an Eagle, a royal Eagle, laid
Almost beyond eye-reach, on such a palm   45
As glitters gilded in thy Book of Hours.
And there was ever haunting round the palm
A lusty youth, but poor, who often saw
The splendour sparkling from aloft, and thought

---

39 ...Yea my son   H-40

40 Were it but of...   H-40
40 An 'twere...   '/ (I)   A-2109
40 (C)   B-II

41 (Omitted H-40;B-IV)
41 ...eyes.   A-2109
41 (C)   T-GP3

42 Nay, nay, my mother, ...   H-40

43 ...lay;   ;/ (I)   A-2109
43 (C)   B-II

Sketch 44 to 46
    An eagle laid on a palm heaven-high
    Such as is blazoned in that book of thine
    Wh tells of how the woman & the man
    Led their captivity captive rest their souls!   H-40

44 For t̸h̸i̸s̸ mother, this a Royal...   B-IV
44 ...Eagle, laid   ,/ (I)   A-2109
44 (C)   B-II

45 ...eyereach, upon a palm   B-IV

46 Such as is blazon'd in...   B-IV

47 ...round the tree   H-40

"An I could climb and lay my hand upon it,   50
Then were I wealthier than a leash of kings,"
But ever when he reached a hand to climb,
One, that had loved him from his childhood, caught
And stayed him, "Climb not lest thou break thy neck,
I charge thee by my love," and so the boy,   55
Sweet mother, neither clomb, nor brake his neck,
But brake his very heart in pining for it,
And past away.'

                    To whom the mother said,
'True love, sweet son, had risked himself and
                            climbed,
And handed down the golden treasure to him.'   60

---

48 ...poor. he when he saw	H-40
48 ...poor; & when he saw who often saw	B-IV
49 The splendor shining in the nest he thought	H-40
49 &	
...aloft, he thought	B-IV
50 If I...	H-40
50 ...my hands upon...	B-IV
50 ...it, ,/ (I)	A-2109
50 (C)	B-II
52 ...when the youth essay'd to climb,	H-40
52 But evermore when he essay'd to climb	B-IV
53 one	
A friend that had loved from his childhood,	H-40
53 ...that loved...	B-IV
54 ...neck, ,/ (I)	A-2109
54 (C)	B-II
55-56 The boy, sweet mother did not break his	
neck	H-40
57 But broke his...	H-40

And Gareth answered her with kindling eyes,
'Gold? said I gold?--ay then, why he, or she,
Or whosoe'er it was, or half the world
Had ventured--<u>had</u> the thing I spake of been
Mere gold--but this was all of that true steel,   65
Whereof they forged the brand Excalibur,
And lightnings played about it in the storm,
And all the little fowl were flurried at it,
And there were cries and clashings in the nest,
That sent him from his senses: let me go.'   70

   Then Bellicent bemoaned herself and said,
'Hast thou no pity upon my loneliness?
Lo, where thy father Lot beside the hearth
Lies like a log, and all but smouldered out!
For ever since when traitor to the King   75

---

62 Ay Ay - had it been gold - why he, or she,		H-40
62 Gold - said I gold - ay - then		
A̸y̸/ A̸y̸/ h̸a̸d̸ t̸h̸i̸s̸ b̸e̸e̸n̸ g̸o̸l̸d̸ - why...		B-IV
62 ...said I gold - ? ay...he, or she,	(?,, I)	A-2109
62 ...gold? - ay/ then, why...	,/	T-GP2
62 (C)		T-GP3

63 ...or all the world	H-40

64 ...the thing we talk about	H-40

65 Been gold - but...that fine steel	H-40

67 ...storm,	,/ (I)	A-2109
67 (C)		B-II

68 ...little birds were frighted at it	H-40
68 ...all the lesser fowl...	B-IV

Alt. following 70
   Live chaste, speak truth, fight well, & serve the

king. \	H-40

71 (Par.) But Bellicent...	B-IV

73 Look how thy...	B-IV
73 Look where thy...	B-IV

He fought against him in the Barons' war,
And Arthur gave him back his territory,
His age hath slowly droopt, and now lies there
A yet-warm corpse, and yet unburiable,
No more; nor sees, nor hears, nor speaks, nor knows.   80
And both thy brethren are in Arthur's hall,
Albeit neither loved with that full love
I feel for thee, nor worthy such a love:
Stay therefore thou; red berries charm the bird,

Sketch 74-80
       like a (1 ?) - extinguished brand
   Lies by the hearth nor speaks nor sees nor
                    hears   H-40

74 ...like a brand now all...   B-IV
74 ...like a brand & all...   B-IV

75   when
   ...since a traitor...   B-IV

78-80 He has droopt & now nor speaks nor hears nor
                       knows   B-IV

80 Nor hears nor sees, nor knows: how lone am I!   B-IV

81 And all thy...   B-IV

82 I love them all & yet m̶y̶ all my love for all   B-IV
82 And they were never loved like thee, my son   B-IV
82 And none of these is loved with that full love B-IV

83-84 Nor worthy of it. Stay with me, my son   B-IV

83 Is overbalanced by my love for thee   B-IV
83 ...a love⁄:   :⁄ (I)   A-2109
83 (C)   B-II

84 My last & noblest. Stay with me, my son   B-IV

84-89 Stay with me son & follow the wild deer   B-IV

84-85   thou art an innocent
     Red berries please the birds & the wars thee B-IV

And thee, mine innocent, the jousts, the wars,   85
Who never knewest finger-ache, nor pang
Of wrenched or broken limb--an often chance
In those brain-stunning shocks, and tourney-falls,
Frights to my heart; but stay: follow the deer
By these tall firs and our fast-falling burns;   90
So make thy manhood mightier day by day;
Sweet is the chase: and I will seek thee out
Some comfortable bride and fair, to grace
Thy climbing life, and cherish my prone year,
Till falling into Lot's forgetfulness   95
I know not thee, myself, nor anything.
Stay, my best son! ye are yet more boy than man.'

    Then Gareth, 'An ye hold me yet for child,
Hear yet once more the story of the child.

Alt. for 85 Nor yearn so madly for the sound of arms.

                                                                B-IV

87   an often
    ...limb, in life (?) a chance   B-IV

88 Brain-stunning tumbles in the tournament   B-IV

Alt. after 88 Blows, bruises   B-IV

89 ...heart:, but...   (, I)   A-2109
89 (C)   B-II

90 By the tall firs & the fast-falling bourn   B-IV

92 And I will close from the noise of arms   B-IV
92 ...chase⁄ : and...   (: I)   A-2109
92 (C)   B-II

93 Find thee some comfortable bride to grace   H-40
93   some   & fair charm
    And find a comfortable bride to g̷r̷a̷c̷e̷   B-IV
93 ...fair, to...   ,/ (I)   A-2109
93 (C)   B-II

95 Till I shall lapse into forgetfulness   H-40
95 Till falling into
    Until I lapse in Lot's forgetfulness,   B-IV

    156

For, mother, there was once a King, like ours.   100
The prince his heir, when tall and marriageable,
Asked for a bride; and thereupon the King
Set two before him. One was fair, strong, armed--
But to be won by force--and many men
Desired her; one, good lack, no man desired.   105
And these were the conditions of the King:
That save he won the first by force, he needs
Must wed that other, whom no man desired,
A red-faced bride who knew herself so vile,
That evermore she longed to hide herself,   110
Nor fronted man or woman, eye to eye--
Yea--some she cleaved to, but they died of her.
And one--they called her Fame; and one,--O Mother,

---

96 I love   myself
    N̸o̸t̸ K̸n̸o̸w̸ m̸y̸s̸e̸l̸f̸ nor thee, nor anything.   B-IV

100 ...ours/   :/ (P)   A-2109
100 ...ours,   B-II
100 ...ours;   :/ (I)   T-GP3
100 ...ours;   72
100 (C)   84

101 Of whom his...   Bd-3
101 Of whom his heir when tall and marriageable   A-2109
101 The prince his heir,   I MS
    A̸n̸d̸ h̸i̸m̸/+/h̸i̸s̸ h̸e̸i̸r̸   I MS
    O̸f̸ w̸h̸o̸m̸ h̸i̸s̸ h̸e̸i̸r̸ when tall and marriageable,
                                      ,/ (I)   T-GP3
101 (C)   72

106 ...King: (: I)   A-2109
106 (C)   B-II

Draft 109 to 112
    A red-faced bride who knew herself so mean
    She look'd nor man nor woman in the f̸a̸c̸e̸ eyes
    But evermore wd long to hide herself
    Yet were they some poor souls to whom she cleaved
    And these died of her or went howling-mad   B-IV

113 ...one, O Mother,   A-2109
113 (C)   73

How can ye keep me tethered to you--Shame.
Man am I grown, a man's work must I do.   115
Follow the deer? follow the Christ, the King,
Live pure, speak true, right wrong, follow the King--
Else, wherefore born?'

                     To whom the mother said,
'Sweet son, for there be many who deem him not,
Or will not deem him, wholly proven King--   120
Albeit in mine own heart I knew him King,
When I was frequent with him in my youth,
And heard him Kingly speak, and doubted him

---

114 ...Shame!   A-2109
114 (C)   86

118 ...born?   A-2109
118 (C)   T-GP3

119 to 120 Sweet son, for there be many within the realm
       Who do not hold him wholly proven king   H-40
119 to 120 there be so many about the realm
       Who hold him not as wholly proven King;   B-IV

121 ...I know him...   H-40

122 For I was...   H-40

123 ...him speak as King   H-40
123 And heard speak as King, & doubted...   B-IV
123 And heard him speak as King, & doubted...   Bd-3
123   kingly   I MS
    And heard him speak, *as King*, and doubted...   S-929
123 (C)   B-II

Sketch c. 124   dropt out of heaven
    So say the people - are the people wise?
    From the great deep another said to me   H-40

124 ...himself, nor dreamd of him   B-IV
124 ...himself,; but...   ;/ (I)   A-2109
124 (C)   B-II

125 Who knows? but wilt thou leave the pleasentness H-40
125 Save as of kin to me; but - dropt from heaven   B-IV

158

No more than he, himself; but felt him mine,
Of closest kin to me: yet--wilt thou leave   125
Thine easeful biding here, and risk thine all,
Life, limbs, for one that is not proven King?
Stay, till the cloud that settles round his birth
Hath lifted but a little. Stay, sweet son.'

    And Gareth answered quickly, 'Not an hour,   130
So that ye yield me--I will walk through fire,
Mother, to gain it--your full leave to go.

Alt. after 125
    So say the people - are the people wise?
    Or 'out of the great deep' some one said
    Who knows? but wilt thou lose the pleasantness (?)
    (see sketch c. 124)   B-IV

126 And ease of living here & risk thine all   H-40

127 ...that hangs about his birth   H-40
127 ...King. ?   ? (I)   S-929
127 (C)   B-II

128 Has cleard itself a little - stay my son   H-40

129   little   (P)
    ...lifted but a m̸o̸m̸e̸n̸t̸. Stay...   Bd-3

Alt. for 130
    I would not stay one moment wh my will
    Let go my will   H-40

131   -I will walk thro' fire
    So that ye yield me your full leave to go.   Bd-3
131   -I will walk thro' fire   I MS
    So that ye yield me y̸o̸u̸r̸ f̸u̸l̸l̸ l̸e̸a̸v̸e̸ t̸o̸ g̸o̸/   S-929
131 (C)   B-II

132 Mother, to gain it
    Not proven, who swept the dust of ruin'd Rome   Bd-3
132   -your full leave to go.   I MS
    Mother, to gain it I̸ w̸i̸l̸l̸ w̸a̸l̸k̸ t̸h̸r̸o̸y̸ f̸i̸r̸e̸.   S-929
132 (C)   B-II

159

Not proven, who swept the dust of ruined Rome
From off the threshold of the realm, and crushed
The Idolaters, and made the people free?   135
Who should be King save him who makes us free?'

    So when the Queen, who long had sought in vain
To break him from the intent to which he grew,
Found her son's will unwaveringly one,
She answered craftily, 'Will ye walk through fire?   140
Who walks through fire will hardly heed the smoke.
Ay, go then, an ye must: only one proof,
Before thou ask the King to make thee knight,
Of thine obedience and thy love to me,
Thy mother,--I demand.'

                         And Gareth cried,   145
'A hard one, or a hundred, so I go.

---

133 Not proven/ , Who...   A-2109
133 (C)   B-II

136 ...free'?   A-2109
136 (C)   T-GP3

137 ...Queen, who...   ,/ (I)   A-2109
137 (C)   B-II

138 ...wh he clung   H-40

Sketch 140 ff
    She answer'd craftily 'ay then, so ye must
    But
    Only this proof of thine obedience
    And love to me thy mother I demand.
    That ere thou ask the king to make thee knight
    Thou shalt abide among the kitchen knaves
    And those that hand the dish across the bar
    And thou shalt serve the king (blot) of meat & drink
    And shalt not tell thy name to anyone
    For one whole moon or else thou shalt not go.   H-40

141 ...smoke.   ./ (I)   S-929
141 (C)   B-II

144 ...me/   (I)   S-929

Nay--quick! the proof to prove me to the quick!"

But slowly spake the mother looking at him,
'Prince, thou shalt go disguised to Arthur's hall,
And hire thyself to serve for meats and drinks   150
Among the scullions and the kitchen-knaves,
And those that hand the dish across the bar.
Nor shalt thou tell thy name to anyone.
And thou shalt serve a twelvemonth and a day.'

For so the Queen believed that when her son   155
Beheld his only way to glory lead
Low down through villain kitchen-vassalage,

---

144 (C)   B-II

145 Thy mother, - I demand.'   (-P)   A-2109
145 Thy mother, I demand.'   -/   T-GP2
145 (C)   72

147 Out with it - quick - what is it? let me try it
      (Added to MS in P by another)   Bd-3
147 Nay   P MS
      Øⱥⱦ wⱦⱦⱨ ⱦⱦ ≠ qⱦⱦⱦⱨ ≠ wⱨⱥⱦ ⱦⱨ ⱦⱦⱦ Lⱥⱦ/wⱦ ⱦⱦⱦ
                              ⱦⱦⱦⱦ
                                                        A-2109
      Nay -   I MS
      Øⱦⱦⱨ! quick! the proof to prove me to the
                              qui.   I MS
      Øⱥⱦ wⱦⱦⱨ ⱦⱦ ≠ qⱦⱦⱦⱨ ≠ wⱨⱥⱦ ⱦⱦ ⱦⱦⱦ/Lⱥⱦ wⱦ ⱦⱦⱦ
                              ⱦⱦⱦⱦ
                                                        T-GP3
147 (C)   72

148 (Par.) Then slowly...   Bd-3
148 (Par.) Then slowly...   A-2109
148   But   I MS
    (Par.) Then slowly...   T-GP3
148 (C)   72

156 Ɫ ⱥ Behold
    Ⱦⱨⱥⱦ øⱦ his only way to glory first   H-40

157 Led low thro'...   H-40
157 ...kitchen - vassalage,   ,/ (I)   A-2109
157 (C)   B-II

Her own true Gareth was too princely-proud
To pass thereby; so should he rest with her,
Closed in her castle from the sound of arms.   160

    Silent awhile was Gareth, then replied,
'The thrall in person may be free in soul,
And I shall see the jousts. Thy son am I,
And since thou art my mother, must obey.
I therefore yield me freely to thy will;   165
For hence will I, disguised, and hire myself
To serve with scullions and with kitchen-knaves;
Nor tell my name to any--no, not the King.'

    Gareth awhile lingered. The mother's eye
Full of the wistful fear that he would go,   170
And turning toward him wheresoe'er he turned,
Perplext his outward purpose, till an hour,
When wakened by the wind which with full voice

---

158 Her Gareth was too princely & too proud   H-40
158 ...was too p̶r̶i̶n̶c̶e̶l̶y̶ ̶&̶ ̶t̶o̶o̶ ̶p̶r̶o̶u̶d̶ [princely--proud]
    (final two words in P MS)   Bd-3

159 ...so sd he stay with her   H-40
159   he   P MS
    ...thereby; &̶ so should stay with her   Bd-3
159   rest   I MS
    ...should he s̶t̶a̶y̶ with her,   (, I)   S-929
159 (C)   B-II

Alt. after 160 And cheer her & charm her solitude   H-40

164 ...mother I must obey   H-40

165 And therefore...   H-40
165 ...will,;   ; (I)   S-929
165 (C)   B-II

166 And I will serve for hire of meat & drink   H-40

167 Among the scullions & the kitchen knaves   H-40

168 Nor will I name my name to anyone   H-40

Alt. after 168 No not thy brother.   H-40

Swept bellowing through the darkness on to dawn,
He rose, and out of slumber calling two   175
That still had tended on him from his birth,
Before the wakeful mother heard him, went.

The three were clad like tillers of the soil.
Southward they set their faces. The birds made
Melody on branch, and melody in mid air,   180
The damp hill-slopes were quickened into green,
And the live green had kindled into flowers,
For it was past the time of Easterday.

So, when their feet were planted on the plain

---

171 ...turning on him...   H-40

173 Then waken'd by a wind that with full voice   H-40

174 ...darkness of the dawn,   H-40
174 ...dawn,   (, I)   A-2109
174 (C)   B-II

175 ~~Unheard~~ ~~arose~~ & ~~call'd~~ his men & went
     Arose, & call'd twain of   H-40
175   ~~summoning~~ calling
     He rose, & ~~summon'd~~ out of slumber two   Bd-3
175   (P corr.)
     He rose, and ~~calling~~ out of slumber two   A-2109
175 (C)   B-II

177 Unnoticed of his mothers wakeful ear.   H-40
177 Before
     ~~And~~ ~~ere~~ the wakeful...   Bd-3

178 ...tillers of the glebe.   H-40

180 Melody on the boughs...   H-40

183 For it was nigh the time of Pentecost.   H-40
183   past   Easterday
     For it was ~~nigh~~ the time of ~~Pentecost~~.   Bd-3

184 And when they set their feet upon the plain   H-40

That broadened toward the base of Camelot,   185
Far off they saw the silver-misty morn
Rolling her smoke about the Royal mount,
That rose between the forest and the field.
At times the summit of the high city flashed;
At times the spires and turrets half-way down   190
Pricked through the mist; at times the great gate shone
Only, that opened on the field below:
Anon, the whole fair city had disappeared.

    Then those who went with Gareth were amazed,
One crying, 'Let us go no further, lord.   195
Here is a city of Enchanters, built
By fairy Kings.' The second echoed him,
'Lord, we have heard from our wise man at home
To Northward, that this King is not the King,
But only changeling out of Fairyland,   200
Who drave the heathen hence by sorcery

---

185 ...broaden'd round the...   H-40

186 ...the misty-silver morn   H-40

187 Go smoking round the Royal Mount. At times   H-40
187   bout
   ...smoke a/r/o/u/n/d the royal...   Bd-3

189 The summit of the high city flash'd: at times   H-40

190 The towers & spires & poplars half way down   H-40

191 ...the great white gate   H-40

192 That open'd on the champaigne, glitter'd   H-40

194 And those...   H-40

196 This is...   H-40
196 Here
    T/h/i/s is a city...   Bd-3

197 ...kings!
       And then that other spake   H-40

198 ...wise men at...   A-2109

And Merlin's glamour.' Then the first again,
'Lord, there is no such city anywhere,
But all a vision.'

                        Gareth answered them
With laughter, swearing he had glamour enow   205
In his own blood, his princedom, youth and hopes,
To plunge old Merlin in the Arabian sea;
So pushed them all unwilling toward the gate.
And there was no gate like it under heaven.
For barefoot on the keystone, which was lined   210
And rippled like an ever-fleeting wave,
The Lady of the Lake stood: all her dress

---

198 (C)		75
199 In Northland		I MS
To Northward, that...		S-929
199 (C)		B-II
200 ...Fairy-land		Bd-3
200 ...of Fairy-land,		A-2109
200 (C)		T-GP3
203 ...anywhere,	(, I)	A-2109
203 (C)		B-II
204 ...Then Gareth...		H-40
204 them		
...answer'd these		Bd-3
205 ...glamour enough		H-40
207 ...Merlin under the Red Sea in the Arabian Sea		H-40
208 So push'd...		H-40
208 ...gate/ .	(⊙ I)	A-2109
208 ...gate/ .	⊙	T-GP2;T-GP3
208 (C)		72
209 And there none such gateway under heaven.		H-40
209 ...heaven/ .	(⊙ I)	A-2109
209 (C)		B-II

Wept from her sides as water flowing away;
But like the cross her great and goodly arms
Stretched under all the cornice and upheld: 215
And drops of water fell from either hand;
And down from one a sword was hung, from one
A censer, either worn with wind and storm;
And o'er her breast floated the sacred fish;
And in the space to left of her, and right,   220
Were Arthur's wars in weird devices done,
√ New things and old co-twisted, as if Time
Were nothing, so inveterately, that men
Were giddy gazing there; and over all
High on the top were those three Queens, the friends 225
Of Arthur, who should help him at his need.

213	sides		
	...her d̸o̸w̸n̸ like water		H-40
213	...away:;	(; I)	S-929
213	(C)		B-II

218	...censer, each was worn...		H-40

· 219	breast floated		
	...her b̸o̸s̸o̸m̸ s̸w̸a̸m̸ the...		H-40

220	And in the field to right & left to her		H-40

224	there		
	...gazing on them; & at the top		H-40
224	...there,; and...	; (I)	A-2109
224	(C)		B-II

225	High over all were...		H-40

227	And those...		H-40

228	...figures, that...	,/ (I)	A-2109
228	(C)		B-II

GARETH AND LYNETTE

Then those with Gareth for so long a space
Stared at the figures, that at last it seemed
The dragon-boughts and elvish emblemings
Began to move, seethe, twine and curl: they called   230
To Gareth, 'Lord, the gateway is alive.'

And Gareth likewise on them fixt his eyes
So long, that even to him they seemed to move.
Out of the city a blast of music pealed.
Back from the gate started the three, to whom   235
From out thereunder came an ancient man,
Long-bearded, saying, 'Who be ye, my sons?'

Then Gareth, 'We be tillers of the soil,
Who leaving share in furrow come to see
The glories of our King: but these, my men,   240

---

229 The dragon's tails & elvish...   H-40

230 Began to move, twine twist & curl...   H-40

232 And Gareth also fixt his eyes so long   H-40

233 Upon them that to him they...   H-40

234 Then came a blast of music from the town.   H-40
234 Out of
     T̸h̸e̸n̸ f̸r̸o̸m̸ the city...   Bd-3

235 Started the three back from the gate, ⱥ t̸h̸e̸n̸
                              to whom   H-40

236   r̸o̸d̸e̸ came
     ...thereunder c̸a̸m̸e̸ an ancient   ¡Bd-3

238 Said Gareth...   H-40

239 ...leaving plough in...   H-40
239   share
     ...leaving p̸l̸o̸u̸g̸h̸ in...   Bd-3

240 ...glories of the king...   H-40

167

(Your city moved so weirdly in the mist)
Doubt if the King be King at all, or come
From Fairyland; and whether this be built
By magic, and by fairy Kings and Queens;
Or whether there be any city at all,   245
Or all a vision: and this music now
Hath scared them both, but tell thou these the truth.'

    Then that old Seer made answer playing on him
And saying, 'Son, I have seen the good ship sail
Keel upward, and mast downward, in the heavens,   250

---

243 ...fairyland & hold the city is built		H-40
243 ...fairyland; & if the city is built		Bd-3
243 and whether this be		P MS
From fairyland; ~~and if the city is built~~		A-2109
243 From fairyland; and...		B-II
243 (C)		75

245 And whether there be any city here   H-40

246 ...& this bugle blast   H-40

247   these   I MS
...tell thou ~~them~~ the truth.'   S-929
247 (C)   B-II

248 And ancient Merlin answer'd playing on him   H-40

250 Keel upward and mast downward in...   A-2109
250 (C)   86

251   turrets
...solid ~~towers~~ topsey-turvey...   Bd-3

253 I tell the truth...   H-40

254 For truly, son, this city was as thou sayest   H-40
254 For truly, son, the city was, as ye say,   Bd-3
254 For truly ~~son the city was as ye say~~   A-2109
254 For truly, as thou sayest, a Fairy...   B-II
254 For truly, as...   72
254 (C)   75

And solid turrets topsy-turvy in air:
And here is truth; but an it please thee not,
Take thou the truth as thou hast told it me.
For truly as thou sayest, a Fairy King
And Fairy Queens have built the city, son;   255
They came from out a sacred mountain-cleft
Toward the sunrise, each with harp in hand,
And built it to the music of their harps.
And, as thou sayest, it is enchanted, son,
For there is nothing in it as it seems   260
Saving the King; though some there be that hold
The King a shadow, and the city real:
Yet take thou heed of him, for, so thou pass
Beneath this archway, then wilt thou become
A thrall to his enchantments, for the King   265
Will bind thee by such vows, as is a shame
A man should not be bound by, yet the which
No man can keep; but, so thou dread to swear,

---

255 W̶a̶s̶ built by a fairy King & fairy Queen   H-40
255 Built by a Fairy king, & Fairy Queens,   Bd-3
255 B̶u̶i̶l̶t̶ b̶y̶ a̶ F̶a̶i̶r̶y̶ K̶i̶n̶g̶, a̶n̶d̶ F̶a̶i̶r̶y̶ Q̶u̶e̶e̶n̶s̶,   A-2109
255 ..., son,;   ;   T-GP2
255 (C)   T-GP3

256 That came...   H-40
256 Who came from...   Bd-3
256 W̶h̶o̶ came...   A-2109
256 (C)   B-II

259 And as thou sayest it is enchanted, son,   A-2109
259 (C)   86

261 ...tho' there be many that hold   H-40

262 The king unreal & the city real: H-40
262   t̶h̶e̶ a shadow
    The King u̶n̶r̶e̶a̶l̶, & the...   Bd-3

263 And take...him, for an thou pass   H-40

264 Beneath this...   H-40

268 ...but if thou...   H-40

Pass not beneath this gateway, but abide
Without, among the cattle of the field.   270
For an ye heard a music, like enow
They are building still, seeing the city is built
To music, therefore never built at all,
And therefore built for ever.'

                    Gareth spake
Angered, 'Old Master, reverence thine own beard   275
That looks as white as utter truth, and seems
Wellnigh as long as thou art statured tall!
Why mockest thou the stranger that hath been
To thee fair-spoken?'

               But the Seer replied,
'Know ye not then the Riddling of the Bards?   280
"Confusion, and illusion, and relation,
Elusion, and occasion, and evasion"?

---

269 ...this gate but...		H-40
269 ...gateway, but...	,/ (I)	A-2109
269 (C)		B-II
270 Here son among...		H-40
270 Without, among...	,/ (P)	A-2109
270 (C)		B-II
271 For, an...		A-2109
271 (C)		75
275 ...reverence thou t̸h̸y̸ o̸w̸n̸ w̸h̸i̸t̸e̸ beard		H-40
275 Anger'd. 'Old...		A-2109
275 (C)		T-GP3
277 ...art s̸t̸a̸t̸u̸r̸e̸d̸ tall. I ask		H-40
278 at strangers these		
Why mockest thou these my two men & me		H-40
279 Who have been fair spoken to thee?		
Merlin said		H-40
279 ...fair-spoken'?		A-2109
279 (C)		T-GP3
281 "Confusion...	"/ (I)	A-2109

I mock thee not but as thou mockest me,
And all that see thee, for thou art not who
Thou seemest, but I know thee who thou art.   285
And now thou goest up to mock the King,
Who cannot brook the shadow of any lie.'

   Unmockingly the mocker ending here
Turned to the right, and past along the plain;
Whom Gareth looking after said, 'My men,   290
Our one white lie sits like a little ghost
Here on the threshold of our enterprise.
Let love be blamed for it, not she, nor I:
Well, we will make amends.'

                   With all good cheer
He spake and laughed, then entered with his twain   295
Camelot, a city of shadowy palaces
And stately, rich in emblem and the work
Of ancient kings who did their days in stone;

---

281 (C)   B-II

282 ...evasion"?   "/ (I)   A-2109
282 (C)   72

284   look on
   And all that see thee, thou art not he   H-40
284   who
   ...art not h̸é   Bd-3

287 ...of a lie.   H-40

295 ...with those twain   H-40
295   w   I MS
   ...his T̸ŕain   S-929
295 (C)   B-II

296 The city, a city of stately palaces   H-40
296 Camelot,
   T̸h̸é ¢ít̸ý, a city...   Bd-3
296 ...palaces,   A-2109
296 ...palaces/   T-GP2;T-GP3
296 (C)   72

297 And shadowy, rich in statues & the work   H-40

171

Which Merlin's hand, the Mage at Arthur's court,
Knowing all arts, had touched, and everywhere   300
At Arthur's ordinance, tipt with lessening peak
And pinnacle, and had made it spire to heaven.
And ever and anon a knight would pass
Outward, or inward to the hall: his arms
Clashed; and the sound was good to Gareth's ear.   305
And out of bower and casement shyly glanced
Eyes of pure women, wholesome stars of love;
And all about a healthful people stept
As in the presence of a gracious king.

   Then into hall Gareth ascending heard   310
A voice, the voice of Arthur, and beheld
Far over heads in that long-vaulted hall
The splendour of the presence of the King
Throned, and delivering doom--and looked no more--
But felt his young heart hammering in his ears,   315
And thought, 'For this half-shadow of a lie
The truthful King will doom me when I speak.'
Yet pressing on, though all in fear to find

---

302 ...made it point to heaven.   H-40

305   good to
  ...was r̸i̸c̸h̸ i̸n̸ Gareth's...   Bd-3
305 Clash'd:; and...   ;/ (I)   A-2109
305 (C)   B-II

306 ...casement sh̸i̸ly glanced   y/ (I)   S-929
306 (C)   B-II

310 Then to the hall...   H-40

Sketch 311 ff.
    The full stream of the voice of Arthur pour
    Thro' open doors [for now the twelfth & last
    Realm freeing battle had been fought] in thanks
    To the High God & praises to his knights
    Who holp him there: & Gareth into hall
    Past on, & watch'd in all the listening eyes   H-40

312   nearest
    Bright over heads of c̸l̸o̸s̸e̸s̸t̸ neighborhood   H-40

Sir Gawain or Sir Modred, saw nor one
Nor other, but in all the listening eyes   320
Of those tall knights, that ranged about the throne,
Clear honour shining like the dewy star
Of dawn, and faith in their great King, with pure
Affection, and the light of victory,
And glory gained, and evermore to gain.   325

    Then came a widow crying to the King,
'A boon, Sir King! Thy father, Uther, reft
From my dead lord a field with violence:
For howsoe'er at first he proffered gold,
Yet, for the field was pleasant in our eyes,   330
We yielded not; and then he reft us of it
Perforce, and left us neither gold nor field.'

---

313 The splendour of the presence of the King   H-40

314 Throned & delivering doom; &...   H-40

315 But heard his...   H-40

318 Yet pressing foreward, fill'd with dread to spy H-40

319 His bretheren in the presence, found no one   H-40

321 ...ranged around the throne   H-40
321 ...knights that...throne,   ,/ (I)   A-2109
321 ...knights,that...   ,/   T-GP2
321 (C)   T-GP3

322 ...honour, shining...   A-2109
322 ...honour/ shining...   T-GP2
322 (C)   T-GP3

323   with
    ...king, & pure   Bd-3

326   n   P MS
    (Par.) There came...   S-929
326 (C)   B-II

330 Yet since the...   H-40

Said Arthur, 'Whether would ye? gold or field?'
To whom the woman weeping, 'Nay, my lord,
The field was pleasant in my husband's eye.'   335

And Arthur, 'Have thy pleasant field again,
And thrice the gold for Uther's use thereof,
According to the years. No boon is here,
But justice, so thy say be proven true.
Accursed, who from the wrongs his father did   340
Would shape himself a right!'

                              And while she past,
Came yet another widow crying to him,
'A boon, Sir King! Thine enemy, King, am I.

---

333 Then Arthur...   H-40
333   Said
    (Par.) T̸h̸e̸n̸ Arthur...   Bd-3

338 ...boon is this   H-40

339 ...say be truly said.   H-40

341 ...a right.!'   ! (I)
                   ...she past   S-929
341 (C)   B-II

342 There came another...   H-40
342 ...to him.   A-2109
342 (C)   T-GP3

343 ...King! I am thine enemy   H-40

345 A knight of Uther in the W̸a̸r̸/w̸h̸e̸n̸/L̸o̸t̸ Baron's
                              war   H-40

346   many another
    When Lot & o̸t̸h̸e̸r̸s̸ i̸n̸ t̸h̸y̸ y̸o̸u̸t̸h̸ árose & fought   H-40

With thine own hand thou slewest my dear lord,
A knight of Uther in the Barons' war,   345
When Lot and many another rose and fought
Against thee, saying thou wert basely born.
I held with these, and loathe to ask thee aught.
Yet lo! my husband's brother had my son
Thralled in his castle, and hath starved him dead;   350
And standeth seized of that inheritance
Which thou that slewest the sire hast left the son.
So though I scarce can ask it thee for hate,
Grant me some knight to do the battle for me,
Kill the foul thief, and wreak me for my son.'   355

    Then strode a good knight forward, crying to him,
'A boon, Sir King! I am her kinsman, I.

---

347 ...wert bastard-born.   H-40
347   basely
    ...wert b̸a̸s̸t̸a̸r̸d̸-born   Bd-3

349 ...brother hath my boy   H-40
349   had
    ...brother h̸a̸t̸h̸ my...   Bd-3

350 ...castle & means to starve him and   H-40
350   hath starved
    ...castle & w̸i̸l̸l̸ s̸t̸a̸r̸v̸e̸ him...   Bd-3

351 That he may sieze on that inheritance   H-40
351   standeth
    And n̸o̸w̸ s̸t̸a̸n̸d̸s̸ siezed...   Bd-3

354 ...knight to fight for me & mine   H-40

355 ...thief, & bring me back my son.'   H-40
355   wreak me for
    ...thief & r̸e̸n̸d̸e̸r̸ m̸e̸ my son.'   Bd-3
355 ...thief, and...   ,/ (I)   A-2109
355 (C)   B-II

356 ...to him   72
356 (C)   73

175

GARETH AND LYNETTE

Give me to right her wrong, and slay the man.'

Then came Sir Kay, the seneschal, and cried,
'A boon, Sir King! even that thou grant her none,   360
This railer, that hath mocked thee in full hall--
None; or the wholesome boon of gyve and gag.'

But Arthur, 'We sit King, to help the wronged
Through all our realm. The woman loves her lord.
Peace to thee, woman, with thy loves and hates!   365
The kings of old had doomed thee to the flames,
Aurelius Emrys would have scourged thee dead,
And Uther slit thy tongue: but get thee hence--
Lest that rough humour of the kings of old
Return upon me! Thou that art her kin,   370
Go likewise; lay him low and slay him not,
But bring him here, that I may judge the right,
According to the justice of the King:

(First draft of Arthur's reply; to follow 358.)
    Then a̶n̶s̶w̶e̶r̶'̶d̶ Arthur Thou has loved thy lord: &
                peace
    Be with thee, woman, & thy like for me.
    Go thou & lay him low, & slay him not
    But bring him hither: I will judge the right.' H-40

360 ...king - t̶h̶i̶s̶ ev'n that...   H-40

361 T̶h̶e̶ w̶o̶m̶a̶n̶ This railer that...   H-40

363 And Arthur, I sit here to help the all wrong'd H-40
363 ...sit, King, to...   A-2109
363 (C)   73

364 ...all my realm...   H-40

365 Peace with thee, woman, & thy hate for me   H-40

368   yet get thee hence
    ...tongue: be thankful thou   H-40

Alt. after 368   I say
    I am Arthur & not Uther: &̶ begone   H-40
Alt. after 368 I am Arthur & not Uther: I say,
               begone   Bd-3

176

Then, be he guilty, by that deathless King
Who lived and died for men, the man shall die.'   375

    Then came in hall the messenger of Mark,
A name of evil savour in the land,
The Cornish king. In either hand he bore
What dazzled all, and shone far-off as shines
A field of charlock in the sudden sun   380
Between two showers, a cloth of palest gold,
Which down he laid before the throne, and knelt,
Delivering, that his lord, the vassal king,
Was even upon his way to Camelot;
For having heard that Arthur of his grace   385
Had made his goodly cousin, Tristram, knight,
And, forhimself was of the greater state,
Being a king, he trusted his liege-lord
Would yield him this large honour all the more;
So prayed him well to accept this cloth of gold,   390
In token of true heart and feālty.

    Then Arthur cried to rend the cloth, to rend
In pieces, and so cast it on the hearth.

---

371 ...low but slay...   H-40

372 And bring him hither I will judge the right   H-40

374 And so his guilt be proven by that king   H-40

Alt. after 375
    (Par.) And many another came as Gareth watcht
    And evermore a knight wd ride away   H-40

382   down
      T̸h̸e̸ Which he...   H-40

383 ...his Lord, the...   A-2109
383 (C)   72

387   for
      And, s̸e̸e̸i̸n̸g̸ himself...   Bd-3

391 ...and fealty.   ··/ (I)   A-2109
391 (C)   B-II

An oak-tree smouldered there. 'The goodly knight!
What! shall the shield of Mark stand among these?'   395
For, midway down the side of that long hall
A stately pile,--whereof along the front,
Some blazoned, some but carven, and some blank,
There ran a treble range of stony shields,--
Rose, and high-arching overbrowed the hearth.   400
And under every shield a knight was named:
For this was Arthur's custom in his hall;
When some good knight had done one noble deed,
His arms were carven only; but if twain
His arms were blazoned also; but if none,   405
The shield was blank and bare without a sign
Saving the name beneath; and Gareth saw
The shield of Gawain blazoned rich and bright,
And Modred's blank as death; and Arthur cried

---

394 An oaktree smoulder'd...   A-2109
394 An oak-tree smoulder'd...   -/ (I MS) T-GP3
394 (C)   72

397 ...pile, - ⟨whereof...front,⫫   (I)   A-2109
397 (C)   B-II

398 ...blank ⫫,   (, I)   S-929
398 (C)   B-II

399 ...shields, ⫽ -   (I)   A-2109
399 (C)   B-II

403 When
    ⫽⫽ some good...   Bd-3

405 ...none   A-2109
405 (C)   73

411 More like am I to...   H-40

412 ...because we call...   H-40

413 ...know ⫽⫽ ⫽⫽⫽⫽ ⫽⫽⫽⫽ ⫽⫽⫽⫽⫽/   Bd-3

414   ...we left them kings
    And only bound them by the common bond
    To break the heathen & uphold the Xt   H-40

To rend the cloth and cast it on the hearth.   410

   'More like are we to reave him of his crown
Than make him knight because men call him king.
The kings we found, ye know we stayed their hands
From war among themselves, but left them kings;
Of whom were any bounteous, merciful,   415
Truth-speaking, brave, good livers, them we enrolled
Among us, and they sit within our hall.
But Mark hath tarnished the great name of king,
As Mark would sully the low state of churl:
And, seeing he hath sent us cloth of gold,   420
Return, and meet, and hold him from our eyes,
Lest we should lap him up in cloth of lead,

---

414 A̶n̶d̶ o̶n̶l̶y̶ s̶t̶a̶y̶'̶d̶ t̶h̶e̶i̶r̶ h̶a̶n̶d̶s̶ f̶r̶o̶m̶ m̶u̶t̶u̶a̶l̶ w̶a̶r̶/   Bd-3

415 And were any among them merciful,   H-40
415 Whereof
     O̶f̶ w̶h̶o̶m̶ were...   Bd-3
415 of whom   I MS
     W̶h̶e̶r̶e̶o̶f̶ were...merciful, /   S-929
415 (C)   B-II

417 ...they sat within...   H-40
417 ...they sắt within...   i / (P)   A-2109
417 (C)   B-II

418 For Mark hath t̶a̶r̶n̶ sullied the...   H-40

419   tarnish
   ...wd sully all the state...   H-40

420 ...sent me cloth...   H-40

421 Depart & meet & stay him from mine eyes   H-40
421 ...& stay him...   H-40;B-II
421   hold   I MS
   ...and s̶t̶a̶y̶ him...   S-929
421 (C)   B-II

422 S̶e̶e̶ t̶h̶a̶t̶ wrap him not in cloth of lead   H-40
422 For fear I lap...   H-40

Silenced for ever—craven—a man of plots,
Craft, poisonous counsels, wayside ambushings--
No fault of thine: let Kay the seneschal   425
Look to thy wants, and send thee satisfied--
Accursed, who strikes nor lets the hand be seen!'

   And many another suppliant crying came
With noise of ravage wrought by beast and man,
And evermore a knight would ride away.   430

   Last, Gareth leaning both hands heavily
Down on the shoulders of the twain, his men,
Approached between them toward the King, and asked,
'A boon, Sir King (his voice was all ashamed),
For see ye not how weak and hungerworn   435
I seem--leaning on these? grant me to serve

---

423 Lest
   A̸n̸d̸ silence h̸i̸m̸ for ever he, a man of plots   H-40

424 And cloudy council, wayside ambushings   H-40
424 And poisonous counsels, wayside ambushings   H-40
424 A̸n̸d̸ Poisonous counsels, wayside ambushings--   Bd-3
424 Craft   P MS
   Poisonous counsels, ...   A-2104
424 (C)   B-II

Alt. after 424 Who dare not beard t̸h̸e̸ his enemy face to
                        face -   H-40
Alt. after 424 Who dares not beard his foeman front to
                        front -   H-40

427 ...seen.!'   (! I)   A-2109
427 (C)   B-II

431 Then Gareth leaning his hands heavily   H-40
431   Last
   (Par.) T̸h̸e̸n̸ Gareth...   Bd-3
431 (Par.) Last Gareth...   A-2109
431 (C)   73

432 ...of those twain...   H-40

For meat and drink among thy kitchen-knaves
A twelvemonth and a day, nor seek my name.
Hereafter I will fight.'

      To him the King,
'A goodly youth and worth a goodlier boon!   440
But so thou wilt no goodlier, then must Kay,
The master of the meats and drinks, be thine.'

He rose and past; then Kay, a man of mien
Wan-sallow as the plant that feels itself
Root-bitten by white lichen,

      'Lo ye now!   445
This fellow hath broken from some Abbey, where,
God wot, he had not beef and brewis enow,

---

433 Advanced between...	H-40
433 ...ask'd	A-2109
433 (C)	T-GP3
434 A boon Sir King!	
A falling homage lived upon his tongue	H-40
438 For one whole moon & ask me not my name	H-40
438 ...nor ask my name.	Bd-3
438 seek	I MS
...nor ~~ask~~ my name.	S-929
438 (C)	B-II
439 To him the King	
...~~The King replied~~	Bd-3
439 ...the King ⁄ . ./ (I)	A-2109
439 ...the King.	B-II
439 (C)	72
441 Yet if thou wilt...	H-40
441 But an thou...	Bd-3
441 But an thou...	A-2109
441 (C)	73
447 ...enow, ,/ (I)	A-2109
447 (C)	B-II

However that might chance! but an he work,
Like any pigeon will I cram his crop,
And sleeker shall he shine than any hog.'   450

    Then Lancelot standing near, 'Sir Seneschal,
Sleuth-hound thou knowest, and gray, and all the
                  hounds;
A horse thou knowest, a man thou dost not know:
Broad brows and fair, a fluent hair and fine,
High nose, a nostril large and fine, and hands   455
Large, fair and fine!--Some young lad's mystery--
But, or from sheepcot or king's hall, the boy
Is noble-natured. Treat him with all grace,
Lest he should come to shame thy judging of him.'

    Then Kay, 'What murmurest thou of mystery?   460

451	...standing near him Seneschal,		Bd-3
451	'Sir		I MS
	...near , K̶i̶m̶, 'Seneschal,	(1st, I)	S-929
451	(C)		B-II

| 452 | ...the hounds,; | ; (I) | S-929 |
| 452 | (C) | | B-II |

| 453 | Being a hunter, & a horse thou knowest - | | W-Pf |

456	Large, fair & fine - a man thou dost not know.		
	There is a mystery in him. Sure am I,		W-Pf
456	...fine! there is a mystery here;		Bd-3
456	-some young lad's mystery -		I MS
	...fine! t̶h̶e̶r̶e̶ i̶s̶ a̶ m̶y̶s̶t̶e̶r̶y̶ h̶e̶r̶e̶		S-929
456	(C)		B-II

457	That, or...		W-Pf
457	...hall, the b̶o̶y̶ lad	(Last word I MS)	S-929
457	(C)		B-II

| 459 | For fear he come to shame thy judgment of him.' | | |
| | | | W-Pf |

| 466 | See thou that thine own fineness, some fine | | |
| | day, | | W-Pf |

Think ye this fellow will poison the King's dish?
Nay, for he spake too fool-like: mystery!
Tut, an the lad were noble, he had asked
For horse and armour: fair and fine, forsooth!
Sir Fine-face, Sir Fair-hands? but see thou to it   465
That thine own fineness, Lancelot, some fine day
Undo thee not--and leave my man to me.'

  So Gareth all for glory underwent
The sooty yoke of kitchen-vassalage;
Ate with young lads his portion by the door,   470
And couched at night with grimy kitchen-knaves.
And Lancelot ever spake him pleasantly,
But Kay the seneschal, who loved him not,
Would hustle and harry him, and labour him
Beyond his comrade of the hearth, and set   475

---

467 ...not, but leave...	W-Pf
469 ...kitchen servitude.	H-40
469 ...of kitchen vassalage;	A-2109
469 (C)	73
470 And ate with lads & grooms beside the door	H-40
471 ...night among the kitchenknaves.	H-40
472 Sir Lancelot...	H-40

Alt. for 473 ff.
    And gave him gold; but Kay the s̶e̶n̶e̶s̶c̶h̶a̶l̶ sour, a
                                      man
    Of visage sallow as the stump that feels
    The touch of some white lichen at the root -   H-40

473 ...seneschal who...not	A-2109
473 (C)	86

474 full of Mistrusting harried & hustled him	H-40

475 ...his comrades of the hearth & set him	H-32
475 ...& set h̶i̶m̶	Bd-3

183

To turn the broach, draw water, or hew wood,
Or grosser tasks; and Gareth bowed himself
With all obedience to the King, and wrought
All kind of service with a noble ease
That graced the lowliest act in doing it.   480
And when the thralls had talk among themselves,

---

476 Hew wood - begone - bring water - turn the
                              broach   H-40
476 ...water, & hew...   H-32;Bd-3

476   or   I MS
    ...water, ⱥⱥⱥ hew...   S-929
476 (C)   B-II

477 And ⱥⱥⱥⱥⱥ coarser tasks: but Gareth smiled &
                              went   H-40
477 And grosser...   H-32;Bd-3
477 ⱥⱥ   I MS
    And grosser...   S-929
477 (C)   B-II

478 Bow'd himself down with all obedience   H-40

479 And wrought all service with a noble ease   H-40
479 And wrought all service in an careful way   H-40
479   ease   I MS
    ...a noble ⱥⱥⱥⱥ   S-929
479 (C)   B-II

480 ...the lowliest deed in...   H-40
480 ...itⱥ,   ,/ (I)   A-2109
480 (C)   B-II

Sketch 481-487
     And often as he workd among the thralls
     Wd hear them talk of that abounding love
     That lived between Sir Lancelot & their King
     Who once had saved Sir Lancelots life & he
     The good kings twice; & Gareth loved to hear   H-40

482 Of that abounding love betwixt the King   H-32
482   one wd praise the   that
    And ⱥⱥⱥⱥⱥ ⱥⱥ ⱥⱥⱥⱥ ⱥⱥⱥⱥⱥⱥ love ⱥⱥⱥⱥⱥ linkt the
                              King   Bd-3

184

And one would praise the love that linkt the King
And Lancelot--how the King had saved his life
In battle twice, and Lancelot once the King's--
For Lancelot was the first in Tournament,   485
But Arthur mightiest on the battle-field--
Gareth was glad. Or if some other told,

---

483 ...Lancelot, for the King...   H-32

484 In battle once & Lancelot, thrice, the Kings,   H-32;
                                                          Bd-3
484   thrice   once   I MS
    In battle ó́ńć́é́, and Lancelot t́h́ŕíć́é́ the King's -
                                                          S-929
484   twice   MS
    ...battle t́h́ŕíć́é́, and...   T-GP2
484 (C)   T-GP3

485-6 (Omitted)   A-2109
485-6 (Added, lined out)   T-GP2
485-6 (C - save below)   T-GP3
486   battlefield   I MS
    ...battle field —   T-GP3
486 ...battlefield -   72
486 (C)   73

Alt. sketch 487 ff
    Or some
    Ańd́ óńé́ wd tell him how the f́óŕé́śt́é́ŕ woodman once
    At dawn on Caer-Eryri found the King
    A naked babe, of whom Sir Merlin spake
    "He passes & is heal'd & will not die"
    Gareth was glad: Bd-3
Sketch 487-491
    And one wd tell him how the foresters
    Át́ d́áẃń on Caer-Eryri found the King
    As naked child of whom Sir Merlin spake   H-32

487   O   I MS
    ...glad; ór if...   S-929
487 (C)   B-II

How once the wandering forester at dawn,
Far over the blue tarns and hazy seas,
On Caer-Eryri's highest found the King,   490
A naked babe, of whom the Prophet spake,
'He passes to the Isle Avilion,
He passes and is healed and cannot die'--
Gareth was glad. But if their talk were foul,
Then would he whistle rapid as any lark,   495
Or carol some old roundelay, and so loud
That first they mocked, but, after, reverenced him.
Or Gareth telling some prodigious tale
Of knights, who sliced a red life-bubbling way

---

490 On C ae r-Eryri's...King,	ae(ae, I)	S-929
490 (C)		B-II
491 ...babe, of whom...spake	(, I)	S-929
491 ...spake		B-II
491 (C)		T-GP3
492 ...the Isle ø̸f̸ Avilion		Bd-3
492 ⫽ 'He...	(' I)	S-929
492 (C)		B-II
493 ...die̸ ⫽ ' -	'/- (I)	A-2109
493 (C)		B-II
494 many a time their talk was foul		H-40
494 or if...		H-40
494 He loved to hear; but if		H-32
494 B		
...glad̸/. but...foul,	(.B, I)	A-2109
494 (C)		B-II
495 ...whistle as any lark in heaven		H-40
495 ...whistle as any lark in air		H-40
495 ...whistle as quick as...		H-32
495 ...whistle as rapid...		Bd-3
495 ...whistle, ̸a̸s̸ rapid...	(, I)	S-929
495 (C)		B-II
496 Or carol some old catch		H-40
497 Till first they mock'd & after reverenced him		H-40

186

Through twenty folds of twisted dragon, held   500
All in a gap-mouthed circle his good mates
Lying or sitting round him, idle hands,
Charmed; till Sir Kay, the seneschal, would come
Blustering upon them, like a sudden wind
Among dead leaves, and drive them all apart.   505
Or when the thralls had sport among themselves,
So there were any trial of mastery,
He, by two yards in casting bar or stone
Was counted best; and if there chanced a joust,
So that Sir Kay nodded him leave to go,   510
Would hurry thither, and when he saw the knights
Clash like the coming and retiring wave,
And the spear spring, and good horse reel, the boy
Was half beyond himself for ecstasy.

---

497 ...him̸.   (. I)   A-2109
497 (C)   B-II

498 ...some long goodly talk   H-40
498 ...some old knightly tale   H-32;Bd-3

Alt. 499-500 Challenge, & blow on blow, & overthrow
                                                     H-32;Bd-3

499   ·   who
       ...knights, ̸t̸h̸a̸t̸ sliced...   Bd-3

501 All in a listening circle held his mates,   H-32
501 All in a gap-mouth'd circle held his mates,   Bd-3

502 ...or standing round...   H-32

507 And were there any trial of mastery   H-40

508 Quoit cast or wrestle or putting bar or stone   H-40

509 & whensoeer a joust   H-40
509 ...best; or if...   H-32

510 Was cried & Kay had given him leave to go,   H-40

513 ...spring, & the horse...   H-40

514 ...himself in ecstasy.   H-40

So for a month he wrought among the thralls;   515
But in the weeks that followed, the good Queen,
Repentant of the word she made him swear,
And saddening in her childless castle, sent,
Between the in-crescent and de-crescent moon,
Arms for her son, and loosed him from his vow.   520

    This, Gareth hearing from a squire of Lot
With whom he used to play at tourney once,
When both were children, and in lonely haunts
Would scratch a ragged oval on the sand,

---

515 ...for one month...   H-32

516   good
    But in that one which follow'd, the b̸a̸d̸ Queen,   H-32
516 But in the one that...   Bd-3
516   weeks   .   I MS
    But in the ø̸n̸e̸ that...   S-929
516 (C)   B-II

517 ...the vow she...   H-32
517   word   P MS
...the ̸v̸o̸w̸ she...   Bd-3

519 Between the increscent and decrescent moon,   S-929
519 (C)   84

520 ...from his ̸v̸o̸w̸ word   (P MS corr)   Bd-3

Sketch 521 ff
    (Par.) These news when Gareth from the lips of one
    With whom ̸t̸o̸ in mimic tilt at home he strove
    To make his boyhood (1 ?), heard, he laughd
    These be fair news - From out the smoke I leap
    At once from Satans foot to Peter's knee.
    So now for Arthurs face to question him
    Then diving found all empty & laugh'd again
    Anon, my friend, anon. These news be mine
    None other's, save one other. Yet (1 ?) down
    Into the city: there (1 ?) & sought   H-32

And each at either dash from either end--   525
Shame never made girl redder than Gareth joy.
He laughed; he sprang. 'Out of the smoke, at once
I leap from Satan's foot to Peter's knee--
These news be mine, none other's--nay, the King's--
Descend into the city;' whereon he sought
The King alone, and found, and told him all.   530

    'I have staggered thy strong Gawain in a tilt

521	Squire of Lot	P MS
	...hearing from a ~~man at arms~~	Bd-3
521	(Par.) This Gareth...	A-2109
521	(Par.) This, Gareth... ,/	T-GP2
521	(C)	T-GP3
522	...tourney/ once, ,/ (I)	A-2109
522	(C)	B-II

Alt. after 528
    So now for Arthur's face to guerdon him!'
    He dived but found all empty & laugh'd again
    'Anon, my friend, anon! these news be mine,
    None others, save one other ev'n the King -   Bd-3
Alt. after 528
    ~~So now for Arthur's face to guerdon himly~~
    ~~He dived, but found/all empty and laugh'd again/~~
    ~~'Anon, my friend, anon!/these news be mine,/~~
    ~~None other, save one other ev'n the King /~~   S-929
Alt. after 528 (Omitted)   B-II

530	whereon	P MS
	...city': ~~thereon~~ he...	Bd-3

Alt. preceding 531
    Then sought for gold to fee the news but found
    All empty & cried anon, my friend, anon.   W-Pf

531 Then sought the King alone, & told him all: W-Pf

532 I staggerd the strong...   H-32

533 For pastime. Modred saw it: ~~and~~ I can fight.   H-32

For pastime; yea, he said it: joust can I.
Make me thy knight--in secret! let my name
Be hidden, and give me the first quest, I spring   535
Like flame from ashes.'

                         Here the King's calm eye
Fell on, and checked, and made him flush, and bow
Lowly, to kiss his hand, who answered him,
'Son, the good mother let me know thee here,
And sent her wish that I would yield thee thine.   540
Make thee my knight? my knights are sworn to vows
Of utter hardihood, utter gentleness,
And, loving, utter faithfulness in love,
And uttermost obedience to the King.'

---

535 Be silent; grant me...   W-Pf

536 And the King replied   W-Pf;Bd-3

537-538
    C̸h̸e̸c̸k̸y̸d̸ G̸a̸r̸e̸t̸h̸y̸s̸ h̸e̸a̸t̸ & h̸a̸s̸t̸e̸, & d̸o̸w̸n̸ h̸e̸ k̸n̸e̸l̸t̸
    L̸o̸w̸l̸y̸, t̸o̸ k̸i̸s̸s̸ h̸i̸s̸ h̸a̸n̸d̸ w̸h̸o̸ a̸n̸s̸w̸e̸r̸y̸d̸ h̸i̸m̸,   Bd-3

539 Fair son, the mother...   W-Pf

540 ...thine̸.   . (I)   A-2109
540 (C)   B-II

541 ...knight? but canst thou hold the vows   H-32
541 ...knight̸ ? my...   (? I)   A-2109
541 (C)   B-II

545 ...Gareth rising lightly from his knees   Bd-3
545   springing   I MS
    ...Gareth, r̸i̸s̸i̸n̸g̸ lightly...   S-929
545 (C)   B-II

547-549 For gentleness, obedience ask of Kay   H-32

548 ...Seneschal̸ ,   ,/ (I)   A-2109
548 (C)   B-II

Then Gareth, lightly springing from his knees,   545
'My King, for hardihood I can promise thee.
For uttermost obedience make demand
Of whom ye gave me to, the Seneschal,
No mellow master of the meats and drinks!
And as for love, God wot, I love not yet,   550
But love˙I shall, God willing.'

                    And the King--
'Make thee my knight in secret? yea, but he,
Our noblest brother, and our truest man,
And one with me in all, he needs must know.'

   'Let Lancelot know, my King, let Lancelot know,   555
Thy noblest and thy truest!'

---

549 ...drinks⁄ !	(! I)	A-2109
549 (C)		B-II

550 ...as to love...		H-32
550 ...wot, I...	,/ (I)	S-929
550 (C)		B-II

551 And the King   P
    T̸h̸e̸ K̸i̸n̸g̸ m̸u̸s̸e̸d̸⁄   Bd-3

552 But if I make thee knight in secret, one,   H-32

553-554
   Lancelot, our noblest brother, one with me
   In all that touches on our Order, knows   H-32
553-554
   And Lancelot needs must know, as one with me
   In all that touches on our Table Round   W-Pf

555 ...know, said he, let...   W-Pf

556 ...& thy best
                Then Arthur Why,   W-Pf
556 ...truest,'   A-2109
556 ...truest⁄!'   !/ (I)   T-GP3
556 (C)   72

And the King--
'But wherefore would ye men should wonder at you?
Nay, rather for the sake of me, their King,
And the deed's sake my knighthood do the deed,
Than to be noised of.'

                    Merrily Gareth asked,   560
'Have I not earned my cake in baking of it?
Let be my name until I make my name!
My deeds will speak: it is but for a day.'
So with a kindly hand on Gareth's arm
Smiled the great King, and half-unwillingly   565

---

557 Son, wilt thy wish that men sd wonder at thee?		W-Pf
557 ...at you,?	(? I)	S-929
557 (C)		B-II
558 Fair nephew? for the...		W-Pf;B-II
558 Nay, rather		I MS
F̸a̸i̸r̸ ̸n̸e̸p̸h̸e̸w̸?̸ ≠ for...King,	(, I)	S-929
558 (C)		B-II
559 And		
For the deed's...		W-Pf
560 Not be babbled of.'		W-Pf
But Gareth said		
560 Not to be...		Bd-3
560 Than		I MS
N̸o̸t̸ to be...		S-929
560 (C)		B-II
561 Uncle, I earn'd my...		W-Pf
562 ...name⁄ until...name,	(, I)	A-2109
562 ...name, !	!⁄	T-GP2
562 (C)		T-GP3
565 So Arthur smiled & half unwillingly		W-Pf
567 Then, after⁄ summoning...	(, P)	A-2109
567 (C)		B-II

Loving his lusty youthhood yielded to him.
Then, after summoning Lancelot privily,
'I have given him the first quest: he is not proven.
Look therefore when he calls for this in hall,
Thou get to horse and follow him far away.   570
Cover the lions on thy shield, and see
Far as thou mayest, he be nor ta'en nor slain.'

   Then that same day there past into the hall
A damsel of high lineage, and a brow
May-blossom, and a cheek of apple-blossom,   575

---

569 ...this in Hall,		,/ (I)	A-2109
569 ...this in Hall,			B-II
569 ...this in Hall,		h/ (I)	T-GP3
569 (C)			72

570 Thou
    Ye get...   Bd-3

571 Not let him spy/ the lions on thy shield		Bd-3
571 And cover thy shield-lions over and see		Bd-3
571 ...shield, and...	,/ (I)	A-2109
571 (C)		B-II

572 And see that he be neither ta'en or slain		Bd-3
572 ...mayest, he...	,/ (I)	A-2109
572 (C)		B-II

573 (Par.) And by & bye there came into the hall   W-Pf
573   Then
   (Par.) And that...   Bd-3

574 ...lineage, with a brow   W-Pf

575 May-white, a cheek of appleblossom, eyes		W-Pf
575 May blossom-white//an appleblossom/cheek/		Bd-3
575 May-blossom...-blossom,	-/,/(P)	A-2109
575 May-blossom, and a cheek of apple-blossom		
	-/,/-/	T-GP2
575 (C)		T-GP3

Hawk-eyes; and lightly was her slender nose
Tip-tilted like the petal of a flower;
She into hall past with her page and cried,

'O King, for thou hast driven the foe without,
See to the foe within! bridge, ford, beset   580
By bandits, everyone that owns a tower
The Lord for half a league. Why sit ye there?
Rest would I not, Sir King, an I were king,
Till even the lonest hold were all as free
From cursed bloodshed, as thine altar-cloth   585
From that best blood it is a sin to spill.'

'Comfort thyself,' said Arthur, 'I nor mine
Rest: so my knighthood keep the vows they swore,

---

576 Hawk-keen; & saucily was her little nose		W-Pf
576 ~~Hawklikes & saucily was her little~~		Bd-3
576 ~~Hawk eyes;~~		Bd-3
576 Hawk-eyes; and...	(-; I)	S-929
576 Hawk-eyes; ...	-/	T-GP2
576 (C)		T-GP3
583 ...king,	,/ (I)	A-2109
583 (C)		B-II
585 ...altar-cloth	-/ (P)	A-2109
585 (C)		B-II
586 ...that blest blood...		Bd-3
588 ...keep their vows a year,		Bd-3
588 they swore		I MS
...keep ~~their~~ vows a year,		S-929
588 ...swore,	,/	T-GP2
588 (C)		T-GP3
589 ~~One year~~ the wastest of region of my realm shall		
be		H-40
592 My name, Lynette, noble; my need, a knight		
~~Lynette my name & noble an I/ my need~~		H-32

The wastest moorland of our realm shall be
Safe, damsel, as the centre of this hall.   590
What is thy name? thy need?'

                              'My name?' she said--
'Lynette my name; noble; my need, a knight
To combat for my sister, Lyonors,
A lady of high lineage, of great lands,
And comely, yea, and comelier than myself.   595
She lives in Castle Perilous: a river
Runs in three loops about her living-place;
And o'er it are three passings, and three knights
Defend the passings, brethren, and a fourth
And of that four the mightiest,holds her stayed   600
In her own castle, and so besieges her
To break her will, and make her wed with him:

---

592 Lineth my...   Bd-3
592 Lynette   I MS
    ~~Lineth~~ my...   S-929
592 (C)   B-II

593   my sister Linors
    ~~A goodly knight warrior~~ to do battle for a maid H-32
593 ...sister Linors   Bd-3
593   y   I MS
    ...sister L~~i~~nors,   S-929
593 (C)   B-II

594   high lineage &
    Lionors, my sister, a lady of great lands,   H-32

597 Flies in three whirls about her castle wall,   H-32
597 Runs   living place   P MS
    ~~Flies~~ in...her ~~castle walls~~   Bd-3

600   among   all keeps her stay'd
    The mightiest ~~of~~ them besieges her,   H-32

601 ...castle and...   A-2109
601 (C)   73

602 ...him: :/ (I)   A-2109
602 (C)   B-II

And but delays his purport till thou send
To do the battle with him, thy chief man
Sir Lancelot whom he trusts to overthrow,   605
Then wed, with glory: but she will not wed
Save whom she loveth, or a holy life.
Now therefore have I come for Lancelot.'

   Then Arthur mindful of Sir Gareth asked,
'Damsel, ye know this Order lives to crush   610
All wrongers of the Realm. But say, these four,
Who be they? What the fashion of the men?'

| 603 | purport | |
| | ...his d́ńd́ till thou śh́d́l̷l̷ send | H-32 |

| 604 | ...chief knight | H-32 |

605	slay, & then	I MS
	...trusts to ǿv́ér̷t́h́r̷ǿẃ	S-929
605	overthrow	MS
	...trusts to śĺd́ý/ d́ńd́ t́h́éń	T-GP2
605	(C)	T-GP3

606	Then	
	D́ńd́ wed	H-32
606	Wed her,	I MS
	T́h́éń ẃéd́, with...	S-929
606	Then wed,	MS
	Ẃéd́ h́ér̷/ with glory; but...	T-GP2
606	...glory; but...	T-GP3
606	(C)	72

608	have	P MS
	...therefore h́ér̷e I come...	S-929
608	(C)	B-II

611	worlds offences	P MS
	The ẃǿḿd́ń ẃr̷ǿńǵér̷. Tell us, these four	
	knights,	Bd-3
611	All wrongers of the realm: but say, these four	I MS
	The world's offences, T́él̷l̷ ús/ these four	
	K̷ń́ı̷ǵh́t́ś/	S-929
611	(C)	B-II

'They be of foolish fashion, O Sir King,
The fashion of that old knight-errantry
Who ride abroad, and do but what they will;   615
Courteous or bestial from the moment, such
As have nor law nor king; and three of these
Proud in their fantasy call themselves the Day,
Morning-Star, and Noon-Sun, and Evening-Star,
Being strong fools; and never a whit more wise   620

Alt. for 614
    ree
    T̸h̸e̸ s̸o̸n̸s̸ o̸f̸ o̸n̸e̸ o̸f̸ o̸t̸h̸e̸r̸'̸s̸ p̸e̸e̸r̸a̸g̸e̸:̸ T̸h̸r̸e̸e̸
    F̸a̸n̸t̸a̸s̸t̸i̸c̸a̸l̸l̸y̸ c̸a̸l̸l̸ t̸h̸e̸m̸s̸e̸l̸v̸e̸s̸ T̸h̸e̸ D̸a̸y̸   Bd-3

615   they
    That rides̸ abroad & dot̸h̸ but what i̸t̸ will;   Bd-3
615 Who   I MS
    T̸h̸a̸t̸ ride abroad and...   S-929
615 ...abroad and...   B-II
615 (C)   86

616 ...bestial, as the mood may fall   Bd-3
616   bestial (l ?) from the moment-men   I MS
    Courteous or b̸r̸u̸t̸a̸l̸, as the mood may fall,
                        ,/ (I)   A-2109
616 Courteous or bestial, as the mood may fall,   B-II
616   from the moment, such   I MS
    Courteous or bestial a̸s̸ t̸h̸e̸ m̸o̸o̸d̸ m̸a̸y̸ f̸a̸l̸l̸,   T-GP3
616 (C)   72

617 Not having law nor King...   Bd-3
617 Not having law...   S-929
617 As have nor   I MS
    N̸o̸t̸ h̸a̸v̸i̸n̸g̸ law...   T-GP3
617 (C)   72

619 Morning-star, and Noon-sun, and Evening-star, A-2109
619   S   S   S   I MS
    Morning-s̸tar, and Noon-s̸un, and Evening-s̸tar,   T-GP3
619 (C)   72

The fourth, who alway rideth armed in black,
A huge man-beast of boundless savagery.
He names himself the Night and oftener Death,
And wears a helmet mounted with a skull,
And bears a skeleton figured on his arms,   625
To show that who may slay or scape the three,
Slain by himself, shall enter endless night.
And all these four be fools, but mighty men,
And therefore am I come for Lancelot.'

    Hereat Sir Gareth called from where he rose,   630

---

621 ...alway arms himself in black.	Bd-3
621 rideth arm'd	I MS
...alway a̶r̶m̶s̶ h̶i̶m̶s̶e̶l̶f̶ in black,	S-929
621 (C)	B-II

622 ...boundless savageness	Bd-3
622 ery	P MS
...boundelss savag̶e̶n̶e̶s̶s̶,. (. I)	S-929
622 (C)	B-II

623 Who oftener	
A̶n̶d̶ names himself the Night & s̶o̶m̶e̶w̶h̶i̶l̶e̶ (?),	
Death	Bd-3
623 He	I MS
W̶h̶o̶ names...	S-929
623 (C)	B-II

624 mounted with	
...helmet f̶a̶s̶h̶i̶o̶n̶d̶ l̶i̶k̶e̶ a skull,	Bd-3

625 ...skeleton painted on...	Bd-3
625 figured	I MS
...skeleton p̶a̶i̶n̶t̶e̶d̶ on his arms, (, I)	S-929
625 (C)	B-II

626 ...the three	S-929
626 (C)	86

627 himself enter endless	
Slain by h̶i̶s̶ h̶a̶n̶d̶ shall p̶a̶s̶s̶ t̶o̶ d̶a̶t̶e̶l̶e̶s̶s̶ night, Bd-3	

A head with kindling eyes above the throng.
'A boon, Sir King--this quest!' then—for he marked
Kay near him groaning like a wounded bull--
'Yea, King, thou knowest thy kitchen-knave am I,
And mighty through thy meats and drinks am I,   635
And I can topple over a hundred such.
Thy promise, King.' and Arthur glancing at him,
Brought down a momentary brow. 'Rough, sudden,
And pardonable, worthy to be knight--
Go therefore,' and all hearers were amazed.   640

    But on the damsel's forehead shame, pride, wrath
Slew the May-white: she lifted either arm,
'Fie on thee, King! I asked for thy chief knight,
And thou hast given me but a kitchen-knave.'
Then ere a man in hall could stay her, turned,   645
Fled down the lane of access to the King,
Took horse, descended the slope street, and past
The weird white gate, and paused without, beside
The field of tourney, murmuring 'kitchen-knave.'

---

627 ...himself shall...night.   ⊙ (I)   S-929
627 ...himself shall...   B-II
627 (C)   86

Sketch for 630 ff
    Then cried the newmade knight from where he rose
    A head with sparkling eyes above the throng
    Mine is the Quest. & after one brief (1 ?)
    Thine, kitchen knave, from Kay the seneschal
    Yea, for   H-32

638   a momentary brow   P MS
    Brought down ~~his brows a little~~. Rough ~~&~~
                    sudden,   Bd-3

Alt. after 638 ~~Yet with the makings of a Knight of mine~~
           ~~But bold & pardonable~~   Bd-3

646 Fled
    ~~Ran~~ down...   Bd-3

648   wierd
    The ~~great~~ white...   Bd-3

Now two great entries opened from the hall,   650
At one end one, that gave upon a range
Of level pavement where the King would pace
At sunrise, gazing over plain and wood;
And down from this a lordly stairway sloped
Till lost in blowing trees and tops of towers;   655
And out by this main doorway past the King.

---

650 ...great doorways opend		H-32
650 ...the Hall,		A-2109
650 ...the H̸all,	h/ (I)	T-GP3
650 (C)		72

651 One at one end, wh gave upon a s̸p̸a̸c̸e̸ range   H-32

653 ...over f̸i̸e̸l̸d̸ & plain...	H-32
653 ...and wood.	A-2109
653 (C)	73

654   lordly
...this a s̸t̸a̸t̸e̸l̸y̸ stairway   Bd-3

655 Till lost in tops of towers & blowing trees.	H-32
655 ...of towers.	A-2109
655 (C)	73

657 And one...hearth, & h̸i̸g̸h̸ huge, rose		H-32
657 But		
A̸n̸d̸ one...		Bd-3
657 ...hearth, and...	,/ (I)	A-2109
657 (C)		B-II

658 Hight that the tallest knight therethro cd ride H-32
658   t̸h̸e̸r̸e̸t̸h̸r̸o̸   helm cd ride
Hight that the highest-crested k̸n̸i̸g̸h̸t̸ t̸h̸e̸r̸e̸/
               t̸h̸r̸o̸/   Bd-3

659 ...by this side-door had fled		H-32
659 Therethro'		
Could ride nor graze: by this side-entry fled		Bd-3
659 ...graze: & by this s̸i̸d̸e̸- entry fled	(& I)	S-929
659 (C)		B-II

But one was counter to the hearth, and rose
High that the highest-crested helm could ride
Therethrough nor graze: and by this entry fled
The damsel in her wrath, and on to this   660
Sir Gareth strode, and saw without the door
King Arthur's gift, the worth of half a town,
A warhorse of the best, and near it stood
The two that out of north had followed him:
This bare a maiden shield, a casque; that held   665
The horse, the spear; whereat Sir Gareth loosed
A cloak that dropt from collar-bone to heel,
A cloth of roughest web, and cast it down,
And from it like a fuel-smothered fire,

---

661 ...saw beside the door   H-32

663   it
     ...& near ~~him~~ stood   Bd-3

664 The twain that came with Gareth from the North   H-32

665 This held a helmet & a shield, & that   H-32
665 This held a burgonet, a shield; & that   Bd-3
665   maiden   I MS
     ~~Waiting~~ This bare a ~~virgin~~ shield, a casque;
                              that held   I MS
     ~~This held a burgonet, a shield, and that~~   A-2109

666 The horse & spear; & Gareth letting fall   H-32

667 Wh vail'd him all from...   H-32

668 A cloak of roughest fabric shone in arms   H-32
668 A cloth of coarsest web, he cast it down   H-32
668 ...down.,   (, I)   A-2109
668 (C)   B-II

Alt. after 668 Beside the door & all complete arms   H-32

669 Shone as breaks out a fuel smotherd fire   H-32
669 ~~Near him, & like/a/fuel smother'd fire~~   Bd-3
669 So like a fuel smother'd fire that lookt   S-929
669 ...fire,   (I)   T-GP2
669 (C)   T-GP3

201

That lookt half-dead, brake bright, and flashed as
those   670
Dull-coated things, that making slide apart
Their dusk wing-cases, all beneath there burns
A jewelled harness, ere they pass and fly.
So Gareth ere he parted flashed in arms.
Then as he donned the helm, and took the shield   675
And mounted horse and graspt a spear, of grain
Storm-strengthened on a windy site, and tipt
With trenchant steel, around him slowly prest

---

670 ...dead, brake out as bright as those	Bd-3
670 Half dead he brake out bright and flashed as those	S-929
670 ...bright, and... (I)	T-GP2
670 (C)	T-GP3

671 Or as the beetle making slide apart	H-32
671 And as the beetle making slide apart	H-32
671 Dull-seeming things,...	Bd-3
671 Dull-seeming things...	S-929
671 coated	I MS
Dull-s̸e̸e̸m̸i̸n̸g̸ things...	T-GP3
671 (C)	72

672 His dark wingcases underneath them shows	H-32
672 His dusk wingcases underneath them shows	H-32

673 A jeweled harness ere he flies away	H-32

674 ...parted shone in arms	H-32

675 took And while he donn'd the helm; & graspt the shield,	H-32
675 And while he donn'd...	Bd-3
675 A̸n̸d̸ l̸e̸t̸t̸i̸n̸g̸ t̸h̸i̸s̸/ a̸ c̸l̸o̸t̸h̸ o̸f̸ x̸ (P MS - facing pg.)	
F̸a̸l̸l̸ f̸r̸o̸m̸ h̸i̸m̸/ l̸i̸k̸e̸ a̸ (P MS - facing pg.)	
A̸n̸d̸ while he...	A-2109
675 Then	I MS
A̸n̸d̸ while...	T-GP2
675 Then while he...	T-GP3
675 (C)	73

The people, while from out of kitchen came
The thralls in throng, and seeing who had worked   680
Lustier than any, and whom they could but love,
Mounted in arms, threw up their caps and cried,
'God bless the King, and all his fellowship!'
And on through lanes of shouting Gareth rode
Down the slope street, and past without the gate.   685

676	graspt	
	...& took a spear...	H-32
678	...steel, about him...	H-32
679	A gaping crowd, & out...	H-32
679	of	
	...from out t̸h̸e̸/kitchen came	Bd-3
679	The people, and from	A-2109
679	(C)	73
681	Lustiest of any...	H-32
682	...cried	A-2109
682	(C)	T-GP3
683	...fellowship̸/' !/ (P)	A-2109
683	(C)	B-II

Alt. after 683 Whereat the people mingled with
                        the cry   H-32

684	And so thro' ...	Bd-3
684	on	P MS
	And s̸o̸ thro' ...	A-2109
684	on	MS
	And s̸o̸ thro' ...	T-GP2
684	(C)	T-GP3
685	Down the slope city & past from out the Gate	H-32
685	...street, and... ,/ (P)	A-2109
685	...street, and... ,/	T-GP2
685·	(C)	T-GP3

    So Gareth past with joy; but as the cur
Pluckt from the cur he fights with, ere his cause
Be cooled by fighting, follows, being named,
His owner, but remembers all, and growls
Remembering, so Sir Kay beside the door   690
Muttered in scorn of Gareth whom he used
To harry and hustle.

                        'Bound upon a quest
With horse and arms--the King hath past his time--
My scullion knave! Thralls to your work again,
For an your fire be low ye kindle mine!   695
Will there be dawn in West and eve in East?
Begone!--my knave!--belike and like enow

Sketch 686 ff
         as   cur   ṃáṣṭéṛṣ ḥíṃ
    But ḻíḳé the ḍóǵ which he that owns him plucks
                   cur   fought   cause
    Plucks from the dog he strove with, ere his rage
       cool'd by fighting
    Ḅé ḟóúǵḥṭ áẃáỵ ḅúṭ follows being call'd,
                   remembering all
    His owner, but he feels the bite & growls
    Remembering so Sir Kay beside the door
                   whom he used to fl
    Mutterd remembering Gareth & the King.
    And hustle, Gareth: Bound on quest
    The kitchen knave   H-32

686 (Par.) Ḃúṭ áṣ ṭḥé ćúṛ ẃḥ ḥé ẃḥó óẃṇṣ íṭ ṗḻúćḳṣ   Bd-3
686 ...joy,; but...   ;/ (I)   S-929
686 (C)   B-II

687 Ṗḻóṃ óḟḟ the cur...   Bd-3

688   named
     ...being ćáḻḻỵá,   Bd-3

691   in scorn of   P MS
     Mutter's ṛéṃéṃḅéṛíṇǵ Gareth...   Bd-3

694-695 Thrall to your work for an your fire be low
         Ye kindle mine. Belike, & like enow   W-Pf

204

Some old head-blow not heeded in his youth
So shook his wits they wander in his prime--
Crazed! How the villain lifted up his voice,   700
Nor shamed to bawl himself a kitchen-knave.
Tut: he was tame and meek enow with me,
Till peacocked up with Lancelot's noticing.
Well--I will after my loud knave,and learn
Whether he know me for his master yet.   705
Out of the smoke he came, and so my lance
Hold, by God's grace, he shall into the mire--
Thence, if the King awaken from his craze,

---

696 ...West and Eve in East?   S-929
696 (C)   72

697 Begone! - my knave! - belike...   -/-/ (I)   A-2109
697 (C)   B-II

698 That old headwound of Badon battle field   H-32
698 Some old head-stroke not...   H-32;W-Pf

699 Has broken out again.   H-32
699 B̶e̶l̶i̶k̶e̶ Shook him, & works   in age upon his wit. H-32
699 ...in his age   W-Pf;Bd-3
699   prime -   I MS
    ...in his a̶g̶e̶ -   S-929
699 (C)   B-II

Alt. after 699 A quest for him! & whence his horse &
                          arms - from him   H-32
                 Crazed
Alt. after 699 The quest, & arms & horse? from whom?
                          the King   W-Pf

700 Crazed - how   W-Pf
700 Crazed/ How...   !/ (P)   A-2109
700 (C)   B-II

706 ...smoke he went & so...   H-32

707 ...shall pass into...   H-32

708 ...if the recovers of his craze   H-32

Into the smoke again.'

                     But Lancelot said,
'Kay, wherefore wilt thou go against the King,   710
For that did never he whereon ye rail,
But ever meekly served the King in thee?
Abide: take counsel; for this lad is great
And lusty, and knowing both of lance and sword.'
'Tut, tell not me,' said Kay, 'ye are overfine   715
To mar stout knaves with foolish courtesies:'
Then mounted, on through silent faces rode
Down the slope city, and out beyond the gate.

But by the field of tourney lingering yet
Muttered the damsel,'Wherefore did the King   720
Scorn me? for, were Sir Lancelot lackt, at least
He might have yielded to me one of those
Who tilt for lady's love and glory here,

---

709 ...again.   A-2109
709 ...again.'   ʘ'/ (I)   T-GP3
709 (C)   72

710 ...wherefore will ye go...   Bd-3
710 ...wherefore will ye go...   S-929
710 (C)   73

712 ...in thee⁄   ?/(P)   A-2109;T-GP3
712 (C)   72

Alt. after 712 Told I thee not there was a mystery
                            here?   Bd-3
Alt. after 712 T̸o̸l̸d̸ I̸ t̸h̸e̸e̸ n̸o̸t̸ t̸h̸e̸r̸e̸ w̸a̸s̸ a̸ m̸y̸s̸t̸e̸r̸y̸
                            h̸e̸r̸e̸?̸   A-2109
Alt. after 712 (Omitted)   B-II

715 'Tut tell...   A-2109
715 'Tut, tell...   ,/   T-GP2
715 (C)   T-GP3

716 T̸o̸ m̸a̸r̸ a̸ w̸h̸o̸l̸e̸s̸o̸m̸e̸ k̸n̸a̸v̸e̸ w̸i̸t̸h̸ a̸n̸   Bd-3
716   stout
   To mar g̸o̸o̸d̸ knaves...   Bd-3
716 ...courtesies.'   A-2109
716 (C)   84

Rather than--O sweet heaven! O fie upon him--
His kitchen-knave.'

                    To whom Sir Gareth drew   725
(And there were none but few goodlier than he)
Shining in arms, 'Damsel, the quest is mine.
Lead, and I follow.' She thereat, as one
That smells a foul-fleshed agaric in the holt,
And deems it carrion of some woodland thing,   730
Or shrew, or weasel, nipt her slender nose
With petulant thumb and finger, shrilling, 'Hence!

---

717 And thro the silent people fuming rode   H-32
717   on
    Then mounted, ~~horse~~ & thro'...   Bd-3

723 ...tilt for ~~glory~~ & lady's love...   Bd-3

724 ...sweet heavens! fie fie upon him -   Bd-3
724   O   P MS
    ...heaven! ~~fie~~ fie...   A-2109
724 (C)   B-II

725   drew   I MS
    ...Gareth ~~then~~   A-2109
725 (C)   B-II

729 That smells a snakeshead agaric...   Bd-3
729   ~~sickening~~ ~~foul~~ ~~fleshed~~   P MS
    That smells a ~~snakeshead~~ agaric...   A-2109
729   ~~hidden~~   stet   MS
    ...smells a ~~snakeshead~~ agaric...   T-GP2
729   foul-flesh'd   I MS
    ...smells a ~~sickening~~ agaric...   T-GP3
729 (C)   72

732 Between thumb & finger crying Hence   Bd-3
732 With petulant   shrilling   I MS
    ~~Between~~ a thumb and finger, ~~crying~~ Hence!
                              !/ (I)   A-2109
732 ~~Between~~ a thumb and finger crying 'Hence!   T-GP2
732 With petulant   shrilling   I MS
    ~~Between~~ a thumb and finger, ~~crying~~, 'Hence! T-GP3
732 (C)   72

207

Avoid, thou smellest all of kitchen-grease.
And look who comes behind,' for there was Kay.
'Knowest thou not me? thy master? I am Kay.   735
We lack thee by the hearth.'

                  And Gareth to him,
'Master no more! too well I know thee, ay--
The most ungentle knight in Arthur's hall.'
'Have at thee then,' said Kay: they shocked, and Kay
Fell shoulder-slipt, and Gareth cried again,   740
'Lead, and I follow,' and fast away she fled.

    But after sod and shingle ceased to fly
Behind her, and the heart of her good horse
Was nigh to burst with violence of the beat,

---

733 Avaunt, thou...		Bd-3
733 Avoid		P MS
A̸v̸a̸u̸n̸t̸, thou...		A-2109
733 (C)		B-II
737 too well yea -		P MS
...more! I know thee w̸e̸l̸l̸ e̸n̸o̸w̸,		Bd-3
737 a		P MS
...thee, y̸e̸a̸		A-2109
737 a		MS
...thee, y̸e̸a̸ -		T-GP2;T-GP3
737 (C)		72
742 But w̸h̸e̸n̸ after...		W-Pf
744 ...burst thro' violence		W-Pf
745 ...overtaken spake.		W-Pf
746 ...thou s̸c̸u̸l̸l̸i̸o̸n̸ here in my companionship		W-Pf
747 Thinkst thou that...thee any the more		W-Pf
748 And love thee better, s̸e̸e̸i̸n̸g̸ that...		W-Pf
750 ...master, K̸a̸y̸. Thou		W-Pf;Bd-3
750 ...master/ K̸a̸y̸/ thou/ -	-/ (I)	A-2109
750 (C)		B-II

Perforce she stayed, and overtaken spoke.   745

'What doest thou, scullion, in my fellowship?
Deem'st thou that I accept thee aught the more
Or love thee better, that by some device
Full cowardly, or by mere unhappiness,
Thou hast overthrown and slain thy master--thou!--   750
Dish-washer and broach-turner, loon!--to me
Thou smellest all of kitchen as before.'

'Damsel,' Sir Gareth answered gently, 'say
Whate'er ye will, but whatsoe'er ye say,
I leave not till I finish this fair quest   755
Or die therefore.'

'Ay, wilt thou finish it?
Sweet lord, how like a noble knight he talks!

---

751 ...turner, lusk & loon. depart but he   W-Pf
751 ...loon! - to me   -/ (P)   A-2109
751 (C)   B-II

Alt. after 751 Made her a   W-Pf

752   all of
   ...smellest ø̸f̸ t̸h̸e̸ kitchen   Bd-3

753 (Par.) Gently Sir Gareth answer'd Damsel, say   Bd-3

Sketch 754
            eer   will   Damsel, say
    Say what ye list, f̸a̸i̸r̸ d̸a̸m̸s̸e̸l̸,̸ a̸n̸s̸w̸e̸r̸d̸ h̸e̸
    But whatsoeer ye say I w̸i̸l̸l̸ n̸ø̸t̸ h̸e̸n̸c̸e̸   W-Pf

755 I part not...   W-Pf
755 ...this thy quest   Bd-3

757   talks
    Good lord, ...he speaks   W-Pf
757 Good Lord, ...   Bd-3
757 Sweet   P MS
    G̸ø̸ø̸d̸ lord, ...   A-2109;T-GP3
757 (C)   72

The listening rogue hath caught the manner of it.
But, knave, anon thou shalt be met with, knave,
And then by such a one that thou for all   760
The kitchen brewis that was ever supt
Shalt not once dare to look him in the face.'

    'I shall assay,' said Gareth with a smile
That maddened her, and away she flashed again
Down the long avenues of a boundless wood,   765
And Gareth following was again beknaved.

    'Sir Kitchen-knave, I have missed the only way
Where Arthur's men are set along the wood;
The wood is nigh as full of thieves as leaves:
If both be slain, I am rid of thee; but yet,   770
Sir Scullion, canst thou use that spit of thine?

---

758 He hath caught the manner of it, listening   Bd-3

759 ...met ⱳⁱⱦⱨⁱⱦ, knave   W-Pf

760 And that by...   W-Pf

761 The kitchenbroth that ever slipt thy throat   W-Pf
761 The kitchen stuff that ever slipt thy throat   Bd-3
761   brewis   was   supp'd   I MS
    The kitchen-ₛⱦ ⱳ ⱦⱦ that ever slipt thy throat   S-929
761 (C)   B-II

763 ...Gareth smiling at her   W-Pf;Bd-3

764 Wh madden'd...   Bd-3

765 And miss'd the main track in a boundless wood   Bd-3
765 Down long
    Along the avenues of...   Bd-3

Sketch 767 ff
    Sir knave, for at the choosing of thee
    We two be here The lion & the stoat
    Will isle together in the time of flood.
    I have missed the way where Arthur's men are set
    The woods are nigh as full of thief as leaf.   H-32

Fight, an thou canst: I have missed the only way.'

    So till the dusk that followed evensong
Rode on the two, reviler and reviled;
Then after one long slope was mounted, saw,   775
Bowl-shaped, through tops of many thousand pines
A gloomy-gladed hollow slowly sink
To westward--in the deeps whereof a mere,
Round as the red eye of an Eagle-owl,

---

771 Friend scullion, ...	H-32
771 Sir	
F̶r̶i̶e̶n̶d̶ Scullion...	Bd-3
772 Fight if thou canst. My God - I have lost the	
way.	H-32
773 So till it darken'd after evensong,	H-32
773 evensong	I MS
...that follow'd e̶v̶e̶n̶i̶n̶g̶	S-929
773 (C)	B-II
774 The two rode on, reviler...	H-32
774 ...reviled:	A-2109
774 (C)	72
775 Then after climbing a great slope they saw	H-32
775 Then after mounting one long slope, beheld	H-32
776-777 A̶ g̶l̶d̶ Bowl-shaped, a gloomy gladed hollow	
sink	H-32
776-777 A gloomy-gladed hollow slowly sink,	
Bowl-shaped, & tops of many thousand pines	H-32
778 To westward, & beneath, a rounded mere	H-32
778 ...a mere, (, I)	A-2109
778 (C)	B-II
779 Red as the round eye...	H-32
779 Glar'd like	
Round as the red...	Bd-3
779 2 1	
Round as the red eye of an Eagle-owl, (, I)	S-929
779 (C)	B-II

Under the half-dead sunset glared; and shouts   780
Ascended, and there brake a servingman
Flying from out of the black wood, and crying,
'They have bound my lord to cast him in the mere.'
Then Gareth, 'Bound am I to right the wronged,
But straitlier bound am I to bide with thee.'   785
And when the damsel spake contemptuously,
'Lead, and I follow,' Gareth cried again,
'Follow, I lead!' so down among the pines

---

780 ...glared in gloom.		H-32
780 ...glared, & from it		H-32
780 & a cry		
...glared; & from it		Bd-3
780 ...glared; & cries		Bd-3
780 ...glared; and cries		A-2109
780 (C)		72

781 And from the mere came shrieks and cries	H-32
781 Ascended shriek & shouting, & a man	H-32
781 from it - & there rush'd a servitor	
Came shrieks & shoutings; & a serving man	Bd-3

782 Then from the black wood came a serving man	
Flying & crying 'They have bound my lord	H-32
782 Flying & crying issued from the wood	H-32
782 from out of the dark wood,	
Flying & crying b̷r̷a̷k̷e̷ f̷r̷o̷m̷ o̷u̷t̷ t̷h̷e̷ w̷o̷o̷d̷	Bd-3

783 Six robbers & will cast him in...	H-32

Alt. after 783 That some may know	H-32

784 ...wrong'd⁄	,⁄ (P)	A-2109
784 (C)		B-II

785 I may not leave thee alone in the black wood	H-32
785 But cannot leave thee alone within the wood'	H-32
785 bide	
...am I to stay with thee'	Bd-3

786 Whereat the damsel...	H-32

212

He plunged; and there, blackshadowed nigh the mere,
And mid-thigh-deep in bulrushes and reed,   790
Saw six tall men haling a seventh along,
A stone about his neck to drown him in it.
Three with good blows he quieted, but three
Fled through the pines; and Gareth loosed the stone
From off his neck, then in the mere beside   795

---

787 ...follow & Gareth...   H-32
787 'Lead and...   A-2109
787 (C)   73

788 ...lead & plunged into the wood.   H-32
788   down
   ...lead' & p̷l̷u̷n̷g̷e̷d̷ among...   Bd-3
788 ...lead! & down...   Bd-3
788 ...lead,' and down...   A-2109
788   so   I MS
   ...lead/' a̷n̷d̷ down...   ! (I) T-GP3
788 (C)   72

789-790 There blackening by the sedges of the mere H-32

789   blackshadow'd by the pool
   ...there blackening in   Bd-3

790   mid thigh deep in bulrushes & reed
   And nigh knee-deep in shallows of the mere Bd-3
790 ...and reeds̷,   ,/ (I) A-2109
790 (C)   B-II

791   tall
   He saw six men...   H-32

792 ...him. At once   H-32
792 ...him there   Bd-3

793 And three with blows he quieted & three H-32
793 ...quieted, & three   H-32

794 ...loosed his bonds   H-32
794 ...pines: then Gareth   H-32

795 ...neck, & in...   H-32

Tumbled it; oilily bubbled up the mere.
Last, Gareth loosed his bonds and on free feet
Set him, a stalwart Baron, Arthur's friend.

'Well that ye came, or else these caitiff rogues
Had wreaked themselves on me; good cause is theirs   800
To hate me, for my wont hath ever been
To catch my thief, and then like vermin here
Drown him, and with a stone about his neck;
And under this wan water many of them
Lie rotting, but at night let go the stone,   805
And rise, and flickering in a grimly light

---

796 Tumbled
      ~~He cast it~~: oilily...   H-32

797   with free   he
     Then ~~freed his~~ hands, & set him on his feet   H-32

798 A hoar but stalwart...   H-32
798 Set him, an ancient Baron,...   Bd-3

799 ...else the catiff-rogues   H-32
799 (Par.) 'Well, that...   A-2109
799 (Par.) 'Well/ that...   T-GP3
799 (C)   72

800   day
     Had wreak'd their vengeance on me here to-night.
                                                        H-32
800   theirs   P MS
     ...is ~~there~~   A-2109
800 (C)   B-II

Sketch 801-804
     I have ever warrd on these thieves & my manner was
     When I had overcome them to tie a stone round their
     necks & drown them in this mere - & there be many
     rotting under this wan water   H-32

801   manner when I caught
     For this hath been my many a day fair Sir Knight
                                                        H-32

214

Dance on the mere. Good now, ye have saved a life
Worth somewhat as the cleanser of this wood.
And fain would I reward thee worshipfully.
What guerdon will ye?'

                          Gareth sharply spake,   810
'None! for the deed's sake have I done the deed,
In uttermost obedience to the King.

802	like vermin here	
	When I had overcomen any of these	H-32
803	To drown him with...	H-32
803	and	P MS
	~~To~~ drown him with...	Bd-3
803	...neck;	(; I) A-2109
803	(C)	B-II

804 ...many of these   H-32

Sketch 805-810
                  (1 ?) for
    Lie rotting. Ye have saved my life Sir Knight
    And fain wd I reward thee worshipfully.
    What will ye for reward.   H-32

805 ~~Lie rotting! Good now, ye have saved a life~~   Bd-3
805   let go
    ...night ~~they slip~~ the stone   Bd-3
805 ...rotting ~~&~~ , but...stone,   (,, I)   A-2109
805 (C)   B-II

806   rise & flicker
    And ~~some have seen them~~ in a grimly light   Bd-3
806 And rise, and...   (, I)   A-2109
806 (C)   B-II

807 Dance onthe ~~pool~~ mere...   Bd-3
807   now   I MS
    ...Good ~~man~~, ye...   S-929
807 (C)   B-II

810 Gareth quickly said
    The new knight said   H-32

But wilt thou yield this damsel harbourage?'

    Whereat the Baron saying, 'I well believe
You be of Arthur's Table,' a light laugh   815
Broke from Lynette, 'Ay, truly of a truth,
And in a sort, being Arthur's kitchen-knave!--
But deem not I accept thee aught the more,
Scullion, for running sharply with thy spit
Down on a rout of craven foresters.   820
A thresher with his flail had scattered them.
Nay--for thou smellest of tne kitchen still.
But an this lord will yield us harbourage,
Well.'

---

813 But will ye yield this...	Bd-3
813 But will ye yield...	A-2109
813 (C)	73

Sketch 814-816
    Ye be of Arthur's table' ask'd the Lord.
    The damsel laught Ay Truly of a truth,   H-32

814 well	
...I d̸o̸ perceive	Bd-3
814 believe	I MS
...saying, 'I d̸o̸ well p̸e̸r̸c̸e̸i̸v̸e̸	S-929
814 (C)	B-II

815 Ye be...	Bd-3
814 Ye be...	A-2109
815 (C)	73

816 Brake from...		Bd-3
816 Lynette		I MS
Broke from L̸y̸n̸e̸t̸h̸ 'Ay...truth,	,/ (I)	S-929
816 ...Lynette 'Ay, ...		B-II
816 (C)		T-GP3

Sketch 818-819
    Deemest thou that I have joy of thee for this
    Or laud to yield for thy performance done
    But think ye I allow you for the deed   H-32

So she spake. A league beyond the wood,
All in a full-fair manor and a rich,   825
His towers where that day a feast had been
Held in high hall, and many a viand left,
And many a costly cate, received the three.
And there they placed a peacock in his pride
Before the damsel, and the Baron set   830
Gareth beside her, but at once she rose.

'Meseems, that here is much discourtesy,
Setting this knave, Lord Baron, at my side.

---

819   for running sharply
       Scullion, b̸e̸c̸a̸u̸s̸e̸ t̸h̸o̸u̸ r̸a̸n̸n̸e̸s̸t̸ with...   Bd-3

820 Wrought on a rout of...   H-32

824 Why,   that were well'
       Well,'   Bd-3

825 ...a rich,   (, I)   A-2109
825 (C)   B-II

826   where that day a feast
       His towers r̸e̸c̸e̸i̸v̸e̸d̸ t̸h̸e̸m̸./ T̸h̸e̸r̸e̸ had been á
                        f̸e̸a̸s̸t̸   Bd-3

827   viand
       ...many a c̸a̸t̸e̸ w̸a̸s̸ left,   Bd-3

828   many a costly cate   received the three
       And v̸i̸a̸n̸d̸s̸ o̸f̸ t̸h̸e̸ g̸o̸o̸d̸l̸i̸e̸s̸t̸, & g̸r̸e̸a̸t̸ c̸h̸e̸e̸r̸.   Bd-3

831 ...her, but...   (, I)   A-2109
831 (C)   B-II

832 (Par.) Lord Baron, ye be too discourteous   W-Pf
832 ...discourtesy,   (, I)   A-2109
832 (C)   B-II

833   kitchen   here;
       To set this knave beside me hear me, thou   W-Pf

Hear me--this morn I stood in Arthur's hall,
And prayed the King would grant me Lancelot   835
To fight the brotherhood of Day and Night--
The last a monster unsubduable
Of any save of him for whom I called--
Suddenly bawls this frontless kitchen-knave,
"The quest is mine; thy kitchen-knave am I,   840

---

834 I stood this day in Arthur's ~~&~~ ~~d$k$$\cancel{y}$d~~ hall   W-Pf
834 Hear - for this...   Bd-3
834   me -   I MS
      Hear $\cancel{f}$ $\cancel{for}$ this...hall,   ,/ (I)   A-2109
834 (C)   B-II

Sketch 835 ff.
      to ask him for a knight who wd do battle with
      Night & Day - yea & none but Lancelot cd do it,
      then this kitchen Knave cries out 'Thy promise, King
      give me the Quest; & the King having gone mad, gives
      it to him, to him - a fellow fitter to stick a
      swine than sit beside a noble gentlewoman.   H-32

835 And asked the King to grant me Lancelot   W-Pf

836 ...Night/ -   (- I)   A-2109
836 (C)   B-II

839 And suddenly cries this shameless kitchenknave   W-Pf
839 ...kitchen-knave   S-929
839 (C)   T-GP3

840 ...mine; I have been thy kitchenknave   W-Pf
840 'The quest...   S-929
840 (C)   T-GP3

841 And lusty with thy...   W-Pf
841 ...am I.'   S-929
841 (C)   T-GP3

842 And Arthur..mad, replied   W-Pf
842 ...replies   S-929
842 (C)   T-GP3

And mighty through thy meats and drinks am I. "
Then Arthur all at once gone mad replies,
"Go therefore," and so gives the quest to him--
Him--here--a villain fitter to stick swine
Than ride abroad redressing women's wrong,   845
Or sit beside a noble gentlewoman.'

　　Then half-ashamed and part-amazed, the lord
Now looked at one and now at other, left
The damsel by the peacock in his pride,
And, seating Gareth at another board,   850
Sat down beside him, ate and then began.

---

843 ...so gave this ϻⅰϱͪͭⅯ quest...   W-Pf
843 'Go therefore,' and...the Quest to...   A-2109
843 (C)   T-GP3

844 ...a fellow fitter...   W-Pf

845 ...redressing human wrong,   W-Pf
845　　　　　　women's
　　...redressing ⅼⅿⅾⅰⅿ wrongⅿ,   Bd-3

847 & the Baron was half amazed & half ashamed   H-32
847 (Par.) ⅿⅿ Then, half amazed, half-shamed, ⅿⅿⅾⅿ
　　　　　　　　　　baron left   W-Pf

Sketch 849-851
　　ⅿ ⅿⅿⅿ ⅿⅿ left the damsel with the peacock in
　　his pride before her & set Gareth at a sideboard
　　& set himself beside him. & said   H-32

849 ...damsel with the peacock...   W-Pf
849 ...pride,   ,/ (I)   A-2109
849 (C)   B-II

850 And, setting Gareth...   Bd-3
850　　　　seating   I MS
　　And, ⅿⅿⅿⅿⅿⅿ Gareth...   A-2109
850 (C)   B-II

'Friend, whether thou be kitchen-knave, or not,
Or whether it be the maiden's fantasy,
And whether she be mad, or else the King,
Or both or neither, or thyself be mad,   855
I ask not: but thou strikest a strong stroke,
For strong thou art and goodly therewithal,
And saver of my life; and therefore now,
For here be mighty men to joust with, weigh
Whether thou wilt not with thy damsel back   860
To crave again Sir Lancelot of the King.
Thy pardon; I but speak for thine avail,
The saver of my life.'

                                    And Gareth said,
'Full pardon, but I follow up the quest,
Despite of Day and Night and Death and Hell.'   865

    So when, next morn, the lord whose life he saved
Had, some brief space, conveyed them on their way
And left them with God-speed, Sir Gareth spake,
'Lead, and I follow.' Haughtily she replied.

852 ...whether ye be...			Bd-3
852 ...whether ye be...			A-2109
852 (C)			73
857 ...therewithal,		(, I)	S-929
857 (C)			B-II
858 ...now,		(, I)	S-929
858 (C)			B-II
862 ...thine avail,		(, I)	S-929
862 (C)			B-II
864 ...the quest,		(, I)	S-929
864 (C)			B-II
865 ...of Day, and Night, and...		(,, I)	S-929
865 (C)			B-II
868 ...with God-speed...		-/ (I)	S-929
868 (C)			B-II

'I fly no more: I allow thee for an hour.   870
Lion and stoat have isled together, knave,
In time of flood. Nay, furthermore, methinks
Some ruth is mine for thee. Back wilt thou, fool?
For hard by here is one will overthrow
And slay thee: then will I to court again,   875
And shame the King for only yielding me
My champion from the ashes of his hearth.'

To whom Sir Gareth answered courteously,
'Say thou thy say, and I will do my deed.
Allow me for mine hour, and thou wilt find   880

---

869 ...follow' & haughtily...   Bd-3
869 'Lead and I follow,' and haughtily she replied ~~/~~ ,
                                        (, I)   S-929
869   H   MS
    'Lead and I follow,' ~~And~~ Ḥaughtily she replied,
                                                                T-GP2
869 'Lead and I...replied,   T-GP3
869 'Lead and I...   72
869 (C)   73

872   N   P MS
    ...of flood~~/~~; nay,...   ;/ (P)   A-2109
872   N   MS
    ...of flood~~/~~ ~~N~~ay,...   T-GP2
872 (C)   T-GP3

873 Some ruth have I for thee. Back wilt thou, fool?
    ~~I have some ruth on thy foolhardiness~~   Bd-3
873   is mine   I MS
    Some ruth ~~have~~ I for thee.   S-929
873 (C)   B-II

875 ...again,   (, I)   A-2109
875 (C)   B-II

880 ~~In thy behalf.~~ Allow me for an hour, and thou
                                wilt find   Bd-3
880 ~~And peradventure, damsel, thou wilt find,~~   Bd-3
880   mine   I MS
    Allow me for ~~an~~ hour...   S-929
880 (C)   B-II

My fortunes all as fair as hers who lay
Among the ashes and wedded the King's son.'

    Then to the shore of one of those long loops
Wherethrough the serpent river coiled, they came.
Rough-thicketed were the banks and steep; the stream 885
Full, narrow; this a bridge of single arc
Took at a leap; and on the further side
Arose a silk pavilion, gay with gold
In streaks and rays, and all Lent-lily in hue,
Save that the dome was purple,and above,   890
Crimson, a slender banneret fluttering.

---

881 ...hers, who...		A-2109
881 (C)		75
882 ...the king's son.'		A-2109
882 ...the K̸ing's son.'	K/ (I)	T-GP3
882 (C)		72
885 Steep were the banks, rough-thicketed; the		
stream		H-32
886 ...narrow; wh a...		H-32
890 ...purple, & thereon,		H-32
890 violet		MS
...was p̸ṵr̸p̸l̸e̸, and...		A-2109
892 ...the bandit-warrior stood,		H-32
892 ...warrior s̸t̸o̸o̸d̸ paced		Bd-3
894 ...champion ye have brought...		H-32;Bd-3
894 ...champion ye have brought...		S-929
894 (C)		73

Sketch 895-898
    To free thy sister' Nay, Sir Morning Star
    His kitchen-page. The King in scorn of me,
    Or thee & thy much folly, hath sent t̸h̸e̸e̸ h̸i̸m̸
    His kitchen knave & look thou to thyself -   H-32

And therebefore the lawless warrior paced
Unarmed, and calling, 'Damsel, is this he,
The champion thou hast brought from Arthur's hall?
For whom we let thee pass.' 'Nay, nay,' she said,   895
'Sir Morning-Star. The King in utter scorn
Of thee and thy much folly hath sent thee here
His kitchen-knave: and look thou to thyself:
See that he fall not on thee suddenly,
And slay thee unarmed: he is not knight but knave.'   900

    Then at his call, 'O daughters of the Dawn,
And servants of the Morning-Star, approach,
Arm me,' from out the silken curtain-folds

---

895 For whom we let thee pass?' ...		72
895 (C)		73
901 when		
At this he cried O...		H-32
901 (No par.) ...call 'O...		A-2109
901 ...call, 'O...	,/ (I)	T-GP3
901 (C)		72
902 ...Morning Star...		A-2109
902 ...Morning-Star...	-/ (I)	T-GP3
902 (C)		72

Sketch for 903 ff
    Arm me. whereat three damsels lightly stept
    From out the gay pavilion, rosy-clad,
    Barefooted & bareheaded & there glanced
    Like sparkles in the stone avanturine
                his
    From dewdrop or f̷r̷o̷m̷ jewel, in their hair.
    Blue arms they brought   W-Pf

903 ...out the silken curtains came		H-32
903 i̷n̷g̷s̷ folds		
...silken curtains̷ f̷o̷l̷d̷s̷		Bd-3
903 ...me' from...curtain-folds	-/ (I)	A-2109
903 ...me' from...		B-II
903 ...me ,' from...	,/ (I)	T-GP3
903 (C)		72

223

Bare-footed and bare-headed three fair girls
In gilt and rosy raiment came: their feet   905
In dewy grasses glistened; and the hair
All over glanced with dewdrop or with gem
Like sparkles in the stone Avanturine.
These armed him in blue arms, and gave a shield
Blue also, and thereon the morning star.   910
And Gareth silent gazed upon the knight,
Who stood a moment, ere his horse was brought,
Glorying; and in the stream beneath him, shone
Immingled with Heaven's azure waveringly,

Sketch 904-907
    In gilt & rosey raiment three fair girls
    Barefooted and bare-headed: their light feet
          thick dews
    Among the d̷e̷w̷d̷r̷o̷p̷s̷ glisten i̷n̷g̷ ed; & there gleamed
    From dewdrops or hid jewel in their hair,   H-32

904 Bare-footed and bare-headed...   -/-/(I)   A-2109
904 (C)   B-II

905   came
   ...raiment their l̷i̷g̷h̷t̷ feet   Bd-3

906 ...glisten'd; & there glanced   Bd-3
906 ...glisten'd; and there glanced   S-929
906 (C)   B-II

907   the
   From dewdrop or hid jewel in t̷h̷e̷i̷r̷ hair,   Bd-3
907 From dewdrop or hid jewel in the hair,   S-929
907 All over glanced with dewdrop or with gem
                          (MS-Not A.T.)
   H̷a̷d̷ s̷p̷a̷r̷k̷l̷e̷s̷ g̷l̷a̷n̷c̷i̷n̷g̷ i̷n̷ i̷t̷ / d̷e̷w̷s̷ o̷r̷ g̷e̷m̷s̷   T-GP2
907 (C)   T-GP3

908   sparkles   (MS-Not A.T.)
   Like s̷t̷a̷r̷l̷e̷t̷s̷ in...   T-GP2
908 (C)   T-GP3

909 ...blue harness, w̷i̷t̷h̷ gave...   W-Pf
909 ...blue harness, gave...   H-32

224

The gay pavilion and the naked feet,   915
His arms, the rosy raiment, and the star.

Then she that watched him, 'Wherefore stare ye so?
Thou shakest in thy fear: there yet is time:
Flee down the valley before he get to horse.
Who will cry shame? Thou art not knight but knave.' 920

Said Gareth, 'Damsel, whether knave or knight,

---

910 ...& thereon
    ...also, wherefrom the morning...   W-Pf

Alt. after 910 Bright-burnishd   H-32

911 And Gareth all in silence gazed on him   H-32

912 He stood...   W-Pf

Alt. after 912
    Burnish'd to blinding. Gareth on him gazed
    As there he stood, until his horse was brought
    Glorying; & in   W-Pf

913 ...shone,   (, I)   A-2109
913 ...shone,   72
913 (C)   75

914   e   I MS
    ...azure wavringly,   (, I)   A-2109
914 (C)   B-II

915 ...feet,   ,/ (I)   A-2109
915 (C)   B-II

917 And she...   H-32

919 ...he gets to...   H-32;Bd-3
919 ...he gets to...   A-2109
919 (C)   B-II

920 None will...   H-32

921 And Gareth Whether...   H-32

Far liefer had I fight a score of times
Than hear thee so missay me and revile.
Fair words were best for him who fights for thee;
But truly foul are better, for they send   925
That strength of anger through mine arms, I know
That I shall overthrow him.'

                    And he that bore
The star, when mounted, cried from o'er the bridge,
'A kitchen-knave, and sent in scorn of me!
Such fight not I, but answer scorn with scorn.   930
For this were shame to do him further wrong
Than set him on his feet, and take his horse

---

922 Far liever had I fight battles   H-32
922 Far liever had...   Bd-3
922 Far liever had...   S-929
922 (C)   72

924 ...for one who...   H-32
924 ...thee;   ;/ (I)   A-2109
924 (C)   B-II

925 But foul perchance are better for they put   H-32
925   truly
    But foul p̸e̸r̸c̸h̸a̸n̸c̸e̸ are better, for they put   Bd-3
925   send   P MS
...they p̸u̸t̸   A-2109
925 (C)   B-II

926 ...anger in mine...   H-32;Bd-3
926   thro'   I MS
...anger i̸n̸ mine...   A-2109
926 (C)   B-II

927 ...Then he...   Bd-3
927   and   I MS
...T̸h̸e̸n̸ he...   A-2109
927   And   (MS-Not A.T.)
...T̸h̸e̸n̸ he...   T-GP2
927 (C)   72

928 The star, being mounted spake beyond the bridge H-32
928 The star, being mounted, ...   Bd-3

226

And arms, and so return him to the King.
Come, therefore, leave thy lady lightly, knave.
Avoid: for it beseemeth not a knave   935
To ride with such a lady.'

                  'Dog, thou liest.
I spring from loftier lineage than thine own.'
He spake; and all at fiery speed the two
Shocked on the central bridge, and either spear
Bent but not brake, and either knight at once,   940
Hurled as a stone from out of a catapult

---

928 The star, being mounted, ...bridge, ,/ (P)   A-2109
928 The star, being mounted, ...   T-GP3
928 (C)   86

929 ...me!   !/ (I)   A-2109
929 (C)   B-II

930 Such   I
    I̶ fight not s̶u̶c̶h̶, but...   Bd-3

931 Then were it shame...   H-32

932 ...feet, and...   ,/ (I)   A-2109
932 (C)   B-II

933-934 And armour: leave thy lady lightly, knave. H-32

937 ...from nobler lineage...   H-32

938 Said Gareth   H-32
938 As Gareth spake - galloping up - the two
    S̶a̶i̶d̶ G̶a̶r̶e̶t̶h̶./ T̶h̶e̶n̶ t̶h̶e̶ t̶w̶o̶/ g̶a̶l̶l̶o̶p̶i̶n̶g̶ u̶p̶/   Bd-3
938 A̶s̶ G̶a̶r̶e̶t̶h̶ s̶p̶a̶k̶e̶ ⊁ g̶a̶l̶l̶o̶p̶i̶n̶g̶ u̶p̶ ⊁ t̶h̶e̶ t̶w̶o̶   A-2109
938   galloping up   (MS-Not A.T.)
    As Gareth spake, the two, w̶i̶t̶h̶ l̶o̶o̶s̶e̶n̶'d̶ r̶e̶i̶n̶s̶, T-GP2
938 He spake; & all at fiery speed the two   I MS
    A̶s̶ G̶a̶r̶e̶t̶h̶ s̶p̶a̶k̶e̶/ g̶a̶l̶l̶o̶p̶i̶n̶g̶ u̶p̶ t̶h̶e̶ t̶w̶o̶   T-GP3
938 (C)   72

Sketch 939-940 & either spear bent & not brake   H-32

940 ...once,   ,/ (P)   A-2109
940 (C)   B-II

Beyond his horse's crupper and the bridge,
Fell, as if dead; but quickly rose and drew,
And Gareth lashed so fiercely with his brand
He drave his enemy backward down the bridge,   945
The damsel crying, 'Well-stricken, kitchen-knave!'
Till Gareth's shield was cloven; but one stroke
Laid him that clove it grovelling on the ground.

   Then cried the fallen, 'Take not my life: I yield.'
And Gareth, 'So this damsel ask it of me   950
Good--I accord it easily as a grace.'
She reddening, 'Insolent scullion: I of thee?
I bound to thee for any favour asked!'
'Then shall he die.' And Gareth there unlaced
His helmet as to slay him, but she shrieked,   955
'Be not so hardy, scullion, as to slay
One nobler than thyself.' 'Damsel, thy charge

Sketch 942-943 Their horses croups beyond the bridge
             Lay as if dead   H-32

943 Fell, as if
    ~~And lay as~~ dead: but both arose & drew   Bd-3
943   quickly   P MS
   ...dead:; but ~~both~~ arose...   ;/ (P)   A-2109
943 (C)   B-II

945 ...bridge,   ,/ (P)   A-2109
945 (C)   B-II

946 ...kitchen-knave'   A-2109
946 ...kitchen-knave!'   !/ (I)   T-GP3
946 (C)   72

947 ...cloven & then one stroke   Bd-3
947   but   P MS
   ...cloven; ~~And then~~ one ···   (; I)   A-2109
947 (C)   B-II

948 ~~Bent down the cleaver grovelling to the ground~~   Bd-3

949   Take not my life
   Then cried the knight 'I yield me: H-32

950 ...Gareth 'let this...   H-32

Is an abounding pleasure to me. Knight,
Thy life is thine at her command. Arise
And quickly pass to Arthur's hall, and say   960
His kitchen-knave hath sent thee. See thou crave
His pardon for thy breaking of his laws.
Myself, when I return, will plead for thee.
Thy shield is mine--farewell; and, damsel, thou,
Lead, and I follow.'

                        And fast away she fled.   965

| 950 | so | P MS |
| | ...Gareth ~~let~~ this... | Bd-3 |

951	will	
	~~And~~ I accord it...	Bd-3
951	Good - I	I MS
	~~I/will~~ accord...	A-2109
951	(C)	B-II

| 952 | She reddening ask it, kitchenknave, of thee | H-32 |

| 953 | ...ask'd of thee! | H-32 |

954	...die, & there unlaced his helm	H-32
954	there	MS
	...Gareth ~~then~~ unlaced	A-2109
954	(C)	B-II

| 955 | As if to slay him; but the damsel shriekd | H-32 |

| 957 | A nobler... | H-32 |

958	Said Gareth is a pleasure to me. Knight	H-32
958	Is an abounding pleasure	
	~~He answered is a pleasure~~ to...	Bd-3

960	And pass...say to him	H-32
960	...hall & tell him	Bd-3
960	say	I MS
	...and ~~tell him~~	A-2109
960	(C)	B-II

| 964 | ...thou, | ,/ (I) | A-2109 |
| 964 | (C) | | B-II |

Then when he came upon her, spake, 'Methought,
Knave, when I watched thee striking on the bridge
The savour of thy kitchen came upon me
A little faintlier: but the wind hath changed:
I scent it twenty-fold.' And then she sang,   970
'"O morning star" (not that tall felon there
Whom thou by sorcery or unhappiness
Or some device, hast foully overthrown),
"O morning star that smilest in the blue,
O star, my morning dream hath proven true,   975
Smile sweetly, thou! my love hath smiled on me."

  'But thou begone, take counsel, and away,
For hard by here is one that guards a ford--
The second brother in their fool's parable--
Will pay thee all thy wages, and to boot.   980
Care not for shame: thou art not knight but knave.'

  To whom Sir Gareth answered, laughingly,
'Parables? Hear a parable of the knave.
When I was kitchen-knave among the rest
Fierce was the hearth, and one of my co-mates   985

---

968 ...of the kitchen...   Bd-3

970 ...it twentyfold.' And...   A-2109
970 (C)   73

971 ...tall fellow there   Bd-3
971   felòn   I MS
    '"O morning star" [not that tall f̷e̷l̷l̷o̷w̷ there]
                    ("" P)   A-2109
971 "O morning...   B-II
971 '"O morning...   '/ (I)   T-GP3
971 (C)   72

974 ...that shinest in the blue,   Bd-3
974 "O morning star that s̷h̷i̷n̷e̷s̷t̷ in... (" P)   A-2109
974 ...that s̷h̷i̷n̷e̷s̷t̷ in...   T-GP2
974   smilest   I MS
    ...that s̷h̷i̷n̷e̷s̷t̷ in...   T-GP3
974 (C)   72

Owned a rough dog, to whom he cast his coat,
"Guard it," and there was none to meddle with it.
And such a coat art thou, and thee the King
Gave me to guard, and such a dog am I,
To worry, and not to flee--and--knight or knave--   990
The knave that doth thee service as full knight
Is all as good, meseems, as any knight
Toward thy sister's freeing.'

                         'Ay, Sir Knave!
Ay, knave, because thou strikest as a knight,
Being but knave, I hate thee all the more.'   995

---

975 O   P
     S̸w̸e̸e̸t̸ star,...   Bd-3

976   sweetly   P MS
    Shine m̸e̸r̸r̸i̸l̸y̸, thou!...   Bd-3
976 S̸h̸i̸n̸e̸ sweetly, ...me."   "/ (P)   A-2109
976 S̸h̸i̸n̸e̸ sweetly, ...   T-GP2
976 Smile   I MS
    S̸h̸i̸n̸e̸ sweetly,...   T-GP3
976 (C)   72

984 F̸i̸e̸r̸c̸e̸ w̸a̸s̸ t̸h̸e̸ h̸e̸a̸r̸t̸h̸ w̸h̸e̸n̸/I̸ w̸a̸s̸ K̸i̸t̸c̸h̸e̸n̸K̸n̸a̸v̸e̸   Bd-3

985 A̸m̸o̸n̸g̸ t̸h̸e̸ r̸e̸s̸t̸ ⁄ &̸ o̸n̸e̸ o̸f̸ m̸y̸ c̸o̸-m̸a̸t̸e̸s̸   Bd-3
985 ...of my good mates   Bd-3
985   co-mates   I MS
    ...my g̸o̸o̸d̸ m̸a̸t̸e̸s̸   A-2109
985 (C)   B-II

986 Own'd rough   P MS
    P̸o̸s̸s̸e̸s̸s̸e̸d̸ a̸ dog, to whom he flung his coat,   Bd-3
986 ...he flung his...   A-2109
986   cast   (MS-Not A.T.)
    ...he f̸l̸u̸n̸g̸ his...   T-GP2;T-GP3
986 (C)   72

987 'Guard it,' and...   S-929
987 (C)   T-GP3

991   full
    ...service as a̸ knight   Bd-3

'Fair damsel, you should worship me the more,
That, being but knave, I throw thine enemies.'

'Ay, ay,' she said, 'but thou shalt meet thy match.'

So when they touched the second river-loop,
Huge on a huge red horse, and all in mail   1000
Burnished to blinding, shone the Noonday Sun
Beyond a raging shallow. As if the flower,
That blows a globe of after arrowlets,
Ten thousand-fold had grown, flashed the fierce shield,
All sun; and Gareth's eyes had flying blots   1005
Before them when he turned from watching him.
He from beyond the roaring shallow roared,
'What doest thou, brother, in my marches here?'
And she athwart the shallow shrilled again,

996	Fair damsel,	
	(Par.) S̸a̸i̸d̸ G̸a̸r̸e̸t̸h̸ ye should...	Bd-3
996	...damsel, ye should...	A-2109
996	(C)	73
999	But as they near'd the river once again,	H-32
1000	High on a huge white horse, in yellow mail	H-32
1000	Huge huge	
	H̸i̸g̸h̸ on a g̸r̸e̸a̸t̸ red horse...	Bd-3
1000	Huge on	I MS
	O̸n̸ a huge red...	S-929
1000	(C)	B-II
1001	...blinding, was the...	H-32
1003	after	P MS
	...globe of A̸u̸t̸u̸m̸n̸ arrowlets,	Bd-3
1006	...then as he turnd from looking at it.	H-32
1006	watching him	P MS
	...turn'd from l̸o̸o̸k̸i̸n̸g̸ a̸t̸ i̸t̸	Bd-3
1008	What do ye brother...	H-32
1009	And back athwart the shallow shrill'd Linette.	H-32
1012	closely vizoring...	H-32

'Here is a kitchen-knave from Arthur's hall   1010
Hath overthrown thy brother, and hath his arms.'
'Ugh!' cried the Sun, and vizoring up a red
And cipher face of rounded foolishness,
Pushed horse across the foamings of the ford,
Whom Gareth met midstream: no room was there   1015
For lance or tourney-skill: four strokes they struck
With sword, and these were mighty; the new knight
Had fear he might be shamed; but as the Sun
Heaved up a ponderous arm to strike the fifth,
The hoof of his horse slipt in the stream, the
                              stream   1020

1012   cried
         'Ugh' s̶a̶i̶d̶ the Sun...   Bd-3

1013 ...foolishness,   ,/ (I)   S-929
1013 (C)   B-II

1014 (3 ?), but all in anger push'd   H-32

1015 ...no use was left   H-32
1015   midstream   P MS
     Whom Gareth m̶i̶d̶w̶a̶y̶ met: no use was there   Bd-3
1015   room   P MS
     ...no u̶s̶e̶ was...   A-2109
1015 (C)   B-II

1016 For spear or...   H-32

1017 ...these so strong, that the...   H-32
1017 ...mighty, the...   A-2109
1017 ...mighty/ the...   ;/ (I)   T-GP3
1017 (C)   72

1018 ...but while the Sun   H-32

1019 Was heaving up his arms up to strike the fifth H-32
1019 Heaved up a ponderous   P MS
     W̶a̶s̶ h̶e̶a̶v̶i̶n̶g̶ u̶p̶ a̶n̶ arm to strike...   Bd-3
1019 ...fifth,   ,/ (P)   A-2109
1019 (C)   B-II

1020 ...horse reel'd in the flood, the flood   H-32

Descended, and the Sun was washed away.

   Then Gareth laid his lance athwart the ford;
So drew him home; but he that fought no more,
As being all bone-battered on the rock,
Yielded; and Gareth sent him to the King.   1025
'Myself when I return will plead for thee.'
'Lead, and I follow.' Quietly she led.
'Hath not the good wind, damsel, changed again?'

1021 ...was rolld away.   H-32

Alt. for 1022
    (Par.) Then Gareth waved a hand of courtesy
    /Lead/ & I followly Quietly she led/
    /Lady/Lynette/ hath not the wind Ø damsel changed
                        again?   Bd-3

1022 Then
    But Gareth laid his lance across the stream   Bd-3
1022   athwart   spray;   I MS
    ...lance across the stream,   (, I)   S-929
1022   ford   MS
    ...the/stream   T-GP2
1022 (C)   T-GP3

1023 And drew him home, but he that wd not fight   Bd-3
1023 So   P MS
    And drew him home,; but he that would not
                      fight,   ;/ (P)   A-2109
1023 ...that would not fight,   B-II
1023 (C)   72

1026 ...thee/.   ./ (P)   A-2109
1026 ...thee.   B-II
1026 (C)   78

Alt. after 1026 And Gareth with a wave of courtesy H-32

1027 Lead, and...   72
1027 (C)   73

'Nay, not a point: nor art thou victor here.
There lies a ridge of slate across the ford;   1030
His horse thereon stumbled--ay, for I saw it.

'"O Sun" (not this strong fool whom thou, Sir Knave,
Hast overthrown through mere unhappiness),
"O Sun, that wakenest all to bliss or pain,
O moon, that layest all to sleep again,   1035
Shine sweetly: twice my love hath smiled on me."

'What knowest thou of lovesong or of love?
Nay, nay, God wot, so thou wert nobly born,

1029 This victory is not thine, Sir Kitchenboy   H-32
1029 ...point: thou art not victor here.   Bd-3
1029   nor art thou   P MS
     ...point: t̸h̸o̸u̸ a̸r̸e̸ n̸o̸t̸ victor here.   A-2109
1029 (C)   B-II

1030 ...ford,;   ;/ (I)   S-929
1030 (C)   B-II

1031 His horse stumbled thereon, &̸ b̸u̸t̸ f̸o̸r̸ t̸h̸i̸s̸ yea
                         for...   H-32
1031 ...saw it.'   S-929
1031 (C)   T-GP3

1032 (Par.) '/ O Sun'/   "/"/ (P)   A-2109
1032 (Par.) "O...   B-II
1032 (Par.) '"O...   '/ (I)   T-GP3
1032 (C)   72

1034 "O Sun,...   (" I)   S-929
1034 (C)   B-II

1035   to   P MS
     ...all i̸n̸ sleep...   Bd-3

1036   sweetly   P MS
     Shine s̸w̸e̸e̸t̸l̸y̸: twice...   Bd-3
1036 ...me."   "/ (P)   A-2109
1036 (C)   B-II

1038 ...wert noble knave   H-32

Thou hast a pleasant presence. Yea, perchance--

  '"O dewy flowers that open to the sun,   1040
O dewy flowers that close when day is done,
Blow sweetly: twice my love hath smiled on me."

  'What knowest thou of flowers, except, belike,
To garnish meats with? hath not our good King
Who lent me thee, the flower of kitchendom,   1045
A foolish love for flowers? what stick ye round
The pasty? wherewithal deck the boar's head?
Flowers? nay, the boar hath rosemaries and bay.

  '"O birds, that warble to the morning sky,

1039 ...presence & belike		H-32
1039 ...presence ≠ yea, perchance, -	-/ (P&I)	A-2109
1039 Y		MS
...presence ≠ ̸Yea, perchance, -	-/	T-GP2
1039 .Y		I MS
...presence - ̸Yea, perchance, -		T-GP3
1039 (C)		72

Alt. after 1039
    Some kitchen-malkin, taken with it
    Hath left her greasy kisses on thy lips   H-32
Alt. after 1039
    Some honest kitchen-malkin taken with it,
    Unwash'd, hath left her kisses on thy lips.'
                       Bd-3;Printed same A-2109
Alt. after 1039 (Printed - lined out)   T-GP2
Alt. after 1039 (C)   T-GP3

1040 (Par.) "O dewey...	"/ (P)	A-2109
1040 (Par.) 'O dewey...		B-II
1040 (Par.) '"O dewey...	'/ (I)	T-GP3
1040 (C)		72

1042 sweetly		P MS
Blow ̶m̶e̶r̶r̶i̶l̶y̶: twice...		Bd-3
1042 ...me."	"/ (P)	A-2109
1042 (C)		B-II

1043 ...except perchance   H-32;Bd-3

O birds that warble as the day goes by,   1050
Sing sweetly: twice my love hath smiled on me."

   'What knowest thou of birds, lark, mavis, merle,
Linnet? what dream ye when they utter forth
May-music growing with the growing light,
Their sweet sun-worship? these be for the snare   1055

1043		belike		I MS
..., except,	p̸é̸r̸c̸h̸á̸n̸c̸é̸			A-2109
1043		belike		MS
..., except,	p̸é̸r̸c̸h̸á̸n̸c̸é̸			T-GP2;T-GP3
1043 (C)				72

1044 To garnish Arthur's meat withal.   The King   H-32

1045-1047 Loves flowers, I hear: how deck the boars-
                   head?   H-32

1048 ...nay for those be rosemaries...   H-32
1048 Flowers? nay,
    M̸á̸y̸ ⫽ f̸ó̸r̸ the boar...   Bd-3
1048 ...and bay.'   A-2109
1048 ...and bay.⫽   T-GP3
1048 (C)   72

1049 (Par.) "O birds...   "⫽ (P)   A-2109
1049 (Par.) "O birds...   B-II
1049 (Par.) '"O birds...   '⫽ (I)   T-GP3
1049 (C)   72

1051   s̸w̸é̸é̸t̸l̸y̸ stet   P MS
   Sing m̸é̸r̸r̸í̸l̸y̸⫽ twice...   Bd-3
1051 Sing m̸é̸r̸r̸í̸l̸y̸⫽ twice...me."   "⫽ (P)   A-2109
1051   sweetly   MS
   Sing m̸é̸r̸r̸í̸l̸y̸; twice...   T-GP2;T-GP3
1051 ...sweetly; twice...   72
1051 (C)   73

1052 ...lark, blackbird, thrush -   H-32

1053 ...they (1 ?) at dawn   H-32

1055 And sweet sun-worship in the solitude
               these be for the snare   H-32

(So runs thy fancy) these be for the spit,
Larding and basting. See thou have not now
Larded thy last, except thou turn and fly.
There stands the third fool of their allegory.'

For there beyond a bridge of treble bow,   1060
All in a rose-red from the west, and all
Naked it seemed, and glowing in the broad
Deep-dimpled current underneath, the knight,
That named himself the Star of Evening, stood.

And Gareth, 'Wherefore waits the madman there   1065
Naked in open dayshine?' 'Nay,' she cried,
'Not naked, only wrapt in hardened skins
That fit him like his own; and so ye cleave
His armour off him, these will turn the blade.'

Then the third brother shouted o'er the bridge,   1070
'O brother-star, why shine ye here so low?
Thy ward is higher up: but have ye slain
The damsel's champion?' and the damsel cried,

1057 ...basting: Larded hast thou, knave   H-32

1058 Thy last & basted, save thou turn & flee.   H-32
1058 ...fly.   A-2109
1058 (C)   84

1060 ...treble arch,   H-32

1061 Red smitten by the lowering Sun that struck   H-32
1061 R̷e̷d̷/̷s̷m̷i̷t̷t̷e̷n̷ b̷y̷ t̷h̷e̷ l̷o̷w̷e̷r̷i̷n̷g̷ s̷u̷n̷/̷&̷ a̷l̷l̷   Bd-3
1061 ...west, and...   ,/ (I)   A-2109
1061 (C)   B-II

Alt. after 1061
    The topmost tower of Castle Perilous, far
    Behind him i̷n̷ priming (?) on the margin, stood H-32

1063 ...dimpled river underneath...   H-32

1064 Called of himself the Evening star stood.   H-32

1065   madman
    Then Gareth...the fellow there   H-32

'No star of thine, but shot from Arthur's heaven
With all disaster unto thine and thee!   1075
For both thy younger brethren have gone down

1066 ...in open day. Linette replied   H-32
1066 ...dayshine'? 'Nay...   S-929
1066 (C)   T-GP3

1067 ...only clothed in...   H-32

1068 ...him as his...   H-32

1069 ...him ~~habits of a life~~ these will turn thy
                                sword   H-32

1070 ...brother haild them from the bridge   H-32
1070 (Par.) Then shouted the third brother across
                                the bridge   Bd-3
1070   shouted oer   I MS
        (Par.) Then ~~shouted~~ the third brother across the
                                bridge.   S-929
1070 ...bridge.   B-II
1070 (C)   T-GP3

1071 ...low,?   ?/ (P)   A-2109
1071 (C)   B-II

1072 ...higher: hast thou tain or slain   H-32

1073 This damsel's...damsel shrill'd   Bd-3
1073 The   cried   I MS
        ~~This~~ damsel's champion'? and the damsel ~~shrilld~~
                                                    A-2109
1073 The damsel's champion'? and the damsel
                                shrill'd.   B-II
1073   cried   I MS
        ...damsel ~~shrilld~~,   T-GP3
1073 (C)   72

1074   is here
        ...of thine but...   H-32

1075-1076 To shame thee: both thy bretheren have
                                gone down   H-32

Before this youth; and so wilt thou, Sir Star;
Art thou not old?'

                  'Old, damsel, old and hard,
Old, with the might and breath of twenty boys.'
Said Gareth, 'Old, and over-bold in brag!   1080
But that same strength which threw the Morning Star
Can throw the Evening.'

               Then that other blew
A hard and deadly note upon the horn.
'Approach and arm me!' With slow steps from out
An old storm-beaten, russet, many-stained   1085

1077 Before this choice of Arthur so wilt thou	H-32
1077 This youth ~~this boy youth~~	
Before him easily - ay, & so	Bd-3
1077 ...Star,; ;/ (P)	A-2109
1077 (C)	B-II

1078 For thou art old. Old & hard	H-32
1078 Art not	
~~For~~ thou ~~art~~ old'...	Bd-3
1078 A	I MS
~~For~~ art thou not old'?	S-929
1078 (C)	B-II
1078 ..., and hard	A-2109
1078 (C)	78

1079 Old, ~~truly~~ with...	H-32
1079 ...the Morning-Star	72
1079 (C)	73

1080 make	
And Gareth wherefore ~~blow~~ ye such a boast?	Bd-3
1080 Said Thou art overbold in brag:	I MS
~~And~~ Gareth, ~~'wherefore make ye such a boast?~~	S-929
1080 Old, &	MS
Said Gareth, '~~Thou~~ ~~art~~ over-bold in brag;	T-GP2
1080 Old, &	I MS
Said Gareth, '~~Thou~~ ~~art~~ over-bold in brag;!!/(I)	T-GP3
1080 (C)	72

1081 The strength that overthrew	P MS
~~Not hard for him that threw~~ the morning star	Bd-3

GARETH AND LYNETTE

Pavilion, forth a grizzled damsel came,
And armed him in old arms, and brought a helm
With but a drying evergreen for crest,
And gave a shield whereon the Star of Even
Half-tarnished and half-bright, his emblem, shone.   1090
But when it glittered o'er the saddle-bow,
They madly hurled together on the bridge;
And Gareth overthrew him, lighted, drew,
There met him drawn, and overthrew him again,

1081 The strength that overthrew the Morning Star   A-2109
1081 But that same strength which threw the Morning-
                              Star   I MS
     T̸h̸e̸ s̸t̸r̸e̸n̸g̸t̸h̸ t̸h̸a̸t̸ o̸v̸e̸r̸t̸h̸r̸e̸w̸ t̸h̸e̸ M̸o̸r̸n̸i̸n̸g̸ S̸t̸a̸r̸ T-GP3
1081 (C)   72

1082 Can
     T̸o̸ throw...   Bd-3

1084 then slowly passing   H-32
1084 & then from out   H-32

1086 Pavilion, came a grizzled damsel, harsh,   H-32
1086 ...came,   ,/ (I)   A-2109
1086 (C)   B-II

1087 Flint-faced & b̸r̸o̸u̸g̸h̸t̸/h̸i̸s̸ armed him in old arms
                              & gave (2 ?)   H-32

Sketch 1088-1090 His shield & there
                 Whereon his emblem shone,
                 Part bright & tarnish'd,   H-32

1092 ...the bridge,:   :/ (I)   A-2109
1092 ...the bridge,   B-II
1092 (C)   72

1093 ...him, alighted, drew,   Bd-3
1093 ...him, a̸lighted, drew,   A-2109
1093 (C)   B-II

1094 M̸e̸t̸ h̸i̸m̸ t̸h̸a̸t̸ d̸r̸e̸w̸/ & o̸v̸e̸r̸t̸h̸e̸w̸ h̸i̸m̸ a̸g̸a̸i̸n̸/   Bd-3
1094 ...drawn, and...again;   (,; I)   S-929
1094 (C)   B-II

241

But up like fire he started: and as oft   1095
As Gareth brought him grovelling on his knees,
So many a time he vaulted up again;
Till Gareth panted hard, and his great heart,
Foredooming all his trouble was in vain,
Laboured within him, for he seemed as one   1100
That all in later, sadder age begins
To war against ill uses of a life,
But these from all his life arise, and cry,
'Thou hast made us lords, and canst not put us down!'

1095   and as oft   P MS
    ...started: ~~As many times~~   Bd-3

1097   a time   P MS
    So many ~~times~~ he...   Bd-3
1097 ...again,;   ;/ (P)   A-2109
1097 (C)   B-II

1098   hard and his great heart   P MS
    ...panted, ~~& he felt his heart/~~   Bd-3

1099 Foredooming all his trouble was in vain   P MS
    ~~Believing all his trouble was in vain/~~   Bd-3
1099   oo   P MS
    Fored~~ee~~ming...   A-2109
1099 (C)   B-II

1100 And Gareth felt as one   H-32

1101   later
    That in his sadder ~~middle~~ age begins   H-32
1101   all in   P MS
    That ~~in his~~ later...   Bd-3

1102 To strive against the habits of...   H-32
1102 warring   ill uses   P MS
    ~~To fight~~ against ~~the habits~~ of a life,   Bd-3
1102 Warring against...   S-929
1102 war   MS
    ~~Warring~~ against...   T-GP2
1102 (C)   T-GP3

1104 Thou...down!   S-929
1104 'Thou...down!'   '/'/(I)   T-GP3

He half despairs; so Gareth seemed to strike   1105
Vainly, the damsel clamouring all the while,
'Well done, knave-knight, well stricken, O good
                         knight-knave--
O knave, as noble as any of all the knights--
Shame me not, shame me not. I have prophesied--
Strike, thou art worthy of the Table Round--   1110
His arms are old, he trusts the hardened skin--
Strike--strike--the wind will never change again.'
And Gareth hearing ever stronglier smote,

1104 (C)   72

Sketch 1105-1106
        ...despairs; for many a time
        Sir Gareth struck him down on his knees
        But ever up a̶s̶ l̶i̶g̶h̶t̶ he lightly sprung again
                                   tumbled up
        And ever as he struck the damsel cried   H-32

1106 Vainly   P MS
     I̶n̶ v̶a̶i̶n̶, the damsel...   Bd-3
1106 ...the while   S-929
1106 (C)   T-GP3

1107 ...knight-knave -   (dash I)   S-929
1107 (C)   B-II

1108 O noble Knave as good as any knight of all the
                         to.   H-32
1108 ...the knights -   (- I)   S-929
1108 (C)   B-II

1109 ...prophesied -   (- I)   S-929
1109 (C)   B-II

1110 ...Round -   (- I)   S-929
1110 (C)   B-II

1111 ...skin -   (- I)   S-929
1111 (C)   B-II

1113 But vainly still Sir Gareth brought him down   H-32

And hewed great pieces of his armour off him,
But lashed in vain against the hardened skin,   1115
And could not wholly bring him under, more
Than loud Southwesterns, rolling ridge on ridge,
The buoy that rides at sea, and dips and springs
For ever; till at length Sir Gareth's brand
Clashed his, and brake it utterly to the' hilt.   1120
'I have thee now;' but forth that other sprang,
And, all unknightlike, writhed his wiry arms
Around him, till he felt, despite his mail,
Strangled, but straining even his uttermost
Cast, and so hurled him headlong o'er the bridge   1125

1114 ...armour off		H-32
1115 And vainly smote against...		H-32
1115 ...skin,	,/ (P)	A-2109
1115 (C)		B-II
1116 But cd not bring him under any more		H-32
1116 And		
Y̶e̶t̶ B̶u̶t̶ could...		Bd-3
1118 dips		I MS
...sea, and s̶l̶i̶p̶s̶ and springs		S-929
1118 (C)		B-II
1120 Met his...it even unto the hilt		H-32
1121 ...other leapt		H-32
1121 that		I MS
...now' but forth t̶h̶e̶ other sprang	,(, I)	S-929
1121 ...now' but...		B-II
1121 ...now;' but...	;/ (I)	T-GP3
1121 (C)		72
1122 ...all unknightly wound his...		H-32
1122 ...unknightlike, wound his...		Bd-3
1122 writhed		P MS
And all unknightlike, w̶o̶u̶n̶d̶ his...		A-2109
1122 And all...		B-II
1122 And, all...	,/ (I)	T-GP3
1122 (C)		72

Down to the river, sink or swim, and cried,
'Lead, and I follow.'

                         But the damsel said,
'I lead no longer; ride thou at my side;

1123 Round him till Gareth felt, for all his mail   H-32
1123 Round him, till Gareth felt despite his mail   Bd-3
1123 A   he   P MS
     Round him, till G̸a̸r̸e̸t̸h̸ felt despite...   A-2109
1123 Around   he   MS
     R̸o̸u̸n̸d̸ him, till G̸a̸r̸e̸t̸h̸ felt, despite...
                                        (2nd, I)   T-GP2
1123 (C)   T-GP3

1124 ...straining all his thewes to cast   H-32
1124   uttermost   P MS
     ...evn his u̸t̸m̸o̸s̸t̸ s̸t̸r̸e̸n̸g̸t̸h̸   Bd-3
1124   ev'n   I MS
     ...straining e̸v̸e̸n̸ his   S-929
1124 (C)   B-II

1125 Cast him, & there flung him suddenly oer...   H-32
1125   hurl'd   P MS
     ...& so f̸l̸u̸n̸g̸ him   Bd-3

1127 But
     T̸h̸e̸n̸ the damsel   Bd-3

Sketch 1128 ff.
     I̸ I̸e̸a̸d̸ n̸o̸ I̸o̸n̸g̸e̸r̸:̸ r̸i̸d̸e̸ t̸h̸o̸u̸ a̸t̸ m̸y̸ s̸i̸d̸e̸
     W̸h̸a̸t̸ a̸i̸l̸s̸ t̸h̸e̸e̸?̸ a̸r̸t̸ t̸h̸o̸u̸ h̸u̸r̸t̸?̸ &̸ G̸a̸r̸e̸t̸h̸/̸s̸a̸i̸d̸
     H̸u̸r̸t̸ t̸h̸a̸t̸ I̸/̸a̸m̸ b̸u̸t̸ p̸r̸o̸v̸e̸n̸ K̸i̸t̸c̸h̸e̸n̸k̸n̸a̸v̸e̸
     I̸ s̸o̸ h̸a̸v̸e̸ h̸o̸l̸p̸e̸n̸ h̸i̸m̸ t̸h̸e̸r̸e̸ f̸r̸o̸m̸ b̸e̸i̸n̸g̸ d̸t̸o̸w̸n̸/̸d̸/̸
     M̸a̸d̸e̸ h̸i̸m̸ t̸o̸ y̸i̸e̸l̸d̸
     F̸o̸u̸g̸h̸t̸ h̸i̸m̸ a̸g̸a̸i̸n̸,̸ &̸ s̸e̸n̸t̸ h̸i̸m̸ t̸o̸ t̸h̸e̸ K̸i̸n̸g̸/̸/̸
     T̸o̸ w̸h̸o̸m̸ t̸h̸e̸ d̸a̸m̸s̸e̸l̸/̸ C̸a̸r̸e̸ n̸o̸t̸/̸ a̸s̸ f̸o̸r̸ h̸i̸m̸/̸
     F̸u̸l̸l̸ o̸f̸t̸e̸n̸ h̸a̸v̸e̸ I̸ s̸e̸e̸n̸ h̸i̸m̸ w̸i̸t̸h̸e̸ h̸i̸m̸s̸e̸l̸f̸
     U̸p̸ t̸h̸e̸ b̸r̸i̸d̸g̸e̸-̸p̸i̸e̸r̸ f̸o̸r̸ s̸p̸o̸r̸t̸/̸ &̸ a̸s̸ f̸o̸r̸ t̸h̸e̸e̸   Bd-3

1128 I lead no longer: yonder be the towers   H-32
1128 I̸ I̸e̸a̸d̸ n̸o̸ I̸o̸n̸g̸e̸r̸/̸ y̸o̸n̸d̸e̸r̸ b̸e̸ t̸h̸e̸ t̸o̸w̸e̸r̸s̸   Bd-3
1128 ...longer,; ride...side;   ;/ (;;I)   A-2109
1128 (C)   B-II

245

Thou art the kingliest of all kitchen-knaves.

'"O trefoil, sparkling on the rainy plain,   1130
O rainbow with three colours after rain,
Shine sweetly: thrice my love hath smiled on me."

'Sir,--and, good faith, I fain had added--Knight,
But that I heard thee call thyself a knave,--
Shamed am I that I so rebuked, reviled,   1135
Missaid thee; noble I am; and thought the King
Scorned me and mine; and now thy pardon, friend,

Alt. after 1129 I have a kitchen-wench's longing to
                              thee--   Bd-3

1130 (Par.) "O trefoil,...   "/ (P)   A-2109
1130 (Par.) "O trefoil,...   B-II
1130 (Par.) '"O trefoil,...   '/ (I)   T-GP3
1130 (C)   72

1132 ...me."   "/ (P)   A-2109
1132 (C)   B-II

1133 Sir
     I fain had added Knight   H-32
1133 ...good sooth I...   Bd-3
1133 (Par.) 'Sir, and good sooth I fain...   A-2109
1133   faith,   I MS
     (Par.) 'Sir, - and, good s̸o̸o̸t̸h̸ I fain ...
                              (2nd, I)   T-GP3
1133 (C)   72

1134 Save that...   H-32
1134 ...a knave.   A-2109
1134 ...a knave.,-   ,-/ (I)   T-GP3
1134 (C)   72

1135 And wd not make thee liar. I have revild   H-32
1135 S   so
     Ashamed am I that I rebuked, reviled   Bd-3
1135 ...rebuked, reviled   A-2109
1135 ...rebuked, reviled,   ,/ (I)   T-GP3
1135 (C)   72

For thou hast ever answered courteously,
And wholly bold thou art, and meek withal
As any of Arthur's best, but, being knave,   1140
Hast mazed my wit: I marvel what thou art.'

'Damsel,' he said, 'you be not all to blame,
Saving that you mistrusted our good King
Would handle scorn, or yield you, asking, one
Not fit to cope your quest. You said your say;   1145
Mine answer was my deed. Good sooth! I hold
He scarce is knight, yea but half-man, nor meet

1140 ...best - & yet a knave.   H-32

1141 Thou hast amazed me I know not what...   H-32
1141   y wit
       ...mazed me m̶u̶c̶h̶: I...   Bd-3

1142 ye be not much to blame   H-32
1142 ...said 'ye be...   Bd-3
1142 ...said, 'ye be...   A-2109
1142 (C)   73

1143 ...that ye mistrusted our great King   H-32
1143 ...that ye mistrusted...   Bd-3;A-2109
1143 (C)   73

1144 ...yield thee, asking...   Bd-3:A-2109
1144 (C)   73

1145 ...cope thy quest. Ye said...   Bd-3;A-2109
1145 (C)   73

1146 Damsel for I hold   H-32
1146 My answer...deed. Sayings? I hold   Bd-3
1146 **My** answer...deed. Sayings? I hold   A-2109
1146 mine   Good sooth!   (MS, not A.T.)
       M̶y̶ answer...deed. S̶a̶y̶i̶n̶g̶s̶?̶ I hold   T-GP2;T-GP3
1146 (C)   72

1147 He is no knight..nor fit   H-32

247

To fight for gentle damsel, he, who lets
His heart be stirred with any foolish heat
At any gentle damsel's waywardness.   1150
Shamed? care not! thy foul sayings fought for me:
And seeing now thy words are fair, methinks
There rides no knight, nor Lancelot, his great self,
Hath force to quell me.'

1148	...for noble damsel, he who lets who shall let	H-32
1148	...for noble damsel, who shall let	Bd-3
1148	...for noble damsel, who shall let	S-929
1148	he	(MS, not A.T.)
	...damsel, who...	T-GP2
1148	gentle he, s	I MS
	...for ńőbĺé damsel, who śh́áĺĺ let	T-GP3
1148	(C)	72

1149	(1 ?)	
	His heart within him move to any wrath heat	H-32

1150	To hear a noble damsels petulency railing at him	H-32
1150	At hearing any damsel's petulency.	Bd-3
1150	gentle waywardness	I MS
	At h́éáŕińǵ any damsel's ṕét́úĺáńćý.	A-2109;T-GP3
1150	(C)	72

1151	Care not: for thy foul words have made me win	H-32
1151	fought for me	P MS
	Care not; for thy foul sayings ḿád́é ḿé ẃíń,	Bd-3
1151	Care not; for thy foul sayings fought for me/ ;/ (P)	A-2109
1151	Shamed? care not!	I MS
	Ćáŕé ńőt́ f́őt́ thy foul sayings fought for me,	T-GP3
1151	(C)	72

                    Nigh upon that hour
When the lone hern forgets his melancholy,   1155
Lets down his other leg, and stretching, dreams
Of goodly supper in the distant pool,
Then turned the noble damsel smiling at him,
And told him of a cavern hard at hand,
Where bread and baken meats and good red wine   1160
Of Southland, which the Lady Lyonors

1152 And now thy words are fair & sweet methinks   H-32
1152 ...fair, meseems   Bd-3;A-2109
1152   thinks   (MS, not A.T.)
     ...fair, me~~seems~~/   T-GP2;T-GP3
1152 (C)   72

1154 Shall have the better of me.   H-32
1154 Nigh upon that hour
     ~~Then about the time~~   Bd-3

1156 ...leg, and, stretching, dreams   ,/(,,, I) A-2109
1156 ...stretching dreams   B-II
1156 (C)   72

Alt. for 1158 ff
     Then - as they rode along a narrow comb
     ~~Wherein were~~
     With slabs of carven rock, the damsel turn'd Bd-3

1159 And told him...   Bd-3
1159 ...hand,   ,/ (P)   A-2109
1159 (C)   B-II

1161 ...Lady L~~y~~onors   y/ (P)   A-2109
1161 (C)   B-II

Had sent her coming champion, waited him.

    Anon they past a narrow comb wherein
Were slabs of rock with figures, knights on horse
Sculptured, and deckt in slowly-waning hues.   1165
'Sir Knave, my knight, a hermit once was here,
Whose holy hand hath fashioned on the rock
The war of Time against the soul of man.

_____

Sketch 1162 ff   - here
        In years agone, the man whose hand hath wrought
        On these great stones, a holy hermit, lived
        To whom the brethren wd confess themselves
        But when he past they feard the King no more
        See ye not whence these four unfurnished fools
        From these damp walls have suck'd their allegory.
                                        as in (1 ?)
        All arm'd as knights, their faces all one way
        Morning star & noonsun & evening star
        Night death wealth & lust & evil doubt (?) & pride
        All running down the soul that like a maid
        Fled as for spiritual succour to the cave.
        Follow the faces till we find it. look
        Who comes behind?   H-32
Sketch 1162 ff ...& here
        There dwelt in older days a holy man
        Whose hand hath fashiond symbols in the rock
        Of time, of life, the passions & the soul -
        All, for he once was knight, like armed men
        The four (unfurnishd?) fools from these damp stones
        Have suck'd their allegory & know no more
        Know ye not these? & Gareth lookd & saw
        Sculpt & in waning colours on the rock
        Morningstar, sun, & eveningstar, & night
        And many more, Wealth, world, lust, habit, pride
        Slab after slab, their faces one way set,
        And running down the soul a shape that fled
        With broken wings, torn raiment, & loose hair
        To seek for help & shelter in the cave
        Follow the faces & we find it. Look   Bd-3

And yon four fools have sucked their allegory
From these damp walls, and taken but the form.   1170
Know ye not these?' and Gareth lookt and read--
In letters like to those the vexillary
Hath left crag-carven o'er the streaming Gelt--

1162 ff ...waited him, '~~but~~ ~~look~~
         ~~who~~ ~~follows~~ ~~there?~~y   Bd-3

1163 ...they reach'd a narrow...   H-32
1163 ...past ~~adown~~ along a narrow comb   H-32

1164 With slabs of carven rock   H-32
1164 ...with armed men on horse   H-32
1164 Where armed men were sculpt on slabs of rock   H-32

1165 Insculpt, & drest in...   H-32

1166 ...here,   (, P)   A-2109
1166 (C)   B-II

1167 ...hath symbolld on the stone   H-32
1167   fashion'd on   P MS
     ...hath ~~wrought~~ ~~upon~~ the rock   Bd-3

1169 ~~know ye not these~~
     And you four fools...   H-32
1169   yon   I MS
     And ~~your~~ four...   S-929
1169 (C)   B-II

1170 ...walls, & misst the lesson there.   H-32

1171 ...& saw   H-32
1171 ...these'? and...   A-2109
1171 (C)   T-GP3

1172-3 Graven beneath five shapes of armed men   H-32
1172-3 In Roman lettering such as that wh lasts
        Tho' worn beside the Southward Roman walls   H-32

'PHOSPHORUS,' then 'MERIDIES'--'HESPERUS'--
'NOX'--'MORS,' beneath five figures, armed men,   1175
Slab after slab, their faces forward all,
And running down the Soul, a Shape that fled
With broken wings, torn raiment and loose hair,
For help and shelter to the hermit's cave.
'Follow the faces, and we find it. Look,   1180
Who comes behind?'

                              For one--delayed at first
Through helping back the dislocated Kay
To Camelot, then by what thereafter chanced,

1174-5   phosphor
          Hesper: meredies: hesper: nox: &:d̸e̸a̸t̸h̸:
                                    mors: H-32

1174 'Phosphorous' then 'Meridies' - 'Hesperus' -   A-2109
1174 'PHOSPHOROUS' then...   B-II
1174 'PHOSPHOROUS,' then...   ,/ (I)   T-GP3
1174 (C)   72

1175 ...five shapes of armed...   H-32
1175   figures
     ...five s̸h̸a̸p̸e̸s̸ o̸f̸ armed...   Bd-3
1175   M   I MS
     'Nox' - 'Thors' beneath five ̸(figures̸), armed
                          men,   ,/ (1st, I) A-2109
1175 ...'MORS' beneath...   B-II
1175 ...'MORS,' beneath...   ,/ (I)   T-GP3
1175 (C)   72

1176 ..faces one line set   H-32
1176 ...slab, with faces...   H-32
1176   their   2   1
     ...slab, w̸i̸t̸h̸ forward faces all,   Bd-3

1177 All running...   H-32

1178 ...hair,   ,/ (P)   A-2109
1178 (C)   72

1181 For Sir Lancelot first delay'd   H-32
1181   one   2   1
     For H̸e̸ - at first delay'd   Bd-3

GARETH AND LYNETTE

```
The damsel's headlong error through the wood--
Sir Lancelot, having swum the river-loops--            1185
His blue shield-lions covered--softly drew
Behind the twain, and when he saw the star
Gleam, on Sir Gareth's turning to him, cried,
'Stay, felon knight, I avenge me for my friend,'
```

1182	holping		
	By tending back...		H-32

1183	...by that wh after chanced,		H-32
1183	...by that which after chanced		Bd-3
1183	what thereafter		
	...by ~~that~~ ~~which~~ ~~after~~ chanced,	(, I)	S-929
1183	...chanced,	,/	T-GP2
1183	(C)		T-GP3

1184	...the wood~~s~~ -	A-2109
1184	(C)	B-II

1185	...having past the passes, came	H-32
1185	swum	
	...having ~~crost~~ the river-loops	Bd-3
1185	...river-loops~~,~~ -	A-2109
1185	(C)	B-II

```
Sketch 1186-1188
        Came on the twàin, & when the morning-star
        At length had (2 ?) him but when he saw
        The morning star on Gareth's turning, cried      H-32
```

1186	~~A~~ ~~cover~~ ~~on~~ ~~the~~ ~~shield,~~ ~~that~~ ~~none~~ ~~might~~ ~~know~~		Bd-3
1186	...shield - lions...	-/ (I)	A-2109
1186	(C)		B-II

1187	~~Drew/to/the/twain//&/when/he/saw/the/star~~		Bd-3
1187	...twain, and...	,/ (P)	A-2109
1187	(C)		T-GP3

1189	Bide Sir Rebel thou hast slain my friend	
	And shamed	H-32
1189	'Stay rebel knight; ...	Bd-3
1189	felon	I MS
	'Stay, ~~rebel~~ knight,...	S-929
1189	(C)	B-II

And Gareth crying pricked against the cry;   1190
But when they closed--in a moment--at one touch
Of that skilled spear, the wonder of the world--
Went sliding down so easily, and fell,
That when he found the grass within his hands
He laughed; the laughter jarred upon Lynette: 1195
Harshly she asked him, 'Shamed and overthrown,
And tumbled back into the kitchen-knave,
Why laugh ye? that ye blew your boast in vain?'

1190	crying	P MS
	And Gareth prick'd against H̶i̶m̶ a̶t̶ the cry	Bd-3
1190	...the cry,;	(; I)	A-2109
1190	(C)		B-II

1191	But	P MS
	T̶h̶e̶n̶ when...	Bd-3
1191	...closed, ⌐ in a moment, - at one touch	
		(- - P)	A-2109
1191	(C)		B-II

| 1192 | ...world/ - | -/ (P) | A-2109 |
| 1192 | (C) | | B-II |

1194	in either	I MS
	...grass w̶i̶t̶h̶i̶n̶ h̶i̶s̶ hands̶	S-929
1194	(C)		B-II

Sketch 1195-1198
    He laugh'd & she was anger'd at it, saying
    Why laugh ye? that your boast hath proven vain?
                                 H-32

1195	Lynette	I MS
	...upon L̶i̶n̶e̶t̶h̶	S-929
1195	(C)		B-II

1196	she ask'd him	
	Harshly d̶e̶m̶a̶n̶d̶i̶n̶g̶' shamed...	Bd-3
1196	...overthrown,	,/ (I)	A-2109
1196	(C)		B-II

| 1197 | ...kitchen-knave, | ,/ (I) | A-2109 |
| 1197 | (C) | | B-II |

'Nay, noble damsel, but that I, the son
Of old King Lot and good Queen Bellicent,⠀⠀⠀⠀⠀1200
And victor of the bridges and the ford,
And knight of Arthur, here lie thrown by whom
I know not, all through mere unhappiness--
Device and sorcery and unhappiness--
Out, sword; we are thrown!' And Lancelot answered,
⠀⠀⠀⠀⠀⠀⠀⠀⠀⠀⠀'Prince,⠀⠀⠀⠀⠀1205
O Gareth--through the mere unhappiness
Of one who came to help thee, not to harm,

1198⠀⠀⠀⠀⠀⠀ye blew your
⠀⠀⠀...that y̸o̸u̸r̸ boast w̸a̸s̸ a̸l̸l̸ in vain?⠀⠀⠀⠀⠀Bd-3
1198 ...vain'?⠀⠀⠀⠀⠀⠀⠀⠀⠀⠀⠀⠀⠀⠀⠀⠀⠀A-2109
1198 (C)⠀⠀⠀⠀⠀⠀⠀⠀⠀⠀⠀⠀⠀⠀⠀⠀⠀⠀⠀⠀⠀T-GP3

Sketch 1199-1203
⠀⠀⠀⠀Nay that I went so easily down - that I
⠀⠀⠀⠀Son of King Lot & good Queen Bellicent
⠀⠀⠀⠀Am overthrown thro' mere unhappiness by this
⠀⠀⠀⠀⠀⠀⠀⠀⠀⠀chance⠀⠀⠀⠀⠀⠀⠀⠀⠀H-32

1199 N̸a̸y̸/ d̸a̸m̸s̸e̸l̸/ s̸u̸r̸e̸l̸y̸ ⫽ b̸u̸t̸ t̸h̸a̸t̸ I̸/ t̸h̸e̸ s̸o̸n̸⠀⠀⠀Bd-3

1201 I̸ v̸i̸c̸t̸o̸r̸ o̸f̸...⠀⠀⠀⠀⠀⠀⠀⠀⠀⠀⠀⠀⠀⠀⠀⠀⠀Bd-3

1202 A̸n̸d̸ K̸n̸i̸g̸h̸t̸ o̸f̸ A̸r̸t̸h̸u̸r̸'s̸ T̸a̸b̸l̸e̸/ h̸e̸r̸e̸ b̸e̸ t̸h̸r̸o̸w̸n̸⠀⠀Bd-3

1203 s̸o̸ e̸a̸s̸i̸l̸y̸/ & t̸h̸r̸o̸/ m̸e̸r̸e̸ u̸n̸h̸a̸p̸p̸i̸n̸e̸s̸s̸⠀⠀⠀⠀⠀Bd-3

Alt. after 1203 B̸y̸ w̸h̸o̸m̸ I̸ K̸n̸o̸w̸ n̸o̸t̸/ A̸n̸d̸ s̸i̸r̸
⠀⠀⠀⠀⠀⠀⠀⠀⠀⠀⠀⠀⠀L̸a̸n̸c̸e̸l̸o̸t̸ s̸a̸i̸d̸⠀⠀⠀⠀⠀⠀Bd-3

1205 ...thrown, !' and...⠀⠀⠀⠀⠀⠀⠀⠀(! I)⠀⠀⠀⠀S-929
1205⠀⠀⠀⠀⠀⠀⠀A⠀⠀⠀⠀⠀⠀⠀⠀⠀⠀⠀⠀⠀⠀⠀I MS
⠀⠀⠀...thrown!' A̸nd...⠀⠀⠀⠀⠀⠀⠀⠀⠀⠀⠀⠀⠀T-GP3
1205 (C)⠀⠀⠀⠀⠀⠀⠀⠀⠀⠀⠀⠀⠀⠀⠀⠀⠀⠀⠀⠀⠀⠀72

1206 O Gareth/ - thro'⠀⠀⠀⠀⠀⠀⠀⠀⠀(- P)⠀⠀⠀A-2109
1206 (C)⠀⠀⠀⠀⠀⠀⠀⠀⠀⠀⠀⠀⠀⠀⠀⠀⠀⠀⠀⠀⠀B-II

1207 ...thee not...⠀⠀⠀⠀⠀⠀⠀⠀⠀⠀⠀⠀⠀⠀⠀A-2109
1207 (C)⠀⠀⠀⠀⠀⠀⠀⠀⠀⠀⠀⠀⠀⠀⠀⠀⠀⠀⠀⠀⠀73

Lancelot, and all as glad to find thee whole,
As on the day when Arthur knighted him.'

Then Gareth, 'Thou--Lancelot!--thine the hand   1210
That threw me? An some chance to mar the boast
Thy brethren of thee make--which could not chance--
Had sent thee down before a lesser spear,

1208   all
      Lancelot, & ńǿẃ as glad...   Bd-3
1208   all
      ..., and ǽǹ as glad...   S-929
1208 (C)   B-II

Sketch 1210 ff   Țħǿṃ   ǵ
    Țħẹǹ Ǧáṛẹțħ /țẹáċħ/ṃẹ țħǿṃ țħẏ ńǿḅĺẹ ħáǹḋ/
    Țħáț țħẹẁ ṃẹ ḅ/ẹț/
    (1 ?) ẘḭḟ Ǧǿḋ/ ḭḟ ṡǿṃẹ ḭṃṗǿṡṡḭḅĺẹ ċħáǹċẹ/
    țǿ ṃáṛ țħẹ ḅĺǿțẏ ḅḟ ḅǿț țáḅĺẹ ṛǿǿǹḋ/
    ħáḋ ċáṡț țħẹẹ ḋǿẃǹ ḅẹḟǿṛẹ á ĺẹṡṡẹṛ ṡṗẹáṛ/
                              ṃẏ áĺĺ țħẹ ṡáḭǹțṡ
    Ṡħáṃẹḋ ħáḋ ḭ ḅẹẹǹ/ & ṡáḋ/ ṃẏ ħáǹḋ/ ṃẏ ħáǹḋ/
    ḭ ṡṗẹáḵ țț·ǿṃ ǹẹțḭ·ẹṡț ħẹáṛț· /ṃẏ ħáǹḋ/ ṃẏ ħáǹḋ·/
    Ẁħẹṛẹáț țħẹ ḅẹṛǿḭáǹț   Bd-3

1210 Then Gareth 'țẹáċħ Thou? reach me the noble   P MS
                                    hand   Bd-3
1210   Lancelot? is thine
     (No Par.) Then Gareth, 'Thouẓ, țẹáċħ ṃẹ țħẹ
                                    the hand   I MS
                              ńǿḅĺẹ ħáǹḋ   (2nd, I)   S-929
1210 (Par.) Then Gareth, 'Thou Lancelot! is thine the
                                    hand   B-II
1210 (C)   T-GP2

1211 ...me - an...   A-2104
1211 (C)   T-GP2

1212 ...make - impossible - ħẹ ċáǹț   (P MS)   Bd-3
1212   wh cd not chance -   MS
     ...make - ḭṃṗǿṡṡḭḅĺẹ ≠ ḭ   S-929
1212 (C)   B-II

Shamed had I been, and sad—O Lancelot--thou!'

   Whereat the maiden, petulant, 'Lancelot,   1215
Why came ye not, when called? and wherefore now
Come ye, not called? I gloried in my knave,
Who being still rebuked, would answer still
Courteous as any knight--but now, if knight,

1213 ...spear   A-2109
1213 ...spear,   ,/ (I)   T-GP3
1213 (C)   72

1214 ...and sad - thy hand - thy hand   (P MS)   Bd-3
1214   O Lancelot - thou!   I MS
    ...been and sad - t̷h̷y̷ h̷a̷n̷d̷ ≠ t̷h̷y̷ h̷a̷n̷d̷/'   S-929
1214 ...been and...thou?   B-II
1214 ...been and...   72
1214 (C)   73

1215   Whereat   2   1   P MS
    (Par.) T̷o̷ w̷h̷o̷m̷ the petulant maiden 'Lancelot   Bd-3

1216 ...when askd come ye now   H-32
1216   & Wherefore
    ...calld? W̷h̷y̷ c̷o̷m̷e̷ y̷e̷ now   Bd-3

Sketch 1217 ff
     Betrayd   am I! I (1 ?) at the knave
     Wh being still (1 ?) rebuked (1 ?)
     Wd even   (2 ?) he answer courteously   H-32

1217 Come ye   gloried in
     Not call'd? I m̷a̷r̷v̷e̷l̷l̷'̷d̷ a̷t̷ my goodly knave   H-32

1218   would answer still   P MS
    ...rebuked, m̷i̷s̷s̷a̷i̷d̷, u̷n̷b̷i̷d̷   Bd-3

1219 Courteous as any knight of all - if knight   P MS
   W̷o̷u̷l̷d̷ s̷t̷i̷l̷l̷ m̷a̷k̷e̷ a̷n̷s̷w̷e̷r̷ c̷o̷u̷r̷t̷e̷o̷u̷s̷ a̷s̷ a̷ k̷n̷i̷g̷h̷t̷ Bd-3
1219   but now   I MS
    ...knight, o̷f̷ a̷l̷l̷ - if knight   (, I)   S-929
1219 ...knight,   ,/   T-GP2
1219 (C)   T-GP3

The marvel dies, and leaves me fooled and tricked   1220
And only wondering wherefore played upon:
And doubtful whether I and mine be scorned.
Where should be truth if not in Arthur's hall,
In Arthur's presence? Knight, knave, prince and fool,
I hate thee and for ever.'

               And Lancelot said,   1225

1220 The marvel dies and leaves me fool'd and trick'd
                                                      P MS
     If Knight, the marvel dies & leaves me trick'd Bd-3
1220 ...dies, and...   ,/ (I)   A-2109
1220 (C)   T-GP3

1221 ...wherefore *I was* play'd   Bd-3

1224 And Arthur's...   H-32

1225 ...thee for ever.   H-32

1227-1229 ...wish: my lance hath borne thee down.
           Borne down was I when young a score of
                    times   H-32

1227   be   P MS
    ...damsel, *are* ye wise   Bd-3
1227 ..., be ye wise   A-2109
1227 (C)   73

1229   God wot   P MS
    ...been, & many a time, *of old*,   Bd-3
1229   nor once, but   I MS
    ...been, *God wot, and* many a time*/*. (⊙ I) S-929
1229   but   MS
    ...once, *and* many a time*/*;   ⊙/   T-GP2
1229 (C)   T-GP3

GARETH AND LYNETTE

'Blessed be thou, Sir Gareth! knight art thou
To the King's best wish. O damsel, be you wise
To call him shamed, who is but overthrown?
Thrown have I been, nor once, but many a time.
Victor from vanquished issues at the last,   1230
And overthrower from being overthrown.
With sword we have not striven; and thy good horse
And thou are weaɪy; yet not less I felt
Thy manhood through that wearied lance of thine.

_____

Alt. after 1229 N̸o̸t̸ a̸l̸w̸a̸y̸s̸ v̸i̸c̸t̸o̸r̸ w̸i̸t̸h̸ m̸y̸ s̸w̸o̸r̸d̸ w̸a̸s̸
                              I̸   Bd-3

1231   er   I MS
   ...overthrow from...   S-929
1231 (C)   B-II

Sketch 1232-1235
                    I say it
   Wd God that   en from mine inmost heart
   Sir Gareth served the King as well as thou!   H-32
Sketch 1232-1235
   ...striven. Thy horse & thou
   Are faint with toil; a lesser than thyself
   Had borne thee down & wd to God that I
   Cd serve the King from inmost heart, in all
   As well as thou hast here. The stream is freed
                                                     H-32
Sketch 1232-1235
   I̸ s̸p̸e̸a̸k̸ t̸o̸o̸ l̸o̸u̸d̸;̸ a̸ l̸e̸s̸s̸e̸r̸ t̸h̸a̸n̸ t̸h̸y̸s̸e̸l̸f̸
   S̸e̸e̸i̸n̸g̸ t̸h̸y̸ /̸h̸o̸r̸s̸e̸ i̸s̸ w̸e̸a̸r̸i̸e̸d̸ &̸ t̸h̸y̸s̸e̸l̸f̸
   W̸i̸t̸h̸ d̸a̸y̸l̸o̸n̸g̸ b̸a̸t̸t̸l̸e̸ m̸i̸g̸h̸t̸ h̸a̸v̸e̸ b̸o̸r̸n̸e̸ t̸h̸e̸e̸ d̸o̸w̸n̸/̸
   W̸o̸u̸l̸d̸ G̸o̸d̸/̸ t̸h̸a̸t̸ I̸ c̸o̸u̸l̸d̸ s̸e̸r̸v̸e̸ t̸h̸e̸ K̸i̸n̸g̸ i̸n̸ a̸l̸l̸
   A̸s̸ w̸e̸l̸l̸ &̸ t̸r̸u̸l̸y̸/̸ G̸a̸r̸e̸t̸h̸/̸ a̸s̸ t̸h̸y̸s̸e̸l̸f̸/̸   Bd-3

1233   e   I MS
   ...thou ar̸t̸ weary...   S-929
1233 (C)   B-II

259

GARETH AND LYNETTE

Well hast, thou done; for all the stream is freed,   1235
And thou hast wreaked his justice on his foes,
And when reviled, hast answered graciously,
And makes merry when overthrown. Prince, Knight,
Hail, Knight and Prince, and of our Table Round!'

Sketch 1235 ff.
Well hast thou done; & we to God that/I
Cd serve the King / from inmost heart / in all
As well as thou in this/ the stream is freed/
Loyally as thou hast here   Bd-3

Alt. for 1235 Well hast thou serve the King and
                        would that I (P MS)   Bd-3

1235 ...done; for...freed,   (; , I)   S-929
1235 (C)   B-II

1236 And
     For thou...   Bd-3

1237 Being revild thou answerest courteously   H-32

1238   makest merry when
     And laughest overthrown. Sir Knight & Prince
                        & Knight   H-32
1238 ...overthrown. Knight, Prince,   Bd-3
1238 ...merry, when...   A-2109
1238 (C)   73

1239   our
     ...of the Table...   Bd-3
1239 ...Round?'   A-2109
1239 ...Round/'   !/ (I)   T-GP3
1239 (C)   72

Sketch 1240 ff.
     (Par.) Then turning to Linette he told the tale
     Of Gareth but she still was wroth & cried
     Well well ay well but he that fights must eat
     Viands & drinks & bread & flint for fire.   H-32

And then when turning to Lynette he told 1240
The tale of Gareth, petulantly she said,
'Ay well--ay well--for worse than being fooled
Of others, is to fool one's self. A cave,
Sir Lancelot, is hard by, with meats and drinks
And forage for the horse, and flint for fire. 1245
But all about it flies a honeysuckle.
Seek, till we find.' And when they sought and found,

1240   Lynette   I MS
  ...to L̷i̷n̷e̷t̷h̷ he...   A-2109

1241 Again the maiden answerd petulantly   H-32

1242   for   I MS
  ...well - f̷a̷r̷ worse...   A-2109
1242 (C)   B-II

1243 By others is to make oneself a fool A cave H-32

1244 Is somewhere hard beside, & meats therein H-32

1245 And wine & flint for fire - but hard to find H-32

1246 ...about flies...   H-32

Alt. after 1246 A̷n̷d̷ v̷e̷i̷l̷s̷ t̷h̷e̷ h̷o̷l̷l̷o̷w̷:̷ t̷h̷a̷t̷ f̷i̷g̷h̷t̷s̷
         m̷u̷s̷t̷ e̷a̷t̷:̷   Bd-3

Sketch alt. for 1247
  Hiding the hollow: here a hermit (1 ?)
  To whom these lawless four confess'd themselves
  And since he died, they care not for the King
    fear
  But shun the cave: & this is hard to find
  The entry but they found & entring   H-32

1247 ...found,   (, I) A-2109
1247 (C)   B-II

Sir Gareth drank and ate, and all his life
Past into sleep; on whom the maiden gazed.
'Sound sleep be thine! sound cause to sleep hast
               thou.   1250
Wake lusty! Seem I not as tender to him
As any mother? Ay, but such a one
As all day long hath rated at her child,
And vext his day, but blesses him asleep--

1248-1249 ...ate & fell & slept
        Then spake the damsel to Sir Lancelot   H-32

1248 ...ate & f̸a̸l̸l̸i̸n̸g̸ s̸l̸e̸p̸t̸ all his life   Bd-3
1248 ...ate, and...   ,/ (I)   A-2109
1248 (C)   B-II

1249   gazed
      ...maiden g̸l̸a̸n̸c̸e̸d̸   Bd-3

1250 Sound be thy sleep: Sound is t̸h̸y̸ cause hast thou
                 for sleep.   H-32

1251 Seem A̸m̸ I not tender as any mother to him?   H-32
1251 ...lusty! s̸eem I...   cap (I MS)   S-929
1251 (C)   B-II

1252 ...mother - ay, but...   ,/ (I)   A-2109
1252 ...mother - ay, but...   B-II
1252 ...mother ≠ a̸y, but...   ?Ay (I)   T-GP3
1252 (C)   72

1253 That all...   H-32
1253 ...child,   ,/ (I)   A-2109
1253 (C)   B-II

1254 ...his life, but...   H-32
1254   day
      ...his l̸i̸f̸e̸, but...   Bd-3

1256 ...if this world...   H-32

Good lord, how sweetly smells the honeysuckle   1255
In the hushed night, as if the world were one
Of utter peace, and love,and gentleness!
O Lancelot, Lancelot'--and she clapt her hands--
'Full merry am I to find my goodly knave
Is knight and noble. See now, sworn have I,   2160
Else yon black felon had not let me pass,
To bring thee back to do the battle with him.
Thus an thou goest, he will fight thee first;
Who doubts thee victor? so will my knight-knave
Miss the full flower of this accomplishment.'   1265

1258 O Lancelot [& she clapt her hands]   H-32

1259 Right merry...   H-32;Bd-3
1259 Full   I MS
     ~~Right~~ merry...   S-929
1259 (C)   B-II

1260 ...now I have sworn   H-32
1260 ...sworn am I   H-32;Bd-3
1260   have   I MS
     ...sworn ~~am~~ I,   S-929
1260 (C)   B-II

Sketch 1261-1265
     To yon black thief that I sd bring thee back
     To fight him: an thou goest he fights with thee
     And thou wilt overthrow him & my knave-knight
     Will not finish this fair quest.   H-32

1262   ~~one~~ do the battle with him   P MS
     ...back ~~with to combat him~~.   Bd-3

1263 So an thou...   Bd-3
1263 Thus, an   I MS
     ~~So ete~~ thou...   S-929
1263 (C)   B-II

1264   thee   so will my knight knave
     Who doubts ~~thou will be~~ victor? ~~& my knave~~   Bd-3

263

Said Lancelot, 'Peradventure he, you name,
May know my shield. Let Gareth, an he will,

1266 And Lancelot the black felon knows my shield   H-32
1266   he, ye name
     ...peradventure t̸h̸i̸s̸ b̸l̸a̸c̸k̸ t̸h̸i̸e̸f̸   Bd-3
1266 ...he, ye name,   A-2109
1266 (C)   73

1267 Let Gareth when he wakes an he will   H-32

1268   his with   &
     Make change of shield with me; take my steed, t̸o̸o̸
     Take it & have my warhorse also - fresh   H-32

1269 Not to be spurr'd loving
     F̸r̸e̸s̸h̸/ o̸n̸e̸ (̸1̸/̸2̸)̸ the battle n̸i̸g̸h̸ a̸s̸ well   H-32

1270 ...him. Utter thanks she said   H-32
1270 ...him. 'Thanks from heart' she said   Bd-3
1270   Lancelot-like   I MS
     ...him.' 'T̸h̸a̸n̸k̸s̸ f̸r̸o̸m̸ h̸e̸a̸r̸t̸/' she said,   S-929
1270 (C)   B-II

1272 ...wakening gladly graspt the shield   Bd-3
1272 ...the shield,;   ;/ (P)   A-2109
1272 (C)   B-II

Sketch 1273 ff   clutch'd
                            hugg'd
     And Gareth wakening fiercely caught the shield:
                                      on
     'Ramp, ye lance-splintering lions, y̸e̸ t̸o̸ whom all
                            spears
        - myself have seen - ye seem agape to roar -
     All spears are rotten sticks - I know you well -
     Yea, ramp & roar at leaving of your lord
     Stet   so well
     C̸a̸r̸e̸ n̸o̸t̸/ g̸o̸o̸d̸ beasts, b̸e̸c̸a̸u̸s̸e̸ I care for you -
     P̸a̸t̸i̸e̸n̸c̸e̸   c̸a̸r̸e̸ n̸o̸t̸;   Bd-3

Change his for mine, and take my charger, fresh,
Not to be spurred, loving the battle as well
As he that rides him.' 'Lancelot-like,' she said,   1270
'Courteous in this, Lord Lancelot, as in all.'

   And Gareth, wakening, fiercely clutched the shield;
'Ramp ye lance-splintering lions, on whom all spears
Are rotten sticks! ye seem agape to roar!
Yea, ramp and roar at leaving of your lord!--   1275
Care not, good beasts, so well I care for you.
O noble Lancelot, from my hold on these
Streams virtue--fire--through one that will not shame
Even the shadow of Lancelot under shield.
Hence: let us go.'

                    Silent the silent field 1280

1274 ...sticks - ye...roar.		S-929
1274 ...sticks - ! ye...roar.!	!/!/	T-GP2
1274 (C)		T-GP3

1275 ...lord/!	! (I)	A-2109
1275 ...lord! -	-/	T-GP2
1275 (C)		T-GP3

1277 Then when
      O Lancelot from the graspings of thy shield   H-32
1277   from
      ...Lancelot, t̸h̸r̸o̸y̸ my...   Bd-3

1278   thine all thro one who will
      Streams virtue & is made mine. I shall not
                         shame   H-32
1278   fire
      ...virtue - t̸h̸i̸n̸e̸ - thro'...   Bd-3

1279 ...Lancelot in his arms   H-32
1279 ...Lancelot i̸n̸ h̸i̸s̸ a̸r̸m̸s̸ under shield.   Bd-3

1280   let us go
      Hence o̸n̸ t̸h̸e̸ m̸o̸m̸e̸n̸t̸   H-32
1280 Silent oer the...   H-32

265

They traversed. Arthur's harp though summer-wan,
In counter motion to the clouds, allured
The glance of Gareth dreaming on his liege.
A star shot: 'Lo,' said Gareth, 'the foe falls!'
An owl whoopt: 'Hark the victor pealing there!'   2185
Suddenly she that rode upon his left
Clung to the shield that Lancelot lent him, crying,
'Yield, yield him this again: 'tis he must fight:

1281 ...Arthurs wain & Arthurs harp		H-32
1281 harp tho summer-wan		P MS
They traversed. A̶r̶t̶h̶u̶r̶'̶s̶ w̶a̶i̶n̶ & A̶r̶t̶h̶u̶r̶'̶s̶		
h̶a̶r̶p̶		Bd-3

1282 Paled aloft, & all beneath was dew.	H-32
1282 Bekend aloft & all the land was dew.	H-32
1282 In counter motion to the clouds allured	P MS
F̶l̶e̶d̶ i̶n̶ & o̶u̶t̶ a̶m̶o̶n̶g̶/t̶h̶e̶ r̶o̶l̶l̶i̶n̶g̶ c̶l̶o̶u̶d̶s̶	Bd-3

1283 The glance of Gareth dreaming on his liege	P MS
A̶ s̶t̶a̶r̶ s̶h̶o̶t̶l̶ t̶h̶e̶n̶ S̶i̶r̶ G̶a̶r̶e̶t̶h̶/ L̶o̶o̶k̶/ h̶e̶ f̶o̶r̶	
f̶a̶l̶l̶s̶y̶	Bd-3
1283 ...Gareth/ dreaming...	A-2109
1283 (C)	B-II

1284 ...shot: & SirGareth'there he falls'		H-32
1284 ..falls' ≠ !	! (I)	A-2109
1284 (C)		B-II

1285 ...hark the hymn of victory!'		H-32
1285 ...there.!	! (I)	A-2109
1285 (C)		B-II

1286 Suddenly, riding on his left, Lynette	H-32

1287 Laid hand upon the shield of Lancelot.	H-32

1288 yield	
Yield it him back Sir Prince oh give it to him	H-32

1289 Cursed be my tongue that all the yesterday	H-32
1289 I curse	
C̶u̶r̶s̶e̶d̶ i̶s̶ the tongue ...	Bd-3

I curse the tongue that all through yesterday
Reviled thee, and hath wrought on Lancelot now   1290
To lend thee horse and shield: wonders ye have done;
Miracles ye cannot: here is glory enow
In having flung the three: I see thee maimed,
Mangled: I swear thou canst not fling tne fourth.'

    'And wherefore, damsel? tell me all ye know.   1295
You cannot scare me; nor rough   face, or voice,

1290 Wd rate thee & now hath wrought on Lancelot   H-32

1291 To lend thee shield & lance. Thou hast glory
                            enow   H-32
1291   ye have
    ...wonders t̸h̸o̸u̸ h̸a̸s̸t̸ done   Bd-3
1291 ...done   A-2109
1291 (C)   T-GP2

Sketch 1292-1294
    Flinging the three thou canst not fling the 4th.
                                      H-32

1292   ye cannot
    Miracles t̸h̸o̸u̸ c̸a̸n̸s̸t̸ n̸o̸t̸/ here...   Bd-3

1294 ...canst fling...   Bd-3
1294   not   I MS
    ...canst fling...   A-2109
1294 (C)   B-II

Sketch 1295 ff
    And wherefore, damsel: fling the fourth I will
    Or die therefore   H-32

1296 I never heard his voice nor saw his face   H-32
1296   rough face or voice   P MS
    Ye cannot scare me,/n̸o̸r̸ b̸r̸u̸t̸e̸ b̸u̸l̸k̸ o̸f̸ l̸i̸m̸b̸   Bd-3
1296 Ye cannot scãre me, nor rough face, or voice
                              (last 2,I)A-2109
1296 Ye cannot scare me,; nor...   ;/   T-GP2
1296 Ye cannot...   T-GP3
1296 (C)   73

Brute bulk of limb, or boundless savagery
Appal me' from the quest.'

                'Nay, Prince,' she cried,
'God wot, I never looked upon the face,
Seeing he never rides abroad by day;   1300
But watched him have I like a phantom pass
Chilling the night: nor have I heard the voice.
Always he made his mouthpiece of a page

1297 Brute bulk of limb or boundless savagery		P MS
~~A tough voice, & a face of savagery~~		Bd-3
1297 ...limb, or...	,/ (I)	A-2109
1297 ...limb;, or...	,/	T-GP2
1297 (C)		T-GP3
1299 ...the face,	,/ (I)	S-929
1299 ...the face,	,	T-GP2
1299 (C)		T-GP3

Sketch 1300 ff
    He never rides by day: I have seen him pass
    Darkling at night: nor ever heard him speak
    His mouthpiece was a puny page who (1 ?)
    Reported him   this reported him
    As having in himself the strength of ten
    He spares not man
    Some hold that he hath swallow'd infant flesh
    Monster   H-32

1300 ...by day,;	; (I)	S-929
1300 ...by day,;	;	T-GP2
1300 (C)		T-GP3
1301 watch'd		P MS
But ~~seen~~ him...		Bd-3
1302 Chilling the		
~~Darkling/by~~ night...		Bd-3
1303 ...mouthpiece ~~always~~ of a page		Bd-3

Who came and went, and still reported him
As closing in himself the strength of ten,   1305
And when his anger tare him, massacring
Man, woman, lad and girl--yea, the soft babe!
Some hold that he hath swallowed infant flesh,
Monster! O Prince, I went for Lancelot first,
The quest is Lancelot's: give him back the shield.' 1310

   Said Gareth laughing, 'An he fight for this,
Belike he wins it as the better man:
Thus--and not else!'

                 But Lancelot on him urged
All the devisings of their chivalry

1306   anger tare him
    ...his w̶r̶a̶t̶h̶ w̶a̶s̶ o̶n̶ h̶i̶m̶ massacring   Bd-3

1307 ...babe -   A-2109
1307 (C)   72

1308 ...flesh,   ,/ (I)   A-2109
1308 (C)   B-II

1309 ...O prince, I...   A-2109
1309 (C)   75

1311 (Par.) And Gareth...fight for i̶t̶ this   Bd-3
1311   Said   I MS
    (Par.) A̶n̶d̶ Gareth...for this   S-929
1311 (C)   B-II

1312   as   P MS
    ...wins it b̶e̶i̶n̶g̶ the better...   Bd-3
1312 ...man/:   :/ (P)   A-2109
1312 (C)   B-II

1313   on him   P MS
    ...Lancelot urged u̶p̶o̶n̶ h̶i̶m̶   Bd-3
1313 ...else'?   A-2109
1313 ...:else?'   T-GP3
1313 (C)   73

1314 The new devisings...   H-32

When one might meet a mightier than himself;   1315
How best to manage horse, lance, sword and shield,
And so fill up the gap where force might fail
With skill and fineness. Instant were his words.

    Then Gareth, 'Here be rules. I know but one--
To dash against mine enemy and to win.   1320
Yet have I watched thee victor in the joust,
And seen thy way.' 'Heaven help thee,' sighed Lynette.

1315	When		P MS
	W̷h̷e̷r̷e̷ one...himself;	(; I)	S-929
1315	Where one...		B-II
1315	(C)		73
1318	...fineness. Earnest were...		Bd-3
1318	Instant		I MS
	...fineness. E̷a̷r̷n̷e̷s̷t̷ were...		S-929
1318	(C)		B-II
1319	Then		P MS
	(Par.) A̷n̷d̷ Gareth...		Bd-3
1319	...Gareth 'Here...one		A-2109
1319	...one -	-/ (I)	T-GP3
1319	(C)		72
1320	mine		
	...against o̷n̷e̷y̷s̷ enemy...		Bd-3
1320	...win.	☉ (I)	A-2109
1320	(C)		B-II
1321	...joust,	(, I)	A-2109
1321	(C)		B-II
1322	Heaven sigh'd		P MS
	...way' 'G̷o̷d̷ help thee' s̷a̷i̷d̷ Lynette.		Bd-3
1322	Lynette		I MS
	...sigh'd L̷y̷n̷e̷t̷t̷.		A-2109
1322	(C)		B-II
1323	(Par.) S̷o̷ t̷h̷r̷o̷ t̷h̷e̷ d̷a̷r̷k̷e̷s̷t̷ h̷o̷u̷r̷ b̷e̷f̷o̷r̷e̷ d̷a̷w̷n̷		Bd-3
1323	...space, and...	,/ (I)	A-2109
1323	(C)		B-II

Then for a space, and under cloud that grew
To thunder-gloom palling all stars, they rode
In converse till she made her palfrey halt,   1325
Lifted an arm, and softly whispered, 'There.'
And all the three were silent seeing, pitched
Beside the Castle Perilous on flat field,
A huge pavilion like a mountain peak
Sunder the glooming crimson on the marge,   1330
Black, with black banner, and a long black horn
Beside it hanging; which Sir Gareth graspt,
And so, before the two could hinder him,

1324 D̸a̸r̸k̸e̸r̸ f̸o̸r̸ c̸l̸o̸u̸d̸ t̸h̸a̸t̸ w̸r̸a̸p̸t̸ a̸l̸l̸ s̸t̸a̸r̸s̸, t̸h̸e̸y̸
                       r̸o̸d̸e̸   Bd-3
1324   thunder   P MS
     To r̸a̸i̸n̸y̸ gloom...   Bd-3
1324 To thunder-gloom...stars, they...   -/(-, I)   S-929
1324 (C)   B-II

1326 ...whisper'd 'There.'   A-2109
1326 (C)   T-GP3

Alt. before 1329 They when they came before the
                              tower beheld   H-32

1329 Huge black
     A black pavilion, like a mountain top,   H-32

1330 Sundering the dusking crimson   H-32
1330 Sunder the...   H-32

1331 ...& a black horn hung   H-32

1332 Before it pendant: wh...   H-32
1332   Beside   P MS
     Before it, hanging...   Bd-3

1333   hinder
     And Gareth ere the two could stay him   H-32
1333 ...so, before...him,   (,, I)   A-2109
1333 (C)   B-II

Sent all his heart and breath through all the horn.
Echoed the walls; a light twinkled; anon   1335
Came lights and lights, and once again he blew;
Whereon were hollow tramplings up and down
And muffled voices heard, and shadows past;
Till high above him, circled with her maids,
The Lady Lyonors at a window stood,   1340
Beautiful among lights, and waving to him
White hands, and courtesy; but when the Prince

1334 He sent his breath & heart into the horn   H-32

1335 A light within from/out/a lower twinkled/ to
                          which   Bd-3
1335 Echoed the walls echod; a light twinkled; &
                          then anon   Bd-3

1336 Came lights & ever lights/ /he blew it again   Bd-3
1336   and once again he blew   P MS
     ...lights. once more he winded it   Bd-3
1336 ...lights; and...blew;   (;; I)   A-2109
1336 (C)   B-II

1337   hollow tramplings up & down
     Whereon were rushings to & fro within   Bd-3

1338 ...hard, and...   (, I)   S-929
1338 (C)   B-II

1339 Till
     And high...   Bd-3

1340   y   I MS
     ...Lyonors...   S-929
1340 (C)   B-II

1343   hush, at last   P MS
     ...long pause/ at length   Bd-3
1343 ...hush/ - at last -   -/ (I&P)   A-2109
1343 (C)   B-II

1344 ...up,   ,/ (I)   A-2109
1344 (C)   B-II

Three times had blown--after long hush--at last--
The huge pavilion slowly yielded up,
Through those black foldings, that which housed
                              therein.   1345
High on a nightblack horse, in nightblack arms,
With white breast-bone, and barren ribs of Death,
And crowned with fleshless laughter--some ten steps--
In the half-light--through the dim dawn--advanced
The monster, and then paused, and spake no word.   1350

   But Gareth spake and all indignantly,

1345	...foldings, that...	,/ (I)	A-2109
1345	(C)		B-II
1346	night- in nightblack arms		
	...a huge black horse, his armour black		H-32
1347	...& naked ribs...		H-32
1348	...laughter/ - some ten steps/ -	(- - I)	A-2109
1348	(C)		B-II
Alt. before 1349	Before a gloomy (1 ?) of the East		H-32
Alt. before 1349	In the dim light in the half dawn		
	approachd		H-32
1349	...light in the dim dawn approachd		H-32
1349	...half-light/ - thro' ...dawn/ - advanced		
		(- - I)	A-2109
1349	(C)		B-II
1350	Gareth said		
	...paused. ~~á ŕáíđéń śćŕééńýá~~		H-32
1350	paused and		P MS
	...& then ~~śŧøød/~~ ~~þúŧ~~ spake no...		Bd-3
1350	...paused, and...	(, I)	A-2109
1350	(C)		B-II
1351	But Gareth cried indignant Treble shame		H-32
1351	~~Ťħéń ŧø ẃħøḿ Śíŕ Ǵáŕéŧħ~~	(P MS)	Bd-3

'Fool, for thou hast, men say, the strength of ten,
Canst thou not trust the limbs thy God hath given,
But must, to make the terror of thee more,
Trick thyself out in ghastly imageries   1355
Of that which Life hath done with, and the clod,
Less dull than thou, will hide with mantling flowers
As if for pity?' But he spake no word;
Which set the horror higher: a maiden swooned;

1352 for we hear thou hast the strength of ten	
Fool, art thou strong of limb	H-32
1352 Upon thee knight. men say thou hast the strength	H-32
1353 And canst not trust the might that God hath given	H-32
Sketch 1354 ff. out these eye-blasting	
O shame to trick thyself in ghastly types	
Of mortal desolation, which kind Earth	
Covers with flowers to make	
Thy terrors greater	
but he spake no word	H-32

1354 ...more,	,/(I)	A-2109
1354 (C)		B-II
1356 ...with, and the clod,	(,, I)	A-2109
1356 (C)		B-II
1357 less than will which even		
N̸o̸t̸ dull a̸s̸ thou a̸r̸t̸, mantles with her flowers		H-32
1357 ...thou, will...	(, I)	A-2109
1357 (C)		B-II
1358 As if she pitiyd		H-32
1358 ...pity'? But...word,;	;/ (P)	A-2109
1358 ...pity'? But...		B-II
1353 (C)		T-GP3

The Lady Lyonors wrung her hands and wept,   1360
As doomed to be the bride of Night and Death;
Sir Gareth's head prickled beneath his helm;
And even Sir Lancelot through his warm blood felt
Ice strike, and all that marked him were aghast.

At once Sir Lancelot's charger fiercely neighed, 1365
And Death's dark war-horse bounded forward with him.
Then those that did not blink the terror, saw

1359 Which m̷a̷d̷e̷ set...   Bd-3

1360   y   I MS
     ...L̷yonors   S-929
1360 (C)   B-II

1361 ...Death;   ; (I)   A-2109
1361 (C)   B-II

1362 Sir Gareth's head
     Perceived his hair prickle beneath the casque H-32
1362 ...helm;   ;/ (P)   A-2109
1362 (C)   B-II

1363   even   thro   warm
    And Lancelot felt his blood was touch of ice H-32

1364 ...that watch'd him were amazed.   H-32
1364   that mark'd him were
    ...& all t̷h̷e̷ g̷a̷z̷e̷r̷s̷ w̷e̷r̷e̷ aghast.   Bd-3

1365 ...neigh'd -   A-2109
1365 (C)   73

1366 Whereon
    At last the black horse...   H-32
1366 At once   P MS
    Whereat the black horse...   Bd-3
1366 At once the black horse...   A-2109
1366 (C)   73

That Death was cast to ground, and slowly rose,
But with one stroke Sir Gareth split the skull.
Half fel'l to right and half to left and lay.   1370
Then with a stronger buffet he clove the helm
As throughly as the skull; and out from this
Issued the bright face of a blooming boy
Fresh as a flower new-born, and crying, 'Knight,
Slay me not: my three brethren bad me do it,   1375
To make a horror all about the house,

1367-1368 And Gareth dash'd against him & he fell.   H-32

1367   the   P MS
     ...blink f̷o̷r̷ terror...   Bd-3

1368 That   P MS
     A̷n̷d̷ Death...   Bd-3

1369 Then with...Gareth clove the skull   H-32
1369 Then with...   Bd-3
1369 But   I MS
     T̷h̷e̷n̷ with...   S-929
1369 (C)   B-II

1371   by with
     And Then with another clove...   H-32

1372 ...& out of this   H-32

1373 Issued the blonde head of a beauteous boy   H-32

1374 Bright as...born. I yield Sir Knight   H-32
1374 ..., & crying I yield   Bd-3
1374   Knight   I MS
     ...crying, 'I̷ y̷i̷e̷l̷d̷   A-2109
1374 (C)   B-II

1375 my brethren made me...   H-32

1376 ...house,   ,/ (P)   A-2109
1376 (C)   B-II

And stay the world from Lady Lyonors.
They never dreamed the passes would be past.'
Answered Sir Gareth graciously to one
Not many a moon his younger, 'My fair child,   1380
What madness made thee challenge the chief knight
Of Arthur's hall?' 'Fair Sir, they bad me do it.
They hate the King, and Lancelot, the King's friend,
They hoped to slay him somewhere on the stream,

1377   stay
       And ~~hold~~ the world...   Bd-3
1377   ...Lionors.   S-929
1377   (C)   B-II

1378   ...the passings cd...   H-32

1379   answerd   P MS
       ~~Then spake~~ Sir...   Bd-3

Alt. for 1380 ff
       Fair child said Gareth thou shall hence with me
       Half-liar as myself have been, to court
       There shalt thou learn the King & not to lie   H-32

Alt. for 1383 ff.
          dearly
       They hate Sir Lancelot, the king's friend,
                    ~~who still~~
       ~~Hath striven to break/that old knight-errantry~~
       ~~Of others like/wd doth but what/it will~~   Bd-3

1383   the King & Lancelot   I MS
       They ~~dearly~~ hate ~~Sir Lancelot~~, the King's
                          friend,   S-929
1383   dearly hate Sir   MS
       They ~~hate the King/ and~~ Lancelot...   T-GP2
1383   (C)   72

1384   slay   P MS
       They hoped to ~~have slain~~ him...   Bd-3
1384   ...stream,   ,/ (P)   A-2109
1384   (C)   B-II

They never dreamed the passes could be past.'   1385

    Then sprang the happier day from underground;
And Lady Lyonors and her house, with dance
And revel and song, made merry over Death,
As being after all their foolish fears
And horrors only proven a blooming boy.   1390
So large mirth lived and Gareth won the quest.

    And he that told the tale in older times
Says that Sir Gareth wedded Lyonors,
But he, that told it later, says Lynette.

| 1385 | ...past.' | (' I) | S-929 |
| 1385 | (C) | | B-II |

| 1386 | ...underground; | ;/ (I) | A-2109 |
| 1386 | (C) | | B-II |

Sketch 1387-1388
    T̸h̸é̸n̸   f̸ṵ̸l̸l̸
    A̸n̸d̸ ̸a̸l̸l̸ ̸t̸h̸é̸ ̸h̸ø̸ṵ̸s̸é̸/m̸a̸d̸é̸ m̸é̸r̸r̸y̸ ø̸v̸é̸r̸ d̸é̸a̸t̸h̸   Bd-3

| 1387 | ...Lionors...house, with... | (, I) | S-929 |
| 1387 | (C) | | B-II |

| 1388 | ...song, made...Death, | (,, I) | A-2109 |
| 1388 | (C) | | B-II |

1390   horrors
    And a̸g̸ø̸n̸i̸é̸s̸ only...   Bd-3

1391 So   lived
    A̸n̸d̸ large mirth r̸é̸i̸g̸n̸d̸ & Gareth   Bd-3

1393	y		I MS
	...Li̸onors,		S-929
1393	(C)		B-II

1394   Lynette   I MS
    But he, that ...later, says L̸i̸n̸é̸t̸h̸ (, , I) A-2109
1394 (C)   B-II

The Marriage of Geraint

The brave Geraint, a knight of Arthur's court,
A tributary prince of Devon, one
Of that great Order of the Table Round,
Had married Enid, Yniol's only child,
And loved her, as he loved the light of Heaven.   5
And as the light of Heaven varies, now
At sunrise, now at sunset, now by night
With moon and trembling stars, so loved Geraint
To make her beauty vary day by day,
In crimsons and in purples and in gems.   10

---

1 The good Geraint...   H-35

3 ...great order of...   F-ENI
3 (C)   73

4 Had wedded Enid...   H-35;Tn-30;T-E
4 Had wedded Enid...   BM-I
4 (C)   62

7 ...night,   F-ENI
7 ...night⁄   BM-I
7 (C)   L-EN2

8 With moon & shaking stars...   H-35
8 ...Geraint,   F-ENI
8 ...Geraint⁄   BM-I
8 (C)   L-EN2

THE MARRIAGE OF GERAINT

And Enid, but to please her husband's eye,
Who first had found and loved her in a state
Of broken fortunes, daily fronted him
In some fresh splendour; and the Queen herself,
Grateful to Prince Geraint for service done,   15
Loved her, and often with her own white hands
Arrayed and decked her, as the loveliest,
Next after her own self, in all the court.
And Enid loved the Queen, and with true heart
Adored her, as the stateliest and the best   20
And loveliest of all women upon earth.
And seeing them so tender and so close,
Long in their common love rejoiced Geraint.

11 And Enid but...		F-ENI
11 And Enid, but...	,/ (I)	L-EN2
11 (C)		L-EN3
13 ...fortunes, met him every day		H-35
14 ...splendour, and...		F-ENI
14 ...splendour,; and...	;/ (I)	L-EN3
14 (C)		F-EN2
16 Loved her & often with her royal hand		H-35
17 Array'd her, & deckt her, ...		H-35
18 Next after own self, of all the court		H-35
18 ...after own...		Tn-30
19 And Enid loved the Queen & in her heart		H-35
20 Almost adored her as the statliest		H-35
21 And loveliest of all creatures upon earth.		H-35
23 And in their...		H-35
28 ...it, and...		F-ENI
28 ...it,; and...	;/ (I)	L-EN3
28 (C)		F-EN2

But when a rumour rose about the Queen,
Touching her guilty love for Lancelot,   25
Though yet there lived no proof, nor yet was heard
The world's loud whisper breaking into storm,
Not less Geraint believed it; and there fell
A horror on him, lest his gentle wife,
Through that great tenderness for Guinevere,   30
Had suffered, or should suffer any taint
In nature: wherefore going to the King,
He made this pretext, that his princedom lay
Close on the borders of a territory,
Wherein were bandit earls, and caitiff knights,   35
Assassins, and all flyers from the hand
Of Justice, and whatever loathes a law:
And therefore, till the King himself should please
To cleanse this common sewer of all his realm,

---

29 A horror fell upon him lest his wife   H-35

30 Considering her strong love for Guinevere,   H-35

31   or had suffered
      Sd suffer taint in nature; o̷r̷ i̷n̷ n̷a̷m̷e̷   H-35

32 ...the king,   F-ENI
32 (C)   73

33 And made this...   H-35

34 Close on the borders of a land wherein   H-35

35 Were bandit earls, & flyers from the law   H-35

36 Of justice, traitors, wrongers of this world
   and
   There to defend his   H-35

38 ...the king himself...   F-ENI
38 (C)   73

39 ...common shore of...   Tn-30;T-F
39 ...common shore of...   F-ENI
39 (C)   L-EN2

281

He craved a fair permission to depart,   40
And there defend his marches; and the King
Mused for a little on his plea, but, last,
Allowing it, the Prince and Enid rode,
And fifty knights rode with them, to the shores
Of Severn, and they past to their own land;   45
Where, thinking, that if ever yet was wife
True to her lord, mine shall be so to me,
He compassed her with sweet observances
And worship, never leaving her, and grew
Forgetful of his promise to the King,   50
Forgetful of the falcon and the hunt,

---

40 He craved the kings permission to return   H-35
40 ...permission to return,   Tn-30

41 & the blameless king   H-35
41 ...the king   F-ENI
41 (C)   73

42-43 Allow'd his plea & he & Enid went   H-35

42 ...but then   Tn-30

43 ...the prince and...   F-ENI
43 (C)   59

44 And fifty knights went with him to the ford   H-35
44 ...to the ford   Tn-30;T-E
44 ...them, to the ford   F-ENI
44 (C)   L-EN2

46 Where thinking...   F-ENI
46 Where, thinking...   ,/ (I)   L-EN2
46 (C)   L-EN3

48-49 He compast her with worship & with love
      Nor ever parted from her & so grew   Tn-30

48 He compast her...   F-ENI
48   compass'd   I MS
   He compast her...   L-EN3
48 (C)   F-EN2

Forgetful of the tilt and tournament,
Forgetful of his glory and his name,
Forgetful of his princedom and its cares.
And this forgetfulness was hateful to her.   55
And by and by the people, when they met
In twos and threes, or fuller companies,
Began to scoff and jeer and babble of him
As of a prince whose manhood was all gone,
And molten down in mere uxoriousness.   60
And this she gathered from the people's eyes:
This too the women who attired her head,
To please her, dwelling on his boundless love,
Told Enid, and they saddened her the more:
And day by day she thought to tell Geraint,   65
But could not out of bashful delicacy;
While he that watched her sadden, was the more

---

50 ...the king,   F-ENI
50 (C)   73

55 ...her: F-ENI
55 ...her/ ☉   (I)   L-ENI
55 (C)   BM-1

Alt. after 55 And yet she did not speak for delicacy. H-35

56-57 At last the people when his name was named   H-35

57 ...threes & fuller...   Tn-30

62 Wh things the women that attired her head   H-35

64 Told Enid & they sadden'd her the more
      These things she heard & they were hateful to her
                              day by day   H-35

65 And evermore she thought to tell Geraint   H-35

66 But did not out of...   H-35

67   den
   ...that saw her sad was áll the more   Tn-30

THE MARRIAGE OF GERAINT

Suspicious that her nature had a taint.

```
     At last, it chanced that on a summer morn
(They sleeping each by either) the new sun          70
Beat through the blindless casement of the room,
And heated the strong warrior in his dreams;
Who, moving, cast the coverlet aside,
And bared the knotted column of his throat,
The massive square of his heroic breast,           75
And arms on which the standing muscle sloped,
As slopes a wild brook o'er a little stone,
Running too vehemently to break upon it.
And Enid woke and sat beside the couch,
Admiring him, and thought within herself,           80
```

```
68  suspicious, that...                              F-ENI
68  suspicious/ that...                              F-EN2
68  (C)                                                  59

69  ...on a summer morn in may                       H-35
69          summer
    ...on a   morn i̸n̸ M̸a̸y̸                         Tn-30

70  ...by other ] the...                          H-35;T-E
70  ...by other ] the...                             F-ENI
70  (C)                                                  69

71  ...blindless casements of...                    Tn-30
71  ...blindless casements of...                     F-ENI
71  ...blindless casement̸s̸ of...        (I)          L-EN3
71  (C)                                              F-EN2

74  ...the column of his knotted throat,        Tn-30;T-E
74              knotted
    And bared the column of his K̸n̸o̸t̸t̸e̸d̸ throat,    L-ENI
74  (C)                                               BM-1

75  The manful square of his...                      H-35
75              2             1
    The massive square of his heroic breast,          T-E
75              2             1                       I MS
    The massive heroic  of his square breast,         L-ENI
75  (C)                                               BM-1
```

284

Was ever man so grandly made as he?
Then, like a shadow, past the people's talk
And accusation of uxoriousness
Across her mind, and bowing over him,
Low to her own heart piteously she said: 85

'O noble breast and all-puissant arms,
Am I the cause, I the poor cause that men
Reproach you, saying all your force is gone?
I am the cause, because I dare not speak
And tell him what I think and what they say.   90

---

76 On either arm the muscle standing sloped   H-35
76 ...sloped   F-ENI
76 ...sloped,   ,/ (I)   L-EN3
76 (C)   F-EN2

77   a brook   little
    As slopes above a   stone x̷ b̷r̷o̷o̷k̷   H-35

78 Running
   T̷h̷a̷t̷ r̷u̷n̷s̷ too violently to...   H-35

79 And Enid woke admiring him & thought   H-35

81 ...so nobly made...   H-35

84 ...her heart & bowing...   H-35

85 ...heart, piteously...said: ⫻   (I)   L-ENI
85 ...heart⫻ piteously...   BM-1
85 (C)   L-EN2

86 ...and all puissant arms,   (, I)   L-ENI
86 ...all-puissant...   -/ (I)   BM-1
86 (C)   L-EN2

88 M̷a̷k̷e̷ s̷h̷a̷m̷e̷f̷u̷l̷ c̷o̷m̷m̷e̷n̷t̷ o̷n̷ t̷h̷e̷ f̷i̷r̷s̷t̷ o̷f̷ m̷e̷n̷   H-35

89 I am the...   ("am" underlined I)   L-ENI
89 ...cause because...   BM-1
89 (C)   73

And yet I hate that he should linger here;
I cannot love my lord and not his name.
Far liefer had I gird his harness on him,
And ride with him to battle and stand by,
And watch. his mightful hand striking great blows   95
At caitiffs and at wrongers of the world.
Far better were I laid in the dark earth,
Not hearing any more his noble voice,
Not to be folded more in these dear arms,
And darkened from the high light in his eyes,   100
Than that my lord through me should suffer shame.
Am I so bold, and could I so stand by,
And see my dear lord wounded in the strife,
Or maybe pierced to death before mine eyes,
And yet not dare to tell him what I think,   105
And how men slur him, saying all his force

-----

91 ...I w̸i̸s̸h̸ hate...   Tn-30
91 ...here̸ ;   (I)   L-ENI
91 (C)   BM-1

Sketch 93 ff   Far rather wd I ride with him to fight
               And help him to horse & stand beside him
               I am the cause because I dare not speak
               And tell him what I think & what they say
               and I wish not he sd linger here
               I̸ c̸a̸n̸n̸o̸t̸ l̸o̸v̸e̸ m̸y̸ l̸o̸r̸d̸/&̸/n̸o̸t̸ h̸i̸s̸ n̸a̸m̸e̸   H-35

93 Far lever had...   Tn-30;T-E
93 Far liever had...   F-ENI
93 (C)   73

94 Ride out with him to battle...   Tn-30

95   hand
   ...mightful a̸r̸m̸s̸/ striking...   Tn-30

99   these
   Not to be folded more in his dear arms,   H-35

100 And darken'd from the sweet light of his eyes   H-35
100   high   in
    ...from the s̸w̸e̸e̸t̸ light o̸f̸ his eyes,   Tn-30

286

THE MARRIAGE OF GERAINT

Is melted into mere effeminacy?
O me, I fear that I am no true wife.'

    Half inwardly, half audibly she spoke,
And the strong passion in her made her weep   110
True tears upon his broad and naked breast,
And these awoke him, and by great mischance
He heard but fragments of her later words,
And that she feared she was not a true wife.
And then he thought, 'In spite of all my care,   115
For all my pains, poor man, for all my pains,
She is not faithful to me, and I see her
Weeping for some gay knight in Arthur's hall.'
Then though he loved and reverenced her too much
To dream she could be guilty of foul act,   120
Right through his manful breast darted the pang
That makes a man, in the sweet face of her

---

102 Am I so bold could I stand by & watch   H-35

103 My dear lord wounded in the strife of arms   H-35

106-107 And what men say of him that all his force
        Is melted into mere uxoriousness
        And all lapsed in effeminacy.   H-35

108 ...I am not a true wife   H-35

110 W̸h̸i̸l̸e̸ the strong...   Tn-30

117 ...her w̸e̸e̸p̸/   Tn-30

118 Weeping
    /1̸/2̸/ h̸i̸m̸/ for...   Tn-30

119 And tho'...   Tn-30;T-E
119 Then   I MS
    A̸n̸d̸ tho' ...   L-ENI
119 (C)   BM-1

120 Right
    Y̸e̸t̸ thro'...   Tn-30

121 Then thro' his manful heart shot the keen pang H-35

287

Whom he loves most, lonely and miserable.
At this he hurled his huge limbs out of bed,
And shook his drowsy squire awake and cried,   125
'My charger and her palfrey;' then to her,
'I will ride forth into the wilderness;

------

123 ...loves best lonely...   H-35

124-125   ~~& had him bring~~
       ~~Then rising up he call'd his squire & said~~ Tn-30

124 ~~At th~~
    Whereon he suddenly snatch'd himself from
                          bed   Tn-30
124 At this he snatch'd his great limbs from
                      the bed   Tn-30;T-E
124 At this he snatch'd his great limbs from
                      the bed,   (, I)   L-ENI
124 At this he snatch'd his great limbs from
                      the bed,   BM-1
124 (C)   59

126 ...palfrey" & to her.   Tn-30
126 ...palfrey,' then to her: F-ENI
126 ...palfrey,' then...   59
126 (C)   73

127 ...wilderness,;   ;/ (I)   L-ENI
127 (C)   BM-1

Alt. after 127 ~~And will do battle with the bandit~~
               ~~earls~~   Tn-30

Alt. after 129 ~~And you shall see it; you shall ride~~
              ~~with me~~
     ~~And we will both begin our lives~~
           ~~afresh.~~   Tn-30

130 And you put on your worst...   Tn-30;T-E
130 And you put on your worst...   F-EN1
130 And you, put on your worst...   L-EN2
130 (C)   73

For though it seems my spurs are yet to win,
I have not fallen so low as some would wish.
And thou, put on thy worst and meanest dress   130
And ride with me.' And Enid asked, amazed,
'If Enid errs, let Enid learn her fault.'
But he, 'I charge thee, ask not, but obey.'
Then she bethought her of a faded silk,
A faded mantle and a faded veil,   135
And moving toward a cedarn cabinet,

131-133 (1 ?)   with me
         (1 ?) ride ~~along~~ and Enid wonder'd at
                       him   Tn-30
131-133 And ride with me.' And Enid wonder'd
                       at him,   Tn-30;T-E
131-133 And ride with me.' And Enid wonder'd
                       at him~~/~~; (I)   L-ENI
131-133 And ride with me.' And Enid wonder'd
                       at him: BM-1
131-133 And ride with me.' And Enid ~~wonder'd at~~
                       ~~him~~:
                       ask~~e~~d amazed.   I MS
        'If Enid errs let Enid learn her fault'   I MS
        But he 'I charge you, ask not but obey'   I MS
                                                         L-EN2
131 ...Enid ask'd, amazed,   ,/,/ (I)
132 ...errs, let...   ,/ (I)
133 (Same)   L-EN3
131-132 (C)   F-EN2
133 ...charge you, ask not but...   F-EN2
133 (C)   73

134 But then bethought...   Tn-30;T-E
134 But then bethought...   F-ENI
134 And then bethought...   BM-1
134 Then she   I MS
     ~~But then~~ bethought...   L-EN2
134 (C)   L-EN3

135 ...faded vestment & ...   Tn-30
135   mantle
     ...faded ~~vestment~~ &...   T-E

THE MARRIAGE OF GERAINT

Wherein she kept them folded reverently
With sprigs of summer laid between the folds,
She took them, and arrayed herself therein,
Remembering when first he came on her   140
Drest in that dress, and how he loved her in it,
And all her foolish fears about the dress,
And all his journey to her, as himself
Had told her, and their coming to the court.

    For Arthur on the Whitsuntide before   145
Held court at old Caerleon upon Usk.
There on a day, he sitting high in hall,
Before him came a forester of Dean,
Wet from the woods, with notice of a hart

---

137   them
    ...kept it folded...   Tn-30

139   them
    ...took i̶t̶ & ...   Tn-30

143 ...her, as...   ,/ (I)   L-ENI
143 (C)   BM-1

144 ...her, and...   ,/ (I)   L-ENI
144 (C)   BM-1

Sketch 145-159
    This is the story of the faded silk
    The year before a forester of Dean
    Wet from the forest, when the blameless king
    Kept court at fair Kaerlon upon Usk,
    Came in with notice of a snowy hart
    Far lordlier than a̶l̶l̶ his fellows of the wood.
                  to let blow
    Then the great king gave order that the horns
    The horns for hunting on the morrow morn.
    And Guinevere
    Lost in sweet dreams forgetful of the hunt   H-35

Alt. before 145 This was the story of the faded silk H-35

145 King Arthur...   H-35

290

Taller than all his fellows, milky-white,   150
First seen that day: these things he told the King.
Then the good King gave order to let blow
His horns for hunting on the morrow morn.
And when the Queen petitioned for his leave
To see the hunt, allowed it easily.   155
So with the morning all the court were gone.
But Guinevere lay late into the morn,
Lost in sweet dreams, and dreaming of her love
For Lancelot, and forgetful of the hunt;

146 ...court at fair Carlon upon...   H-35
146 ...Usk/ ☉   (I)   L-ENI
146 (C)   BM-1

147 Where
    A/n/d/ on...   Tn-30

148 And in there came a forester...   H-35

149 ...the wood & telling of a hart   H-35

151 ...the king:☉   (I)   L-ENI
151 ...the king.   BM-1
151 (C)   73

152 ...the great King gave...   H-35
152 So
    T/h/e/n/ the good...   Tn-30
152 ...good king gave...   F-ENI
152 (C)   73

153 The horns to hunting...   H-35
153 The horns...   Tn-30

154 And when   petition'd for his
    T/h/e/n/ s/a/i/d/ the Queen, M/y/ l/o/r/d/ I/ p/r/a/y/ y/o/u/r/
                        leave   Tn-30

155   allow'd it w/i/t/h/ a/l/l/ e/a/s/e/ easily
    To see thi/s/ hunt/i/n/g/ & gave it (I ?) easily Tn-30
155 ...hunt, allow'd...   (, I)   L-ENI
155 (C)   BM-1

291

But rose at last, a single maiden with her,   160
Took horse, and forded Usk, and gained the wood;
There, on a little knoll beside it, stayed
Waiting to hear the hounds; but heard instead
A sudden sound of hoofs, for Prince Geraint,
Late also, wearing neither hunting-dress   165
Nor weapon, save a golden-hilted brand,
Came quickly flashing through the shallow ford
Behind them, and so galloped up the knoll.
A purple scarf, at either end whereof
There swung an apple of the purest gold,   170

---

160 But rose at last
   ~~And~~ ~~rising~~ ~~late~~, a single...   Tn-30

161 ...Usk and...   F-ENI
161 ...Usk, and...   ,/ (I)   L-EN3
161 (C)   F-EN2

Alt. 162-163
   ~~And/Listen'd~~ ~~for~~ ~~the~~ ~~baying~~ ~~of~~ ~~the~~ ~~hounds~~
   ~~Then~~ ~~stood~~ ~~&~~ ~~waited/~~ ~~&~~ ~~behind~~ ~~her~~ ~~rose~~   Tn-30

162 There on...it stay'd   F-ENI
162 There, on...it, stay'd   ,/,/ (I)   L-EN2
162 (C)   L-EN3

163 ...hounds,; but...   ;/   L-ENI
163 (C)   BM-1

164 ...Geraint,   ,/ (I)   L-ENI
164 (C)   BM-1

165 ...hunting - dress   -/ (I)   L-ENI
165 (C)   BM-1

166 ...hilted ~~sword~~ brand   Tn-30

Swayed round about him as he galloped up
To join them, glancing like a dragon-fly
In summer suit and silks of holiday.
Low bowed the tributary Prince, and she,
Sweetly and statelily, and with all grace   175
Of womanhood and queenhood, answered him.
'Late, late, Sir Prince,' she said, 'later than we!'
'Yea, noble Queen,' he answered, 'and so late
That I but come like you to see the hunt,

---

168 ...them ~~twain~~ & so...   Tn-30

171   up
       ...gallop'd ~~to~~ ~~the~~ ~~Queen~~   Tn-30

174 ...she   F-ENI
174 ...she,   ,/ (I)   L-EN3
174 (C)   F-EN2

175 ...statelily and...   F-ENI
175 ...statelily, and...   ,/ (I)   L-EN3
175 (C)   F-EN2

176 ...queenhood answer'd him: /   L-ENI
176 ...queenhood answer'd...   BM-1
176 ...queenhood, answer'd...   ,/ (I)   L-EN3
176 (C)   F-EN2

177 Late I ate
       Sir Prince ~~you~~ ~~are~~ late' she...   Tn-30
177 You are late, Sir Prince, she said, as well
                             as we.   Tn-30

178 Yes noble...   Tn-30

179 I have but come to see not join the hunt   Tn-30

Not join it.' 'Therefore wait with me,' she said;   180
'For on this little knoll, if anywhere,
There is good chance that we shall hear the hounds;
Here often they break covert at our feet.'

   And while they listened for the distant hunt,
And chiefly for the baying of Cavall,   185
King Arthur's hound of deepest mouth, there rode
Full slowly by a knight, lady, and dwarf;
Whereof the dwarf lagged latest, and the knight
Had vizor up, and showed a youthful face,
Imperious, and of haughtiest lineaments.   190
And Guinevere, not mindful of his face

---

180   me
    ...with ~us~' she...   Tn-30

180-183 'Then wait with me here on this ~knoll~ little
                        knoll she said
        Replied the Queen for here if anywhere there
                          is good chance   Tn-30

181 For
   ~here~, on...   Tn-30

183 Here sometimes they...   Tn-30

184 (No printed par. indent.; but indent. symbol.) L-ENI
184 (C)   BM-1

189 ...vizor ~lifted~ up...   Tn-30

190 ...of haughty lineaments   H-35

191 ...of the face   H-35

192 In the king's hall desired
   ~And she desired to learn~ his name...   H-35
192 ...the king's hall,...   F-ENI
192 (C)   73

193 ...of the ~knight~ dwarf   H-35
193 ...demand of...   Tn-30

THE MARRIAGE OF GERAINT

In the King's hall, desired his name, and sent
Her maiden to demand it of the dwarf;
Who being vicious, old and irritable,
And doubling all his master's vice of pride,   195
Made answer sharply that she should not know.
'Then will I ask it of himself,' she said.
'Nay, by my faith, thou shalt not,' cried the dwarf;
'Thou art not worthy even to speak of him;'
And when she put her horse toward the knight,   200
Struck at her with his whip, and she returned
Indignant to the Queen; whereat Geraint
Exclaiming, 'Surely I will learn the name,'

---

194 ...being old vicious & ...   H-35

195 With twice his...   H-35

196 Gave churlish answer that...   H-35

Alt. after 196 Who was not worthy evn to speak
                                  of him.   H-35

197 ...himself said she   Tn-30
197 ...himself s̸a̸i̸d̸ she said   T-E

198 ...not answer'd he   H-35
198 ...not said the dwarf   Tn-30
198   cried
    ...not s̸a̸i̸d̸ the dwarf   T-E

199 ...speak to him,   Tn-30;T-E
199 ...speak to him.'   F-ENI
199 (C)   L-EN2

200 ...she moved her palfrey to the knight   H-35

202 ...Queen; at which Geraint   H-35;Tn-30;T-E
202 ...Queen; at which Geraint   F-ENI
202 (C)   69

203 ...learn his name   H-35

Made sharply to the dwarf, and asked it of him,
Who answered as before; and when the Prince   205
Had put his horse in motion toward the knight,
Struck at him with his whip, and cut his cheek.
The Prince's blood spirted upon the scarf,
Dyeing it; and his quick, instinctive hand
Caught at the hilt, as to abolish him: 210

---

204 Made for the dwarf & put the question to him   H-35
204   it of him
    ...dwarf & asked t̸h̸e̸ n̸a̸m̸e̸   Tn-30

205 ...before he sd not know.   H-35

206 And when he moved his charger to the knight   H-35

207 ...cut his face   H-35

208   red   spirted upon
    And the blood f̸l̸o̸w̸e̸d̸ ̸&̸ ̸d̸y̸e̸d̸ the scarf h̸e̸ w̸o̸r̸e̸   H-35
208   T Prince's
    T̸i̸l̸l̸ the r̸e̸d̸ blood...   Tn-30
208   T
    T̸i̸l̸l̸ the Prince's...   T-E

209   warrior   his hand
    At this the prince laid hold unthinking   H-35

210 On the sword hilt as if to...   H-35
210 ...him. :   :/ (P)   L-ENI
210 (C)   BM-1

211 But out of his...   H-35
211   he, from
    But ø̸u̸t̸ ø̸f̸ his...   Tn-30

212 ...nobility of temper, check'd   H-35

213-214 His wrath refraining even from a word.
                      at such an insect & returnd
        To Guinevere & with all calmness said   H-35

But he, from his exceeding manfulness
And pure nobility of temperament,
Wroth to be wroth at such a worm, refrained
From even a word, and so returning said:

    'I will avenge this insult, noble Queen,   215
Done in your maiden's person to yourself:
And I will track this vermin to their earths:
For though I ride unarmed, I do not doubt
To find, at some place I shall come at, arms
On loan, or else for pledge; and, being found,   220
Then will I fight him, and will break his pride,

---

213 Wroth to be wroth at such a worm, refrain'd
    H̶e̶ ̶c̶h̶e̶c̶k̶t̶ ̶h̶i̶m̶s̶e̶l̶f̶,̶ ̶r̶e̶t̶a̶i̶n̶i̶n̶g̶ ̶f̶r̶o̶m̶ ̶o̶n̶e̶ ̶w̶o̶r̶d̶   Tn-30
213   at
   ...wroth w̶i̶t̶h̶ such...   T-E

214 From evn a word & so   ing
    T̶o̶ ̶s̶u̶c̶h̶ ̶a̶n̶ ̶i̶n̶s̶e̶c̶t̶ & return'd &̶ said   Tn-30

215 ...insult to the Queen   H-35

216 Done to her in the person of her man.   H-35
216   your maiden's   to yourself
    Done t̶o̶ y̶o̶u̶ in t̶h̶e̶ person o̶f̶ y̶o̶u̶r̶ m̶a̶i̶d̶   Tn-30
216 ...yourself;:   :/ (P)   L-ENI
216 (C)   BM-1

217 ...earths. :   :/ (P)   L-ENI
217 (C)   BM-1

Alt. after 217 T̶h̶e̶n̶ ̶w̶i̶l̶l̶ ̶I̶ ̶f̶i̶g̶h̶t̶ ̶h̶i̶m̶ ̶&̶ ̶w̶i̶l̶l̶ ̶b̶r̶e̶a̶k̶
                        h̶i̶s̶ ̶p̶r̶i̶d̶e̶   Tn-30

218 And tho...   H-35

219 ...find in some...   H-35

220 ...pledge & so farewell.   H-35

221 ...fight with him & break...   H-35

And on the third day will again be here,
So that I be not fallen in fight. Farewell.'

   'Farewell, fair Prince,' answered the stately Queen.
'Be prosperous in this journey, as in all;   225
And may you light on all things that you love,
And live to wed with her whom first you love:
But ere you wed with any, bring your bride,
And I, were she the daughter of a king,
Yea, though she were a beggar from the hedge,   230
Will clothe her for her bridals like the sun.'

   And Prince Geraint, now thinking that he heard
The noble hart at bay, now the far horn,

---

222 And the third day I will return   H-35
222 ...day, will...here~~/~~,   (2nd, I)   L-ENI
222 ...day, will...   BM-1
222 (C)   73

224 Farewell Sir Prince...   Tn-30
224   fair
   'Farewell ~~Sir~~ Prince'...   T-E
224 (No par. indent. printed; MS indent. symbol)   L-ENI
224 (C)   BM-1

227 ...you love ~~look~~ ~~at~~   Tn-30

228 ...bring ~~her~~ ~~here~~ ~~&~~ ~~I~~ your...   Tn-30

Sketch for 232 ff.
     And all the summer morning Prince Geraint
     Behind the three that rose & dipt & rose
     By hill & hollow, follow'd, vext at heart.
     Losing the hunt; but when the oak became
     Thrice shorter than its shadow   H-35

235 A little at the vile occasion
    ~~Altho he had but come to watch it~~, rode   Tn-30

298

THE MARRIAGE OF GERAINT

```
A little vext at losing of the hunt,
A little at the vile occasion, rode,                    235
By ups and downs, through many a grassy glade
And valley, with fixt eye following the three.
At last they issued from the world of wood,
And climbed upon a fair and even ridge,
And showed themselves against the sky, and sank.    240
And thither came Geraint, and underneath
Beheld the long street of a little town
In a long valley, on one side whereof,
White from the mason's hand, a fortress rose;
And on one side a castle in decay,                      245
Beyond a bridge that spanned a dry ravine:
And out of town and valley came a noise
As of a broad brook o'er a shingly bed
Brawling, or like a clamour of the rooks
At distance, ere they settle for the night.             250
```

```
239 And rose upon a long & even ridge            H-35
239     climb'd
        And r̸o̸s̸e̸ upon...                        Tn-30

241 And after them Geraint r̸o̸s̸e̸ & b̸e̸h̸e̸l̸d̸     H-35
241              c̸l̸i̸m̸b̸d̸ came
        And t̸h̸e̸ then r̸o̸s̸e̸ Geraint...           Tn-30

243-249 In a long valley, out of wh arose
        A clamour like the crying of the rooks   H-35

243 ...side of which                         Tn-30;T-E
243 ...side of which,                            F-ENI
243 (C)                                            69

246 ...ravine.                                   F-ENI
246 (C)                                          L-EN2

250 At distance ere...                           F-ENI
250 (C)                                          L-EN2
```

299

THE MARRIAGE OF GERAINT

And onward to the fortress rode the three,
And entered, and were lost behind the walls.
'So,' thought Geraint, 'I have tracked him to his
earth.'

---

251 And downward
    ~~Then~~ to the fortress...   H-35

Alt. after 251 There ~~And~~ after trumpet blown &
                        let down
                        ~~drawbridge falln~~   H-35
Alt. after 251 Where after trumpet blown &
                        bridge let down   Tn-30
Alt. after 251 (Cancelled)   T-E

252 They enter'd & were...   H-35
252 They enter'd & were...   Tn-30
252 And
    ~~They~~ enter'd...   T-E

253 Then thought...   H-35
253 ...earth;'   (; I)   BM-1
253 (C)   L-EN2

Sketch 254-256 And
             ~~Then~~ down the long street rode; he
                        wearily
             Beheld each
             Saw every hostel full, & heard the clink
             Of horses being shoed, & the hot
                        hiss   H-35

256 Clink of hammer'd   I MS
    ~~Was hammer laid to~~ hoof, and...   BM-1
256 (C)   L-EN2

257 ...of the squire who...   H-35;Tn-30;T-E
257 ...of the squire who...   F-ENI
257   youth   I MS
    ...of the ~~squire~~ who...   L-EN3
257 (C)   F-EN2

300

And down the long street riding wearily,
Found every hostel full, and everywhere   255
Was hammer laid to hoof, and the hot hiss
And bustling whistle of the youth who scoured
His master's armour; and of such a one
He asked,'What means the tumult in the town?'
Who told him, scouring still, 'The sparrow-hawk!'   260
Then riding close behind an ancient churl,
Who, smitten by the dusty sloping beam,
Went sweating underneath a sack of corn,

---

258   arms   asking one of the   I MS
     His master's a̶r̶m̶o̶u̶r̶; and o̶f̶ s̶u̶c̶h̶ a̶ o̶n̶e̶   BM-1
258 (C)   L-EN2

259 He ask'd what meant the hubub of the town   H-35
259 'What means the noise & hurly burly here?'   I MS
     H̶e̶ a̶s̶k̶'̶d̶ w̶h̶a̶t̶ m̶e̶a̶n̶s̶/̶t̶h̶e̶ t̶u̶m̶u̶l̶t̶ i̶n̶ t̶h̶e̶ t̶o̶w̶n̶?̶   BM-1
259 (C)   L-EN2

260 Who said You ask that know 'The Sparrow Hawk!,   H-35
260 Who said 'The sparrow-hawk: you ask that
                              know'   Tn-30;T-E
260 Who said, 'The sparrow-hawk, you ask that
                              know.'   F-ENI
260 Was answer'd O fair lord, the sparrow-hawk'   I MS
     W̶h̶o̶ s̶a̶i̶d̶ '̶T̶h̶e̶ s̶p̶a̶r̶r̶o̶w̶-̶h̶a̶w̶k̶/̶ y̶o̶u̶ a̶s̶k̶ t̶h̶a̶t̶
                              k̶n̶o̶w̶l̶y̶   BM-1
260   told him 'O fair Lord,   I MS
     Who s̶a̶i̶d̶, 'The sparrow-hawk;' ! y̶o̶u̶ a̶s̶k̶ t̶h̶a̶t̶
                              k̶n̶o̶w̶l̶y̶   (! I)   L-EN2
260   scouring still 'The   I MS
     Who told him, 'O̶ f̶a̶i̶r̶ L̶o̶r̶d̶,/̶t̶h̶e̶ sparrow-
                              hawk!'   L-EN3
260 ...still 'The...   F-EN2
260 (C)   73

261 Then rode g behind an ancient churl w̶h̶o̶ w̶a̶l̶k̶'̶d̶
                                                           H-35

263 Who
    And sweated underneath a sack of wheat   H-35

Asked yet once more what meant the hubbub here?
Who answered gruffly, 'Ugh! the sparrow-hawk.'   265
Then riding further past an armourer's,
Who, with back turned, and bowed above his work,
Sat riveting a helmet on his knee,
He put the self-same query, but the man
Not turning round, nor looking at him, said: 270

265	gruffly Ugh the	
	Who render'd niggard answer Sparrow Hawk	H-35
265	He answer'd...	Tn-30;T-E
265	He answer'd...	F-ENI
265	And had for answer	I MS
	H̸é̸ ̸a̸n̸s̸w̸é̸r̸'̸d̸ ̸g̸r̸u̸f̸f̸l̸y̸, 'Ugh!...	BM-1
265	Who	I MS
	H̸é̸ answer'd...	L-EN2
265	(C)	L-EN3
266	...an armourer's/ booth,	(/booth, I)	BM-1
266	(C)	L-EN2
267	Who s̸a̸t̸ with back turn'd & bowing oe'r his work	H-35
267	Who / with back turn'd, and...	(, I)	L-ENI
267	(C)	BM-1
268	Sat	
	W̸á̸s̸ riveting a skullcap on...	H-35
268	...riveting a skullcap on...	Tn-30;T-E
268	...riveting a skullcap on...	F-ENI
268	helmet	I MS
	...riveting a s̸k̸u̸l̸l̸c̸a̸p̸ on...	L-EN2
268	(C)	L-EN3
269	...selfsame question but...	H-35
270	..., said:	:/ (I)	L-ENI
270	(C)	BM-1
271	Friend	
	s̸á̸i̸d̸ he that does work for...	H-35

'Friend, he that labours for the sparrow-hawk
Has little time for idle questioners.'
Whereat Geraint flashed into sudden spleen:
'A thousand pips eat up your sparrow-hawk!
Tits, wrens, and all winged nothings peck him dead!   275
Ye think the rustic cackle of your bourg
The murmur of the world! What is it to me?
O wretched set of sparrows, one and all,
Who pipe of nothing but of sparrow-hawks!

---

273 Then flush'd Geraint into a fit of spleen   H-35
273 At this Geraint...   Tn-30;T-E
273 Whereat   I MS
    A̸t̸ t̸h̸i̸s̸ Geraint...spleen:̸   L-ENI
273 (C)   BM-1

274
    ...pips devour your...   H-35
274 ...sparrow-hawk!   (! I)   L-ENI
274 (C)   BM-1

275 (Omitted; written in I MS)   L-ENI
275 (C)   BM-1

276 Who think...   Tn-30;T-E
276 You   I MS
    W̸h̸o̸ think...   L-ENI
276 You think...   BM-1
276   e   I MS
    Y̸o̸u̸ think...   L-EN2
276 (ᵕ)   L-EN3

278-281 Why what a lot of sparrows are you all
          To talk of nothing but of sparrowhawk
          Where can I get a lodging for the night?   H-35

278 A wretched set of sparrows, all & one   Tn-30
278 O   I MS
    A̸ wretched   L-ENI
278 (C)   BM-1

Speak, if ye be not like the rest, hawk-mad,   280
Where can I get me harbourage for the night?
And arms, arms, arms to fight my enemy? Speak!'
Whereat the armourer turning all amazed
And seeing one so gay in purple silks,
Came forward with the helmet yet in hand   285
And answered, 'Pardon me, O stranger knight;
We hold a tourney here tomorrow morn,
And there is scantly time for half the work.
Arms? truth! I know not: all are wanted here.

280	Speak	
	B̸ǘt̸ if you be...	Tn-30
280	...if you be...	T-E
280	..., if you be..., hawk-mad -/ (I)	L-ENI
280	..., if you be...	BM-1
280	(C)	<u>69</u>
281	...night?'	F-ENI
281	(C)	BM-1
282	(Omitted; included in I MS.)	L-ENI
282	(C)	BM-1
283	At this the armourer turning half amazed	H-35
283	At this the armourer...	Tn-30;T-E
283	At this the armourer...	F-ENI
283	(C)	73
284	And seeing ő̸ń̸é̸ a gay knight in...	H-35
285	skull-cap	I MS
	...the h̸é̸l̸m̸é̸t̸ yet...	BM-1
285	helmet	I MS
	...the s̸k̸ǘl̸l̸-c̸ǎ̸p̸ yet...	L-EN2
285	(C)	L-EN3
286	Sir stranger. I.	
	...Pardon, I perceive you strange	H-35
286	...knight,; ;/ (I)	L-ENI
286	said he pardon me	I MS
	And ǎ̸n̸s̸w̸é̸r̸é̸d̸, P̸ǎ̸r̸d̸ő̸n̸ m̸é̸, O stranger knight;	BM-1
286	(C)	L-EN2

Harbourage? truth, good truth, I know not, save,   290
It may be, at Earl Yniol's, o'er the bridge
Yonder.' He spoke and fell to work again.

    Then rode Geraint, a little spleenful yet,
Across the bridge that spanned the dry ravine.
There musing sat the hoary-headed Earl,   295

Alt. after 286 The truth is - lodging nay I know
                            not where   H-35

287 We have a tourney here at early dawn   H-35
287 ...here tomorrow morn,   (, I)   L-ENI
287 ...tomorrow...   BM-1
287 (C)   73

288 ...is hardly time...   H-35

289 (Omitted; included in I MS)   L-ENI
289 Arms? truth! I...   (! I)   BM-1
289 (C)   L-EN2

290 Lodging? indeed I know not where except   H-35
290 Lodging, in truth...   Tn-30;T-E
290 Harbourage?   I MS
    ~~Lodging~~ ~~in~~ truth, ...   L-ENI
290 (C)   BM-1

291 At old earl Yniol's yonder oer...   H-35
291 ...at ~~old~~ earl...   Tn-30

292 So saying to his work he fell again.   H-35

293 And Prince Geraint a...   H-35

294 Past oer the bridge that...   H-35

295-298   [his dress
    There sat the hoary-headed earl & said
    a suit of fray'd magnificence]
    'Whither, fair son? & Geraint answer'd him   H-35

295 There musing
    ~~Upon~~ ~~it~~ sat...   Tn-30

305

(His dress a suit of frayed magnificence,
Once fit for feasts of ceremony) and said:
'Whither, fair son?' to whom Geraint replied,
'O friend, I seek a harbourage for the night.'
Then Yniol, 'Enter therefore and partake   300
The slender entertainment of a house
Once rich, now poor, but ever open-doored.'
'Thanks, venerable friend,' replied Geraint;
'So that ye do not serve me sparrow-hawks
For supper, I will enter, I will eat   305
With all the passion of a twelve hours' fast.'
Then sighed and smiled the hoary-headed Earl,
And answered, 'Graver cause than yours is mine

---

297 ...ceremony], and...   F-ENI
297 ...ceremony]⁄ and...   -   L-EN3
297 (C)   F-EN2

299 'My friend, I...   H-35

300 ...therefore. you shall have   H-35

301 The   of
    T̸x̸ø̸x̸h̸ slender entertainment ø̸ß̸ x̸n̸ ø̸ʉ̸x̸ß̸ a house   H-35

303 O venerable...   H-35

304 Thanks; if you will not...   H-35
304 ...that you do...   Tn-30;T-E
304 ...that you do...   F-ENI
304 (C)   69

305   I will
    ...enter, x̸é̸ß̸x̸ & eat   H-35

307 And sighing smild...   H-35

309 ...sparrow-hawk ⁄ :   :⁄ (I)   L-ENI
309 (C)   BM-1

310 ...save yourself x̸é̸q̸ʉ̸é̸ß̸x̸ desire it   H-35
310 ...it   F-ENI
310 (C)   59

THE MARRIAGE OF GERAINT

To curse this hedgerow thief, the sparrow-hawk:
But in, go in; for save yourself desire it,   310
We will not touch upon him even in jest.'

    Then rode Geraint into the castle court,
His charger trampling many a prickly star
Of sprouted thistle on the broken stones.
He looked and saw that all was ruinous.   315
Here stood a shattered archway plumed with fern;
And here had fallen a great part of a tower,
Whole, like a crag that tumbles from the cliff,
And like a crag was gay with wilding flowers:

---

311 ...ev'n in sport. /talk   H-35
311 ...ev'n in game.   Tn-30;T-E
311   jest   I MS
    ...ev'n in g̸a̸m̸e̸/'   L-ENI
311 (C)   BM-1

312 (No par. indent; MS par. symbol.)   L-ENI
312 (C)   BM-1

313-314 T̸h̸e̸ s̸t̸a̸r̸l̸i̸k̸e̸ t̸h̸i̸s̸t̸l̸e̸ p̸r̸i̸c̸k̸l̸y̸ s̸t̸a̸r̸ o̸f̸ t̸h̸e̸
                              /n̸e̸w̸ t̸h̸i̸s̸t̸l̸e̸   H-35

315 ...ruinous̸   ☉   (I)   L-ENI
315 (C)   BM-1

316 For here there stood a statue plumed...   Tn-30
316   shatter'd archway
    F̸o̸r̸ here t̸h̸e̸r̸e̸ stood a s̸t̸a̸t̸u̸e̸ plumed...   T-E
316 ...fern,;   ;/ (I)   L-ENI
316 (C)   BM-1

317   part
    ...a great p̸i̸e̸c̸e̸ of a tower   H-35

318   tumbles
    ...that t̸o̸p̸p̸l̸e̸s̸ from...   T-E

319 ...flowers;:   :/ (I)   L-ENI
319 (C)   BM-1

And high above a piece of turret stair,   320
Worn by the feet that now were silent, wound
Bare to the sun, and monstrous ivy-stems
Claspt the gray walls with hairy-fibred arms,
And sucked the joining of the stones, and looked
A knot, beneath, of snakes, aloft, a grove.   325

    And while he waited in the castle court,
The voice of Enid, Yniol's daughter, rang
Clear through the open casement of the hall,
Singing; and as the sweet voice of a bird,
Heard by the lander in a lonely isle,   330
Moves him to think what kind of bird it is
That sings so delicately clear, and make
Conjecture of the plumage and the form;

---

323 ...arms,	(, I)	L-ENI
323 (C)		BM-1
325 Beneath a knot of snakes...		H-35
326 ...court,	,/ (I)	L-ENI
326 (C)		BM-1
327 Yniol's ǿńƚȳ daughter...		T-E
328 ...the Hall,		F-ENI
328 (C)		73
329 Singing, and...		F-ENI
329 Singing,; and...	;/ (I)	L-EN3
329 (C)		F-EN2
332 ...delicatly & to make		H-35
333 ...& the ѕħáṕé form		H-35

THE MARRIAGE OF GERAINT

So the sweet voice of Enid moved Geraint;
And made him like a man abroad at morn   335
When first the liquid note beloved of men
Comes flying over many a windy wave
To Britain, and in April suddenly
Breaks from a coppice gemmed with green and red,
And he suspends his converse with a friend,   340
Or it may be the labour of his hands,
To think or say, 'There is the nightingale;'
So fared it with Geraint, who thought and said,
'Here, by God's grace, is the one voice for me.'

    It chanced the song that Enid sang was one   345
Of Fortune and her wheel, and Enid sang:

---

334 ...Geraint,;	;/ (I)	L-ENI
334 (C)		BM-1
335 And took him ear & heart; or as a man		H-35
335 O̸r̸ a̸s̸ a̸ l̸a̸b̸o̸u̸r̸e̸r̸ i̸n̸ t̸h̸e̸ m̸o̸r̸n̸i̸n̸g̸ f̸i̸e̸l̸d̸		Tn-30
340 Awhile suspends the currents of his thoughts		H-35
340 his converse with friend		
...suspends the labour of his hands		Tn-30
343 So was it with Geraint...		H-35
344 Here by the rood is...		H-35
345 (No par. indent.; MS par. symbol.)		L-ENI
345 (C)		BM-1
346 ...wheel & t̸h̸u̸s̸ s̸h̸e̸ s̸a̸n̸g̸ Enid...		Tn-30
346 ...sang: /̸		L-ENI
346 (C)		BM-1

THE MARRIAGE OF GERAINT

(Enid's Song.)
(Rejected stanza, first draft.)
    gay, be gay
Be ~~rich in heart~~ when Fortune makes thee poor
And smile at Fortune when she smiles no more
~~Be rich in heart & rich is thine estate~~
Thy smile may win her's back however late   Tn-30

(Rejected stanza, second draft.)
  Be gay be gay
~~Come in come in~~ for who shall count as poor
Who smile at Fortune till she frowns no more
    But (I ?)
Herself will smile at last however late.   Tn-30

(Rejected stanza, third draft.)
  Be gay be gay for how sd those be poor
Who smile at Fortune till she frowns no more
But gives them smile for smile however late.   Tn-30

(Another rejected stanza, first draft.)
  Let health be wealth & old possessions go
And care not friend if our estate be low
We have not fallen low ~~as~~ with our estate   H-71a

(Another rejected stanza, second draft.)
  If our estate have slipt from high to low
Content is rich when old possessions go
And health is wealth in much or mean estate.   H-71a

(Another rejected stanza.)
  Smile Smile
Shine Shine fair sun our fortunes are but pale
               not
But tho thou smile, none shall hear us wail
Tho poor the house yet open is the gate   H-35

(First full draft of the Song.)

Come in the ford is roaring on the plain
The distant hills are pale across the rain
Come in, come in for open is the gate
    Come in, poor man & let the tempest blow

310

THE MARRIAGE OF GERAINT

Let fortune frown & old possessions go
But health is wealth in high or low estate
   Tho fortune frown thou shalt not hear us rail
The frown of Fortune never turn'd us pale
For man is man & master of his Fate.
   Turn, Fortune, turn thy wheel with smile or
                     frown
With thy false wheel we go not up or down
Our hoard is little but our hearts are great
   Smile and we smile the lords of many lands
Frown & we smile the lords of our own hands
For man is man & master of his fate.
   The river ford will fall on yonder plain
The flying rainbow chase the flying rain
                 at last
The sun will smile again however late
   Come in come in whoever lingers there
Nor scorn the ruin'd house & homely fare
The house is poor but open is the gate.   H-71a

(Second full draft of the Song.)
   ~~Come in / the hills are pale across the rain /~~
   ~~Come in / the ford is roaring on the plain~~
   ~~Come in / come in / for open is the gate /~~
     ~~Come in / poor man / & /let the tempest blow /~~
  ~~And fortune frown / & whirl & glory go /~~
  ~~For health is wealth in high or low estate.~~
   Turn, fortune, turn thy wheel with smile
               or frown,
On   at wild
~~With~~ thy ~~false~~ wheel we go not up or down
Our hoard is little but our hearts are great.
   Smile, & we smile the lords of many lands,
Frown, & we smile the lords of our own hands,
For man is man & master of his fate.
    ~~Fall, fall wild/ fall, be still on yonder plain/~~
  ~~Come/ rainbow/ come & chase the flying rain/~~
  ~~Smile/ smile at last/ fair sun/ however late~~
   ~~Smile/ smile fair sun/ our fortunes look but~~
               ~~pale~~
~~But they thou smile not/ none shall hear us rail~~
~~For man is man & master of his fate/~~
   ~~Come in/ come in/whoever lingers there,~~
~~The house is poor & simple is the gate~~ (Continued)

311

'Turn, Fortune, turn thy wheel and lower the
proud;
Turn thy wild wheel through sunshine, storm, and cloud;
Thy wheel and thee we neither love nor hate.

'Turn, Fortune, turn thy wheel with smile or
frown;   350
With that wild wheel we go not up or down;
Our hoard is little, but our hearts are great.

(Second full draft of the Song.) (Cont'd)

~~The house is good but open is the gate;~~

~~Smile, smile at Fortune when she smiles no more;~~

~~She turns her wheel & makes the wealthy poor;~~

~~The wheel may turn again, however late;~~

(Then 350-355 c)
      Smile, smile at Fortune, when she makes thee poor
Smile, smile at Fortune, till she frowns no more.
But turns her wheel again, however late.
(Then 356-358,c)   Tn-30

347 (Par.) Turn, ...proud,   F-ENI
347 (Par.) 'Turn, ...proud,;   ('; I)   BM-1
347 (Par.) Turn, ...proud,   L-EN2
347 (Par.) 'Turn Fortune, turn/ thy wheel and lower
                        the proud; ,/;/ (I)   L-EN3
347 (Par.) 'Turn Fortune,...   F-EN2
347 (C)   59

350 O turn thy wheel false Fate & smile or frown   H-35
350   Fortune
      Turn turn thy wheel, False ~~Fate~~ & smile or frown Y-II
350 (Par.) Turn, ...frown,   F-ENI
350 (Par.) Turn, ...frown,;   (; I)   BM-1
350 (Par.) Turn, ...frown,   L-EN2
350 (Par.) Turn,...   L-EN3
350 (C)   59

351 With thy false wheel we go not up or down Y-II;H-35
351 ...down,;   ;/ (I)   L-ENI
351 (C)   BM-1

352 ...little but...   F-ENI
352 ...little, but...   ,/ (I)   L-EN3
352 (C)   F-EN2

'Smile and we smile, the lords of many lands;
Frown and we smile, the lords of our own hands;
For man is man and master of his fate.   355

'Turn, turn thy wheel above the staring crowd;
Thy wheel and thou are shadows in the cloud;
Thy wheel and thee we neither love nor hate.'

'Hark, by the bird's song ye may learn the nest,'

353	(Par.) Smile...smile, the...lands,	(1st, I)	L-ENI
353	(Par.) Smile...lands,;	(; I)	BM-1
353	(Par.) Smile...lands,		L-EN2
353	(Par.) Smile...		L-EN3
353	(C)		59

354	...smile & labour with our hands		H-35
354	...smile the...hands,;	;/ (I)	L-ENI
354	(C)		BM-1

355	master of his fate		
	...man & m̸a̸s̸t̸e̸r̸ h̸i̸s̸ o̸w̸n̸ e̸s̸t̸a̸t̸e̸		H-35

356	(Par.) Turn,...crowd,		F-ENI
356	(Par.) Turn,...crowd,;	(; I)	BM-1
356	(Par.) Turn,...crowd,		L-EN2
356	crowd		I MS
	(Par.) Turn,...staring c̸l̸o̸u̸d̸;		L-EN3
356	(C)		F-EN2

357	thou		
	...and t̸h̸e̸e̸ are...		L-ENI
357	(C)		BM-1

358	...hate.		F-ENI
358	...hate.'	(' I)	BM-1
358	...hate.		L-EN2
358	(C)		L-EN3

359	learn		
	...song you may f̸i̸n̸d̸ the nest'		Tn-30
359	...song, you may...		T-E
359	...song you may...nest'		F-ENI
359	(C)		73

Said Yniol; 'enter quickly.' Entering then,   360
Right o'er a mount of newly-fallen stones,
The dusky-raftered many-cobwebbed hall,
He found an ancient dame in dim brocade;
And near her, like a blossom vermeil-white,
That lightly breaks a faded flower-sheath,   365
Moved the fair Enid, all in faded silk,
Her daughter. In a moment thought Geraint,
'Here by God's rood is the one maid for me.'
But none spake word except the hoary Earl:
'Enid, the good knight's horse stands in the court; 370
Take him to stall, and give him corn, and then

---

360 ...Yniol; 'Enter...then   F-ENI
360 ...Yniol; 'Enter...   L-EN3
360 (C)   59

361 (Omitted)   F-ENI
361 Right o'er   MS
    Ø¢¢¢ a mount of newly-fallen .stones,   L-EN3
361 (C)   F-EN2

362 ...-rafter'd & much-cobwebb'd...   H-35
362 ...many-cobwebb'd Hall,   F-ENI
362 (C)   73

363 ...brocade,;   ;/ (I)   L-ENI
363 (C)   BM-1

364 And near like a blossom seemed while   H-35

365 ...flower-sheath,   (, I)   L-ENI
365 ...flower-sheath   BM-1
365 (C)   L-EN2

369 But no one spake...   H-35

Alt. before 370 Rest, friend: the maiden serves:
                    it is her wont   (I MS)   BM-1

370 ...court,;   ;/ (I)   L-ENI
370 ...court,   L-EN2
370 (C)   L-EN3

314

THE MARRIAGE OF GERAINT

Go to the town and buy us flesh and wine;
And we will make us merry as we may.
Our hoard is little, but our hearts are great.'

He spake: the Prince, as Enid past him, fain   375
To follow, strode a stride, but Yniol caught
His purple scarf, and held, and said, 'Forbear!
Rest! the good house, though ruined, O my son,

---

371 ...stall & after that yourself	H-35
371 ...stall and...	F-ENI
371 food ce	I MS
...stall and give him ~~corn~~, and then	BM-1
371 ...stall and...	L-EN2
371 (C)	L-EN3
373 ...may~~/~~ ◉ (I)	L-ENI
373 ...may,	L-EN2
373 (C)	L-EN3
375-381 (Omitted)	F-ENI
375-381 (Added w. following variants, L-EN3)	
375 fain	I MS
...him, ~~moved~~	L-EN3
375 (C)	F-EN2
376 To follow, strode a stride, but	I MS
~~All fain to follow/~~ ~~had not~~ Yniol caught	L-EN3
376 (C)	F-EN2
377 held, & said 'forbear!	I MS
...scarf, and ~~added smiling May~~ –	L-EN3
377 ...said 'forbear!	F-EN2
377 ...said 'Forbear!	59
377 (C)	73
378 son	I MS
...my ~~friend~~,	L-EN3
378 ..., O my son,	F-EN2
378 (C)	73

Endures not that her guest should serve himself.'
And reverencing the custom of the house   380
Geraint, from utter courtesy, forbore.

    So Enid took his charger to the stall;
And after went her way across the bridge,
And reached the town, and while the Prince and Earl
Yet spoke together, came again with one,   385
A youth, that following with a costrel bore
The means of goodly welcome, flesh and wine.

---

381   from   I MS
    Geraint, ~~throy~~ utter courtesy, forebore. (,,I) L-EN3
381 (C)   F-EN2

382 Then Enid took the knight's horse to the
                              stall   H-35;T-E
382 (Par.) Then Enid took the knight's horse to
                              the stall   .   F-ENI
382 (C)   L-EN3

Alt. after 382
    And litter'd him & gave him hay & corn   Tn-30;T-E
Alt. after 382
    And litter'd him and gave him hay and corn; F-ENI
Alt. after 382 (C)   L-EN3

383 And after
    ~~Then Enid~~ went...   H-35

384 And reach ~~into~~ the town, & while the knight
                              & Earl   H-35

385 ...together, came...   (, I)   L-ENI
385 (C)   BM-1

386 ...following in a costrel...   H-35;Tn-30;T-E
386 ...following in a costrel...   F-ENI
386 (C)   L-EN3

387   goodly
    The means of ~~happy~~ welcome...   H-35

And Enid brought sweet cakes to make them cheer,
And in her veil enfolded, manchet bread.
And then, because their hall must also serve   390
For kitchen, boiled the flesh, and spread the board,
And stood behind, and waited on the three.
And seeing her so sweet and serviceable,
Geraint had longing in him evermore
To stoop and kiss the tender little thumb,   395
That crost the trencher as she laid it down:
But after all had eaten, then Geraint,
For now the wine made summer in his veins,
Let his eye rove in following, or rest
On Enid at her lowly handmaid-work,   400
Now here, now there, about the dusky hall;

390-391 And after boild the flesh & spread the
                        board   H-35

391 ...board,   (, I)   L-ENI
391 (C)   BM-1

392 And meekly stood behind & waited on them.   H-35
392 ...behind, and...   ,/ (I)   L-ENI
392 (C)   BM-1

394 A̸n̸d̸/e̸v̸e̸r̸m̸o̸r̸e̸ Geraint had longing in him
                        evermore   H-35

395   tender
    To stoop , & kiss the l̸i̸t̸t̸l̸e̸ thumb t̸h̸a̸t̸ l̸a̸y̸   H-35
395 ...thumb   F-ENI
395 (C)   L-EN3

396 That crost   laid
    U̸p̸o̸n̸ the trencher as she p̸u̸t̸ it down   H-35
396 ...down/:   (: I)   L-ENI
396 (C)   BM-1

399 ...following, or...   , (I)   L-ENI
399 (C)   BM-1

401 Now here, now there, about...hall,; (,,;I)   L-ENI
401 (C)   BM-1

317

Then suddenly addrest the hoary Earl:

'Fair Host and Earl, I pray your courtesy;
This sparrow-hawk, what is he? tell me of him.
His name? but no, good faith, I will not have it: 405
For if he be the knight whom late I saw
Ride into that new fortress by your town,
White from the mason's hand, then have I sworn
From his own lips to have it--I am Geraint
Of Devon--for this morning when the Queen   410

---

403 ...courtesy:;	; (I)	L-ENI
403 (C)		BM-1

404 ...he, tell...	.	F-ENI
404 (C)		73

draft, 406-414
    Yet if he be the tall K̸h̸ man whom I saw
    R̸i̸d̸e̸ ̸w̸i̸t̸h̸ ̸a̸ ̸d̸a̸m̸e̸ ̸&̸
    Ride into that near fortress near your town
    White from the masons hand - if this be he
    Then by Gods death I will not learn his name
    Except from his own lips at point of sword
    For the Queen this morning sent
    Her maiden to demand it of his dwarf
    And when she moved to ask it of the knight
    Struck at her with his whip & she returnd
    Indignant to the Queen   H-35

406 ...whom I beheld	H-35

407 ...town,	,/ (I)	L-ENI
407 (C)		BM-1

410 Devon	I MS
Of D̸e̸v̸o̸n̸ - for...	L-ENI
410 (C)	BM-1

411 (Blot) sent her maiden to demand h̸i̸s̸ ̸n̸a̸m̸e̸,
                it of him   H-35

Sent her own maiden to demand the name,
His dwarf, a vicious under-shapen thing,
Struck at her with his whip, and she returned
Indignant to the Queen; and then I swore
That I would track this caitiff to his hold,   415
And fight and break his pride, and have it of him.
And all unarmed I rode, and thought to find
Arms in your town, where all the men are mad;
They take the rustic murmur of their bourg
For the great wave that echoes round the world;   420
They would not hear me speak: but if ye know
Where I can light on arms, or if yourself
Should have them, tell me, seeing I have sworn
That I will break his pride and learn his name,

---

416 ...him, ⊙	(I)	L-ENI
416 (C)		BM-1

Alt. after 416 Avenging his great insult done the
                              Queen.   Tn-30

417 ...rode, and...	(, I)	L-ENI
417 (C)		BM-1

418 ...town, but all the men...		H-35
418 ...mad,;	;/ (I)	L-ENI
418 (C)		BM-1

419 And take the rustic...   H-35

420 ...world.	F-ENI
420 (C)	BM-1

421 ...if you know		H-35;Tn-30;T-E
421 ...speak;: but if you know	:/ (I)	L-ENI
421 ...if you know		BM-1
421 (C)		69

423 Should have them, let me know tell me...   H-35

424 To break his pride, God's death, & learn his
                              name.   H-35

319

Avenging this great insult done the Queen.'   425

    Then cried Earl Yniol, 'Art thou he indeed,
Geraint, a name far-sounded among men
For noble deeds? and truly I, when first
I saw you moving by me on the bridge,
Felt ye were somewhat, yea, and by your state   430
And presence might have guessed you one of those

---

425   done
    ...insult ~~to~~ the Queen...   Tn-30

426   cried   Art thou he
    (Par.) Then spake Earl Yniol, ~~Truly are~~
                indeed
                ~~you be~~   Tn-30
426 ...Yniol. 'Art...   F-ENI
426 (C)   73

428 ...when ~~at~~ first   Tn-30
428 ...deeds! and...   F-ENI
428 (C)   L-EN3

430 Felt   were   judging
    I ~~thought~~ you somewhat, yea & by your state   Tn-30
430 Felt you were...   T-E
430 Felt you were somewhat, yea and...   F-ENI
430 (C)   73

431   that you must be
    ...might have guess'd you...   Tn-30

433 ...flattery,;   ;/(I)   L-ENI
433 (C)   BM-1

434 Prince
    ~~And~~ this...   Tn-30
434 For
    ~~Prince~~ this...   T-E

435 ...paused/   L-ENI
435 (C)   BM-1

That eat in Arthur's hall at Camelot.
Nor speak I now from foolish flattery;
For this dear child hath often heard me praise
Your feats of arms, and often when I paused   435
Hath asked again, and ever loved to hear;
So grateful is the noise of noble deeds
To noble hearts who see but acts of wrong:
O never yet had woman such a pair
Of suitors as this maiden; first Limours,   440
A creature wholly given to brawls and wine,
Drunk even when he wooed; and be he dead

---

436 ...again, and...   (, I)   L-ENI
436 (C)   BM-1

Sketch 437-439   And
    ~~To hear of such is grateful~~ where we see
                            To hear of thee is grateful
    But acts of violence; such a ~~noble~~ pair   Tn-30
Sketch 437-439
    For but to hear of these is grateful to us
    ~~And where we see but acts of violence~~
    Who see but acts of violence
    ~~To hear of these is grateful~~; such a pair   T-E
437-439 For but to hear of these is grateful to us
        Who see but acts of violence; such a pair   F-ENI
437-439 So grateful is the noise of noble deeds   I MS
    ~~For but to hear of these is grateful to us~~
    To those who suffer wrong, &   I MS
    ~~Who see but acts of violence;~~ such a pair   BM-1
437-439 For but to hear of these is grateful to us
        Who see but acts of violence; such a pair   L-EN2
437-439 (C)   L-EN3

Alt. before 440 Nor ever hath she seen a noble
                            Knight   H-35

440 Tho' there were two, her suitors; one, Limours H-35
440 ...suitors had this...   Tn-30;T-E
440 ...suitors had this...   F-ENI
440 (C)   L-EN3

441 An earl, but wholly given...   H-35

321

I know not, but he past to the wild land.
The second was your foe, the sparrow-hawk,
My curse, my nephew--I will not let his name   445
Slip from my lips if I can help it--he,
When I that knew him fierce and turbulent
Refused her to him, then his pride awoke;
And since the proud man often is the mean,
He sowed a slander in the common ear,   450

---

443 ...but he went to the...   H-35

445 My plague, my...   H-35
445 ...nephew. /- I...   (- I)   L-ENI
445 (C)   BM-1

446 ...I can let it] he,   H-35
446 ...it/ - he, .   (- I)   L-ENI
446 (C)   BM-1

449 And since the proud man is the mean one,
                          spread   H-35
449 ...mean,   (, I)   L-ENI
449 (C)   BM-1

450 All kinds of slanders   H-35
450 ...in the p̸e̸o̸p̸l̸e̸s̸ common...   Tn-30

451 Affirming   his
    A̸s̸s̸e̸r̸t̸i̸n̸g̸ that m̸y̸ father...   Tn-30
451 ...gold   F-ENI
451 ...gold,   ,/ (I)   BM-1
451 ...gold   L-EN2
451 (C)   L-EN3

452   wh was render'd
    ...charge, not g̸i̸v̸e̸n̸ to him; h̸e̸ l̸i̸e̸d̸.   Tn-30
452 ...to him,;   ;/ (I)   L-ENI
452 (C)   BM-1

453   served
    ...who hung   Tn-30

322

Affirming that his father left him gold,
And in my charge, which was not rendered to him;
Bribed with large promises the men who served
About my person, the more easily
Because my means were somewhat broken into   455
Through open doors and hospitality;
Raised my own town against me in the night
Before my Enid's birthday, sacked my house;
From mine own earldom foully ousted me;
Built that new fort to overawe my friends,   460
For truly there are those who love me yet;
And keeps me in this ruinous castle here,
Where doubtless he would put me soon to death,

---

454 About my person
    Upon my favor, the...   Tn-30

456 ...hospitality;   ;/ (I)   BM-1
456 (C)   L-EN2

457   night
    ...in one d̸a̸y̸;   Tn-30
457   the
    ... in o̸n̸e̸ night,   T-E

460   ousted me
    From my own earldom, built the fort you saw   H-35

461 To overawe those friends who love me yet   H-35

462 And set me in...   H-35
462 And placed me...   Tn-30;T-E
462   keeps   I MS
    And p̸l̸a̸c̸e̸d̸ me...   L-ENI
462 (C)   BM-1

463 Where surely he put me soon to death   H-35
463   doubtless
    Where s̸u̸r̸e̸l̸y̸ he...   Tn-30
463 ...death   F-ENI
463 ...death,   ,/ (I)   L-EN3
463 (C)   F-EN2

But that his pride too much despises me:
And I myself sometimes despise myself;   465
For I have let men be, and have their way;
Am much too gentle, have not used my power:
Nor know I whether I be very base
Or very manful, whether very wise
Or very foolish; only this I know,   470
That whatsoever evil happen to me,

---

464 Save that his...		H-35
464 ...me⸍ :	(: I)	L-ENI
464 (C)		BM-1

Sketch c. 465 ff.
    Why friend I fear I have misused my life
    And that is past rejecting - I am old
    I thought to do my duty by all men
    By letting them alone   H-35

467 Am much	
H̶a̶v̶e̶ b̶e̶e̶n̶ too...	Tn-30

Alt. before 470 I cannot tell if I be very wise   H-35

470 Or very foolish only this I know   H-35

471 Or seem to know, whatever comes to me		H-35
471 ...me,	(, I)	L-ENI
471 (C)		BM-1

472 I suffer nothing or in heart or limb		H-35
472 ...limb,	(, I)	L-ENI
472 (C)		BM-1

473 But do endure it very manfully   H-35

474 W true heart	
/Y̶e̶a̶/ y̶e̶a̶/ well said replied...	Tn-30
474 ...heart' replied Geraint 'but arms:	F-ENI
474 ...'but arms:	59
474 (C)	73

I seem to suffer nothing heart or limb,
But can endure it all most patiently.'

   'Well said, true heart,' replied Geraint, 'but arms,
That if the sparrow-hawk, this nephew, fight   475
In next day's tourney I may break his pride.'

   And Yniol answered, 'Arms, indeed, but old
And rusty, old and rusty, Prince Geraint,
Are mine, and therefore at thine asking, thine.
But in this tournament can no man tilt,   480
Except the lady he loves best be there.
Two forks are fixt into the meadow ground,
And over these is placed a silver wand,

---

475 That if, as I suppose your nephew fights	Tn-30;T-E
475 That if, as I suppose, your nephew fights	F-ENI
475 (C)	69

477 ...answer'd 'arms,...	F-ENI
477 ...answer'd 'Arms,...	59
477 (C)	73

479 at your asking	
...therefore, ~~as~~ ~~you~~ ~~ask~~ ~~them~~, yours	Tn-30
479 ...at your asking, yours	T-E
479 ...at your asking, yours.	F-ENI
479 (C)	73

480 ...tilt		F-ENI
480 ...tilt,	,/(I)	L-EN3
480 (C)		F-EN2

482 fixt	
...are ~~stuck~~ into...	Tn-30

483 laid	
...is ~~placed~~ a silver...	Tn-30
483 ...is laid a silver...	T-E
483 ...is laid a silver...	F-ENI
483 (C)	73

And over that a golden sparrow-hawk,
The prize of beauty for the fairest there.   485
And this, what knight soever be in field
Lays claim to for the lady at his side,
And tilts with my good nephew thereupon,
Who being apt at arms and big of bone
Has ever won it for the lady with him,   490
And toppling over all antagonism
Has earned himself the name of sparrow-hawk.
But thou, that hast no lady, canst not fight.'

   To whom Geraint with eyes all bright replied,
Leaning a little toward him, 'Thy leave!   495
Let me lay lance in rest, O noble host,
For this dear child, because I never saw,

484	is placed the	
	...that ~~a gilded~~ sparrowhawk.	Tn-30
484	...that is placed the sparrowhawk	T-E
484	...that is placed the sparrow-hawk,	F-ENI
484	(C)	73

485	The prize of beauty	
	~~This is proclaim'd as~~ for...	Tn-30

487	...side.,	,/(I)	L-ENI
487	(C)		BM-1

490-491	And ing	
	2 ~~Hath~~ toppl~~ed~~ over all anatagonis~~ts~~ ism	
	Has	
	1 ~~And~~ ever won it for the lady with him,	Tn-30

492	Has	
	~~And~~ earn'd...	Tn-30

493	But you, that have no lady, cannot fight.	Tn-30;T-E
493	But you, that have no lady, cannot fight.'	F-ENI
493	(C)	73

494	...replied	F-ENI
494	(C)	59

Though having seen all beauties of our time,
Nor can see elsewhere, anything so fair.
And if I fall her name will yet remain   500
Untarnished as before; but if I live,
So aid me Heaven when at mine uttermost,
As I will make her truly my true wife.'

    Then, howsoever patient, Yniol's heart
Danced in his bosom, seeing better days.   505
And looking round he saw not Enid there,

---

495 ...him 'Your leave!		Tn-30;T-E
495 ...him 'Your leave!		F-ENI
495 ...him, 'Your leave!		59
495 (C)		73
496 Let me lay...	(Ital. I)	L-ENI
496 (C)		BM-1
497 this child because		
For ẏóúŕ d́éáŕ d́áúǵh́t́éŕ f́óŕ I...		Tn-30
497 ...saw,	(, I)	L-ENI
497 (C)		BM-1
498 ...time,	(, I)	L-ENI
498ₑ (C)		BM-1
499 ...elsewhere, anything...	(, I)	L-ENI
499 (C)		BM-1
500-501 Áńd́ íf́ Í f́áll Í f́áll/ b́úŕ íf́ Í lív́é		Tn-30
501 ...live,	(, I)	L-ENI
501 (C)		BM-1
502 aid me Heaven, áńd́ when		
So ḿáẏ ǵód́ h́élṕ ḿé at...		Tn-30
502 ...uttermost,	(, I)	L-ENI
502 (C)		BM-1
503 As will		
T́h́éń ẃíll Í make...		Tn-30

(Who hearing her own name had stolen away)
But that old dame, to whom full tenderly
And folding all her hand in his he said,
'Mother, a maiden is a tender thing,   510
And best by her that bore her understood.
Go thou to rest, but ere thou go to rest
Tell her, and prove her heart toward the Prince.'

So spake the kindly-hearted Earl, and she
With frequent smile and nod departing found,   515
Half disarrayed as to her rest, the girl;

---

507 ...had slipt away]		T-E
507 ...had slipt away]		F-ENI
507 (C)		84
510 ...thing:		F-ENI
510 ...thing⫽	,/ (MS)	BM-1
510 ...thing:		L-EN2
510 (C)		L-EN3
513 ...her and...		F-ENI
513 ...her, and...	,/ (I)	L-EN3
513 (C)		F-EN2
514 (No par.; par. symbol.) ...the kindly hearted Earl, and...		L-ENI
514 ...the kindly-hearted earl, and...		L-EN3
514 (C)		59
515 ...found,	(, I)	L-ENI
515 (C)		BM-1
516 ...girl;	(; I)	L-ENI
516 (C)		BM-1
517 on either cheek ...kissed f̶u̶l̶l̶ m̶o̶t̶h̶e̶r̶l̶i̶k̶e̶ & then		Tn-30
517 ...cheek, and...	(, I)	L-ENI
517 (C)		BM-1
518 ...shoulder/ laid a hand,	,/ (I)	L-ENI
518 (C)		BM-1

Whom first she kissed on either cheek, and then
On either shining   shoulder laid a hand,
And kept her off and gazed upon her face,
And told her all their converse in the hall,   520
Proving her heart: but never light and shade
Coursed one another more on open ground
Beneath a troubled heaven, than red and pale
Across the face of Enid hearing her;
While slowly falling as a scale that falls,   525
When weight is added only grain by grain,
Sank her sweet head upon her gentle breast;
Nor did she lift an eye nor speak a word,
Rapt in the fear and in the wonder of it;
So moving without answer to her rest   530

---

519 ...fare,		(, I)	L-ENI
519 (C)			BM-1
523 ...heaven, than...		(, I)	L-ENI
523 (C)			BM-1
524 ...her:;		; (I)	L-ENI
524 (C)			BM-1
525 ...falls,		(, I)	L-ENI
525 (C)			BM-1
526 ...grain,		(, I)	L-ENI
526 (C)			BM-1
527 ...breast:;		(; I)	L-ENI
527 (C)			BM-1
528 ...word,		(, I)	L-ENI
528 (C)			BM-1
529 ...it,			F-ENI
529 ...it,;		;/ (I)	BM-1
529 ...it,			L-EN2
529 (C)			L-EN3
530 rest			I MS
...her l̸e̸s̸t̸			L-ENI
530 (C)			BM-1

329

She found no rest, and ever failed to draw
The quiet night into her blood, but lay
Contemplating her own unworthiness;
And when the pale and bloodless east began
To quicken to the sun, arose, and raised   535
Her mother too, and hand in hand they moved
Down to the meadow where the jousts were held,
And waited there for Yniol and Geraint.

And thither came the twain, and when Geraint
Beheld her first in field, awaiting him,   540

532 ...blood, but	(, I)	L-ENI
532 (C)		BM-1
533 ...unworthiness.;	;/ (I)	L-ENI
533 (C)		BM-1
534 But when...		Tn-30
534 And		
B̸u̸t̸ when...		T-E
535 ...sun, arose, and...	(2nd, I)	L-ENI
535 (C)		BM-1
537 ...held		F-ENI
537 (C)		BM-1
540 Beheld her there before him in the field		Tn-30;T-E
540 Beheld her there before him in the field		F-ENI
540 Beheld her there before him in the field,		
	,/ (I)	L-EN3
540 (C)		F-EN2
541 ...force,	(, I)	L-ENI
541 (C)		BM-1
546 ...and by̸e̸ the...		L-ENI
546 (C)		BM-1
547 ...in and...		F-ENI
547 (C)		L-EN3

He felt, were she the prize of bodily force,
Himself beyond the rest pushing could move
The chair of Idris. Yniol's rusted arms
Were on his princely person, but through these
Princelike his bearing shone; and errant knights   545
And ladies came, and by and by the town
Flowed in, and settling circled all the lists.
And there they fixt the forks into the ground,
And over these they placed the silver wand,
And over that the golden sparrow-hawk.   550
Then Yniol's nephew, after trumpet blown,
Spake to the lady with him and proclaimed,
'Advance and take, as fairest of the fair,
What I these two years past have won for thee,

---

548   re
     And th~~en~~ they...   Tn-30

549 ...they laid a silver...   Tn-30
549   placed
     ...they ~~laid~~ a silver...   T-E
549 ...placed a silver...   F-ENI
549 ...placed a silver wand   F-EN2
549 (C)   73

550 ...that they placed the sparrowhawk.   Tn-30
550   a golden
     ...that ~~they~~ ~~placed~~ ~~the~~ sparrowhawk.   T-E
550 ...that a golden...   F-ENI
550 (C)   73

552 ...proclaim'd   F-ENI
552 (C)   L-EN3

553 ...take as...fair~~y~~,   (, I)   L-ENI
553 ...take as...   BM-1
553 (C)   86

554 For I...won it for...   Tn-30;T-E
554 For I...won it for thee,   (, I)   L-ENI
554 For I...won it for...   BM-1
554 (C)   86

The prize of beauty.' Loudly spake the Prince,   555
'Forbear: there is a worthier,' and the knight
With some surprise and thrice as much disdain
Turned, and beheld the four, and all his face
Glowed like the heart of a great fire at Yule,
S̓o burnt he was with passion, crying out,   560
'Do battle for it then,' no more; and thrice
They clashed together, and thrice they brake their
                  spears.
Then each, dishorsed and drawing, lashed at each
So often and with such blows, that all the crowd
Wondered, and now and then from distant walls   565

---

555 ...Prince		F-ENI
555 ...Prince.		L-EN3
555 ...Prince,	,/ (I)	F-EN2
555 (C)		59

Sketch 558-560 A̶t̶ E̶n̶i̶d̶ &̶ G̶e̶r̶a̶i̶n̶t̶ g̶l̶a̶n̶c̶i̶n̶g̶ r̶e̶p̶l̶i̶e̶d̶

                                                        Tn-30

558 Turn'd and...		F-ENI
558 (C)		BM-1

559 ...Yule,	(, I)	L-ENI
559 (C)		BM-1

560 crying out,		
...passion, &̶ h̶e̶ c̶r̶i̶e̶d̶		T-E

562 ...together and...		F-ENI
562 ...together, and...	,/ (I)	F-EN2
562 (C)		59

563 ...each, dishorsed and drawing, lash'd		
	(,, I)	L-ENI
563 (C)		BM-1

564 ...blows that...		F-ENI
564 ...blows, that...	,/ (I)	L-EN3
564 (C)		F-EN2

There came a clapping as of phantom hands.
So twice they fought, and twice they breathed, and still
The dew of their great labour, and the blood
Of their strong bodies, flowing, drained their force.
But either's force was matched till Yniol's cry,   570
'Remember that great insult done the Queen,'
Increased Geraint's, who heaved his blade aloft,
And cracked the helmet through, and bit the bone,
And felled him, and set foot upon his breast,
And said, 'Thy name?' To whom the fallen man   575
Made answer, groaning,'Edyrn, son of Nudd!
Ashamed am I that I should tell it thee.
My pride is broken: men have seen my fall.'
'Then, Edyrn, son of Nudd,' replied Geraint,
'These two things shalt thou do, or else thou diest. 580
First, thou thyself, with damsel and with dwarf,

567	...fought, and...breathed, and...	(,, I)	L-ENI
567	(C)		BM-1
568	...labour and...		F-ENI
568	...labour, and...	,/ (I)	L-EN3
568	(C)		F-EN2
569	...bodies flowing drain'd...		F-ENI
569	...bodies, flowing, drain'd...	,/,/(I)	L-EN3
569	(C)		F-EN2
573	...the skull cap thro'...		Tn-30;T-E
573	And crackt the skull-cap thro,'...		F-ENI
573	(C)		L-EN3
575	...said, 'thy...		F-ENI
575	(C)		59
577	I am ashamed that...		Tn-30
577	am I		
	I̸ A̸m̸ ashamed that...		T-E
581	...thyself thy lady & thy dwarf		Tn-30;T-E
581	...thyself, thy lady, and thy dwarf,		F-ENI
581	(C)		73

Shalt ride to Arthur's court, and coming there,
Crave pardon for that insult done the Queen,
And shalt abide her judgment on it; next,
Thou shalt give back their earldom to thy kin.   585
These two things shalt thou do, or thou shalt die.'
And Edyrn answered, 'These things will I do,
For I have never yet been overthrown,
And thou hast overthrown me, and my pride
Is broken down, for Enid sees my fall!'   590
And rising up, he rode to Arthur's court,
And there the Queen forgave him easily.
And being young, he changed and came to loathe

---

582 ...court & being there   Tn-30;T-E
582 ..., and being there,   F-ENI
582 (C)   73

593 ...himself & t̸h̸r̸o̸v̸e̸ grew   Tn-30
593 ...changed himself & grew   T-E
593 ...changed himself, and grew   F-ENI
593 (C)   69

Alt. after 593
    I̸n̸ f̸a̸v̸o̸u̸r̸ w̸i̸t̸h̸/a̸l̸l̸ m̸e̸n̸ & a̸f̸t̸e̸r̸ f̸e̸l̸l̸   Tn-30;T-E
(followed by 596-c.)

594 To hate the sin that seem'd so like his own   Tn-30;
                                                T-E;F-ENI
594 (C)   69

595 Of Modred Arthur's nephew & fell at last   Tn-30;T-E
595 Of Modred,Arthur's nephew, and fell at last   F-ENI
595 (C)   69

596 ...the king.   F-ENI
596 (C)   73

Sketch 598 ff.
    Beneath the swelling bosom of the cloud
    Had cast her golden zone along the dark
    Rose Enid to ride with him & to be
    At fair Caerleon upon Usk by him
    [For so the Prince had warn'd her yestereve]
    Presented to the stately Guinevere.   H-35

His crime of traitor, slowly drew himself
Bright from his old dark life, and fell at last   595
In the great battle fighting for the King.

But when the third day from the hunting-morn
Made a low splendour in the world, and wings
Moved in her ivy, Enid, for she lay
With her fair head in the dim-yellow light,   600
Among the dancing shadows of the birds,
Woke and bethought her of her promise given
No later than last eve to Prince Geraint--
So bent he seemed on going the third day,
He would not leave her, till her promise given--   605
To ride with him this morning to the court,
And there be made known to the stately Queen,
And there be wedded with all ceremony.
At this she cast her eyes upon her dress,
And thought it never yet had looked so mean.   610
For as a leaf in mid-November is
To what it was in mid-October, seemed
The dress that now she looked on to the dress
She looked on ere the coming of Geraint.
And still she looked, and still the terror grew   615

598-599 Made a low splendour, Enid, for she lay   Tn-30
598-599 (C)   T-E

602   bethought her of her promise given
     Woke & remember'd how she bound herself   Tn-30

603 ...Geraint/ -   (- I)   L-ENI
603 (C)   BM-1

605 ..., till she bound herself   Tn-30
605   her promise given
     ...till she bound herself   T-E
605 ...given -   (- I)   L-ENI
605 (C)   BM-1

609 And when she cast her...   H-71a

610 It never yet had seem'd so mean & bare   H-71a

615 She lookt again & still the horror grew   Tn-30

335

Of that strange bright and dreadful thing, a court,
All staring at her in her faded silk:
And softly to her own sweet heart she said:

'This noble prince who won our earldom back,
So splendid in his acts and his attire,   620
Sweet heaven, how much I shall discredit him!
Would he could tarry with us here awhile,
But being so beholden to the Prince,
It were but little grace in any of us,
Bent as he seemed on going this third day,   625
To seek a second favour at this hands.

---

621 Sweet heavens, how...   T-E;F-ENI
621 (C)   L-EN2

(The second and third fascicle of L-EN2 offer a
problem. Page 32 (2nd fascicle) ends with line 621;
page 33 (3rd fascicle) begins with line 619.)

622 ...he but rest with us a day or twain-   Tn-30
622   tarry   o
    ...he but /r/e/s/t/ with us a day or tw/a/i/n/-   T-E
622 Would he but tarry with us a day or two;   F-ENI
622 ...awhile,   L-EN2
622 ...awhile!   L-EN3
622 (C)   73

627 ...but rest a breathing while   Tn-30
627   day or two
    ...but rest /a/ /b/r/e/a/t/h/i/n/g/ /w/h/i/l/e/   T-E
627 Yet if he would but rest a day or two,   F-ENI
627 (C)   L-EN2

628 ...work my fingers to the bone   Tn-30;T-E
628 ...work my fingers to the bone,   F-ENI
628   eye dim, & finger lame,   I MS
    ...work /m/y/ /f/i/n/g/e/r/s/ /t/o/ /t/h/e/ /b/o/n/e/,   L-EN2
628 (C)   L-EN3

629 Far rather than...   Tn-30;T-E
629 Far rather than...him.'   '/ (I)   L-ENI
629 Far rather than...   BM-1
629   liefer   I MS
    Far /r/a/t/h/e/r/ than...   L-EN2
629 (C)   L-EN3

Yet if he could but tarry a day or two,
Myself would work eye dim, and finger lame,
Far liefer than so much discredit him.'

Sketch 630-647
    And then she wish'd the Prince had found her first
    While yet her father was the ruling earl,
    And yet they lived in their old palace, burnt
    That fearful night in which arose the cry
    That Edeyrn's men were on them, & they fled
    With little save some jewels in a purse
    Which being sold & sold had bought them bread.
    Then she remembered how she used to watch.   Tn-30

Sketch 630-647 (Repeated in T-E save for the sixth line
               reading:)...jewels they had on   T-E

Second sketch 630-647
    And then she fell in longing for a dress
    Wh once her mother gave her, years ago,
    Three years ago - so costly was the work.
    Her gift on Yniol's birthday to be worn
    Who touch'd next morning on his sixtieth year.
    Her nurse had brought it in at close of day
    And lights were lit that they might look at it
    And while the three well-pleased were looking at
    And turning & admiring it - the work
    Appear'd so costly, there arose the cry
    That Edeyrn's men were on them & they fled
    With little save some jewels in a purse
    Wh being sold & sold had bought them life;
    And Edeyrn's men had caught them in their flight
    And placed them in the ruinous castle here
                   her
    In which the Prince had found t̶h̶e̶m̶ & she wish'd
    The Prince had found her in her ancient home
    Where everything was rich & orderly
    And where Limours had wooed her - that wild earl.
    Here was amother man; & after this
    She let her fancy flit across the past
    To roam the goodly places wh she knew
    And, last, remember'd   Tn-30

And Enid fell in longing for a dress   630
All branched and flowered with gold, a costly gift
Of her good mother, given her on the night
Before her birthday, three sad years ago,
That night of fire, when Edyrn sacked their house,
And scattered all they had to all the winds: 635
For while the mother showed it, and the two
Were turning and admiring it, the work

---

630 (No par. indent.; par. indent. symbol)   L-ENI
630 (C)   BM-1

632 Of   given
    W̸h̸ her...mother g̸a̸v̸e̸ her   Tn-30

633 ...ago̸,   (, I)   L-ENI
633 (C)   BM-1

634 That dreadful night when Edeyrn came upon them Tn-30
634   of fire   sack'd their house
    That d̸r̸e̸a̸d̸f̸u̸l̸ night when Edeyrn c̸a̸m̸e̸ u̸p̸o̸n̸ t̸h̸e̸m̸   T-E

636 And while
    T̸h̸e̸n̸ f̸i̸r̸s̸t̸ her mother...   Tn-30

637   it
    ...admiring r̸o̸s̸e̸ a̸ c̸r̸y̸ the work   Tn-30

Alt. before 638 And then she wish'd the prince had
                         found her first   H-71a

638 While yet they lived in their old palace, burnt
    That dreadful night on wh there rose the cry   H-71a
638 ...costly, the cry rose   Tn-30

639 ...were coming and...   H-71a

640 ...save some jewels in a purse.   H-71a

641 ...bread;   F-ENI
641 (C)   59

To both appeared so costly, rose a cry
That Edyrn's men were on them, and they fled
With little save the jewels they had on,   640
Which being sold and sold had bought them bread:
And Edyrn's men had caught them in their flight,
And placed them in this ruin; and she wished
The Prince had found her in her ancient home;
Then let her fancy flit across the past,   645
And roam the goodly places that she knew;
And last bethought her how she used to watch,
Near that old home, a pool of golden carp;
And one was patched and blurred and lustreless
Among his burnished brethren of the pool;   650

Alt. for 642 And Edyrn had not slain them in
                    his pride   H-71a

642 ...in their flight   Not ital. (I MS Instruction)
                                                   L-ENI
642 (C)   BM-1

643 But put them in the guarded castle hall   H-71a

Alt. after 643
        And made them wait tho noble on themselves
        And loved to see them poor & beggerly.   H-71a

646 ...knew/;   ;/ (I)   L-ENI
646 (C)   BM-1

647 ...watch   F-ENI
647 ...watch,   ,/ (I)   L-EN3
647 (C)   F-EN2

648 And then remember'd how she...   H-71a
648 ...carp, ;   ;/ (I)   L-ENI
648 (C)   BM-1

Alt. for 649 And one of these had lost her golden mail
                    And now she passed it   it movd
                    All blurred & hueless with dim disuse H-71a

650 ...pool.;   ;/ (I)   L-ENI
650 (C)   BM-1

And half asleep she made comparison
Of that and these to her own faded self
And the gay court, and fell asleep again;
And dreamt herself was such a faded form
Among her burnished sisters of the pool;   655
But this was in the garden of a king;
And though she lay dark in the pool, she knew
That all was bright; that all about were birds
Of sunny plume in gilded trellis-work;
That all the turf was rich in plots that looked   660
Each like a garnet or a turkis in it;

Draft 651 ff. She made a fanciful comparison
              [Tho' falling back to sleep] of that
                        & these
              With her own faded self & the gay court.
              Then slept again, for it was early morn.
                                                Tn-30
Draft 651 ff. (Repeated, cancelled, corrected)   T-E

653 ...again:;   ;/ (I)   L-ENI
653 (C)   BM-1

655   her
    Among ƭⱨҿ burnish'd...   T-E
655 ...pǫol.;   (; I)   L-ENI
655 (C)   BM-1

656 ...king:;   ;/ (I)   L-ENI
656 (C)   BM-1

657 ...pool, she...   (, I)   L-ENI
657 (C)   BM-1

658 ...bright, that...   F-ENI
658 ...bright,; that...   ;/ (I)   F-EN2
658 (C)   59

659 ...trellis - work:;   (; I)   L-ENI
659 (C)   BM-1

340

And lords and ladies of the high court went
In silver tissue talking things of state;
And children of the King in cloth of gold
Glanced at the doors or gamboled down the walks;   665
And while she thought 'They will not see me,' came
A stately queen whose name was Guinevere,
And all the children in their cloth of gold
Ran to her, crying, 'If we have fish at all

---

660 And fresh the turf, & beds of blossom glow'd   H-71a
660 The turf was rich in blossom beds that...   Tn-30
660   at all the   plots
    Th~~e~~ turf was rich in ~~blossom~~ ~~beds~~ that...   T-E

661 ...it:;   (: I)   L-ENI
661 (C)   BM-1

663 ...state:;   (: I)   L-ENI
663 (C)   BM-1

664 ...in cloth of gold   H-71a
664 ...the king in...   F-ENI
664 (C)   73

665 Glanced from the walls & gambol'd on the
                      walks   H-71a
665 ...walks:;   (; I)   L-ENI
665 (C)   BM-1

666   They will not see me come
    And while she thought Shall I hide in the pool H-71a
666 ...thought 'they...   F-ENI
666 (C)   73

667   whose name was
  ~~There~~ ~~came~~ a stately Queen ~~like~~ Guinevere   H-71a

669 ...her crying, 'if we...   F-ENI
669 ...her, crying, 'if we...   ,/(1st, I) L-EN2
669 ...crying, 'if we...   F-EN2
669 (C)   73

Let them be gold; and charge the gardeners now   670
To pick the faded creature from the pool,
And cast it on the mixen that it die.'
And therewithal one came and seized on her,
And Enid started waking, with her heart
All overshadowed by the foolish dream,   675
And lo! it was her mother grasping her
To get her well awake; and in her hand
A suit of bright apparel, which she laid
Flat on the couch, and spoke exultingly:

'See here, my child, how fresh the colours look   680

---

670 ...& tell the gardeners...   H-71a;Tn-30
670   charge
   ...gold: & ṭéḻḻ the gardeners...   T-E
670 ...gold;' and...   BM-1
670 (C)   L-EN3

671 To pick the hueless thing from out the pool   H-71a

674 ...started/ awaking,...   L-ENI
674 (C)   BM-1

Sketch 678 A gift & on her bidding to be worn
            Her mothers gift three years   H-35

679 ...couch and...   F-ENI
679 ...couch, and...   ,/ (I)   L-EN3
679 (C)   F-EN2

680   gay
   ...how ḟṛéṣḥ the colours...   H-71a

Alt. after 680
      It is my gift: we   not shame
      We would ǹóṭ ẃiḻḻiṅǵḻý ḍiṣǵṛáċé the Prince
      To whom we are beholden; & my self,
      For this long time   H-35

How fast they hold like colours of a shell
That keeps the wear and polish of the wave.
Why not? It never yet was worn, I trow:
Look on it, child, and tell me if ye know it.'

And Enid looked, but all confused at first,   685
Could scarce divide it from her foolish dream:
Then suddenly she knew it and rejoiced,
And answered, 'Yea, I know it; your good gift,
So sadly lost on that unhappy night;
Your own good gift!' 'Yea, surely,' said the dame,   690
'And gladly given again this happy morn.

---

681 **They** hold as fast as colours of a shell		H-71a
681 ...hold, like...		F-ENI
681 (C)		67
683 ...not? it...worn, I trow,		F-ENI
683 ...not? it...worn, I trow,:	:/ (I)	BM-1
683 ...not? it...		L-EN2
683 (C)		59
684 ...child, see if you know it		H-71a
684 Look to it...if you know...		Tn-30
684 ...if you know...		T-E
684 ...if you know...		F-ENI
684 (C)		69
686 ...dream/ :	(: I)	L-ENI
686 (C)		BM-1
687 ...rejoiced,	(, I)	L-ENI
687 (C)		BM-1
688 ...answer'd Is it not your gift to me,		Tn-30
688 Yea I know it: your good		
...answer'd. Y̶I̶s̶ i̶t̶ n̶o̶t̶ y̶o̶u̶r̶ gift, t̶o̶ m̶e̶		T-E
688 O̶h̶,		I MS
...answer'd, 'Y̶e̶a̶ I...		BM-1

For when the jousts were ended yesterday,
Went Yniol through the town, and everywhere
He found the sack and plunder of our house
All scattered through the houses of the town;   695
And gave command that all which once was ours
Should now be ours again: and yester-eve,

Alt. after 692   with

Last night when you were talking the prince
Came the & brought it, seeking favour of us,
Because we have but eat from back again,
And told me of a hundred other things
Which once were ours & will be ours again
All scatter'd thro' the houses in the town
And yesterevening I would/not tell you of it
But kept it for a sweet surprise at morn.
So take it now.
Because/you must have next your tender heart
In thanking that you bless no shame the prince   Tn-30

695 ...town: F-ENI
695 (C)   59

696 ...ours,   F-ENI
696 (C)   73

697 ...again; and...   F-ENI
697 (C)   59

698 While you were talking sweetly to the prince H-71a
698 While you were...   Tn-30;T-E;F-ENI
698 (C)   73

699 Came one who brought it whether bought or found
    How come by   H-71a
699 Came one who brought it seeking favour of us H-71a

700 For truly there are those who love us yet   H-71a

Alt. after 700
    And told me of a hundred other things
    That once were ours, all scatter'd thro' the house
                    in this corner or in that   H-71a

THE MARRIAGE OF GERAINT

While ye were talking sweetly with your Prince,
Came one with this and laid it in my hand,
For love or fear, or seeking favour of us,   700
Because we have our earldom back again.
And yester-eve I would not tell you of it,
But kept it for a sweet surprise at morn.
Yea, truly is it not a sweet surprise?
For I myself unwillingly have worn   705
My faded suit, as you, my child, have yours,
And howsoever patient, Yniol his.
Ah, dear, he took me from a goodly house,
With store of rich apparel, sumptuous fare,
And page, and maid, and squire, and seneschal,   710

---

702 And this I did not tell you yesterday
    But wishd to wake you with a sweet surprise (?)
                                                            H-71a

705 I know right well unwittingly have worn   'H-35

706 My   as you
    T̸h̸e̸s̸e̸ faded clothes ̸& ̸s̸o̸ my child have yours   H-35

Sketch 708-726
    Who took me truly from a noble house,
    Where there was goodly fare, & splendid (1 ?)
    And page & maid & seneschal & all
    That appertains to noble maintenance
    But come, my child, array yourself in this
    For tho mine own
    For let no damsel think, however fair
    She is not fairer in new clothes than old
    Nor must the great court ladies say the Prince
                        pick'd
    Has found a pretty beggar from the hedge
    Then were you shamed & worse wd shame the Prince
                                                            H-35

708 ...from a noble house   H-35
708   took
    ...he brought me...   Tn-30

709 ...apparel, goodly fare,   H-35

345

And pastime both of hawk and hound, and all
That appertains to noble maintenance.
Yea, and he brought me to a goodly house;
But since our fortune swerved from sun to shade,
And all through that young traitor, cruel need   715
Constrained us, but a better time has come;
So clothe yourself in this, that better fits
Our mended fortunes and a Prince's bride:
For though ye won the prize of fairest fair,
And though I heard him call you fairest fair,   720
Let never maiden think, however fair,
She is not fairer in new clothes than old.
And should some great court-lady say, the Prince
Hath picked a ragged-robin from the hedge,
And like a madman brought her to the court,   725

---

713 ...house /;	(; I)	L-ENI
713 (C)		BM-1
714 ...fortune slipt from...		H-35;Tn-30;T-E
714 ...fortune slipt from...		F-ENI
714 (C)		84
715 ...all thro' young...		H-35
718 ...fortunes & the prince's...		H-35
718 ...bride;		F-ENI
718 ...bride;:	:/ (I)	L-EN3
718 (C)		F-EN2
719 ...tho' you won...		H-35;Tn-30;T-E
719 ...tho' you won...		F-ENI
719 (C)		69
724 ...pick'd a pretty beggar from...		H-35;Tn-30;T-E
724 ...pickt a pretty beggar from...		F-ENI
724 ragged-robin		I MS
...pick'd a p̷r̷e̷t̷t̷y̷ b̷e̷g̷g̷a̷r̷ from...		L-EN3
724 (C)		F-EN2
726 ...were you shamed...		H-35;Tn-30;T-E

Then were ye shamed, and, worse, might shame the
               Prince
To whom we are beholden; but I know,
When my dear child is set forth at her best,
That neither court nor country, though they sought
Through all the provinces like those of old   730
That lighted on Queen Esther, has her match.'

Here ceased the kindly mother out of breath;
And Enid listened brightening as she lay;
Then, as the white and glittering star of morn
Parts from a bank of snow, and by and by   735
Slips into golden cloud, the maiden rose,
And left her maiden couch, and robed herself,
Helped by the mother's careful hand and eye,
Without a mirror, in the gorgeous gown;

---

726 ...were you shamed...   F-ENI
726 (C)   <u>69</u>

729 ...tho men sought   H-35

730 ...provinces as those of yore   H-35

732 ...breath,   F-ENI
732 ...breath,;   ;/ (I)   L-EN3
732 (C)   F-EN2

Sketch 733-739
      ~~listened brightening as she lay~~
~~And Enid but half-heard her in her joy~~
    ~~T~~   ~~& glittering~~
~~And rising then as the white morning star of morn~~
~~Parts from a bank of snow & by & by~~
~~That rising slips into a golden cloud/~~
~~Slips into golden cloud/the/maiden rose~~
~~Clothed all her beauty with her mother's eye~~
~~And left her maiden couch & robed herself~~
~~And hand to help her in the gorgeous gown/~~ Tn-30

734 Then as...   F-ENI
734 Then, as...   ,/ (I)   BM-1
734 (C)   L-EN2

Who, after, turned her daughter round, and said,   740
She never yet had seen her half so fair;
And called her like that maiden in the tale,
Whom Gwydion made by glamour out of flowers
And sweeter than the bride of Cassivelaun,
Flur, for whose love the Roman Caesar first   745
Invaded Britain, 'But we beat him back,
As this great Prince invaded us, and we,
Not beat him back, but welcomed him with joy
And I can scarcely ride with you to court,
For old am I, and rough the ways and wild;   750
But Yniol goes, and I full oft shall dream

---

740 ...round & r̸o̸u̸n̸d̸ & said   Tn-30
740 Who after turn'd her daughter round, and
                        said   (, I)   L-ENI
740 Who after turn'd...   BM-1
740 Who, after, turn'd...   ,/,/(I)   L-EN2
740 (C)   L-EN3

741 ...fair,;   ;/ (I)   L-ENI
741 (C)   BM-1

742 ...like the woman of old times   Tn-30
742   at maiden in the Tale
    ...like th̸e̸ w̸o̸m̸a̸n̸ o̸f̸ o̸l̸d̸ t̸i̸m̸e̸s̸   T-E

743   wy
    ...Gø̸ø̸dion...   Tn-30
743 /Whom...   L-ENI
743 (C)   BM--1

744   u   I MS
    ...of Cassivelaẃn,   L-ENI
744 (C)   BM-1

745 'Flur...   (' I)   L-ENI
745 'Flur...   BM-1
745 (C)   L-EN3

746 ...Britain, but...   F-ENI
746 (C)   67

THE MARRIAGE OF GERAINT

I see my princess as I see her now,
Clothed with my gift, and gay among the gay.'

   But while the women thus rejoiced, Geraint
Woke where he slept in the high hall, and called   755
For Enid, and when Yniol made report
Of that good mother making Enid gay
In such apparel as might well beseem
His princess, or indeed the stately Queen,
He answered: 'Earl, entreat her by my love,   760

---

747 ...us, but we   Tn-30
747   and   I MS
    ...great prince invaded us, b̸u̸t̸ we   L-ENI
747 ...great prince invaded...we   BM-1
747 ...great prince invaded...we,   ,/ (I)   L-EN2
747 ...great prince invaded...   L-EN3
747 (C)   73

750   I am
    For I̸ a̸m̸ old, & rough ̸& w̸i̸l̸d̸ the ways
                      & wild,   Tn-30

751 ...full oft̸e̸n̸ h̸e̸r̸e̸ shall dream   Tn-30

752   my princess   her
    s̸h̸a̸l̸l̸ t̸h̸i̸n̸k̸ I see y̸o̸u̸ as I see y̸o̸u̸ now   Tn-30

756 So said she: but when Yinol told Geraint   H-35

758   apparel   well beseem
    In such a dress as might b̸e̸c̸o̸m̸e̸ h̸i̸s̸ b̸r̸i̸d̸e̸   Tn-30

759 ...queen̸/',   ,/ (I)   L-ENI
759 ...stately queen,   BM-1
759 (C)   73

760 He answerd But entreat her, all of you,   H-35
760 ...entreat by...   Tn-30;T-E
760 ...answer'd,; 'Earl,...   (; I)   L-ENI
760 ...answer'd; 'Earl...   BM-1
760 (C)   73

349

```
Albeit I  give no reason but my wish,
That she ride with me in her faded silk.'
Yniol with that hard message went; it fell
Like flaws in summer laying lusty corn:
For Enid, all abashed she knew not why,              765
Dared not to glance at her good mother's face,
But silently, in all obedience,
Her mother silent too, nor helping her,
Laid from her limbs the costly-broidered gift,
And robed them in her ancient suit again,            770
And so descended.  Never man rejoiced
```

```
761 Yea, by my love, I have no reason for it.       H-35
761 I give no reason weightier than my w̶i̶s̶h̶ love
        But beg her by the love I bear to her        Tn-30
761  albeit           no
        I w̶i̶l̶l̶ n̶o̶t̶ give a̶ m̶y̶ reason, but my wish,   Tn-30
761 ...reason, but...                                F-ENI
761 ...reason/ but...                                BM-1
761 ...wish,                              ,/ (I)     L-EN2
761 (C)                                              L-EN3

762 That she ride...                                 H-35

Sketch 763 ff as he
        And Yniol took the message [& he] heard
        His own good consort laugh in merriment
        Before he enter'd & the message came          Tn-30

763 ...went, which fell,                             Tn-30
763          it
        ...went; w̶h̶i̶c̶h̶ fell                          T-E
763 ...fell,                                         F-ENI
763 (C)                                                73

764 ...corn/:                              :/ (I)    L-ENI
764 (C)                                              BM-1

Alt. after 764 On those two laughers high in merri-
                                      ment:          Tn-30
```

More than Geraint to greet her thus attired;
And glancing all at once as keenly at her
As careful robins eye the delver's toil,
Made her cheek burn and either eyelid fall,   775
But rested with her sweet face satisfied;
Then seeing cloud upon the mother's brow,
Her by both hands he caught, and sweetly said,

---

765   d
    And Enid hear*ing* with all humility,   H-35
765 And Enid...   Tn-30
    For
    And Enid...   T-E
765 ...Enid all...   F-ENI
765 (C)   73

Sketch 769-834
    Laid from her limbs her mothers wedding gift
    And robed them in her ancient silk again
    And rode to fair Caerleon where the Queen
    Embraced with all welcome as a friend   H-35

769 ...limbs her mother's glittering gift   Tn-30
769   the costly-braided
    ...limbs *her mother's glittering* gift   T-E
769 ...the costly-braided gift,   F-ENI
769 (C)   L-EN2

773 And glancing at her with as keen an eye   Tn-30
773   all at once as keenly at her
    And glancing *at her with as keen an eye*   T-E
773 ...her,   F-ENI
773 (C)   73

777 But seeing...   Tn-30
777 Then
    But seeing...   T-E

778 ...caught and sweetly said.   F-ENI
778 ...caught, and sweetly said.   ,/ (I)   L-EN2
778 ...said.   L-EN3
778 (C)   73

'O my new mother, be not wroth or grieved
At thy new son, for my petition to her.   780
When late I left Caerleon, our great Queen,
In words whose echo lasts, they were so sweet,
Made promise, that whatever bride I brought,
Herself would clothe her like the sun in Heaven.

---

779 Dear dame, I pray you be not wroth or grieve		H-35
779 (Par.) O mother, be not vext or wroth or		
	grieved	Tn-30
779 my new		
(Par.) O Mother be not ~~vext~~ ~~or~~ wroth...		T-E
779 (Par.) 'O~~r~~ my...		L-ENI
779 (C)		BM-1

780 Nor vext with me for...		H-35
780 At your new...		Tn-30;T-E
780 At your new...		F-ENI
780 (C)		73

783 ...promise that...		F-ENI
783 ...promise, that...	,/ (I)	L-EN2
783 (C)		L-EN3

785 ...ruin'd hold		Tn-30;T-E
785 ...this ruin'd hold,	(, I)	L-ENI
785 ...this ruin'd hold,		BM-1
785 (C)		73

786 And I, seeing one...		Tn-30
786 Beholding		
~~I~~ ~~seeing~~ one...		T-E

787		
Vow'd, could I gain her love, that		
our kind queen,		
~~our~~ ~~kind~~ ~~Queen~~		Tn-30
787...our kind Queen,		F-ENI
787 (C)		73

Thereafter, when I reached this ruined hall,   785
Beholding one so bright in dark estate,
I vowed that could I gain her, our fair Queen,
No hand but hers, should make your Enid burst
Sunlike from cloud--and likewise thought perhaps,
That service done so graciously would bind   790
The two together; fain I would the two
Should love each other: how can Enid find
A nobler friend? Another thought was mine;
I came among you here so suddenly,
That though her gentle presence at the lists   795
Might well have served for proof that I was loved,

---

791 The two together
      Ø𝑛é 𝑡ø 𝑡𝘩é ø𝑡𝘩é𝑡, for I wish the two   Tn-30
791 ...together, for I wish the two   T-E
791 ...together,; for I wish the two   ;/ (I)   L-ENI
791 ...together; for I wish the two   BM-1
791 (C)   73

792 To love each other: Enid cannot find   Tn-30;T-E
792 To love each other.; Enid cannot find ;/(I)   L-ENI
792 To love each other; Enid cannot find   BM-1
                      how sd
      To love each other;: Enid ¢𝑎𝑛𝑛ø𝑡 find :/(I)   L-EN3
792 To love each other: how should Enid find   F-EN3
792 (C)   73

793 ...thought I had   Tn-30;T-E
793   A   I MS
      A nobler friend⁄ 𝑎nother thought I had,; ⊙
                                    (; ⊙ I)   L-ENI
793 A nobler friend. Another thought I had;   BM-1
793 ...friend.? Another thought I had;   ?/ (I)   L-EN3
793 ...thought I had;   F-EN2
793 (C)   73

Alt. after 794 I told my love for her so suddenly,
                              T-E;F-EN1;L-ENI
Alt. after 794 (C)   BM-1

```
I doubted whether daughter's tenderness,
Or easy nature, might not let itself
Be moulded by your wishes for her weal;
Or whether some false sense in her own self          800
Of my contrasting brightness, overbore
Her fancy dwelling in this dusky hall;
And such a sense might make her long for court
And all its perilous glories: and I thought,
That could I someday prove such force in her         805
```

```
797 ...whether ~~pliability~~ filial softenss in her   Tn-30
797 ...whether filial softness in her                  T-E
797 I doubted whether filial softness in her,          F-ENI
797                          tenderness                I MS
    I doubted whether filial ~~softness in her~~,      BM-1
797 I doubted whether filial tenderness,               L-EN2
797 (C)                                                73

798      waxen nature
    Or ~~softness~~ in her had not...                  Tn-30
798 Or waxen nature had not...                         T-E
798      easy                                          I MS
    Or ~~waxen~~ nature had not let itself             L-ENI
798 Or easy nature had not let itself                  BM-1
798 Or easy nature, did not let itself    ,/ (I)       L-EN2
798 Or easy nature, did not let itself                 L-EN3
798 (C)                                                73

799 ...for ~~your~~ her...                             Tn-30
799 ...weal ~~/~~ ;                        {; I)       L-ENI
799 (C)                                                BM-1

802          dusky hall
    ...this ~~dusky hold~~                             Tn-30
802 ...hall,;                              ;/ (I)      L-ENI
802 (C)                                                BM-1

803 And that same sense might           Tn-30;T-E
803      such a                                        I MS
    And ~~that same~~ sense might...                   L-ENI
803 (C)                                                BM-1
```

Linked with such love for me, that at a word
(No reason given her) she could cast aside
A splendour dear to women, new to her,
And therefore dearer; or if not so new,
Yet therefore tenfold dearer by the power   810

---

804   its dangerous
     And all ~~the~~ ~~glories~~ ~~in~~ ~~its~~ &...   Tn-30
804 ...its dangerous glories...   T-E
804 ...its dangerous glories: and...   :/ (I)   F-ENI
804 ...its dangerous glories: and...   BM-1
804 (C)   73

805 I thought if I could prove that force in her   H-35
805 ...prove that force...   Tn-30;T-E;
                                                       F-ENI
805 (C)   L-EN2

807 Without a reason she wd scatter (?) from her
     As calmly (?) as woods their worn leaves,   H-35

808 ...her   F-ENI
808 (C)   L-EN2

Sketch 809-821   then not   I sd rest
     And therefore dearer. now, tho I remain
     sure of her faith &   do rest
     A prophet sure of mine own prophecy
              never
     That shadow of mistrust can come
     Between us; & this also will I say
     That when you flow in your old course again
     And we (I ?) you she shall wear your gifts
                                her
     By your own hearth with maybe on ~~your~~ knees
     Another gift of the high God.   H-35

809 ...dearer,; or...new   (; I)   L-ENI
809 ...new   BM-1
809 ...new,   ,/ (I)   L-EN2
809 (C)   L-EN3

355

Of intermitted usage; then I felt
That I could rest, a rock in ebbs and flows,
Fixt on her faith. Now, therefore, I do rest,
A prophet certain of my prophecy,
That never shadow of mistrust can cross   815
Between us. Grant me pardon for my thoughts:
And for my strange petition I will make
Amends hereafter by some gaudy-day,
When your fair child shall wear your costly gift

---

811 Of intermitted custom, ~~I~~ ~~saw~~ ~~that~~ ~~I~~ then I
                              felt,   Tn-30
811 Of intermitted custom, then...   T-E
811 Of intermitted custom,; then...   ;/ (I)   L-ENI
811   knew   I MS
    Of intermitted custom; then I ~~felt~~   BM-1
811 Of intermitted custom; then I felt   L-EN2
811 (C)   73

812 ...rest a rock...   F-ENI
812 (C)   L-EN2

813 ...faith: now therefore I...   F-ENI
813 ...Now, therefore, I...   ,/,/(I)   L-EN2
813 (C)   L-EN3

815 ...can ~~come~~ cross   Tn-30

816 ...thought   Tn-30
816 ...thoughts,   F-ENI
816 (C)   L-EN2

817-820
    I have not kept them long. I promise you
    That when we come once more, as come we shall
    To see you, she shall wear your noble gift
    Here at your own warm hearth, with, on her
                      knee   Tn-30;T-E
817-820
    I have not kept them long. I promise you
    That when we come once more, as come we shall,
    To see you, she shall wear your noble gift,
    Here at your own warm hearth, with, on her
                      knee,   F-ENI

THE MARRIAGE OF GERAINT

Beside your own warm hearth, with, on her knees,   820
Who knows? another gift of the high God,
Which, maybe, shall have learned to lisp you thanks.'

He spoke: the mother smiled, but half in tears,
Then brought a mantle down and wrapt her in it,

817-820

        I pledge my faith   I MS
I have not kept them long. ~~I promise you~~
That Enid, when we come, some golden day,   I MS
~~That when we come once more/ as come/we shall/~~
As come we will,   I MS
~~To see you/ she~~ shall wear your noble gift/
Here at your own warm hearth, with, on her
        knee,   BM-1
817-820 (C)   L-EN2

822 Which maybe shall...   F-ENI
822 Which, maybe, shall...   ,/,/ (I)   L-EN2
822 (C)   L-EN3

Sketch 823-825 Then smiled the mother pleased & half
        in tears
        To hear him talk so solemnly & well
        And kiss'd her Enid & they rode
        away.   Tn-30

Sketch 823-825 (Same as Tn-30 save following for
    line 825) And claspt & kiss'd her
        ~~And kiss'd her Enid~~ & ...   T-E

823 & alt. after 823
    Then smiled the mother, pleased, and half in tears
    To hear him talk so solemnly and well: F-ENI
823 & alt. after 823
    Then smiled the mother, pleased and half in
        tears,   (final, I)
    ~~To hear him talk so solemnly and well/~~   L-EN2
823 & alt. after 823 (C)   L-EN3

824 And brought...   F-ENI
824 (C)   L-EN2

And claspt and kissed her, and they rode away.   825

    Now thrice that morning Guinevere had climbed
The giant tower, from whose high crest, they say,
Men saw the goodly hills of Somerset,
And white sails flying on the yellow sea;
But not to goodly hill or yellow sea   830
Looked the fair Queen, but up the vale of Usk,
By the flat meadow, till she saw them come;
And then descending met them at the gates,
Embraced her with all welcome as a friend,
And did her honour as the Prince's bride,   835
And clothed her for her bridals like the sun;
And all that week was old Caerleon gay,

---

826 Now on that morning...   Tn-30;T-E
826 (Par.) Now on that...   F-ENI
826   thrice   I MS
     (Par.) Now on that...   L-EN2
826 (C)   L-EN3

827 The summit of that tower from wh they say Tn-30;T-E
827 The summit of that tower from which they say F-ENI
827 ...tower from...crest they say   BM-1
827 ...tower, from...crest they say   ,/ (I)   L-EN2
827 ...crest they say   L-EN3
827 (C)   59

832 ...come,;   ;/ (I)   L-ENI
832 (C)   BM-1

833 ...gates/,   (, I)   L-ENI
833 (C)   BM-1

836 ...clothed for...   H-35

THE MARRIAGE OF GERAINT

For by the hands of Dubric, the high saint,
They twain were wedded with all ceremony.

And this was on the last year's Whitsuntide.   840
But Enid ever kept the faded silk,
Remembering how first he came on her,
Drest in that dress, and how he loved her in it,
And all her foolish fears about the dress,
And all his journey toward her, as himself   845
Had told her, and their coming to the court.

And now this morning when he said to her,
'Put on your worst and meanest dress,' she found
And took it, and arrayed herself therein.

_____

839 And there were...   H-35

840 ...on the Whitsuntide before.   H-35

843 ...it/ ,   (, I)   L-ENI
843 (C)   BM-1

844 ...dress/ ,   (, I)   L-ENI
844 (C)   BM-1

845 ...her, as...   ,/ (I)   L-ENI
845 (C)   BM-1

848 'Put...dress,' she...   ('' I)   L-ENI
848 (C)   BM-1

849 ...it and...   F-ENI
849 ...it, and...   ,/ (I)   L-EN3
849 (C)   F-EN3

359

Geraint and Enid

O purblind race of miserable men,
How many among us at this very hour
Do forge a life-long trouble for ourselves,
By taking true for false, or false for true;
Here, through the feeble twilight of this world   5
Groping, how many, until we pass and reach
That other, where we see as we are seen!

    So fared it with Geraint, who issuing forth
That morning, when they both had got to horse,
Perhaps because he loved her passionately,   10

---

3 ...for themselves   Tn-30;T-E
3   our   I MS
  ...for ~~them~~selves,   L-ENI
3 (C)   BM-1

4 ...taking false for true, or true for false, Tn-30;T-E
4   2   1   I MS
  By taking false for true, or true for false; L-ENI
4 (C)   BM-1

5 Here thro...world/   L-ENI
5 Here thro...   BM-1
5 Here, thro...   ,/ (I)   L-EN2
5 (C)   L-EN3

7 ...seen. !   (! I)   L-ENI
7 (C)   BM-1

And felt that tempest brooding round his heart,
Which, if he spoke at all, would break perforce
Upon a head so dear in thunder, said:
'Not at my side. I charge thee ride before,
Ever a good way on before; and this   15
I charge thee, on thy duty as a wife,
Whatever happens, not to speak to me,
No, not a word!' and Enid was aghast;
And forth they rode, but scarce three paces on,
When crying out, 'Effeminate as I am,   20
I will not fight my way with gilded arms,
All shall be iron;' he loosed a mighty purse,
Hung at his belt, and hurled it toward the squire.
So the last sight that Enid had of home

---

11 ...heart		F-ENI
11 ...heart,	,/ (I)	L-EN2
11 (C)		L-EN3

12 Which if...all would		F-ENI
12 Which, if...all, would	,/,/ (I)	L-EN2
12 (C)		L-EN3

13 ...dear, in...said:	:/ (I)	L-ENI
13 ...dear, in...		BM-1
13 ...dear/ in...		L-EN3
13 (C)		F-EN2

14 N̷o̷t̷ a̷t̷ m̷y̷ s̷i̷d̷e̷ I charge you r̷i̷d̷e̷ b̷e̷f̷o̷r̷e̷ ride not at
                              my side
   Ride e̷v̷e̷r̷ o̷n̷ a̷ s̷p̷a̷c̷e̷ b̷e̷f̷o̷r̷e̷ m̷e̷ &̷ t̷h̷i̷s̷   Tn-30
14 Not at my side! I charge you ride before,
   I̷ c̷h̷a̷r̷g̷e̷ y̷o̷u̷ r̷i̷d̷e̷ n̷o̷t̷ a̷t̷ m̷y̷ s̷i̷d̷e̷   T-E
14 ...side! I charge you ride...   F-ENI
14 (C)   73

15 But ever a good way before & this s̷t̷i̷l̷l̷   Tn-30
15   way on
   B̷u̷t̷ Ever a good s̷p̷a̷c̷e̷ before; & this   T-E

16 ...charge you on your duty...   Tn-30;T-E
16 ...charge you, on your duty...   F-ENI
16 (C)   73

362

Was all the marble threshold flashing, strown   25
With gold and scattered coinage, and the squire
Chafing his shoulder: then he cried again,
'To the wilds!' and Enid leading down the tracks
Through which he bad her lead him on, they past
The marches, and by bandit-haunted holds,   30
Gray swamps and pools, waste places of the hern,
And wildernesses, perilous paths, they rode:
Round was their pace at first, but slackened soon:
A stranger meeting them had surely thought
They rode so slowly and they looked so pale,   35

---

18 was aghast		
...Enid w̶o̶n̶d̶e̶r̶'d̶ a̶t̶ him.		Tn-30
18 ...aghast a̶t̶ h̶i̶m̶		T-E
18 No not...aghast.		F-ENI
18 No, not...aghast.;	,/;/(I)	L-EN2
18 (C)		L-EN3
20 ...out 'Effeminate...		F-ENI
20 (C)		73
22 ...iron; ' he...	'/ (I)	**L-ENI**
22 (C)		BM-1
23 toward		
...it a̶t̶ the squire.		Tn-30
25 ...marble ̸ threshold...		L-ENI
25 (C)		BM-1
32 ...paths, they rode.	,/ (I)	L-ENI
32 ...rode.		BM-1
32 ...rode. :	(: I)	L-EN2
32 (C)		L-EN3
33 (Omitted)		F-ENI
33 (I MS, correct)		L-EN2
33 (C)		L-EN3
34 ...thought,		F-ENI
34 (C)		67
35 So slow their pace was & they...		H-35

That each had suffered some exceeding wrong.
For he was ever saying to himself,
'O I that wasted time to tend upon her,
To compass her with sweet observances,
To dress her beautifully and keep her true'--   40
And there he broke the sentence in his heart
Abruptly, as a man upon his tongue
May break it, when his passion masters him.
And she was ever praying the sweet heavens
To save her dear lord whole from any wound.   45

```
37 ...himself                                          F-ENI
37 (C)                                                    73


38 ...tend on her                                       H-35


39 That compast her with all observances               H-35


40              true
   ...keep her f̶a̶i̶r̶ -                                  H-35


41 ...true̶'̶ -                           -/ (I)        L-ENI
41 (C)                                                  BM-1


42 ...heart̷                                           L-ENI
42 (C)                                                  BM-1


47 Accusing her sweet self, examining how
   For some unthought-of failing in herself            H-35
47 ...herself                                          F-ENI
47 (C)                                                  BM-1


48 That made...                                         H-35


49 Then the...                                          H-35
49        G      P                                      I MS
   ...the g̷reat p̷lover's...                           L-ENI
49 ...the Great Plover's...                             BM-1
49 (C)                                                  F-EN2


50 ...& looking round...                                H-35
50 ...waste̷ she...                                    L-ENI
50 (C)                                                  BM-1
```

364

And ever in her mind she cast about
For that unnoticed failing in herself,
Which made him look so cloudy and so cold;
Till the great plover's human whistle amazed
Her heart, and glancing round the waste she feared   50
In every wavering brake an ambuscade.
Then thought again, 'If there be such in me,
I might amend it by the grace of Heaven,
If he would only speak and tell me of it.'

But when the fourth part of the day was gone,   55
Then Enid was aware of three tall knights
On horseback, wholly armed, behind a rock

```
52 ...again. if such a fault there be                    H-35
52 And even thought...                                   H-35
52 ...again 'if...me,                      ,/ (I)        L-ENI
52 ...again 'if...                                       BM-1
52 (C)                                                   73

53 ...of heaven,                           ,/ (I)        L-ENI
53 ...of heaven,                                         BM-1
53 (C)                                                   73

54          wd only
   Wd he but speak & tell me: [ so she thought.]         H-35

55 ...the third part...                                  H-35
55          fourth
   ...the t̸h̸i̸r̸d̸ part...                                 Tn-30

56          tall
   ...three a̸r̸m̸d̸ men                                    H-35

57-58          all in arms          behind a rock
      On horseback, waiting for them, varlets all;
      In shadow,                                         H-35
57-58          wholly arm'd, behind a rock
      On horseback, waiting for them, valets all;
      In shadow                                          Tn-30
57 ...horseback, wholly arm'd, behind a rock/
                       (first 2 commas I)                L-ENI
57 (C)                                                   BM-1
```

365

In shadow, waiting for them, caitiffs all;
And heard one crying to his fellow, 'Look,
Here comes a laggard hanging down his head,   60
Who seems no bolder than a beaten hound;
Come, we will slay him and will have his horse
And armour, and his damsel shall be ours.'

    Then Enid pondered in her heart, and said:
'I will go back a little to my lord,   65
And I will tell him all their caitiff talk;
For, be he wroth even to slaying me,
Far liefer by his dear hand had I die,
Than that my lord should suffer loss or shame.'

    Then she went back some paces of return,   70
Met his full frown timidly firm, and said;

58	...them, varlets all;	F-ENI
58	caitiffs	I MS
	...them, ~~varlets~~ all;	L-EN3
58	(C)	F-EN2
59	his fellow	
	...crying to the other look	H-35
60	...laggard with his head full low	H-35
61	Who looks no bolder...	H-35
62	...will take his...	H-35
64	in	
	...ponder'd ~~with~~ her...	Tn-30
64	...said,;	;/ (I)	L-ENI
64	...said;	BM-1
64	(C)	73
65	I will abide the coming of my lord	H-35
65	'I...	(' I)	L-ENI
65	(C)	BM-1
67	For be...	F-ENI
67	For, be...	,/ (I)	L-EN2
67	(C)	L-EN3

'My lord, I saw three bandits by the rock
Waiting to fall on you, and heard them boast
That they would slay you, and possess your horse
And armour, and your damsel should be theirs.'   75

   He made a wrathful answer: 'Did I wish
Your warning or your silence? one command
I laid upon you, not to speak to me,
And thus ye keep it! Well then, look--for now,

---

68 Far liever by...		H-35;T-E
68 Far liever by...die		F-ENI
68 Far liever by...die,	,/ (I)	L-EN2
68 Far liever by...		L-EN3
68 (C)		73
69 ...shame.'	(' I)	L-ENI
69 (C)		BM-1
70 some paces of return		
...back, ~met~ ~his~ ~full~ ~frown~ ~&~ ~said~		Tn-30
71 ...said:		F-ENI
71 (C)		78
74 ...you, and...	,/ (I)	L-ENI
74 (C)		BM-1
76 Did I wish		
...answer '~I~ ~desired~		Tn-30
76 ...answer. 'Did...		F-ENI
76 (C)		73
77 Your silence, not your warning: one...		Tn-30
77 Your silence or your warning? one...		T-E
77 Your silence or your warning? one...		F-ENI
77 (C)		62
79 ...thus you keep...		Tn-30;T-E
79 ...thus you keep...now		F-ENI
79 ...thus you keep...now,	,/	BM-1
79 ...thus you keep...		L-EN2
79 (C)		73

Whether ye wish me victory or defeat,⠀⠀⠀⠀⠀⠀⠀⠀80
Long for my life, or hunger for my death,
Yourself shall see my vigour is not lost.'

⠀⠀Then Enid waited pale and sorrowful,
And down upon him bare the bandit three.
And at the midmost charging, Prince Geraint⠀⠀⠀⠀85
Drave the long spear a cubit through his breast
And out beyond; and then against his brace
Of comrades, each of whom had broken on him
A lance that splintered like an icicle,
Swung from his brand a windy buffet out⠀⠀⠀⠀⠀90
Once, twice, to right, to left, and stunned the twain
Or slew them, and dismounting like a man
That skins the wild beast after slaying him,
Stript from the three dead wolves of woman born
The three gay suits of armour which they wore,⠀⠀95

---

80 Whether you wish...⠀⠀⠀⠀⠀⠀⠀⠀⠀⠀⠀⠀⠀⠀⠀⠀⠀Tn-30;T-E
80 Whether you wish..defeat ≠ ,⠀⠀⠀⠀⠀⠀⠀(, I)⠀⠀⠀⠀L-ENI
80 Whether you wish...⠀⠀⠀⠀⠀⠀⠀⠀⠀⠀⠀⠀⠀⠀⠀⠀⠀⠀BM-1
80 (C)⠀⠀⠀⠀⠀⠀⠀⠀⠀⠀⠀⠀⠀⠀⠀⠀⠀⠀⠀⠀⠀⠀⠀⠀⠀⠀⠀⠀73

83 ...sorrowful,⠀⠀⠀⠀⠀⠀⠀⠀⠀⠀⠀⠀⠀⠀(, I)⠀⠀⠀⠀L-ENI
83 (C)⠀⠀⠀⠀⠀⠀⠀⠀⠀⠀⠀⠀⠀⠀⠀⠀⠀⠀⠀⠀⠀⠀⠀⠀⠀⠀BM-1

84 And downward on him...⠀⠀⠀⠀⠀⠀⠀⠀⠀⠀⠀⠀⠀H-35

86 ...spear a shaft (1 ?) thro' his...⠀⠀⠀⠀H-35

87 And out behind him. Then against...⠀⠀⠀H-35

91 ...to left to right...⠀⠀⠀⠀⠀⠀⠀⠀⠀⠀⠀⠀⠀⠀H-35
91 Once more to...⠀⠀⠀⠀⠀⠀⠀⠀⠀⠀⠀⠀⠀⠀⠀⠀⠀⠀T-E
91⠀⠀⠀⠀⠀twice,⠀⠀⠀⠀⠀⠀⠀⠀⠀⠀⠀⠀⠀⠀⠀⠀⠀⠀⠀I MS
⠀⠀Once, m̶o̶r̶e̶ to right..⠀⠀⠀⠀⠀⠀⠀⠀(, I)⠀⠀⠀⠀L-ENI
91 (C)⠀⠀⠀⠀⠀⠀⠀⠀⠀⠀⠀⠀⠀⠀⠀⠀⠀⠀⠀⠀⠀⠀⠀⠀⠀⠀BM-1

And let the bodies lie, but bound the suits
Of armour on their horses, each on each,
And tied the bridle-reins of all the three
Together, and said to her, 'Drive them on
Before you;' and she drove them through the waste.　100

　　He followed nearer; ruth began to work
Against his anger in him, while he watched
The being he loved best in all the world,
With difficulty in mild obedience
Driving them on: he fain had spoken to her,　　　105
And loosed in words of sudden fire the wrath
And smouldered wrong that burnt him all within;
But evermore it seemed an easier thing
At once without remorse to strike her dead,
Than to cry 'Halt,' and to her own bright face　　110
Accuse her of the least immodesty:

| 95 ...wore, | (, I) | L-ENI |
| 95 (C) | | BM-1 |

| 96 ...lie;, but... | ,/ (I) | L-ENI |
| 96 (C) | | BM-1 |

Sketch for 101 and ff. Read every other line for se-
　　　　　　　　quence)
　　　　　　　　　nearer:　in scarce longer time
　　He follow'd still, but nearer:　ere an hour
　　Than at Caeleron the full-tided Usk
　　Had vanish'd, she that kept a watch, beheld
　　Before he turn to fall seaward again
　　In the first shallow shade of a deep wood,
　　Pauses did she that kept a watch
　　Before a grove of stubborn-shafted oaks　　H-35

105 ...on ~~before her &~~ he...		Tn-30
105 ...on, : he...her,	:/(:, I)	L-ENI
105 (C)		BM-1

Sketch 106-107 ~~Had spoken & have loosed his wrath &~~
　　　　　　　　　　~~wrong~~　　　　　　　　　　　Tn-30

| 110 ...cry halt, and... | F-ENI |
| 110 (C) | L-EN2 |

And thus tongue-tied, it made him wroth the more
That she <u>could</u> speak whom his own ear had heard
Call herself false: and suffering thus he made
Minutes an age: but in scarce longer time   115
Than at Caerleon the full-tided Usk,
Before he turn to fall seaward again,
Pauses, did Enid, keeping watch, behold
In the first shallow shade of a deep wood,
Before a gloom of stubborn-shafted oaks,   120
Three other horsemen waiting, wholly armed,
Whereof one seeméd far larger than her lord,
And shook her pulses, crying, 'Look, a prize!
Three horses and three goodly suits of arms,
And all in charge of whom? a girl: set on.'   125
'Nay,' said the second, 'yonder comes a knight.'
The third, 'A craven; how he hangs his head.'
The giant answered merrily, 'Yea, but one?
Wait here, and when he passes fall upon him.'

---

112 ...tongue-tied it...			F-ENI
112 ...tongue-tied, it...		,/ (I)	L-EN2
112 (C)			L-EN3

114 Call	& suffering	made	
A̸c̸c̸u̸s̸é herself ø̸f̸ false (1 ?) : thus he p̸á̸s̸t̸			Tn-30

115 Minutes			
An age ø̸f̸ p̸á̸i̸n̸; but...			Tn-30
115 ...age;: but...		:/ (I)	L-ENI
115 (C)			BM-1

124 Three horsemen & ...	Tn-30

125 ...charge of a mere girl:	set...	H-35;Tn-30;T-E	
125 ...charge of a mere girl:	set on.'	F-ENI	
125	whom? a	I MS	
...charge of á̸ m̸é̸r̸é̸ girl:	set on.'	L-EN2	
125 (C)		L-EN3	

126 Another said but yonder...	H-35
126 'Nay' said...	F-ENI
126 (C)	62

And Enid pondered in her heart and said,   130
'I will abide the coming of my lord,
And I will tell him all their villainy.
My lord is weary with the fight before,
And they will fall upon him unawares.
I needs must disobey him for his good;   135
How should I dare obey him to his harm?
Needs must I speak, and though he kill me for it,
I save a life dearer to me than mine.'

And she abode his coming, and said to him
With timid firmness, 'Have I leave to speak?'   140
He said, 'Ye take it, speaking,' and she spoke.

'There lurk three villains yonder in the wood,
And each of them is wholly armed, and one
Is larger-limbed than you are, and they say

127	a craven how		
	...third 'h̸e̸ w̸i̸l̸l̸ n̸o̸t̸ f̸i̸g̸h̸t̸, he...		Tn-30
128 To whom the giant answerd Yea but one			H-35
128	merrily		
	T̸o̸ w̸h̸o̸m̸ the Giant answer'd, 'Yea...		Tn-30
128 ...one ̸ ?		(? I)	L-ENI
128 (C)			BM-1
131 ...lord			F-ENI
131 ...lord,		,/ (I)	L-EN3
131 (C)			F-EN2
134 ...unawares ̸ .		(. I)	L-ENI
134 (C)			BM-1
137 ̸I needs...			Tn-30
141 ...said 'you take...			Tn-30;T-E
141 ...said, 'You take...			F-ENI
141 (C)			69
144 Is larger limb'd than...			F-ENI
144 Is larger-limb'd than...		(- MS)	BM-1
144 (C)			L-EN2

That they will fall upon you while ye pass.'   145

    To which he flung a wrathful answer back:
'And if there were an hundred in the wood,
And every man were larger-limbed than I,
And all at once should sally out upon me,
I swear it would not ruffle me so much   150
As you that not obey me. Stand aside,
And if I fall, cleave to the better man.'

    And Enid stood aside to wait the event,
Not dare to watch the combat, only breathe
Short fits of prayer, at every stroke a breath.   155
And he, she dreaded most, bare down upon him.
Aimed at the helm, his lance erred; but Geraint's,
A little in the late encounter strained,
Struck through the bulky bandit's corselet home,
And then brake short, and down his enemy rolled,   160

---

145 ...while you pass'		Tn-30;T-E
145 ...while you pass.'		F-ENI
145 (C)		<u>69</u>
147 ...were a hundred...		Tn-30
148 ...were larger limb'd than...		F-ENI
148 ...were larger-limb'd than...	(- MS)	BM-1
148 (C)		L-EN2
152 ...fall cleave...		F-ENI
152 ...fall, cleave...	,/ (I)	L-EN3
152 (C)		F-EN2
153 And Enid drew a little on one side		H-35
154 To watch nor dared to watch the issue of it		H-35
155 And breathe short prayers with every...		H-35
155 ...breath,	(. I)	L-ENI
155 (C)		BM-1
156 And down came the Giant: his long lance		H-35
156 ...him/	(. I)	L-ENI
156 (C)		BM-1

And there lay still; as he that tells the tale
Saw once a great piece of a promontory,
That had a sapling growing on it, slide
From the long shore-cliff's windy walls to the beach,
And there lie still, and yet the sapling grew: 165
So lay the man transfixt. His craven pair
Of comrades making slowlier at the Prince,
When now they saw their bulwark fallen, stood;
On whom the victor, to confound them more,
Spurred with his terrible war-cry; for as one,   170
That listens near a torrent mountain-brook,
All through the crash of the near cataract hears
The drumming thunder of the huger fall
At distance, were the soldiers wont to hear
His voice in battle, and be kindled by it,   175
And foemen scared, like that false pair who turned
Flying, but, overtaken, died the death
Themselves had wrought on many an innocent.

  Thereon Geraint, dismounting, picked the lance

---

157 Erred from his enemy's helm but Prince Geraint   H-35
157 ...helm/ , his lance err'd, but...   (, I)   L-ENI
157 (C)   BM-1

158 Tho somewhat in the last encounter straind   H-35

160 ...roll'd   F-ENI
160 ...roll'd,   ,/ (I)   BM-1
160 (C)   L-EN2

161 ...still, as...tale,   F-ENI
161 ...tale,   L-EN2
161 (C)   73

163 ...it, slip   Tn-30;T-E
163 ...it, slip   F-ENI
163 (C)   73

167 ...comrades, making...   F-ENI
167 (C)   84

170 ...one,   (, I)   L-ENI
170 (C)   BM-1

That pleased him best, and drew from those dead
                     wolves   180
Their three gay suits of armour, each from each,
And bound them on their horses, each on each,
And tied the bridle-reins of all the three
Together, and said to her, 'Drive them on
Before you,' and she drove them through the wood.   185

   He followed nearer still: the pain she had
To keep them in the wild ways of the wood,
Two sets of three laden with jingling arms,
Together, served a little to disedge
The sharpness of that pain about her heart: 190
And they themselves, like creatures gently born
But into bad hands fallen, and now so long
By bandits groomed, pricked their light ears, and felt
Her low firm voice and tender government.

   So through the green gloom of the wood they past, 195
And issuing under open heavens beheld

---

195 ...they w̶e̶n̶t̶ past   Tn-30;T-E

197 A little thorpe with...   H-35

198 And underneath a meadow gemlike set   H-35
198 ...beneath, a...   (, I)   L-ENI
198 (C)   BM-1

199 In the brown waste and...   H-35

201 ...youth who in...   H-35

202-206 ...and the Prince
    Called to him as he past The damsel here
    Is faint for food I pray you let her eat   H-35

203 ...pale;:   :/ (I)   L-ENI
203 (C)   BM-1

204 Then
    A̶n̶d̶ moving...   Tn-30

A little town with towers, upon a rock,
And close beneath, a meadow gemlike chased
In the brown wild, and mowers mowing in it:
And down a rocky pathway from the place   200
There came a fair-haired youth, that in his hand
Bare victual for the mowers: and Geraint
Had ruth again on Enid looking pale:
Then, moving downward to the meadow ground,
He, when the fair-haired youth came by him, said,   205
'Friend, let her eat; the damsel is so faint.'
'Yea, willingly,' replied the youth; 'and thou,
My lord, eat also, though the fare is coarse,
And only meet for mowers;' then set down
His basket, and dismounting on the sward   210
They let the horses graze, and ate themselves.
And Enid took a little delicately,
Less having stomach for it than desire
To close with her lord's pleasure; but Geraint
Ate all the mowers' victual unawares,   215

---

207 ...the youth & you   H-35;T-E
207 ...replied the ~~fair/haired~~ youth'& you,   Tn-30
207 ...; 'and you,   F-ENI
207 (C)   73

208 Sir Knight eat...   H-35
208 My lord,
    ~~And you~~ eat...   Tn-30

210 And they twain dismounting on the grass   H-35

211 Let all the horses graze...   H-35
211 ...themselves~~,~~.   (. I)   L-ENI
211 (C)   BM-1

212 ...Enid ate a little...   H-35

Alt. after 212 And drank a little also but the
                              Prince   H-35

213-214 Less   than desire
        ~~Not~~ having stomach for it~~,~~ ~~but Geraint her~~
                      ~~lord~~ Geraint
        To close with her lord's pleasure   Tn-30

And when he found all empty, was amazed;
And 'Boy,' said he, 'I have eaten all, but take
A horse and arms for guerdon; choose the best.'
He, reddening in extremity of delight,
'My lord, you overpay me fifty-fold.'   220
'Ye will be all the wealthier,' cried the Prince.
'I take it as free gift, then,' said the boy,
'Not guerdon; for myself can easily,
While your good damsel rests, return, and fetch
Fresh victual for these mowers of our Earl;   225
For these are his, and all the field is his,

---

216 ...amazed.;   ;/ (I)   L-ENI
216 (C)   BM-1

Alt. after 216 At his own work   H-35

217   'boy' said he 'I have eaten all but take
    And ~~cried My boy as guerdon of as gift~~   Tn-30

218 A horse & arms for guerdon
    ~~Take thou a horse and/arms~~ choose the best.   Tn-30

219   extremity of delight
    ...in ~~his pleasure & surprise~~   Tn-30

221 You will...   Tn-30;T-E
221 'You will...   F-ENI
221 (C)   <u>69</u>

222 He answerd I receive it then as gift   Tn-30
222   take it as free gift said the boy
    ~~He answer'd~~ 'I ~~receive it~~ then as ~~gift~~   T-E

223   for myself
    ...guerdon & can easily ~~return~~   Tn-30

224-225 While your good damsel rests return & fetch
    ~~And fetch~~ fresh victual for these mowers ~~here~~ of
                            our earl   Tn-30

376

And I myself am his; and I will tell him
How great a man thou art: he loves to know
When men of mark are in his territory:
And he will have thee to his palace here,   230
And serve thee costlier than with mowers' fare.'

    Then said Geraint, 'I wish no better fare:
I never ate with angrier appetite
Than when I left your mowers dinnerless.
And into no Earl's palace will I go.   235
I know, God knows, too much of palaces!

---

226 ...his & I am also his all...   Tn-30

227 And I am also his & I will tell him
    And I will tell out lord/who loves to know   Tn-30
227 I am his servant & this field is his   Tn-30
227 ...I am also his...   T-E
227   myself   I MS
    And I am also his;...   L-ENI
227 (C)   BM-1

228 ...man you are...   Tn-30;T-E
228 ...man you are - he...   F-ENI
228 ...man you are: he...   L-EN2
228 (C)   73

229 What men...   Tn-30

230 ...have you to...   Tn-30;T-E;F-ENI
230 (C)   73

231 ...serve you costlier...   Tn-30;T-E;F-ENI
231 (C)   73

232 ...fare;:   (: I)   L-ENI
232 (C)   BM-1

235   palace   P MS
    ...Earl's place will...   L-ENI
235 (C)   BM-1

And if he want me, let him come to me.
But hire us some fair chamber for the night,
And stalling for the horses, and return
With victual for these men, and let us know.'   240

   'Yea, my kind lord,' said the glad youth, and went,
Held his head high, and thought himself a knight,
And up the rocky pathway disappeared,
Leading the horse, and they were left alone.

   But when the Prince had brought his errant eyes   245
Home from the rock, sideways he let them glance
At Enid, where she droopt: his own false doom,
That shadow of mistrust should never cross

---

237 ...me×́ .	(. I)	L-ENI
237 (C)		BM-1
239 And stabling for...		Tn-30;T-E
239 And stabling for...		F-ENI
239 stalling		I MS
And s̸t̸a̸b̸l̸i̸n̸g̸ for...		L-EN2
239 (C)		L-EN3
241 kind said glad		
...my f̸a̸i̸r̸ lord', r̸e̸t̸u̸r̸n̸d̸ the youth...		Tn-30
245-251 (Par.) He cast a side glance on her where she sat		
saw (?)		
Then t̸h̸o̸u̸g̸h̸t̸ (?) the mowers labouring dinner-		
less		Tn-30
245-251 (Par.) H̸e̸ c̸a̸s̸t̸ a̸ s̸i̸d̸e̸ g̸l̸a̸n̸c̸e̸ a̸t̸ her w̸h̸e̸r̸e̸ she s̸a̸t̸		
Then mark'd the mowers labouring dinnerless		T-E
247 ...Enid where...		F-ENI
247 ...Enid, where...	,/ (I)	L-EN2
247 (C)		L-EN3
250 (Omitted)		F-ENI
250 (C)		BM-1

378

Betwixt them, came upon him, and he sighed;
Then with another humorous ruth remarked   250
The lusty mowers labouring dinnerless,
And watched the sun blaze on the turning scythe,
And after nodded sleepily in the heat.
But she, remembering her old ruined hall,
And all the windy clamour of the daws   255
About her hollow turret, plucked the grass
There growing longest by the meadow's edge,
And into many a listless annulet,
Now over, now beneath her marriage ring,
Wove and unwove it, till the boy returned   260
And told them of a chamber, and they went;
Where, after saying to her, 'If ye will,
Call for the woman of the house,' to which
She answered, 'Thanks, my lord;' the two remained

---

251 Then mark'd the mowers labouring dinnerless,   F-ENI
251 (C)   BM-1

261 ...went.:   :/ (I)   L-ENI
261 ...went: BM-1
261 ...went:;   ;/ (I)   L-EN2
261 ...went: L-EN3
261 (C)   F-EN2

262 ...If you will   Tn-30;T-E
262 Where after..., 'If you will,   F-ENI
262 Where, after..., 'If you will,   (1st, I)   L-EN2
262 ..., 'If you will,   L-EN3
262 (C)   69
                                                        ——

263 ...house;' to...   F-ENI
263 (C)   L-EN2

264-265 ...lord' They rested mute   Tn-30;T-E
264   two remain'd   I MS
                s̸a̸t̸ a̸p̸a̸r̸t̸   I MS
                t̸h̸e̸r̸e̸   I MS
      ...lord: 'they r̸e̸s̸t̸e̸d̸ m̸u̸t̸e̸,   L-ENI
264 ...lord: 'the...   BM-1
264 (C)   L-EN2

Apart by all the chamber's width, and mute   265
As creatures voiceless through the fault of birth,
Or two wild men supporters of a shield,
Painted, who stare at open space, nor glance
The one at other, parted by the shield.

On a sudden, many a voice along the street,   270
And heel against the pavement echoing, burst
Their drowse; and either started while the door,
Pushed from without, drave backward to the wall,
And midmost of a rout of roisterers,
Femininely fair and dissolutely pale,   275
Her suitor in old years before Geraint,

------

265 And sunder'd by the whole breadth of the room,   T-E
(265 - this line omitted in F-ENI and L-ENI. Following
269 appears this version of 265 in print:)
      And sunder'd by the whole breadth of the room. F-ENI
(This line is struck out in L-ENI and, inserted between
264 and 266 in I MS is:)
      Divided by the chamber's width & mute   L-ENI
(This same line is printed in BM-1)
265 (C)   L-EN2

266 Like creatures voiceless from the fault...   T-E
266 As   by   I MS
      L̸i̸k̸e̸ creatures voiceless f̸r̸o̸m̸ the fault...   L-ENI
266 ...voiceless by the...   BM-1
266 (C)   L-EN2

267 Like two...   Tn-30
267 Or
      L̸i̸k̸e̸ two...   T-E
267 ...shield,   (, I)   L-ENI
267 (C)   BM-1

380

GERAINT AND ENID

Entered, the wild lord of the place, Limours.
He moving up with pliant courtliness,
Greeted Geraint full face, but stealthily,
In the mid-warmth of welcome and graspt hand,   280
Found Enid with the corner of his eye,
And knew her sitting sad and solitary.
Then cried Geraint for wine and goodly cheer

---

269 One at the other, parted...		Tn-30
269 The		
One at ~~the~~ other, parted...		T-E
269 ...shield.	(. I)	L-ENI
269 (C)		BM-1
272 ...drowze,; and...	;/ (I)	L-ENI
272 (C)		BM-1
273 ...to the ~~chamber~~ wall,		Tn-30
273 ...wall.,	,/ (I)	L-ENI
273 (C)		BM-1
277 & Lo it was her suitor earl Limours		H-35
Alt. after 277 He with followers entering in		H-35
279 He greeted him full...		H-35
280 ...hand,	,/ (I)	L-ENI
280 (C)		BM-1
283 Then call'd Geraint...		Tn-30;T-E;F-ENI
283 cried		I MS
Then ~~call'd~~ Geraint...		L-EN2
283 (C)		L-EN3

381

To feed the sudden guest, and sumptuously
According to his fashion, bad the host   285
Call in what men soever were his friends,
And feast with these in honour of their Earl;
'And care not for the cost; the cost is mine.'

And wine and food were brought, and Earl Limours
Drank till he jested with all ease, and told   290
Free tales, and took the word and played upon it,
And made it of two colours; for his talk,

---

elision 284-290 ...guest, & Earl Limours
                    Drank...   Tn-30;T-E
elision 284-290 ...guest, and Earl Limours
                    Drank...   F-ENI
Sketch for 284-290   & bad the host
              men soever   were
        Call in what ₵₵₵₵ ₥ₑ₦ he ₵₳₴₵ ₦₳₥ₑ₵ his friends,
        past with these
        And ₥₳₭ₑ ₍₣₥ₑ₥₣₥ ₣ₑ₳₴₵ in honour of their earl;
        'And care not for the cost; the cost is mine.'
        And wine & food were brought & Earl L
                                        I MS in L-ENI
(284-290 first printed in BM-1 with following variants.)
284-285 To feed the sudden guest, and bad the host BM-1
284-285 (C)   L-EN2

287 ...of their earl;   BM-1
287 (C)   73

289 (no par. indent.)   BM-1
289 (par. indent. symbol)   L-EN2
289 (C)   L-EN3

293 When wine & boon companions...   H-35

296 ...his menay to...   Tn-30;T-E
296   comrades   I MS
    ...his ₥ₑ₦₳₵ to...   L-ENI
296 (C)   BM-1

GERAINT AND ENID

When wine and free companions kindled him,
Was wont to glance and sparkle like a gem
Of fifty facets; thus he moved the Prince   295
To laughter and his comrades to applause.
Then, when the Prince was merry, asked Limours,
'Your leave, my lord, to cross the room, and speak
To your good damsel there who sits apart,
And seems so lonely?' 'My free leave,' he said;   300
'Get her to speak: she doth not speak to me.'
Then rose Limours, and looking at his feet,

---

297   askt Limours
    ...the Prince~~'s~~ ~~heart~~ ~~who~~ was merry in him   Tn-30
297 And when...   T-E
297 Then,   I MS
    ~~And~~ when...Limours,   (, I)   L-ENI
297 (C)   BM-1

298 Have I your leave, my lord, to cross, & speak
                                              Tn-30;T-E
298   Y   the room   I MS
    '~~Have~~ ~~I~~ your leave, my lord, to cross, and
                                    speak   L-ENI
298 (C)   BM-1

299 ...apart,   ,/ (I)   L-ENI
299 (C)   BM-1

300 ...leave' he said,   ,/ (I)   L-ENI
300 ...leave' he ...   BM-1
300 (C)   73

301 ...she does not...   Tn-30;T-E
301 ...she does not...   F-ENI
301 (C)   73

302 ...Limours and...feet,   (, I)   L-ENI
302 ...Limours and...   BM-1
302 (C)   73

Like him who tries the bridge he fears may fail,
Crost and came near, lifted adoring eyes,
Bowed at her side and uttered whisperingly: 305

   'Enid, the pilot star of my lone life,
Enid, my early and my only love,
Enid, the loss of whom hath turned me wild--

303	Like one that tries new ice if it will bear	Tn-30;T-E
303	old	I MS
	Like one that tries n̸e̸w̸ ice if it will bear,	L-ENI
303	Like one that tries old ice if it will bear,	BM-1
303	old	
	Like one that tries y̸o̸u̸n̸g̸ ice if it will bear,	L-EN2
303	him who the bridge he fears may fail	I MS
	Like o̸n̸e̸ t̸h̸a̸t̸ tries o̸l̸d̸ i̸c̸e̸ i̸f̸ i̸t̸ w̸i̸l̸l̸ b̸e̸a̸r̸,	L-EN3
303	(C)	F-EN2

| 305 | ...whisperingly: :/ (I) | L-ENI |
| 305 | (C) | BM-1 |

306	The lodestar of my crushed life	H-35
306	(no par. indent.; indent. symbol.)	L-ENI
306	(C)	BM-1

307	Enid my only & my early love	Lo-1
307	Enid my...	F-ENI
307	(C)	73

308	...whom has turned...	Lo-1;Tn-30;T-E
308	Enid the...whom has turn'd...	F-ENI
308	(C)	73

| 309 | ...is it I find you here? | Lo-1 |

310	at last	
	You are in my power, s̸w̸e̸e̸t̸ g̸i̸r̸l̸, you are...	Tn-30
310	You are...	T-E
310	You are...power,.	(. I)	L-ENI
310	You are...	BM-1
310	(C)	73

What chance is this? how is it I see you here?
Ye are in my power at last, are in my power.   310
Yet fear me not: I call mine own self wild,
But keep a touch of sweet civility
Here in the heart of waste and wilderness.
I thought, but that your father came between,
In former days you saw me favourably.   315
And if it were so do not keep it back:
Make me a little happier: let me know it:
Owe you me nothing for a life half-lost?
Yea, yea, the whole dear debt of all you are.

----

311 ...not.: I...wild,   (: , I)   L-ENI
311 (C)   BM-1

Sketch 312 ff.   touch of
      I have a little sweet civility
      Yet living in the rudest of wilderness.
      I think you wd (I ?) to tell me of it.
      Owe you me nothing for a life half lost?
      And here the tender sound of his own voice
      Made his eye moist & answering his own self
      The whole dear debt, he said, of all you are
      Oh Enid he & you - I see it with joy -
      I saw it when I enterd all at once   Lo-1

315 In olden days...   H-35
315 In former years you...   Lo-1
315 ...favourably/   (. I)   L-ENI
315 (C)   BM-1

316   hold
      ...do not keep it back   Lo-1
316 And it were...   Tn-30
316 ...back,   F-ENI
316 (C)   BM-1

317 ...little happy. let...   Tn-30
317 (Omitted; but included C, I MS)   L-ENI
317 (C)   BM-1

319 You owe me the dear debt of your whole self.   Tn-30
319 ...of /o/u/ all...   Tn-30

And, Enid, you and he, I see with joy,   320
Ye sit apart, you do not speak to him,
You come with no attendance, page or maid,
To serve you--doth he love you as of old?
For, call it lovers' quarrels, yet I know
Though men may bicker with the things they love,   325
They would not make them laughable in all eyes,

_____

Sketch 320-341
    Enid your lord & you, I see it with joy,
    You come with no attendance, maid or page
    To serve you, - yea, you are at variance
                 ring him round
    Speak but the word; my followers are all here
    He sits unarm'd - I mean no violence, none
    But I will take & dungeon him so close   Tn-30

320 Enid your lord & you, I see with joy,   H-35
320 For Enid, he & you, I see it with joy,   Tn-30
320 ...see it with...   T-E;F-ENI
320 (C)   73

Alt. for 321 I saw it when I entered - you were here
             Sitting apart - I knew it - & besides Tn-30

321 You sit...   Lo-1;Tn-30;T-E
321 You sit...   F-ENI
321 (C)   73

322 You came with no attendants, nor one maid   H-35

Sketch 323-328 To serve you, yea you are at variance.
                  look
        Your   alone
        This wretched dress, an insult to you,
             speaks   Tn-30

323 To wait upon you, are at variance   H-35
323 ...you - does he...   Lo-1;Tn-30;T-E
323 ...you - does he...   F-ENI
323 (C)   73

Not while they loved them; and your wretched dress,
A wretched insult on you, dumbly speaks
Your story, that this man loves you no more.
Your beauty is no beauty to him now: 330
A common chance--right well I know it--palled--

---

324 For call...		F-ENI
324 (C)		L-EN2

325 ...with things...		Lo-1
325 ...love		F-ENI
325 ...love,	,/ (I)	L-EN2
325 (C)		L-EN3

326 They wd not have them common laughing (? stock) Lo-1
326   laughable in all eyes
   ...them ~~the worlds ridicule~~   T-E
326 ...eyes   F-ENI
326 (C)   L-EN2

328 ...you cries aloud   Lo-1
328 ...you, tells your tale   Tn-30
328   dumbly shrieks
   ...you, ~~tells your tale~~   T-E
328   speaks   I MS
   ...dumbly ~~shrieks~~   L-ENI
328 (C)   BM-1

329 In all men's eyes that this man loves you not   Lo-1
329 In all mens eyes that this man loves no more. Tn-30
329 Your story   you
   ~~In all men's eyes~~ that this man loves no more.   T-E

330 Your beauty has no more a beauty for him   Lo-1
330 ...is to him beauty no more.   Tn-30;T-E
330   no   to him now: I MS
   Your beauty is ~~to/him~~ beauty ~~no more~~   L-ENI
330 (C)   BM-1

331 ...common case: right...   Lo-1;Tn-30

387

For I know men: nor will ye win him back,
For the man's love once gone never returns.
But here is one who loves you as of old;
With more exceeding passion than of old: 335
Good, speak the word: my followers ring him round:
He sits unarmed; I hold a finger up;
They understand: nay; I do not mean blood:
Nor need ye look so scared at what I say:

Alt. after 331
    With sweetness pall'd: he cannot love, for tho'
    We sometimes bicker with the things we love
    We would not make the world's (1 ?)
    Not while we loved them: but he loves you not:
    He may have loved you but he loves no more   Tn-30

332 ...will you win...   Tn-30;T-E
332 ...will you win...back,   ,/ (I)   L-ENI
332 ...will you win...   BM-1
332 (C)   70

333 And the man's...   Lo-1;Tn-30

334 Yet lives there one who loves you...   Lo-1
334 ...old;   ;/ (I)   L-ENI
334 (C)   BM-1

335 More tenfold more almost to madness. sweet,   Tn-30

336-341 Speak but the word - I mean no violence
        But I will prison him so close, my love   H-35

336 Speak but the word: my...   Tn-30

337 ...unarm'd:; I...up;   ;/;/(I)   L-ENI
337 (C)   BM-1

338 ...understand - No, I...   Tn-30;T-E
338 ...understand, : no,; I...   :/ (;:I)   L-ENI
338 ...understand: no; I...   BM-1
338 (C)   73

My malice is no deeper than a moat,   340
No stronger than a wall: there is the keep;
He shall not cross us more; speak but the word:
Or speak it not; but then by Him that made me
The one true lover whom you ever owned,
I will make use of all the power I have.   345
O pardon me! the madness of that hour,
When first I parted from thee, moves me yet.'

At this the tender sound of his own voice

---

339 You need not look...   T-E
339 Nor   you   I MS
    Y̶o̶u̶ need n̶o̶t̶ look...   L-ENI
339 ...need you look...   BM-1
339 (C)   73

341 ...wall. There...   F-ENI
341 (C)   L-EN2

342 ...more:; speak...   ;/ (I)   L-ENI
342 (C)   BM-1

343 ...then God who made me   H-35

344 ...lover which you ever had,   H-35;Tn-30;T-E
344 ...lover which you ever had,   F-ENI
344 (C)   73

345 ...of the power wh I have.   H-35

347 ...from you moves...   H-35;Tn-30;T-E
347 ...from you moves...   F-ENI
347 ...from you, moves...   ,/ (I)   L-EN3
347 ...from you, moves...   F-EN2
347 (C)   73

348 (No par. indent.; indent. symbol in I MS)   L-ENI
348 (C)   BM-1

And sweet self-pity, or the fancy of it,
Made his eye moist; but Enid feared his eyes,   350
Moist as they were, wine-heated from the feast;
And answered with such craft as women use,
Guilty or guiltless, to stave off a chance
That breaks upon them perilously, and said:

    'Earl, if you love me as in former years,   355
And do not practise on me, come with morn,
And snatch me from him as by violence;
Leave me tonight: I am weary to the death.'

Alt. before 349 He spoke
                And Enid glanced on him ø̸n̸c̸e̸ m̸ø̸r̸e̸
                      & saw   Lo-1

349 That sweet...   Lo-1

350   once more but
    Made his eye moist; &̸ y̸ḙt̸ s̸h̸ḙ fear'd his eyes   Lo-1
350 And Enid lookt at him & fear'd his eyes   H-35;
                                  Tn-30;T-E

351 Hot from the banquet   H-35
351 Evn in their tears, wineheated from the feast.   Lo-1
351 Wineheated from the revel as she thought   Tn-30;T-E

352 She
    Then answerd E̸n̸i̸d with the craft wh women use   H-35
352 ...with that craft wh women...   Tn-30
352   such   as
    ...with t̸h̸a̸t̸ craft w̸h̸i̸c̸h̸ women...   T-E

353 ...off the chance   H-35

354 Which breaks...   H-35
354 ...said,   F-ENI
354 (C)   L-EN2

355 ...former days   H-35
355 ...years   F-ENI
355 ...years,   ,/ (I)   L-EN2
355 (C)   L-EN3

Low at leave-taking, with his brandished plume
Brushing his instep, bowed the all-armorous Earl,   360
And the stout Prince bad him a loud good-night.
He moving homeward babbled to his men,
How Enid never loved a man but him,
Nor cared a broken egg-shell for her lord.

But Enid left alone with Prince Geraint,   365
Debating his command of silence given,
And that she now perforce must violate it,
Held commune with herself, and while she held

---

357 ...violence,;   ;/ (I)   L-ENI
357 (C)   BM-1

358 To night I am quite weary & worn out' H-35;Tn-30;T-E
358 To-night I am quite weary and worn out.'   F-ENI
358 (Variant cancelled & I MS correction)   L-EN2
358 (C)   L-EN3

Alt. after 358 And i̶f̶ do not feign, come then
                        tomorrow morn   H-35

361 ...good night.   F-ENI
361 ...good-night.   -/ (I)   L-EN2
361 (C)   L-EN3

362 And moving...   Tn-30
362 He
      A̶n̶d̶ moving...   T-E
362 ...moving homewards babbled...men   F-ENI
362 ...moving homeward̶s̶ babbled...men   BM-1
362 ...men,   ,/ (I)   L-EN2
362 (C)   L-EN3

366 ...w̶i̶t̶h̶ h̶e̶r̶s̶e̶l̶f̶ his command...   H-35

367 W̶h̶ y̶e̶t̶ s̶h̶e̶ And that she n̶e̶e̶d̶s̶ m̶u̶s̶t̶ break it held
                        nor perforce must violate it
                                                    H-35

368 Held commune with...   H-35

391

He fell asleep, and Enid had no heart
To wake him, but hung o'er him, wholly pleased   370
To find him yet unwounded after fight,
And hear him breathing low and equally.
Anon she rose, and stepping lightly, heaped
The pieces of his armour in one place,
All to be there against a sudden need;   375
Then dozed awhile herself, but overtoiled
By that day's grief and travel, evermore
Seemed catching at a rootless thorn, and then
Went slipping down horrible precipices,
And strongly striking out her limbs awoke;   380

---

369 He fell in sleep...   H-35

371 ...fight   F-ENI
371 (C)   L-EN2

373 ...& slipping gently p̸a̸s̸t̸ heap'd   H-35
373 ...rose and...lightly heap'd   F-ENI
373 ...rose, and...lightly heap'd   ,/ (I)   L-EN2
373 ...lightly, heap'd   ,/ (P)   L-EN3
373 (C)   F-EN2

374 ...place,   ,/ (I)   L-ENI
374 (C)   BM-1

375 To be at hand against a perilous chance   H-35
375 To be at hand against...   T-E
375 All to be there   I MS
    T̸o̸ b̸e̸ a̸t̸ h̸a̸n̸d̸ against...need,;   ;/ (I)   L-ENI
375 (C)   BM-1

376-377 By that day's grief & travail/ overtoiled
                                    herself
        Then dozed a little while   but evermore
                                                          H-35

380 And wildly striking out...   H-35
380 ...awoke.;   ;/ (I)   L-ENI
380 (C)   BM-1

381 Anon she heard the...   H-35

392

Then thought she heard the wild Earl at the door,
With all his rout of random followers,
Sound on a dreadful trumpet, summoning her;
Which was the red cock shouting to the light,
As the gray dawn stole o'er the dewy world,   385
And glimmered on his armour in the room.
And once again she rose to look at it,
But touched it unawares: jangling, the casque
Fell, and he started up and stared at her.
Then breaking his command of silence given,   390
She told him all that Earl Limours had said,
Except the passage that he loved her not;
Nor left untold the craft herself had used;
But ended with apology so sweet,

---

383 Sound with a dreadful...   H-35

385 And the gray...   H-35

387 And once again she rose & (heapt?) his arms   H-35

388   it unawares
    His armour wh she touch'd; jangling, the casque H-35
388 ...unawares;: jangling the...   :/(I)   L-ENI
388 ...jangling the...   BM-1
388 (C)   L-EN2

389 ...up & h̸e̸ stared...   Tn-30
389 Fell, and...   ,/ (I)   L-ENI
389 (C)   BM-1

Alt. after 389 A̸n̸d̸ t̸i̸m̸o̸r̸o̸u̸s̸l̸y̸ w̸i̸t̸h̸ l̸o̸w̸ a̸p̸o̸l̸o̸g̸i̸e̸s̸   H-35

390 Then f̸o̸r̸ breaking...   H-35
390 ...given,   (, I)   L-ENI
390 (C)   BM-1

393   told
    ...left unsaid the craft...   Tn-30

394 ...sweet   F-ENI
394 ...sweet,   ,/ (I)   L-EN2
394 (C)   L-EN3

Low-spoken, and of so few words, and seemed 395
So justified by that necessity,
That though he thought 'was it for him she wept
In Devon?' he but gave a wrathful groan,
Saying, 'Your sweet faces make good fellows fools
And traitors. Call the host and bid him bring 400

---

395 So worded & of... Tn-30
395 Low spoken
ₛₒ ₘₒᵣₐₑₐ & of... T-E
395 Low spoken and... F-ENI
395 Low-spoken and... - / (MS) BM-1
395 Low-spoken, and... (, I) L-EN2
395 (C) L-EN3

398 ...gave an angry groan Tn-30
398 wrathful I MS
...gave an ₐₙₒᵣᵧ/groan, L-ENI
398 (C) BM-1

399 sweet
...your pretty faces... Tn-30
399 Saying 'your... F-ENI
399 (C) 73

400 C I MS
...traitors; . ₵all the... ⊙ (I) L-ENI
400 (C) BM-1

401 My charger & your palfrey. Enid went Tn-30;T-E
401 My charger & your palfrey.' Enid went: F-ENI
401 My charger & her palfrey.' Out she stole Y-III
401 (I MS correct) L-ENI
401 (C) BM-1

402-407 He arm'd ₕᵢₘₛₑₗ & issuing found the host
& cried Tn-30
402-407 He arm'd, and issuing found the host and
cried, T-E;F-ENI

(Lines 402-406, omitted in earlier versions, now appear
in MS in Y-III and L-ENI, w. following variants.)

Charger and palfrey.' So she glided out
Among the heavy breathings of the house,
And like a household Spirit at the walls
Beat, till she woke the sleepers, and returned:
Then tending her rough lord, though all unasked,   405
In silence, did him service as a squire;
Till issuing armed he found the host and cried,
'Thy reckoning, friend?' and ere he learnt it, 'Take

403	But like a household...	Y-III
403	(I MS, correct)	L-ENI
403	...household spirit at...	BM-1
403	(C)	L-·EN2

404	Around the sleepers, told her princes will,	Y-III
404	(I MS, correct)	L-ENI
404	(C)	BM-1

405	And so returning, served him as page	Y-III
405	Then tho' he had not ask'd her, tending him (I MS)	L-ENI
405	Then tho' he had not ask'd her, tending him	BM-1
405	Then, tho' he had not ask'd her, tending him	L-EN2
405	tending her rough lord, tho' all unask'd,	I MS
405	Then, t̶h̶o̶'̶ h̶e̶ h̶a̶d̶ n̶o̶t̶ a̶s̶k̶e̶d̶/̶h̶e̶r̶/̶ t̶e̶n̶d̶i̶n̶g̶ h̶i̶m̶	L-EN3
405	(C)	F-EN2

406	In silence, with her eyes upon the floor.	Y-III
406	(I MS, correct)	L-ENI
406	(C)	BM-1

407	Till arm'd he	I MS
	h̶e̶ a̶r̶m̶'̶d̶,̶/̶a̶n̶d̶ issuing found...	L-ENI
407	(C)	BM-1

408	ere it Your reckoning friend & w̶h̶e̶n̶ he learnt Take	Tn-30
408	'Your reckoning...	T-E
408	'Your reckoning, friend,' and...	F-ENI
408	Thy ? ?/ (I MS)	
	'Y̶o̶u̶r̶ reckoning, friend,' and...	L-EN3
408	(C)	F-EN2

395

GERAINT AND ENID

Five horses and their armours;' and the host
Suddenly honest, answered in amaze,   410
'My lord, I scarce have spent the worth of one!'

---

409 ...armours: then the host   Tn-30;T-E
409   and   I MS
   ...armours,' ̷t̷h̷e̷n̷ the host,   (, I) L-ENI
409 ... the host,   BM-1
409 (C)   84

410-411 Amazed I have not spent the worth of one.
                                              Tn-30;T-E
410-411 (410 in I MS)
        'My Lord,   I MS
        ̷A̷m̷a̷z̷e̷d̷/ 'I have not spent the worth of one'
                                      (! I)   L-ENI
410 (C)   BM-1
411 ...lord, I have not spent the worth...   BM-1
411   scarce   I MS
    'My lord, I have ̷n̷o̷t̷ spent...   L-EN2
411 (C)   L-EN3

I MS, rejected alt. for 410
    ̷H̷e̷ ̷w̷a̷s̷ ̷s̷o̷ ̷a̷m̷a̷z̷e̷d̷ ̷h̷e̷ ̷a̷n̷s̷w̷e̷r̷'̷d̷ ̷h̷o̷n̷e̷s̷t̷l̷y̷;'   L-ENI

412 You will...wealthier cried the Prince   Tn-30;T-E
412   said   I MS
    'You will...wealthier' ̷c̷r̷i̷e̷d̷ the Prince., (, I)L-ENI
412 'You will...wealthier' said...   BM-1
412 (C)   73

413 ...foreward & I ̷c̷h̷a̷r̷g̷e̷ ̷y̷o̷u̷ to day   Tn-30
413 ...'Forward, ! and...   ! (I) L-ENI
413 (C)   BM-1

415 That whatsoever thing you see or hear   Tn-30;T-E
415 That whatsoever thing you see or hear   F-ENI
415 What   soever may   or see   I MS
    ̷T̷h̷a̷t̷ ̷w̷h̷a̷t̷s̷o̷e̷v̷e̷r̷ thing you ̷s̷e̷e̷ ̷o̷r̷ hear BM-1
415 ...soever you may...   L-EN2
415 (C)   69

396

'Ye will be all the wealthier,' said the Prince,
And then to Enid, 'Forward! and today
I charge you, Enid, more especially,
What thing soever ye may hear, or see,   415
Or fancy (though I count it of small use
To charge you) that ye speak not but obey.'

    And Enid answered, 'Yea, my lord, I know
Your wish, and would obey; but riding first,
I hear the violent threats you do not hear,   420

---

417 ...that you speak...   Tn-30;T-E
417 ...that you speak...   F-ENI
417 (C)   <u>69</u>

418 (No par. indent.)   F-ENI
418 (C)   BM-1

Sketch 419-423
    ~~But this is hard to me your wife~~ I hear these vio-
                      lent men
~~Threaten your life~~
Your wish & would obey ~~it where I can~~. but riding
                      first
~~But this is hard~~. I hear the violent threats ~~against~~
                    ~~your life~~
                    you do not hear,
~~Of evil men against your noble life~~
          danger which
I see the peril   you do not see -
~~Perhaps you see it & I do not know~~
~~Pray pardon me / but not to speak of it~~ -
Then Not to
~~Not to~~ give you any warning, that seems hard,
Almost beyond me: yet I would obey
~~(Likelyly) I would obey you when I can~~.   Tn-30

419 ...obey,; but riding first   ;/ (I)   L-ENI
419 ...first   BM-1
419 ...first,   ,/ (P)   L-EN3
419 (C)   F-EN2

I see the danger which you cannot see:
Then not to give you warning, that seems hard;
Almost beyond me: yet I would obey.'

  'Yea so,' said he, 'do it: be not too wise;
Seeing that ye are wedded to a man,   425
Not all mismated with a yawning clown,
But one with arms to guard his head and yours,
With eyes to find you out however far,
And ears to hear you even in his dreams.'

  With that he turned and looked as keenly at her   430
As careful robins eye the delver's toil;
And that within her, which a wanton fool,

---

421 cannot		
...you d̸o̸ n̸o̸t̸ see -		T-E
421 ...see ≠ :	(: I)	L-ENI
421 (C)		BM-1
422 ...hard,		F-ENI
422 ...hard,;	;/ (MS)	BM-1
422 (C)		L-EN2
425 ...that you are...	Tn-30;T-E;F-ENI	
425 (C)		69
426 Not quite mismated...	Tn-30;T-E;F-ENI	
426 (C)		73
432 ...wh an easy fool		Tn-30;T-E
432 wanton		I MS
...her which an e̸a̸s̸y̸ fool		L-ENI
432 ...her which...fool		BM-1
432 ...her, which...fool	,/ (I)	L-EN3
432 (C)		F-EN2
433 ...have h̸a̸d̸d̸ call'd...		Tn-30
434 ...fall,.	(. I)	L-ENI
434 (C)		BM-1

Or hasty judger would have called her guilt,
Made her cheek burn and either eyelid fall.
And Geraint looked and was not satisfied.   435

    Then forward by a way which, beaten broad,
Led from the territory of false Limours
To the waste earldom of another earl,
Doorm, whom his shaking vassals called the Bull,
Went Enid with her sullen follower on.   440
Once she looked back, and when she saw him ride
More near by many a rood than yestermorn,
It wellnigh made her cheerful; till Geraint

---

435   Geraint
      And H̸e̸ look'd...   T-E

436   way
      Then onward by a ɍo̸a̸d̸ wh beaten broad   H-35
436 (No par. indent.; indent symbol I MS) ...which,
                        beaten...   ,/ (I)   L-ENI
436 (C)   BM-1

437   false
      ...of ɇa̸r̸l̸ Limours   H-35
437 ...Limours∕   L-ENI
437 (C)   BM-1

438 To the green earldom...   H-35

439 ...whom his foes shaking...   H-35

440 ...sullen follower.   H-35

442 By many a rood more near than yestermorn   Tn-30;T-E
442 ...yester-morn,   F-ENI
442 (C)   84

443 It well nigh...cheerful,; still...   ;/ (I)   L-ENI
443   wellnigh   MS
      It well nigh...   BM-1
443 (C)   L-EN2

Waving an angry hand as who should say
'Ye watch me,' saddened all her heart again.   445
But while the sun yet beat a dewy blade,
The sound of many a heavily-galloping hoof
Smote on her ear, and turning round she saw
Dust, and the points of lances bicker in it.
Then not to disobey her lord's behest,   450
And yet to give him warning, for he rode
As if he heard not, moving back she held
Her finger up, and pointed to the dust.
At which the warrior in his obstinacy,
Because she kept the letter of his word,   455

---

445 'You watch...		Tn-30;T-E
445 'You watch...		F-ENI
445 (C)		69
446 And when the Sun...		H-35
448 Beat on...		H-35
448 ...round/ she...		L-ENI
448 (C)		BM-1
449 Dust, and...	(, I)	L-ENI
449 (C)		BM-1
450 And not to...		H-35
451 ...him notice, for...		H-35
453 ...up, and...	,/ (I)	L-ENI
453 (C)		BM-1
455 ...word		F-EN2
455 (C)		73
456 ...pleased and turning stood.		F-ENI
456 ...pleased, and turning, stood.	,/,/(I&P)	L-EN3
456 (C)		F-EN2
457 And in a moment...		H-35

Was in a manner pleased, and turning, stood.
And in the moment after, wild Limours,
Borne on a black horse, like a thunder-cloud
Whose skirts are loosened by the breaking storm,
Half ridden off with by the thing he rode,   460
And all in passion uttering a dry shriek,
Dashed on Geraint, who closed with him, and bore
Down by the length of lance and arm beyond
The crupper, and so left him stunned or dead,
And overthrew the next that followed him,   465
And blindly rushed on all the rout behind.
But at the flash and motion of the man
They vanished panic-stricken, like a shoal
Of darting fish, that on a summer morn
Adown the crystal dykes at Camelot   470

---

458 ...horse, like a thunder-cloud⁄   (, I)   L-ENI
458 (C)   BM-1

459 ...storm –   F-ENI
459 (C)   L-EN2

462 ...who hurtled with...   H-35;Tn-30;T-E
462   closed
    ...who h̶u̶r̶t̶l̶e̶d̶ with him, and bore   ,⁄ (I)   L-ENI
462 (C)   BM-1

465 Then overthrew...   H-35
465 ...him,   (, I)   L-ENI
465 (C)   BM-1

466   rushed
    Then t̶u̶r̶n̶d̶ himself against the rout behind   H-35

469   f̶l̶i̶c̶k̶e̶r̶i̶n̶g̶ stars
    Of l̶i̶t̶t̶l̶e̶ fish...   H-35
469 ...fish that...   F-ENI
469 ...fish, that...   ,⁄ (I)   L-EN3
469 (C)   F-EN2

401

Come slipping o'er their shadows on the sand,
But if a man who stands upon the brink
But lift a shining hand against the sun,
There is not left the twinkle of a fin
Betwixt the cressy islets white in flower;   475
So, scared but at the motion of the man,
Fled all the boon companions of the Earl,
And left him lying in the public way;
So vanish friendships only made in wine.

Then like a stormy sunlight smiled Geraint,   480
Who saw the chargers of the two that fell
Start from their fallen lords, and wildly fly,

---

471 Come -ping
        slip over ~~their own~~ shadows on the sand   H-35

Alt. after 471 ~~Among the cressy islets white in~~
                    ~~flower~~   H-35

472 ...man that stands...   H-35
472 ...upon the bank   T-E; F-ENI
472   brink   I MS
    ...upon the ~~bank~~   BM-1
472 (C)   L-EN2

473   lifts   shining
        But holds up a ~~whole~~ hand...   H-35

475 ...flower: F-ENI
475 ...flower;   (; I)   BM-1
475 (C)   L-EN2

476 So scared...man   F-ENI
476 So, scared...man,   ,/,/ (I)   L-EN3
476 (C)   F-EN2

481 Who saw
    ~~Seeing~~ the chargers of the fallen men   T-E

Mixt with the flyers. 'Horse and man,' he said,
'All of one mind and all right-honest friends!
Not a hoof left: and I methinks till now   485
Was honest--paid with horses and with arms;
I cannot steal or plunder, no nor beg:

---

482 Start masterless from their mute lords & fly   T-E
482   from their fallen   wildly   I MS
     Start ~~masterless~~ ~~from~~ ~~their~~ ~~mute~~ lords and fly, L-ENI
482 (C)   BM-1

483 Mixt   O right-honest friends
    ~~Fly~~ with the flyers. '~~Not~~ ~~a~~ ~~hoof~~ ~~left,~~~~he~~ ~~said.~~   T-E
483 ...flyers. 'Honest friends!' he said   T-E
483   'Horse and man' he said   I MS
    ...flyers. ~~Honest~~ ~~friendsly~~ ~~he~~ ~~said,~~   L-ENI
483 (C)   BM-1

Alt. for 484 'Almost as honest as a weeping wife.
                                         T-E;F-ENI
484 (I MS, correct)   L-ENI
484 (C)   BM-1

Alt. after 484 Wellnigh   I MS
           '~~Almost~~ as honest as a weeping wife.;
                           (; I)   L-ENI
Alt. after 484 Wellnigh as honest as a weeping wife;
                                           BM-1
Alt. after 484 (printed; cancelled in I MS) L-EN3
Alt. after 484 (C)   F-EN2

485 ...left~~,~~ : and...   :/ (I)   L-ENI
485 (C)   BM-1

486 ~~Will~~ ~~not~~ too honest -- I that paid with arms
    I ~~cannot~~ ~~plunder~~ & ~~I~~ ~~cannot~~ ~~steal--~~   T-E

487 And horses - cannot plunder, steal   or beg,
    ~~I~~ ~~paid~~ ~~with~~ ~~arms,&~~ ~~horses~~ ~~+~~ ~~no,~~ ~~nor~~ ~~beg,~~   T-E

403

And so what say ye, shall we strip him there
Your lover? has your palfrey heart enough
To bear his armour? shall we fast, or dine?   490
No?--then do thou, being right honest, pray
That we may meet the horsemen of Earl Doorm,
I too would still be honest.' Thus he said:
And sadly gazing on her bridle-reins,
And answering not one word, she led the way.   495

    But as a man to whom a dreadful loss
Falls in a far land and he knows it not,
But coming back he learns it, and the loss

---

488 What say you? shall we strip your lover there?	T-E
488 What say you therefore? shall....	T-E
488 And so what	I MS
W̸h̸a̸t̸ say you t̸h̸e̸r̸e̸f̸o̸r̸e̸? shall...	L-ENI
488 ...say you? shall...	BM-1
488 ...say you, shall...	L-EN3
488 (C)	69

489 And has your palfrey heart enough to bear	T-E

490 His casque & cuirass? shall...	T-E

491 ...do you, being...	T-E
491 ...do you, being right-honest, pray	F-ENI
491 ...do you, being...	L-EN3
491 (C)	73

493 ...too wd fain be...	T-E

494 And m̸e̸e̸k̸l̸y̸ sadly...	T-E

498 But coming home he knows it & the loss	H-35

500 ...who slightly prickd	H-35

501 ...followers of the Earl	H-35
501 ...of the Earl	Tn-30;T-E
501 ...of the Earl,	F-ENI
501 (C)	F-EN2

So pains him that he sickens nigh to death;
So fared it with Geraint, who being pricked   500
In combat with the follower of Limours,
Bled underneath his armour secretly,
And so rode on, nor told his gentle wife
What ailed him, hardly knowing it himself,
Till his eye darkened and his helmet wagged;   505
And at a sudden swerving of the road,
Though happily down on a bank of grass,
The Prince, without a word, from his horse fell.

And Enid heard the clashing of his fall,
Suddenly came, and at his side all pale   510
Dismounting, loosed the fastenings of his arms,

---

502 Beneath his armour bleeding secretly   H-35
502 ...secretly   F-ENI
502 (C)   L-EN2

503 Rode on nor told his guileless wife   H-35

505 ...his helmet lower wagg'd   H-35

507 Tho haply down...   H-35

508 The Prince without a word from   F-ENI
508 (C)   F-EN2

509   afar   fled
    And Enid heard the clashing fall, & came   H-35

510   Came
    Suddenly Full quickly back, & at his side all
                         pale   H-35

511 Dismounting, for his armour's buckles   H-35
511 Dismounting forced his armour-buckles back,   Tn-30
511   loosed the fastenings of his arms
    Dismounting f̷o̷r̷c̷e̷d̷ h̷i̷s̷ a̷r̷m̷o̷u̷r̷-̷b̷u̷c̷k̷l̷e̷s̷ b̷a̷c̷k̷/̷   T-E

Alt. after 511 A̷n̷d̷ s̷h̷e̷ f̷o̷u̷n̷d̷/̷t̷h̷e̷ b̷a̷t̷t̷l̷e̷ w̷o̷u̷n̷d̷ t̷h̷a̷t̷
                        d̷r̷a̷i̷n̷'̷d̷ h̷i̷s̷ l̷i̷f̷e̷   H-35

405

Nor let her true hand falter, nor blue eye
Moisten, till she had lighted on his wound,
And tearing off her veil of faded silk
Had bared her forehead to the blistering sun,   515
And swathed the hurt that drained her dear lord's life.
Then after all was done that hand could do,
She rested, and her desolation came
Upon her, and she wept beside the way.

And many past, but none regarded her,   520

---

512 Nor did her white hand falter or sweet eye   H-35
512   let
     Nor d̸i̸d̸ her...falter, or her eye   Tn-30
512 ...nor her eye   T-E
512   N   blue   I MS
     ...falter, or h̸e̸r̸ eye   (, I)   L-ENI
512 (C)   BM-1

513 Moisten, before she lighted...   H-35
513 ...his h̸e̸a̸r̸t̸ wound   Tn-30

514 And wound it with her veil...   H-35

516 ...life̸   (. I)   L-ENI
516 (C)   BM-1

517 And then when all was done that she could do   H-35
517 ...do,   (, I)   L-ENI
517 (C)   BM-1

518 She let the grip of desolation work   H-35

519 Upon her & her loneliness return
     Upon her & she wept beside the way   H-35
519 ...her and...   F-ENI
519 ...her, and...   ,/ (I)   L-EN3
519 (C)   F-EN2

521 ...that land of...   H-35

522 ...for a murdered lord   H-35

406

For in that realm of lawless turbulence,
A woman weeping for her murdered mate
Was cared as much for as a summer shower:
One took him for a victim of Earl Doorm,
Nor dared to waste a perilous pity on him: 525
Another hurrying past, a man-at-arms,
Rode on a mission to the bandit Earl;
Half whistling and half singing a coarse song,

---

525 ...him,:   :/ (I)   L-ENI
525 (C)   BM-1

Sketch 526-530
    For now there came a whistling man at arms
    And drove the dust against her veilless eyes
    Another flying from his anger made (followed by 532)
                                                  H-35

Sketch 526-529
    Another past, a whistling man-at-arms
    Bound on a mission to the bandit earl
    And drove the dust against her veilless eyes;
                                        Tn-30;T-E
First printed version 526-529
    Another past, a whistling man-at-arms
    Bound on a mission to the bandit earl,
    And drove the dust against her veilless eyes; F-ENI
(Corrections, line by line, follow.)
526   hurried   I MS
         ȶ̶r̶o̶ȶ̶ȶ̶e̶d̶ p̶a̶s̶ȶ̶   I MS
    Another past, a w̶h̶i̶s̶ȶ̶ȴ̶i̶n̶g̶ man-at-arms   L-ENI
526   pass'd   who rode   I MS
    Another h̶u̶ȶ̶ȶ̶i̶e̶d̶ p̶a̶s̶ȶ̶, a man-at-arms,   BM-1
526 (C)   L-EN2

527 Bound on a mission to the bandit earl,   BM-1
527 ...earl;   L-EN2
527 (C)   59

528 (included, I MS)   L-ENI
528 (C)   BM-1

He drove the dust against her veilless eyes:
Another, flying from the wrath of Doorm   530
Before an ever-fancied arrow, made
The long way smoke beneath him in his fear;
At which her palfrey whinnying lifted heel,
And scoured into the coppices and was lost,
While the great charger stood, grieved like a man.   535

But at the point of noon the huge Earl Doorm,

---

529 And drove the dust against her veilless eyes⫻ :
                                    (: I)   L-ENI
529 And drove...   BM-1
529 (C)   L-EN2

530 Another, flying...Doorm⫻   (, I)   L-ENI
530 (C)   BM-1

531 ...arrow, made   (, I)   L-ENI
531 (C)   BM-1

Alt. after 532 But none spoke to her   H-35

533 ...heel,   (, I)   L-ENI
533 (C)   BM-1

535 ...stood, grieved...   ,/ (I)   L-ENI
535 (C)   BM-1

536 ...the broad Earl Doorm   H-35

538 Bent on a...   H-35

539 ...lances by.   H-35

Alt. for 540 And seeing Enid weeping by the way   H-35

540   like one that hails a ship
    But a̶l̶m̶o̶s̶t̶ ere he came t̶o̶ w̶h̶e̶r̶e̶ s̶h̶e̶ s̶a̶t̶   Tn-30

541 Cried out   a
    And spoke in great voice...   H-35

Broad-faced with under-fringe of russet beard,
Bound on a foray, rolling eyes of prey,
Came riding with a hundred lances up;
But ere he came, like one that hails a ship,   540
Cried out with a big voice, 'What, is he dead?'
'No, no, not dead!' she answered in all haste.
'Would some of your kind people take him up,
And bear him hence out of this cruel sun?
Most sure am I, quite sure, he is not dead.'   545

    Then said Earl Doorm: 'Well, if he be not dead,
Why wail ye for him thus? ye seem a child.

Alt. after 541 And she lookt up & answer'd hastily   H-35

542 Oh no no no, he faints from lack of blood   H-35
542 Not so, not...   Tn-30
542 'Not so; not dead!' she...   F-ENI
542 No, no,   I MS
    'N̸o̸t̸ s̸o̸; not...   L-EN3
542 (C)   F-EN2

543   wd
    If some...people w̸o̸d̸ l̸e̸t̸ take...   H-35

544 ...sun: F-ENI
544 (C)   73

545 He is not dead I am quite sure of that   H-35

546 Then spake Earl...   H-35
546 ...Doorm,; 'Well,...   ;/ (I)   L-ENI
546 ...Doorm; 'Well,...   BM-1
546 (C)   73

547 ...wail you for..thus? you seem...   Tn-30;T-E
547   y   I MS
    ...wail you for...thus? Y̸ou seem a child̸. (.I)L-ENI
547 ...wail you for...thus? you seem...   BM-1
547 (C)   69

And be he dead, I count you for a fool;
Your wailing will not quicken him: dead or not,
Ye mar a comely face with idiot tears.   550
Yet, since the face _is_ comely--some of you,
Here, take him up, and bear him to our hall:
An if he live, we will have him of our band;
And if he die, why earth has earth enough
To hide him. See ye take the charger too,   555
A noble one.'

            He spake, and past away,
But left two brawny spearmen, who advanced,
Each growling like a dog, when his good bone
Seems to be plucked at by the village boys

---

548 And if he be, I...		Tn-30
548　　　　dead		
And ȷ́f́ he be, I...		T-E
548　　　　he		I MS
And ȷ́f́ h́é́ be dead...fool,;	(; I)	L-ENI
548 (C)		BM-1

549 ...not help him:　either way		Tn-30;T-E
549　　　quicken　　dead or not,		I MS
...not h́é́ĺṕ him:　é́ít́h́é́ŕ ẃá́ý		L-ENI
549 (C)		BM-1

550 You spoil a pretty face with	(? such childish)	
tears		H-35
550 You spoil a comely face with crying for him.		
		Tn-30;T-E
550　　mar　　　　　　idiot tears		I MS
You śṕó́íĺ a comely face with ćŕ́ýíń́ǵ/f́ó́ŕ/h́íḿ.		L-ENI
550 You mar...		BM-1
550 (C)		_69_

551 ...face _is_ comely...you,.	(ital. and , I)	L-ENI
551 (C)		BM-1

552 Go take...		H-35

553 An		I MS
Áń́d́ if he...		L-ENI
553 (C)		BM-1

Who love to vex him eating, and he fears   560
To lose his bone, and lays his foot upon it,
Gnawing and growling: so the ruffians growled,
Fearing to lose, and all for a dead man,
Their chance of booty from the morning's raid,
Yet raised and laid him on a litter-bier,   565
Such as they brought upon their forays out
For those that might be wounded; laid him on it
All in the hollow of his shield, and took
And bore him to the naked hall of Doorm,
(His gentle charger following him unled)   570
And cast him and the bier in which he lay
Down on an oaken settle in the hall,

---

555 ...See you take...		Tn-30
555 ...See you take...		F-ENI
555 ye		I MS
...See y̸ø̸u̸ take...		L-EN3
555 (C)		F-EN2

562 ...growling: l̸i̸k̸e̸ ₐ d̸ø̸g̸/so...   T-E

564 ...raid;	F-ENI
564 ...raɪd,	73
564 (C)	75

567 those that	
For s̸u̸c̸h̸ a̸s̸ might...	Tn-30
567 ...it,	F-ENI
567 (C)	L-ENI

570 ...following of itself]	Tn-30
570 all unled	
...following ø̸f̸ i̸t̸s̸e̸l̸f̸]	T-E
570 ...following all unled]/	L-ENI
570 ...following all unled]	BM-1
570 (C)	L-EN2

571-572 And laid him on a settle in the hall,   Tn-30;
                                         T-E;F-ENI

571-572 And cast him & the bier on wh he lay   I MS
    A̸n̸d̸ l̸a̸i̸d̸ h̸i̸m̸ ø̸n̸ a̸ s̸e̸t̸t̸l̸e̸ i̸n̸ t̸h̸e̸ h̸a̸l̸l̸
    Down on an oaken settle in the hall (I MS) BM-1

571-572 (C)   L-EN2

And then departed, hot in haste to join
Their luckier mates, but growling as before,
And cursing their lost time, and the dead man,   575
And their own Earl, and their own souls, and her.
They might as well have blest her: she was deaf
To blessing or to cursing save from one.

So for long hours sat Enid by her lord,
There in the naked hall, propping his head,   580
And chafing his pale hands, and calling to him.
Till at the last he wakened from his swoon,
And found his own dear bride propping his head,
And chafing his faint hands, and calling to him;

---

573 ...departed i̶n̶ hot...   Tn-30

575 ...time, and...   ,/ (I)   L-ENI
575 (C)   BM-1

576 ...Earl, and...   ,/ (I)   L-ENI
576 (C)   BM-1

579   for love
    And many an hour sat...   H-35
579   So
    (Par.) A̶n̶d̶ for...   Tn-30

582 And at...   H-35;Tn-30;F-ENI
582 (C)   73

583 And felt his own dear love propping...   H-35
583   ound
    And felt his...   Tn-30

585 And felt her warm tears...   H-35

586 ...heart, 'she...   F-ENI
586 (C)   73

589 ...heart 'she...   F-ENI
589 (C)   73

And felt the warm tears falling on his face;   585
And said to his own heart, 'She weeps for me:'
And yet lay still, and feigned himself as dead,
That he might prove her to the uttermost,
And say to his own heart, 'She weeps for me.'

But in the falling afternoon returned   590
The huge Earl Doorm with plunder to the hall.
His lusty spearmen followed him with noise:
Each hurling down a heap of things that rang
Against the pavement, cast his lance aside,
And doffed his helm: and then there fluttered in,   595
Half-bold, half-frighted, with dilated eyes,
A tribe of women, dressed in many hues,
And mingled with the spearmen: and Earl Doorm

---

590 And in the falling...   H-35

591 The broad Earl...   H-35
591 ...Doorm/ with plunder/ to...   L-ENI
591 (C)   BM-1

592 And all his lusty...   H-35
592 ...noise/:   :/ (I)   L-ENI
592 (C)   BM-1

593 And casting down...   H-35
593   hurling
     Each dashing down...   Tn-30

594 ...pavement: each (? sat) by his lance   H-35

595 ...helm;: and...   :/ (I)   L-ENI
595 (C)   BM-1

596 A tribe of women with...   H-35

597 Half bold half frightend, drest...   H-35

598 ...spearmen;: and Earl Doorm,   :/ (I)   L-ENI
598 ...Doorm,   BM-1
598 ...Doorm/   L-EN3
598 (C)   F-EN2

413

Struck with a knife's haft hard against the board,
And called for flesh and wine to feed his spears.   600
And men brought in whole hogs and quarter beeves,
And all the hall was dim with steam of flesh:
And none spake word, but all sat down at once,
And ate with tumult in the naked hall,
Feeding like horses when you hear them feed;   605
Till Enid shrank far back into herself,
To shun the wild ways of the lawless tribe.
But when Earl Doorm had eaten all he would,
He rolled his eyes about the hall, and found

---

599 Then with a knife's haft struck against...   H-35

600 ...feed his men.   H-35

601 ...hogs & halves of beeves   H-35

603 And so none spoke one word but all sat down   H-35

604 And so they ate...   H-35

605 ...like horses, you could hear them eat   H-35

606 And Enid...   H-35
606 Till
    But Enid...   Tn-30

607 To shun
    N̶o̶t̶ s̶a̶w̶ the wild...   Tn-30

608 But
    A̶n̶d̶ when...   Tn-30

611 ...wept.;   ;/ (I)   L-ENI
611 (C)   BM-1

612 ...there flow'd a power...   Tn-30;T-E
612   came
    ...there f̶l̶o̶w̶'̶d̶ a...him,;   ;/ (I)   L-ENI
612 (C)   BM-1

A damsel drooping in a corner of it.   610
Then he remembered her, and how she wept;
And out of her there came a power upon him;
And rising on the sudden he said, 'Eat!
I never yet beheld a thing so pale.
God's curse, it makes me mad to see you weep.   615
Eat! Look yourself. Good luck had your man,
For were I dead who is it would weep for me?
Sweet lady, never since I first drew breath
Have I beheld a lily like yourself.
And so there lived some colour in your cheek,   620
There is not one among my gentlewomen
Were fit to wear your slipper for a glove.
But listen to me, and by me be ruled,
And I will do the thing I have not done,

Alt. after 612 ~~Which lasted but a minute yet it came~~
                                                       Tn-30

614 ...pale~~,~~ .   (. I)   L-ENI
614 (C)   BM-1

615 ...me ~~sad~~ mad...   Tn-30

Alt. before 618
    Then spake Earl Doorm your good man is dead
    That put your beauty to such flout & scorn.
    By hiding it in rags.   H-35

618 ...breath,   F-ENI
618 (C)   73

620 ...lived more colour...   Tn-30
620   some
    ...lived ~~more~~ colour...   T-E

623 And listen...   Tn-30
623 But
    ~~And~~ listen...   T-E

Alt. after 623
    For I am taken with your faithfulness   Tn-30;T-E

415

For ye shall share my earldom with me, girl,   625
And we will live like two birds in one nest,
And I will fetch you forage from all fields,
For I compel all creatures to my will.'

    He spoke: the brawny spearman let his cheek
Bulge with the unswallowed piece, and turning
                          stared;   630
While some, whose souls the old serpent long had drawn
Down, as the worm draws in the withered leaf
And makes it earth, hissed each at other's ear
What shall not be recorded--women they,
Women, or what had been those gracious things,   635

---

625 And you shall...with me, dame   H-35;Tn-30
625 For   girl
    ~And~ you sha~l~l...me ~dame~   T-E
625 For you shall...   F-ENI
625 (C)   62

627 ...will bring you forage from the fields   H-35

628 For compel all...   H-35

629   the   ~turning~ let his cheek
    He spoke. his brawny spearman ~stared,~ & ~some~ Tn-30

630 ...and turning/ stared,   L-ENI
630 ...stared;   ;/ (MS)   BM-1
630 (C)   L-EN2

631 While
    ~And~ some...   Tn-30
631 ...some whose...drawn/   L-ENI
631 ...some whose...   BM-1
631 (C)   L-EN2

633 ...hiss'd ~at~ each...   Tn-30

644 ...himself has done...   Tn-30

But now desired the humbling of their best,
Yea, would have helped him to it: and all at once
They hated her, who took no thought of them,
But answered in low voice, her meek head yet
Drooping, 'I pray you of your courtesy,   640
He being as he is, to let me be.'

    She spake so low he hardly heard her speak,
But like a mighty patron, satisfied
With what himself had done so graciously,
Assumed that she had thanked him, adding, 'Yea,   645
Eat and be glad, for I account you mine.'

    She answered meekly, 'How should I be glad
Henceforth in all the world at anything,
Until my lord arise and look upon me?'

    Here the huge Earl cried out upon her talk,   650

---

645 ...adding, 'yea,		F-ENI
645 (C)		59

Sketch 647-652
    (Par) ~~Then Enid~~ ~~Yeat~~ ~~I~~ ~~cannot/~~ ~~not~~ ~~be~~ ~~glad~~
~~Henceforth~~ ~~in~~ ~~all/the~~ ~~world~~ ~~at~~ ~~anything~~
~~Unless~~
~~Except~~ ~~this~~ ~~man~~ ~~arise~~ ~~&~~ ~~look~~ ~~upon~~ ~~mely~~
~~He~~ ~~swore~~ ~~a~~ ~~great~~ ~~oath~~   ~~coaly~~
~~Ynot~~ ~~eat/he~~ ~~cried/~~ ~~&~~ ~~by~~ ~~the~~ ~~blackfaced~~ ~~King~~
~~Who~~ ~~first~~ ~~made~~ ~~woman~~ ~~eat~~ ~~the~~ ~~thing~~ ~~he~~ ~~would~~
~~I~~ ~~swear~~ ~~that~~ ~~you~~
~~That~~ ~~she~~ ~~so~~ ~~eat~~   ~~&~~ ~~sitting~~ ~~on~~ ~~her~~   Tn-30

648 ...anything		F-ENI
648 ...anything,	,/ (I)	L-EN3
648 (C)		F-EN2
649 ...me.?'	(?' I)	L-ENI
649 (C)		BM-1
650 ...talk,	(, I)	L-ENI
650 (C)		BM-1

417

As all but empty heart and weariness
And sickly nothing; suddenly seized on her,
And bare her by main violence to the board,
And thrust the dish before her, crying, 'Eat.'

    'No, no,' said Enid, vext, 'I will not eat   655
Till yonder man upon the bier arise,
And eat with me.' 'Drink, then,' he answered. 'Here!'
(And filled a horn with wine and held it to her,)
'Lo! I, myself, when flushed with fight, or hot,

---

652 ...her,	(, I)	L-ENI
652 (C)		BM-1
653 And		
H̸e̸ bare...		Tn-30
654 ...her & said eat.		Tn-30
654 crying		
...her &̸/s̸a̸i̸d̸ 'Eat'		T-E
655 Not so' she said 'by heaven I...		Tn-30
655 No, no, said Enid vext		
(Par.) N̸o̸t̸ s̸o̸ s̸h̸e̸ s̸a̸i̸d̸ b̸y̸ h̸e̸a̸v̸e̸n̸ I...		T-E
655 v		I MS
...Enid, v̸ext, 'I...		L-ENI
655 (C)		BM-1
655 ...eat,		F-EN2
655 (C)		73
656 ...man arise from off the bier		Tn-30
656 upon the bier		
...man arise f̸r̸o̸m̸ o̸f̸f̸ t̸h̸e̸/b̸i̸e̸r̸		T-E
656 ...arise		F-ENI
656 ...arise,	,/ (I)	L-EN3
656 (C)		F-EN2
657 ...answer'd here,		F-ENI
657 'H		I MS
...answer'd. H̸ere!	(.! I)	BM-1
657 ...'Here!		L-EN2
657 (C)		F-EN2

God's curse, with anger--often I myself,   660
Before I well have drunken, scarce can eat:
Drink therefore and the wine will change your will.'

'Not so,' she cried, 'by Heaven, I will not drink
Till my dear lord arise and bid me do it,
And drink with me; and if he rise no more,   665
I will not look at wine until I die.'

At this he turned all red and paced his hall,
Now gnawed his under, now his upper lip,

Alt. after 658 This talk is all from sickly weanness
                                                        Tn-30

659 For I, when fresh from hunt or foray, I.   Tn-30
659 óttéń
    For I...   T-E
659 Lo!   I MS
    'Fóx I, myself,...   L-ENI
659 (C)   BM-1

660 Or hot God's curse with anger I myself   Tn-30
660 Óx Hóx, God's...   T-E
660 ...I, myself,   F-ENI
660 (C)   L-EN2

661 Oft till I...   Tn-30

662 Drink, therefore, and...   F-ENI
662 Drink/ therefore, and...   L-EN3
662 ...therefore, and...   F-EN2
662 (C)   73

663 ...heaven, I...   ,/ (I)   L-ENI
663 (C)   BM-1
663 ...drink,   F-EN2
663 (C)   67

667   At this he turn'd all red & paced
    (Par.) Tńéń śtŕódé tńé ńúǵé éáŕl úṕ & dóẃń his
                        hall   Tn-30

419

And coming up close to her, said at last:
'Girl, for I see ye scorn my courtesies,   670
Take warning: yonder man is surely dead;
And I compel all creatures to my will.
Not eat nor drink? And wherefore wail for one,
Who put your beauty to this flout and scorn
By dressing it in rags? Amazed am I,   675
Beholding how ye butt against my wish,
That I forbear you thus: cross me no more.
At least put off to please me this poor gown,

---

669 Then spake the brute earl Doorm contemptuously H-35
669 ...last,;   ;/ (I)   L-ENI
669 ...last;   BM-1
669 (C)   73

670 I see that you disdaine my courtesies.   H-35
670 Dame, for I see you scorn...   H-35
670   for
    (Par.) Girl, s̸i̸n̸c̸e̸ I see you scorn...   Tn-30
670 ...see you scorn...   T-E
670 ...see you scorn my courtesies -   F-ENI
670 ...see you scorn...   L-EN2
670 (C)   69

671 Be friendly with me: your good man is gone.   H-35
671 ...dead,;   ;/ (I)   L-ENI
671 (C)   BM-1

672 Take counsel: I can force you to my will.   H-35

673 Not eat nor drink?
    C̸r̸o̸s̸s̸ m̸e̸ n̸o̸ m̸o̸r̸e̸: & wherefore...   Tn-30
673   1   I MS
    ...wherefore wai̸t̸ for...   L-ENI
673 (C)   BM-1

675   amazed am I
    ...rags - n̸o̸t̸ e̸a̸t̸ n̸o̸t̸ d̸r̸i̸n̸k̸   Tn-30
675 ...rags. ̸/ Amazed...   L-ENI
675 ...rags. Amazed...   BM-1
675 (C)   59

This silken rag, this beggar-woman's weed:
I love that beauty should go beautifully: 680
For see ye not my gentlewomen here,
How gay, how suited to the house of one
Who loves that beauty should go beautifully?

---

676 Beholding how you butt against my wish
    ~~I am amazed I beat with you so long.~~   Tn-30
676 ...how you butt...   T-E
676 ...how you butt...wish   F-ENI
676 ...how you butt...wish,   ,/ (I)   F-EN2
676 ...how you butt...   59
676 (C)   <u>69</u>

679 At least to please me (3 ?) silk   H-35
679 Put off this silken tatters that you wear
    This beggar maid's weed   H-35
679 ...weed.   F-ENI
679 ...weed.:   :/ (I)   L-EN3
679 (C)   F-EN2

680 That beauty should be suited beautifully   H-35
680 ...beautifully,;   ;/ (I)   L-ENI
680 ...beautifully;   BM-1
680 ...beautifully;:   :/ (I)   L-EN3
680 (C)   F-EN2

681 And see you not...   Tn-30
681 For
    ~~And~~ see you not...   T-E
681 ...see you not...here   F-ENI
681 ...see you not...here,   ,/ (I)   F-EN2
681 ...see you not...   59
681 (C)   <u>69</u>

682 ...one,   ,/ (I)   L-ENI
682 ...one,   BM-1
682 (C)   75

683 ...beautifully.   F-ENI
683 ...beautifully.!   !/ (I)   L-EN3
683 ...beautifully~~/~~?   ?/ (I)   F-EN2
683 ...beautifully!   59
683 (C)   73

Rise therefore; robe yourself in this: obey.'

He spoke, and one among his gentlewomen   685
Displayed a splendid silk of foreign loom,
Where like a shoaling sea the lovely blue
Played into green, and thicker down the front
With jewels than the sward with drops of dew,
When all night long a cloud clings to the hill,   690
And with the dawn ascending lets the day
Strike where it clung: so thickly shone the gems.

But Enid answered, harder to be moved
Than hardest tyrants in their day of power,

---

684 ...therefore clothe yourself...		Tn-30
684 robe		
...therefore ¢l̸ø̸t̸h̸¢ yourself...		T-E
684 ...therefore,; robe...	;/ (I)	L-ENI
684 (C)		BM-1
685 He spake &...		H-35
686 ...silk of (Corbly?)		H-35
686 ...silk of costliest loom		Tn-30;T-E
686 foreign		I MS
...silk of ¢ø̸s̸t̸l̸i̸e̸s̸t̸ loom,		L-ENI
686 (C)		BM-1
689 ...jewels, than...dew		F-ENI
689 ...jewels/ than...dew,	(, I)	L-EN2
689 (C)		L-EN3
690 ...hill		F-ENI
690 (C)		L-EN2
691 ...lets the sun		H-35;Tn-30
691 day		
...lets the s̸u̸n̸		T-E
692 where it couch'd		
Strike on the r̸ø̸ø̸f̸s̸ s̸l̸ø̸p̸¢		H-35
694 Than hardest rulers in...		H-35
694 ...power		F-ENI
694 ...power,	,/ (I)	L-EN3

With life-long injuries burning unavenged,   695
And now their hour has come; and Enid said:

   'In this poor gown my dear lord found me first,
And loved me serving in my father's hall:
In this poor gown I rode with him to court,
And there the Queen arrayed me like the sun: 700
In this poor gown he bad me clothe myself,

----

694 (C)   F-EN2

695 With ancient injuries unavenged, & said   H-35
695   lifelong
   With a̸n̸c̸i̸e̸n̸t̸ injuries...   Tn-30
695 ...unavenged,   (, I)   L-ENI
695 (C)   BM-1

696 ...come,; and...   ;/ (I)   L-ENI
696 (C)   BM-1

697 ...Lord loved me first   H-35
697 ...first   F-ENI
697 (C)   L-EN2

698 When first I met him in my father's hall   H-35
698 ...hall;   F-ENI
698 ...hall;:   :/ (I)   L-EN3
698 (C)   F-EN2

699 In this I followd him to Arthurs court   H-35

700 ...the sun;   F-ENI
700 ...the sun;:   :/ (I)   L-EN3
700 (C)   F-EN2

701 In this my dear Lord bade me clothe myself   H-35
701 ...myself   F-ENI
701 (C)   L-EN2

When now we rode upon this fatal quest
Of honour, where no honour can be gained:
And this poor gown I will not cast aside
Until himself arise a living man,   705
And bid me cast it. I have griefs enough:
Pray you be gentle, pray you let me be:
I never loved, can never love but him:
Yea, God, I pray you of your gentleness,
He being as he is, to let me be.'   710

---

703 ...can be won:			Tn-30
703 gain'd;			
...can be w̸o̸n̸,			T-E
703 ...gain'd;			F-ENI
703 ...gain'd;:	:/	(I)	L-EN3
703 (C)			F-EN2

704 And I will never lay it from my limbs   H-35

706 And bid me cast it from me. let me be			H-35
706 ...grief...			Tn-30
706 ...enough/:	:/	(I)	L-ENI
706 (C)			BM-1

707 If you...	Tn-30
707 Pray	
I̸f̸ you...	T-E

708 ...him,;	(;	I)	L-ENI
708 ...him;			BM-1
708 ...him;:	:/	(I)	L-EN3
708 (C)			F-EN2

709 Yea, God., I...	,/	(I)	L-ENI
709 (C)			BM-1

710 ...me be.'	(.	I)	BM-1
710 (C)			L-EN2

712 ...teeth,	F-ENI
712 (C)	L-EN2

Then strode the brute Earl up and down his hall,
And took his russet beard between his teeth;
Last, coming up quite close, and in his mood
Crying, 'I count it of no more avail,
Dame, to be gentle than ungentle with you;   715
Take my salute,' unknightly with flat hand,
However lightly, smote her on the cheek.

Then Enid, in her utter helplessness,
And since she thought, 'He had not dared to do it,
Except he surely knew my lord was dead,'   720
Sent forth a sudden sharp and bitter cry,

---

713   earl
   Then the brute came close & in his mood   H-35
713 Then coming...   Tn-30
713 Last
   T̸h̸e̸n̸ coming...   T-E

714 Crying s̸a̸y̸i̸n̸g̸ I count it...   H-35

716   my salute
   Take t̸h̸i̸s̸ w̸h̸i̸c̸h̸ m̸i̸g̸h̸t̸ b̸e̸ h̸a̸r̸d̸e̸r̸ with flat hand H-35

717 However lightly yet unknightly struck   H-35

718 (No par. indent.; indent. symbol I)   L-ENI
718 (C)   BM-1

719 ...thought, he...   F-ENI
719 ...thought, 'he   '/ (I)   L-EN3
719 ...thought, 'he   F-EN2
719 (C)   73

720 ...my lord were dead'   H-35
720 ...dead,   F-ENI
720 ...dead, '   '/ (I)   L-EN3
720 (C)   F-EN2

721 Sent out a...   H-35
721 ...cry   F-ENI
721 (C)   59

425

As of a wild thing taken in the trap,
Which sees the trapper coming through the wood.

    This heard Geraint, and grasping at his sword,
(It lay beside him in the hollow shield),   725
Made but a single bound, and with a sweep of it
Shore through the swarthy neck, and like a ball
The russet-bearded head rolled on the floor.
So died Earl Doorm by him he counted dead.
And all the men and women in the hall   730
Rose when they saw the dead man rise, and fled
Yelling as from a spectre, and the two
Were left alone together, and he said:

    'Enid, I have used you worse than that dead man;
Done you more wrong: we both have undergone   735
That trouble which has left me thrice your own;

---

722 ...trap,	,/ (I)	L-ENI
722 (C)		BM-1
724 That heard...		H-35
724 ...sword		F-ENI
724 (C)		59
725 Beside him in the hollow of his shield		H-35
725 ...shield]		F-ENI
725 (C)		F-EN2
729 ...dead⁄ .	(. I)	L-ENI
729 (C)		BM-1
732 Shrieking as from a phantom & he spoke		H-35
Alt. before '734 To Enid (?) I have done you		
wrong,		H-35
734 Enid, more cruel wrong than that dead man,		H-35
734 I have done far more wrong than that dead man		H-35

Henceforward I will rather die than doubt.
And here I lay this penance on myself,
Not, though mine own ears heard you yestermorn--
You thought me sleeping, but I heard you say,   740
I heard you say, that you were no true wife:
I swear I will not ask your meaning in it:
I do believe yourself against yourself,
And will henceforward rather die than doubt.'

   And Enid could not say one tender word,   745
She felt so blunt and stupid at the heart:

---

736 ...I am thrice your own   H-35
736 That   which has left me
   M̶u̶c̶h̶ trouble: E̶n̶i̶d̶ I̶ a̶m̶ thrice your own   Tn-30

738 And I will lay...   H-35;Tn-30
738   here
   And I w̶i̶l̶l̶ lay...   T-E

739 Yea tho'...   H-35
739 ...yester-morn--   F-ENI
739 (C)   84

741 Saying   you were no true wife   H-35

742 That I will never ask what those words meant   H-35
742 ...it;:   :/ (I)   L-ENI
742 (C)   BM-1

743 But will believe...   H-35

744 ...doubt.   F-ENI
744 (C)   L-EN2

746 ...at her heart   H-35

427

She only prayed him, 'Fly, they will return
And slay you; fly, your charger is without,
My palfrey lost.' 'Then, Enid, shall you ride
Behind me.' 'Yea,' said Enid, 'let us go.'   750
And moving out they found the stately horse,
Who now no more a vassal to ·the thief,
But free to stretch his limbs in lawful fight,
Neighed with all gladness as they came, and stooped
With a low whinny toward the pair: and she   755

747-750 She only answer'd ~~pray you~~ Fly my lord at once
         Before these thieves return & murder you
         Your charger is without, my palfrey lost.
         Then shall you ride behind me said the Prince
                                                  Tn-30
747-750   pray'd him
         She only ~~answer'd~~ 'Fly my lord at once
         Before these thieves return & murder you
         Your charger is without; my palfrey lost'
         ~~/Then shall you ride behind me/ said the Prince~~
                                                  T-E
747-749 ...him, 'Fly my lord at once
         Before these thieves return and murder you.
         Your charger is without, my palfrey lost
         For ever.' 'Then,' he answer'd, 'shall you
                       ride   F-ENI
747-750 (Corrected save for following alternate) L-EN2
Alternate after 748
         ~~Before these thieves return and murder you.~~
Alt. after 748 (C)   L-EN3

749 For ever. Then' he answer'd 'shall you ride   T-E

751   horse
     ...the stately ~~steed~~,   Tn-30

754 ~~Neigh'd as they neard & stoopt his noble front~~
     ~~Turnd with all gladness when they came & stoopd~~
     Neigh'd with all gladness ~~toward the/pair~~ as they
                               came & stoopt   Tn-30

Kissed the white star upon his noble front,
Glad also; then Geraint upon the horse
Mounted, and reached a hand, and on his foot
She set her own and climbed; he turned his face
And kissed her climbing, and she cast her arms   760
About him, and at once they rode away.

And never yet, since high in Paradise
O'er the four rivers the first roses blew,
Came purer pleasure unto mortal kind
Than lived through her, who in that perilous hour   765

---

755   the pair
   ...toward t̸h̸e̸m̸, &...   Tn-30
755   whinny   I MS
   ...low w̸h̸i̸n̸i̸n̸g̸ towards the...   L-ENI
755 ...towards̸ the...   BM-1
755 (C)   L-EN2

757   Geraint upon
   ...then h̸e̸ s̸e̸t̸ h̸e̸r̸ o̸n̸ the croupe   Tn-30
757   horse
   ...upon the c̸r̸o̸u̸p̸e̸   T-Ė

758-761 Set her &   cast
        A̸n̸d̸ mounted, & she f̸l̸u̸n̸g̸ her f̸a̸i̸t̸h̸f̸u̸l̸ arms
        bout
        A̸r̸o̸u̸n̸d̸ him, & at once they rode away.   Tn-30
758-761 Set her & mounted & she cast her arms
        About him, & at once they rode away.   T-E

758 Mounted, and lent an arm, and...   T-E;F-ENI
758   reach'd a hand   I MS
            h̸i̸s̸ h̸a̸n̸d̸   I MS
    Mounted, and l̸e̸n̸t̸ a̸n̸ a̸r̸m̸, and...   BM-1
758 (C)   L-EN2

765 Than Enid felt, who...   Tn-30;T-E
765   proved   I MS
    Than Enid f̸e̸l̸t̸, who...   L-ENI
765   lived thro' her   I MS
    Than E̸n̸i̸d̸ p̸r̸o̸v̸e̸d̸, who...   BM-1
765 (C)   L-EN2

Put hand to hand beneath her husband's heart,
And felt him hers again: she did not weep,
But o'er her meek eyes came a happy mist
Like that which kept the heart of Eden green
Before the useful trouble of the rain: 770
Yet not so misty were her meek blue eyes
As not to see before them on the path,
Right in the gateway of the bandit hold,
A knight of Arthur's court, who laid his lance
In rest, and made as if to fall upon him.   775
Then, fearing for his hurt and loss of blood,
She, with her mind all full of what had chanced,
Shrieked to the stranger   'Slay not a dead man!'

---

766 ...heart   F-ENI
766 (C)   BM-1

(Alt. passage inserted in line 767 between "again" and
                        "she")
                 She cd not speak.
    Not even to her own self in silent words,
    And shadows of a sound: I MS
                         (In both L-ENI; BM-1)
767 (C)   L-EN2

770 ...rain;:   :/ (I)   L-ENI
770 (C)   BM-1

775 ...him:.   (. I)   L-ENI
775 (C)   BM-1

778 Shriek'd
    c̶r̶i̶e̶d̶ to...   Tn-3C
778 ...stranger, 'slay...   F-ENI
778 ...stranger, 'Slay...   5⁹
778 (C)   7³

780 ...Edeyrn...   Tn-3C
780 ...Nudd,   ,/ (I)   L-EN]
780 (C)   BM-]

781   shriekd
    ...& c̶r̶i̶e̶d̶ again   Tn-3C

430

'The voice of Enid,' said the knight; but she,
Beholding it was Edyrn son of Nudd,   780
Was moved so much the more, and shrieked again,
'O cousin, slay not him who gave you life.'
And Edyrn moving frankly forward spake:
'My lord Geraint, I greet you with all love;
I took you for a bandit knight of Doorm;   785
And fear not, Enid, I should fall upon him,
Who love you, Prince, with something of the love
Wherewith we love the Heaven that chastens us.
For once, when I was up so high in pride
That I was halfway down the slope to Hell,   790
By overthrowing me you threw me higher.
Now, made a knight of Arthur's Table Round,
And since I knew this Earl, when I myself
Was half a bandit in my lawless hour,

---

783 ...Edeyrn...   Tn-30

786 ...not, Enid, I...   (, , I)   L-ENI
786 (C)   BM-1

787 ...love yon prince with   F-ENI
787   you,   I MS
      ...love y̶o̶n̶ prince, with   BM-1
787 (C)   L-EN2

789   once
      For y̶o̶u̶, when...   Tn-30
789 ...once when...   F-ENI
789 (C)   L-EN2

792 ...Round,   F-ENI
792 (C)   84

793 ...this earl, when...   F-ENI
793 (C)   59

794 ...lawless days,   Tn-30;T-E
794 ...lawless days,   F-ENI
794   hour   MS
      ...lawless d̶a̶y̶s̶,   BM-1
794 (C)   L-EN2

431

GERAINT AND ENID

I come the mouthpiece of our King to Doorm   795
(The King is close behind me) bidding him
Disband himself, and scatter all his powers,
Submit, and hear the judgment of the King.'

    'He hears the judgment of the King of kings,'
Cried the wan Prince; 'and lo, the powers of Doorm   800
Are scattered,' and he pointed to the field,
Where, huddled here and there on mound and knoll,
Were men and women staring and aghast,

---

795 ...our king to...   F-ENI
795 (C)   59

796 ...me], bidding...   F-ENI
796 ...me]/ bidding...   BM-1
796 (C)   L-EN2

798 Submitting to the judgment of...   Tn-30;T-E
798 Submitting to the judgment of the king.'   F-ENI
798 ...the king.'   L-EN2
798 (C)   59

799 'Doorm is disbanded by the King of Fears,
    And suffers judgment from the King of Kings'
                                                   Tn-30;T-E
799 (No par. indent.) 'Doorm is disbanded by the King
                          of Fears,
    And suffers judgment from the King of Kings,'   F-ENI

799 (Alternates cancelled)   L-ENI
799 (Par.) 'He hath submitted to the King of
                          Kings,'   BM-1
799 ...of Kings,'   L-EN2
799 (C)   73

800 Answer'd Geraint & lo...   Tn-30
800 Cried the wan Prince
    A̶n̶s̶w̶e̶r̶'̶d̶ ̶G̶e̶r̶a̶i̶n̶t̶ &...   T-E
800 ...lo the...   F-ENI
800 (C)   73

432

```
While some yet fled; and then he plainlier told
How the huge Earl lay slain within his hall.          805
But when the knight besought him, 'Follow me,
Prince, to the camp, and in the King's own ear
Speak what has chanced; ye surely have endured
Strange chances here alone;' that other flushed,
And hung his head, and halted in reply,               810
```

```
803 Were
        ~~Stood~~ men...staring, others yet              Tn-30
803          & aghast
    ...staring, ~~others~~ ~~yet~~                        T-E

804 Flying aghast, & then...                             Tn-30
804 While some yet fled
    ~~Flying~~ ~~aghast,~~ &...                           T-E

805 ...huge earl lay...                                  F-ENI
806 (C)                                                  59

806-810
    But on the knight's beseeching him to ride
    Back with him to the blameless king & speak
    All that he knew, the other hung his head
    A little flush'd & halted in reply               Tn-30

807 ...the king's own...                                 F-ENI
807 (C)                                                  59

808 ...chanced:  you surely...             Tn-30;T-E
808 ...chanced; ; you surely...        (; I)            L-ENI
808 ...chanced; you surely...                            BM-1
808 (C)                                                  69

809             that other flush'd
    ...alone: ~~he~~ ~~hung~~ ~~his~~ ~~head~~            T-E
809 ...alone:;' that...flush'd,        ;/,/ (I)          L-ENI
809 ...flush'd,                                           BM-1
809 (C)                                                  69

810 And hung his head
    ~~A~~ ~~little~~ ~~flush'd~~ & halted...              T-E
```

GERAINT AND ENID

Fearing the mild face of the blameless King,
And after madness acted question asked:
Till Edyrn crying, 'If ye will not go
To Arthur, then will Arthur come to you,'
'Enough,' he said, 'I follow,' and they went.   815
But Enid in their going had two fears,
One from the bandit scattered in the field,
And one from Edyrn. Every now and then,
When Edyrn reined his charger at her side,
She shrank a little. In a hollow land,   820
From which old fires have broken, men may fear
Fresh fire and ruin. He, perceiving, said:

   'Fair and dear cousin, you that most had cause
To fear me, fear no longer, I am changed.

---

811 ...blameless king,   F-ENI
811 (C)   59

Alt. after 812 ~~At last they were accorded &/they/~~
                             ~~went/~~   Tn-30
813 Till
     ~~But~~ Edeyrn...'if you will...   Tn-30
813 ..., 'If you will...   T-E;F-ENI
813 (C)   69

814 ...you.,'   ,/ (I)   L-ENI
814 (C)   BM-1

816 But Enid/ in their going had two fears, /   L-ENI
816 (C)   BM-1

818 ...Edyrn/ . every...   E   (.E I)   L-ENI
818 (C)   BM-1

821 ...broken, one may...   Tn-30
821   men
    ...broken, /one/ may...   T-E

822 ...ruin/ He, ...   (. I)   L-ENI
822 (C)   BM-1

Yourself were first the blameless cause to make   825
My nature's prideful sparkle in the blood
Break into furious flame; being repulsed
By Yniol and yourself, I schemed and wrought
Until I overturned him; then set up
(With one main purpose ever at my heart)   830
My haughty jousts, and took a paramour;
Did her mock-honour as the fairest fair,
And, toppling over all antagonism,
So waxed in pride, that I believed myself
Unconquerable, for I was wellnigh mad: 835
And, but for my main purpose in these jousts,
I should have slain your father, seized yourself.
I lived in hope that sometime you would come
To these my lists with him whom best you loved;

823-824 Fair & dear cousin, fear not, I am
                    changed.   H-71a;Tn-30;T-E
823-824 (Par.) 'Fair and dear cousin, fear not, I
                    am changed.   F-ENI
823-824 (Corr. in I MS)   L-ENI
823-824 (C)   BM-1

828-829 I overturned Earl Yniol & set up   H-71a

828 ...I plotted, wrought   Tn-30;T-E
828   schemed &   I MS
    ...yourself, I p̸l̸o̸t̸t̸e̸d̸, wrought   L-ENI
828 (C)   BM-1

830 ...purpose burning in   H-71a

835 ...well-nigh...   F-ENI
835 (C)   73

836 And but that my...   H-71a

Alt. after 836 Was yet unanswered I had scarcely
                    faild   H-71a

837 To slay your father & to sieze yourself. H-71a

838 ...you might come   H-71a

And there, poor cousin, with your meek blue eyes,   840
The truest eyes that ever answered Heaven,
Behold me overturn and trample on him.
Then, had you cried, or knelt, or prayed to me,
I should not less have killed him. And you came,--
But once you came,--and with your own true eyes   845
Beheld the man you loved (I speak as one
Speaks of a service done him) overthrow
My proud self, and my purpose three years old,
And set his foot upon me, and give me life.
There was I broken down; there was I saved: 850
Though thence I rode all-shamed, hating the life

---

840 ...eyes -		F-ENI
840 ...eyes ⚹ ,	(, I)	L-EN3
840 (C)		F-EN2
841 ...answer'd heaven -		F-ENI
841 ...answer'd heaven ⚹ ,	(, I)	L-EN3
841 ...answer'd heaven,		F-EN2
841 (C)		73
842 ...him⚹ .	(. I)	L-ENI
842 (C)		BM-1
844 I think I sd have...		Tn-30;T-E
844 *Í&&Í* stet not less		I MS
I *t̸h̸i̸n̸k̸* I should have kill'd him...		L-ENI
844 I *t̸h̸i̸n̸k̸* I should...		BM-1
844 (C)		L-EN2
846 ...loved [I speak of it		
As of a service done me, overthrow		H-71a
848 My purpose three-years old & my proud self		H-71a
850 ...down,; ⚹ there...saved;:	;/:/(I)	L-ENI
850 (C)		BM-1
851 And thence I...hating my life;		H-71a
851 Tho' *r̸i̸d̸i̸n̸g̸* thence...		Tn-30;T-E

He gave me, meaning to be rid of it.
And all the penance the Queen laid upon me
Was but to rest awhile within her court;
Where first as sullen as a beast new-caged,   855
And waiting to be treated like a wolf,
Because I knew my deeds were known, I found,
Instead of scornful pity or pure scorn,
Such fine reserve and noble reticence,
Manners so kind, yet stately, such a grace   860
Of tenderest courtesy, that I began
To glance behind me at my former life,
And find that it had been the wolf's indeed:
And oft I talked with Dubric, the high saint,
Who, with mild heat of holy oratory,   865
Subdued me somewhat to that gentleness,
Which, when it weds with manhood, makes a man.

---

854 ...court.   F-ENI
854 (C)   L-EN2

855 First was I sullen like a beast new-caged.   H-71a;
                                                    Tn-30;T-E
855 Where first all -   I MS
    F̶i̶r̶s̶t̶ w̶a̶s̶ I̶ sullen, like a beast new-caged,
                                        -/ (I)   L-ENI
855 ...first all-sullen, like a beast...   BM-1
855 (C)   L-EN2

857 Because they knew my deeds found instead   H-71a
857 Because they knew my doings; but I found   Tn-30;T-E
857   I knew   deeds l̶i̶f̶e̶/   I MS
    Because they knew my d̶o̶i̶n̶g̶s̶/ b̶u̶t̶ I found,   L-ENI
857 Because I know they knew my deeds, I found,   BM-1
857 (C)   L-EN2

860 Such noble forms of manners, such a grace   H-71a

Alt. for 862 To cast mine eyes upon my behind   H-71a

865 And he with heat of holy oratory   H-71a

866 ...me s̶l̶o̶w̶l̶ somewhat...   Tn-30

437

And you were often there about the Queen,
But saw me not, or marked not if you saw;
Nor did I care or dare to speak with you,   870
But kept myself aloof till I was changed;
And fear not, cousin; I am changed indeed.'

He spoke, and Enid easily believed,
Like simple noble natures, credulous
Of what they long for, good in friend or foe,   875
There most in those who most have done them ill.
And when they reached the camp the King himself
Advanced to greet them, and beholding her

---

868 And you were there but still about the Queen   H-71a

869 And saw...   H-71a

870 ...did I wish nor dare to speak with you   H-71a
870 ...you:,   (, I)   L-ENI
870 (C)   BM-1

871 (Omitted; added in I MS)   L-ENI
871 (C)   BM-1

872 But fear...   H-71a;Tn-30;T-E
872 And
      ~But~ fear...   L-ENI
872 (C)   BM-1

875-876 In those they most have suffer'd from, of
                                   good.   H-71a

877 And so they rode to Arthur's camp & he,   H-71a
877 ...camp/ the king himself   L-ENI
877 .·..the king himself   BM-1
877 (C)   59

878 The King advanced to meet them & withdrew   H-71a
878 ...and/ beholding her/   L-ENI
878 (C)   BM-1

880 With Edyrn for a minute & returnd   H-71a

438

Though pale, yet happy, asked her not a word,
But went apart with Edyrn, whom he held   880
In converse for a little, and returned,
And, gravely smiling, lifted her from horse,
And kissed her with all pureness, brother-like,
And showed an empty tent allotted her,
And glancing for a minute, till he saw her   885
Pass into it, turned to the Prince, and said:

   'Prince, when of late ye prayed me for my leave
To move to your own land, and there defend
Your marches, I was pricked with some reproof,

---

881 ...for a minute & ...   Tn-30
881   little
     ...for a m̸i̸n̸u̸t̸e̸ & ...   T-E

884 ...showd a vacant tent   H-71a
884 ...her;,   ,/ (I)   L-ENI
884 (C)   BM-1

885 ...a moment where she past   H-71a

886 Into the tent, turnd...   H-71a

Sketch 887-891
     Prince that petition wh of late you made
     That you press to your land & there
     Defend your marches prick'd me like reproof
     Since it well suits a king not quite to see
     Thro' others eyes or hear thro' alien ears   H-71a

887   you pray'd me for my leave
     Prince, when y̸o̸u̸ m̸a̸d̸e̸ of late t̸h̸a̸t̸ p̸r̸a̸y̸e̸r̸   H-71a
887 ...late you pray'd...   Tn-30;T-E;F-ENI
887   ye   I MS
     ...late y̸o̸u̸ pray'd...   L-EN3
887 ...late you pray'd...   F-EN2
887 (C)   69

888 To pass to your land, ...   H-71a

As one that let foul wrong stagnate and be,   890
By having looked too much through alien eyes,
And wrought too long with delegated hands,
Not used mine own: but now behold me come
To cleanse this common sewer of all my realm,
With Edyrn and with others: have ye looked   895
At Edyrn? have ye seen how nobly changed?
This work of his is great and wonderful.
His very face with change of heart is changed.
The world will not believe a man repents:
And this wise world of ours is mainly right.   900
Full seldom doth a man repent, or use

---

890 As one that let
    For letting this foul...   Tn-30
890 ...be   F-ENI
890 (C)   L-EN2

891   look'd
    As having s̸e̸e̸n̸ too...   H-71a

894 ...common shore of...   H-71a;Tn-30;T-E
894 ...common shore of...realm,   ,/ (I)   L-ENI
894 ...common shore of...   BM-1
894 (C)   L-EN2

895 ...have you look'd   H-71a;Tn-30;T-E
895 ...have you look'd   F-ENI
895   ye   I MS
    ...have y̸o̸u̸ look'd   L-EN3
895 ...have you look'd   F-EN2
895 (C)   69

896 ...have you seen...   H-71a;Tn-30;T-E
896 ...have you seen...   F-ENI
896   ye   I MS
    ...have y̸o̸u̸ seen...   L-EN3
896 ...have you seen...   F-EN2
896 (C)   69

Both grace and will to pick the vicious quitch
Of blood and custom wholly out of him,
And make all clean, and plant himself afresh.
Edyrn has done it, weeding all his heart   905
As I will weed this land before I go.
I, therefore, made him of our Table Round,
Not rashly, but have proved him everyway
One of our noblest, our most valorous,
Sanest and most obedient: and indeed   910
This work of Edyrn wrought upon himself
After a life of violence, seems to me
A thousand-fold more great and wonderful
Than if some knight of mine, risking his life,
My subject with my subjects under him,   915
Should make an onslaught single on a realm
Of robbers, though he slew them one by one,
And were himself nigh wounded to the death.'

Alt. before 899 This work of his is great & wonderful.
                                      H-71a

901 ...seldom does a man...   Tn-30
901 ...seldom does a man...   T-E; F-ENI
901 (C)   73

904 ...all clear & plant...   Tn-30

905   cleansing all his heart
    Edyrn has done it.   I have watchd him well   H-71a
905 Edeyrn...   Tn-30

906 As I shall cleanse my land before I go   H-71a

907 I A̶n̶d̶ therefore...   H-71a

911 ...Edeyrn...   Tn-30

914 ...if a knight...   H-71a; Tn-30; T-E
914 ...if a knight...   F-ENI
914 (C)   59

918 ...wounded unto death   H-71a

GERAINT AND ENID

So spake the King; low bowed the Prince, and felt
His work was neither great nor wonderful,   920
And past to Enid's tent; and thither came
The King's own leech to look into his hurt;
And Enid tended on him there; and there
Her constant motion round him, and the breath
Of her sweet tendance hovering over him,   925
Filled all the genial courses of his blood
With deeper and with ever deeper love,
As the south-west that blowing Bala lake
Fills all the sacred Dee. So past the days.

---

919 (Par.) Low bowd the tributary Prince & felt		H-71a
919 ...the king; low...		F-ENI
919 (C)		59
921 And past into the tent appointed him.		H-71a
922 The king's own...hurt,;	;/ (I)	L-ENI
922 The king's own...		BM-1
922 (C)		59
925 Of her sweet tendance oer him seem'd to fill		H-71a
926 His heart & all the courses of his blood		H-71a
927 With love that seem'd to deepen, hour by hour		H-71a
930 And while Geraint...		H-35
931 ...forth & set his eyes		H-35
931 ...blameless king went...		F-ENI
931 (C)		59
932 On whom his father Uther...		H-35;Tn-30;T-E
932 On whom his father Uther...		F-ENI
932 (C)	'	69

But while Geraint lay healing of his hurt,   930
The blameless King went forth and cast his eyes
On each of all whom Uther left in charge
Long since, to guard the justice of the King:
He looked and found them wanting; and as now
Men weed the white horse on the Berkshire hills   935
To keep him bright and clean as heretofore,
He rooted out the slothful officer
Or guilty, which for bribe had winked at wrong,
And in their chairs set up a stronger race

---

933 ...since, to...the king: ,/ (I)   L-ENI
933 ...the king: BM-1
933 (C)   59

934   wanting
    And look'd & found them & as men   H-35
934   found them
    He look'd & ád̶l̶l̶ ẃ̶ér̶é̶ wanting; & as men   Tn-30
934 ...as men   T-E
934   now   I MS
    ...wanting,; and as m̶é̶n̶   (; I)   L-ENI
934 (C)   BM-1

935 Weed the white horse upon the Wiltshire hills   Tn-30
935 Weed the white horse upon the Berkshire hills   T-E
935 Men w   on   I MS
    W̶eed the white horse úṕóń the Berkshire hills   L-ENI
935 (C)   BM-1

936   as heretofore
    ,...clean from year to year   H-35

938   for bribes
    ...which h̶á̶d̶ winkd at ṕú̶b̶l̶í̶c̶ wrong   H-35

939   a newer race
    And put ńéẃ ḿéń into their chairs with hands   H-35

With hearts and hands, and sent a thousand men   940
To till the wastes, and moving everywhere
Cleared the dark places and let* in the law,
And broke the bandit holds and cleansed the land.

Then, when Geraint was whole again, they past
With Arthur to Caerleon upon Usk.   945
There the great Queen once more embraced her friend,
And clothed her in apparel like the day.
And though Geraint could never take again
That comfort from their converse which he took
Before the Queen's fair name was breathed upon,   950
He rested well content that all was well.
Thence after tarrying for a space they rode,
And fifty knights rode with them to the shores
Of Severn, and they past to their own land.

Sketch 940 ff
    With hearts & hands & eye;
    To guard the rights of men & everywhere
    With limbs & hands[, & moving elsewhere
    To till the wastes] & sent his workmen in   H-35

952 There after...   Tn-30

953 ...to the ford   Tn-30;T-E
953 ...to the ford   F-ENI
953 (C)   L-EN2

955 ...the king   F-ENI
955 (C)   59

957 ...& the slanderous whisper...   Tn-30
957   spiteful
    ...& the s̸l̸a̸n̸d̸e̸r̸o̸u̸s̸ whisper...   T-E

958 ...chase   F-ENI
958 (C)   59

And there he kept the justice of the King   955
So vigorously yet mildly, that all hearts
Applauded, and the spiteful whisper died:
And being ever foremost in the chase,
And victor at the tilt and tournament,
They called him the great Prince and man of men.   960
But Enid, whom her ladies loved to call
Enid the Fair, a grateful people named
Enid the Good; and in their halls arose
The cry of children, Enids and Geraints
Of times to be; nor did he doubt her more,   965
But rested in her fealty, till he crowned
A happy life with a fair death, and fell

---

961   her   loved to
...whom ~~the palace~~ ladies call'~~d~~   Tn-30
961 But   I MS
~~And~~ Enid,...   L-ENI
961 (C)   BM-1

963-965 Enid the good; nor did he doubt her
                        more.   (Tn-30;T-E cancelled)

965 ...more   F-ENI
965 (C)   73

966   crown'd
...till he/~~fell closed~~   Tn-30
966 ...fealty, till...   (, I)   L-ENI
966 (C)   BM-1

Sketch 967-969
    ~~With glory after many a year of bliss~~
    ~~At Longport/fighting for the blameless King.~~   Tn-30

967   happy   fair
    A ~~noble~~ life with a ~~great~~ death...   Tn-30

445

Against the heathen of the Northern Sea
In battle, fighting for the blameless King.

968-969 At Longport fighting for the blameless
        King   Tn-30;T-E
968-969 At Longport, fighting for the blameless
        king.   F-ENI
968-969 ~~At Longport, fighting for the blameless~~
        ~~King.~~
  ~~In battle with the swarming heathen hordes.~~ I MS
  Against the heathen of the Northern Sea   I MS
  In battle, fighting for the blameless
        King.   (I MS)   L-EN2
968-969 (C)   L-EN3

Balin and Balan

(Prose draft)

Pellam the King who held & lost with Lot had his realm render'd tributary, & he had no child, but Sir Garlon, his heir, was his nephew. And Sir Garlon hated K. A. because the King had refused to make him of his Round Table, knowing him & many times in his anger he had sworn that come what might come he wd pay the tribute no more.

And it chanced on a time that he sat drinking red wine in Lyonesse with King Mark for these were close friends & King (?) spoke of the great King, who hoped to bring the world right by **swearing** his Knights to vows of perfect obedience & perfect purity: & either laugh'd & scorned at the phantasy of so many mighty knights being pure.

And there was with him a damsel of that court Little-held (?) who besotted men with her beauty. & she said What wilt thou wager, Sir King with me that I do not go to the court of His & bring back loveblind from there pure ones, yea, both (?) were it curl from the golden beard of Arthur. Have we not heard that this Lancelot worships no unwedded damsel but the Queen herself, to show forsooth, his utter selflessness, swears by her, & fights in her name. here be snakes in the grass, wh methinks I can stir till they sting.

Go an thou wilt said Mark the King & an thou canst make a mischief among them there is nothing I will not grant thee.

Then spake Sir Garlon. I ride in the tomorrow back to the Castle of King Pellam on thy way to Arthur. Ride thou with me. ~~but when they came~~ & she took with her a squire whom now she treated as a lover & now she mocked as a child. & the boy was besotted with her. But King Pellam thrust her from the gates. & there she dwelt among the woods awhile waiting for Garlon to go with her. And Garlon ever kept the tribute from being paid.

BALIN AND BALAN

(The first opening for the poem, present in the two
sketches below, incorporates material later used in
II. 9-20.)

Opening. 1st Sketch.
   (Par.) There came a sound to Arthur of two knights
   Who sat near Camelot at a fountain side
   A mile beneath the beechwood, challenging
   And overthrowing every knight who past,
   For Lancelot and the mightier were away.
   (Par.) These things were told the king, & one
                       fair dawn
   Early, the spirit of his youth return'd
   On Arthur, till he arm'd himself & rode
   Beneath   H-32

Opening. 2nd Sketch.
   (Par.) There came a sound to Arthur of two Knights
   Who sat near Camelot at a fountain side,
   A mile beneath the forest, challenging
   And overthrowing every knight who past,
   For Lancelot & the mightier were away.
   (Par.) These things were told the King, & one
                       fair dawn
   Tho Early, the spirit of his youth return'd
   On Arthur, till he arm'd, & rode away;   HM-1323

449

BALIN AND BALAN

Pellam the King, who held and lost with Lot
In that first war, and had his realm restored
But rendered tributary, failed of late
To send his tribute; wherefore Arthur called
His treasurer, one of many years, and spake,   5
'Go thou with him and him and bring it to us,
Lest we should set one truer on his throne.
Man's word is God in man.'
                                His Baron said
'We go but harken: there be two strange knights
Who sit near Camelot at a fountain-side,   10
A mile beneath the forest, challenging
And overthrowing every knight who comes.

---

1 Pelles a king, who held the side of Lot   HM-1323
1   & lost with
...who held t̸h̸e̸ s̸i̸d̸e̸ ø̸f̸ Lot   Tn-31
1 ...the king, who...   L-Bl
1 (C)   L-B2

2 In that first battle, had his realm restored   HM-1323

3 But r̸e̸n̸d̸e̸r̸'̸d̸ tributary, having fail'd of late HM-1323

4 To send the tribute owing, Arthur call'd   HM-1323

5 A r̸e̸v̸e̸r̸e̸n̸t̸ man of many years, his treasurer,
                              saying   HM-1323
5 ...spake,   ,/ (I)   L-Bl
5 (C)   L-B2

7 Lest I sd...   HM-1323
7 ...throne ⊙   (I)   L-Bl
7 (C)   L-B2

10 ...fountain side,   L-Bl
10 (C)   85

12   every knight who comes
   And overthrowing a̸l̸l̸ t̸h̸e̸ k̸n̸i̸g̸h̸t̸s̸ w̸h̸o̸ p̸a̸s̸s̸.   HM-1323

450

BALIN AND BALAN

Wilt thou I undertake them as we pass,
And send them to thee?'
                    Arthur laughed upon him,
'Old friend, too old to be so young, depart,   15
Delay not thou for aught, but let them sit,
Until they find a lustier than themselves.'

  So these departed. Early, one fair dawn,
The light-winged spirit of his youth returned
On Arthur's heart; he armed himself and went,   20
So coming to the fountain-side beheld
Balin and Balan sitting statuelike,
Brethren, to right and left the spring, that down,
From underneath a plume of lady-fern,
Sang, and the sand danced at the bottom of it.   25
And on the right of Balin Balin's horse

---

13 ...thou we undertake...   HM-1323

14 ...him.   ⊙ (I)   L-B1
14 (C)   L-B2

15 Blessed the land whose old men keep their
                     youth   HM-1323

16 But stay not thou for aught; & let them sit HM-1323

21 And coming...   H-32

23 Bretheren, on either side the spring, that rose H-32
23 ...spring that s̸a̸n̸g̸ down   HM-1323

24 ...lady-fern,   ,/(-, I)   L-B1
24 (C)   L-B2

25 And at the bottom danced the silver sand   H-32
25 Sang, & the
   T̸h̸e̸ s̸i̸l̸v̸e̸r̸ sand danced...   HM-1323

28 ...Balan's by a poplar...   H-32

29 ...Sirs' said Arthur 'wherefore...   L-B1
29 ...Sirs,' said Arthur', wherefore... (,, I) L-B2
29 (C)   85

BALIN AND BALAN

Was fast beside an alder, on the left
Of Balan Balan's near a poplartree.
'Fair Sirs,' said Arthur, 'wherefore sit ye here?'
Balin and Balan answered 'For the sake   30
Of glory; we be mightier men than all
In Arthur's court; that also have we proved;
For whatsoever knight against us came
Or I or he have easily overthrown.'
'I too,' said Arthur, 'am of Arthur's hall,   35
But rather proven in his Paynim wars
Than famous jousts; but see, or proven or not,
Whether me likewise ye can overthrow.'
And Arthur lightly smote the brethren down,
And lightly so returned, and no man knew.   40

---

30   F   I MS
   ...answer'd 'for...   L-B1
30 (C)   L-B2

31 ...be better knights than all   H-32;HM-1323

32 ...have we proven.   H-32;Tn-31

33 ...knight c̸a̸m̸e̸ f̸o̸r̸t̸h̸ against us came   H-32

34 Or I or he (1 ?)
   H̸i̸m̸ h̸e̸r̸e̸/w̸e̸ overthrown...   H-32

35 Said Arthur I too am of Arthur's hall   H-32
35 ...too' said Arthur 'am...   L-B1
35 ...too,'said Arthur, 'am...   (,, I)   L-B2
35 (C)   85

37 Than famous in his jousts. such as I am   H-32
37 Than in his jousts; but such, or proven or not,
                                                 HM-1323

38 See whether me too ye can overthrow.   H-32;HM-1323
38 ...overthrow.'   (.' I)   L-B1
38 (C)   L-B2

39 But Arthur...   HM-1323

452

BALIN AND BALAN

Then Balin rose, and Balan, and beside
The carolling water set themselves again,
And spake no word until the shadow turned;
When from the fringe of coppice round them burst
A spangled pursuivant, and crying, 'Sirs,   45
Rise, follow! ye be sent for by the King,'
They followed; whom when Arthur seeing asked

---

41   So
   (Par.) ~~Then~~ Balin...   HM-1323
41 ...rose, and Balan, and...   ,/,/(I)   L-B1
41 (C)   L-B2

42 The laughing water...   H-32
42 The warbling water...   HM-1323
42 ...again,   ,/ (I)   L-B1
42 (C)   L-B2

44 And,   them
   Then from the fringing coppice round ~~the twain~~
                        burst   H-32
44 Then from the fringing coppice...   HM-1323

46 ...the king,'   ,/ (P)   L-B1
46 (C)   L-B2

47 ...whom the king beholding ask'd   H-32

48 ...names' whereon in words   H-32

50   A   A I MS
   Saying 'am   L-B1
50 (C)   L-B2

51 Balin, the Savage, I: ~~he here hi~~ king & this
                        man here   H-32
51 Balin the Savage I - the addition, thine,   HM-1323
51 ...Savage, I - the addition...   Tn-31
51   at   I MS
   Balin, "the Savage" - the addition... (,"" I) L-B1
51 (C)   L-B2

453

'Tell me your names; why sat ye by the well?'
Balin the stillness of a minute broke
Saying 'An unmelodious name to thee,   50
Balin, "the Savage"--that addition thine--
My brother and my better, this man here,
Balan. I smote upon the naked skull
A thrall of thine in open hall, my hand
Was gauntleted, half slew him; for I heard   55
He had spoken evil of me; thy just wrath
Sent me a three-years' exile from thine eyes.
I have not lived my life delightsomely:
For I that did that violence to thy thrall,
Had often wrought some fury on myself,   60
Saving for Balan: those three kingless years
Have past--were wormwood-bitter to me. King,

52-53 Balan my brother, & my better   H-32

52 ...here,   ,/ (, P)   L-B1
52 (C)   L-B2

53 ...naked head   H-32

54 A thrall of thine in hall my hand   H-32

55 Was gauntleted, nigh slew him: thy just wrath H-32
55 ...slew him: thy just wrath   HM-1323

56 He had spoken evil of me   HM-1323

57 Madest me a...   H-32

60 Often had wrought some violence on myself   H-32
60   fury on
   ...some v̸i̸o̸l̸e̸n̸c̸e̸ t̸o̸ myself   HM-1323
60 ...myself,   L-B1
60 (C)   L-B2

62 ...me. Sire   HM-1323;Tn-31
62   King   I MS
   ...me. S̸i̸r̸e̸   L-B1
62 (C)   L-B2

Methought that if we sat beside the well,
And hurled to ground what knight soever spurred
Against us, thou would'st take me gladlier back,   65
And make, as ten-times worthier to be thine
Than twenty Balins, Balan knight.   I have said.
Not so--not all. A man of thine today
Abashed us both, and brake my boast. Thy will?'
Said Arthur 'Thou hast ever spoken truth;   70
Thy too fierce manhood would not let thee lie.
Rise, my true knight. As children learn, be thou
Wiser for falling! walk with me, and move
To music with thine Order and the King.
Thy chair, a grief to all the brethren, stands   75

64	And overthrew what knight soever came		H-32
64	...soever prickt		HM-1323
65	...back,	,/ (I)	L-B1
65	(C)		L-B2
66	...worthier to be knight		H-32
68	...all: a knight of thine...		HM-1323
68	...thine to-day		L-B1
68	(C)		85
69	...both, and...	,/ (I)	L-B1
69	(C)		L-B2
70	(Par. Indent.)		Tn-31
70	T		I MS
	...Arthur 'thou...truth;	;/ (I)	L-B1
70	(C)		L-B2
72	Arise my knight: be stronger for thy fall.		HM-1323
72	wiser		
	Rise, my true knight; the ~~stronger~~ for thy fall		HM-1323
73	As children are, & walk henceforth with me.		HM-1323
73	Wiser for falling!		
	~~The wiser for thy fall~~ & walk...		Tn-31
73	...me, and...	,/ (I)	L-B1
73	(C)		L-B2

455

Vacant, but thou retake it, mine again!'

    Thereafter, when Sir Balin entered hall,
The Lost one Found was greeted as in Heaven
With joy that blazed itself in woodland wealth
Of leaf, and gayest garlandage of flowers,   80
Along the walls and down the board; they sat,
And cup clashed cup; they drank and some one sang,
Sweet-voiced, a song of welcome, whereupon

---

74 ...the king.			L-B1
74 (C)			L-B2
75 ...bretheren, stands		,/ (I)	L-B1
75 (C)			L-B2
76		mine again.'	
Vacant in hall: resume it - ⱥłł łⱥ wełł.'			HM-1323
77 (Par.) Thereafter, when...hall,		,/,/(I)	L-B1
77 (C)			L-B2
78 ...was welcomed as...			H-32
78 greeted			
...was wełⱥⱥⱥⱥⱥⱥ as...			HM-1323
78 H			I MS
...in heaven			L-B1
78 (C)			L-B2
79 to 81 With such a joy as blazed itself in wealth			
Of woodland leaf & gayest garlandage			
Of blossom on the table & the walls			H-32
80 ...leaf, and...flowers,		,/,/(I)	L-B1
80 (C)			L-B2
81 ...they satⱥ,			L-B1
81 (C)			L-B2
82 ...sang,		,/ (I)	L-B1
82 (C)			L-B2
83 whereupon			
...of welcome, ⱥⱥⱥⱥⱥ wⱥⱥⱥⱥ			HM-1323

Their common shout in chorus, mounting, made
Those banners of twelve battles overhead   85
Stir, as they stirred of old, when Arthur's host
Proclaimed him Victor, and the day was won.

Then Balan added to their Order lived
A wealthier life than heretofore with these
And Balin, till their embassage returned.   90

'Sir King' they brought report 'we hardly found,
So bushed about it is with gloom, the hall
Of him to whom ye sent us, Pellam, once
A Christless foe of thine as ever dashed
Horse against horse; but seeing that thy realm   95
Hath prospered in the name of Christ, the King
Took, as in rival heat, to holy things;

---

84 The   voice in
   A common shout of chorus...   HM-1323

85   ose
   The banners...   HM-1323

86 ...Arthur's hosts   HM-1323

Sketch 88 ff
   (Par.) So Balan, added to their Table, stood
   Before the King, to whom one day there came
   An ancient Baron sent from him to claim
   Tribute of Pelles, one who l̸o̸s̸t̸ the side
   Of Lot, when Arthur w̸o̸n̸ ̸ winning, took his realm
   Gave it again but made it tributary.   H-37

88 (Par.) So Balan, added to their Table, lived   H-37
88 to 136 (Par.) Then Balan, added to the Table took
          A quest that came, & rode away; but
                         first   HM-1323
(HM-1323 has this elision; then continues with 136 ff.)

89 A richer life than...   H-37

90 ...Balin, till   ,/ (I)   L-B1
90 (C)   L-B2

457

And finds himself descended from the Saint
Arimathaean Joseph; him who first
Brought the great faith to Britain over seas;   100

Prose and Verse Sketch for 91 ff
    We got the tribute with much ado. for the King is
                      old & hath
fallen into dreams, & his brother, Sir Garlon rules
                    him & his
& he would fain be holier than thou art & so hath put
his wife away, & lets not dame or damsel enter his
                    castle,
holding them a pollution, & hath let all things go
                    to wrack
& we past into his chapel, & saw
        Thorns of the crown & shivers of the cross
        Rich arcs with precious bone of martyrdom
& Sir Garlon hates thee & thine, & cried out a-
                  gainst the
tribute.
& thus we saw the spear wherewith the soldier Longus
pierced our Lord & which he said was inherited from
his ancestor Joseph of Aromat - (1 ?) is he in his
fantasies (?)
But I will tell thee another thing. In the woods
nigh Pelles castle we found a knight of thine speared
thro' the back & again another whom we buried
& whether this be the work of a bandit or Sir Garlon
it behoves thee to look to it   H-37

91 ...report' we found with pain,   H-37
91 'Sir king'...found,   (, I)   L-Bl
91 (C)   L-B2

92 So grown about it is...   H-37

93 ...us, Pelles, once...   H-37

94 As fierce a foe of thine,...   H-37

96 Was made, & prospered thro' the name of Xt   H-37
96 ...the king   L-Bl
96 (C)   L-B2

458

He boasts his life as purer than thine own;
Eats scarce enow to keep his pulse abeat;
Hath pushed aside his faithful wife, nor lets
Or dame or damsel enter at his gates
Lest he should be polluted. This gray King   105
Showed us a shrine wherein were wonders--yea--
Rich arks with priceless bones of martyrdom,
Thorns of the crown and shivers of the cross,
And therewithal (for thus he told us) brought
By holy Joseph hither, that same spear   110
Wherewith the Roman pierced the side of Christ.
He much amazed us; after, when we sought

_____

101 And boasts...   H-37

105 ...gray king   L-Bl
105 (C)   L-B2

106   wonders - yea
    ...were ~~wonderous things~~   H-37

107 ...with precious bones...   H-37;Tn-31
107   k   I MS
    Rich arcs with ~~precious~~ bones...   (Corr. I)   L-Bl
107 (C)   L-B2

109-110 And therewithal the spear [for thus he said]H-37

112 Wh made us marvel much, but when we sought   H-37

113 The tribute, told us, he had quite forgone   H-37
113 ...answer'd 'I...   L-Bl
113 (C)   92

114 ...Garlon, his heir   H-37
114 ...heir   85
114 (C)   88

115 ...this Garlon paid (1 ?)   H-37
115 ...it,' which...   L-Bl
115 (C)   92

The tribute, answered "I have quite foregone
All matters of this world: Garlon, mine heir,
Of him demand it," which this Garlon gave   115
With much ado, railing at thine and thee.

'But when we left, in those deep woods we found
A knight of thine spear-stricken from behind,
Dead, whom we buried; more than one of us
Cried out on Garlon, but a woodman there   120
Reported of some demon in the woods
Was once a man, who driven by evil tongues
From all his fellows, lived alone, and came
To learn black magic, and to hate his kind
With such a hate, that when he died, his soul   125
Became a Fiend, which, as the man in life
Was wounded by blind tongues he saw not whence,

---

116 ...at thee & thine.'		H-37
117 (Par.) But...		L-B1
117 (C)		92
119 ...buried: there were some of us		H-37
121 some ...of a demon...		H-37
122 ...man, who...	,/ (I)	L-B1
122 (C)		L-B2
123 From all men, lived alone, & ~~learnt~~ came to learn		H-37
123 ...alone, and...	,/ (I)	L-B1
123 (C)		L-B2
124 Black magic, & to hate ~~his~~ fellowmen his kind		H-37
126 Became a demon, & as he in life		H-37
126 Fiend Became a ~~devil~~, which, ...		Tn-31
127 ...whence ~~/~~ ,	,/ (I)	L-B1
127 (C)		L-B2

Strikes from behind. This woodman showed the cave
From which he sallies, and wherein he dwelt.
We saw the hoof-print of a horse, no more.'   130

    Then Arthur, 'Let who goes before me, see
He do not fall behind me: foully slain
And villainously! who will hunt for me
This demon of the woods?' Said Balan, 'I'!

---

128 Strikes from behind. I have seen the flash of him
      The woodman said, & pointed out the cave   H-37

130 We ⱦ saw...   H-37

Alt. after 130 (Par.) Sir Balin when they spake of evil
                              tongues
                  Beheld his brother's face   H-37

131   L   I MS
    ...Arthur 'let...   L-Bl
131 ...Arthur, 'Let...   Comma (I MS)   L-B2
131 (C)   85

132-134 ...me. Who will hunt
        This demon of the woods?'...   H-37

134 ...,'I'!   !/ (P)   L-Bl
134 (C) (I.e., as corrected above)   L-B2

135   q   I MS
    ...the guest...first,   ,/ (I)   L-Bl
135 (C)   L-B2

136 ...Balin., 'Good...hear!   ,/!/(I)   L-Bl
136 ...'Good, my...   comma (I MS)   L-B2
136 (C)   92

137 ...prevail, when...   ,/ (I)   L-Bl
137 (C)   L-B2

138 ...them: yea believe them fiends   HM-1323
138 ...fiends,   ,/ (I)   L-Bl
138 (C)   L-B2

461

So claimed the quest and rode away, but first,   135
Embracing Balin, 'Good my brother, hear!
Let not thy moods prevail, when I am gone
Who used to lay them! hold them outer fiends,
Who leap at thee to tear thee; shake them aside,
Dreams ruling when wit sleeps! yea, but to dream   140
That any of these would wrong thee, wrongs thyself.
Witness their flowery welcome. Bound are they
To speak no evil. Truly save for fears,
My fears for thee, so rich a fellowship
Would make me wholly blest: thou one of them,   145

---

140 ruling when wit sleeps - yea but to dream   HM-1323

141 To dream that these will wrong thee wrongs
                        thyself   HM-1323

142-3   way of
        Witness their flowery welcome. Save for fears ø̸f̸
                        t̸h̸ø̸ø̸   HM-1323
142-3 Witness their flowery welcome. Save for fears
                                                      HM-1323

142 Witness their flowery...   Not Ital.(I MS)   L-Bl
142 (C)   L-B2

143   T   I MS
    ...evil. truly...   ⊙ (I)   L-Bl
143 (C)   L-B2

144 Most blessed in such a fellowship   HM-1323
144 ...thee, so sweet a fellowship   HM-1323

Sketch 145 ff
    Would make one blest. for no hatred lives
    Nor no more insult than in heaven itself
    No more of jealousy than in Paradise
    (Par.) Wilt thou consider them
    Their common bond of love, their courtesies
    Art thou not one of them?   HM-1323

145 Makes me all blest: an thou be one of these HM-1323
145 ...thou, ḁ̸l̸l̸ one of them,   Tn-31

Be one indeed: consider them, and all
Their bearing in their common bond of love,
No more of hatred than in Heaven itself,
No more of jealousy than in Paradise.'

    So Balan warned, and went; Balin remained: 150
Who--for but three brief moons had glanced away
From being knighted till he smote the thrall,
And faded from the presence into years
Of exile--now would strictlier set himself
To learn what Arthur meant by courtesy,   155
Manhood, and knighthood; wherefore hovered round
Lancelot, but when he marked his high sweet smile

146	Brother, be one indeed: consider them,		HM-1323
146	...consider <u>them</u>, and...	Not Ital. (I MS)	L-B1
146	(C)		L-B2

147	...bearing & their...		HM-1323
147	...love,	,/ (I)	L-B1
147	(C)		L-B2

Alt. after 147 And all their courtesies - no insult,
                      scorn-   HM-1323

150	But Balin wd not hurry himself ~~away~~		H-32
150	But Balin wd not hurry from the court		H-32
150	(Par.) So Balan warn'd & went: but he re-main'd;		HM-1323
150	...warn'd, and...	,/ (I)	L-B1
150	(C)		L-B2

151	a month had scarcely glanced away		H-32
151	For seeing that but one moon had glanced away		H-32
151	...three short moons		HM-1323

| 152 | ...thrall, | ,/ (I) | L-B1 |
| 152 | (C) | | L-B2 |

| 154 | Of exile, he would set himself to learn | | H-32 |

In passing, and a transitory word
Make knight or churl or child or damsel seem
From being smiled at happier in themselves--   160
Sighed, as a boy lame-born beneath a height,
That glooms his valley, sighs to see the peak
Sun-flushed, or touch at night the northern star;
For one from out his village lately climbed
And brought report of azure lands and fair,   165
Far seen to left and right; and he himself
Hath hardly scaled with help a hundred feet
Up from the base: so Balin marvelling oft
How far beyond him Lancelot seemed to move,

---

155 What the great king might mean by knightliness H-32

156 Manhood & courtesy;...   H-32
156 ...knighthood; therefore hover'd...   HM-1323

157 ...but - when...   L-B1
157 (C)   L-B2

159 Make knight & damsel even thrall & churl   H-32
159 Make knight & churl & child & damsel...   HM-1323

162 That darkens 𝑎𝑙𝑙 half his valley, sees the peak H-32

163 Sun-flush'd, or...   ,/ (I)   L-B1
163 (C)   L-B2

164 And one from...   H-32;HM-1323

165 ...of goodly lands...   H-32

166 Far seen to west & East - ...   H-32

167 Has hardly...   H-32

169 ...far above him...   HM-1323

Groaned, and at times would mutter, 'These be
                            gifts,   170
Born with the blood, not learnable, divine,
Beyond <u>my</u> reach. Well had I foughten--well--
In those fierce wars, struck hard--and had I crowned
With my slain self the heaps of whom I slew--
So--better!--But this worship of the Queen,   175
That honour too wherein she holds him--this,
This was the sunshine that hath given the man
A growth, a name that branches o'er the rest,
And strength against all odds, and what the King
So prizes--overprizes--gentleness.   180

```
170 He moan'd & marvell'd thinking 'These be gifts   H-32
170 Moan'd & at...                                  HM-1323
170           T                                      I MS
    ...mutter 'these...                              L-B1
170 ...mutter, 'These...          comma (I MS)       L-B2
170 (C)                                              85


172 ...reach:  I might have foughten well            HM-1323


176 ...him - these                                   HM-1323
176 ... - this,                      ,/(I)           L-B1
176 (C)                                              L-B2


Alt. before 177               Lancelot
    Surely that worship which he gives the Queen
    And all that honour [to himself he said]
    In which she holds him, these have wrought upon him,
    Still gazing on her grace & stateliness,         H-32


177     the sweet
    Until sunshine gave the man                      H-32
177 These were the sunshine...                       HM-1323


178 Growth & a name that branches o'er the rest.     H-32
178         a
    Growth & name...                                 HM-1323
178 Growth, & a name...                              Tn-31
178 A g                                              I MS
    G̸r̸owth, a̸n̸d̸ a name...                           L-B1
178 (C)                                              L-B2
```

Her likewise would I worship an I might.
I never can be close with her, as he
That brought her hither. Shall I pray the King
To let me bear some token of his Queen
Whereon to gaze, remembering her--forget   185
My heats and violences? live afresh?
What, if the Queen disdained to grant it! nay
Being so stately-gentle, would she make
My darkness blackness? and with how sweet grace
She greeted my return! Bold will I be--   190
Some goodly cognizance of Guinevere,
In lieu of this rough beast upon my shield,
Langued gules,and toothed with grinning savagery.'

And Arthur, when Sir Balin sought him, said

---

179 ...the king   L-B1
179 (C)   L-B2

180 A̶n̶d̶ w̶h̶a̶t̶ t̶h̶e̶ K̶i̶n̶g̶ s̶o̶ p̶r̶i̶z̶e̶s̶; gentleness.
    So prizes - overprizes   HM-1323

181 ...likewise will I ...an I may.   H-32

Alt. after 181 Forget my violences, & live anew - H-32

183 ...the king   L-B1
183 (C)   L-B2

Alt. after 184 S̶o̶m̶e̶ f̶a̶i̶r̶ d̶e̶v̶i̶c̶e̶   HM-1323

186 ...violences, & live...   HM-1323
186 ...violences - ? live afresh. ?   ??/(I)   L-B1
186 (C)   L-B2

187 But if the Queen denied it. Wd she nay   HM-1323

192 In place of...   H-32
192 ...shield,   ,/ (I)   L-B1
192 (C)   L-B2

193 ...gules, and...   ,/ (I)   L-B1
193 (C)   L-B2

'What wilt thou bear?' Balin was bold, and asked   195
To bear her own crown-royal upon shield,
Whereat she smiled and turned her to the King,
Who answered 'Thou shalt put the crown to use.
The crown is but the shadow of the King,
And this a shadow's shadow, let him have it,   200
So this will help him of his violences!'
'No shadow' said Sir Balin 'O my Queen,
But light to me! no shadow, O my King,
But golden earnest of a gentler life!'

So Balin bare the crown, and all the knights   205
Approved him, and the Queen, and all the world
Made music, and he felt his being move
In music with his Order, and the King.

The nightingale, full-toned in middle May,
Hath ever and anon a note so thin   210

---

195 will ye bear
   What token, knight. Balin...   HM-1323

196   upon
  .. crown-royal ø̸ǿ t̸h̸ǿ shield   HM-1323
196 ...shield,   ,/ (I) L-B1
196 (C)   L-B2

197 ...the king,   ,/ (I) L-B1
197 (C)   L-B2

199 ...the king,   L-B1
199 (C)   L-B2

201   is
   So that will...   HM-1323

203 ...my king   L-B1
203 (C)   92

204   gentler
  ...of a loftier life.'   HM-1323

208 ...the king.   L-B1
208 (C)   L-B2

It seems another voice in other groves;
Thus, after some quick burst of sudden wrath,
The music in him seemed to change, and grow
Faint and far-off.
                              And once he saw the thrall
His passion half had gauntleted to death,   215
That causer of his banishment and shame,
Smile at him, as he deemed, presumptuously:
His arm half rose to strike again, but fell:
The memory of that cognizance on shield
Weighted it down, but in himself he moaned: 220

        'Too high this mount of Camelot for me:
These high-set courtesies are not for me.
Shall I not rather prove the worse for these?
Fierier and stormier from restraining, break
Into some madness even before the Queen?   225

        Thus, as a hearth lit in a mountain home,
And glancing on the window, when the gloom
Of twilight deepens round it, seems a flame

---

209 ...nightingale, full -...May,	, ,/(I)	L-B1
209 (C)		L-B2
212 ...wrath,	,/(I)	L-B1
212 (C)		L-B2
213 ...change, and...	,/(I)	L-B1
213 (C)		L-B2
220 ...moan'd.:	:/ (P)	L-B1
220 (C)		L-B2
224 ...stormier/ from restraining, break ,/(I)		L-B1
224 (C)		L-B2
225 e'vn		I MS
...madness e'en before...		L-B1
225 ...madness e'vn before...		L-B2
228 ...twilight saddens round...		Tn-31
228 deepens		I MS
...twilight s̸a̸d̸d̸e̸n̸s̸ round...		L-B1
228 (C)		L-B2

That rages in the woodland far below,
So when his moods were darkened, court and King   230
And all the kindly warmth of Arthur's hall
Shadowed an angry distance: yet he strove
To learn the graces of their Table, fought
Hard with himself, and seemed at length in peace.

Then chanced, one morning, that Sir Balin sat   235
Close-bowered in that garden nigh the hall.
A walk of roses ran from door to door;
A walk of lilies crost it to the bower:
And down that range of roses the great Queen
Came with slow steps, the morning on her face;   240
And all in shadow from the counter door
Sir Lancelot as to meet her, then at once,
As if he saw not, glanced aside, and paced
The long white walk of lilies toward the bower.
Followed the Queen; Sir Balin heard her 'Prince,   245

---

230 ...and king   L-B1
230 (C)   L-B2

235 (Par.) It chanced...   HM-1323
235 ...chanced, one...   ,/(I)   L-B1
235 (C)   L-B2

239 And thro' the range...   HM-1323

240   with slow steps,
    Came s̷l̷o̷w̷l̷y̷, w̷i̷t̷h̷ the morning in her face   HM-1323
240 ...face,;   ;/ (I)   L-B1
240 (C)   L-B2

242 Sir
    Came Lancelot...   HM-1323

244   the long
    Down that white walk...   HM-1323
244 ...bower.   ⊙ (I)   L-B1
244 (C)   L-B2

246 Art so little...   HM-1323

247 ...without goodmorrowing to the Queen?   HM-1323

BALIN AND BALAN

Art thou so little loyal to thy Queen,
As pass without good morrow to thy Queen?'
To whom Sir Lancelot with his eyes on earth,
'Fain would I still be loyal to the Queen?'
'Yea so' she said 'but so to pass me by--   250
So loyal scarce is loyal to thyself,
Whom all men rate the king of courtesy.
Let be: ye stand, fair lord, as in a dream.'

    Then Lancelot with his hand among the flowers
'Yea--for a dream. Last night methought I saw   255
That maiden Saint who stands with lily in hand
In yonder shrine. All round her prest the dark,
And all the light upon her silver face
Flowed from the spiritual lily that she held.

---

248 ...earth,   ,/ (I)   L-B1
248 (C)   L-B2

250 Yea so she said but so
    He answerd 'yet Sir Prince, to pass me by -   HM-1323

253 ~~Let her what dream ye by the lilies here~~   HM-1323

254 (Par.) ~~Said Lancelot~~   HM-1323
254 (Par.) And Lancelot, with his eyes on earth
                            replied   HM-1323

First draft 255 ff
    ~~He answer'd 'I had fall'n into a dream/~~
    ~~Of one who died for perfect purity~~
    ~~That virgin saint who holds a lily in hand~~
    ~~There in our shrine / how pure / the slightest flush~~
    ~~Wd mar for me this charm/of maidenhood.~~   HM-1323

255 ...dream: for yesternight I saw   HM-1323

257 There in our shrine. The dark night round
                        her stood   HM-1323

258 ...her holy face   HM-1323
258   silver
    ...her ~~holy~~ face   Tn-31

BALIN AND BALAN

Lo! these her emblems drew mine eyes--away: 260
For see, how perfect-pure! As light a flush
As hardly tints the blossom of the quince
Would mar their charm of stainless maidenhood.'

  'Sweeter to me' she said 'this garden rose
Deep-hued and many-folded! sweeter still   265
The wild-wood hyacinth and the bloom of May.

---

260 Now these, her emblem, drew mine eyes -from
                      thee.   HM-1323

261 For look how...   HM-1323

262   briar
    That sometime hardly tints the ~~whitest~~ rose HM-1323

Sketch 264 ff
    ~~'Better' she said 'I love this garden. rose~~
    ~~Deep-hued & many-folded. See thy hand~~
    ~~Is kindled with the glowing dust of these~~
    ~~Thy maiden emblems have a heart as. warm~~
    ~~As other maids who look as white as they.~~
    ~~All white is/rare in aught that lives. in snow~~
    ~~We find it. but the firstlings of the snow-~~
    ~~Fair-maids of February. as we say -~~
    ~~Flame in them./look'd to close. a spark/of fire.~~
    ~~And this a damsel. seven small summers old.~~
    ~~Show'd/me at Camelierde + when first we met.~~ H-33

264 (Par.) I better love the garden rose she said HM-1323

Alt. for 265 ff
    Deep-hued & many-folded. See thy hand
    Is kindled with the glowing dust of these
    Thy maiden-emblems have a heart as warm
    As other maids, which are as white as they
          all   is (1 ?)
    No utter white in what hath life - in snow
    We find it; but the firstlings of the snow -
    Fair maids of February as we say
    Have in them - lookt at close - a spark of fire.
                              HM-1323

471

BALIN AND BALAN

Prince, we have ridden before among the flowers
In those fair days--not all as cool as these,
Though season-earlier. Art thou sad? or sick?
Our noble King will send thee his own leech--   270
Sick? or for any matter angered at me?'

    Then Lancelot lifted his large eyes; they dwelt
Deep-tranced on hers, and could not fall: her hue
Changed at his gaze: so turning side by side
They past, and Balin started from his bower.   275

    'Queen? subject? but I see not what I see.

---

266 ...wild-wood...   (- I)   L-Bl
266 (C)   L-B2

267 We have ridd'n heretofore among the flowers HM-1323

269 ...-earlier. Pray thee art thou sad?   HM-1323

270 ...noble king will...   L-Bl
270 (C)   L-B2

271 ...me?'   '/ (P)   L-Bl
271 (C)   L-B2

272 (Par.) She spake; he raised his large gray eyes:
                        they dwelt   HM-1323
272 ...eyes,; they...   ;/ (I)   L-Bl
272 (C)   L-B2

273 ...fall: a bloom   HM-1323

274 Flash'd on her face; so...   HM-1323

275   Balin
    ..., & ¢á́x́é́x́h́ started...   Tn-31

276   but   not what
    ...subject? ¢á́x́ I see the things I see.   Hm-1323
276 (Par.) 'Queen,? subject...   ? (? I)   L-Bl
276 (C)   L-B2

Damsel and lover? hear not what I hear.
My father hath begotten me in his wrath.
I suffer from the things before me, know,
Learn nothing; am not worthy to be knight;   280
A churl, a clown!' and in him gloom on gloom
Deepened: he sharply caught his lance and shield,
Nor stayed to crave permission of the King,
But, mad for strange adventure, dashed away.

He took the selfsame track as Balan, saw   285
The fountain where they sat together, sighed
'Was I not better there with him?' and rode
The skyless woods, but under open blue

---

277 ...lover? I hear...   HM-1323

279 ...things before. I know   HM-1323

280 Nothing. I am not...   HM-1323

281 ...clown.' & gloom in him on gloom   HM-1323
281   gloom
    ...clown'! & g̶l̶o̶o̶m̶ in him   on gloom   Tn-31

283 ...the king,   L-Bl
283 (C)   92

285 (Par.) He took the track that Balan went on,
                        p̶a̶s̶t̶ saw   HM-1323
285   road
    Taking the w̶a̶y̶ that Balan took, & saw   HM-1323

286 ...they twain had sat, & sighed   HM-1323

287 ...him & past   HM-1323
287 ...him & thro'   HM-1323

288 The forest issuing, in an open shade   HM-1323

289 And found the hoary woodman hewing at a bough
                                                       HM-1323

BALIN AND BALAN

Came on the hoarhead woodman at a bough
Wearily hewing. 'Churl, thine axe!' he cried,   290
Descended, and disjointed it at a blow:
To whom the woodman uttered wonderingly
'Lord, thou couldst lay the Devil of these woods
If arm of flesh could lay him.' Balin cried
'Him, or the viler devil who plays his part,   295
To lay that devil would lay the Devil in me.'

---

290 ...hewing 'Give me thine axe' he said	HM-1323
290 ...hewing 'Give me thine axe' he cried	HM-1323
290 Churl,	
...hewing 'G̸i̸v̸e̸ m̸e̸ thine...	Tn-31
290 ...hewing., 'Churl, thine axe' he cried,	
,/,/,/ (P&I)	L-B1
290 ...axe! he... !/ (I)	L-B2
290 (C)	86

291 And clave it at one stroke.	HM-1323
291 And so descending cleft it at a stroke	HM-1323
291 Descended & disjointed it at a blow,	
A̸n̸d̸ s̸o̸ d̸e̸s̸c̸e̸n̸d̸i̸n̸g̸ c̸l̸e̸f̸t̸ i̸t̸ a̸t̸ a̸ s̸t̸r̸o̸k̸e̸	Tn-31

293-294 If any' said the woodman 'thou art he	
To quell the Demon of our woods	HM-1323
293-294 To whom the hoarhead woodman wonderingly	
laid by strength	
An our wood-devil cd be stricken down	
By fleshly prowess thou art he to do it.	HM-1323

293 Knight, thou...	HM-1323

294 ...Balin said	HM-1323

295 And Balin ay or he who apes him - here	HM-1323
295 ...part., ,/ (P)	L-B1
295 (C)	L-B2

Alt. for 296 Perchance this craven Garlon or	
another.	HM-1323

'Nay' said the churl, 'our devil is a truth,
I saw the flash of him but yestereven.
And some <u>do</u> say that our Sir Garlon too
Hath learned black magic, and to ride unseen.　　　　300
Look to the cave.' But Balin answered him
'Old fabler, these be fancies of the churl,

297　Nay - said the woodman Devil he is a true　　HM-1323
297　...said the man 'Our...　　　　　　　　　　　　HM-1323
297　　　　said the churl
　　　Nay, ~~Lord Sir Knight~~, our...　　　　　　　　Tn-31

299　Howbeit some say that our Sir Garlon too　　　HM-1323
299　Howbeit some do say Sir Garlon too　　　　　　HM-1323
299　...say this Garlon too -　　　　　　　　　　　　HM-1323

300　Hath magic & can ride invisible　　　　　　　　HM-1323

302　But old Jester
　　　He answering these be fancies of the churl!　　H-37

303　~~So they parted,~~
　　　　ook　　　　　　　　　　& so left him there
　　　Luck to thy woodcraft!　Balin parted from him　H-37

306　...brow thro' the dark woods he rode.　　　　　H-32
306　...brow thro' the deep woods, he rode;　　　　HM-1323

Alt. after 306 There on a day when Balin deaf to
　　　　　　　　　　　　　　all　　　　　　　　　　　　H-32

307　　　　　　　　　　Upon his right
　　　Nor mark'd a cavern yawn
　　　Arching a gloom　　　　　　　　　　　　　　　　H-37

308-309　　　　　　not for within　　chasm
　　　...died but dying show'd sharp rocks　　　　　H-37

308　　　　　　nor　　　　　　　　　　　　　　　　　　I MS
　　　...where, ~~not~~ far...　　　　　　　　　　　　L-B1
308 (C)　　　　　　　　　　　　　　　　　　　　　　　L-B2

Look to thy woodcraft,' and so leaving him,
Now with slack rein and careless of himself,
Now with dug spur and raving at himself,   305
Now with droopt brow down the long glades he rode;
So marked not on his right a cavern-chasm
Yawn over darkness, where, nor far within,
The whole day died, but, dying, gleamed on rocks
Roof-pendent, sharp; and others from the floor,   310
Tusklike, arising, made that mouth of night
Whereout the Demon issued up from Hell.
He marked not this, but blind and deaf to all
Save that chained rage, which ever yelpt within,

---

309 ...died; but,...		L-B1
309 ...died;, but,...	,/ (I)	L-B2
309 (C)		85

310 Roofpendent; others from the craggy floor		H-37
310 ...floor,	,/ (I)	L-B1
310 (C)		L-B2

311 Toothlike, ascending, made a mouth of night	H-37
311 Toothlike, arising...	HM-1323

312   up from
    From wh the Demon issued ø̸f̸ Hell.   H-37
312 Whereout
    From which the Demon...   HM-1323

Alt. after 312 And down a narrow slide between the
                             stems   H-37

313 But while Sir Balin blind & deaf
    H̸é̸ m̸á̸r̸k̸/d̸ i̸t̸ n̸ó̸t̸ b̸ú̸t̸ d̸é̸á̸f̸ to all   H-37
313 He saw not...   HM-1323
313 ...far within   85
313 (C)   86

314 Ex. the voices at his heart till all at once   H-37
314 Except the moody voices in his heart   H-32
314 Except the voices brooding at his heart   HM-1323

Past eastward from the falling sun. At once   315
He felt the hollow-beaten mosses thud
And tremble, and then the shadow of a spear,
Shot from behind him, ran along the ground.
Sideways he started from the path, and saw,
With pointed lance as if to pierce, a shape,   320
A light of armour by him flash, and pass
And vanish in the woods; and followed this,
But all so blind in rage that unawares
He burst his lance against a forest bough,
Dishorsed himself, and rose again, and fled   325
Far, till the castle of a King, the hall
Of Pellam, lichen-bearded, grayly draped
With streaming grass, appeared, low-built but strong;

---

315 ...sun, he h̸e̸a̸r̸d̸ felt   H-32
315 ...sun, he saw at once   H-37

316 The hollow beaten moss behind him thud   H-32

317 And shudder & the shadow of a spear   H-32

319 He prickt his horse & started from the way   H-32
319 ...from the track & saw   H-37

320-322 And one all-armed with lance as if to charge
        Past like a flash & vanish'd thro' the trees
        A̸n̸d̸ Stay bandit Balin cried, & following
                          fled   H-32

320 ...pointed spear as...   H-37

321 In armour like a sudden lightning flash   H-37
321 ...armour, past him flash & pass   HM-1323

322 Past in the wood   H-37
322 ...woods, & following fled   HM-1323
322 & follow'd him   HM-1323
322 ...this,   ,/ (I)   L-B1
322 (C)   L-B2

326 ...a king, the...   L-B1
326 (C)   L-B2

The ruinous donjon as a knoll of moss,
The battlement overtopt with ivytods,   330
A home of bats, in every tower an owl.

   Then spake the men of Pellam crying 'Lord,
Why wear ye this crown-royal upon shield?'
Said Balin 'For the fairest and the best
Of ladies living gave me this to bear.'   335
So stalled his horse, and strode across the court,
But found the greetings both of knight and King
Faint in the low dark hall of banquet: leaves
Laid their green faces flat against the panes,
Sprays grated, and the cankered boughs without   340
Whined in the wood; for all was hushed within,

---

327 ...bearded, moss'd, draped   H-32

332 ...Pellam saying Lord   HM-1323
332 ...crying 'Lord,   ,/ (I)   L-Bl
332 (C)   L-B2

Alt. after 333 ~~And when they gave at feast sir Garlon~~
                    ~~askt~~
           ~~Why wear ye that~~   HM-1323

334 Because the purest and the best, he said,   HM-1323
334 ...'for the purest &...   HM-1323
334   F   I MS
   ...Balin   'for...   L-Bl
334 (C)   L-B2

335 ...living gave it me to bear.   HM-1323

337 ...and king   L-Bl
337 (C)   L-B2

339 Their flat green faces on the quarrel-panes   HM-1323

341 Whined in the woods for all the hall was hush'd
                                                           HM-1323
341 ...within,   ,/ (I)   L-Bl
341 (C)   L-B2

Till when at feast Sir Garlon likewise asked
'Why wear ye that crown-royal?' Balin said
'The Queen we worship, Lancelot, I, and all,
As fairest, best and purest, granted me   345
To bear it!' Such a sound (for Arthur's knights
Were hated strangers in the hall) as makes
The white swan-mother, sitting, when she hears
A strange knee rustle through her secret reeds,
Made Garlon, hissing; then he sourly smiled.   350
'Fairest I grant her: I have seen; but best,

---

342 So
    And likewise at the feast Sir Garlon ask'd   HM-1323
342 So likewise at the feast Sir Garlon ask'd   HM-1323
342   when
    Till at ~~the~~ feast...   Tn-31
342 ...at ~~the~~ feast...   L-B1
342 (C)   L-B2

343 ...crownroyal? She, Sir Knight,   HM-1323

344   our great
    Whom I & Lancelot worship as the best   HM-1323
344 'The Queen whom I, Sir Lancelot, all of us HM-1323
344 ...all,   ,/ (I)   L-B1
344 (C)   L-B2

345 And purest of all ladies granted me   HM-1323
345 Worship as best...   HM-1323

346 Our Queens to bear it   sourly   HM-1323
               Garlon ~~grimly~~ smiled
346 To bear it' Grimly smiling Garlon spoke,   HM-1323

Alt. before 348-350
               Such a sound as makes
  The white swan-mother on her nest, who sees
  Some strange knee rustling thro' her secret reeds
  So hiss'd Sir Garlon   HM-1323

348 ...-mother, sitting, when...   ,/,/(I)   L-B1
348 (C)   L-B2

Best, purest? thou from Arthur's hall, and yet
So simple! hast thou eyes, or if, are these
So far besotted that they fail to see
This fair wife-worship cloaks a secret shame?   355
Truly, ye men of Arthur be but babes.'

---

350   sourly
     Garlon g̸x̸ı̸m̸l̸y̸ smiled   HM-1323
350   sourly   I MS
     ...he smiled.   L-Bl
350 (C)   L-B2

351 I grant her fairest. I have seen her once   HM-1323
351 ...seen; h̸e̸x̸ ø̸n̸c̸e̸ but...   Tn-31

352 Best? purest? ḁ̸x̸x̸ t̸h̸ø̸ṵ fresh from Arthur's court
                            & yet   HM-1323
352 ...hall, and...   ,/ (I)   L-Bl
352 (C)   L-B2

Alt. for 352 But fair & false have run in couples,
                            friend
Alt. for 352 Since first the (1 ?) gleam'd & faded.
                     But   HM-1323

353   thou neither
     Art thou so simple? hast nor eyes nor ears   HM-1323

354   fail to
     So far Assotted, that thy see not this fair
                          plea   HM-1323
354 ...far assotted that...   Tn-31
354   be   I MS
     ...far ḁ̸s̸sotted...   L-Bl
354 (C)   L-B2

355 To have knowest not this womaness cloaks the
                          shame   HM-1323
355   this fair wife
     Of woman worship...   HM-1323

Alt. after 355 T̸h̸é̸ s̸é̸c̸x̸é̸x̸ s̸h̸ḁ̸m̸é̸ t̸h̸ḁ̸x̸ g̸x̸ø̸w̸s̸ b̸é̸x̸w̸é̸é̸n̸
                     them both   HM-1323

BALIN AND BALAN

    A goblet on the board by Balin, bossed
With holy Joseph's legend, on his right
Stood, all of massiest bronze: one side had sea
And ship and sail and angels blowing on it: 360
And one was rough with wattling, and the walls
Of that low church he built at Glastonbury.
This Balin graspt, but while in act to hurl,
Through memory of that token on the shield
Relaxed his hold: 'I will be gentle' he thought   365
'And passing gentle' caught his hand away,

----

356 ...ye knights of...   HM-1323

357 A goblet
    There stood upon the board by Balin, rough   HM-1323
357   bo͞ss'd
    ...Balin, ̷r̷o̷u̷g̷h̷   Tn-31

358 With Arimethean Joseph's history   HM-1323
359   thereof
    A goblet, heavy bronze: one side had sea   HM-1323

361 And one stood out with poles & scaffolding   HM-1323
361   was rough
    ...one ̷s̷t̷o̷o̷d̷ ̷o̷u̷t̷ with...   Tn-31
361 ...rough with pole and scaffoldage   L-B1
361 (C)   86

363 ...graspt, & while...   HM-1323
363 ...hurl,   ,/ (I)   L-B1
363 (C)   L-B2

364 The memory of that bearing on his shield   HM-1323
364 ...shield̸   (I)   L-B1
364 (C)   L-B2

365-6 Relaxt his hold, he caught his hand away   HM-1323

366 'And...   '/ (I)   L-B1
366 (C)   L-B2
366 ...away,   85
366 (C)   88

BALIN AND BALAN

Then fiercely to Sir Garlon 'Eyes have I
That saw today the shadow of a spear,
Shot from behind me, run along the ground;
Eyes too that long have watched how Lancelot
                    draws   370
From homage to the best and purest, might,
Name, manhood, and a grace, but scantly thine,
Who, sitting in thine own hall, canst endure
To mouth so huge a foulness--to thy guest,
Me, me of Arthur's Table. Felon talk!   375
Let be! no more!'
                    But not the less by night
The scorn of Garlon, poisoning all his rest,
Stung him in dreams. At length, and dim through leaves

---

367 To whom Sir Balin fiercely Eyes have I   HM-1323
367 ...Garlon 'eyes...   L-Bl
367 (C)   92

368 ...spear,   ,/ (I)   L-Bl
368 (C)   L-B2

369 ...me glance along...   HM-1323

370   too long
    Eyes also wh have mark'd how Lancelot draws   HM-1323

372 Name, A̸n̸d̸ manhood...   HM-1323
372 ...thine,   ,/ (I)   L-Bl
372 (C)   L-B2

373 Who canst endure, sitting in thine own hall   HM-1323

374 ...so great a foulness unto me,   HM-1323

375 Thy guest, of Arthur's...   HM-1323

376 ...less at night   HM-1323

377 Those words of Garlon poison'd all...   HM-1323
377 ...Garlon, poisoning...   ,/ (I)   L-Bl
377 (C)   L-B2

378 And stung him ev'n in dreams, till dim thro'
                    leaves   HM-1323

482

Blinkt the white morn, sprays grated, and old boughs
Whined in the wood. He rose, descended, met   380
The scorner in the castle court, and fain,
For hate and loathing, would have past him by;
But when Sir Garlon uttered mocking-wise;
'What, wear ye still that same crown-scandalous?'
His countenance blackened, and his forehead veins   385
Bloated, and branched; and tearing out of sheath
The brand, Sir Balin with a fiery 'Ha!
So thou be shadow, here I make thee ghost,'
Hard upon helm smote him, and the blade flew

---

379 Blinkt the sad morn, sprays grated, & white stems
                                              HM-1323

380 Whined in the forest. Up he rose & met   HM-1323

381 That scorner...   HM-1323
381 ...and/ fain,   ,/ (I)   L-B1
381 (C)   L-B2

382 ...hate/ and...by;   ;/ (I)   L-B1
382 (C)   L-B2

383 ...utter'd mockingly   HM-1323
383 ...mocking-wise;   (- I)   L-B1
383 (C)   L-B2

386 Bloated & branch'd he ground his teeth &
                             crying   H-32

387 ...with a sudden 'ha!   HM-1323
387   H   I MS
    ...fiery 'Ha!   L-B1
387 (C)   L-B2

388 ...shadow, I will make...   H-32
388 ...ghost.,'   ,/ (I)   L-B1
388 (C)   L-B2

Alt. after 388 And on the sudden drawing sword from
                             sheath   H-32

Splintering in six, and clinkt upon the stones.   390
Then Garlon, reeling slowly backward, fell,
And Balin by the banneret of his helm
Dragged him, and struck, but from the castle a cry
Sounded across the court, and--men-at-arms,
A score with pointed lances, making at him--   395
He dashed the pummel at the foremost face,
Beneath a low door dipt, and made his feet
Wings through a glimmering gallery, till he marked
The portal of King Pellam's chapel wide
And inward to the wall; he stept behind;   400
Thence in a moment heard them pass like wolves
Howling; but while he stared about the shrine,
In which he scarce could spy the Christ for Saints,

---

390 Shatter'd & falling clinkt upon the stones   H-32

391 While Garlon tumbled backward stunned or dead   H-32
391 Sir Garlon...   HM-1323
391 Then Garlon≠, reeling ≠ slowly≠ backward, fell,
    ,/,/ (I)   L-B1
391 (C)   L-B2

393 ...struck: out of the castle...   HM-1323
393   but from
  ...struck, ø̸u̸t̸ ø̸f̸ the castle...   Tn-31

395 ...lances came upon him.   HM-1323
395   making at
        c̸o̸m̸i̸n̸g̸ o̸n̸
  ...lances, c̸a̸m̸e̸ u̸p̸o̸n̸ him -   Tn-31
395 ...him -   -/ (I)   L-B1
395 (C)   L-B2

397 Under a low...   HM-1323
397 Beneath
  U̸n̸d̸e̸r̸ a low...   Tn-31

398 Wings down a glimmering...   HM-1323

400 Flung inward toward the wall, & stept behind, HM-1323

Beheld before a golden altar lie
The longest lance his eyes had ever seen,   405
Point-painted red; and seizing thereupon
Pushed through an open casement down, leaned on it,
Leapt in a semicircle, and lit on earth;
Then hand at ear, and harkening from what side
The blindfold rummage buried in the walls   410
Might echo, ran the counter path, and found
His charger, mounted on him and away.
An arrow whizzed to the right, one to the left,
One overhead; and Pellam's feeble cry
'Stay, stay him! he defileth heavenly things   415
With earthly uses'--made him quickly dive

---

404 There lying upon a table diaper'd
        With branch'd imagining & device, beheld   HM-1323
404 Behold before   lie
        B̸é̸f̸ø̸ŕ̸é̸ a golden altar s̸t̸á̸n̸d̸í̸n̸g̸, s̸á̸ẃ   Tn-31

405 ...eyes had lookt upon,   HM-1323

407 Thrust thro' an open casement, leant upon
                        it,   HM-1323
407 Push'd   down
        D̸ø̸ẃń thro' an open casement t̸h̸ŕ̸ú̸s̸t̸, lean'd
                        on it,   Tn-31

408 ...Saints,   ,/ (I)   L-B1
408 (C)   L-B2

409 Then, ear in hand, &...   HM-1323

415 ...defileth holy things   HM-1323

416 For earthly...him quicklier dive   HM-1323

417-419 For many a weary league
        Beneath the boughs, & on for many a league
        Until his goodly charger faild for breath
        And rising wearily at a...   HM-1323

418 ...horse,   ,/ (I)   L-B1
418 (C)   L-B2

419 ...oak,   ,/ (I)   L-B1

485

Beneath the boughs, and race through many a mile
Of dense and open, till his goodly horse,
Arising wearily at a fallen oak,
Stumbled headlong, and cast him face to ground.   420

   Half-wroth he had not ended, but all glad,
Knightlike, to find his charger yet unlamed,
Sir Balin drew the shield from off his neck,
Stared at the priceless cognizance, and thought
'I have shamed thee so that now thou shamest me,   425
Thee will I bear no more,' high on a branch
Hung it, and turned aside into the woods,
And there in gloom cast himself all along,
Moaning 'My violences, my violences!'

   But now the wholesome music of the wood   430
Was dumbed by one from out the hall of Mark,
A damsel-errant, warbling, as she rode

----

419 (C)   L-B2

421   had
   ...he ~~was~~ not...   Tn-31

Sketch 423 ff
       He rose; he felt & found
       But Then the crownroyal burnt his eyes; he loosed
       And hung the shield upon a branch, & said
       Thee will I bear no more; so turn'd aside
       Into the gloom & cast him all along
       Groaning 'my violences, my violences
       I go to Arthurs hall no more here lie
       Savage among the savage woods, here die.   HM-1323

428 ...along,   ,/ (I)   L-B1
428 (C)   L-B2

429   M   I MS
    Moaning 'my...   L-B1
429 (C)   L-B2

430 But hear the wholesome music of the birds   H-47

432 ...errant carolling as...   H-47

BALIN AND BALAN

The woodland alleys, Vivien, with her Squire.

'The fire of Heaven has killed the barren cold,
And kindled all the plain and all the wold.   435
The new leaf ever pushes off the old.
The fire of Heaven is not the flame of Hell.

'Old priest, who mumble worship in your quire--
Old monk and nun, ye scorn the world's desire,
Yet in your frosty cells ye feel the fire!   440
The fire of Heaven is not the flame of Hell.

'The fire of Heaven is on the dusty ways.

_____

435 ...wold.   ⊙ (I)   L-B1
435 (C)   L-B2

Alt. before 436
    A̶n̶d̶ c̶a̶r̶e̶ n̶o̶t̶ t̶h̶o̶u̶ b̶u̶t̶ i̶n̶ t̶h̶y̶ y̶o̶u̶t̶h̶ b̶e̶ b̶o̶l̶d̶
                        can warm
    The fire of heaven l̶e̶t̶ warmed no sullen world   H-47

436 The new leaf ever pushes off the old   H-47
436 ...old.   ⊙ (I)   L-B1
436 (C)   L-B2

Alt. after 436
    And be bold, I care not, boy, if overbold.
                        is
    The fire's of heaven are not the flame's of Hell   H-47

438 (Par.) Old...   L-B1
438 (C)   92

442 ...on our dusty...   H-47
442 (Par.) The...ways/   ⊙ (I)   L-B1
442 (Par.) The...   L-B2
442 (C)   92

443 The wayside blossom opens to the blaze   H-47
443 ...blaze/   ⊙ (I)   L-B1
443 (C)   L-B2

487

The wayside blossoms open to the blaze.
The whole wood-world is one full peal of praise.
The fire of Heaven is not the flame of Hell.   445

'The fire of Heaven is lord of all things good,
And starve not thou this fire within thy blood,
But follow Vivien through the fiery flood!
The fire of Heaven is not the flame of Hell!'

Then turning to her Squire 'This fire of Heaven,   450
This old sun-worship, boy, will rise again,

444	peal	
	...one full p̶u̶s̶h̶ of praise	H-47
444	...praise⁄ . ⊙ (I)	L-Bl
444	(C)	L-B2
444	...praise	85
444	(C)	92

445	is	
	The fires̶ of heaven a̶r̶e̶ not the flames̶ of Hell.	H-47

446	The fire of Heaven has given us all things good	H-47
446	(Par.) The...	L-Bl
446	(C)	92

447	And follow thou the pleasure of the blood	H-47
447	And chill not thou that fire within thy blood	H-47

448	And bathe with Vivian in the fiery flood	H-47
448	But bathe with Vivian in the fiery flood	H-47

449	...Hell!' '/ (I)	L-Bl
449	(C)	L-B2

450	Then Vivian turning to her Squire Sir Boy	H-47
450	T	I MS
	...squire 't̶his...	L-Bl
450	(C)	L-B2

451	That old Sun-worship of the world will w̶a̶k̶e̶	
	rise	H-47

And beat the cross to earth, and break the King
And all his Table.'
                   Then they reached a glade,
Where under one long lane of cloudless air
Before another wood, the royal crown   455
Sparkled, and swaying upon a restless elm
Drew the vague glance of Vivien, and her Squire;
Amazed were these; 'Lo there' she cried--'a crown--

---

452 Once more against the Cross & break the king   H-47
452 ...the king   L-B1
452 (C)   L-B2

454 Where, underneath a lane of living blue   H-47
454 ...cloudless blue,   Tn-31
454   air   I MS
    ...cloudless b̶l̶u̶e̶   L-B1
454 (C)   L-B2

1st Sketch 455 ff
    Meanwhile t̶h̶e̶ s̶h̶i̶e̶l̶d̶ in open sun. the royal crown
                         swaying with the branch
    Sparkled &
    A wandering damsel Vivian & her Squire
    Amazed they stood   HM-1323

2nd Sketch 455 ff
    Meanwhile in open sun the royal crown
    Sparkled, & swaying in the heavens lured
    An errant damsel, Vivian & her squire   H-33

3rd Sketch 455 ff
    S̶h̶e̶ c̶e̶a̶s̶e̶d̶:̶ i̶n̶ o̶p̶e̶n̶ s̶u̶n̶ t̶h̶e̶ R̶o̶y̶a̶l̶ C̶r̶o̶w̶n̶
    S̶p̶a̶r̶k̶l̶e̶d̶ &̶ s̶w̶a̶y̶i̶n̶g̶ u̶p̶o̶n̶/ a/ r̶e̶s̶t̶l̶e̶s̶s̶/ e̶l̶m̶/
                     b̶l̶a̶n̶c̶e̶
    D̶r̶e̶w̶ t̶h̶e̶ v̶a̶g̶u̶e̶ e̶y̶e̶s̶ o̶f̶ V̶i̶v̶i̶a̶n̶ &̶ h̶e̶r̶ S̶q̶u̶i̶r̶e̶   H-47

455   r   I MS
    ...the R̶oyal crown   L-B1
455 (C)   L-B2

457 ...Squire,;   ;/ (P)   L-B1
457 (C)   L-B2

Borne by some high lord-prince of Arthur's hall,
And there a horse! the rider? where is he?   460
See, yonder lies one dead within the wood.
Not dead; he stirs!--but sleeping. I will speak.
Hail, royal knight, we break on thy sweet rest,
Not, doubtless, all unearned by noble deeds.
But bounden art thou, if from Arthur's hall,   465
To help the weak. Behold, I fly from shame,
A lustful King, who sought to win my love
Through evil ways: the knight, with whom I rode,

---

458 look a crown -   HM-1323
458   L   I MS
    ...these; 'X̷o there'...   L-B1
458 (C)   L-B2

459 ...hall.,   ,/ (P)   L-B1
459 (C)   L-B2

460   the rider?
    ...horse: where is he (1 ?) ẍ́ s̷ẻ́ẻ́   HM-1323
460   Where is he?
    ...horse! b̷ủ̷t̷ w̷h̷ẻ́r̷ẻ́ the rider? s̷ẻ́ả́r̷ċ̷h̷ -   Tn-31

461   yonder   2   1
    Lo where there lies one dead...   HM-1323

462 He moves: he is but sleeping: I must speak HM-1323
462   will
    ...I m̷ủ́ś̷t̷ speak.   Tn-31

463 All h̷ả́ỉ̷l̷ s̷ẃ̷ẻ́ẻ́t̷ noble lord, we   HM-1323
463 Sweet lord she cried we break...   HM-1323

Alt. after 465 To succor damsels in distress.   HM-1323

467 From Mark the king, who sought to win me to
                        him   HM-1323
467 From Mark the King, who...   Tn-31
467 A lustful   I MS
    F̷r̷ớ̷m̷ M̷ả́r̷k̷ t̷h̷ẻ́ king...   L-B1
467 (C)   L-B2

468 By evil...   HM-1323

Hath suffered misadventure, and my squire
Hath in him small defence; but thou, Sir Prince,   470
Wilt surely guide me to the warrior King,
Arthur the blameless, pure as any maid,
To get me shelter for my maidenhood.
I charge thee by that crown upon thy shield,
And by the great Queen's name, arise and hence.'   475

    And Balin rose, 'Thither no more! nor Prince
Nor knight   am I, but one that hath defamed
The cognizance she gave me: here I dwell
Savage among the savage woods, here die--
Die: let the wolves' black maws ensepulchre   480
Their brother beast, whose anger was his lord.
O me, that such a name as Guinevere's,
Which our high Lancelot hath so lifted up,

---

471 ...warrior king,		L-B1
471 (C)		L-B2
473 ...for mine innocence.		Tn-31
473 my maidenhood.		I MS
...shelter for m̸i̸n̸e̸ i̸n̸n̸o̸c̸e̸n̸c̸e̸.		L-B1
473 (C)		L-B2
474 ...that coronet on thy...		HM-1323
476 ...Thither I go no more!...		HM-1323
476 T		I MS
...rose, '̸thither...		L-B1
476 (C)		L-B2
477 r but one that hath		
No p̸r̸i̸n̸c̸e̸/am I, no knight. I have (1 **?**) defamed		
		HM-1323
480 Die & the wolves'...		HM-1323
482 ...as our great Queens		HM-1323
482 O me,		I MS
ø̸n̸c̸e̸, that ...Guinevere's,	,/ (I)	L-B1
482 (C)		L-B2

And been thereby uplifted, should through me,
My violence, and my villainy, come to shame.'   485

   Thereat she suddenly laughed and shrill, anon
Sighed all as suddenly. Said Balin to her
'Is this thy courtesy--to mock me, ha?
Hence, for I will not with thee.' Again she sighed
'Pardon, sweet lord! we maidens often laugh   490
When sick at heart, when rather we should weep.
I knew thee wronged. I brake upon thy rest,
And now full loth am I to break thy dream,
But thou art man, and canst abide a truth,
Though bitter. Hither, boy--and mark me well.   495
Dost thou remember at Caerleon once--
A year ago--nay, then I love thee not--
Ay, thou rememberest well--one summer dawn--
By the great tower--Caerleon upon Usk--
Nay, truly we were hidden: this fair lord,   500
The flower of all their vestal knighthood, knelt
In amorous homage--knelt--what else?--O ay

---

484 And been uplifted sd thru me   HM-1323

486 Thereat the damsel suddenly laugh'd & shrill   HM-1323

487 And then as suddenly sign'd; but Balin said   HM-1323

488 ...me, girl   HM-1323
488 ...me, g̸i̸r̸l̸ ha?   Tn-31

Sketch 489 to 496
   for I will not with thee. Again she sighd
   Hence, & again she sighed full oft we laugh
   When rather we sd weep. I broke upon thy rest
   Pardon, sweet lord
   And now full loath am I to break thy dreams
   But harken! Hither boy & mark me well   HM-1323

496 Dost For thou...   HM-1323

498 ...well - on Sunday morn   HM-1323

502 In amorous homage - knelt - what else - O ay,
   K̸n̸e̸l̸t̸ ̸ ̸&̸ ̸h̸i̸s̸ ̸h̸a̸n̸d̸ ̸&̸ ̸h̸e̸r̸s̸ ̸ ̸w̸h̸a̸t̸ ̸e̸l̸s̸e̸ ̸ ̸O̸ ̸a̸y̸   Tn-31

BALIN AND BALAN

Knelt, and drew down from out his night-black hair
And mumbled that white hand whose ringed caress
Had wandered from her own King's golden head,   505
And lost itself in darkness, till she cried--
I thought the great tower would crash down on both- -
"Rise, my sweet King, and kiss me on the lips,
Thou art my King." This lad, whose lightest word

503-506 Knelt mouthing her white hand; whereat she
                              cried   HM-1323

503   night-black hair
    ...his ~~raven curls~~   Tn-31

505 ...own king's golden...   L-Bl
505 (C)   L-B2

506   till
    ...darkness, ~~&~~ she...   Tn-31

508 ...sweet lord & ...   HM-1323
508 'Rise, my sweet king, and...   L-Bl
508 (C)   L-B2

509 ...This boy was witness I   HM-1323
509 ...my king.' This...   L-Bl
509 (C)   L-B2

Sketch after 509
     I lookt to see the great house all at once
     Crash down on both. this boy beheld it too.
     I swear as I am maiden undefiled
     I swear on all the four Ev.
     And by the gates of heaven & jaws of Hell
     I speak whole truth. (1 ?)
     So ride with me. Thou canst
     Do these
     And I have set thee now on vantage-ground
     And our great Queen when knowing that thou knowest
     Will fear thee, and so honour thee the more. HM-1323

493

Is mere white truth in simple nakedness,   510
Saw them embrace: he reddens, cannot speak,
So bashful, he! but all the maiden Saints,
The deathless mother-maidenhood of Heaven,
Cry out upon her. Up then, ride with me!
Talk not of shame! thou canst not, an thou would'st, 515
Do these more shame than these have done themselves.'

    She lied with ease; but horror-stricken he,
Remembering that dark bower at Camelot,
Breathed in a dismal whisper 'It is truth.'

    Sunnily she smiled 'And even in this lone wood,   520
Sweet lord, ye do right well to whisper this.
Fools prate, and perish traitors. Woods have tongues,

---

510   in simple
    ...truth, ~~white even to~~ nakedness   Tn-31

511   he reddens, cannot speak
    ...embrace. ~~what noted why speak her falset~~ Tn-31
511 ...embrace~~/~~: he reddens, cannot speak,
                                :/,/,/ (I)   L-Bl
511 (C)   L-B2

512 So bashful, he!
    ~~She never wronged her~~ but...   Tn-31
512 ...,he~~?~~! but...   ! (I)   L-Bl
512 (C)   L-B2

513 ...Heaven   L-Bl
513 (C)   85

515 'Sweet lord' she cried 'ye cd not an ye wd   HM-1323

517 (No par. indent. but I corr. symbol)   L-Bl
517 (C)   L-B2

520   A   I MS
    ...smiled 'and...wood   L-Bl
520 ...wood   L-B2
520 (C)   92

494

As walls have ears: but thou shalt go with me,
And we will speak at first exceeding low.
Meet is it the good King be not deceived.   525
See now, I set thee high on vantage ground,
From whence to watch the time, and eagle-like
Stoop at thy will on Lancelot and the Queen.'

    She ceased; his evil spirit upon him leapt,
He ground his teeth together, sprang with a yell,   530
Tore from the branch, and cast on earth, the shield,
Drove his mailed heel athwart the royal crown,
Stampt all into defacement, hurled it from him
Among the forest weeds, and cursed the tale,
The told-of, and the teller.
                            That weird yell,   535
Unearthlier than all shriek of bird or beast,
Thrilled through the woods; and Balan lurking there
(His quest was unaccomplished) heard and thought
'The scream of that Wood-devil I came to quell!'
Then nearing 'Lo! he hath slain some brother-knight, 540
And tramples on the goodly shield to show
His loathing of our Order and the Queen.
My quest, meseems, is here. Or devil or man
Guard thou thine head.' Sir Balin spake not word,
But snatched a sudden buckler from the Squire,   545
And vaulted on his horse, and so they crashed

---

525 ...good king be...		L-B1
525 (C)		L-B2
535 (Indent.) B̸u̸t̸ That...		Tn-31
540 L		I MS
∴..nearing 'lo! ...		L-B1
540 (C)		L-B2
553   back
Rolling i̸n̸ upon...		Tn-31
555 ...'Fools.!'	! (I)	L-B1
555 (C)		L-B2
556 ...Queen: θ	(I)	L-B1
556 (C)		L-B2

495

BALIN AND BALAN

In onset, and King Pellam's holy spear,
Reputed to be red with sinless blood,
Reddened at once with sinful, for the point
Across the maiden shield of Balan pricked   550
The hauberk to the flesh; and Balin's horse
Was wearied to the death, and, when they clashed,
Rolling back upon Balin, crushed the man
Inward, and either fell, and swooned away.

    Then to her Squire muttered the damsel 'Fools!   555
This fellow hath wrought some foulness with his Queen:
Else never had he borne her crown, nor raved
And thus foamed over at a rival name:
But thou, Sir Chick, that scarce hast broken shell,
Art yet half-yolk, not even come to down--   560
Who never sawest Caerleon upon Usk--
And yet hast often pleaded for my love--
See what I see, be thou where I have been,
Or else Sir Chick--dismount and loose their casques
I fain would know what manner of men they be.'   565
And when the Squire had loosed them, 'Goodly!
                    --look!
They might have cropt the myriad flower of May,
And butt each other here, like brainless bulls,
Dead for one heifer!'
                    Then the gentle Squire
'I hold them happy, so they died for love: 570
And, Vivien, though ye beat me like your dog,
I too could die, as now I live, for thee.'

    'Live on, Sir Boy,' she cried, 'I better prize

---

558 ...name⁄:   :/ (I)   L-Bl
558 (C)   L-B2

566 ...'Goodly ⁄ ! -/ look!   ! (I)   L-Bl
566 (C)   L-B2

568 ...bulls,   ,/ (I)   L-Bl
568 (C)   L-B2

570 ...love: :/ (I)   L-Bl
570 (C)   L-B2

The living dog than the dead lion: away!
I cannot brook to gaze upon the dead.'   575
Then leapt her palfrey o'er the fallen oak,
And bounding forward 'Leave them to the wolves.'

But when their foreheads felt the cooling air,
Balin first woke, and seeing that true face,
Familiar up from cradle-time, so wan,   580
Crawled slowly with low moans to where he lay,
And on his dying brother cast himself
Dying; and <u>he</u> lifted faint eyes; he felt
One near him; all at once they found the world,
Staring wild-wide; then with a childlike wail,   585
And drawing down the dim disastrous brow
That o'er him hung, he kissed it, moaned and spake;

'O Balin, Balin, I that fain had died
To save thy life, have brought thee to thy death.
Why had ye not the shield I knew? and why   590
Trampled ye thus on that which bare the Crown?'

Then Balin told him brokenly, and in gasps,

---

574 ...lion,: away!	:/ (I)	L-Bl
574 (C)		L-B2
577 L		I MS
...forward 'leave...		L-Bl
577 (C)		L-B2
583 ...and he lifted... (Underlined "he" I; "ital" I		
on margin)		L-Bl
583 (C)		L-B2
592 ...brokenly, and in gasps,	,/,/(I)	L-Bl
592 (C)		L-B2
594 ...hall:	:/ (I)	L-Bl
594 (C)		L-B2
596 E		I MS
...said "ǵat in...he,	,/ (I)	L-Bl
596 (C)		L-B2

BALIN AND BALAN

All that had chanced, and Balan moaned again.

'Brother, I dwelt a day in Pellam's hall:
This Garlon mocked me, but I heeded not.   595
And one said "Eat in peace! a liar is he,
And hates thee for the tribute!" this good knight
Told me, that twice a wanton damsel came,
And sought for Garlon at the castle-gates,
Whom Pellam drove away with holy heat.   600
I well believe this damsel, and the one
Who stood beside thee even now, the same.
"She dwells among the woods" he said "and meets
And dallies with him in the Mouth of Hell."
Foul are their lives; foul are their lips; they
                              lied.   605
Pure as our own true Mother is our Queen.'

'O brother' answered Balin 'woe is me!
My madness all thy life has been thy doom,
Thy curse, and darkened all thy day; and now
The night has come. I scarce can see thee now.   610
Goodnight! for we shall never bid again
Goodmorrow--Dark my doom was here, and dark
It will be there. I see thee now no more.
I would not mine again should darken thine,
Goodnight, true brother.'

------

598 ...came,	,/ (I)	L-Bl
598 (C)		L-B2
603 "She...woods" he said "and...	"/"/"/(I)	L-Bl
603 (C)		L-B2
604 ...of Hell."	⊙("⊙ I)	L-Bl
604 (C)		L-B2

607   'Peace brother' answer'd Balin 'Woe is me!
     (Par.) T̸h̸e̸n̸ a̸f̸t̸e̸r̸ a̸ l̸o̸n̸g̸ s̸i̸l̸e̸n̸c̸e̸ B̸a̸l̸i̸n̸   Tn-31
607   O   I MS
     (Par.) 'T̸r̸u̸e̸ brother...   L-Bl
607 (C)   L-B2

610   thee now.
     ...see t̸h̸y̸ f̸a̸c̸e̸   Tn-31

                498

                              Balan answered low   615
'Goodnight, true brother here! goodmorrow there!
We two were born together, and we die
Together by one doom:' and while he spoke
Closed his death-drowsing eyes, and slept the sleep
With Balin, either locked in either's arm.   620

---

618 ...doom' & s̸i̸l̸e̸n̸t̸ t̸h̸e̸n̸ while   Tn-31
618 ...doom:' and...spoke̸   :/ (I)   L-B1
618 (C)   L-B2

Merlin and Vivien

A storm was coming, but the winds were still,
And in the wild woods of Broceliande,
Before an oak, so hollow, huge and old
It looked a tower of ivied masonwork,
At Merlin's feet the wily Vivien lay.   5

For he that always bare in bitter grudge
The slights of Arthur and his Table, Mark
The Cornish King, had heard a wandering voice,
A minstrel of Caerleon by strong storm
Blown into shelter at Tintagil, say   10
That out of naked knightlike purity
Sir Lancelot worshipt no unmarried girl
But the great Queen herself, fought in her name,
Sware by her--vows like theirs, that high in heaven
Love most, but neither marry, nor are given   15
In marriage, angels of our Lord's report.

He ceased, and then--for Vivien sweetly said
(She sat beside the banquet nearest Mark),
'And is the fair example followed, Sir,
In Arthur's household?'--answered innocently: 20

'Ay, by some few--ay, truly--youths that hold
It more beseems the perfect virgin knight

---

6 (Par.) Whence came she? One that bare...	H-34
6 (Par.) Whence came she? One that bore...	H-34
6 (Par.) Whence came she? One that bare...	Y-I
6 (Par.) Whence came she? One that bare in bitter grudge	74
6 (C)	86

7 The scorn of Arthur...	H-34
7 The scorn of Arthur...	Y-I
7 The scorn of Arthur and his Table, Mark	74
7 (C)	86

9   by strong storm
...Caerleon, s̸i̸n̸g̸ & s̸a̸y̸   H-34

13 ...name   74
13 (C)   78

14 elided to 33
    Sware by her 'here be snakes within the grass;   H-34
14 elided to 33
    Sware by her 'Here are snakes within the grass   H-34

17 ...then to Vivian's questioning   H-34

To worship woman as true wife beyond
All hopes of gaining, than as maiden girl.
They place their pride in Lancelot and the Queen.   25
So passionate for an utter purity
Beyond the limit of their bond, are these,
For Arthur bound them not to singleness.
Brave hearts and clean! and yet--God guide them--
                    young.'

    Then Mark was half in heart to hurl his cup   30
Straight at the speaker, but forbore: he rose
To leave the hall, and, Vivien following him,
Turned to her: 'Here aré snakes within the grass;
And you methinks, O Vivien, save ye fear
The monkish manhood, and the mask of pure   35
Worn by this court, can stir them till they sting.'

    And Vivien answered, smiling scornfully,
'Why fear? because that fostered at <u>thy</u> court

---

21 (Par.) 'By five or six - ay; surely-youths...   H-34

28 For Arthur sware them...   H-34

31-33 Hard at the speaker, but forebore & turnd
       Whispering 'here be   H-34

31 ...forebore, & rose   Y-I

33 ...her: 'Here...   74
33 (C)   78

35 This monkish knighthood, & that mask of pure   H-34
35 The mummeries, & the pretty mask of pure   H-34

36 This Arthur, you can stir...   H-34
36 Worn at this...   H-34
36 Worn at their court...   H-34
36 ...sting."   74
36 (C)   78

38 Was I not nurtured in <u>thy</u> court, Sir Mark,   H-34
38 'Was I not nurtured at <u>thy</u> court, Sir Mark,   H-34

```
I savour of thy--virtues? fear them? no.
As Love, if Love be perfect, casts out fear,          40
So Hate, if Hate be perfect, casts out fear.
My father died in battle against the King,
My mother on his corpse in open field;
She bore me there, for born from death was I
Among the dead and sown upon the wind--              45
And then on thee! and shown the truth betimes,
That old true filth, and bottom of the well,
Where Truth is hidden.  Gracious lessons thine
And maxims of the mud! "This Arthur pure!
```

```
39 And mingled with thy - virtues? fear? not I.      H-34
39 And batten'd on thy - virtues? fear? not I.       H-34

43 ...his corse in...                                 H-34

Alt. after 45
    I hate the man that wears the mask of pure
    I front him with a countermask of pure;
    For Nature thro' the flesh herself hath made
    Gives him the lie:  there is no being pure
    And saith not holy writ the same.  I go.          H-34

46 Then cast on thee.  Who wears the mask of pure,    H-34

47 That most true...                                  Y-I

51 Gives him the lie! A̶g̶a̶i̶n̶ ̶/̶ ̶t̶h̶a̶t̶ ̶e̶v̶i̶l̶ ̶d̶a̶y̶
    W̶h̶e̶n̶ ̶N̶a̶t̶u̶r̶e̶ ̶s̶h̶o̶w̶l̶d̶ ̶s̶u̶p̶e̶r̶f̶l̶o̶u̶s̶ ̶b̶a̶s̶h̶f̶u̶l̶n̶e̶s̶s̶ ̶/̶
    T̶a̶p̶p̶i̶n̶g̶ ̶m̶y̶ ̶c̶h̶e̶e̶k̶ "There is no being pure,     Y-I

52 Man - woman :  saith not Holy Writ the same?       H-34

54 Come kiss me for old sake!  I bring thee back      H-34
54 Come, kiss me for old sake!  I bring thee back     Y-I

56 ...all the Table in...                             H-34
56 ...all this Order in...                            H-34
```

Great Nature through the flesh herself hath made   50
Gives him the lie! There is no being pure,
My cherub; saith not Holy Writ the same?"--
If I were Arthur, I would have thy blood.
Thy blessing, stainless King! I bring thee back,
When I have ferreted out their burrowings,   55
The hearts of all this Order in mine hand--
Ay--so that fate and craft and folly close,
Perchance, one curl of Arthur's golden beard.
To me this narrow grizzled fork of thine
Is cleaner-fashioned--Well, I loved thee first,   60
That warps the wit.'

                              Loud laughed the graceless Mark.

---

57 Yea - so that fortune, craft & folly close   H-34
57 Yea, so that fate & craft & folly join,   H-34

58 ...curl from Arthur's...   H-34

59 To me this little grizzly one of thine   H-34
59 And yet to me this little grizzled one   H-34
59 And yet to me this little grizzled one   Y-I

60 ...fashioned, ~~for~~ truly I...   H-34

First half 61 Wh warps the wit.
            ~~And none beside~~   H-34

61 ff   Loud laugh'd the graceless King
        And like a long stilt-walker of the fens,
        More wood than man, shambled away to sleep.   H-34
61 ff   ~~To whom the graceless King~~
        ~~With a hard laugh said so, sweetheart, let~~
                ~~thy love~~
        ~~Still warp thy wit to serve thine ends & mine,~~ Y-I
61 ff   Loud laugh'd the graceless King.
        ~~And like a long stilt-walker of the fens,~~
        ~~More wood than man shambled away to sleep~~   Y-I

505

MERLIN AND VIVIEN

But Vivien, into Camelot stealing, lodged
Low in the city, and on a festal day
When Guinevere was crossing the great hall
Cast herself down, knelt to the Queen, and wailed.   65

    'Why kneel ye there? What evil have ye wrought?

Sketch 62 ff
    (Par.) Stealthily she sped then to Arthur's hall
    Took the dead hair, & the besotted boy
    And batter'd shield, & came before the Queen;
    Knelt lowly then, and bidden rise arose,   H-33

62 (Par.) Stealthily then she sped to Arthur's
                       court,   H-34
62 Stealthily then she sped to A̶r̶t̶h̶u̶r̶'̶s̶ c̶o̶u̶r̶t̶
                       Camelot,   H-34

63 Dwelt in...   H-34

64 While the great Queen was passing thro' the hall
Alt. after 64 Gave one sharp shriek, claspt hands
                     above her head,   H-34
64   the great hall
   When Guinevere was crossing p̶a̶s̶s̶i̶n̶g̶ t̶h̶r̶o̶ the hall
Alt. after 64 G̶a̶v̶e̶ o̶n̶e̶ s̶h̶a̶r̶p̶ s̶h̶r̶i̶e̶k̶,̶ c̶l̶a̶s̶p̶t̶ h̶a̶n̶d̶s̶
                  a̶b̶o̶v̶e̶ h̶e̶r̶ h̶e̶a̶d̶   Y-I

65 ...& wept.   H-34

72 ...his body in...   H-33

Alt. after 72
    Brake her true heart. An orphan maid am I,
    For what small share of beauty may be mine
    Pursued by Mark the King; - yea - & by one
    Sir Tristram - of the Table - nay perchance
    I wrong him, being fearful, full of shame;
    The Cornish manners be so rough; but lo
    I bring thee here a message from the dead.
    And therewithal showing Sir Balan's hair
    Know ye not this? not so, belike; but this
    A most strange red, is easier known. The Queen
                       (Continued)

506

Rise!' and the damsel bidden rise arose
And stood with folded hands and downward eyes
Of glancing corner, and all meekly said,
'None wrought, but suffered much, an orphan maid!   70
My father died in battle for thy King,
My mother on his corpse--in open field,

Alt. after 72, Continued
   Took the dead hair & slightly shuddering ask'd
   Sir Balin's?is he slain? Yea, noble Queen
   Likewise his brother, Balan: for they fought,
   Not knowing - some miss vision of their shields -
   I know not what. I found them side by side -
   And wounded to the death, unlaced their helms,
   And gave them air & water, held their heads,
   Wept with them; & thy Balin joy'd my heart
             stainless
   Calling their p̸e̸r̸f̸e̸c̸t̸ wife & perfect Queen
   Heaven's white Earth-angel; then they bad me clip
   One
   A̸ tress from either head, & bring it thee,
   Proof that my message is not feign'd; & pray'd
   King Arthur would dispatch some holy man,
   As these had lain together in one g̸r̸a̸v̸e̸ womb,
   To give them burial in a single grave -
   Sent their last blessings to their King & thee,
   And therewithal their dying wish, that thou,
   For that good service I had done thy knights,
   Wouldst yield me shelter for mine innocency.
   To whom the Queen made answer 'we must hear
   Thy story further; thou shalt bide the while.'
       thy maidens'
   Among my d̸a̸m̸s̸e̸l̸s̸ Damsel' said the Queen
   I know no more of thee than that thy tale
   Hath chill'd me to the heart. Ghastly mischance,
   Enough to make all childless motherhood
   Fain so to bide for ever! Where do they lie?
   And Vivian's voice was broken answering her.
   Dead in a nameless corner of the woods
   Each lockd in either's arms. I know the place,
   But scarce can word it plain for thee to know.'
   And therefore damsel shalt thou ride at once
   With Arthur's knights & guide them thro' the woods
                         (Continued)

The sad sea-sounding wastes of Lyonnesse--
Poor wretch--no friend!--and now by Mark the King
For that small charm of feature mine, pursued--   75
If any such be mine--I fly to thee.
Save, save me thou--Woman of women--thine
The wreath of beauty, thine the crown of power,
Be thine the balm of pity, O Heaven's own white
Earth-angel, stainless bride of stainless King--   80
Help, for he follows! take me to thyself!
O yield me shelter for mine innocency
Among thy maidens!'

Alt. after 72, Continued
    Thy wish, & these dead men's, if such were theirs
    Must bide mine answer till we meet again.'
        After when Vivian on returning came
    To Guinevere & spake I saw the twain
    Buried; & wept above their woodland grave
    But grant me now my wish & theirs' The Queen
    All-glittering like may-sunshine ø𝑛 among leaves
    In green & gold, & plumed with green, replied
        A moiety of thy tale is proven true;
    Yet must we test thee more; but even now
Picks up 93   H-33

73 ...sad sea-moaning wastes...   H-34

74 ...Mark the s̸c̸u̸r̸r̸u̸l̸o̸u̸s̸ King   H-34

75 P̸u̸r̸s̸u̸e̸d̸ for that small charm of favour mine pur-
                                sued   H-34

77 Save me from Mark - woman of women - thine   H-34
77 Save me, thou
   S̸a̸v̸e̸ m̸e̸ f̸r̸o̸m̸ M̸a̸r̸k̸, Woman of Women, thine   H-34

Alt. after 77 No help but flight & thou, great
                        Queen who wearest   H-34

78   thine
   ...beauty, & the crown   H-34

508

```
                    Here her slow sweet eyes
Fear-tremulous, but humbly hopeful, rose
Fixt on her hearer's, while the Queen who stood          85
All glittering like May sunshine on May leaves
In green and gold, and plumed with green replied,
'Peace, child! of overpraise and overblame
We choose the last.  Our noble Arthur, him
Ye scarce can overpraise, will hear and know.          90
Nay--we believe all evil of thy Mark--
Well, we shall test thee farther; but this hour
We ride a-hawking with Sir Lancelot.
He hath given us a fair falcon which he trained;
We go to prove it.  Bide ye here the while.'           95
```

---

79 Be thou the ~~save~~ balm of pity
  ~~this satan~~
  ~~save me from Mark's desire~~ - Heaven's own white   H-34

80 Earth- angel
  ~~Archangel~~, stainless...   Y-I

84 ...- tremulous, & humbly   H-34

85 ...her hearer, while...   H-34

89 ff We choose the last: our noble king, in whom
     We place our pride, will shield thee from all
                        wrong
     In his own city. See - we know thee not.   H-34

89   Our noble Arthur - him
  ...last. Tell thou thy tale the morn   H-34

90 ~~To Arthur, whom~~ ye scarce can overpraise - will
                        hear & judge   H-34

92 Well, we shall
  ~~Yet must we~~ test...   H-34

94 ...given me a...   H-33

95 ...to fly her. Bide thou here...   H-33

MERLIN AND VIVIEN

She past; and Vivien murmured after 'Go!
I bide the while.' Then through the portal-arch
Peering askance, and muttering broke-wise,
As one that labours with an evil dream,
Beheld the Queen and Lancelot get to horse.   100

'Is that the· Lancelot? goodly--ay, but gaunt:
Courteous--amends for gauntness—takes her hand--
That glance of theirs, but for the street, had been
A clinging kiss—how hand lingers in hand!

---

96 She past; & Vivian looking after thought   H-34
96 ...after her   H-34
96 ...murmur'd after ~~her~~ 'Go!   Y-I

98 ...muttering brokenwise,   74
98 (C)   84

100 ...Lancelot as they met.'   H-34

103 ...theirs but for the common stare   H-34

104 Had been a kiss - how...   H-34

Alt. after 104 Bruise not the little fingers,
                             courtesy -   H-34

105 ...last - ~~&~~ ~~so~~ they...   H-34

106 For waterfowl - royaller game is mine.
~~They hawk for fowls & I for Queens & Kings.~~   H-34

Alt. after 106
~~Not possible that such a bond/could live~~
~~Betwixt the man & woman in their might~~
~~As that gray cricket chirpt of in our hall.~~
Lies! Lies! for which   - yea
~~Hypocrisies~~ - I hate the world ~~&~~ him
                    hate   tho' he spake the truth -
That made me ~~know~~ it, when a tender child
~~Nay~~ - ~~but~~   perchance   for he
~~And yet~~ him least - ~~o~~ fool! - ~~who~~ wrong'd me
                             most.   H-34

```
Let go at last!--they ride away--to hawk            105
For waterfowl.  Royaller game is mine.
For such a supersensual sensual bond
As that gray cricket chirpt of at our hearth--
Touch flax with flame--a glance will serve--the liars!
Ah little rat that borest in the dyke               110
Thy hole by night to let the boundless deep
Down upon far-off cities while they dance--
Or dream--of thee they dreamed not--nor of me
```

```
107 For such a supersexual sexless bond              H-34
107              sensual, sensual
    For such a super~~sexual//sexless~~ bond          Y-I
```

```
Alt. after 108              of life
    ~~When all~~ the heat & force were out of him -   H-34
```

```
109 Touch flax with fire - a glance will do - no
                               more.                 H-34
109              flame              serve - the liars!
    Touch flax with ~~fire~~ - a glance will ~~do~~ - ~~no more~~
                                                     Y-I
```

```
Alt. after 109
    Liars! I know the world & hate - yes, him
    By whom I knew it - tho he spake the truth
    Him least, perchance - fool, for he wrong'd me
                               most.                 Y-I
```

```
First sketch 110 ff          ~~O the little rat~~
    ~~That bores/the wound & lets the boundless deep~~
    ~~Down on the distant cities while they dance/~~
    ~~I love him~~                                     H-34
```

```
110 O little rat,  that borest in the dank dyke      H-34
```

```
111                        tideful
    ...night letting the boundless deep              H-34
111 ...the tideful deeps                             H-34
```

```
112 Down on far cities while they drink & dance -    H-34
```

```
113 They dreamd of thee - nay nor these of me        H-34
113 ...they dreamt not...                            H-34
```

These--ay, but each of either: ride, and dream
The mortal dream that never yet was mine--   115
Ride, ride and dream until ye wake--to me!
Then, narrow court and lubber King, farewell!
For Lancelot will be gracious to the rat,
And our wise Queen, if knowing that I know,
Will hate, loathe, fear--but honour me the more.'   120

    Yet while they rode together down the plain,
Their talk was all of training, terms of art,
Diet and seeling, jesses, leash and lure.
'She is too noble' he said 'to check at pies,
Nor will she rake: there is no baseness in her.'   125
Here when the Queen demanded as by chance
'Know ye the stranger woman?' 'Let her be,'

Alt. 114 But these shall more than dream - shall ride
                         & ride   H-34

114 These - nay but...   H-34

115 The goodly dream...   H-34

Alt. 116 Until at length they stumble into the (1?) H-34

116 And dream & ride until...   H-34

118 Then tentimes courteous will this Lancelot be   H-34
118 Then Lancelot will be courteous to the rat   H-34
118 For   gracious
    T̸h̸e̸n̸ Lancelot will be c̸o̸u̸r̸t̸e̸o̸u̸s̸ to the rat   H-34

120   hate &
    Will fear me & s̸o̸ honour me the more.   H-34
120   loathe, but
    Will hate, b̸u̸t̸ fear, s̸o̸ honour me the more.   H-34

121-122 (Par.) Yet while she rode with Lancelot
                  down the plain
                  all their talk   H-34
121-122 But when she rode with Lancelot down the
                    plains   H-33

Said Lancelot and unhooded casting off
The goodly falcon free; she towered; her bells,
Tone under tone, shrilled; and they lifted up   130
Their eager faces, wondering at the strength,
Boldness and royal knighthood of the bird
Who pounced her quarry and slew it. Many a time
As once--of old--among the flowers--they rode.

   But Vivien half-forgotten of the Queen   135
Among her damsels broidering sat, heard, watched
And whispered: through the peaceful court she crept
And whispered: then as Arthur in the highest
Leavened the world, so Vivien in the lowest,
Arriving at a time of golden rest,   140
And sowing one ill hint from ear to ear,
While all the heathen lay at Arthur's feet,

---

123 Was diet, seeling...   H-34
123 Seeling, & diet, jesses...   H-33

126 And when she saw Sir Lancelot askt him saying   H-33

128 Said L. & as Arthur in the highest (elides w. 138)
                                                      H-37
128 ...casting from him   H-33

129 ...falcon loose; she...   H-33

135 Said Lancelot; half-forgotten by the Queen   H-33
135   Many a time
   They rode; & half-forgotten of the Queen   H-33

136 Among her maidens broidering Vivian sat   H-33

137 Thro' the still court with wistful (?) eyes
                              she crept   H-33

140 And Arriving in an hour of golden peace   H-37
140 Arriving in a...   H-33

141 And sowing one coarse tale from ear to ear   H-37

142 When all...   H-37

And no quest came, but all was joust and play,
Leavened his hall. They heard and let her be.

Thereafter as an enemy that has left   145
Death in the living waters, and withdrawn,
The wily Vivien stole from Arthur's court.

---

143 ...came & sowing one
Alt. after 143 Among the younger   H-37
143 When no quest...
Alt. after 143 And all the heathen lay at Arthur's
                        feet.   H-33

144 Leaven'd the K. They heard...   H-37
144 Leaven'd his court.   H-37

147   wileful
     (Par.) The w̶a̶n̶t̶o̶n̶ Nimuë...   Lo-1
147 (Par.) The wileful Nimuë stole from Arthur's
                        court: BM-1
147 (Par.) The...   ...court: F-II
147 (C)   74

148 (No par.) ...because they seemd   HM-1326
148 (No par.) ...because she deem'd   Lo-1
148 (No par.) She hated all the knights because
                        she deem'd   BM-1
148 (No par.) She hated all the knights, b̶e̶c̶a̶u̶s̶e̶ s̶h̶e̶
                        & heard in thought   I MS
                        d̶e̶e̶m̶'̶d̶   L-II
148 (No par.)   F-II
148 (C)   74

149 To jest & wink whenever she was named.   HM-1326
149 They wink'd & jested when her name was named.   Lo-1
149 They wink'd and jested when her name was named. BM-1
149 Their scornful laughter   I MS
     T̶h̶e̶y̶ w̶i̶n̶k̶'̶d̶ a̶n̶d̶ j̶e̶s̶t̶e̶d̶ when her name was named. L-II
149 (C)   F-II

514

    She hated all the knights, and heard in thought
Their lavish comment when her name was named.
For once, when Arthur walking all alone,   150
Vext at a rumour issued from herself
Of some corruption crept among his knights,
Had met her, Vivien, being greeted fair,
Would fain have wrought upon his cloudy mood
With reverent eyes mock-loyal, shaken voice,   155
And fluttered adoration, and at last
With dark sweet hints of some who prized him more

----

150 For once when Arthur, walking all alone   BM-1
150 ...Arthur, walking all alone   F-II
150 (C)   59

151-2 And troubled in his heart about the Queen,   BM-1
151-2 Vext at ẃít́h́ a rumour rife   I MS
      Ánd́ t́ŕóúb́ĺéd́ íń h́íś h́éáŕt́ about the Queen,   L-II
151-2 Vext at a rumour rife about the Queen,   F-II
151-2 (C)   73

153 Had met her, she had spoken to the King   BM-1
153 Had met her, Nimuë; being greeted fair,   I MS
    H́ád́ ḿét́ h́éŕ/ śh́é h́ád́ śṕóḱéń/t́ó/t́h́é Ḱíń́ǵ   F-I
153 Had met her, Nimuë, being greet fair,   L-I
153 (C)   F-II

154 (Omitted)   BM-1
154 Would fain have wrought upon his cloudy mood
                                        (I MS)   F-I
154 (C)   F-II

155 ...eyes, mock-loyal shaken...   BM-1
155 ...eyes/ mock-loyal, shaken...   ,/ (I)   F-I
155 (C)   L-I

157 Had hinted at the some who...   BM-1
157 With dark sweet hints of   I MS
    H́ád́ h́íńt́éd́ át́ t́h́é some...   F-I
157 (C)   L-I

515

Than who should prize him most; at which the King
Had gazed upon her blankly and gone by:
But one had watched, and had not held his peace: 160
It made the laughter of an afternoon
That Vivien should attempt the blameless King.
And after that, she set herself to gain
Him, the most famous man of all those times,
Merlin, who knew the range of all their arts,   165
Had built the King his havens, ships, and halls,
Was also Bard, and knew the starry heavens;
The people called him Wizard; whom at first
She played about with slight and sprightly talk,
And vivid smiles, and faintly-venomed points   170
Of slander, glancing here and grazing there;
And yielding to his kindlier moods, the Seer

158 ...most: at...		BM-1
158 ...most:; at...	(; I)	F-I
158 (C)		L-I
159 ...by;		BM-1
159 ...by;:	(: I)	F-I
159 (C)		L-I
160 ...peace;		BM-1
160 ...peace;:	(: I)	F-I
160 (C)		L-I
164 ...times		BM-1
164 ...times,	(, I)	F-I
164 (C)		L-I
166 ..., ships and		F-I
166 (C)		L-II
169 ...talk;		BM-1
169 ...talk/ ,	(, I)	F-I
169 (C)		L-I
170-171 (Omitted)		BM-1
170-171 (Added, C, I MS)		F-I
170-171 (C)		L-I

Would watch her at her petulance, and play,
Even when they seemed unloveable, and laugh
As those that watch a kitten; thus he grew   175
Tolerant of what he half disdained, and she,
Perceiving that she was but half disdained,
Began to break her sports with graver fits,
Turn red or pale, would often when they met
Sigh fully, or all-silent gaze upon him   180
With such a fixt devotion, that the old man,
Though doubtful, felt the flattery, and at times
Would flatter his own wish in age for love,
And half believe her true: for thus at times
He wavered; but that other clung to him,   185

---

173 ...play		BM-1
173 ...play,	,/ (I)	L-I
173 (C)		L-II
176 ...she		BM-1
176 ...she,	(, I)	F-I
176 (C)		L-I
177 (Omitted)		BM-1
177 (Added I, MS, C.)		F-I
177 (C)		L-I
180 ...or all silent gaze...		BM-1
180 ...or all-silent gaze...	(- I)	F-I
180 (C)		L-I
183 ...love		BM-1
183 ...love,	(, I)	F-I
183 (C)		L-I
184 ...true; for...		BM-1
184 ...true;: for...	:/ (I)	F-I
184 (C)		L-I
185 ...waver'd, but...		BM-1
185 ...waver'd,; but...	;/ (I)	F-I
185 (C)		L-I

517

MERLIN AND VIVIEN

Fixt in her will, and so the seasons went.

Then fell on Merlin a great melancholy;
He walked with dreams and darkness, and he found
A doom that ever poised itself to fall,
An ever-moaning battle in the mist,   190
World-war of dying flesh against the life,
Death in all life and lying in all love,
The meanest having power upon the highest,
And the high purpose broken by the worm.

So leaving Arthur's court he gained the beach;   195
There found a little boat, and stept into it;
And Vivien followed, but he marked her not.
She took the helm and he the sail; the boat
Drave with a sudden wind across the deeps,

1st draft 187 ff with shapes
    He walkd ~~in gulfs~~ of darkness where he found
                             lying
    Death in all life & ~~falsehood~~ in all love,   6
    ~~World war of flesh against the Spiritual King~~/7
    The meanest having power upon the highest,   6
    And the high purpose broken by the worm.   2
    A wave that ever poised itself to fall,   3
    An ever-moaning battle in the mist,   4
    Faint cries for him who fainted in his path,
    And dimly felt the King who cannot die.
    World war of dying flesh against the life   5 H-39

187 Then fell upon him a great melancholy (Jump to 195)
                                            Lo-1
187 (No par.) Then fell upon him a great melancholy,
                                          BM-1
187 (No par.) Then fell upon him a great melancholy,;
                              ;/ (I)   F-I
187 (No par.) Then fell upon him a great melancholy; L-I
187 (C)   73

188-194 (Omitted)   BM-1
188-194 (C)   73

518

And touching Breton sands, they disembarked.   200
And then she followed Merlin all the way,
Even to the wild woods of Broceliande.
For Merlin once had told her of a charm,
The which if any wrought on anyone
With woven paces and with waving arms,   205
The man so wrought on ever seemed to lie
Closed in the four walls of a hollow tower,
From which was no escape for evermore;
And none could find that man for evermore,
Nor could he see but him who wrought the charm   210
Coming and going, and he lay as dead
And lost to life and use and name and fame.
And Vivien ever sought to work the charm
Upon the great Enchanter of the Time,
As fancying that her glory would be great   215
According to his greatness whom she quenched.

---

195   Arthur's
   And flying ~~from~~ ~~the~~ court...   Lo-1
195 (No par.) And leaving...   BM-1
195 (C)   73

196 There   stept into it
   ~~And~~ found a little boat & ~~entered it~~   Lo-1
196 ...it,   BM-1
196 ...it, ;   ;/ (I)   F-I
196 (C)   L-I

201 And so she...   HM-1326;Lo-1
201 And so she...   BM-1
201   Then   I MS
   And ~~so~~ she...   F-I
201 (C)   L-I

203 ...charm   BM-1
203 ...charm,   ,/ (I)   F-I
203 (C)   L-I

207 Shut in...   HM-1326

209 ...cd see that man that evermore   HM-1326

There lay she all her length and kissed his feet,
As if in deepest reverence and in love.
A twist of gold was round her hair; a robe
Of samite without price, that more exprest   220
Than hid her, clung about her lissome limbs,
In colour like the satin-shining palm
On sallows in the windy gleams of March:
And while she kissed them, crying, 'Trample me,

---

217 ...feet		BM-1
217 ...feet,	,/ (I)	F-I
217 (C)		L-I
218 ...if in reverence...love: a robe		HM-1326
220 ...samite, beyond price...		HM-1326
222 ...colour, like...		BM-1
222 ...colour/ like...	(I)	F-I
222 (C)		L-I
223 ...March.		BM-1
223 ...March.:	:/ (I)	F-I
223 (C)		L-I
227 ...it,' he was mute.		BM-1
227 ...it,;' he was mute.	;/ (I)	F-I
227 ...mute/ :	:/ (I)	L-I
227 ...mute;		L-II
227 (C)		59
228 ...brain		BM-1
228 ...brain,	,/ (I)	F-I
228 (C)		L-I
231 ...silence: therefore when...		HM-1326
231 ...wherefore when...		BM-1
231 ...wherefore, when...	,/ (I)	L-I
231 (C)		L-II

Dear feet, that I have followed through the world,   225
And I will pay you worship; tread me down
And I will kiss you for it;' he was mute:
So dark a forethought rolled about his brain,
As on a dull day in an Ocean cave
The blind wave feeling round his long sea-hall   230
In silence: wherefore, when she lifted up
A face of sad appeal, and spake and said,
'O Merlin, do ye love me?' and again,
'O Merlin, do ye love me?' and once more,
'Great Master, do ye love me?' he was mute.   235
And lissome Vivien, holding by his heel,
Writhed toward him, slided up his knee and sat,
Behind his ankle twined her hollow feet
Together, curved an arm about his neck,

---

232 As if in sad appeal, her face & said   HM-1326

233 ...do you love...   HM-1326;Lo-1
233 ...do you love...   BM-1
233 (C)   <u>69</u>

234 ...do you love...   HM-1326;Lo-1
234 ...do you love...   BM-1
234 (C)   <u>69</u>

235 ...do you love...   HM-1326;Lo-1
235 'Great Master, do you love...   BM-1
235 "Great Master, do you love...   <u>69</u>
235 (C)   84

236 She along the ground   H-152a
236 She, holding...   HM-1326

237 ...him, glided up...   H-152a

238 Behind his ancle turned her silver feet   H-152a
238   hollow
    Behind his ancle twined her t̶e̶n̶d̶e̶r̶ feet   HM-1326
238 ...his ancle twined...   Lo-1
238 ...his ancle twined...   BM-1
238 (C)   59

Clung like a snake; and letting her left hand   240
Droop from his mighty shoulder, as a leaf,
Made with her right a comb of pearl to part
The lists of such a beard as youth gone out
Had left in ashes: then he spoke and said,
Not looking at her, 'Who are wise in love   245

---

240 ...snake & while she let one hand   H-152a
240 ...snake, and...   BM-1
240 ...snake,; and...   ;/ (I)   F-I
240 (C)   L-I

241 ...shoulder like a leaf   H-153a;HM-1326

242 The other made a comb of pearl to part   H-152a

243 The ~~silver~~ lists...   HM-1326

Sketch 244 ff
    Had left in ashes. Crying then before
    I argue with the ~~wise~~ let me clothe
    Myself with wisdom, over her rapt heart
    And bosom   H-153a

244 ~~Burnt out~~, had left in ashes: then he lookt at
                          her.   HM-1326

Sketch 245 ff   Who love most
    O wit ye well, fair damsel, ~~Merlin said~~
    He spoke, say least: and Nimuë answerd him
    Why then sweet love hath neither eyes nor tongue
                                                   HM-1326

245 ...her, 'who are...   BM-1
245 (C)   73

246 ...least,;' and...   ;/ (I)   L-I
246 (C)   L-II

247 ...Elfgod without eyes   HM-1326

Love most, say least,' and Vivien answered quick,
'I saw the little elf-god eyeless once
In Arthur's arras hall at Camelot:
But neither eyes nor tongue--O stupid child!
Yet you are wise who say it; let me think   250
Silence is wisdom: I am silent then,
And ask no kiss;' then adding all at once,
'And lo, I clothe myself with wisdom,' drew
The vast and shaggy mantle of his beard
Across her neck and bosom to her knee,   255
And called herself a gilded summer fly
Caught in a great old tyrant spider's web,
Who meant to eat her up in that wild wood

---

248 ...Camelot.			BM-1
248 ...Camelot.:	:/ (I)		F-I
248 (C)			L-I

250 But you are...		HM-1326;Lo-1	
250 But you... ...it. Let...		BM-1	
250 Yet 1		I MS	
B̸u̸t̸ you... ...it.; L̸et...	;/1/ (I)	F-I	
250 (C)		L-I	

251 ...wisdom - I ...then		BM-1	
251 :	:/ (I)		
...wisdom - I...then		F-I	
251 ...then		L-I	
251 (C)		73	

253 ...myself in wisdom' ...		HM-1326	
253 'And lo I...		BM-1	
253 'And lo, I...	,/ (I)	F-I	
253 'And lo I...		L-I	
253 (C)		L-II	

256 ...herself 'a...		BM-1
256 ...herself /a...		F-I
256 (C)		L-I

257 Caught in huge old...	HM-1326
257 ...old s̸p̸i̸d̸e̸r̸y̸s̸ tyrant spider's web,	Lo-1

523

Without one word. So Vivien called herself,
But rather seemed a lovely baleful star   260
Veiled in gray vapour; till he sadly smiled:
'To what request for what strange boon,' he said,
'Are these your pretty tricks and fooleries,
O Vivien, the preamble? yet my thanks,
For these have broken up my melancholy.'   265

   And Vivien answered smiling saucily,
'What, O my Master, have ye found your voice?
I bid the stranger welcome. Thanks at last!
But yesterday you never opened lip,
Except indeed to drink: no cup had we: 270
In mine own lady palms I culled the spring
That gathered trickling dropwise from the cleft,

---

259 ...word' for so she call'd...   HM-1326
259 ...word.' So...   BM-1
259 ...word.⟋ So...   F-I
259 (C)   L-I

260   glittered like a baleful star
   In a grey cloud   H-152a

262-263 'To what strange boon are these, he said,
      your tricks   HM-1326

267 ...have you found...   H-153a;HM-1326;Lo-1
267 ...have you found your voice?   BM-1
267 (C)   <u>69</u>

269 ...open'd lips   H-153a
269 ...lip   BM-1
269 ...lip,   ,⟋ (I)   F-I
269 ...lip   L-I
269 (C)   F-II

270 Except indeed to drink   H-153a
270 ...drink: we had no cup: HM-1326

271 But when I cull'd in mine lady palms   H-153a

MERLIN AND VIVIEN

And made a pretty cup of both my hands
And offered you it kneeling: then you drank
And knew no more, nor gave me one poor word;   275
O no more thanks than might a goat have given
With no more sign of reverence than a beard.
And when we halted at that other well,
And I was faint to swooning, and you lay
Foot-gilt with all the blossom-dust of those   280
Deep meadows we had traversed, did you know
That Vivien bathed your feet before her own?
And yet no thanks: and all through this wild wood
And all this morning when I fondled you:

---

272 The spring that trickled f̶r̶o̶m̶ dropwise from the
                              cleft   H-153a

274 ...kneeling; then...   BM-1
274 ...kneeling;: then...   :/ (I)   F-I
274 (C)   L-I

275   recompenced
    And knew no more; & n̶e̶v̶e̶r̶ t̶h̶a̶n̶k̶e̶d̶ my pain   H-153a
275 ...word.   BM-1
275 ...word.;   ;/ (I)   F-I
275 (C)   L-I

276 With no more thanks than might an ancient goat
                                                   H-153a

277 Whose only sign of reverence is his beard   H-153a
277 With no sign...   HM-1326

279 I faint almost to swooning...   H-153a

280 Foot-gilted with...   H-153a

281 ...we had come thro' did you know   H-153a
281 ...had wander'd, did...   HM-1326

283 ...all thro' wild wood   H-153a

284 ...when I woo'd you - Boon   HM-1326

525

Boon, ay, there was a boon, one not so strange--   285
How had I wronged you? surely ye are wise,
But such a silence is more wise than kind.'

   And Merlin locked his hand in hers and said:
'O did ye never lie upon the shore,
And watch the curled white of the coming wave   290

---

285 Boon O why yes & not in truth so strange.   H-153a
285 O yes there was a boon & not...   HM-1326
285 Boon, yes there...   Lo-1
285 Boon, yes, there...   BM-1
285 (C)   73

286 ...surely you are...   H-153a;HM-1326;Lo-1
286 ...surely you are...   BM-1
286 (C)   73

287 ...silence were more...   HM-1326

288 ...said,   BM-1
288 ...said,;   ;/ (I)   F-I
288 ...said;   L-I
288 (C)   73

289 O did you never...   H-153a;HM-1326;Lo-1
289 ...did you never... ...shore   BM-1
289 ...did you never... ...shore, (,I)   F-I
289 ...did you never...   L-I
289 (C)   73

290   curl'd white
   And watch the ~~white~~ ~~curl'd~~ ~~crest~~ of the coming
                wave   H-153a

292 O
   ~~Yon~~ such a wave, but not so sunny, dark   H-153a
292 ...not so sunny, dark   HM-1326

Glassed in the slippery sand before it breaks?
Even such a wave, but not so pleasurable,
Dark in the glass of some presageful mood,
Had I for three days seen, ready to fall.
And then I rose and fled from Arthur's court   295
To break the mood. You followed me unasked;
And when I looked, and saw you following still,
My mind involved yourself the nearest thing
In that mind-mist: for shall I tell you truth?
You seemed that wave about to break upon me   300
And sweep me from my hold upon the world,
My use and name and fame. Your pardon, child.

---

293 And darkly mirror'd on a (ends)   H-153a

294 Have I these three...   HM-1326
294   d   ̶f̶o̶r̶ for
       Ha̶v̶e̶ I the̶s̶e̶ three..   Lo-1

296 ...follow'd one unasked   HM-1326

297 I lookt & still I saw you following me: HM-1326
297 I lookd, & when I saw you following still,   Lo-1
297 I look'd, and when I saw...   BM-1
297 And when   I MS
    I look'd, and ̶w̶h̶e̶n̶ ̶I̶ saw...   F-I
297 (C)   L-I

298   envolved
    And I confused yourself...   HM-1326

299   mind-mist
    With that dark mood, for...   HM-1326
299 In
    ̶W̶i̶t̶h̶ that...   Lo-1

Alt. before 300 And I saw that still you follow'd
                          me   H-153a

300 ...wave ready to break...   H-153a

302 My uses & my glory. Pardon me   H-153a

Your pretty sports have brightened all again.
And ask your boon, for boon I owe you thrice,
Once for wrong done you by confusion, next   305
For thanks it seems till now neglected, last
For these your dainty gambols: wherefore ask;
And take this boon so strange and not so strange.'

---

303 Your pretty play has brightened me again   H-153a
303 ...pretty sport has made me light again   HM-1326
303   en'd all
    ...have m̷a̷d̷e̷ m̷e̷ bright   again.   Lo-1

304 And let me know this boon that is so strange
    Yet not so strange; because I owe you twice   H-153a
304 ..boon; a boon...   HM-1326

305 ...done to you in thought again   H-153a

306 ...seems neglected. Speak & ask   H-153a

309 ...mournfully,   BM-1
309 ...mournfully,,;   ;/ (I)   F-I
309 ...mournfully;   L-I
309 (C)   73

Sketch 310 ff
    Yea, not so strange, not strange at least to you
    My begging for it: you yourself are strange
    I want some proof to know you are not strange
    Strange was this mood. I sweep you from the world
    O Heavens my seer, My silverstar of eve
    My Lord, My Merlin. I
        Merlin's fame & shame not Nimuë's too   H-153a

310 Not half so strange as...   H-153a
310 Yea, not...   HM-1326
310 O
    Y̷e̷a̷, not...   Lo-1

311 Nor half so strange as...   H-153a
311 Nor yet...   HM-1326
311   yourself   y̷o̷u̷r̷s̷e̷l̷f̷
    Nor yet so strange as you y̷o̷u̷r̷s̷e̷l̷f̷ are strange Lo-1

528

And Vivien answered smiling mournfully:
'O not so strange as my long asking it,   310
Not yet so strange as you yourself are strange,
Nor half so strange as that dark mood of yours.
I ever feared ye were not wholly mine;
And see, yourself have owned ye did me wrong.
The people call you prophet: let it be: 315
But not of those that can expound themselves.

---

311 Nor yet...   BM-1
311 (C)   67

312 ...as this strange mood of yours.   H-153a
312 ...that strange mood...   HM-1326
312   dark
    ...that s̸t̸r̸a̸n̸g̸e̸ mood...   Lo-1

Alt. for 313 Mistrust, mistrust for evermore mis-
                    trust   HM-1326

313 ...fear'd you were...   Lo-1
313 ...fear'd you were...   ...mine,   BM-1
313 ...fear'd you were...   mine,;   ;/ (I)   F-I
313 ...fear'd you were...   L-I
313 (C)   69

314 ...own'd you did...   HM-1326;Lo-1
314 And see yourself have own'd you did...   BM-1
314 And see, yourself have own'd you did... ,/ (I)   F-I
314 ...own'd you did...   L-I
314 (C)   69

315 Men call you prophet. prophet you may be
    Prophet you may be in great things of state   H-153a
315   p̸r̸o̸p̸h̸e̸t̸
    Men call you prophet. You may be so   H-30
315 You may be prophet as they call you   HM-1326

316 But as to this presageful gloom of yours   H-30

529

Take Vivien for expounder; she will call
That three-days-long presageful gloom of yours
No presage, but the same mistrustful mood
That makes you seem less noble than yourself,   320

---

317 M̸y̸s̸e̸l̸f̸ am fairest prophet, calling it
    I count myself the best interpreter   H-153a
317 Take Nimuё for expounder. She will call it   H-30

318 But touching this presageful gloom of yours   H-153a

319 No presage but the same suspicious gloom   H-153a
319 No presage but the same suspicious mood   H-30

320 Wh makes you seem less noble than yourself   H-153a
320 Which makes...   H-30;HM-1326

321   Whenever I have askt you this one boon
    Alt. after 321 To teach me how to do this foolish
                      charm   H-153a
321 ...boon   BM-1
321 (C)   59

322 Now ask'd again. for see you not my love   H-30
322 ...again; for...   BM-1
322 ...again/: for...   :/ (I)   F-I
322 (C)   L-I

324 ...when you saw...   H-30;HM-1326
324 ...when you saw...   BM-1
324 (C)   73

Alt. before 325   Nay she said you know
    This foolish charm wh is to make a̸l̸l̸ you mine
    Not that I wish to make you mine
    By glamour, but to feel that you are mine
    For if you trust me I shall know you mine.
    I gather from this mood you are not changed   H-153a

Whenever I have asked this very boon,
Now asked again: for see you not, dear love,
That such a mood as that, which lately gloomed
Your fancy when ye saw me following you,
Must make me fear still more you are not mine,   325
Must make me yearn still more to prove you mine,
And make me wish still more to learn this charm
Of woven paces and of waving hands,

Alt. before 325 But these your moods confirm my
                          wish   H-153a

325 So then I ever fear we are not one   H-153a
325 They make me fear still more you are not mine H-153a
325 I want some proof that you are wholly mine   H-153a
325   still
     Must make me fear the more you are not mine   H-30

326 But ever yearn to prove it to myself   H-153a
326 I yearn to prove it to myself you are   H-153a
326 I yearn to prove to myself you are   H-153a
326 Must make me yearn still more to prove
                          you mine   H-30

327   & want to do this charm
     I wish to learn this charm wh   H-153a
327 And wish the more to learn this foolish charm H-153a
327 And make me wish the more to learn this charm   H-30
327 Must make me...   HM-1326
327 And
     M̸ṵ̸s̸t̸ make...   Lo-1

Alt. after 327
     Whereof you said that learnt a child cd do it
     Since if you gave me   H-153a

328 Of woven paves & of waving hands   H-30
328 ...hands   BM-1
328 ...hands,   ,/ (I)   L-I
328 ...hands   L-II
328 (C)   59

531

As proof of trust. O Merlin, teach it me.
The charm so taught will charm us both to rest.   330
For, grant me some slight power upon your fate,
I, feeling that you felt me worthy trust,
Should rest and let you rest, knowing you mine.
And therefore be as great as ye are named.
Not muffled round with selfish reticence.   335
How hard you look and how denyingly!

---

329 ...O, Merlin, teach...   BM-1
329 (C)   75

330 Wh charm so taught will charm us both to rest   H-30

331 For if you gave me power upon your fate   H-153a
331 For - give me some slight power upon your fate   H-30

332 I then sd know you felt me worthy trust   H-153a

333 And knowing that sd know you wholly mine   H-153a
333 And knowing that sd rest & know you mine   H-153a

334 O master, be as great as you are named   H-30;HM-1326
334 ...as you are...   Lo-1
334 ...as you are...   BM-1
334 (C)   73

Alt. after 334 I yearn to prove it to myself you are
                                                     H-30

337 But if you think, you surely do not think   H-153a
337 ...think that wickedness...   H-30
337   is
    ...think thǎt wickedness, that I   HM-1326
337   is
    ...think thǎt wickedness...   Lo-1

338 I mean to try it on you unawares   H-153a
338 That I sd try it on you unawares   H-30
338 ...should try it...   HM-1326
338 ...unawares,   59
338 (C)   73

532

```
O, if you think this wickedness in me,
That I should prove it on you unawares,
That makes me passing wrathful; then our bond
Had best be loosed for ever:  but think or not,          340
By Heaven that hears I tell you the clean truth,
As clean as blood of babes, as white as milk:
O Merlin, may this earth, if ever I,
If these unwitty wandering wits of mine,
```

Alt. after 338 That were not noble, no nor true nor	
kind	H-153a
Alt. after 338 To make you lose your use & name &	
fame,	Lo-1
Alt. after 338 To make you lose your use and name	
and fame,	BM-1
Alt. after 338 (C)	73

339	If that, our bonds had best be loosed at once.	H-30
339	...me too indignant: then...	HM-1326;Lo-1
339	That makes me too indignant. Then our bond	BM-1
339	t	I MS
	That makes me too indignant.; 𝑇hen our bond	
	; (I)	F-I
339	That makes me too indignant; then our bond	L-I
339	most	I MS
	That makes me 𝑡𝑜𝑜 indignant; then our bond	L-II
339	That makes me most indignant; then our bond	F-II
339	(C)	73

340	...or not	BM-1
340	...or not, ,/ (P)	L-II
340	(C)	F-II

341 But think or not I tell you the clean truth	H-30

342	Truth white as milk. O heaven if ever I	H-30
342	...milk;	BM-1
342	...milk𝑓: : (I)	F-I
342	(C)	L-I

Alt. before 344 O Heavens if ever my Power	H-153a

344	Or these...	H-153a
344	Of these...	H-30

Even in the jumbled rubbish of a dream,   345
Have tript on such conjectural treachery--
May this hard earth cleave to the Nadir hell
Down, down, and close again, and nip me flat,
If I be such a traitress. Yield my boon,
Till which I scarce can yield you all I am;   350
And grant my re-reiterated wish,
The great proof of your love: because I think,
However wise, ye hardly know me yet.'

   And Merlin loosed his hand from hers and said,
'I never was less wise, however wise,   355
Too curious Vivien, though you talk of trust,
Than when I told you first of such a charm.

---

345 ...rubbish of the night   H-153a

349 ...Yield this boon   H-30
349 ...traitress - will you yield -   HM-1326

350 Till then I scarce can yield you all myself   H-30
350 ...arm,   BM-1
350 ...arm,;   ;/ (I)   F-I
350 (C)   L-I

351 Grant me my long-reiterated desire   H-30

352 The great proof of your love because I think   H-30
352 ...I fear   HM-1326

353 However wise you hardly know me yet.   H-30
353 ...wise, you hardly...   HM-1326;Lo-1
353 ...wise, you hardly...yet.   BM-1
353 ...wise, you hardly...   L-II
353 (C)   69

354 And Merlin loosed his hold from hers & said   H-153a

355 I was not wise, never so little wise   H-153a
355 Ah wit you well however wise I am
      I never w̸a̸ less was wise than when I spoke HM-1326
355 H̸ø̸w̸ė̸v̸ė̸r̸ w̸į̸s̸ė̸, I never was less wise, however
                                    wise   HM-1326

                    534

Yea, if ye talk of trust I tell you this,
Too much I trusted when I told you that,

Draft 356 ff
      Too curious, child, of such a charm at all.
      I call you child & yet no child are you
      Your face is subtle - this long life of mine
      Long versed in faces well can spell the lines
      This neck (?) of yours has ruin'd mighty states
      As first it ruind man for howsoever
      In children ø/ø/ø/ a great curiousness be good
      Who have to learn themselves & all the world
      And also good in afterlife if men
      Were like the child & sought to learn themselves
      And Nature, yet in you that are no child
      Howeer you call yourself the summer fly
      I ẃíĺĺ can ćá but deem it great (1 ?)
      And well cd wish some cobweb for the gnat
      That settles beaten back & beaten back
      Settles till one cd yield for weariness
      And ever breaks the just beginning sleep
      With (1 ?) hung the one bloodsucking note -
      I will not yield
      Çøńśúĺẗ ǵøød. for I will not let you know it.
      And if you talk of trust I tell you this
      I trusted too much when I told you that.
                  in
      Trust me believe me: it may be right
      There may be reasons why you sd not know.
      Why will you never ask some other boon.   HM-1326

356   talk of trust
     ...tho' you ṕẗáẗé ǿẗ ṕẗǿǿẗ́ś,   HM-1326

357 As when I told such was a charm   H-153a

358 ...if you talk...   HM-1326;Lo-1
358 ...if you talk...   BM-1
358 (C)   <u>69</u>

359 I trusted too much, when...   HM-1326
359 ...trusted, when...   BM-1
359 (C)   73

And stirred this vice in you which ruined man   360
Through woman the first hour; for howsoe'er
In children a great curiousness be well,
Who have to learn themselves and all the world,
In you, that are no child, for still I find
Your face is practised when I spell the lines, 365
I call it,--well, I will not call it vice:

Sketch 360 ~~This vice of yours hath ruined states/ killed kings~~

  361 ~~As first it ruined man~~ for howsoe'er HM-1326

362 ...well   BM-1
362 ...well,   ,/ (I)   F-I
362 (C)   L-I

Alt. after 363
 And also well in afterlife if men
 Were childlike seeking but to teach themselves
               HM-1326

364 From nature, yet in you, that are no child HM-1326

365 ...practiced, I can spell your lines HM-1326
365 ...spell your lines   HM-1326
365 ...practised, when...   BM-1
365 (C)   73

366 ...it, well, I will...   BM-1
366 ...it, - well, ...   -/ (I)   F-I
366 (C)   L-I

367 You call yourself the little gilded fly H-153a

368 ...gnat   BM-1
368 ...gnat,   ,/ (I)   F-I
368 (C)   L-I

Alt. after 368 That ever breaks the just beginning
         rest   HM-1326

369 Settles & breaks the just beginning dream H-153a
369 And settles...   HM-1326

But since you name yourself the summer fly,
I well could wish a cobweb for the gnat,
That settles, beaten back, and beaten back
Settles, till one could yield for weariness: 370
But since I will not yield to give you power
Upon my life and use and name and fame,
Why will ye never ask some other boon?
Yea, by God's rood, I trusted you too much.'

   And Vivien, like the tenderest-hearted maid   375
That ever bided tryst at village stile,
Made answer, either eyelid wet with tears:
'Nay, Master, be not wrathful with your maid;

Alt. after 369
   With twang twang twang in one bloodsucking note
   I will not teach you
   I trusted you too much in telling that   H-153a

Draft 371 ff
   I will not yield; I will not let you know
   Trust? trust in me there may reasons for
   There may be things
   And wherefore   HM-1326

373 For mine own peace & yours ask me some other
               boon   H-153a
373 Why will you never...   Lo-1
373 ...will you never...   BM-1
373 (C)   73

376 ...tryst by village...   HM-1326
376 ...stile   BM-1
376 ...stile,   ,/ (I)   F-I
376 (C)   L-I

377 ...tears.   BM-1
377 (C)   73

378 ...your slave,   H-153a
378 'Nay, master, be...   BM-1
378 (C)   73

Caress her: let her feel herself forgiven
Who feels no heart to ask another boon.   380
I think ye hardly know the tender rhyme
Of "trust me not at all or all in all."
I heard the great Sir Lancelot sing it once,
And it shall answer for me. Listen to it.

    "In Love, if Love be Love, if Love be ours,   385
Faith and unfaith can ne'er be equal powers:

---

379 ...feel she is forgiven   HM-1326

380 I have no heart to...   H-153a

381 But did you never hear the tender rhyme   H-153a;
                                                               HM-1326
381 I think you hardly...   Lo-1
381 ...think you hardly...   BM-1
381 (C)   73

382 O trust me not all or all in all   H-31
382 Of 'trust...in all.'   BM-1
382 (C)   73

384 It shall make answer for me. Listen. this, H-153a
384 That rhyme shall answer for me. will you hear
                                                               HM-1326

385 ...love, & love be ours   H-153a
385 (Par.) In Love...   BM-1
385 (Par.) "In Love...   ("I)   F-I
385 (C)   L-I

Sketch for song 385
     O trust me not at all or all in all
     The least unhurt in love is lack of love   H-153a

386 ...powers.   BM-1
386 ...powers.:   :/ (I)   F-I
386 (C)   L-I

Alt. before 387 For when we love, in love, if love
                              be love   H-153a

538

Unfaith in aught is want of faith in all.

"It is the little rift within the lute,
That by and by will make the music mute,
And ever widening slowly silence all.   390

"The little rift within the lover's lute
Or little pitted speck in garnered fruit,
That rotting inward slowly moulders all.

"It is not worth the keeping: let it go:

388 Tis like the little rift within a lute		H-153a
388 It is		
(Par.) 𝜡𝜤𝜮 𝜤𝜤𝜥𝜮 the little...		HM-1326
388 (Par.) It is...lute		BM-1
388 (Par.) It is...lute,	,/ (I)	F-I
388 (Par.) It is...		L-I
388 (Par.) "It is...	"/ (I)	L-II
388 (C)		F-II

391 ...within a lover's...		H-153a;HM-1326
391 (Par.) The little...lute,		BM-1
391 (Par.) "The little...lute,	"/ (I)	L-II
391 ...lute,		F-II
391 (C)		73

392 And like the pitted...	H-153a

393 Wh by & by will rot it to the core,	H-153a

Alt. after 393
    And make it not having - it must go
    O trust me not at all in all. O master we shall
                     have to throw it out. H-153a

394 (Par.) It is...	BM-1
394 (Par.) "It is...	"/ (I) L-II
394 (C)	F-II

Alt. after 394 And shall we live to serve our passion
                      So   H-153a

But shall it? answer, darling, answer, no.   395
And trust me not at all or all in all."

O Master, do ye love my tender rhyme?'

   And Merlin looked and half believed her true,
So tender was her voice, so fair her face,
So sweetly gleamed her eyes behind her tears   400
Like sunlight on the plain behind a shower:
And yet he answered half indignantly:

   'Far other was the song that once I heard

---

395 We will not do it: answer, answer, no   H-153a

396 ...trust not me at...   H-153a
396 ...all.'   BM-1
396 ...all."   "/ (I)   F-I
396 (C)   L-I

397 ..., do you love...   Lo-1
397 O, master, do you love...   BM-1
397 O, master, do ye love...   <u>69</u>
397 (C)   73

398 ...believed her l̷o̷v̷e̷. true,   Lo-1
398 (No par. indent.)   BM-1
398 (MS, I indent sign)   F-I
398 (C)   L-I

401 Shone sweetly like the sunlight on a field
    Behind a shower: H-153a
401   plain
   ...on the f̷i̷e̷l̷d̷ behind...   Lo-1

402 ...indignantly.   BM-1
402 (C)   73

404 By this huge oak   nearly
  I̷n̷ t̷h̷e̷s̷e̷ w̷i̷l̷d̷ w̷o̷o̷d̷s̷, sung where we sit   HM-1326
404 ...sit.   BM-1
404 ...sit.:   :/ (I)   F-I
404 (C)   L-I

540

MERLIN AND VIVIEN

By this huge oak, sung nearly where we sit:
For here we met, some ten or twelve of us,   405
To chase a creature that was current then
In these wild woods, the hart with golden horns.
It was the time when first the question rose
About the founding of a Table Round,
That was to be, for love of God and men   410
And noble deeds, the flower of all the world.
And each incited each to noble deeds.
And while we waited, one, the youngest of us,
We could not keep him silent, out he flashed,
And into such a song, such fire for fame,   415
Such trumpet-blowings in it, coming down
To such a stern and iron-clashing close,
That when he stopt we longed to hurl together,

-----

407 ...horns.   BM-1
407 (C)   84

408 It was the time   first
    ~~About that season~~ (?) when the question rose HM-1326

409 ...Round   BM-1
409 (C)   59

410   for love of God & men
to   That was to be the flower of all the world
411 And noble deeds   HM-1326

Sketch 414-415
     Flash'd into such a song, such lust of fame HM-1326

416 ~~Such fire of fame~~, such trumpet blowings in it,
                              that ever came HM-1326
416 ...it - coming...   BM-1
416 ...it ~~,~~ coming...   ,/(I)   F-I
416 (C)   L-I

417 To such a stern   d
    ~~That when he reach'd~~ an iron clashing close HM-1326

418 That when he stopt
    We long'd to hurl together, ~~horse to horse~~, HM-1326

541

And should have done it; but the beauteous beast
Scared by the noise upstarted at our feet,   420
And like a silver shadow slipt away
Through the dim land; and all day long we rode
Through the dim land against a rushing wind,
That glorious roundel echoing in our ears,
And chased the flashes of his golden horns   425
Until they vanished by the fairy well
That laughs at iron--as our warriors did--
Where children cast their pins and nails, and cry,
"Laugh, little well!" but touch it with a sword,

---

419 ...it, but...		BM-1
419 ...it,; but...	;/ (I)	F-I
419 (C)		L-I
420 ...feet		BM-1
420 ...feet,	,/ (I)	F-I
420 (C)		L-I

422 ...land: & all the day ~~till~~ ~~the~~/we rode   HM-1326

424   at
    The song of glory ringing in our ears   HM-1326

425 And
    We chased...   HM-1326

428   & nails
  ~~I~~ ~~near~~ the well where children cast their pins
                                            HM-1326

429 'Laugh, little' well,' but...sword		BM-1
429 'Laugh, little well,' but...sword,	,/ (I)	F-I
429 'Laugh, little well,' but...		L-I
429 (C)		73
430 It dances madly round...		HM-1326
430 It buzzes wildly round...		Lo-1
430 ...buzzes wildly round...		BM-1
430 (C)		73

It buzzes fiercely round the point; and there   430
We lost him: such a noble song was that.
But, Vivien, when you sang me that sweet rhyme,
I felt as though you knew this cursèd charm,
Were proving it on me, and that I lay
And felt them slowly ebbing, name and fame.'   435

    And Vivien answered smiling mournfully:
'O mine have ebbed away for evermore,
And all through following you to this wild wood,
Because I saw you sad, to comfort you.
Lo now, what hearts have men! they never mount   440

---

431 ...such a song...   HM-1326

434   it
      Were proving them upon me & I lay   HM-1326
434 ...it upon me...   Lo-1
434 ...it upon me, ...   BM-1
434   on   I MS
    ...it ᴜᴘᴏᴺ me, ...   F-I
434 (C)   L-I

435 ...fame.   BM-1
435 (C)   L-II

Draft 436 ff
    (Par.) I your poor Nimuë sweep you from the world
    I, master, who have left the world for you!
    I make you lose your use & name & fame,
                        name
    Who lost mine own good in following you -
    I now remember yet one other verse
    In that sweet rhyme   the lady speaks   HM-1326

436 ...mournfully,   BM-1
436 ...mournfully,;   ;/ (I)   F-I
436 ...mournfully;   L-I
436 (C)   59

440 But men are all the same: they...   HM-1326

As high as woman in her selfless mood.
And touching fame, howe'er ye scorn my song,
Take one verse more--the lady speaks it--this:

   '"My name, once mine, now thine, is closelier mine,
For fame, could fame be mine, that fame were thine, 445
And shame, could shame be thine, that shame were mine.
So trust me not at all or all in all."

---

442 ...fame I well remember now	HM-1326
442 ..., howe'er you scorn...	Lo-1
442 ...howe'er you scorn my song	BM-1
442 (C)	<u>69</u>

Alt. before 443 I your poor Nimuĕ sweep you from the
                          world
            I make you lose your use & name &
                        fame   H-153a

443 Stay there is one more little		H-153a
443 One other verse, the lady...		HM-1326
444 (Par.) My name...		BM-1
444 (Par.) "My name...	(" I)	F-I
444 (Par.) "My name...		L-I
444 (C)		70
447 ...in all.		BM-1
447 ...in all."	(" I)	F-I
447 (C)		L-I
449 ...Queen		BM-1
449 ...Queen,	,/ (I)	F-I
449 (C)		L-II
450 ...dancing, when the pearls		HM-1326
450 ...spilt,		BM-1
450 ...spilt,;	(; I)	F-I
450 (C)		L-II

MERLIN AND VIVIEN

'Says she not well? and there is more--this rhyme
Is like the fair pearl-necklace of the Queen,
That burst in dancing, and the pearls were spilt;   450
Some lost, some stolen, some as relics kept.
But nevermore the same two sister pearls
Ran down the silken thread to kiss each other
On her white neck--so is it with this rhyme:
It lives dispersedly in many hands,   455
And every minstrel sings it differently;
"Man dreams of Fame while woman wakes to love."

---

451 Some lost some stolen some...		BM-1
451 Some lost, some stolen, some...	,/,/	F-I
451 (C)		L-II
454 On the Queen's neck: ...		HM-1326
455 That lives dispersedly in many mouths		HM-1326
455 lives		
It ís dispersedly...		Lo-1
455 ...hands		BM-1
455 ...hands,	,/ (I)	F-I
455 (C)		Y-VIII
456 ...differently,		BM-1
456 ...differently,;	;/ (I)	F-I
456 (C)		Y-VIII
457 But there is one...		HM-1326
457 ...pearls,		BM-1
457 ...pearls,;	;/ (I)	F-I
457 ...pearls;		Y-VIII
457 (C)		73
458 Men dream of fame while women wake to love.		H-153a
458 ...fame but woman...		HM-1326
458 'Man...love,'		BM-1
458 "Man...love."	"/⊙/"/(I)	F-I
458 (C)		Y-VIII

Yea! Love, though Love were of the grossest, carves
A portion from the solid present, eats   460
And uses, careless of the rest; but Fame,
The Fame that follows death is nothing to us;
And what is Fame in life but half-disfame,
And counterchanged with darkness? ye yourself
Know well that Envy calls you Devil's son,   465
And since ye seem the Master of all Art,
They fain would make you Master of all vice.'

---

459 For love, L   let it be the grossest, carves HM-1326
459 True: Love, ...   Lo-1
459 True: Love...   BM-1
459 (C)   73

461 And uses careless...Fame   BM-1
461 And uses, careless...Fame,   ,/,/(I)   F-I
461 (C)   Y-VIII

Draft 462 ff
Men think so much of fame. They cannot mount
As high as woman in her selfless mood.
See, Merlin, I have lost mine own fame
And have to leave it here in this wild woods
And all thro following you. I saw you sad
And meant to /N/ /?/ you.   HM-1326

462 ...death. What is it? a dream   HM-1326
462 ...us,   BM-1
462 ...us,;   ;/ (I)   F-I
462 (C)   Y-VIII

463 ...is fame in...   BM-1
463 (C)   59

464 ...darkness: you yourself   HM-1326;Lo-1
464 ...darkness? you yourself   BM-1
464 (C)   73

465 You know that...   HM-1326

466 ...since you seem...   HM-1326;Lo-1

```
     And Merlin locked his hand in hers and said,
     'I once was looking for a magic weed,
     And found a fair young squire who sat alone,          470
     Had carved himself a knightly shield of wood,
     And then was painting on it fancied arms,
     Azure, an  Eagle rising or, the Sun
```

---

466 ...since you seem...   BM-1
466 (C)   73

467 ...of all Vice.'   BM-1
467 (C)   73

First draft 470 ff
    To make fame nothing. Agramant a knight
    Of Arthur once came to me with a shield,
    An eagle volant, noir in azure, on it,
    What motto? so he ask'd me. follow fame.
    I counselld him to blot his eagle out
    And paint a gardener putting in a gaff
    The motto under this. not use but fame   HM-1326

Second draft 470 ff
    I stole behind a fair young squire
    The boy had carved himself a knightly shield
    Of wood
    And there was painting on it his fancied arms
    A̸n̸d̸ An eagle noir in azure v̸o̸l̸a̸n̸t̸ flying high
    And underneath a scroll I follow fame.
    (475-477 same)
                              use   fame
    Beneath for motto Rather f̸a̸m̸e̸ than use.   HM-1326

473 An Eagle, noir in azure, volant, armed   Lo-1
473 An Eagle, noir in azure, volant, armed   BM-1
473 Azure, an Eagle rising or, the Sun   I MS
    A̸ g̸o̸l̸d̸e̸n̸ E̸a̸g̸l̸e̸t̸ o̸n̸ a̸n̸ a̸z̸u̸r̸e̸ f̸i̸e̸l̸d̸/   I MS
    A̸n̸ E̸a̸g̸l̸e̸/ n̸o̸i̸t̸/i̸n̸ a̸z̸u̸r̸e̸/ v̸o̸l̸a̸n̸t̸/ a̸r̸m̸e̸d̸   F-I
473 Argent,   a̸r̸m̸s̸ sable, arm'd   I MS
    A̸z̸u̸r̸e̸, an Eagle rising o̸r̸/ t̸h̸e̸ s̸u̸n̸   Y-VIII
473 (C)   L-II

547

In dexter chief; the scroll "I follow fame."
And speaking not, but leaning over him,   475
I took his brush and blotted out the bird,
And made a Gardener putting in a graff,
With this for motto, "Rather use than fame."
You should have seen him blush; but afterwards
He made a stalwart knight. O Vivien,   480
For you, methinks you think you love me well;
For me, I love you somewhat; rest: and Love
Should have some rest and pleasure in himself,

---

474 Gules; & a scroll beneath 'I follow fame'		Lo-1
474 Gules; and a scroll beneath 'I follow fame.'		BM-1
474 In dexter chief; the scroll 'I follow fame.'		I MS
/~~Volant in bend, the scroll~~		I MS
~~Gules, and/a scroll beneath 'I follow famely~~		F-I
474 And member'd gules;		I MS
~~In dexter chief,~~ the scroll 'I follow fame.'		Y-VIII
474 ...scroll 'I...fame.'		L-II
474 (C)		59

475 And speaking not but leaning over him		BM-1
475 ...not, but... ...him,	,/,/(I)	F-I
475 (C)		Y-VIII

477 ...gaff		BM-1
477 ...gaff,	,/ (I)	F-I
477 (C)		Y-VIII

478 ...motto, 'Rather...fame.'		BM-1
478 (C)		59

481 Nimuë, methinks...		HM-1326

482 For me I...		BM-1
482 For me, I...	,/ (I)	F-I
482 (C)		Y-VIII

483 And Love sd take some pleasure in itself		HM-1326

486 Of him you say you love. conversely, Fame		HM-1326
486 Of him you say you love: ...		Lo-1
486 Of him you say you love: ...		BM-1
486 (C)		73

Not ever be too curious for a boon,
Too prurient for a proof against the grain   485
Of him ye say ye love: but Fame with men,
Being but ampler means to serve mankind,
Should have small rest or pleasure in herself,
But work as vassal to the larger love,
That dwarfs the petty love of one to one.   490
Use gave me Fame at first, and Fame again
Increasing gave me use. Lo, there my boon!
What other? for men sought to prove me vile,
Because I fain had given them greater wits:
And then did Envy call me Devil's son: 495
The sick weak beast seeking to help herself
By striking at her better, missed, and brought

---

487 Fame is but ampler means to help mankind   HM-1326

488 Should t̸a̸k̸e̸ have small rest or pleasure in
                                herself   HM-1326

489 ...love   BM-1
489 ...love,   ,/ (I)   F-I
489 (C)   L-I

490 Wh dwarfs...   HM-1326

492 ...use. what proof of trust,   HM-1326

493 What boon had I. they sought...   HM-1326

494 Because I ever wish'd to lift them higher.   HM-1326
494 Because I wish'd to give them greater minds: Lo-1
494 Because I wish'd to give them greater minds: BM-1
494 (C)   73

497 And striking at a greater than herself
to And missing did but bring her own claw back
498 And strike at her own heart. That other
                                fame   HM-1326

497 ...miss'd and...   BM-1
497 ...miss'd, and...   ,/ (I)   F-I
497 (C)   L-I

549

Her own claw back, and wounded her own heart.
Sweet were the days when I was all unknown,
But when my name was lifted up, the storm   500

---

498 ...back and...		BM-1
498 ...back, and...	,/ (I)	F-I
498 (C)		L-I
499 ...unknown		BM-1
499 ...unknown,	,/ (I)	F-I
499 (C)		L-I
501 Broke on...		Lo-1
501 Broke on...		BM-1
501 (C)		73

503   needs must
     Yet ~~must/I~~ work...   Lo-1

505 ...unborn of the grave   HM-1326

506 Allured not me. a single...   HM-1326

507 That is the...   HM-1326;Lo-1
507 That is...   BM-1
507 (C)   F-II

508 Which looks a sword...   HM-1326

First draft 511 ff (N.B. This connects with first
                    draft 470 ff.)
     ~~He did/not do it. Wherefore if I fear/~~
     ~~However well you think you love me now/~~
            ~~play~~
     ~~That you/may me falsely having power/~~
     ~~As loyal youths/ living in pupillage~~
     ~~Have often proved but tyrants/ having power~~
     ~~I do but dread/the loss of use + so you~~
     ~~From some quick turn of anger/ even a mood~~
     ~~Of overstrained affection it may be/~~
     ~~Or some quick spurt of woman jealousy~~
     ~~So work this charm on whom you say you love/~~ HM-1326

Brake on the mountain and I cared not for it.
Right well know I that Fame is half-disfame,
Yet needs must work my work. That other fame,
To one at least, who hath not children, vague,
The cackle of the unborn about the grave,   505
I cared not for it: a single misty star,
Which is the second in a line of stars
That seem a sword beneath a belt of three,
I never gazed upon it but I dreamt
Of some vast charm concluded in that star   510
To make fame nothing. Wherefore, if I fear,
Giving you power upon me through this charm,
That you might play me falsely, having power,
However well ye think ye love me now
(As sons of kings loving in pupilage   515
Have turned to tyrants when they came to power)

Second draft 512 ff
 Be teaching you this charm & in it power
 Upon me, you
 However well you may seem to love me now
 That you might play me falsely having power
 As royal children sweet in pupillage
 Have d̸f̸t̸e̸r̸ turned to tyrants having come to power
 I rather fear to lose my use than fame
 By giving you power on me thro' this charm HM-1326

514 ...well you think you love...   HM-1326;Lo-1
514 ...well you think you love...   BM-1
514 (C)   73

515 [As royal youths loving...   HM-1326
515 ...pupillage   BM-1
515 STET r̸o̸y̸a̸l̸ c̸h̸i̸l̸d̸r̸e̸n̸/ s̸w̸e̸e̸t̸ I MS
  A̸s̸ s̸o̸n̸s̸ o̸f̸ K̸i̸n̸g̸s̸ l̸o̸v̸i̸n̸g̸ i̸n̸ p̸u̸p̸i̸l̸l̸a̸g̸e̸/ F-I
515 (C)   L-I

516 Have d̸f̸t̸e̸r̸ turn'd...   HM-1326
516 STET M̸a̸y̸   I MS
  H̸a̸v̸e̸ t̸u̸r̸n̸'d̸ t̸o̸ t̸y̸r̸a̸n̸t̸s̸ w̸h̸e̸n̸ t̸h̸e̸y̸ c̸o̸m̸e̸ t̸o̸ p̸o̸w̸e̸r̸ F-I
516 (C)   L-I

I rather dread the loss of use than fame;
If you--and not so much from wickedness,
As some wild turn of anger, or a mood
Of overstrained affection, it may be,   520
To keep me all to your own self,--or else
A sudden spurt of woman's jealousy,--
Should try this charm on whom ye say ye love.'

    And Vivien answered smiling as in wrath:
'Have I not sworn? I am not trusted. Good!   525
Well, hide it, hide it; I shall find it out;
And being found take heed of Vivien.

521 ...own self, or else		BM-1
521 (C)		73
522 ...jealousy,		BM-1
522 (C)		67
523 ...him you say you love.		HM-1326
523 ...whom you say you love.'		Lo-1
523 ...whom you say you love.'		BM-1
523 (C)		73
524 ...smiling wrathfully		HM-1326
524 ...wrath.		BM-1
524 (C)		73
526 ...it. I shall...		BM-1
526 ...it.; I shall...	(; I)	F-I
526 (C)		L-I

527   being
    And having found it then beware of me. take heed
                       of Nimuë then   HM-1326
527 ...heed of Nimuë then.   BM-1
527 (C)   F-II

Alt. after 527 For this will ever echo in mine ear
                                HM-1326

528 A woman being
    I̸ w̸a̸s̸ not trusted. Doubtless, I m̸a̸y̸ f̸e̸e̸l̸ HM-1326

A woman and not trusted, doubtless I
Might feel some sudden turn of anger born
Of your misfaith; and your fine epithet   530
Is accurate too, for this full love of mine
Without the full heart back may merit well
Your term of overstrained. So used as I,
My daily wonder is, I love at all.
And as to woman's jealousy, O why not?   535

---

529 May feel...   HM-1326
529 ight
     Máy̶ feel...   Lo-1

530   faith   fine epithet
     Of your mistrust, & your t̶e̶r̶m̶ t̶o̶o̶/ o̶v̶e̶r̶s̶t̶r̶a̶i̶n̶y̶d̶
                                                           HM-1326

531 ...this full hearted love...   HM-1326
531   love
    ...this full h̶e̶a̶r̶t̶ of mine   Lo-1

532   may well deserve
     Without the whole heart back i̶s̶ o̶v̶e̶r̶s̶t̶r̶a̶i̶n̶e̶d̶
                              what (1 ?)   HM-1326
532 Without the whole heart...   Lo-1
532 ...the whole heart...   BM-1
532   full   I MS
    ...the w̶h̶o̶l̶e̶ heart...   L-I
532 (C)   L-II

533   daily
to The name of overstrained. My wonder is so used as I
534 B̶e̶i̶n̶g̶ s̶o̶ t̶r̶e̶a̶t̶e̶d̶ t̶h̶a̶t̶ I love at all.   HM-1326

535 And touching woman - spurts of jealousy   HM-1326
535 And
    B̶u̶t̶ as to woman s̶p̶u̶r̶t̶s̶ o̶f̶ jealousy O why not?   Lo-1
535 ...to woman jealousy...   BM-1
535 (C)   L-II

Alt. after 535 O̶ w̶i̶c̶k̶e̶d̶/o̶n̶e̶ f̶o̶r̶ a̶l̶l̶ y̶o̶u̶r̶ y̶e̶a̶r̶s̶/ I̶ a̶s̶k̶
                                                           Lo-1

O to what end, except a jealous one,
And one to make me jealous if I love,
Was this fair charm invented by yourself?
I well believe that all about this world

---

536 O wicked one I ask to what end
    Except a jealous one   HM-1326
536 O to
    T̸ó/what f̸i̸n̸é end, except a jealous one,   Lo-1

539 Right well I know that all about the world   HM-1326

540 You hold a pretty cageling here...   HM-1326
540 You cage a pretty captive...   Lo-1
540 You cage a pretty captive...   BM-1
540   buxom
    You cage a p̸r̸é̸t̸t̸ý captive...   F-I
540 You cage...   L-I
540 (C)   69

541 ...tower,   BM-1
541 (C)   L-I

First draft 543 ff
    Then answerd the great master merrily
    Not mine the charm.
    Loves have I had full many in golden youth
    But needed then no charm to keep them mine
    Save youth & happy spirits   HM-1326

Second draft 543 ff
    And Merlin answerd merrily 'Nay, not mine
    The inventor or the practice é̸t̸é̸t̸, then or now.
    Full many a love in loving youth was mine
    I needed no charm but love & youth
    To keep them mine. of those that wrought it first -
    The wrist is parted from the hand that waved
    The feet unsolder'd from their ancle bones
    Who paced it first: but listen you shall hear
    The legend as a guerdon for your rhymes.   HM-1326

Ye cage a buxom captive here and there,   540
Closed in the four walls of a hollow tower
From which is no escape for evermore.'

  Then the great Master merrily answered her:
'Full many a love in loving youth was mine;
I needed then no charm to keep them mine   545
But youth and love; and that full heart of yours
Whereof ye prattle, may now assure you mine;
So live uncharmed. For those who wrought it first,
The wrist is parted from the hand that waved,
The feet unmortised from their ankle-bones   550
Who paced it, ages back: but will ye hear
The legend as in guerdon for your rhyme?

---

543 ...her.	BM-1
543 (C)	73
544 ...mine,	BM-1
544 (C)	73
547 Whereof you prattle...	Lo-1
547 Whereof you prattle...mine,	BM-1
547 Whereof you prattle...mine,; ;/ (I)	F-I
547 Whereof you prattle...	L-I
547 (C)	73
550 The feet unsolder'd from their anclebones	Lo-1
550 The feet unsolder'd from their ancle-bones	BM-1
550 unmortised	I MS
The feet ⱥⱥ⸝⸝ⱥⱥⱥ⸝ⱥⱥ from their ancle-bones	L-II
550 ...their ancle-bones	F-II
550 (C)	59
551 ...will you hear	Lo-1
551 ...will you hear	BM-1
551 (C)	69
552 ...rhyme.	BM-1
552 ...rhyme.? ?/ (I)	F-I
552 (C)	L-I

'There lived a king in the most Eastern East,
Less old than I, yet older, for my blood
Hath earnest in it of far springs to be.   555
A tawny pirate anchored in his port,
Whose bark had plundered twenty nameless isles;
And passing one, at the high peep of dawn,
He saw two cities in a thousand boats

553	King	
	There lived a K̶h̶a̶n̶ in...	H-153a
553 (No par. indent.)	...East	BM-1
553 (No par. indent.)	(Par. indent symbol) ...East,	
	,/ (I)	F-I
553 (Par.) 'There...	'/ (I)	L-I
553 (C)		L-II

555 ...for years to come.	H-153a
555 Has earnest...	HM-1326

556 There came a tawny pirate to his port	H-153a;HM-1326
556 ...port	BM-1
556 ...port, ,/ (I)	F-I
556 (C)	L-I

558 ...one, (1 ?) before	HM-1326

560 ...woman in the sea.	HM-1326

562	is	
	He scatter'd t̶h̶e̶m̶ with ease, & brought her	
	home.	HM-1326

563 ...arrow-slain.	BM-1
563 ...arrow-slain.; ;/ (I)	F-I
563 (C)	L-I

564 He brought a maid so white so wonderful	H-153a
564 ...so smooth so white so wonderful,	BM-1
564 ...so smooth, so white, so wonderful, ,/,/	L-I
564 (C)	L-II

All fighting for a woman on the sea.   560
And pushing his black craft among them all,
He lightly scattered theirs and brought her off,
With loss of half his people arrow-slain;
A maid so smooth, so white, so wonderful,
They said a light came from her when she moved: 565
And since the pirate would not yield her up,
The King impaled him for his piracy;
Then made her Queen: but those isle-nurtured eyes
Waged such unwilling though successful war
On all the youth, they sickened; councils thinned,   570
And armies waned, for magnet-like she drew
The rustiest iron of old fighters' hearts;

---

565 ...moved.		BM-1
565 ...moved.:	:/ (I)	F-I
565 (C)		L-I

Alt. after 565 ~~The Courtliers of the court went mad~~
                                  ~~for her~~   H-153a

567 The king impaled...	BM-1
567 (C)	59

568 And made...those delicious eyes	HM-1326
568 crown'd	I MS
Then ~~made~~ her...	F-I
568 crown'd	I MS
Then ~~made~~ her...	L-I
568 (C)	L-II

569 Waged	
~~Made~~ such...	HM-1326
569 Made such...	BM-1
569 Waged	I MS
~~Made~~ such...	L-I
569 (C)	L-II

570-571 The young went mad for one who even drew	H-153a
570 ...sicken'd - nay she drew	HM-1326

572 The rusty iron of old warrior's hearts	H-153a

557

And beasts themselves would worship; camels knelt
Unbidden, and the brutes of mountain back
That carry kings in castles, bowed black knees   575
Of homage, ringing with their serpent hands,
To make her smile, her golden ankle-bells.
What wonder, being jealous, that he sent
His horns of proclamation out through all

---

573 The camel bowed unbidden when she gazed   H-153a
573 The very beasts did homage: camels knelt   HM-1326
573 ...themselves did homage; camels...   Lo-1
573 ...themselves did homage; camels...   BM-1
573   wd worship;   I MS
    ...themselves d̸i̸d̸ h̸o̸m̸a̸g̸e̸ camels...   F-I
573 (C)   L-I

574 And the black bulk that carries kings in towers
                                                      H-153a
574 Unbidden & the mountain-backs, the beasts   HM-1326
574 Unbidden & the beasts of mountain...   Lo-1
574 ...and the beasts of mountain bulk   BM-1
574   brutes   back   I MS
    ...and the b̸e̸a̸s̸t̸s̸ of mountain b̸u̸l̸k̸   F-I
574 (C)   L-I

575 That in those climates carry kings in towers HM-1326

576 Would kneel & tinkle with his serpent hand   H-153a
576 Adored her, tinkling with...   HM-1326
576 ...hands   BM-1
576 ...hands,   ,/ (I)   F-I
576 (C)   L-I

577 ...golden ancle-bells.   Lo-1
577 ...ancle-bells.   BM-1
577 (C)   59

578 H̸e̸ c̸o̸u̸l̸d̸ n̸o̸t̸ b̸u̸t̸ b̸e̸ jealous
    What marvel he was jealous, that he sent   H-153a
578 What wonder he was jealous, that...   HM-1326

579 Voices of proclamation out thro' all   H-153a

558

The hundred under-kingdoms that he swayed   580
To find a wizard who might teach the King
Some charm, which being wrought upon the Queen
Might keep her all his own: to such a one
He promised more than ever king has given,
A league of mountain full of golden mines,   585
A province with a hundred miles of coast,
A palace and a princess, all for him:
But on all those who tried and failed, the King

---

581   search of someone
      To f̶i̶n̶d̶ some w̶i̶z̶a̶r̶d̶ who might teach & a charm H-153a
581 In search of some enchanter who cd teach   HM-1326
581 ...the king   BM-1
581 (C)   59

582-3   the king sd
      Whereby t̶o̶ keep the Queen his own   H-153a
582-3 The king a charm whereby to keep the Queen
          His, heart & soul, for ever: & to such an
                                  one   HM-1326

584 And promised unto who taught the charm   H-153a
584 As cd do this, he promised a reward   HM-1326

585 A mountain with a mine of gold half-wrought   H-153a
585 ...mountain with goldmines half-wrought   HM-1326

587 A palace & a princess - his own child   H-153a
587 ...princess, h̶i̶s̶ o̶w̶n̶ c̶h̶i̶l̶d̶ all...   HM-1326

588 to But if he failed to prove he was not one
592   Who men might play with, he should lose his
                              head.   H-153a

588 Who might enchant her but on those who faild HM-1326
588 ...fail'd the king   BM-1
588 ...fail'd, the king   ,/ (I)   F-I;L-I
588 ...the king   L-II
588 (C)   59

Pronounced a dismal sentence, meaning by it
To keep the list low and pretenders back,   590
Or like a king, not to be trifled with--
Their heads should moulder on the city gates.
And many tried and failed, because the charm
Of nature in her overbore their own:
And many a wizard brow bleached on the walls: 595
And many weeks a troop of carrion crows
Hung like a cloud above the gateway towers.'

---

589 The King pronounced a sentence, meaning t̶h̶e̶r̶e̶b̶y̶
                        by it   HM-1326

591 ...not to play'd with - this   HM-1326

593 And many faild & many a wizard's brow   H-153a

595 Bleach'd on the city gates, a cloud   H-153a
595 ...the wall   HM-1326

597 Hung over the gateway towers.   H-153a

599 ...honey, yet...   BM-1
599 ...honey,; yet...   ;/ (I)   F-I
599 (C)   L-I

600 Your tongue...ask yourself.   Lo-1
600 Your tongue...little - ask yourself.   BM-1
600 Your tongue...little -: ask yourself!   :/(I)   F-I
600 Your tongue...ask yourself   L-I
600 (C)   73

Alt. before 601
        Say on, say on she answer'd. O my love
        Yet tell me for I find a little doubt   H-153a

601 You say the lady waged unwilling war   H-153a

602 With those fine eyes: is that believeable?   H-153a
602 ...in it.   BM-1
602   t̶h̶a̶t̶   I MS
        ...had her pleasure in it.   F-I
602 (C)   L-I

And Vivien breaking in upon him, said:
'I sit and gather honey; yet, methinks,
Thy tongue has tript a little: ask thyself.   600
The lady never made <u>unwilling</u> war
With those fine eyes: she had her pleasure in it,
And made her good man jealous with good cause.
And lived there neither dame nor damsel then
Wroth at a lover's loss? were all as tame,   605
I mean, as noble, as the Queen was fair?
Not one to flirt a venom at her eyes,
Or pinch a murderous dust into her drink,
Or make her paler with a poisoned rose?
Well, those were not our days: but did they find   610

---

603 (Omitted)   BM-1
603 ~~Wh made her good man jealous with good cause~~
                                        (All I MS)   F-I
603 (Complete, I MS)   L-I
603 (C)   L-II

604 And was neither dame nor damsel, all   H-153a

605 ...loss - were...   BM-1
605 ...loss ≠ were...   ?/ (I) L-I
605 (C)   L-II

606 Were all as good as she ~~to~~ was fair?   not one H-153a

607   at
    ...a venom ~~in~~ her...   Lo-1

608 To put a venom'd pinch into her cup   H-153a

609 Or pale her beauty with a poison'd rose   H-153a

610 Well those were ancient days: H-153a
610 Well those were ancient days: but...   Lo-1
610 Well those were ancient days: ...   BM-1
610 Well, those were ancient days: ...   ,/ (I)   F-I
610 ...were ancient days: ...   L-I
610   not our   I MS
    ...were ~~ancient~~ days: ...   L-II
610 (C)   F-II

A wizard? Tell me, was he like to thee?'

    She ceased, and made her lithe arm round his neck
Tighten, and then drew back, and let her eyes
Speak for her, glowing on him, like a bride's
On her new lord, her own, the first of men.   615

    He answered laughing, 'Nay, not like to me.
At last they found--his foragers for charms--

---

611 ...to thee?		Lo-1
611 ...thee?		BM-1
611 ...thee?'	'/ (I)	L-I
611 (C)		F-II

612 No.' And she made her little arm...		Lo-1
612 (No par. indent.) 'No.' And she made...		BM-1
612	She ceased,& I MS	
(No par. indent.) (Indent Symbol I) Y̶N̶o̶L̶Y̶ A̶n̶d̶ s̶h̶e̶		
made...		F-I
612 (C)		L-I

613 ...back and...		BM-1
613 ...back, and...	(, I)	F-I
613 (C)		L-I

615 Who thinks her new lord is the first of men		Lo-1
615 Who thinks her new lord is the first of men.		BM-1
615 On her own,		I MS
W̶h̶o̶ t̶h̶i̶n̶k̶s̶ her new lord, is the first of men.		F-I
615 (C)		L-I

616 (No par. indent.)		BM-1
616 (No par. indent.) (Indent symbol I MS)		F-I
616 (C)		L-I

618 ...man		BM-1
618 ...man,	(, I)	F-I
618 (C)		L-I

619 He lived...	H-153a

620 He had but one book, only read in that	H-153a
620 Had but...	HM-1326

MERLIN AND VIVIEN

A little glassy-headed hairless man,
Who lived alone in a great wild on grass;
Read but one book, and ever reading grew   620
So grated down and filed away with thought,
So lean his eyes were monstrous; while the skin
Clung but to crate and basket, ribs and spine.
And since he kept his mind on one sole aim,
Nor ever touched fierce wine, nor tasted flesh,   625

---

621   filed off   to the bone
       For he was filed & grated down with thought   H-153a
621   down & filed away with thought
       So fíléd áwáy & grated tó thé bóné   HM-1326
621 ...thought   BM-1
621 ...thought,   (, I)   F-I
621 (C)   L-I

622 His eyes were monstrous, but his leathern skin H-153a
622 So lean   the
    Wíth thóúght his eyes were monstrous but híś
                          skin   HM-1326
622 ...monstrous, but the skin   Lo-1
622 So lean, his eyes were monstrous, but the skin   BM-1
622   while   I MS
    So lean/ his eyes were monstrous,; búf the
                          skin   ;/ (I)   F-I
622 (C)   L-I

623 Mere crate & basket, only ribs & spine: H-153a

624 And since he fixt his mind but on one thing   H-153a
624 But since...   HM-1326;Lo-1
624 But since...   BM-1
624 And   I MS
    Búf since...   F-I
624 (C)   L-I

625 And since he touched no wine, nor tasted
                          flesh,   H-153a
625   fierce
    ...touch'd wíld wine...   HM-1326

563

Nor owned a sensual wish, to him the wall
That sunders ghosts and shadow-casting men
Became a crystal, and he saw them through it,
And heard their voices talk behind the wall,
And learnt their elemental secrets, powers   630
And forces; often o'er the sun's bright eye
Drew the vast eyelid of an inky cloud,
And lashed it at the base with slanting storm;
Or in the noon of mist and driving rain,
When the lake whitened and the pinewood roared,   635
And the cairned mountain was a shadow, sunned
The world to peace again: here was the man.

---

626 Nor *én*' had a sensual wish, to him the wall   H-153a
626 Nor *háá* own'd...   HM-1326

627 The wall that parts our world & that of ghosts
                                                     H-153a
627 That parts the shadowcasting man & ghosts   H-153a
627 That sunders shadow casting man & ghosts   HM-1326

628 Became as chrystal to him, & he saw
      Their faces   H-153a
628 ...chrystal and...   BM-1
628 ...chrystal, and...   ,/ (I)   F-I
628 (C)   L-I

629 And heard their voices there behind the wall   H-153a

630 And learnt their secrets & acquird the power
      Of genii, often   H-153a
630   elemental
    ...their   secrets, *élémentál* powers   HM-1326

631   sun's
    ...the *móóńý́s* bright...   HM-1326

633 ...storm,   BM-1
633 ...storm,;   ;/ (I)   F-I
633 (C)   L-I

635 ...roar'd   BM-1
635 ...roar'd,   (, I)   F-I
635 (C)   L-I

And so by force they dragged him to the King.
And then he taught the King to charm the Queen
In such-wise, that no man could see her more,   640
Nor saw she save the King, who wrought the charm,
Coming and going, and she lay as dead,
And lost all use of life: but when the King
Made proffer of the league of golden mines,
The province with a hundred miles of coast,   645
The palace and the princess, that old man
Went back to his old wild, and lived on grass,
And vanished, and his book came down to me.'

    And Vivien answered smiling saucily:

---

638 ...the king.		BM-1
638 (C)		59
639 ...the king...		BM-1
639 (C)		59
641 ...the king who...the charm		BM-1
641 ...the king, who...the charm,	,/,/(I)	F-I
641 ...the king, who...		L-I
641 (C)		59
642 ...dead		BM-1
642 ...dead,	,/ (I)	F-I
642 (C)		L-I
643 ...life; but...the king		BM-1
643 ...life;: but...the king	:/ (I)	F-I
643 ...the king		L-I
643 (C)		59
647 ...wild and...grass		BM-1
647 ...wild, and...grass,	,/,/(I)	F-I
647 (C)		L-I
649 ...saucily,		BM-1
649 ...saucily,;	;/ (I)	F-I
649 ...saucily;		L-I
649 (C)		73

'Ye have the book: the charm is written in it:　　　650
Good: take my counsel: let me know it at once:
For keep it like a puzzle chest in chest,
With each chest locked and padlocked thirty-fold,
And whelm all this beneath as vast a mound
As after furious battle turfs the slain　　　　　　655
On some wild down above the windy deep,
I yet should strike upon a sudden means
To dig, pick, open, find and read the charm:
Then, if I tried it, who should blame me then?'

　　And smiling as a master smiles at one　　　　　660

---

650 You have...charm is in it. Good.　　　　HM-1326
650 You have...　　　　　　　　　　　　　　　Lo-1
650 'You have...　　　　　　　　　　　　　　BM-1
650 (C)　　　　　　　　　　　　　　　　　　73

651 My counsel is at once to let me know it.　HM-1326

653 ...-fold　　　　　　　　　　　　　　　　BM-1
653 ... - fold,　　　　　　　　　　(, I)　　F-I
653 (C)　　　　　　　　　　　　　　　　　　L-I

654 ...all these beneath...　　　　　　　　HM-1326

655 ...battle hides men's bones　　　　　　HM-1326

657-658 I yet wd dig, pick, open, read the
　　　　　　　　　　　　　　　　charm　　　HM-1326
657　　　　　　　a
　　...upon s̸o̸m̸e̸ sudden...　　　　　　　　　Lo-1

659 And if I tried it...　　　　　　　　　HM-1326

660 ...a Master smiles...　　　　　　　　　BM-1
660 (C)　　　　　　　　　　　　　　　　　　73

661 ...school nor...　　　　　　　　　　　　BM-1
661 ...school, nor...　　　　　　　　,/ (I)　F-I
661 (C)　　　　　　　　　　　　　　　　　　L-I

662 But t̸a̸l̸k̸s̸ o̸f̸ a̸l̸l̸　　　　　　　　　　　HM-1326

That is not of his school, nor any school
But that where blind and naked Ignorance
Delivers brawling judgments, unashamed,
On all things all day long, he answered her:

'Thou read the book, my pretty Vivien!   665
O ay, it is but twenty pages long,
But every page having an ample marge,
And every marge enclosing in the midst
A square of text that looks a little blot,
The text no larger than the limbs of fleas;   670
And every square of text an awful charm,
Writ in a language that has long gone by.

---

663 ...judgments unashamed   BM-1
663 ...judgments, unashamed,   ,/,/ (I)   F-I
663 (C)   L-I

664 ...long; he answer'd her.   BM-1
664 (C)   73

665 (Par.) 'You read...   Lo-1
665 (Par.) 'You read...   BM-1
665 (C)   73

666   twenty
     A dreadful volume but 20 pages long   H-153a

667 And every...   H-153a

Alt. for 667 A̶n̶d̶ e̶v̶e̶r̶y̶ p̶a̶g̶e̶ h̶a̶s̶ a̶ g̶r̶e̶a̶t̶ m̶a̶r̶g̶i̶n̶   H-153a

668 ...enclosing itself in the midst   H-153a

670 ...the l̶e̶g̶s̶ limbs of fleas   H-153a
670 ...fleas,   BM-1
670 ...feas,;   (; I)   F-I
670 (C)   L-I

672 ...gone by,   BM-1
672 ...gone by (blot)   (, I)   F-I
672 ...gone by,   L-I
672 (C)   L-II

So long, that mountains have arisen since
With cities on their flanks--thou read the book!
And every margin scribbled, crost, and crammed   675
With comment, densest condensation, hard
To mind and eye; but the long sleepless nights
Of my long life have made it easy to me.
And none can read the text, not even I;
And none can read the comment but myself;   680
And in the comment did I find the charm.

---

673 ...long that...   BM-1
673 ...long, that...since,   ,/,/ (I)   F-I
673 ...since,   L-I
673 (C)   L-II

674 ...flanks - you read...   Lo-1
674 ...flanks - you read...   BM-1
674 (C)   73

675 And every margin scribbled oer & oer   H-153a

677   in sleepless nights
    To mind & eye but I have mastered that: H-153a
677 ...eye, but...   BM-1
677 ...eye,; but...   ;/ (I)   F-I
677 (C)   L-I

679   one
    In And no d̸y̸é̸ n̸ǿẃ d̸ĺʲ̸ẁ̸é̸ can read the text not
                    even I   H-153a
679 ...text - not even I;   BM-1
679 ...text ≠ , not even I;   ,/ (I)   F-I
679 (C)   L-I

680 ...myself,   BM-1
680 ...myself,;   ;/ (I)   F-I
680 (C)   L-I

681   in
    And from the comment have I learnt the charm H-153a
681 ...charm: BM-1
681 ...charm.   ⊙ (I)   F-I
681 (C)   L-I

O, the results are simple; a mere child
Might use it to the harm of anyone,
And never could undo it: ask no more:
For though you should not prove it upon me,   685
But keep the oath ye sware, ye might, perchance,
Assay it on some one of the Table Round,
And all because ye dream they babble of you.'

    And Vivien, frowning in true anger, said:
'What dare the full-fed liars say of me?   690

---

682 And the result so simple that a child   H-153a
682 ...simple: a...   BM-1
682 ...simple:; a...   ;/ (I)   F-I
682 (C)   L-I

683 Might work it to the harm   H-153a

685 And tho' you might not...   HM-1326
685 For
    A̸n̸d̸ tho' you...   Lo-1

686 ...oath you swore, you might...   HM-1326;Lo-1
686 ...oath you swore, you might...   BM-1
686 (C)   73

688 ...because you dream...   HM-1326;Lo-1
688 ...because you dream...   BM-1
688 (C)   73

689 ...said.   BM-1
689 ...said.:   :/ (I)   F-I
689 (C)   L-I

690 'The filthy swine! what do they say of me?   Lo-1
690 'The filthy swine! what do they say of me?   BM-1
690   W   the stall-fed liars   I MS
    'T̸h̸e̸ f̸i̸l̸t̸h̸y̸ s̸w̸i̸n̸e̸! W̸hat do t̸h̸e̸y̸ say of me?   L-I
690 T̸h̸e̸ s̸t̸a̸l̸l̸ f̸e̸d̸ T   ! what do they say I MS
    'W̸h̸a̸t̸ d̸o̸   the stall-fed liars say of me?   L-II
690 (C)   F-II

They ride abroad redressing human wrongs!
They sit with knife in meat and wine in horn!
They bound to holy vows of chastity!
Were I not woman, I could tell a tale.
But you are man, you well can understand   695
The shame that cannot be explained for shame.
Not one of all the drove should touch me: swine!

    Then answered Merlin careless of her words:
'You breathe but accusation vast and vague,

Sketch, 691 ff
    They sworn to vows of chastity
    They ride abroad redressing human wrongs
    Were she not woman
    But he was man & he cd understand
    The shame that could not be explained for shame
    Not one of them touch her
    And each has nothing that is not all yours
    And there was nothing wild or strange
    Or seeming shameful for what shame in trust
    So love be pure, she would not do
    To pleasure one she was wont to love
    The grand old man
    Who yet denied
    But men   ever be the first of men
    Were so much less in matter of the heart   H-30

692 ...horn.   BM-1
692 (C)   73

697 Not one of them should touch me: filthy swine!'Lo-1
697 Not one of them should touch me: filthy swine!'BM-1
697   all the drove sd   I MS
    Not one of ~~them~~ ~~should~~ touch me: filthy swine!' L-I
697 (C)   L-II

698 ...words.   BM-1
698 (C)   73

699 This is but...   HM-1326

Spleen-born, I think, and proofless. If ye know,   700
Set up the charge ye know, to stand or fall!'

   And Vivien answered frowning wrathfully:
'O ay, what say ye to Sir Valence, him
Whose kinsman left him watcher o'er his wife
And two fair babes, and went to distant lands;   705
Was one year gone, and on returning found
Not two but three? there lay the reckling, one
But one hour old! What said the happy sire?

---

700 ...If you know,   HM-1326;Lo-1
700 ...If you know,   BM-1
700 (C)   <u>69</u>

701   thing
   Speak out the charge you, to...   HM-1326
701 ...charge you know...   Lo-1
701 ...charge you know...   BM-1
701 (C)   <u>69</u>

702 ...wrathfully.   BM-1
702 (C)   73

703   Valence, him
   What say ye to the good Sir V̷a̷l̷e̷n̷   HM-1326

704 Whose
   H̷i̷s̷ kinsman left him guardian to two babes
   And their fair mother, went to distant lands HM-1326

706 ...& coming home he found   HM-1326

707-708 ...three. What said the happy man   HM-1326

707 ...three: there...   BM-1
707 (C)   73

708 ...old. What...   BM-1
708 (C)   F-II

A seven-months' babe had been a truer gift.
Those twelve sweet moons confused his fatherhood.'   710

   Then answered Merlin, 'Nay, I know the tale.
Sir Valence wedded with an outland dame:
Some cause had kept him sundered from his wife:
One child they had: it lived with her: she died:
His kinsman travelling on his own affair   715
Was charged by Valence to bring home the child.
He brought, not found it therefore: take the truth.'

---

709 ...been a sweeter gift		HM-1326
709 'A seven months'...gift,'		BM-1
709'A seven months'...gift,.'	☉ (I)	F-I
709 'A seven months...		L-I
709 (C)		73

710 Those fair moons	
Ⱥ twelvem̶o̶n̶t̶h̶s̶ babe confused...	HM-1326

711 ...Merlin 'Nay I...	BM-1
711 (C)	73

712 Sir Urien married in a distant land.		HM-1326
712 'Sir...dame.		BM-1
712 ...dame.:	:/ (I)	F-I
712 (C)		L-I

713 ...kept separate from...		HM-1326
713 ...kept him separate from...		Lo-1
713 ...him separate from his wife.		BM-1
713 sunder'd		I MS
...him s̶e̶p̶a̶r̶a̶t̶e̶ from his wife.:	: (I)	F-I
713 (C)		L-I

714 it lived with her	
...had: she died. H̶i̶s̶ K̶i̶n̶s̶m̶a̶n̶	HM-1326

715 ...kinsman, voyaging on his own affairs	HM-1326

716 ...by Urien to...	HM-1326

717 And brought...therefore. This is true	HM-1326

'O ay,' said Vivien, 'overtrue a tale.
What say ye then to sweet Sir Sagramore,
That ardent man? "to pluck the flower in season,"   720
So says the song, "I trow it is no treason."
O Master, shall we call him overquick
To crop his own sweet rose before the hour?'

And Merlin answered, 'Overquick art thou
To catch a loathly plume fallen from the wing   725
Of that foul bird of rapine whose whole prey
Is man's good name: he never wronged his bride.

---

719 ...ye to the good Sir Eglemour   HM-1326

720 ...man. 'I know it is no treason   HM-1326
720 ...man? to...season;   BM-1
720 ...man? "to...season;"   "/" (I)   F-I
720 ...season;"   L-I
720 (C)   73

721 The ballad says to crop the flower in season. HM-1326
721 ...song, I...treason.   BM-1
721 ...song, "I...treason."   "/" (I)   F-I
721 (C)   L-I

722-723 He pluck'd his own sweet rose before the
                    time.   HM-1326

724 ...overquick are you   HM-1326;Lo-1
724 ...answer'd 'Overquick are you   BM-1
724 (C)   73

725 ...a filthy plume...   HM-1326;Lo-1
725 ...catch a filthy plume...   BM-1
725   loathly   I MS
        ~~loathsome~~   I MS
...catch a ~~filthy~~ plume...   F-I
725 (C)   L-I

727 ...good fame. he...   HM-1326

I know the tale. An angry gust of wind
Puffed out his torch among the myriad-roomed
And many-corridored complexities   730
Of Arthur's palace: then he found a door,
And darkling felt the sculptured ornament
That wreathen round it made it seem his own;
And wearied out made for the couch and slept,
A stainless man beside a stainless maid;   735
And either slept, nor knew of other there;
Till the high dawn piercing the royal rose
In Arthur's casement glimmered chastely down,
Blushing upon them blushing, and at once
He rose without a word and parted from her: 740
But when the thing was blazed about the court,
The brute world howling forced them into bonds,

---

728 ...tale. A gust of wind at night		HM-1326
730 ...many corridor'd...		BM-1
730 ...many-corridor'd...	-/ (I)	F-I
730 (C)		L-I
731 ...palace: ~~&~~ then...		HM-1326
731 ...door		BM-1
731 (C)		73
732 And ~~Look it~~ darkling...ornaments		HM-1326
732 ...sculptured ornaments		BM-1
732 ...sculptured ornament~~s~~		F-I
732 (C)		L-I
733 That graven round...		HM-1326
Alt. for 733 ~~And look it for his /own/ & found~~		HM-1326
734 Crept to the couch & being wearied out		HM-1326
~~And so~~ lay down & slept his sleep & knew no more,		
734 ...out crept to the couch...		Lo-1
734 ...out crept to the...slept		BM-1
734 made for		I MS
...out ~~crept to~~ the:...slept,	(, I)	F-I
734 (C)		L-I

574

And as it chanced they are happy, being pure.'

    'O ay,' said Vivien, 'that were likely too.
What say ye then to fair Sir Percivale   745
And of the horrid foulness that he wrought,
The saintly youth, the spotless lamb of Christ,
Or some black wether of St Satan's fold.
What, in the precints of the chapel-yard,
Among the knightly brasses of the graves,   750
And by the cold Hic Jacets of the dead!'

    And Merlin answered careless of her charge,

---

735 ...maid,		BM-1
735 ...maid,;	(; I)	F-I
735 (C)		L-I
736 And neither woke or knew another there		HM-1326
736 ...slept; nor...there,		BM-1
736 ...slept/, nor...there,;	,/;/ (I)	F-I
736 (C)		L-I
739 at once		
...blushing & he rose:		HM-1326
745 ...ye to the good Sir Percival		HM-1326
747 ...youth, is he the lamb of Xt		HM-1326
748 Or the black...		HM-1326
749 ...the precint of...		HM-1326
751 And oer the...		HM-1326
751 ...cold hic jacets of...		BM-1
751 H J		I
...cold Hic Jacets of...		F-I
751 (C)		L-I
752 ...charge.		BM-1
752 (C)		67

'A sober man is Percivale and pure;
But once in life was flustered with new wine,
Then paced for coolness in the chapel-yard;   755
Where one of Satan's shepherdesses caught
And meant to stamp him with her master's mark:
And that he sinned is not believable;
For, look upon his face!--but if he sinned,
The sin that practice burns into the blood,   760

---

753   sober   ~~fair~~ ~~six~~   & pure
       A ~~temperate~~ man is Percivale, ~~but~~ ~~once~~   HM-1326

754 But being once in life was flusterd
    ~~his~~ ~~head~~ ~~was~~ ~~loverlily~~ with new wine   HM-1326

755 And
    ~~He~~ paced...   HM-1326

756 And one...   HM-1326

757   meant   stamp
    And sought to ~~brand~~ him...   HM-1326

758   that   were scarce believable
    And ~~if~~ he sinn'd - ~~but~~ look upon his face   HM-1326
758 ...sinn'd, is...   BM-1
758 (C)   73

759   for
    ~~And~~ ~~then~~ ~~believe~~ ~~it~~ - if he sinn'd   HM-1326
759 ...face, - but...   BM-1
759 ...face/! - but...   ! (I)   F-I
759 (C)   L-I

761   one dark
    ...the ~~one~~ ~~half~~-hour that brings...   HM-1326

762 Will stamp us...   HM-1326
762 ...be.   BM-1
762 ...be.:   :/ (I)   F-I
762 (C)   L-I

And not the one dark hour which brings remorse,
Will brand us, after, of whose fold we be:
Or else were he, the holy king,whose hymns
Are chanted in the minster, worse than all.
But is your spleen frothed out, or have ye more?'   765

   And Vivien answered frowning yet in wrath:
'O ay; what say ye to Sir Lancelot, friend
Traitor or true? that commerce with the Queen,
I ask you, is it clamoured by the child,
Or whispered in the corner? do ye know it?'   770

---

766 ...answer'd, frowning...wrath,		BM-1
766 ...answer'd, frowing...wrath,;	;/ (I)	F-I
766 ...answer'd, frowning...wrath;		L-I
766 ...wrath;		59
766 (C)		73

767   friend?
   ...Sir Lancelot'~~s~~ love,   HM-1326
767 'O, ay; ...friend?   BM-1
767 ...friend?   59
767 (C)   73

768 Traitor or ~~friend?~~ true?
   ~~The long and traitorous~~ commerce...   HM-1326

769 What say you? is it patent to the child   HM-1326
769 ...is it patent to the child,   Lo-1
769 ...you, is it patent to the child,   BM-1
769   clamourd by   I MS
   ...you, is it ~~patent to~~ the child,   F-I
769 (C)   L-I

770 ...in a corner? do you know...   HM-1326
770 ...do you know...   Lo-1
770 ...corner? - do you know it?'   BM-1
770 ...corner? / do you know it?'   F-I
770 ...do you know...   L-I
770 (C)   73

577

To which he answered sadly, 'Yea, I know it.
Sir Lancelot went ambassador, at first,
To fetch her, and she watched him from her walls.
A rumour runs, she took him for the King,
So fixt her fancy on him: let them be.   775
But have ye no one word of loyal praise
For Arthur, blameless King and stainless man?'

She answered with a low and chuckling laugh:

---

771 And Merlin answerd with some (?) sadness
                            Yea   HM-1326

772 I know it. Lancelot went ~~to bring her~~ am-
                            bassador   HM-1326

773-774 To fetch her, & she took him for the King
                                        HM-1326;Lo-1
773-774 To fetch her, and she took him for the king;
                                                    BM-1
773-774 To fetch her, and she took him for the King; 62
773-774 (C)   73

775 So
    ~~And~~ fixt...let it be   HM-1326
775 ...let him be.   Lo-1
775 ...him; let him be.   BM-1
775 ...him;: let him be.   :/ (I)   F-I
775 ...let him be.   L-I
775 (C)   73

Alt. after 775 There yet is nothing proved against the
                            Queen   HM-1326

776 ...have you no...   HM-1326;Lo-1
776 ...have you no...   BM-1
776 (C)   73

777 ...blameless king and...   BM-1
777 (C)   59

578

'Man! is he man at all, who knows and winks?
Sees what his fair bride is and does, and winks?   780
By which the good King means to blind himself,
And blinds himself and all the Table Round
To all the foulness that they work. Myself
Could call him (were it not for womanhood)
The pretty, popular name such manhood earns,   785
Could call him the main cause of all their crime;

---

778 And Nimuë laugh'd a...   HM-1326
778 ...answer'd, with...laugh,   BM-1
778 ...answer'd, with...laugh,;   ;/ (I)   F-I
778 ...answer'd, with...laugh;   L-I
778 ...laugh;   59
778 (C)   73

779 Him! is he...   HM-1326;Lo-1
779 'Him? is...   BM-1
779 (C)   73

780 ...fair queen does & winks a wink   HM-1326

Sketch 781 ff
        That coward
And ŧ𝘩̸𝘢̸ŧ̸ ø̸𝘯̸ḗ̸/wink has ruind all his court   HM-1326

781 ...he only means...   HM-1326
781 ...the good king...himself -   BM-1
781 ...the good king...himself ≠ ,   (, I)   F-I
781 ...the good king...   L-I
781 (C)   73

782-783 But blinds the Table Round to all they do.
                                            HM-1326

784 I call...   HM-1326

785   such
...name ḫ̸𝘪̸s̸ manhood...   HM-1326

786   her work
    Could call him our main cause of our vice   HM-1326

Yea, were he not crowned King, coward, and fool.'

   Then Merlin to his own heart, loathing, said:
'O true and tender! O my liege and King!
O selfless man and stainless gentleman,   790
Who wouldst against thine own eye-witness fain
Have all men true and leal, all women pure;
How, in the mouths of base interpreters,
From over-fineness not intelligible
To things with every sense as false and foul   795
As the poached filth that floods the middle street,
Is thy white blamelessness accounted blame!'

---

787 And him [except he were crown'd King] a fool.
    Yea, call him [were he not   HM-1326
787 ...crown'd king, coward...   BM-1
787 (C)   73

788 And Merlin...   HM-1326
788 ...said,   BM-1
788 ...said,;   ;/ (I)   F-I
788 ...said;   L-I
788 (C)   73

789 'O, true and tender! O, my liege and king! BM-1
789 ...and king!   59
789 (C)   73

791   thine own eyesight
    ...against the p̸r̸o̸o̸f̸ o̸f̸ e̸y̸e̸s̸i̸g̸h̸t̸ fair   HM-1326

792   each man   all
    Have everyman true friend, e̸a̸c̸h̸ woman pure, HM-1326
792 ...leal, - all...   BM-1
792 ...leal, / all...   F-I
792 (C)   L-I

795   with
    ...things w̸h̸o̸s̸e̸ every...   HM-1326

796 ...poach'd mud that lines the middle...   HM-1326

But Vivien, deeming Merlin overborne
By instance, recommenced, and let her tongue
Rage like a fire among the noblest names,   800
Polluting, and imputing her whole self,
Defaming and defacing, till she left
Not even Lancelot brave, nor Galahad clean.

Her words had issue other than she willed.
He dragged his eyebrow bushes down, and made   805
A snowy penthouse for his hollow eyes,
And muttered in himself, 'Tell <u>her</u> the charm!

---

798 (Par.) But Nimuë deeming...   BM-1
798 (C)   62

800 ...the noblest   HM-1326

801 Polluting and...   BM-1
801   whole   I MS
    Polluting, and imputing her ø̷w̷n̷ self, (1st,I)   F-I
801 (C)   L-I

803 ...brave or Galahad...   HM-1326

804 She shot beyond her mark   wisht
    Her words had issue other than she meant   HM-1326

805 He drew his bushy eyebrows down & made
    B̷u̷t̷/M̷e̷r̷l̷i̷n̷ d̷r̷a̷w̷i̷n̷g̷ d̷o̷w̷n̷   H-30
805 ...down and...   BM-1
805 ...down, and...   ,/ (I)   F-I
805 (C)   L-I

806 A snowy penthouse for his hollow eyes   H-30

807 Then muttering in himself 'man did she say?
    I think it matters little what she says   H-30
807 ...himself, 'tell...   BM-1
807 (C)   73

So, if she had it, would she rail on me
To snare the next, and if she have it not
So will she rail. What did the wanton say?   810
"Not mount as high;" we scarce can sink as low:
For men at most differ as Heaven and earth,
But women, worst and best, as Heaven and Hell.
I know the Table Round, my friends of old;
All brave, and many generous, and some chaste.   815

First sketch 808 ff
    So would she rail on me to snare the rest
    Face-flatterers & back biters are one race
             these knights/ my noble friends /
    Sweet soul//I think you tempted them & fally'd
    A shameful loathsome shame to cloak defeat with/liesy
           for art/may fail
    Thoy harlots paint their talk as well as/face
    With colours of the heart that are not theirs   H-30

Alt. after 808
    And so/ if she have it not/ so will she/rail   HM-1326

809 ...not,   ,/ (I)   F-I
809 ...not,   L-I
809 (C)   84

811 We mount as high we scarce can sink as low
    Tact, craft & malice working to one end -   H-31
811 Not mount as high, we...   BM-1
811 "Not mount as high,;" we...   (";" I)   F-I
811 (C)   L-I

812 Man & men, the best & worst
    Differ as Heaven & earth: but women vary   H-31
812 In men the best & worst differ as Heaven from
                 earth   H-31

813 As Heaven & Hell. These knights are   H-31
813 But women best & worst as Heaven from Hell   H-31
813 But women, best & worst, as Heaven & Hell.   H-30

814 I hear her at it - but these knights I know   H-30

582

She cloaks the scar of some repulse with lies;
I well believe she tempted them and failed,
Being so bitter: for fine plots may fail,
Though harlots paint their talk as well as face
With colours of the heart that are not theirs.   820
I will not let her know: nine tithes of times
Face-flatterer and backbiter are the same.
And they, sweet soul, that most impute a crime

---

816 I think she cloaks the wounds of loss with lies   Lo-1
816 I think she cloaks the wounds of loss with lies;
                                                      BM-1
816 (C)   73

817 And you sweet soul have tempted them & fail'd   H-31
817 Sweet soul, I think you tempted & faild   H-30
817 I do believe...   Lo-1
817 I do believe she...   BM-1
817 (C)   73

818   plots
    You are so bitter: for fine ~~all~~ may fail   H-30
818 She is so bitter...   Lo-1
818 She is so...fail   BM-1
818 She is so...fail,   ,/ (I)   F-I
818 She is so...   L-I
818 (C)   73

819 The harlot paints her talk as well as face   H-31

820 ...are not hers   H-31;H-30

821 But this I tell you that nine tithes of times   H-30

822 Face-flatterers & backbiters are one race   H-31
822 Face-flatterers & backbiters are the same.   H-30
822 Face-flatterers and backbiters are...   Lo-1
822 Face-flatterers and backbiters are...   BM-1
822 (C)   73

823 And those who most impute a crime to any   H-31
823 I find that those who most impute a crime   H-31
823 And surely those who most impute a crime   H-30

583

```
Are pronest to it, and impute themselves,
Wanting the mental range; or low desire              825
Not to feel lowest makes them level all;
Yea, they would pare the mountain to the plain,
To leave an equal baseness; and in this
Are harlots like the crowd, that if they find
Some stain or blemish in a name of note,             830
Not grieving that their greatest are so small,
Inflate themselves with some insane delight,
And judge all nature from her feet of clay,
Without the will to lift their eyes, and see
Her godlike head crowned with spiritual fire,        835
And touching other worlds.  I am weary of her.'
```

He spoke in words part heard, in whispers part,

---

824 A̶s̶ Impute themselves then   H-30

825 From a mind-narrowing malice & desire   H-31
825 They want a mental range or low desire   H-31
825 They want the mental range, or low desire   H-30
825 ...range, or...   BM-1
825 ...range,; or...   ;/ (I)   F-I
825 (C)   L-I

826 Not to be left,
    Wh   H-31

827 Yet could they, pare the mountain to the plain   H-30

833 ...clay, -   BM-1
833 ...clay, ⁄   F-I
833 (C)   L-I

834 And want the will...   Lo-1
834 And want the will to lift their eyes and see   BM-1
834 Without the will   I MS
    W̶i̶t̶h̶o̶u̶t̶ o̶n̶e̶ w̶i̶s̶h̶   I MS
    A̶n̶d̶ w̶a̶n̶t̶ t̶h̶e̶ w̶i̶l̶l̶ to lift their eyes, and see
                                        (, I)   F-I
834 (C)   L-I

Half-suffocated in the hoary fell
And many-wintered fleece of throat and chin.
But Vivien, gathering somewhat of his mood,   840
And hearing 'harlot' muttered twice or thrice,
Leapt from her session on his lap, and stood
Stiff as a viper frozen; loathsome sight,
How from the rosy lips of life and love,
Flashed the bare-grinning skeleton of death!   845
White was her cheek; sharp breaths of anger puffed
Her fairy nostril out; her hand half-clenched
Went faltering sideways downward to her belt,
And feeling; had she found a dagger there
(For in a wink the false love turns to hate)   850
She would have stabbed him; but she found it not:
His eye was calm, and suddenly she took
To bitter weeping like a beaten child,
A long, long weeping, not consolable.
Then her false voice made way, broken with sobs: 855

Sketch 838-849
        Part suffocated in the hoary fell
        Of cheek of chin
        But Nimuë hearing harlot once or twice
        Leapt from her session on his lap, & stood
        Stiff as a viper when you pinch its neck
        Her pale hand faltered downward to her belt
        Feeling, & had she found a dagger there   H-153a

843 Stiff like a snake nipt by the neck   H-31

849 ...feeling, had...   BM-1
849 ...feeling,; had...   ;   (I)   F-I
849 (C)   L-I

850 ...hate],   BM-1
850 (C)   59

854   not
        A long long weeping unconsolable   H-153a

855 ...way broken...sobs.   BM-1
855 (C)   73

'O crueller than was ever told in tale,
Or sung in song! O vainly lavished love!
O cruel, there was nothing wild or strange,
Or seeming shameful--for what shame in love,

856-7 'Cruel, the love that I have wasted on you'
                                           H-153a;Lo-1
856-7 (No par. indent.) 'Cruel, the love that I have
                        wasted on you!   BM-1
856-7 (Par. symbol I)   F-I
856-7   'O Crueller than was ever told in tale, I MS
      (Par.) ~~Cruel, the love that I have wasted on~~
             ~~you~~   L-I
856-7 (C)   L-II

858 Or sung in song! O vainly lavish'd love!   I MS
    ~~O cruel, there was nothing wild or strange,~~
                                    Stet   L-I
858 (C)   L-II

859 ...shame in trust   H-153a;Lo-1
859 ...shameful, for what shame in trust,   BM-1
859   love   P MS
    ...shameful, for what shame in ~~trust~~,   L-II
859 ...shameful, for...   F-II
859 (C)   73

860 If love be pure & not...   H-153a

861 Poor Nimuё had not done to pleasure him H-153a;Lo-1
861 ...done to pleasure him   BM-1
861   win his trust   P MS
    ...done to ~~pleasure~~ ~~him~~   L-II
861 (C)   F-II

Alt. after 861 Her grand old man, her silver star of eve
               Her God, her Merlin - nothing - H-153a

862 He call'd her what he call'd her.   H-153a

So love be true, and not as yours is--nothing   860
Poor Vivien had not done to win his trust
Who called her what he called her--all her crime,
All--all--the wish to prove him wholly hers.'

She mused a little, and then clapt her hands

---

863   master-
    The wish to prove him wholly - w̶h̶o̶l̶l̶y̶ - hers'   Lo-1
863 The master-wish to prove him wholly hers.'   BM-1
863   wholly   I MS
    The m̶a̶s̶t̶e̶r̶ wish to prove him wholly hers.'   F-I
863 All-all-the   I MS
    T̶h̶e̶ wish to prove him w̶h̶o̶l̶l̶y̶ wholly hers.'   L-I
863 (C)   L-II

Two Sketches for 864 ff.

First sketch 864 ff
    S̶h̶e̶ ̶t̶h̶o̶u̶g̶h̶t̶ ̶a̶ ̶l̶i̶t̶t̶l̶e̶/̶ ̶t̶h̶e̶n̶ ̶b̶r̶o̶k̶e̶ ̶o̶u̶t̶ ̶a̶f̶r̶e̶s̶h̶/̶
        f̶o̶u̶n̶d̶
    Ø̶ ̶I̶ ̶t̶h̶a̶t̶ ̶f̶e̶l̶t̶ ̶a̶l̶l̶ ̶m̶e̶n̶ ̶b̶y̶ ̶y̶o̶u̶ ̶w̶e̶r̶e̶ ̶d̶a̶r̶k̶ ̶i̶n̶ ̶y̶o̶u̶r̶
        l̶i̶g̶h̶t̶/̶
    A̶n̶d̶ ̶m̶a̶d̶e̶ ̶t̶h̶e̶m̶ ̶d̶a̶r̶k̶e̶r̶ ̶b̶y̶ ̶c̶o̶m̶p̶a̶r̶i̶s̶o̶n̶s̶ ̶l̶o̶v̶e̶d̶
        t̶o̶ ̶m̶a̶k̶e̶ ̶t̶h̶e̶m̶ ̶d̶a̶r̶k̶e̶r̶ ̶t̶h̶a̶n̶ ̶t̶h̶e̶y̶
    B̶e̶c̶a̶u̶s̶e̶ ̶o̶f̶ ̶t̶h̶a̶t̶ ̶g̶r̶e̶a̶t̶ ̶p̶l̶e̶a̶s̶u̶r̶e̶ ̶w̶h̶ ̶I̶ ̶t̶o̶o̶k̶
    T̶o̶ ̶s̶e̶a̶t̶ ̶y̶o̶u̶ ̶s̶o̶l̶e̶ ̶u̶p̶o̶n̶ ̶t̶h̶e̶ ̶p̶e̶d̶e̶s̶t̶a̶l̶
    Ø̶f̶ ̶w̶o̶r̶s̶h̶i̶p̶ ̶+̶ ̶s̶u̶r̶e̶l̶y̶ ̶y̶o̶u̶ ̶w̶i̶l̶l̶ ̶b̶r̶e̶a̶k̶ ̶m̶y̶ ̶h̶e̶a̶r̶t̶
    W̶i̶t̶h̶ ̶s̶u̶c̶h̶ ̶u̶n̶u̶t̶t̶e̶r̶a̶b̶l̶e̶ ̶u̶n̶k̶i̶n̶d̶l̶i̶n̶e̶s̶s̶/̶   Lo-1

Second sketch 864 ff
    S̶h̶e̶ ̶p̶a̶u̶s̶e̶d̶ ̶a̶ ̶l̶i̶t̶t̶l̶e̶/̶ ̶t̶h̶e̶n̶ ̶b̶r̶a̶k̶e̶ ̶o̶u̶t̶ ̶a̶f̶r̶e̶s̶h̶
    Ø̶ ̶I̶ ̶t̶h̶a̶t̶ ̶f̶l̶a̶t̶t̶e̶r̶i̶n̶g̶ ̶m̶y̶ ̶o̶w̶n̶ ̶f̶a̶n̶c̶y̶/̶ ̶s̶a̶w̶
    T̶h̶e̶ ̶k̶n̶i̶g̶h̶t̶s̶/̶ ̶t̶h̶e̶ ̶ ̶ ̶ ̶t̶h̶e̶ ̶k̶i̶n̶g̶
    K̶i̶n̶g̶/̶ ̶c̶o̶u̶r̶t̶/̶ ̶&̶ ̶T̶a̶b̶l̶e̶ ̶R̶o̶u̶n̶d̶/̶ ̶d̶a̶r̶k̶ ̶i̶n̶ ̶y̶o̶u̶r̶ ̶l̶i̶g̶h̶t̶/̶+̶
    W̶h̶o̶ ̶l̶o̶v̶e̶d̶ ̶t̶o̶ ̶t̶h̶i̶n̶k̶ ̶t̶h̶e̶m̶ ̶d̶a̶r̶k̶e̶r̶ ̶t̶h̶a̶n̶ ̶t̶h̶e̶y̶/̶a̶r̶e̶
        p̶a̶s̶s̶i̶o̶n̶
    B̶e̶c̶a̶u̶s̶e̶ ̶o̶f̶ ̶t̶h̶a̶t̶ ̶g̶r̶e̶a̶t̶ ̶p̶l̶e̶a̶s̶u̶r̶e̶ ̶w̶h̶ ̶I̶ ̶f̶e̶l̶t̶
    T̶o̶ ̶s̶e̶a̶t̶ ̶y̶o̶u̶ ̶s̶o̶l̶e̶ ̶u̶p̶o̶n̶ ̶m̶y̶ ̶p̶e̶d̶e̶s̶t̶a̶l̶
    Ø̶f̶ ̶w̶o̶r̶s̶h̶i̶p̶ ̶+̶ ̶I̶ ̶a̶m̶ ̶a̶n̶s̶w̶e̶r̶d̶ ̶&̶ ̶m̶y̶ ̶d̶r̶e̶a̶m̶
    I̶s̶ ̶b̶r̶o̶k̶e̶n̶ ̶w̶i̶t̶h̶ ̶a̶n̶ ̶i̶n̶s̶u̶l̶t̶ ̶+̶ ̶n̶o̶t̶h̶i̶n̶g̶ ̶l̶e̶f̶t̶ ̶t̶o̶ ̶m̶e̶

                          (Continued)

Together with a wailing shriek, and said: 865
'Stabbed through the heart's affections to the heart!
Seethed like the kid in its own mother's milk!
Killed with a word worse than a life of blows!
I thought that he was gentle, being great:
O God, that I had loved a smaller man!   870
I should have found in him a greater heart.
O, I, that flattering my true passion, saw
The knights, the court, the King, dark in your light,
Who loved to make men darker than they are,

Second sketch 864 ff., Continued

~~But into some low cave to creep/&/die there/~~
~~If the wolf spares me/ weep my life away//~~
~~Killed with unutterable/unkindliness/~~
(Par.) ~~With that she turn'd her back & hung her~~
~~head.//~~
~~And Merlin look'd & thoy he knew her well/~~
~~And could have told another/what she was/~~
~~(knew?) her so (ill?)/ he half believed her love/~~

Lo-1

864   mused   &   ~~she~~ clapt her hands
           She ~~thought~~ a little, then~~brake out anew~~   Lo-1
864 (No par. indent.)   BM-1
864 (No par. indent.)   (Indent symbol I)   F-I
864 (C)   L-I

865 Together, with a ~~sudden~~ wail, shriek & said: Lo-1

866 ...the best affections...   BM-1
866   heart's   I MS
     ...the ~~best~~ affections...   F-I
866 (C)   L-I

870   that
     O God, ~~if~~ I had...   Lo-1

872   my
     ...flattering ~~a~~ true   Lo-1
872 O, I that, flattering...   BM-1
872 O, I, that~~/~~ flattering...   ,/ (2nd,I)   F-I
872 (C)   L-I

Because of that high pleasure which I had   875
To seat you sole upon my pedestal
Of worship--I am answered, and henceforth
The course of life that seemed so flowery to me
With you for guide and master, only you,
Becomes the sea-cliff pathway broken short,   880
And ending in a ruin--nothing left,
But into some low cave to crawl, and there,
If the wolf spare me, weep my life away,
Killed with inutterable unkindliness.'

    She paused, she turned away, she hung her head,   885
The snake of gold slid from her hair, the braid
Slipt and uncoiled itself, she wept afresh,

---

873 ...the king, dark...	BM-1
873 (C)	73

875 ...which I ~~felt~~ had   Lo-1

879 With ~~only~~ you ~~for~~ ~~master~~ & ~~for~~ guide & master,
                    only you   Lo-1

881 ...left		BM-1
881 ...left,	(, I)	F-I
881 (C)		L-I

884 ...with unutterable unkindliness.'	BM-1
884 i	I MS
...with ~~u~~nutterable unkindliness.'	F-I
884 (C)	L-I

885   hung ~~away~~ her head   ~~aloud~~
    (Par.) She paused, she ~~turn'd~~ ~~her~~ ~~back~~, she ~~wept~~
                    openly afresh   Lo-1
885 (Par.) She paused, she hung her head, she wept
                    afresh;   BM-1
885 (I MS C)   L-I
885 (C)   L-II

886-7 (Omitted)   BM-1
886-7 (I-MS-C)   L-I
886-7 (C)   L-II

And the dark wood grew darker toward the storm
In silence, while his anger slowly died
Within him, till he let his wisdom go   890
For ease of heart, and half believed her true:

Sketch 888 ff (canceled)
                    he look'd, & in him
        In silence & ~~his anger slowly~~ died
        His anger, & he half-believed her true.
        And he (1 ?) when one armed with thrice her hair
        Yea & with thrice her beauty might have proved
        Less perilous, look'd & let his anger die
                    & he look'd &
        Within him, ~~till he~~ half believed ~~her true~~
        He, where the current ran so low that ev'n
        Dim eyes cd see the bottom, let his will
        Drift & lookd on & half believed her true   Lo-1

889-891 In silence, and he look'd, and in him died
            His anger, and he half believed her true,   BM-1
889-891 (I-MS-ċ)   L-I
889-891 (C)   L-II

892-893 (Omitted)   BM-1
892-893 (I-MS-C)   L-I
892-893 (C)   L-II
893 ...storm' and...   F-II
893 (C)   73

Alt. before 894 (Par.) And ~~Merlin look'd & half-her~~
                        ~~lieved her love,~~   Lo-1

894 Pitied the heaving...   HM-1326;Lo-1
894 Pitied the heaving shoulder and the face,   BM-1
894 (I-MS-C)   L-I
894 (C)   L-II

895   for utmost grief
        ...as if in sorrow or shame   HM-1326
895 ...shame,   BM-1
895 ...shame,;   ;(I)   F-I
895 (C)   L-I

Called her to shelter in the hollow oak,
'Come from the storm,' and having no reply,
Gazed at the heaving shoulder, and the face
Hand-hidden, as for utmost grief or shame;   895
Then thrice essayed, by tenderest-touching terms,
To sleek her ruffled peace of mind, in vain.
At last she let herself be conquered by him,
And as the cageling newly flown returns,
The seeming-injured simple-hearted thing   900
Came to her old perch back, and settled there.

Alt. after 895 C̸a̸l̸l̸'̸d̸ h̸e̸r̸ t̸o̸ s̸h̸e̸l̸t̸e̸r̸ i̸n̸ t̸h̸e̸ h̸o̸l̸l̸o̸w̸
                        t̸r̸e̸e̸,̸   (I MS)   L-I

896 And long in vain with tender touching vows   HM-1326
896   thrice
    And long essay'd...   Lo-1
896 And thrice essay'd by...terms   BM-1
896 And thrice essay'd, by...terms   ,/ (I)   F-I
896 Then   I MS
    A̸n̸d̸ thrice...terms   L-I
896 ...terms   L-II
896 (C)   73

897 Essayd to sleek her ruffled peace of mind   HM-1326
897 ...mind in...   BM-1
897 ...mind, in...   ,/ (I)   F-I
897 (C)   L-I

899 ...as caged bird, newly...   HM-1326

900 ...seeming - guileless simple-hearted...   HM-1326;
                                                   Lo-1
900 The seeming-guileless simple-hearted thing   BM-1
900   injured   I MS
    The seeming-g̸u̸i̸l̸e̸l̸e̸s̸s̸ simple-hearted thing   F-I
900 (C)   L-I

901 ...& nested there   HM-1326

Alt. after 901
    And as he watched the rare tear & closed eyes
                                                   HM-1326

591

There while she sat, half-falling from his knees,
Half-nestled at his heart, and since he saw
The slow tear creep from her closed eyelid yet,
About her, more in kindness than in love,   905
The gentle wizard cast a shielding arm.
But she dislinked herself at once and rose,
Her arms upon her breast across, and stood,
A virtuous gentlewoman deeply wronged,
Upright and flushed before him: then she said: 910

  'There must be now no passages of love
Betwixt us twain henceforward evermore;

---

902 And while...   HM-1326;Lo-1
902 And while she...   BM-1
902 There   P MS
    A̶n̶d̶ while she...   L-II
902 (C)   F-II

903 And nestled at his heart, & while he saw
                             watch'd   HM-1326

904 ...eyelid down,   HM-1326

905 Around her waist in pity not in love   HM-1326;Lo-1
905 Around her waist in pity, not in love,   BM-1
905 About   more in kindness than   I MS
    A̶r̶o̶u̶n̶d̶ her, w̶a̶i̶s̶t̶ i̶n̶ p̶i̶t̶y̶/ n̶o̶t̶ in love, (1st,I)   L-I
905 (C)   L-II

907 ...she dislockt herself at once & s̶t̶o̶o̶d̶ like HM-1326

908 ...stood   BM-1
908 (C)   73

Alt. after 909
    Stood up & spoke
    And Merlin lookd & half believed her love
    And set himself to sleek her ruffled peace   HM-1326

910 Flush'd & upright before...   HM-1326

MERLIN AND VIVIEN

Since, if I be what I am grossly called,
What should be granted which your own gross heart
Would reckon worth the taking? I will go.   915
In truth, but one thing now--better have died

Draft 911 ff
        I bear
    M̸y̸ f̸a̸u̸l̸t̸, my fate must be to love you still,
    I cannot help it, whether fate or fault
    Since if I be what I am grossly call'd
    I cannot grant you aught wh your gross heart
    Wd reckon (1 ?)
    Holds worth the granting. I will go
    But there must be no passage of love
    Between us from henceforth for evermore.   HM-1326

912 ...evermore.   BM-1
912 (C)   73

914 I cannot grant you aught which your gross heart Lo-1
914 I cannot grant you aught which your gross heart BM-1
914 What sd I̸ be granted   own   I MS
    I̸ c̸a̸n̸n̸o̸t̸ g̸r̸a̸n̸t̸/y̸o̸u̸/a̸u̸g̸h̸t̸ which your gross heart L-I
914 (C)   L-II

915 Would reckon worth acceptance. I will go   Lo-1
915 Would reckon worth acceptance. I will go.   BM-1
915   the taking?   I MS
    Would reckon worth a̸c̸c̸e̸p̸t̸a̸n̸c̸e̸. I will go.   L-I
915 (C)   L-II

Sketch c. 916 ff
    fear not: I will die a dozen deaths
    But I̸ w̸d̸
    All cruel thou demand it once again,
    The one poor proof of heart, so often ask'd
    Thou   Y-III
Sketch 916 ff
    But Fear not: & I will die a dozen deaths
    All hard as you ere I d̸e̸m̸a̸n̸d̸ ask it now
    The one poor proof so often asked in vain,
    How justly   Y-III

593

Thrice than have asked it once--could make me stay--
That proof of trust--so often asked in vain!
How justly, after that vile term of yours,
I find with grief! I might believe you then,   920
Who knows? once more. Lo! what was once to me
Mere matter of the fancy, now hath grown
The vast necessity of heart and life.
Farewell; think gently of me, for I fear
My fate or folly, passing gayer youth   925
For one so old, must be to love thee still.
But ere I leave thee let me swear once more

916-7 In truth but one thing now could make me stay;
                                           Lo-1

916-7 In truth, but one thing now could make me
                      stay;   BM-1

916-7   -better have died   I MS
      In truth, but one thing now cou*ld* *make* *me*
                  stay   L-I
      Thrice than have ask'd it once - cd make me
                  stay -   I MS

916-7 (C)   L-II

---

917 There is but one thing now cd...   HM-1326

---

918 ...askt of you   HM-1326
918 ...trust so often justly ask'd,   Lo-1
918 That proof of trust so often justly ask'd,   BM-1
918   -   in vain I MS
      That proof of trust so often *justly* ask'd/   L-I
918 (C)   L-II

---

919 How justly: /*now* *I* find: after that vile name of
                        yours   HM-1326
919 ...after that vile name of yours   Lo-1
919 ...justly after that vile name of yours   BM-1
919   term   I MS
      ...justly, after that vile *name* of yours, (,,I) L-I
919 (C)   L-II

---

920 ...grief: I...   BM-1
920 ...grief*:*! I...   ! (I)   L-I
920 (C)   L-II

That if I schemed against thy peace in this,

---

921 What
  for proof to me
  That wish was once   HM-1326
921 ...more. O what...   Lo-1
921 Who knows, once more. O,what...   BM-1
921 Who knows, once more. O, what... ? (I) F-I
921 ...more. O, what...   L-I
921 (C)   73

922 ...now has grown   HM-1326;Lo-1
922 ...now has grown   BM-1
922 (C)   73

Alt. after 923 I might believe you then, (1 ?): but
            now   HM-1326

924 ...think kindly of...   HM-1326;Lo-1
924 Farewell, - think kindly of me, for I fear BM-1
924 Farewell,; ≠ think kindly of... ;/ (I) F-I
924 ...think kindly of...   L-I
924 (C)   73

925-926 ...or fault must be to love you still. HM-1326
925 My fate or fault, omitting gayer youth Lo-1
925 My fate or fault, omitting gayer youth BM-1
925 (C)   73

926 ...love you still.   Lo-1
926 ...love you still.   BM-1
926 (C)   73

927 ...leave you, let...   HM-1326;Lo-1
927 ...leave you let...   BM-1
927 (C)   73

928 ...against your peace...   HM-1326;Lo-1
928 ...against your peace...   BM-1
928 (C)   73

May yon just heaven, that darkens o'er me, send
One flash, that, missing all things else, may make   930
My scheming brain a cinder, if I lie.'

   Scarce had she ceased, when out of heaven a bolt
(For now the storm was close above them) struck,
Furrowing a giant oak, and javelining
With darted spikes and splinters of the wood   935
The dark earth round. He raised his eyes and saw
The tree that shone white-listed through the gloom.
But Vivien, fearing heaven had heard her oath,

---

929   yonder heaven   send
    May that huge cloud that darkens oer me ~~miss~~   HM-1326
929 ...darkens ~~send~~ o'er me, send   Lo-1

930 ...one. And flash...   HM-1326
930 ...flash that, missing...   BM-1
930 ...flash, that~~/~~ missing...   ,/ (I)   F-I
930 ...flash, that missing...   L-I
930 (C)   59

932   ceased   out of heaven a bolt
   She scarce had ~~spoken~~ when ~~a/bolt from heaven~~
                                                 HM-1326
932 (Par.) She scarce had ceased, when...   Lo-1;BM-1
932   S   she   I MS
    (Par.) She ~~s~~carce had ceased, when...   L-II
932 (C)   F-II

933   them] struck
...above ~~their heads~~   HM-1326

934   F   a giant
~~struck~~, ~~f~~urrowing ~~down an~~ oak & javelining   HM-1326

935   darted spikes
With ~~sharp~~ & ~~sudden~~ splinters ~~darted~~ from the
                                      wood   HM-1326

937   that shone
~~Then shone~~ the tree white listed...   HM-1326

```
And dazzled by the livid-flickering fork,
And deafened with the stammering cracks and claps      940
That followed, flying back and crying out,
'O Merlin, though you do not love me, save,
Yet save me!' clung to him and hugged him close;
And called him dear protector in her fright,
Nor yet forgot her practice in her fright,              945
But wrought upon his mood and hugged him close.
The pale blood of the wizard at her touch
Took gayer colours, like an opal warmed.
She blamed herself for telling hearsay tales:
She shook from fear, and for her fault she wept         950
Of petulancy; she called him lord and liege,
Her seer, her bard, her silver star of eve,
```

---

938 But
    A̸ṉ̸d̸ Nimuë...   HM-1326

939   livid flickering fork
    And dazzled with the t̸h̸e̸ b̸l̸i̸n̸d̸i̸n̸g̸ b̸l̸a̸z̸e̸   HM-1326

941   flying back to Merlin waild
    That followd overhead & crying out   HM-1326
941 ...out: BM-1
941 ...out̸ ,   ,/ (I)   L-II
941 (C)   F-II

943   hugged him close
    O save me, clung to him & n̸e̸s̸t̸l̸e̸d̸ t̸o̸ h̸i̸m̸   HM-1326

947   of the wizard
    The pale blood at her touch the wizards blood
                                        HM-1326

951 Of petulancy. She calld him dearer (1 ?)
    From fancied (1 ?), calld him lord & love   HM-1326

952 Her grand old man, her silver...   HM-1326
952   seer, her sage
    Her g̸r̸a̸n̸d̸ o̸l̸d̸ m̸a̸n̸, her...   Lo-1
952 ...seer, her sage, her...   BM-1
952   bard   I MS
    ...seer, her s̸a̸g̸e̸, her...   F-I
952 (C)   L-I

Her God, her Merlin, the one passionate love
Of her whole life; and ever overhead
Bellowed the tempest, and the rotten branch   955
Snapt in the rushing of the river-rain
Above them; and in change of glare and gloom
Her eyes and neck glittering went and came;
Till now the storm, its burst of passion spent,
Moaning and calling out of other lands,   960
Had left the ravaged woodland yet once more
To peace; and what should not have been had been,
For Merlin, overtalked and overworn,
Had yielded, told her all the charm, and slept.

Then, in one moment, she put forth the charm   965
Of woven paces and of waving hands,
And in the hollow oak he lay as dead,
And lost to life and use and name and fame.

Then crying 'I have made his glory mine,'
And shrieking out 'O fool!' the harlot leapt   970
Adown the forest, and the thicket closed
Behind her, and the forest echoed 'fool.'

---

957 Above them   &
    A̶n̶d̶ e̶v̶e̶r̶ in t̶h̶e̶ changing...   HM-1326

963 And Merlin...   HM-1326
963 For
    A̶n̶d̶ Merlin...   Lo-1

965   one
    ...in a moment...   HM-1326
965 (Par.) Then in one moment she...   BM-1
965 (Par.) Then, in one moment, she...   (,, I)   L-I
965 (C)   L-II

966 ...paces of...   HM-1326

967 and he lay as dead   HM-1326

970 ...out the fool, ...   HM-1326
970   O
    ...out T̶h̶e̶ fool...   Lo-1

MERLIN AND VIVIEN

<u>Rejected Passages</u>:

And Merlin tho' he strove against the king
And ever told him his great plan to feel
Yet ~~we~~ since he cleaved to it went forth - search'd
Thro many lands for all great haunts there   H-31

So Vivian spake, & with the dead mens hair
The batter'd shield, & the besotted boy
Fled lightly back to Mark & Lyonesse.   H-33

To what request are all your wicked tricks   H-153a
A prea

Dear feet that I have followed thro the world   H-153a

599

Lancelot and Elaine

    Elaine the fair, Elaine the loveable,
Elaine, the lily maid of Astolat,
High in her chamber up a tower to the east
Guarded the sacred shield of Lancelot;
Which first she placed where morning's earliest ray   5
Might strike it, and awake her with the gleam;
Then fearing rust or soilure fashioned for it
A case of silk, and braided thereupon
All the devices blazoned on the shield
In their own tinct, and added, of her wit,   10
A border fantasy of branch and flower,

Alt. after 2   seeing save
            Far from all human ̷e̷y̷e̷s̷ ̷e̷x̷c̷e̷p̷t̷ her own,   V

3 ...the East   BM-2
3 (C)   59

5 And first She placed it where the rathest beam
            ̷o̷f̷ ̷d̷a̷w̷n̷   V

6 Might strike it when she woke & awake her: then
                            she made   V

7 Then fearing rust or soilure for it made   V

10 .. & added ̷t̷h̷e̷r̷e̷u̷n̷t̷o̷ of her wit,   V

And yellow-throated nestling in the nest.
Nor rested thus content, but day by day,
Leaving her household and good father, climbed
That eastern tower, and entering barred her door,   15
Stript off the case, and read the naked shield,
Now guessed a hidden meaning in his arms,
Now made a pretty history to herself
Of every dint a sword had beaten in it,
And every scratch a lance had made upon it,   20
Conjecturing when and where: this cut is fresh;
That ten years back; this dealt him at Caerlyle;

---

12 And ~~hid in nest with~~ yellow ~~gaping~~ throated
                          nestling
                       ~~fledgling~~ in the nest.   V

13 ...but ~~every~~ day by day   V
13 ...day   BM-2
13 (C)   73

14   & good father
     Leaving ~~her father~~ & her brethren climbd   V
14 ...her brethren &...   Tn-39
14 ...her bretheren and...father climb'd   BM-2
14 ...father climb'd   L-II
14 (C)   73

15 The eastern...   V
15 ...tower and...   BM-2
15 (C)   L-II

16   t   case &   naked
    ~~And~~ strip~~ping~~ off the ~~cover~~, read the shield   V

18 And made...   V

19 of
    ~~And~~ every dint...   V

22   dealt
    ...this ~~given~~ at him at Caerlyle   V
22 ...Caerlyle,   BM-2
22 (C)   L-II

602

LANCELOT AND ELAINE

That at Caerleon; this at Camelot:
And ah God's mercy, what a stroke was there!
And here a thrust that might have killed, but God   25
Broke the strong lance, and rolled his enemy down,
And saved him: so she lived in fantasy.

    How came the lily maid by that good shield
Of Lancelot, she that knew not even his name?
He left it with her, when he rode to tilt   30
For the great diamond in the diamond jousts,

―――――――――
23   at
    This at Caerleon, t̸h̸a̸t̸ a̸t̸ this at Camelot: V
23 ...Caerleon, this at Camelot;   BM-2
23 (C)   L-II
          God's
24 And Ah mercy, what a stroke was there, s̸h̸e̸ t̸h̸o̸u̸g̸h̸t̸/ V
24 .. mercy what...there   BM-2
24 ...mercy what...   L-II
24 (C)   73

Alt. after 24 But
              G̸o̸d̸ bless the goodly shield that warded
                    it   V

25 ...might have r̸e̸a̸c̸h̸d̸ h̸i̸s̸ h̸e̸a̸r̸t̸ kill'd, but G̸o̸d̸   V

26   strong
   G̸o̸d̸ broke the lance...   V

27 A̸n̸d̸ s̸o̸ s̸h̸e̸ w̸o̸r̸e̸ h̸e̸r̸ d̸a̸y̸s̸ i̸n̸ f̸a̸n̸t̸a̸s̸y̸.
   And saved him. So she lived in fantasy   V

28 ...maid o̸f̸ A̸s̸t̸o̸l̸a̸t̸ by that...   V

30   tilt
   ...to j̸o̸u̸s̸t̸   Tn-39
30 ...her when...   BM-2
30 (C)   L-II

31 ...jousts   BM-2
31 (C)   L-II

603

Which Arthur had ordained, and by that name
Had named them, since a diamond was the prize.

    For Arthur, long before they crowned him King,
Roving the trackless realms of Lyonnesse,   35
Had found a glen, gray boulder and black tarn.
A horror lived about the tarn, and clave
Like its own mists to all the mountain side:
For here two brothers, one a king, had met
And fought together; but their names were lost;   40
And each had slain his brother at a blow;

---

32 ...ordain'd and...   BM-2
32 (C)   L-II

34 & 35 (Par.) For Arthur when none knew from whence he
                        came,
   Long ere the people chose him for their king,   Tn-39

34 (Par.) For Arthur when none knew from whence he
                      came,   BM-2
34 (Par.) For Arthur long before they crown'd him
                      king,   69
34 (C)   73

Alt. after 34 Long ere the people chose him for their
                      king,   BM-2
Alt. after 34 (C)   69

Alt before 36 on a dreary glen   V

36 Came suddenly on a black mere & crags.   V

37 There is̸ a horror   V

39 Two kings that were two brothers here had met̸ ̸
                    fought   V

Sketch 40-44
    Without a witness in the dreary pass.
    For each (1 ?) was mad to have his brother's bride
                    brother
    And each had slain his enemy̸ & they lay
    For ages there, till all their bones were bleach'd
    And lichen'd to one colour...   V

And down they fell and made the glen abhorred:
And there they lay till all their bones were bleached,
And lichened into colour with the crags:
And he, that once was king, had on a crown   45
Of diamonds, one in front, and four aside.
And Arthur came, and labouring up the pass,
All in a misty moonshine, unawares
Had trodden that crowned skeleton, and the skull
Brake from the nape, and from the skull the crown   50
Rolled into light, and turning on its rims
Fled like a glittering rivulet to the tarn:

---

40 ...lost.		BM-2
40 (C)		73
41 ...blow,		BM-2
41 (C)		73
45 And one of them had on a diamond crown		V
45	the	
And one of these, ∦ king, had...		Tn-39
45 And one of these, the king, had...		BM-2
45 And he that once was king had...		62
45 (C)		67
47	came	& climbing up the pass
And Arthur as he mounted unawares		V
47 ...came and...pass		BM-2
47 ...pass		F
47 (C)		62
48 Beneath a misty moonshine		V
48 All in		
B̶e̶n̶e̶a̶t̶h̶ a misty...		Tn-39
49 Set foot on that crownd skeleton, & the skull		V
49 ...skeleton and...		BM-2
49 (C)		F
50 ...nape and...		BM-2
50 (C)		F
52 ...rivulet to the meer.		V

And down the shingly scaur he plunged, and caught,
And set it on his head, and in his heart
Heard murmurs, 'Lo, thou likewise shalt be King.'   55

   Thereafter, when a King, he had the gems
Plucked from the crown, and showed them to his
                knights,
Saying, 'These jewels, whereupon I chanced
Divinely, are the kingdom's, not the King's--

---

53 And Arthur follow'd down the scattering (screes ?)   V
Alt. for 53 (canceled)
   And Arthur follow'd down the whispering scree
   And caught it in a bed of fragrant gale   Tn-39

54   in a bed of fragrant gale
  And caught it & a voice within his heart   V
54   head
...his brow & in...   Tn-39

55 Spake saying Lo a sign thou shalt be King.   V
55 ...murmurs 'lo thou...be king.'   BM-2
55 ...murmurs 'lo, thou...be king.'   (, I)   L-II
55 (C)   73

Alt. after 55 And sat it on his head & in his heart
          Heard murmurs Lo a sign thou shalt be
                King.   V

56 Thereafter when he made the Table Round   V
56 (Par.) Thereafter when a king he...   BM-2
56 (Par.) Thereafter, when a king, he... (,, I)   L-II
56 ...a king, he...   F
56 (C)   73

57 ...crown and...knights   BM-2
57 (C)   L-II

58ff   These diamonds came
    By chance divine & are for public use
    Not private. so for every diamond here
    We purpose every year to hold a joust
    For one of these
    So shall we learn our worthiest knight, & grow

For public use: henceforward let there be,   60
Once every year, a joust for one of these:
For so by nine years' proof we needs must learn
Which is our mightiest, and ourselves shall grow
In use of arms and manhood, till we drive
The heathen, who, some say, shall rule the land   65
Hereafter, which God hinder.' Thus he spoke:
And eight years past, eight jousts had been, and still
Had Lancelot won the diamond of the year,
With purpose to present them to the Queen,
When all were won; but meaning all at once   70
To snare her royal fancy with a boon
Worth half her realm, had never spoken word.

58ff, Continued
     In use of arms
     Of manhood, till we break
     The Heathen, tho' some say, that these shall
                      win   V

58 Saying 'these jewels whereupon...   BM-2
58 Saying 'these...   L-II
58 (C)   73

59 Divinely are the kingdom's not the king's -   BM-2
59 ...the king's -   L-II
59 ...the kingdom's not the king's -   F
59 ...the king's -   59
59 (C)   73

63   our
  ...is t̸h̸e̸ mightiest...   Tn-39

65 The Heathen, who...   BM-2
65 (C)   73

67   went   and now
  Eight years h̸a̸d̸ p̸a̸s̸t̸, eight jousts had been, & still
                                      V

69   Bent   all
  W̸i̸t̸h̸ p̸u̸r̸p̸o̸s̸e̸ to present them to the Queen   V

Now for the central diamond and the last
And largest, Arthur, holding then his court
Hard on the river nigh the place which now   75
Is this world's hugest, let proclaim a joust
At Camelot, and when the time drew nigh
Spake (for she had been sick) to Guinevere,
'Are you so sick, my Queen, you cannot move
To these fair jousts?' 'Yea, lord,' she said, 'ye
                              know it.'   80

---

73 (Par.) ~~And/now/the/Arthur/let/proclaim/a/mighty~~
                    ~~jousts~~
    Now For the ~~great~~ central diamond & the last   V

74   largest
    And ~~greatest~~, Arthur...   Tn-39
74 ..., Arthur holding...   BM-2
74 (C)   L-II

75 Hard on
    ~~Upon~~ the river...   Tn-39

76 The king let cry a joust at Camelot,   V
76 And greatest did the king let cry a joust   V
76   hugest
    ...worlds ~~greatest~~, let...   Tn-39

77   near
    At Camelot   & when the days drew ~~nigh~~
    Within to hold it, tenderly the King   V
77 And when the days drew nigh to hold it in   V

78 .. to Guinevere   BM-2
78 (C)   73

79 'Are ye so sick, my Queen, ye cannot move   V
79 'Are ye so...Queen, ye cannot...   Tn-39
79 (Same)   BM-2
79 (C)   F

80 .. said, 'You know it.   V
80 ...said, 'you know...   F
80 (C)   73

'Then will ye miss,' he answered, 'the great deeds
Of Lancelot, and his prowess in the lists,
A sight ye love to look on.' And the Queen
Lifted her eyes, and they dwelt languidly
On Lancelot, where he stood beside the King.   85
He thinking that he read her meaning there,
'Stay with me, I am sick; my love is more
Than many diamonds,' yielded; and a heart
Love-loyal to the least wish of the Queen
(However much he yearned to make complete   90
The tale of diamonds for his destined boon)

---

81 Then will ye miss,' he answer'd, ~~that fair sight~~
     ~~Wh most ye love to look on~~, the great deeds   V
81 ...will you miss   F
81 (C)   <u>69</u>

83 .. sight you love   F
83 (C)   <u>69</u>

84 Lifted her ~~languid~~ eyes & ~~let~~ they dwelt languidly   V

85-6 And Lancelot understood them & replied   V

85 ...the king.   BM-2
85 (C)   59

86 ...read the meaning...   V

88 ....,yielded, and a heart,   BM-2
88 ...yielded, and...   59
88 (C)   73

89 Love loyal...   BM-2
89 (C)   L-II

90   much he yearn'd   make
  [However ~~great his yearning~~ to complete   Tn-39

91   destined
  ...his ~~purposed~~ boon]   Tn-39

Urged him to speak against the truth, and say,
'Sir King, mine ancient wound is hardly whole,
And lets me from the saddle;' and the King
Glanced first at him, then her, and went his way.   95
No sooner gone than suddenly she began:

   'To blame, my lord Sir Lancelot, much to blame!
Why go ye not to these fair jousts? the knights
Are half of them our enemies, and the crowd
Will murmur, "Lo the shameless ones, who take   100
Their pastime now the trustful King is gone!"'

---

92 Moved him to...	V
92 ...the truth and say	BM-2
92 (C)	L-II

94 I may not well be present' & the King	V
94 ...the king	BM-2
94 (C)	59

95   him   her
  ...at ~~her~~, then ~~him~~, & ...   Tn-39

96 No sooner gone than hastily ~~at once~~ she began.	V
96 ...began.	BM-2
96 (C)	73

97 ~~Cut brake the Queen to blame, Sir Lancelot~~
   To blame, Sir Lancelot, you are much to blame ye
                   know   V

97 ...to blame.	BM-2
97 (C)	73

98 ...go you not...jousts: the crowd	V
98 ..go you not	F
98 (C)	<u>69</u>

99 We have enemies enough & all   V

100 ...ones, they take	V
100 ...murmur, lo...	BM-2
100 (C)	73

101 ...trustful king is gone.   BM-2

Then Lancelot vext at having lied in vain:
'Are ye so wise? ye were not once so wise,
My Queen, that summer, when ye loved me first.
Then of the crowd ye took no more account   105
Than of the myriad cricket of the mead,
When its own voice clings to each blade of grass,
And every voice is nothing. As to knights,
Them surely can I silence with all ease.
But now my loyal worship is allowed   110
Of all men: many a bard, without offence,
Has linked our names together in his lay,

---

101 ...trustful king is gone!   F
101 (C)   73

102 (Par.) Then answer'd Lancelot the chief of knights V

103 ...wise   BM-2
103 'Are you so wise? you were...wise   F
103 'Are you so wise? you **were**...   <u>69</u>

104 In that first summer when we loved so well   V
104 ...when you loved...   F
104 (C)   <u>69</u>

105 And of the crowd why take ye more account   V
105 ...crowd you took...   F
105 (C)   <u>69</u>

106 Than of the cricket whining in the field   V

107 When every blade of grass hath its own voice   V

108 And every voice is nothing: & besides   V

Alt. 108 And wh be they that slander you? if knights V

110-111 My worship of the fairest is allow'd
             By all men   V

110   now
        But K̸n̸o̸w̸ my...   Tn-39

112 Has mixt our names together in his chant   V

611

LANCELOT AND ELAINE

Lancelot, the flower of bravery, Guinevere,
The pearl of beauty: and our knights at feast
Have pledged us in this union, while the King   115
Would listen smiling. How then? is there more?
Has Arthur spoken aught? or would yourself,
Now weary of my service and devoir,
Henceforth be truer to your faultless lord?'

   She broke into a little scornful laugh: 120
'Arthur, my lord, Arthur, the faultless King,
That passionate perfection, my good lord--
But who can gaze upon the Sun in heaven?

---

113 ...the flower of knighthood, Guinevere   V

114 The pearl of Queens & oft, the knights at feast   V

115 ...us in this fashion when the king   V
115 ...the king   BM-2
115 (C)   73

116 Has smiled to hear them...   V

117 Hath the King spoken aught? a̶n̶d̶ wd yourself   V

118 Now wearied of...   V
118 ...devoir   BM-2
118 (C)   L-II

119 B̶e̶ henceforth be loyal to the faultless king   V
119   truer
    ...be c̶l̶o̶s̶e̶r̶ to...   Tn-39

120   scornful
    (Par.) She brake into a little p̶a̶s̶s̶i̶o̶n̶a̶t̶e̶ laugh.
                                                        Tn-39
120 ...laugh.   BM-2
120 (C)   73

121 ...faultless king,   BM-2
121 (C)   59

122 That passionless perfection...   V

123 ...can look upon...   V

612

He never spake word of reproach to me,
He never had a glimpse of mine untruth,   125
He cares not for me: only here today
There gleamed a vague suspicion in his eyes:
Some meddling rogue has tampered with him--else
Rapt in this fancy of his Table Round,
And swearing men to vows impossible,   130
To make them like himself: but, friend, to me
He is all fault who hath no fault at all:
For who loves me must have a touch of earth;
The low sun makes the colour: I am yours,
Not Arthur's, as ye know, save by the bond.   135
And therefore hear my words: go to the jousts:
The tiny-trumpeting gnat can break our dream

Alt. after 123 ~~He hath all faults who hath no fault~~
                              ~~at all.~~   V

125   glimpse
...had a ~~dream~~ of mine...   V

128   s
Some meddling rogue ha~~th put it in his head~~
                    tampered...   V

130 And swearing men to vows impossible ~~rapt in an~~
                    ~~idle dream~~   V

131   wd
To make...   V

133   For
~~But~~ who...   V

135 Not Arthur's, as ~~methinks~~, ~~full well~~ ye know...   V
135 ...as you know...   F
135 (C)   69

137   tiny
The little ~~nightly~~ trumpeting of the gnat can break
                    (blot) dreams   V

137 .   can
...gnat ~~may~~ break...   V

613

When sweetest; and the vermin voices here
May buzz so loud--we scorn them, but they sting.'

　　　Then answered Lancelot, the chief of knights:　　140
'And with what face, after my pretext made,
Shall I appear, O Queen, at Camelot, I
Before a King who honours his own word,
As if it were his God's?'

　　　　　　　'Yea,' said the Queen,
'A moral child without the craft to rule,　　　　　145
Else had he not lost me: but listen to me,
If I must find you wit: we hear it said
That men go down before your spear at a touch,

---

138 When sweetest
　　　Our (vows ?)　Can vex us, &...　　　　　　　　V

139　　　　　　　so loud -
　　　May w̶a̶k̶e̶ & buzz, we scorn...　　　　　　　　V

140 ...knights.　　　　　　　　　　　　　　　　　BM-2
140 (C)　　　　　　　　　　　　　　　　　　　　73

Sketch 141 ff　　　after my pretext made
　　　And with what face, O noble Queen, shall I
　　　Show myself at this joust　　can I appear
　　　Of that old mind appear
　　　Better I (2 ?), my Queen, before a king
　　　Who worships his own word, as it were God's.
　　　Tilting at Camelot　　　　　　　　　　　　V

143 ...who worships his...　　　　　　　　　　　V
143 ...a king who...　　　　　　　　　　　　　　BM-2
143 (C)　　　　　　　　　　　　　　　　　　　　73

146 He had not lost me else.　but hear me friend　V

147 ...wit.　I hear...　　　　　　　　　　　　　V

148 ...your lance at a touch　　　　　　　　　　V
148 ...a touch　　　　　　　　　　　　　　　　BM-2
148 (C)　　　　　　　　　　　　　　　　　　　73

But knowing you are Lancelot; your great name,
This conquers: hide it therefore; go unknown: 150
Win! by this kiss you will: and our true King
Will then allow your pretext, O my knight,
As all for glory; for to speak him true,
Ye know right well, how meek soe'er he seem,
No keener hunter after glory breathes.   155
He loves it in his knights more than himself:
They prove to him his work: win and return.'

    Then got Sir Lancelot suddenly to horse,
Wroth at himself. Not willing to be known,
He left the barren-beaten thoroughfare,   160

---

149 ...name   BM-2
149 (C)   L-II

150 Conquers: but hide it go unknown, & win   V
150   &   therefore
    Conquers: b̸u̸t̸ hide it, go unknown; ̸& ̸w̸i̸n̸   Tn-39
150 Conquers: and hide it, therefore go unknown;   BM-2
150 (C)   L-II

151 So by this kiss, you will & our true king   V
151 Win -
    A̸s̸ by...   Tn-39
151 Win - by this kiss you will; and our true king   BM-2
151 ...true king   F
151 (C)   73

152 ...knight   BM-2
152 ...knight,   ,/ (I)   L-II
152 (C)   F

154 You know...   F
154 (C)   69

155 He honours manhood as one with truth   V
155 No ̸k̸̸e̸̸e̸̸e̸̸r̸ keener hunter...   V

159 ...himself: not...   BM-2
159 (C)   73

Chose the green path that showed the rarer foot,
And there among the solitary downs,
Full often lost in fancy, lost his way;
Till as he traced a faintly-shadowed track,
That all in loops and links among the dales   165
Ran to the Castle of Astolat, he saw
Fired from the west, far on a hill, the towers.
Thither he made, and blew the gateway horn.
Then came an old, dumb, myriad-wrinkled man,
Who let him into lodging and disarmed.   170
And Lancelot marvelled at the wordless man;
And issuing found the Lord of Astolat
With two strong sons, Sir Torre and Sir Lavaine,

---

161 ...foot	BM-2
161 (C)	F
163 ...way,	BM-2
163 (C)	F
164 Then while he...	V
168　　　　winding	
...made, & b̸l̸o̸w̸i̸n̸g̸ the great horn	V
168 Thither he rode & wound the horn.　There came	V
168 ...made & wound the gateway...	Tn-39
168 ...made and wound the...	BM-2
168 (C)	73
169 A dumb old deaf & myriadwrinkled man	V
169 ...came a deaf, dumb...	Tn-39
169 Then came a deaf, dumb myriad-wrinkled...	BM-2
169 (C)	F
170 Enter'd, & went to lodging, & disarm'd.	V
170 Who led him...	V
171 ...man.	BM-2
171 .. man:	F
171 (C)	59
172 Thence issuing...	V
172 And	
T̸h̸e̸n̸c̸e̸ issuing...	Tn-39

Moving to meet him in the castle court;   175
And close behind them stept the lily maid
Elaine, his daughter: mother of the house
There was not: some light jest among them rose
With laughter dying down as the great knight
Approached them: then the Lord of Astolat:
'Whence comest thou, my guest, and by what name   180
Livest between the lips? for by thy state
And presence I might guess thee chief of those,
After the King, who eat in Arthur's halls.
Him have I seen: the rest, his Table Round,
Known as they are, to me they are unknown.'   185

     Then answered Lancelot, the chief of knights:
'Known am I, and of Arthur's hall, and known,
What I by mere mischance have brought, my shield.
But since I go to joust as one unknown
At Camelot for the diamond, ask me not,   190
Hereafter ye shall know me--and the shield--
I pray you lend me one, if such you have,
Blank, or at least with some device not mine.'

---

174 ...court: BM-2
174 (C)   59

177-179 There was not: then the Lord of Astolat.   V

179 Approach'd t̶h̶e̶m̶
      b̶l̶e̶w̶ n̶e̶a̶r̶ t̶h̶e̶m̶ then...   Tn-39
179 ...Astolat.   BM-2
179 (C)   73

183 ...the king, who...   BM-2
183 (C)   73

186 ...knights.   BM-2
186 ...knights   70
186 (C)   73

191 Hereafter you shall...   F
191 (C)   73

192 ...such ye have,   Tn-39
192 ...such ye have,   BM-2
192 (C)   F

Then said the Lord of Astolat, 'Here is Torre's:
Hurt in his first tilt was my son, Sir Torre.   195
And so, God wot, his shield is blank enough.
His ye can have.' Then added plain Sir Torre,
'Yea, since I cannot use it, ye may have it.'
Here laughed the father saying, 'Fie, Sir Churl,
Is that an answer for a noble knight?   200
Allow him! but Lavaine, my younger here,
He is so full of lustihood, he will ride,
Joust for it, and win, and bring it in an hour,
And set it in this damsel's golden hair,
To make her thrice as wilful as before.'   205

---

194 ...Astolat' Here...	BM-2
194 (C)	59
197 ...Torre	BM-2
197 His you can..Torre	F
197 His you can...	59
197 (C)	69
198 'Yea since...	BM-2
198 'Yea since..it, you may...	F
198 'Yea since...	69
198 (C)	73
199 Here T̶h̶e̶n̶ laugh'd...	Tn-39
199 ...saying 'Fie, ...	BM-2
199 (C)	73
201 ...him: but...	BM-2
201 (C)	73
202 ...ride	BM-2
202 (C)	67

203 ...it and win and...hour   BM-2
203 ...it, and win, and...hour   (,, I)   L-II
203 ...hour   F
203 (C)   73

204   hair,
    ...golden g̶o̶l̶d̶s̶   Tn-39

618

'Nay, father, nay good father, shame me not
Before this noble knight,' said young Lavaine,
'For nothing. Surely I but played on Torre:
He seemed so sullen, vext he could not go:
A jest, no more! for, knight, the maiden dreamt   210
That some one put this diamond in her hand,
And that it was too slippery to be held,
And slipt and fell into some pool or stream,
The castle-well, belike; and then I said
That _if_ I went and _if_ I fought and won it   215
(But all was jest and joke among ourselves)
Then must she keep it safelier. All was jest.
But, father, give me leave, an if he will,
To ride to Camelot with this noble knight:
Win shall I not, but do my best to win: 220

---

207 ...knight' said young Lavaine   BM-2
207 (C)   73

210   the
   ...knight, ~~this~~ maiden...   Tn-39
210 ...more: for, ...   BM-2
210 (C)   73

213 And ~~that~~ slipt...   Tn-39

216   jest   joke
   ...was ~~jape~~ & ~~jest~~ among...   Tn-39

217   safer
   Then she must keep it ~~better~~. All... Tn-39
217 ...it safer. All...   BM-2
217   lier
   ...it saf~~er~~. All...   L-II
217 (C)   F

218 But father give...   BM-2
218 (C)   73

220 Win shall I   but
   ~~And they~~ not, win, ~~yet~~ do...   Tn-39
220 ...to win,   BM-2
220 (C)   L-II

LANCELOT AND ELAINE

Young as I am, yet would I do my best.'

　　'So ye will grace me,' answer$_e$d Lancelot,
Smiling a moment,'with your fellowship
O'er these waste downs whereon I lost myself,
Then were I glad of you as guide and friend:　　　　225
And you shall win this diamond,--as I hear
It is a fair large diamond,--if ye may,
And yield it to this maiden, if ye will.'
'A fair large diamond,' added plain Sir Torre,

---

221 ...am, I̷ yet...　　　　　　　　　　　　　　　　Tn-39

222 (Par.) So you will...　　　　　　　　　　　　　Tn-39
222 (Par.) 'So you will grace me' answer'd Lancelot BM-2
222 (Par.) 'So you will..　　　　　　　　　　　　　59
222 (C)　　　　　　　　　　　　　　　　　　　　　69

223　　　　　　moment
　　Smiling a l̷i̷t̷t̷l̷e̷ with your g̷o̷o̷d̷ fellowship　　Tn-39
223 ...moment' with...　　　　　　　　　　　　　　BM-2
223 (C)　　　　　　　　　　　　　　　　　　　　　59

224　　　　　　waste
　　...these w̷i̷l̷d̷ downs...　　　　　　　　　　　　Tn-39

225 ...friend;　　　　　　　　　　　　　　　　　BM-2
225 (C)　　　　　　　　　　　　　　　　　　　　73

226 And ye shall...　　　　　　　　　　　　　　　Tn-39
226 And ye shall...diamond - as...　　　　　　　　BM-2
226 ...diamond - as...　　　　　　　　　　　　　　F
226 (C)　　　　　　　　　　　　　　　　　　　　84

227 ...if you may,　　　　　　　　　　　　　　　F
227 (C)　　　　　　　　　　　　　　　　　　　　69

228 ...if you will.'　　　　　　　　　　　　　　　F
228 (C)　　　　　　　　　　　　　　　　　　　　69

229　　　　　　answerd
　　...diamond' added plain...　　　　　　　　　　Tn-39
229 ...diamond' added...Torre　　　　　　　　　　BM-2

'Such be for queens, and not for simple maids.'   230
Then she, who held her eyes upon the ground,
Elaine, and heard her name so tost about,
Flushed slightly at the slight disparagement
Before the stranger knight, who, looking at her,
Full courtly, yet not falsely, thus returned: 235
'If what is fair be but for what is fair,
And only queens are to be counted so,
Rash were my judgment then, who deem this maid
Might wear as fair a jewel as is on earth,
Not violating the bond of like to like.'   240

   He spoke and ceased: the lily maid Elaine,
Won by the mellow voice before she looked,
Lifted her eyes, and read his lineaments.
The great and guilty love he bare the Queen,
In battle with the love he bare his lord,   245
Had marred his face, and marked it ere his time.
Another sinning on such heights with one,

---

229 (C)   59

230 ...for Queens and...   BM-2
230 (C)   73

235 ...return'd.   BM-2
235 (C)   73

237 ...only Queens are...   BM-2
237 (C)   73

238   were   then
     Rash m̸ṵ̸s̸t̸ my judgment s̸e̸e̸m̸, who...   Tn-39

241 ...Elaine   BM-2
241 (C)   L-II

246 ...face and...   BM-2
246 (C)   L-II

247 Another sinning in so high a place   V
247 (Same)   BM-2
247 (C)   F

LANCELOT AND ELAINE

The flower of all the west and all the world,
Had been the sleeker for it: but in him
His mood was often like a fiend, and rose   250
And drove him into wastes and solitudes
For agony, who was yet a living soul.
Marred as he was, he seemed the goodliest man
That ever among ladies ate in hall,
And noblest, when she lifted up her eyes.   255
However marred, of more than twice her years,
Seamed with an ancient swordcut on the cheek,
And bruised and bronzed, she lifted up her eyes
And loved him, with that love which was her doom.

Then the great knight, the darling of the court,   260
Loved of the loveliest, into that rude hall
Stept with all grace,and not with half disdain

---

248 With one esteem'd the blossom of her age	BM-2
248 ...the West and...	F
248 (C)	59
250 ...fiend and...	BM-2
250 (C)	L-II
251 And drove into...	V
253 ...was he...man,	BM-2
253 ...man,	L-II
253 (C)	73
254 ...in Hall,	BM-2
254 (C)	73
256 ~~almost thrice~~	
...of more than twice...	Tn-39
258 And bronzed and bruised, she...	Tn-39
258 And bronzed and bruised,...	BM-2
258 i	I MS
And bru s̸ed and bronzed...	L-II

Hid under grace, as in a smaller time,
But kindly man moving among his kind:
Whom they with meats and vintage of their best   265
And talk and minstrel melody entertained.
And much they asked of court and Table Round,
And ever well and readily answered he:
But Lancelot, when they glanced at Guinevere,
Suddenly speaking of the wordless man,   270
Heard from the Baron that, ten years before,
The heathen caught and reft him of his tongue.

---

258 (C)		F
259 ...him with...		BM-2
259 (C)		L-II
263 ...grace as...		BM-2
263 (C)		L-II
267 ...Round		BM-2
267 (C)		L-II
268 ...he;		BM-2
268 (C)		L-II
269-270 And Lancelot touching on the wordless man		V
269 ...Lancelot when...Guinevere		BM-2
269 (C)		L-II
270 ...man		BM-2
270 (C)		L-II
271 to Learnt that the heathen in a sudden raid		
272 Ten years before had reft him of his tongue		V
271 Learnt from...		Tn-39
271 Learnt from the Baron that...before		BM-2
271 (C)		L-II

'He learnt and warned me of their fierce design
Against my house, and him they caught and maimed;
But I, my sons, and little daughter fled   275
From bonds or death, and dwelt among the woods
By the great river in a boatman's hut.
Dull days were those, till our good Arthur broke
The Pagan yet once more on Badon hill.'

---

273 ff Because he warn'd us of them & we fled
        Else had been slain & hid us in the woods
        And dwelt beside the river. weary days
             by the great river   V

273 ff he being subtle in his master's house
        For that he gave his lord of Astolat
        Forwarning of the raid premeditated
        Against the castle & him they caught & maim'd
        But we, ~~that else had suffered death or bonds~~
        My sons, & little daughter, ~~else~~ fled   V

273 He learnt &   their fierce design
     ~~Because he~~ warn'd me of ~~a raid of theirs~~   Tn-39
273 He...   BM-2
273 (C)   L-II

274   house &
     ...my ~~castle~~ him...   Tn-39
274 ...house and...   BM-2
274 (C)   F

275 But I my sons and...   BM-2
275 (C)   73

276 From death or bonds, & dwelt among the woods   V
276 ...death and   BM-2
276 (C)   L-II

278 [So spake the Baron] till King Arthur broke   V

279 The heathen, once for all on Badon hill.   V
279 Till Arthur broke them at Mt. Badon-Ken   V

624

LANCELOT AND ELAINE

'O there, great lord, doubtless,' Lavaine said,
          rapt   280
By all the sweet and sudden passion of youth
Toward greatness in its elder, 'you have fought.
O tell us--for we live apart--you know
Of Arthur's glorious wars.' And Lancelot spoke
And answered him at full, as having been   285
With Arthur in the fight which all day long
Rang by the white mouth of the violent Glem;

---

280 'And doubtless O fair lord' began Lavaine   V
280   'O there   Lord, doubtless   said,
    (Par.) W̸h̸e̸r̸e̸, Ø great K̸n̸i̸g̸h̸t̸ s̸a̸i̸d̸ Lavain, s̸a̸t̸i̸n̸g̸/
               rapt
               a̸t̸ h̸i̸m̸   Tn-39
280 ...great Lord, doubtless...   BM-2
280 (C)   73

281 siezed   swift
    Rapt by rash-adoring passion of youth   V
281   By   the sweet & sudden
    A̸n̸d̸ r̸a̸p̸t̸ b̸y̸ all l̸o̸y̸a̸l̸ passion of youth   Tn-39

282 For greatness in the elder 'ye were there   V
282 ...elder 'ye have....   Tn-39
282 ...elder 'ye have...   BM-2
282 ...elder 'you...   F
282 (C)   59

283 ...us; for...   BM-2
283 ...us; for...apart, you...   F
283 (C)   67

284 ...wars: and...   BM-2
284 (C)   L-II

285   him
    ...answer'd t̸h̸e̸m̸ at...   Tn-39

287 ...Glem,   BM-2
287 (C)   F

And in the four loud battles by the shore
Of Duglas; that on Bassa; then the war
That thundered in and out the gloomy skirts   290
Of Celidon the forest; and again
By castle Gurnion, where the glorious King
Had on his cuirass worn our Lady's Head,
Carved of one emerald centered in a sun
Of silver rays, that lightened as he breathed;   295
And at Caerleon had he helped his lord,

288-289 And in the four wild battles on Duglass,
        And that by Bassas, & the furious war   Tn-39

288 And in the four wild battles on Duglass,   BM-2
288   ments by the shore   I MS
    ...four wild battles ~~on Duglass~~,   L-II
288 ...four wild battles...   F
288 (C)   73

289 And that by Bassas, and the furious war   BM-2
289 Of Duglas, that on Bassa, then the war   I MS
    ~~And that by Bassas, and the furious war~~   L-II
289 (C)   F

291 Of Cehoron the...   BM-2
291 (C)   L-II

292 Before the castle Gurnion where the king   Tn-39
292 Before the castle Gurnion where the king   BM-2
292   glorious   I MS
    ...Gurnion where the ~~glorious~~ king   L-II
292 ...Gurnion where the glorious king   F
292 ...Gurnion where...   59
292 (C)   73

293 ...Head   BM-2
293 (C)   L-II

294 ...emerald, center'd   F
294 (C)   73

When the strong neighings of the wild white Horse
Set every gilded parapet shuddering;
And up in Agned-Cathregonion too,
And down the waste sand-shores of Trath Treroit,   300
Where many a heathen fell; 'and on the mount
Of Badon I myself beheld the King
Charge at the head of all his Table Round,
And all his legions crying Christ and him,
And break them; and I saw him, after, stand   305
High on a heap of slain, from spur to plume
Red as the rising sun with heathen blood,

295	...rays that...	BM-2
295	(C)	L-II

299	up in Agned-Cathregonion too,	
	And ~~by the woody slopes of Cat Bregoin/~~	Tn-39
299	...Agned Cathregonion...	BM-2
299	(C)	73

301	& on the hill	V
301	...on the ~~hill~~ mount	Tn-39
301	...fell; and...	BM-2
301	(C)	F

302	...the king	BM-2
302	(C)	59

305	(2 ?)	
	He broke them & I saw him, after, ~~fight~~ stand	V
305	...them and...	BM-2
305	(C)	L-II

308	...he cried with a great voice	V
308	...me, he cried with a great voice	Tn-39
308	...he cried with a great voice	BM-2
308	And seeing me, he cried with a great voice	
	(I MS)	L-II
308	...cried	F
308	(C)	73

And seeing me, with a great voice he cried,
"They are broken, they are broken!" for the King,
However mild he seems at home, nor cares   310
For triumph in our mimic wars, the jousts--
For if his own knight cast him down, he laughs
Saying, his knights are better men than he--
Yet in this heathen war the fire of God
Fills him: I never saw his like: there lives   315
No greater leader.'

            While he uttered this,
Low to her own heart said the lily maid,
'Save your great self, fair lord;' and when he fell
From talk of war to traits of pleasantry--
Being mirthful he, but in a stately kind--   320
She still took note that when the living smile
Died from his lips, across him came a cloud
Of melancholy severe, from which again,
Whenever in her hovering to and fro

---

309 'They are broken, they are broken' for the king,

                                    BM-2

309 .. are broken" for...   59
309 (C)   73

310 However meek he seem...   V

313 And says his knights...   V

315   his
     ...saw t̶h̶e̶ like   V

316 .. leader'   BM-2
316 (C)   L-II

317 ...maid   BM-2
317 (C)   73

318 ...lord' and...   BM-2
318 (C)   L-II

320 Mirthful he was but stately in his mirth   V
320 ...he but...   BM-2
320 (C)   73

628

The lily maid had striven to make him cheer,   325
There brake a sudden-beaming tenderness
Of manners and of nature: and she thought
That all was nature, all, perchance, for her.
And all night long his face before her lived,
As when a painter, poring on a face,   330
Divinely through all hindrance finds the man
Behind it, and so paints him that his face,
The shape and colour of a mind and life,
Lives for his children, ever at its best
And fullest; so the face before her lived,   335
Dark-splendid, speaking in the silence, full
Of noble things, and held her from her sleep.
Till rathe she rose, half-cheated in the thought
She needs must bid farewell to sweet Lavaine.
First as in fear, step after step, she stole   340
Down the long tower-stairs, hesitating:

Alt. after 320 Not double-sided in a decent phrase
               Nor dipping into mud for graceless
                               tales   V

321   oft
     But s̸t̸i̸l̸l̸ she mark'd, that...   V

328 ...perchance, f̸o̸r̸ h̸e̸r̸   V

Alt. after 328 She cd not tell - it might be all for
                               her.   V

330 a limner poring on a face   V
330 ...painter poring...face   BM-2
330 (C)   L-II

332 B̸e̸h̸i̸n̸d̸ it & so paints   V

333 ...colour of his mind...   V

338 halfcheated in the thought   V

339 That she must bid farewell to sweet Lavaine   V

341 ...tower-stairs; hesitating: BM-2
341 (C)   L-II

Anon, she heard Sir Lancelot cry in the court,
'This shield, my friend, where is it?' and Lavaine
Past inward, as she came from out the tower.
There to his proud horse Lancelot turned, and
                    smoothed   345
The glossy shoulder, humming to himself.
Half-envious of the flattering hand, she drew
Nearer and stood. He looked, and more amazed
Than if seven men had set upon him, saw
The maiden standing in the dewy light.   350
He had not dreamed she was so beautiful.
Then came on him a sort of sacred fear,
For silent, though he greeted her, she stood
Rapt on his face as if it were a God's.
Suddenly flashed on her a wild desire,   355

---

342 ...court	BM-2
342 (C)	L-II
343 Where is this shield my friend	V
344 ...inward as...	BM-2
344 (C)	L-II
345 There by the proud horse Lancelot stood & smoothed	V
348 ...stood: he turn'd & ...	V
348 ...look'd and...	BM-2
348 (C)	L-II
349 Than if three men had set on him beheld	V
352 Then stole on him a sort of sacred fear	V
353 For silent after greeting given she stood	V
Alt. before 355 Him when she saw, so busied with his horse	V
355 There suddenly woke in her a wild desire	V
356 ...her token at...	V

That he should wear her favour at the tilt.
She braved a riotous heart in asking for it.
'Fair lord, whose name I know not--noble it is,
I well believe, the noblest--will you wear
My favour at this tourney?' 'Nay,' said he,   360
'Fair lady, since I never yet have worn
Favour of any lady in the lists.
Such is my wont, as those, who know me, know.'
'Yea, so,' she answered; 'then in wearing mine
Needs must be lesser likelihood, noble lord,   365
That those who know should know you.' And he turned
Her counsel up and down within his mind,
And found it true, and answered, 'True, my child.

Alt. before 358 T̸h̸e̸n̸ s̸a̸i̸d̸ t̸h̸e̸ l̸i̸l̸y̸ m̸a̸i̸d̸ t̸o̸ L̸a̸n̸c̸e̸l̸o̸t̸   V

358-359   (1 ?) name
        Fair (Lord?) S̸i̸r̸ K̸n̸i̸g̸h̸t̸ w̸h̸o̸m̸ y̸e̸t̸ I know not,
                                  will ye wear   V

359 ...will ye wear   Tn-39
359 ...will ye wear   BM-2
359 (C)   F

361   lady
     Fair d̸a̸m̸s̸e̸l̸...   V

363 Such is my wont as they that know me know!
     I̸t̸ h̸a̸t̸h̸ n̸o̸t̸ b̸e̸e̸n̸ m̸y̸ w̸o̸n̸t̸.   V

365 Ø̸ n̸o̸b̸l̸e̸ K̸n̸i̸g̸h̸t̸ -
            Needs must there be
     If (1 ?) t̸h̸e̸r̸e̸ w̸i̸l̸l̸ b̸e̸ a̸l̸l̸ t̸h̸e̸ lesser liklihood   V

366   those who
     Then m̸e̸n̸ s̸h̸o̸u̸l̸d̸ know you. (T̸r̸u̸e̸ ?) said he   V

367 ...mind   BM-2
367 (C)   L-II

368 ...answer'd 'true, my...   BM-2
368 ..., 'true,...   59
368 (C)   73

Well, I will wear it: fetch it out to me:
What is it?' and she told him 'A red sleeve   370
Broidered with pearls,' and brought it: then he bound
Her token on his helmet, with a smile
Saying, 'I never yet have done so much
For any maiden living,' and the blood
Sprang to her face and filled her with delight;   375
But left her all the paler, when Lavaine

---

369 Will
    A̶n̶d̶ I wear it. (fetch ?) m̶e̶ l̶o̶o̶k̶ u̶p̶o̶n̶ it better
                to me.   V

370 What is it. And she answer'd 'a red sleeve   V
370 ...it? and...him 'a red...   BM-2
370 ...him 'a red...   F
370 (C)   73

371 ...it & he wound   V
371 ...he wound   Tn-39
371 ...pearls' and...he wound   BM-2
371 ...pearls' and...   L-II
371 (C)   59

372   with a smile
    Her token round his helmet s̶h̶e̶ (l ?) s̶a̶y̶i̶n̶g̶ t̶o̶ h̶e̶r̶ V
372 ...token round his...   Tn-39
372 Her token round his helmet with...   BM-2
372 (C)   L-II

373 N̶e̶v̶e̶r̶ Saying I...   V
373 Saying 'I...   BM-2
373 (C)   59

374 For any damsel living & her blood   V
374 ...living' and...   BM-2
374 (C)   59

375 ...delight,   BM-2
375 (C)   L-II

376-377 Then came Lavaine bearing the shield of Torre V

Returning brought the yet-unblazoned shield,
His brother's; which he gave to Lancelot,
Who parted with his own to fair Elaine:
'Do me this grace, my child, to have my shield   380
In keeping till I come.' 'A grace to me,'
She answered, 'twice   today. I am your squire!'
Whereat Lavaine said, laughing, 'Lily maid,
For fear our people call you lily maid
In earnest, let me bring your colour back;   385
Once, twice, and thrice: now get you hence to bed:'

---

378 His brother wh...   V
378   which
    ...brother's; t̸h̸i̸s̸ he...   Tn-39

379 ...Elaine   BM-2
379 ...Elaine;   L-II
379 (C)   73

380   - fair child
    ...grace to b̸e̸a̸r̸ have...   V

381   a grace, to me
    ...come, Yea, lord she said -   V
381 ...me'   BM-2
381 (C)   59

382 Ä̸ g̸r̸a̸c̸e̸ t̸o̸ m̸e̸   Said fair Elaine - if I may be (1 ?)
    You leave me happy in so great a charge   V
382 ...answer'd 'twice...your Squire.'   BM-2
382 ...your Squire.'   59
382 (C)   73

383 At which Lavaine...   Tn-39
383 At which Lavaine said laughing 'lily maid,   BM-2
383 ...said laughing 'lily maid,   L-II
383 (C)   59

385 ...back,   BM-2
385 (C)   L-II

386   hence
    ...you b̸a̸c̸k̸ to...   Tn-39

So kissed her, and Sir Lancelot his own hand,
And thus they moved away: she stayed a minute,
Then made a sudden step to the gate, and there--
Her bright hair blown about the serious face   390
Yet rosy-kindled with her brother's kiss--
Paused by the gateway, standing near the shield
In silence, while she watched their arms far-off
Sparkle, until they dipt below the downs.
Then to her tower she climbed, and took the shield, 395
There kept it, and so lived in fantasy.

     Meanwhile the new companions past away
Far o'er the long backs of the bushless downs,
To where Sir Lancelot knew there lived a knight
Not far from Camelot, now for forty years   400
A hermit, who had prayed, laboured and prayed,

---

387 Then young Lavaine kiss'd her, & Lancelot waved   V

388 His hand in passing, & she made three steps   V
388   us
    And th̷e̷n̷ they...   Tn-39
388 And then they...   BM-2
388 (C)   L-II

389 Behind them to the gate & long remained   V

392 There in the gateway standing by the shield   V
392 ...standing by the shield   Tn-39
392 Paused in the gateway, standing by the shield   BM-2
392 (C)   73

393 And watch'd them growing less & saw their arms   V

395   she climb'd
    (Par.) Then ¢l̷i̷m̷b̷'d̷ she to her tower & took...
                                                         Tn-39
395 (Par.) Then...shield,   BM-2
395 ...shield   62
395 (C)   84

397   past
    ...companions p̷a̷s̷t̷ away   Tn-39

634

And ever labouring had scooped himself
In the white rock a chapel and a hall
On massive columns, like a shorecliff cave,
And cells and chambers: all were fair and dry;   405
The green light from the meadows underneath
Struck up and lived along the milky roofs;
And in the meadows tremulous aspen-trees
And poplars made a noise of falling showers.
And thither wending there that night they bode.   410

But when the next day broke from underground,
And shot red fire and shadows through the cave,
They rose, heard mass, broke fast, and rode away: •
Then Lancelot saying, 'Hear, but hold my name
Hidden, you ride with Lancelot of the Lake,'   415
Abashed Lavaine, whose instant reverence,
Dearer to true young hearts than their own praise,

401 ...pray'd		BM-2
401 (C)		73
405 ...dry.		BM-2
405 (C)		L-II
407 ...roofs,		BM-2
407 (C)		L-II
408 And all about it tremulous...		Tn-39
408 And all about it tremulous aspen trees		BM-2
408 (C)		L-II
410 moving		
...thither ~~making~~ there...		Tn-39
410 ...thither moving there...		BM-2
410 (C)		L-II
414 And Lancelot...		Tn-39
414 And Lancelot...saying 'hear,...		BM-2
414 ...saying 'hear,...		F
414 (C)		73
415 ...the lake,'		BM-2
415 (C)		59

But left him leave to stammer, 'Is it indeed?'
And after muttering 'The great Lancelot,'
At last he got his breath and answered, 'One,   420
One have I seen--that other, our liege lord,
The dread Pendragon, Britain's King of kings,
Of whom the people talk mysteriously,
He will be there--then were I stricken blind
That minute, I might say that I had seen.'   425

So spake Lavaine, and when they reached the lists
By Camelot in the meadow, let his eyes
Run through the peopled gallery which half round
Lay like a rainbow fallen upon the grass,
Until they found the clear-faced King, who sat   430
Robed in red samite, easily to be known,
Since to his crown the golden dragon clung,
And down his robe the dragon writhed in gold,
And from the carven-work behind him crept

---

418 ...stammer 'is...   BM-2
418 ...stammer, 'is...   59
418 (C)   73

419 And, after, muttering 'the great Lancelot'   BM-2
419 And/ after/ muttering 'the great Lancelot' (I)   L-II
419 ...muttering 'the great Lancelot'   F
419 (C)   73

420 ...answer'd 'One   BM-2
420 ...answer'd 'One,   L-II
420 (C)   73

422 ...Britain's king of...   BM-2
422 (C)   73

429   mead
    ...upon the g̸r̸a̸s̸s̸   Tn-39
429 ...fall'n upon the mead   BM-2
429 (C)   L-II

430 ...clear-faced king, who...   BM-2
430 (C)   59

439 ...themselves   BM-2
439 (C)   L-II

636

Two dragons gilded, sloping down to make   435
Arms for his chair, while all the rest of them
Through knots and loops and folds innumerable
Fled ever through the woodwork, till they found
The new design wherein they lost themselves,
Yet with all ease, so tender was the work: 440
And, in the costly canopy o'er him set,
Blazed the last diamond of the nameless king.

   Then Lancelot answered young Lavaine and said,
'Me you call great: mine is the firmer seat,
The truer lance: but there is many a youth   445
Now crescent, who will come to all I am
And overcome it; and in me there dwells
No greatness, save it be some far-off touch
Of greatness to know well I am not great:
There is the man.' And Lavaine gaped upon him   450
As on a thing miraculous, and anon

---

441 And in...set   BM-2
441 (C)   L-II

443 (No par. indent.)   BM-2
443 (C)   73

Draft 444 ff
    Why do you call me great? there bides in me
    No greatness, save it be a far-off touch
    Of greatness, that I know I am not great.
    Mine as the K̸i̸n̸g̸ o̸f̸ thro' all our Table Round
    For Mine a̸s̸ the firmer seat, the truer lance
    In all our idle jousts & tournaments
    Mere luck & practice
    But (l ?) great I am as far from t̸h̸a̸t̸ great, my
                         child,
    As our lord king is from all littleness
    Of n̸a̸t̸u̸r̸e̸.   V

444 'Me ye call..   Tn-39
444 'Me ye call...   BM-2
444 (C)   F

449 ...great;   BM-2
449 (C)   L-II

637

The trumpets blew; and then did either side,
They that assailed, and they that held the lists,
Set lance in rest, strike spur, suddenly move,
Meet in the midst, and there so furiously   455
Shock, that a man far-off might well perceive,
If any man that day were left afield,
The hard earth shake, and a low thunder of arms.
And Lancelot bode a little, till he saw
Which were the weaker; then he hurled into it   460
Against the stronger: little need to speak
Of Lancelot in his glory! King, duke, earl,
Count, baron--whom he smote, he overthrew.

    But in the field were Lancelot's kith and kin,
Ranged with the Table Round that held the lists,   465
Strong men, and wrathful that a stranger knight
Should do and almost overdo the deeds
Of Lancelot; and one said to the other, 'Lo!

---

458 ...shake and...	BM-2
458 (C)	F
462 ...Glory: King...	BM-2
462 (C)	73
464 (No par. indent.)	BM-2
464 (C)	L-II
468 ...other 'Lo!	BM-2
468 (C)	73
469 ...alone,	BM-2
469 (C)	73
470 ...man -	BM-2
470 (C)	73
471 ...Lancelot!' 'When...	BM-2
471 (C)	73
474 ...siezed on them,	Tn-39
474 ...siezed on them,	BM-2
474 (C)	73

What is he? I do not mean the force alone--
The grace and versatility of the man!   470
Is it not Lancelot?' 'When has Lancelot worn
Favour of any lady in the lists?
Not such his wont, as we, that know him, know.'
'How then? who then?' a fury seized them all,
A fiery family passion for the name   475
Of Lancelot, and a glory one with theirs.
They couchèd their spears and prickèd their steeds,
                                           and thus,
Their plumes driven backward by the wind they made
In moving, all together down upon him
Bare, as a wild wave in the wide North-sea,   480
Green-glimmering toward the summit, bears, with all
Its stormy crests that smoke against the skies,
Down on a bark, and overbears the bark,
And him that helms it, so they overbore
Sir Lancelot and his charger, and a spear   485
Down-glancing lamed the charger, and a spear
Pricked sharply his own cuirass, and the head

---

477 ...steeds and...	BM-2
477 (C)	73
479 In motion, all...	Tn-39
479 In motion, all...him,	BM-2
479 In motion, all...	L-II
479 (C)	F
483 ...bark and...	BM-2
483 (C)	L-II
484 ...it, as they...	BM-2
484 (C)	F
486 ...charger and...	BM-2
486 (C)	L-II
487 his own	
..sharply t̷h̷r̷o̷y̷ h̷i̷s̷ hawberk & ...	Tn-39
487 ...own hawberk and...	BM-2
487 (C)	L-II

Pierced through his side, and there snapt, and remained.

Then Sir Lavaine did well and worshipfully;
He bore a knight of old repute to the earth,   490
And brought his horse to Lancelot where he lay.
He up the side, sweating with agony, got,
But thought to do while he might yet endure,
And being lustily holpen by the rest,
His party--though it seemed half-miracle   495
To those he fought with,--drave his kith and kin,

---

488 ...snapt and...   BM-2
488 (C)   L-II

489 (No. par. indent.)   BM-2
489 (Par. symbol I)   L-II
489 (C)   F

490   bore
        He ~~smote~~ a knight...   Tn-39

492 He
        ~~Who~~ up...   Tn-39

494 ...rest   BM-2
494 (C)   L-II

495 ...party [tho' ...   BM-2
495 (C)   L-II

496   he fought with
        ...those ~~that saw it~~]drave...   Tn-39
496 ...with]drave...   BM-2
496 ...with - drave...   L-II
496 (C)   73

498-501   blew
        Back to the barrier, & the heralds ~~cried~~
                            who wore the sleeve
        Proclaiming his the prize; & all the knights
        Of scarlet & the pearls
                    cried
        His party, ~~said~~ 'Advance & take your prize   Tn-39

640

And all the Table Round that held the lists,
Back to the barrier; then the trumpets blew
Proclaiming his the prize, who wore the sleeve
Of scarlet, and the pearls; and all the knights,   500
His party, cried   'Advance and take thy prize
The diamond;' but he answered, 'Diamond me
No diamonds! for God's love, a little air!
Prize me no prizes, for my prize is death!
Hence will I, and I charge you, follow me not.'   505

    He spoke, and vanished suddenly from the field
With young Lavaine into the poplar grove.
There from his charger down he slid, and sat,
Gasping to Sir Lavaine, 'Draw the lance-head:'
'Ah my sweet lord Sir Lancelot,' said Lavaine,   510

---

498 ...barrier, and the heralds blew	BM-2
498 ...barrier; then the heralds blew	L-II
498 (C)	73
500 ...knights	BM-2
500 (C)	L-II
501 ...take your prize	BM-2
501 ...'Advance, and take your prize	F
501 (C)	73
502 The diamond' but he answer'd 'diamond me	BM-2
502 ...answer'd 'diamond me	59
502 (C)	73
505 ...I and...	BM-2
505 (C)	73
506 ...spoke and...	BM-2
506 (C)	L-II
509 ...Lavaine 'draw...	BM-2
509 (C)	73
510 ...Lancelot' said Lavaine	BM-2
510 ...Lancelot' said...	L-II
510 (C)	59

'I dread me, if I draw it, you will die.'
But he, 'I die already with it: draw--
Draw,'--and Lavaine drew, and Sir Lancelot gave
A marvellous great shriek and ghastly groan,
And half his blood burst forth, and down he sank   515
For the pure pain, and wholly swooned away.
Then came the hermit out and bare him in,
There stanched his wound; and there, in daily doubt
Whether to live or die, for many a week
Hid from the wide world's rumour by the grove   520
Of poplars with their noise of falling showers,
And ever-tremulous aspen-trees, he lay.

---

511 dread	
I *fear* me...it, ye will...	Tn-39
511 ...it, ye will...	BM-2
511 (C)	F
512 ...he, 'I ...	BM-2
512 ...he "I...	F
512 ...he 'I...	59
512 (C)	73
513 ...drew & that other gave	Tn-39
513 Draw' - and Lavaine drew and that other gave	BM-2
513 Draw' - and Lavaine drew, and that other gave	L-II
513 Draw,' - and Lavaine drew, and that other gave	67
513 (C)	73
522 ...aspen trees, ...	BM-2
522 (C)	L-II
525 ...isles	BM-2
525 (C)	L-II
526 ...round the great...	Tn-39
526 ...round the great...him	BM-2
526 ...him	L-II
526 (C)	73
527 'So, Sire, our knight thro' ...day	BM-2
527 ...knight thro' ...day	L-II
527 (C)	73

LANCELOT AND ELAINE

But on that day when Lancelot fled the lists,
His party, knights of utmost North and West,
Lords of waste marches, kings of desolate isles,   525
Came round their great Pendragon, saying to him,
'Lo, Sire, our knight, through whom we won the day,
Hath gone sore wounded, and hath left his prize
Untaken, crying that his prize is death.'
'Heaven hinder,' said the King, 'that such an one,   530
So great a knight as we have seen today--
He seemed to me another Lancelot--
Yea, twenty times I thought him Lancelot--
He must not pass uncared for. Wherefore, rise,
O Gawain, and ride forth and find the knight.   535
Wounded and wearied needs must he be near.
I charge you that you get at once to horse.
And, knights and kings, there breathes not one of you

---

530 ...the king 'that...   BM-2
530 (C)   73

534 ...for. Rise, Gawaine,   Tn-39
534 ...for. Rise, Gawaine,   BM-2
534   Gawaine, rise,   I MS
    ...for. R̸i̸s̸e̸, G̸a̸w̸a̸i̸n̸e̸,   L-II
534 ...for. Gawaine, rise,   F
534 (C)   69

535 My nephew, & ride...   Tn-39
535 My nephew, and ride...   BM-2
535 (C)   69

536   he
    ...wearied h̸e̸ must needs be...   Tn-39

537 ...horse,   BM-2
537 (C)   L-II

538   & kings
    And n̸o̸b̸l̸e̸ knights   there is not...   Tn-39
538 And knights and kings there is not...   BM-2
538   breathes   I MS
    And, knights and kings, there i̸s̸ not...   L-II
538 (C)   F

643

LANCELOT AND ELAINE

Will deem this prize of ours is rashly given:
His prowess was too wondrous. We will do him   540
No customary honour: since the knight
Came not to us, of us to claim the prize,
Ourselves will send it after. Rise and take
This diamond, and deliver it, and return,
And bring us where he is, and how he fares,   545
And cease not from your quest until ye find.'

So saying, from the carven flower above,

---

539 Will think this...   Tn-39
539 Will think this...   BM-2
539   deem   I MS
    Will t̷h̷i̷n̷k̷ this...   L-II
539 (C)   F

540 ...wonderous. we will...   BM-2
540 (C)   L-II

543   after
    ...it t̷o̷ h̷i̷m̷. Wherefore take   Tn-39
543 ...after. Wherefore take   BM-2
543 (C)   69

545 ...us what he...   Tn-39
545 ...us what he is and...   BM-2
545 (C)   69

546 ...quest, until...   BM-2
546 ...quest, until you find.'   F
546 (C)   73

547 ...saying from...   BM-2
547 (C)   73

551 ...heart, Gawaine,   Tn-39
551 ...heart, Gawain,   BM-2
551   a t̷h̷e̷ Prince   I MS
    ...heart,/G̷a̷w̷a̷i̷n̷e̷/   L-II
551 (C)   F

To which it made a restless heart, he took,
And gave, the diamond: then from where he sat
At Arthur's right, with smiling face arose,   550
With smiling face and frowning heart, a Prince
In the mid might and flourish of his May,
Gawain, surnamed The Courteous, fair and strong,
And after Lancelot, Tristram, and Geraint
And Gareth, a good knight, but therewithal   555
Sir Modred's brother, and the child of Lot,
Nor often loyal to his word, and now
Wroth that the King's command to sally forth
In quest of whom he knew not, made him leave
The banquet, and concourse of knights and kings.   560

---

552 (Omitted)   BM-2
552 (C, I MS)   L-II
552 (C)   F

553 Surnamed the courteous & the golden tongue,   Tn-39
553 Surnamed the courteous and the golden tongue,   BM-2
553 (C, I MS)   L-II
553 (C)   F

Alt. for 554 ~~And after four great names the greatest~~
                                ~~/Knight~~   I MS L-II

555 And Lamorack, a strong knight...   Tn-39
555 And Lamorack, a strong knight, ...   BM-2
Alt. for 555 No more than twenty summers, fair &
                                strong   I MS L-II
555 And Lamorack, a good...   F
555 (C)   73

556 ...brother, of a crafty house,   Tn-39
556 ...brother, of a crafty house,   BM-2
556 (C)   73

558 ...the king's command...   BM-2
558 (C)   73

560 The banquet ~~& the jewels/ & the smiles~~
     ~~Of Ladies~~, & concourse of knights & Kings   Tn-39

```
      So all in wrath he got to horse and went;
While Arthur to the banquet, dark in mood,
Past, thinking  'Is it Lancelot who hath come
Despite the wound he spake of, all for gain
Of glory, and hath added wound to wound,            565
And ridden away to die?' So feared the King,
And, after two days' tarriance there, returned.
Then when he saw the Queen, embracing asked,
'Love, are you yet so sick?' 'Nay, lord,' she said.
'And where is Lancelot?' Then the Queen amazed,    570
```

561 (No par. indent.) ...went	BM-2
561 (C)	L-II
563 ...who has come	Tn-39
563 ...thinking 'is...who has come	BM-2
563 (C)	73
564 Despite the he spake of, all	
~~Máńgŕé Hís~~ wound,/~~Wŕóńgíńg Hís Lífé~~ for gain	Tn-39
565 ...& has added...	Tn-39
565 ...and has added...wound	BM-2
565 ...and has added...	L-II
565 (C)	73
566 And past away...	Tn-39
566 And past away...the king,	BM-2
566 ...the king,	F
566 (C)	59
567 And there two days he tarried, then return'd.	Tn-39
567 And there two days he tarried, then return'd.	BM-2
567 after , tarriance there,	
And, ~~ŧħéŕé~~ two days ~~ħé ŧáŕŕíéd ŧħéń~~ return'd.	
(1st, I)	L-II
567 (C)	F
568 And when...embracing her,	Tn-39
568 And when...embracing her,	BM-2
568 Then	I MS
~~Áńd~~ when...	L-II
568 (C)	F

LANCELOT AND ELAINE

'Was he not with you? won he not your prize?'
'Nay, but one like him.' 'Why that like was he.'
And when the King demanded how she knew,
Said, 'Lord, no sooner had ye parted from us,
Than Lancelot told me of a common talk   575
That men went down before his spear at a touch,
But knowing he was Lancelot; his great name
Conquered; and therefore would he hide his name

---

569 Ask'd 'are ye yet...   Tn-39
569 Ask'd 'are ye yet...   BM-2
569 'Love, are ye yet...   L-II
569 (C)   F

570 ...Lancelot?' then the...amazed   BM-2
570 ...amazed   59
570 (C)   73

571 ...not the prize?'   Tn-39
571 ...not the prize?'   BM-2
571 (C)   L-II

572-574   ''why that like was he'
    'Nay, but one like him ~~won it and she cried~~
    ~~Why that was Lancelot: his own self & then to him~~
    And then the king demanded how she knew
    ~~Demanding how she knew it answer'd this:~~
    Said 'Lord
    ~~My Liege~~, no sooner...   Tn-39

573 ...the king demanded   BM-2
573 (C)   59

574 Said 'Lord...   BM-2
574 Said 'Lord...had you parted...   F
574 Said 'Lord...   69
574 (C)   73

578   would he hide his
    ...therefore ~~will I hide my~~ name   Tn-39

From all men, even the King, and to this end
Had made the pretext of a hindering wound,   580
That he might joust unknown of all, and learn
If his old prowess were in aught decayed;
And added, "Our true Arthur, when he learns,
Will well allow my pretext, as for gain
Of purer glory."'

                        Then replied the King: 585
'Far lovelier in our Lancelot had it been,

---

579   ev'n the king
  ...men, ~~so he/said~~, &...   Tn-39
579 ...the king, and...   BM-2
579 (C)   73

580   a hindering
  ...pretext of ~~mine ancient~~ wound,   Tn-39

581   he
  That ~~I~~ might...   Tn-39

582   his   were
  If ~~mine~~ old prowess ~~be~~ in...   Tn-39
582 ...decay'd:'   BM-2
582 ...decay'd: L-II
582 (C)   59

583   added "
  And ~~doubtless~~ our...   Tn-39
583 ...added, 'our...   BM-2
583 ...added, "our...   L-II
583 (C)   73

584 ...pretext as...   BM-2
584 ...pretext, as...   ,/ (I)   L-II
584 (C)   F

585 ...glory.'
        ...the king   BM-2
585 ...glory."
        ...the king: L-II
585 the king: F
585 (C)   59

In lieu of idly dallying with the truth,
To have trusted me as he hath trusted thee.
Surely his King and most familiar friend
Might well have kept his secret. True, indeed,   590
Albeit I know my knights fantastical,
So fine a fear in our large Lancelot
Must needs have moved my laughter: now remains
But little cause for laughter: his own kin--
Ill news, my Queen, for all who love him, this!--   595
His kith and kin, not knowing, set upon him;
So that he went sore wounded from the field:

---

586 Far
    ~~It had been~~ lovelier...   Tn-39
586 Far...   BM-2
586 (C)   L-II

587 ...truth   BM-2
587 (C)   L-II

588 ...he has trusted you.   Tn-39
588 ...he has trusted you.   BM-2
588 (C)   73

589 ...his king and...   BM-2
589 (C)   73

593 Must needs have moved my laughter: ~~& methinks~~
    ~~Moved me to laugh it down. but~~ now remains   Tn-39

595   for all who love him, these
    ...Queen, ~~are these for all his friends~~ -   Tn-39
595 ...him, these   BM-2
595 ...him, these!   !/ (I)   L-II
595 ...him, these!   F
595 (C)   73

596 ...him: BM-2
596 (C)   L-II

597 ...field.   BM-2
597 (C)   L-II

Yet good news too: for goodly hopes are mine
That Lancelot is no more a lonely heart.
He wore, against his wont, upon his helm   600
A sleeve of scarlet, broidered with great pearls,
Some gentle maiden's gift.'

                'Yea, lord,' she said,
'Thy hopes are mine,' and saying that, she choked,
And sharply turned about to hide her face,
Past to her chamber, and there flung herself   605
Down on the great King's couch, and writhed upon it,
And clenched her fingers till they bit the palm,
And shrieked out 'Traitor' to the unhearing wall,
Then flashed into wild tears, and rose again,
And moved about her palace, proud and pale.   610

    Gawain the while through all the region round
Rode with his diamond, wearied of the quest,

| 600 | upon | |
| | ...wont, a̶b̶o̶u̶t̶ his... | Tn-39 |

603 Your hopes...		Tn-39
603 'Your hopes...that she...		BM-2
603 (C)		73

605 Moved to...		Tn-39
605 Moved to her chamber and...		BM-2
605 Moved to her chamber, and...	(, I)	L-II
605 Moved to her...		F
605 (C)		<u>69</u>

606 ...great king's couch and...		BM-2
606 ...great king's couch, and...	(, I)	L-II
606 ...great king's couch...		F
606 (C)		59

| 608 ...out 'traitor' to... | | BM-2 |
| 608 (C) | | 73 |

611 (Par.) Meanwhile Gawain thro'...		Tn-39
611 (Par.) Meanwhile Gawain thro'...		BM-2
611 Gawain the while		I MS
(Par.) M̶e̶a̶n̶w̶h̶i̶l̶e̶ G̶a̶w̶a̶i̶n̶ thro'...		L-II
611 (C)		F

Touched at all points, except the poplar grove,
And came at last, though late, to Astolat:
Whom glittering in enamelled arms the maid   615
Glanced at, and cried, 'What news from Camelot, lord?
What of the knight with the red sleeve?' 'He won.'
'I knew it,' she said. 'But parted from the jousts
Hurt in the side,' whereat she caught her breath;
Through her own side she felt the sharp lance go;   620
Thereon she smote her hand: wellnigh she swooned:
And, while he gazed wonderingly at her, came
The Lord of Astolat out, to whom the Prince
Reported who he was, and on what quest
Sent, that he bore the prize and could not find   625
The victor, but had ridden a random round

---

614 ...Astolat;		BM-2
614 (C)		L-II
616 ...at and cried 'What..., lord,		BM-2
616 ...at, and cried 'What...	,/ (I)	L-II
616 ...cried 'What...		F
616 (C)		73
617 red sleeve		
...with the ~~blank~~ ~~shield~~?' 'he...		Tn-39
619 ...breath,		BM-2
619 (C)		L-II
620 sharp		
...the ~~long~~ lance...		Tn-39
620 ...go -		BM-2
620 (C)		L-II
621 Thereon smote		
~~Thereto~~ she ~~clapt~~ her...		Tn-39
621 ...well-nigh...		BM-2
621 (C)		73
623 The lord of...		BM-2
623 (C)		F
626 .. ridden wildly round		Tn-39
626 ...had ridden wildly round		BM-2
626 (C)		73

To seek him, and had wearied of the search.
To whom the Lord of Astolat, 'Bide with us,
And ride no more at random, noble Prince!
Here was the knight, and here he left a shield; 630
This will he send or come for: furthermore
Our son is with him; we shall hear anon,

---

627 ...& was wearied... Tn-39
627 ...him and was wearied... BM-2
627 ...and was wearied... L-II
627 (C) 73

628 To whom
  And then the Lord... Tn-39
628 ...Astolat 'Bide... BM-2
628   ye there I MS
 ...Astolat 'Bide with us, L-II
628 ...Astolat 'Bide... F
628 (C) 73

629 And ride no longer
 In lieu of riding/wildly, noble... Tn-39
629 ...no longer wildly, noble prince! BM-2
629 (C) 73

630 The knight was here & here... Tn-39
630 The knight was here and... BM-2
630 Here was the knight, I MS
 The knight was here and... L-II
630 (C) F

631 This will he
 Wh he will send... Tn-39
631 ...or come - for, furthermore BM-2
631 (C) L-II

632 My son... Tn-39
632 My son...anon BM-2
632 Our I MS
 My son... L-II
632 (C) F

Needs must we hear.' To this the courteous Prince
Accorded with his wonted courtesy,
Courtesy with a touch of traitor in it,   635
And stayed; and cast his eyes on fair Elaine:
Where could be found face daintier? then her shape
From forehead down to foot, perfect--again
From foot to forehead exquisitely turned:
'Well--if I bide, lo! this wild flower for me!'   640
And oft they met among the garden yews,
And there he set himself to play upon her
With sallying wit, free flashes from a height

---

633 Needs   we
    W̶e̶ n̶e̶e̶d̶s̶ must hear' to this the bland Gawain   Tn-39
633 ...this the bland Gawain   BM-2
633   this the courteous Prince   I MS
    ...t̶h̶i̶s̶ t̶h̶e̶ b̶l̶a̶n̶d̶ G̶a̶w̶a̶i̶n̶   L-II
633 (C)   F

636 ...eyes upon the girl -   Tn-39
636 ...eyes upon the girl -   BM-2
636   on fair Elaine   I MS
    ...eyes u̶p̶o̶n̶ t̶h̶e̶ g̶i̶r̶l̶/̶-̶   L-II
636 (C)   F

637   daintier
    ...face p̶r̶e̶t̶t̶i̶e̶r̶? then...   Tn-39

638 ...foot perfect - ...   BM-2
638 (C)   73

641 (Omitted)   BM-2
641 (C)   L-II

642 And then he...   Tn-39
642 And then he...her,   BM-2
642 (C)   L-II

643 With merry talk, & stories from...   Tn-39
643 With merry talk, and stories from a height   BM-2
643   sallying wit, free flashes   I MS
    With m̶e̶r̶r̶y̶ t̶a̶l̶k̶/̶/̶a̶n̶d̶/̶s̶t̶o̶r̶i̶e̶s̶ from a height   L-II
643 (C)   F

Above her, graces of the court, and songs,
Sighs, and slow smiles, and golden eloquence   645
And amorous adulation, till the maid
Rebelled against it, saying to him, 'Prince,
O loyal nephew of our noble King,
Why ask you not to see the shield he left,
Whence you might learn his name? Why slight your
                                  King,   650
And lose the quest he sent you on, and prove
No surer than our falcon yesterday,

644	glories	I MS
	...her, g̶l̶a̶c̶e̶s̶ of the...	L-II
648	...noble king,	BM-2
648	(C)	59
649	...ask ye not...	Tn-39
649	...ask ye not...left?	BM-2
649	...ask ye not...left̶/̶, (, I)	L-II
649	(C)	F

650   why
    Thence might ye learn his name - y̶e̶ slight... Tn-39
650 Thence might ye learn his name. why slight
                      your king.   BM-2
650 Whence ye   ? Why   I MS
    T̶h̶e̶n̶c̶e̶ might y̶e̶ learn his name. Y̶o̶u̶ slight
                      your king,   (, I)   L-II
650 ...your king,   F
650 (C)   59

651 Why   & prove
    A̶n̶d̶ lose...on, a̶s̶ m̶u̶c̶h̶   Tn-39
651 Why lose...   BM-2
651 And   I MS
    W̶h̶y̶ lose...   L-II
651 (C)   F

652 No surer than our
    A̶s̶ d̶i̶d̶ m̶y̶ f̶a̶t̶h̶e̶r̶'̶s̶ falcon...   Tn-39

Who lost the hern we slipt her at, and went
To all the winds?' 'Nay, by mine head,' said he,
'I lose it, as we lose the lark in heaven,   655
O damsel, in the light of your blue eyes;
But an ye will it let me see the shield.'
And when the shield was brought, and Gawain saw

---

653 ...slipt him at, ...   Tn-39
653 ...slipt him at,...   BM-2
653 (C)   84

654 ...winds.' Say rather' added he   Tn-39
654 ...winds?' 'Say rather, ' added he,   BM-2
654   'Nay, by mine head' said he   I MS
    ...winds?' /S̸a̸y̸ r̸a̸t̸h̸e̸r̸/y̸ a̸n̸s̸w̸e̸r̸/y̸d̸ h̸e̸/   L-II
654 .. head' said he   F
654 (C)   59

655   se   we lose the
    I lo̸s̸t̸ it, as t̸h̸e̸ lark i̸s̸ l̸o̸s̸t̸ in...   Tn-39

656 Sweet damsel, ...   Tn-39
656 Sweet damsel, ...eyes.   BM-2
656 O
    S̸w̸e̸e̸t̸ damsel, ...eyes.:   :/ (I)   L-II
656 ...eyes: F
656 (C)   59

657 ...shield'   BM-2
657 ...an you will.. .   F
657 (C)   69

658 .. brought, he smote his thigh   Tn-39
658 ...brought, he smote his thigh   BM-2
658   & Gawain said   I MS
    ...brought, h̸e̸ s̸m̸o̸t̸e̸ h̸i̸s̸ t̸h̸i̸g̸h̸   L-II
658 (C)   F

Alt. after 658 Right was the King! that old knave,
                     Lancelot'   BM-2
Alt. after 658 (Cancelled, I, L-II)
Alt. after 658 (C)   F

Sir Lancelot's azure lions, crowned with gold,
Ramp in the field, he smote his thigh, and mocked   660
'Right was the King! our Lancelot! that true man!'
'And right was I,' she answered merrily, 'I,
Who dreamed my knight the greatest knight of all.'
'And if I dreamed,' said Gawain, 'that you love
This greatest knight, your pardon! lo, ye know it!   665
Speak therefore: shall I waste myself in vain?'
Full simple was her answer, 'What know I?

659-661 (Omitted)   BM-2
659-661 (Added in I MS to L-II)
659 Sir Lancelot's azure lions, crown'd with
                          gold,   (I MS)   L-II

660 ...mock'd;   F
660 (C)   73

661 Right was the King
    T̸h̸e̸ K̸i̸n̸g̸ w̸a̸s̸ r̸i̸g̸h̸t̸:   that old knave, Lancelot' Tn-39

662   was I
    And I̸ w̸a̸s̸ right' she...   Tn-39

663 ...dream'd he was the greatest...   Tn-39
663 ...dream'd he was the greatest...   BM-2
663   my knight   I MS
    ...dream'd h̸e̸ w̸a̸s̸ the greatest...   L-II

664-666
    'So, so' said he 'ye love this greatest knight?'
    Ye know ye love him: wherefore speak the truth
    I charge you: shall I...   Tn-39
664-666
    'So, so,' said he 'ye love this greatest knight?
    Ye know ye love him: wherefore speak the truth
    I charge you: shall I...   BM-2
664-666 (Printed same as above L-II. I MS
      corrections written in, and C save for
      following:)

664 ...that ye love   (I MS)   L-II
664 ...dream'd, said...   F
664 (C)   59

LANCELOT AND ELAINE

My brethren have been all my fellowship;
And I, when often they have talked of love,
Wished it had been my mother, for they talked,   670
Meseemed, of what they knew not; so myself--
I know not if I know what true love is,
But if I know, then, if I love not him,
I know there is none other I can love.'

---

665 ..lo, you know...   F
665 (C)   73

666 Speak therefore: I MS
     I̸ c̸h̸a̸r̸g̸e̸ y̸o̸u̸: shall...   L-II
666 (C)   F

667 She made a simple answer...   Tn-39
667 She made a simple answer 'What...   BM-2
667   Full   was her   I MS
     S̸h̸e̸ m̸a̸d̸e̸ a̸ simple answer 'What...   L-II
667 ...answer 'What   F
667 (C)   73

668 ...fellowship,   BM-2
668 (C)   73

669 ...of love   BM-2
669 (C)   L-II

670 ...talk'd   BM-2
670 (C)   L-II

671 Meseem'd of...   BM-2
671 (C)   F

672 ...is   BM-2
672 (C)   L-II

673 ...then if.. him   BM-2
673 (C)   L-II

674 Methinks
     There is...love, m̸y̸ l̸o̸r̸d̸   Tn-39
674 Methinks there is none...   BM-2
674 (C)   73

LANCELOT AND ELAINE

'Yea, by God's death,' said he, 'ye love him well,   675
But would not, knew ye what all others know,
And whom he loves.' 'So be it,' cried Elaine,
And lifted her fair face and moved away:
But he pursued her, calling, 'Stay a little!

---

675 (Par.) Yea yea said he by God ye ..   Tn-39
675 (Par.) 'Yea, yea,' said he, 'by God ye love
                      him well.   BM-2
675 Not a separate par. by God's death'   I MS
   (Par.) 'Yea, ~~yea~~,' said he, 'ye, ~~doubtless~~, love
              him well,   ,/ (last, I) L-II
675 ...he, 'you love...   F
675 (C)   69

676 'Ye would not an ye knew him as I do   Tn-39
676 Ye would not an ye knew him as I do   BM-2
676 But   ye what all others know,   I MS
   ~~Ye~~ would not, ~~an~~ ~~ye~~ knew ~~him~~ ~~as~~ ~~I~~ ~~do~~, (1st, I) L-II
676 ...knew you what...   F
676 (C)   69

677 ...it 'answer'd she   Tn-39
677 ...be it, answer'd she   BM-2
677   cried Elaine   I MS
   ...be it,' ~~answer'd~~ ~~she~~   L-II
677 ...Elaine   F
677 (C)   59

678 ...away   BM-2
678 (C)   L-II

679   thinking 'may it be so?
   He wore her sleeve' &
   But he pursued her calling 'stay a little,   Tn-39
679 But he pursued her thinking 'may it be so?
   He wore her sleeve' and calling 'stay a little, BM-2
679   calling 'Bide a while!   I MS
   But he pursued her ~~thinking~~ ~~'may~~ ~~it~~ ~~be~~ ~~so?~~
   He ~~wore~~ ~~her~~ ~~sleeve'~~ ~~and~~ ~~calling~~ ~~'stay~~ ~~a~~ ~~little,~~ L-II
679 ...her calling 'Bide a while!   F
679 ...her calling 'Stay...   59
679 (C)   73

LANCELOT AND ELAINE

One golden minute's grace! he wore your sleeve: 680
Would he break faith with one I may not name?
Must our true man change like a leaf at last?
Nay--like enow: why then, far be it from me
To cross our mighty Lancelot in his loves!
And, damsel, for I deem you know full well   685
Where your great knight is hidden, let me leave
My quest with you; the diamond also: here!
For if you love, it will be sweet to give it;
And if he love, it will be sweet to have it
From your own hand; and whether he love or not,   690

680-683
    One Golden
    L̸i̸s̸t̸e̸n̸s̸ á minute's grace: far be it from me   Tn-39
680-683 One golden minute's grace: far be it
                              from me   BM-2
680   he wore your sleeve: I MS
    One golden minute's grace: f̸a̸t̸/b̸e̸/i̸t̸/f̸t̸o̸m̸/m̸e̸   L-II
680 ...grace: he...   F
680 (C)   73

681-682 (Added, C, in I MS at page bottom)   L-II

683 May it be so? why then, far be it from me (I MS
                              page bottom)   L-II
683 May it be so? why...   F
683 Nay - like enough: why...   67
683 (C)   73

684 ...loves   BM-2
684 (C)   L-II

685 ...for belike ye know full...   Tn-39
685 ...for belike ye know...   BM-2
685 (C)   F

Alt. after 687 A̸c̸c̸e̸p̸t̸ i̸t̸ f̸i̸n̸d̸ h̸i̸m̸ o̸u̸t̸ & g̸i̸v̸e̸ i̸t̸ t̸o̸ h̸i̸m̸/
                                                         Tn-39

688 ...give it   BM-2
688   ye   I MS
    ...if y̸o̸u̸ love, ...   L-II
688 (C)   F

659

A diamond is a diamond. Fare you well
A thousand times!--a thousand times farewell!
Yet, if he love, and his love hold, we two
May meet at court hereafter: there, I think,
So ye will learn the courtesies of the court,   695
We two shall know each other.'

---

691 ...Fare ye well   Tn-39
691 ...Fare ye well.   BM-2
691 (C)   F

692 ...times! a thousand...   BM-2
692 (C)   L-II

Alt. after 692
    I pray you do not prattle of all this/
                        daintiest
    You seem to me the prettiest maid alive
                        why two
    And so ye win this Lancelot we may meet   Tn-39

693 Yet if...hold we...   BM-2
693 (C)   L-II

694 May meet
    perhaps at...   Tn-39
694 ...there I think   BM-2
694 (C)   L-II

695 So you will...   Tn-39
695 So you will...court   BM-2
695   e   I MS
    So you will...   L-II
695 So you will...   F
695 (C)   73

696   we shall   each other
    That you will know me better.   Tn-39
696 That we shall...
                    ...Thus he said,   BM-2
696 Then he gave,   I MS
    ...Thus he said/   L-II
696 (C)   F

660

                              Then he gave,
And slightly kissed the hand to which he gave,
The diamond, and all wearied of the quest
Leapt on his horse, and carolling as he went
A true-love ballad, lightly rode away.   700

    Thence to the court he past; there told the King
What the King knew, 'Sir Lancelot is the knight.'
And added, 'Sire, my liege, so much I learnt;
But failed to find him, tho' I rode all round
The region: but I lighted on the maid   705
Whose sleeve he wore; she loves him; and to her,

697-698 (Omitted)	BM-2
697-698 (I MS, C, in)	L-II
697-698 (C)	F
699 ...& whistling as...	Tn-39
699 ...and whistling as...	BM-2
699 carolling	I MS
...and w̶h̶i̶s̶t̶l̶i̶n̶g̶ as...	L-II
699 (C)	F
701 ...the king	BM-2
701 (C)	59
702 ...the king knew 'Sir...	BM-2
702 ...knew 'Sir...	59
702 (C)	73
703 ...added 'Sire, ...learnt.	BM-2
703 ...added 'Sire, ...	L-II
703 (C)	73
704 ...him tho' ...	BM-2
704 (C)	84
705 ...the maid,	F
705 (C)	73
706 &	
...him, w̶e̶l̶l̶ to her,	Tn-39
706 ...wore: she...	BM-2
706 (C)	L-II

LANCELOT AND ELAINE

Deeming our courtesy is the truest law,
I gave the diamond: she will render it;
For by mine head she knows his hiding-place.'

    The seldom-frowning King frowned, and replied,   710
'Too courteous truly! ye shall go no more
On quest of mine, seeing that ye forget
Obedience is the courtesy due to kings.'

    He spake and parted. Wroth, but all in awe,
For twenty strokes of the blood, without a word,   715
Lingered that other, staring after him;
Then shook his hair, strode off, and buzzed abroad
About the maid of Astolat, and her love.

---

707 ...law	BM-2
707 (C)	F

708 ...diamond to be given to him.	Tn-39
708 ...diamond to be given to him	BM-2
708 she will ~~give it him~~ render it;	I MS
...diamond: ~~to be given to him~~ (: I)	L-II
708 (C)	F

709 Here he ceased.	
She knows where he is hidden, ~~as I think.~~	Tn-39
709 She knows where he is hidden.' Here he ceased,	BM-2
709 (Printed same as above, with I MS C version	
above.)	L-II
709 (C)	F

710-711	
The seldom-frowning King frown'd & replied	
~~Then spake the King. Thenceforth~~ ye ~~move~~ no more	
'Too courteous truly! shall go	Tn-39

710 (No par.) ...-frowning king, frown'd and...	BM-2
710 ...-frowning king frown'd...	F
710 (C)	59

711 ...truly! you shall...	F
711 (C)	69

712 ...that you forget	F
712 (C)	69

662

LANCELOT AND ELAINE

All ears were pricked at once, all tongues were loosed:
'The maid of Astolat loves Sir Lancelot,   720
Sir Lancelot loves the maid of Astolat.'
Some read the King's face, some the Queen's, and all
Had marvel what the maid might be, but most
Predoomed her as unworthy. One old dame
Came suddenly on the Queen with the sharp news.   725
She, that had heard the noise of it before,

Sketch 714-717
   The seldom-frowning King frown'd & Gawain
   Astounded, slipt away then buzzed abroad   Tn-39

714 ...but half in...   Tn-39
714 (No par.) ...Wroth but half in awe,   BM-2
714 He spake and went. parted   (Last word I MS)
                        W   but all   I MS
              Half Wroth and Half in awe,   L-II
714 ...Wroth but..   F
714 (C)   73

719 ...ears was prick'd at once: all...loosed.   BM-2
719 (C)   L-II

720 ...Lancelot   BM-2
720 (C)   F

722   all
    ...Queens, & some   Tn-39

723 Had
    Made marvel...   Tn-39

724   doom'd
    Prejudged her...   Tn-39
724 ...unworthy: one old...   BM-2
724 (C)   F

726   who had
    She, Having heard before the rumour of it,   Tn-39
726 She, who had heard before the rumour of it,   BM-2
726   that   noise before,   I MS
    She, who had heard before the rumour of it/   L-II
726 (C)   F

663

But sorrowing Lancelot should have stooped so low,
Marred her friend's aim with pale tranquillity.
So ran the tale like fire about the court,
Fire in dry stubble a nine-days' wonder flared: 730
Till even the knights at banquet twice or thrice
Forgot to drink to Lancelot and the Queen,
And pledging Lancelot and the lily maid
Smiled at each other, while the Queen, who sat
With lips severely placid, felt the knot   735
Climb in her throat, and with her feet unseen
Crushed the wild passion out against the floor

---

727   ing
        But sorrow'ø Lancelot...   Tn-39

728 ...friend's point with...   Tn-39
728 ...friend's point with...   BM-2
728 (C)   73

730 ...nine days'...   BM-2
730 (C)   73

734 ...other while the Queen who...   BM-2
734 ...Queen who...   L-II
734 (C)   73

735 ...placid felt...   BM-2
735 (C)   73

738 ...banquet where...   BM-2
738 (C)   L-II

740 (No par.)   BM-2
740 (C)   L-II

741 ...that sacred kept   V

743 ...father when Gawain had gone,   V
743 ...father, when Gawaine had gone,   Tn-39
743 ...father, when Gawain had gone,   BM-2
743   while he mused alone   I MS
    ...father, ẅhéń Ǵáẃáíń ḱád́ ǵóńé,   L-II
743 (C)   F

664

Beneath the banquet, where the meats became
As wormwood, and she hated all who pledged.

But far away the maid in Astolat,   740
Her guiltless rival, she that ever kept
The one-day-seen Sir Lancelot in her heart,
Crept to her father, while he mused alone,
Sat on his knee, stroked his gray face and said,
'Father, you call me wilful, and the fault   745
Is yours who let me have my will, and now,
Sweet father, will you let me lose my wits?'
'Nay,' said he, 'surely.' 'Wherefore, let me hence,'
She answered, 'and find out our dear Lavaine.'
'Ye will not lose your wits for dear Lavaine: 750

---

744 ...said.   BM-2
744 (C)   67

745 Father ye call...   V
745 'Father ye call....   Tn-39
745 'Father, ye call...   BM-2
745 (C)   F

746 ...now   BM-2
746 (C)   L-II

747 ...will ye let...   V
747 ...will ye let...   Tn-39
747 ...will ye let...   BM-2
747 (C)   F

748 Nay nay said he surely my poor Elaine.   V
748   'Wherefore let me
    ...'surely' 'T̸h̸e̸n̸ I̸ n̸e̸e̸d̸s̸ m̸u̸s̸t̸ hence'   Tn-39
748 ...'Wherefore let...   BM-2
748 (C)   61

749 ...Lavaine   BM-2
749 (C)   L-II

750 'You will...   F
750 (C)   69

665

Bide,' answered he: 'we needs must hear anon
Of him, and of that other.' 'Ay,' she said,
'And of that other, for I needs must hence
And find that other, wheresoe'er he be,
And with mine own hand give his diamond to him,   755
Lest I be found as faithless in the quest
As yon proud Prince who left the quest to me.
Sweet father, I behold him in my dreams
Gaunt as it were the skeleton of himself,
Death-pale, for lack of gentle maiden's aid.   760
The gentler-born the maiden, the more bound,
My father, to be sweet and serviceable

---

753 ...other & I...	Tn-39
753 ...other, and I needs...	BM-2
753 (C)	L-II
757 ...proud prince who...	BM-2
757 (C)	59
758 And I am haunted with a vision of him	Tn-39
758 And I am haunted with a vision of him	BM-2
758 o	I MS
...beheld...	L-II
758 (C)	F
759 ...himself	BM-2
759 (C)	L-II
760 Death pale, ...	BM-2
760 (C)	L-II
761 ...maiden the more bound	BM-2
761 (C)	L-II
762 ...father to...	BM-2
762 (C)	L-II
763 ..., as you know,	F
763 (C)	69
765 ...said	BM-2
765 ...her Father nodding said	F
765 (C)	59

666

LANCELOT AND ELAINE

To noble knights in sickness, as ye know
When these have worn their tokens: let me hence
I pray you.' Then her father nodding said,   765
'Ay, ay, the diamond: wit ye well, my child,
Right fain were I to learn this knight were whole,
Being our greatest: yea, and you must give it--
And sure I think this fruit is hung too high
For any mouth to gape for save a queen's--   770
Nay, I mean nothing: so then, get you gone,
Being so very wilful you must go.'

    Lightly, her suit allowed, she slipt away,
And while she made her ready for her ride,
Her father's latest word hummèd in her ear,   775

---

766 Ay ay the diamond well my poor Elaine   V
766 ...diamond. well my poor Elaine   Tn-39
766 ...diamond. well my poor Elaine   BM-2
766   my child,   I MS
    ...diamond.: S̸o̸o̸t̸h̸/ a̸n̸d̸ wit ye well,   (: I)   L-II
766 ...: wit you well, ...   F
766 (C)   73

767 Right glad were I to hear this...   V
767 Right glad were...   Tn-39
767 Right glad were...   BM-2
767 (C)   L-II

768 ...greatest - good & ye must give it.   V
768 ...greatest. good & ye must...   Tn-39
768 ...greatest. good, and ye must...   BM-2
768 ...and ye must...   L-II
768 (C)   F

769 Elaine I think...   V

770 ...a Queen's -   BM-2
770 (C)   73

771 Nay I mean nothing by it - get you gone   V
771 ...nothing. so then get...   BM-2
771 (C)   L-II

773 ...away.   BM-2
773 (C)   59

'Being so very wilful you must go,'
And changed itself and echoed in her heart,
'Being so very wilful you must die.'
But she was happy enough and shook it off,
As we shake off the bee that buzzes at us;   780
And in her heart she answered it and said,
'What matter, so I help him back to life?'
Then far away with good Sir Torre for guide
Rode o'er the long backs of the bushless downs
To Camelot, and before the city-gates   785
Came on her brother with a happy face
Making a roan horse caper and curvet
For pleasure all about a field of flowers:

---

777 ...heart		BM-2
777 (C)		L-II
779 ...it off		BM-2
779 (C)		L-II
780 ...at us.		BM-2
780 (C)		L-II
781 ...said		BM-2
781 (C)		L-II
783 far		
Then l̸o̸s̸t̸ away...		Tn-39
785 & before		
To Camelot - h̸a̸r̸d̸ & n̸i̸g̸h̸ the city-gates		Tn-39
786 ...with a rosy face		Tn-39
786 ...brother with a rosy face		BM-2
786 (C)		L-II
787 a red curvet		
Making h̸i̸s̸ horse caper & s̸o̸m̸e̸r̸s̸e̸t̸		Tn-39
787 Making a red horse...		BM-2
787 (C)		L-II
789 ...saw 'Lavaine' she cried 'Lavaine		BM-2
789 ...'Lavaine' she cried 'Lavaine,		L-II
789 (C)		59

668

Whom when she saw, 'Lavaine,' she cried, 'Lavaine,
How fares my lord Sir Lancelot?' He amazed,   790
'Torre and Elaine! why here? Sir Lancelot!
How know ye my lord's name is Lancelot?'
But when the maid had told him all her tale,
Then turned Sir Torre, and being in his moods
Left them, and under the strange-statued gate,   795
Where Arthur's wars were rendered mystically,
Past up the still rich city to his kin,
His own far blood, which dwelt at Camelot;
And her, Lavaine across the poplar grove
Led to the caves: there first she saw the casque   800
Of Lancelot on the wall: her scarlet sleeve,

---

792 ...know you my...	F
792 (C)	<u>69</u>
793 ...her tale	BM-2
793 (C)	L-II

Sketch 794-800
 Then past Sir Torre into the city-gates
 To blood of his which dwelt at Camelot;
 But her Lavaine up thro' the poplar grove
 Led to the cave   Tn-39

Alt. 794 Then past Sir Torre beneath the gates to
                         friends   Tn-39

797 ...city to his friends   Tn-39

798 ...blood which...Camelot,	BM-2
798 (C)	L-II
799 ...Lavaine up thro' the poplar...	Tn-39
799 And her Lavaine up thro' the...	BM-2
799 ...her Lavaine...	L-II
799 (C)	67
800 ...caves; there...	BM-2
800 (C)	L-II
801 ...Lancelot hanging & her...	Tn-39
801 Of Lancelot hanging and her scarlet sleeve,	BM-2
801 (C)	L-II

669

Though carved out and cut, and half the pearls away,
Streamed from it still; and in her heart she laughed,
Because he had not loosed it from his helm,
But meant once more perchance to tourney in it.   805
And when they gained the cell wherein he slept,
His battle-writhen arms and mighty hands
Lay naked on the wolfskin, and a dream
Of dragging down his enemy made them move.
Then she that saw him lying unsleek, unshorn,   810
Gaunt as it were the skeleton of himself,
Uttered a little tender dolorous cry.
The sound not wonted in a place so still

---

803 Yet wound about it.   Then she laugh'd in
                                     heart,   Tn-39
803 Yet wound about it.   then she laugh'd in
                                     heart,   BM-2
803 (C)   L-II

804 ...helm   BM-2
804 (C)   L-II

805 But meant perchance once more to joust in it   Tn-39
805 But meant perchance once more to joust in it   BM-2
805 (C)   L-II

806 ...cell in wh he...   Tn-39
806 ...cell in which he slept   BM-2
806 ...cell in which he slept,   L-II
806 ...cell in which he...   F
806 (C)   73

808 ...wolfskin and...   BM-2
808 (C)   L-II

810 ...unsleek unshorn   BM-2
810 (C)   L-II

811 ...himself   BM-2
811 (C)   L-II

812 She gave a little...   V

Woke the sick knight, and while he rolled his eyes
Yet blank from sleep, she started to him, saying,   815
'Your prize the diamond sent you by the King:'
His eyes glistened: she fancied 'Is it for me?'
And when the maid had told him all the tale
Of King and Prince, the diamond sent, the quest
Assigned to her not worthy of it, she knelt   820
Full lowly by the corners of his bed,
And laid the diamond in his open hand.

814-815 Wh woke him: then she started to his side   V

814 ...knight and...   BM-2
814 (C)   L-II

815 ..., saying   BM-2
815 (C)   73

816 ...the king,   BM-2
816 ...the king:'   L-II
816 (C)   59

817 ...fancied 'is it...   BM-2
817 (C)   73

Alt. for 818 The Prince Gawain (1 ?) by the king
          Gave it to me to give (thee ?) noble
                lord.   V

819-820 Then to the couch she stole, knelt on one knee V

819 Of king and prince, the...   BM-2
819 (C)   59

820   her
   ...to ø̸n̸ø̸ not...   Tn-39

821 Then by the border of his bed she knelt   V
821 ...his bed   BM-2
821 (C)   L-II

822 And softly laid the diamond in his hand.   V

Her face was near, and as we kiss the child
That does the task assigned, he kissed her face.
At once she slipt like water to the floor.   825
'Alas,' he said, 'your ride hath wearied you.
Rest must you have.' 'No rest for me,' she said;

---

823   That does the thing we bid him or beyond
      That wh we hoped of him wd do kissd his thanks   V
823   ...near and...   BM-2
823   (C)   L-II

824   .. task al̸l̸o̸t̸e̸d̸ assign'd...   V
824   ...assign'd he...   BM-2
824   (C)   L-II

825   ye   much
         Alas said he why put me to t̸h̸i̸s̸ pain?
                                much   ness
         'And that' she said were t̸o̸o̸ ungrateful i̸n̸ m̸e̸,   V

826   Alas said he your ride hath sickend you   V
826   .. ride has wearied...   Tn-39
826   'Alas' he said 'your ride has wearied you.   BM-2
826   ...ride has wearied...   59
826   (C)   73

827   Ye must have rest   no   for me
                   N̸o̸ n̸e̸e̸d̸ o̸f̸ rest she said   V
827   ...must ye have.' 'What rest...   Tn-39
827   ...must ye have.' 'What rest for me?' she said   BM-2
827   ...must ye have.' 'No rest for me;' she said;
                              (2nd ; I)   L-II
827   ...me;' she...   F
827   (C)   59

828   Lord, seeing that near you I am at rest.'   V
828   None, seeing that near you I am rest   V
828   None, for...   Tn-39
828   'None, for near...   BM-2
828   'Nay, for...   '/ (I)   L-II
828   (C)   F

672

'Nay, for near you, fair lord, I am at rest.'
What might she mean by that? his large black eyes,
Yet larger through his leanness, dwelt upon her,   830
Till all her heart's sad secret blazed itself
In the heart's colours on her simple face;
And Lancelot looked and was perplext in mind,
And being weak in body said no more;
But did not love the colour; woman's love,   835
Save one, he not regarded, and so turned
Sighing, and feigned a sleep until he slept.

   Then rose Elaine and glided through the fields

---

829 What may ye mean by that?		
this...	V	
829 ...eyes	BM-2	
829 (C)	L-II	
830 .. larger from his...	V	
830 ...leanness dwelt...	BM-2	
830 (C)	L-II	
831 ff The sad secret of her heart (1 ?)		
Till over brow & bosom whence she stood		
In the hearts colours blazond all her face		
Brake the sad cloud of maiden truthfulness	V	
833 And Lancelot seeing was perplext in mind	V	
835 He did not love the colour & so turnd	V	
835 ...love	BM-2	
835 (C)	L-II	
836 Save one's he...	BM-2	
836 (C)	L-II	
837 Sighing...	V	
837 ...feign'd to sleep...	Tn-39	
837 .. feign'd a sleep...	BM-2	
837 (C)	F	
838 ...through ye fields	Tn-39	
838 ...the fields	BM-2	
838 (C)	L-II	

And past beneath the weirdly-sculptured gates
Far up the dim rich city to her kin;   840
There bode the night: but woke with dawn, and past
Down throúgh the dim rich city to the fields,
Thence to the cave: so day by day she past
In either twilight ghost-like to and fro
Gliding, and every day she tended him,   845
And likewise many a night: and Lancelot
Would, though he called his wound a little hurt
Whereof he should be quickly whole, at times
Brain-feverous in his heat and agony, seem
Uncourteous, even he: but the meek maid   850
Sweetly forbore him ever, being to him
Meeker than any child to a rough nurse,
Milder than any mother to a sick child,
And never woman yet, since man's first fall,
Did kindlier unto man, but her deep love   855
Upbore her; till the hermit, skilled in all

---

839 ...beneath the wildly-sculptured...   Tn-39
839 ...the wildly-sculptured...   BM-2
839 (C)   73

840 ...kin.   BM-2
840 (C)   L-II

841 ...night but...dawn and...   BM-2
841 (C)   L-II

842 ...fields   BM-2
842 (C)   L-II

843 Thence ú̸p̸w̸a̸r̸d̸ to...   Tn-39

845 . .him   BM-2
845 (C)   L-II

847   wound
    Would s̸o̸m̸e̸t̸i̸m̸e̸s̸, tho he call'd his h̸u̸r̸t̸ a
                       little hurt
                       s̸c̸r̸a̸t̸c̸h̸   Tn-39
847 Would tho..hurt,   BM-2
847 (C)   L-II

674

The simples and the science of that time,
Told him that her fine care had saved his life.
And the sick man forgot her simple blush,
Would call her friend and sister, sweet Elaine,   860
Would listen for her coming and regret
Her parting step, and held her tenderly,
And loved her with all love except the love
Of man and woman when they love their best,
Closest and sweetest, and had died the death   865
In any knightly fashion for her sake.
And peradventure had he seen her first
She might have made this and that other world
Another world for the sick man; but now
The shackles of an old love straitened him,   870
His honour rooted in dishonour stood,
And faith unfaithful kept him falsely true.

  Yet the great knight in his mid-sickness made
Full many a holy vow and pure resolve.
These, as but born of sickness, could not live: 875
For when the blood ran lustier in him again,

---

852 Meeker than any babe to a rough nurse   V

853 ...mother to a first babe   V

854 For ~~And~~ never...   V

855 ...man, for her...   V

858 Told him
    ~~Told h~~ that...   Tn-39

862   &
    ...parting ~~foot~~step, held...   Tn-39

864 ...best   BM-2
864 (C)   73

868   & that ~~at~~ other
    ...this ~~1/2~~ world ~~to come~~   Tn-39

876 ...again   BM-2
876 (C)   L-II

675

Full often the bright image of one face,
Making a treacherous quiet in his heart,
Dispersed his resolution like a cloud.
Then if the maiden, while that ghostly grace   880
Beamèd on his fancy, spoke, he answered not,
Or short and coldly, and she knew right well
What the rough sickness meant, but what this meant
She knew not, and the sorrow dimmèd her sight,
And drave her ere her time across the fields   885
Far into the rich city, where alone
She murmured, 'Vain, in vain: it cannot be.
He will not love me: how then? must I die?'
Then as a little helpless innocent bird,

---

877 ...often the sweet image...		Tn-39
877 ...the sweet image of one face		BM-2
877 ...the sweet image of one face,		L-II
877 ...the sweet image...		F
877 (C)		73
878 ...heart		BM-2
878 (C)		L-II
880 ghostly grace		
...that s̸h̸a̸d̸o̸w̸y̸ f̸a̸c̸e̸		Tn-39
881 Beam'd on		
g̸l̸o̸w̸d̸ i̸n̸ his...		Tn-39
881 ...not		BM-2
881 (C)		L-II
887 ...murmur'd 'vain, ...		BM-2
887 (C)		73
888 ...die.'		BM-2
888 (C)		73
889 ...bird		BM-2
889 (C)		L-II
890 plain		
...one b̸r̸i̸e̸f̸ passage...		Tn-39
890 ...notes		BM-2
890 (C)		L-II

That has but one plain passage of few notes,   890
Will sing the simple passage o'er and o'er
For all an April morning, till the ear
Wearies to hear it, so the simple maid
Went half the night repeating, 'Must I die?'
And now to right she turned, and now to left,   895
And found no ease in turning or in rest;
And 'Him or death,' she mutterèd, 'death or him,'
Again and like a burthen, 'Him or death.'

But when Sir Lancelot's deadly hurt was whole,
To Astolat returning rode the three.   900
There morn by morn, arraying her sweet self

---

891 ...oer ~~again~~   Tn-39

894 ...repeating, 'must I...   BM-2
894 (C)   73

895   she turn'd
   ...right & now to left ~~she turn'd~~   Tn-39
895 ...turn'd and...left   BM-2
895 (C)   L-II

897 And 'him or death' she... him'   BM-2
897 And 'him or death' she...   59
897 (C)   73

898 ...burthen, 'him...   BM-2
898 (C)   73

899   ~~deadly~~
   ...Lancelot's ~~deathly~~ hurt...   Tn-39
899 ...Lancelot's hurt...   BM-2
899 (C)   L-II

901   morn   morn
   There ~~day~~ by ~~day~~ arraying...   Tn-39
901 ...morn arraying...   BM-2
901 (C)   L-II

In that wherein she deemed she looked her best,
She came before Sir Lancelot, for she thought
'If I be loved, these are my festal robes,
If not, the victim's flowers before he fall.'   905
And Lancelot ever prest upon the maid
That she should ask some goodly gift of him
For her own self or hers; 'and do not shun
To speak the wish most near to your true heart;
Such service have ye done me, that I make   910
My will of yours, and Prince and Lord am I
In mine own land, and what I will I can.'
Then like a ghost she lifted up her face,
But like a ghost without the power to speak.
And Lancelot saw that she withheld her wish,   915

---

902 ...best   BM-2
902 (C)   L-II

903   before Sir Lancelot
    ...came &̸ s̸t̸o̸o̸d̸ b̸e̸f̸o̸r̸e̸ h̸i̸m̸, for...   Tn-39

908 ...hers; and...   BM-2
908 (C)   L-II

909 ...heart   BM-2
909 (C)   L-II

Sketch c. 910
    So sd I all repay your service done
    When I was sick, & all your brother's love   V

910 ...me, that/̸ E̸l̸a̸i̸n̸e̸/̸ I...   Tn-39
910 ...have you done...   F
910 (C)   69

911   being
    ...yours & I̸ a̸m̸ Prince...   Tn-39
911 ...yours and...   BM-2
911 (C)   L-II

912   t̸h̸a̸t̸ w̸h̸
    ...land, &̸ w̸h̸a̸t̸ I̸...   Tn-39

LANCELOT AND ELAINE

Sketch c 913

    I speak to Lancelot not to little souls
Wretches who seem to me like little apes
Chuckling & boasting but to you who are great
Your   breaks my modesty
Where greatness ~~almost~~ (2 ?) - to whom
I need not seem the most unmaidenly
            living &
Of any maiden now alive - I say
I love you & I cannot hide my love
Have mercy on me
            (blot) with her glass
Took counsel & (blot) her sweet self
In that wherein she thought she lookd her best
So came to him whose heart was full of her
Who was not his & innocently said
    You are going: we shall never meet again
Have pity on me fair Sir Lancelot.
I must not die for want of effort made.
Not tho' I seem the most unmaidenly
Of any maiden living - yet are you
The noblest man alive - forgive me for it -
I know you are beyond me every way.
I love you ~~& I cannot hide~~ with no power to hide
        my love
No power to live if you sd say me nay
Have mercy one me: take me for your wife.
Then answer'd he - nay - nay it is a flash
(1 ?) maiden, merely - but a flash of youth.
Yourself will live to smile at your own self
And as for me, I never mean to wed.
(1 ?) you not wed she answered (2 ?) not
Then let me as your page, vassal or slave
Follow you thro' the world & wait on you.
That (1 ?) of the (commonplace ?) of -?- that beast
All ear & eye with such a (stupid ?) heart
To interpret its own eye & ear - the world
(3 ?) it do but damn us both   V

915 ...wish   BM-2
915 (C)   L-II

And bode among them yet a little space
Till he should learn it; and one morn it chanced
He found her in among the garden yews,
And said, 'Delay no longer, speak your wish,
Seeing I go today:' then out she brake: 920
'Going? and we shall never see you more.
And I must die for want of one bold word.'
'Speak: that I live to hear,' he said, 'is yours.'
Then suddenly and passionately she spoke:
'I have gone mad. I love you: let me die.'   925
'Ah, sister,' answered Lancelot, 'what is this?'
And innocently extending her white arms,

---

916 And there among them bode a little...   Tn-39
916 And there among them bode a little space BM-2
916 (C)   L-II

917 ...it, and...   BM-2
917 (C)   L-II

919 ...said 'delay...wish   BM-2
919 (C)   59

920 ...I must go...   Tn-39
920 Seeing I must go to-day:' ...brake.   BM-2
920 Seeing I must go to-day:' ...brake;   L-II
920 (C)   73

Sketch 921 ff
  You are going. I shall never see you more.
  I must not die for want of one bold word.
  Have mercy ~~on~~ ~~me~~, noble Lancelot, for I know
  I speak to Lancelot not to little souls,
  Monsters, who seem to me like little apes
  Chattering & chuckling - but to one so great
  His greatness breaks my modesty - to whom
  I need not seem the most unmaidenly
  Of any maiden living when I say
  I love you with no power to hide my love.
  No power to live if you deny me, lo!
  Have mercy on me. Then Sir Lancelot said   V

923 ...hear' he said 'is...   BM-2
923 (C)   59

'Your love,' she said, 'your love--to be your wife.'
And Lancelot answered, 'Had I chosen to wed,
I had been wedded earlier, sweet Elaine: 930
But now there never will be wife of mine.'
'No, no,' she cried, 'I care not to be wife,
But to be with you still, to see your face,
To serve you, and to follow you through the world.'
And Lancelot answered, 'Nay, the world, the world,   935

---

926 What would you have, my sister, what is this?   V
926 'Ah sister' answer'd Lancelot 'what is this,'   BM-2
926 'Ah sister' answer'd Lancelot 'what is this?'   L-II
926 'Ah sister,'...   59
926 (C)   70

927   innocently
    And p̷i̷t̷e̷o̷u̷s̷l̷y̷ extending...   Tn-39

928 Your love' she said your love make me your wife. V
928 ...love' she said 'your...   BM-2
928 (C)   59

929   had I chosen to
    Then answerd Lancelot I shall never wed   V
929 ...answer'd 'had...   BM-2
929 (C)   59

931 But now there
    F̷a̷i̷r̷ s̷i̷s̷t̷e̷r̷ never...   V

932 No wife? she said I care...   V
932 ...cried 'I...   BM-2
932 (C)   59

934 O let me then your page vassal or slave
    Follow you thro the world & wait on you   V
934 To w̷a̷i̷t̷ o̷n̷ serve you & to follow
    F̷o̷l̷l̷o̷w̷ you thro' the world/ & w̷a̷i̷t̷ o̷n̷ y̷o̷u̷   Tn-39

935 ...world, that beast   Tn-39
935 ...world, that beast,   BM-2
935 (C)   L-II

All ear and eye, with such a stupid heart
To interpret ear and eye, and such a tongue
To blare its own interpretation--nay,
Full ill then should I quit your brother's love,
And your good father's kindness.' And she said,   940
'Not to be with you, not to see your face--
Alas for me then, my good days are done.'
'Nay, noble maid,' he answered, 'ten times nay!
This is not love: but love's first flash in youth,
Most common: yea, I know it of mine own self: 945
And you yourself will smile at your own self

---

938 ...-nay	BM-2
938 (C)	L-II
939 ...love	BM-2
939 (C)	L-II
940 ...said	BM-2
940 (C)	73
943 ...maid, said Lancelot 'ten...	V
943 'Nay noble maid' he answer'd 'ten times nay	BM-2
943 'Nay noble maid' he answer'd 'ten times nay!	L-II
943 'Nay noble maid' he answer'd 'ten...	F
943 (C)	59

Alt. after 943 ~~Be happy many days good days are~~
~~yours~~   Tn-39

Sketch for 944
    ~~A flash of youth~~
    Nay noblemaid
    Be happy. this is love's first flash in youth
    Not ~~he~~ love himself & passes. Many days
    Many good days are yours   V
943-944 Nay nay and he it is a flash of youth   V
944 Live & be happy - this is love's first flash   V
944 ...youth   BM-2
944 (C)   L-II

Alt. after 944   no
    They leave one miserable enough but pass
    The sweet disease of gentle natures   V

LANCELOT AND ELAINE

Hereafter, when you yield your flower of life
To one more fitly yours, not thrice your age:
And then will I, for true you are and sweet
Beyond mine old belief in womanhood,   950

Sketch 945 ff
    Myself have had such flashes in my (1 ?) youth
    But you will live to love (blot) - another knight
    Then will I, damsel, should your knight be poor
    Endow him with broad land (1 ?)
    To keep you in all joyance   V

945 ...common. Yea I...self   BM-2
945 ...common. Yea I...self;   F
945 ...common: yea I...   59
945 (C)   73

946   will live   & I forsee
    That your own self will smile at your own self   V

947 Hereafter when you yield
    D̸e̸l̸i̸v̸e̸r̸i̸n̸g̸ u̸p̸ your flower of life t̸o̸ o̸n̸e̸   V
947 When you deliver your fair flower of life   V

948 To one, not thrice your age, some noble knight   V
Sketch 948 ff
    To one more fitly yours
    Not thrice your age. s̸o̸m̸e̸ n̸o̸b̸l̸e̸ k̸n̸i̸g̸h̸t̸
    And make me happy in your happiness
    For A̸n̸d̸ then will I for your good service done   V

Alt. after 948 I shall be happy in your happiness
            Then will   V

949 ...for you are true & sweet   Tn-39
949 ..., for you are true and sweet   BM-2
949 (C)   F

950   hood
    ...in womank̸i̸n̸d̸ -   Tn-39
950 ...womanhood -   BM-2
950 (C)   59

More specially should your good knight be poor,
Endow you with broad land and territory
Even to the half my realm beyond the seas,
So that would make you happy: furthermore,
Even to the death, as though ye were my blood,   955
In all your quarrels will I be your knight.
This will I do, dear damsel, for your sake,
And more than this I cannot.'

                    While he spoke
She neither blushed nor shook, but deathly-pale
Stood grasping what was nearest, then replied: 960
'Of all this will I nothing;' and so fell,
And thus they bore her swooning to her tower.

---

951 More specially sd he you love be poor	V	
952 Endow him with...	V	
954 To keep you all in joyance. furthermore	V	
954 If that...	Tn-39	
955 ...tho you were...	V	
955 ...tho' you were...	Tn-39	
955 (Same)	BM-2	
955 (C)	69	
957 ...your love	V	
957 ...sake	BM-2	
957 (C)	L-II	
958 and more...	BM-2	
958 (C)	L-II	
960 ...replied	BM-2	
960 ...replied;	L-II	
960 (C)	73	
961 ...nothing' and so fell	BM-2	
961 ...nothing' and so fell,	L-II	
961 ...nothing' and...	F	
961 (C)	59	

Then spake, to whom through those black walls of yew
Their talk had pierced, her father:'Ay, a flash,
I fear me, that will strike my blossom dead.   965
Too courteous are ye, fair Lord Lancelot.
I pray you, use some rough discourtesy
To blunt or break her passion.'

                              Lancelot said,
'That were against me: what I can I will;'
And there that day remained, and toward even   970
Sent for his shield: full meekly rose the maid,

963	(Par.) T̸h̸e̸n̸ s̸a̸i̸d̸ t̸h̸e̸ L̸o̸r̸d̸ o̸f̸ A̸s̸t̸o̸l̸a̸t̸ 'ay...	Tn-39
963	(No par. indent.)	BM-2
963	(C)	L-II

964	pierced	
	...had r̸e̸a̸c̸h̸d̸, her...	Tn-39
964	...father. 'Ay, a flash	BM-2
964	(C)	73

965	...my daughter dead.	Tn-39
965	...my daughter dead.	BM-2
965	(C)	F

966	For courteous...	BM-2
966	(C)	L-II
966	...are you, fair...	F
966	(C)	73

968	...said	BM-2
968	(C)	L-II

969	...will.'		BM-2
969	...will;'	;/ (I)	L-II
969	(C)		F

971	...shield, & meekly...		Tn-39
971	Sent in for his shield, and meekly rose the		
	maid		BM-2
971	full		I MS
	...shield; : a̸n̸d̸ meekly...	:/ (I)	L-II
971	(C)		F

Stript off the case, and gave the naked shield;
Then, when she heard his horse upon the stones,
Unclasping flung the casement back,and looked
Down on his helm, from which her sleeve had gone.   975
And Lancelot knew the little clinking sound;
And she by tact of love was well aware
That Lancelot knew that she was looking at him.
And yet he glanced not up, nor waved his hand,
Nor bad farewell, but sadly rode away.   980
This was the one discourtesy that he used.

So in her tower alone the maiden sat:
His very shield was gone; only the case,
Her own poor work, her empty labour, left.
But still she heard him, still his picture formed   985
And grew between her and the pictured wall.

972	...off her case...		Tn-39
972	Stript off her case and...shield.		BM-2
972	the		I MS
	...off h̸e̸r̸ case, and...	,/ (I)	L-II
972	(C)		F

973	...horse go on the stones		Tn-39
973	Then when...horse go on the stones		BM-2
973	(C)		L-II

975	...helm from...		BM-2
975	...helm, from...	(, I)	L-II
975	(C)		F

982	...sat:		BM-2
982	(C)		92

984	..., left:		BM-2
984	(C)		L-II

987	...father saying...tones		BM-2
987	...tones		59
987	(C)		73

988	...comfort' whom...		BM-2
988	(C)		59

Then came her father, saying in low tones,
'Have comfort,' whom she greeted quietly.
Then came her brethren saying, 'Peace to thee,
Sweet sister,' whom she answered with all calm.   990
But when they left her to herself again,
Death, like a friend's voice from a distant field
Approaching through the darkness, called; the owls
Wailing had power upon her, and she mixt
Her fancies with the sallow-rifted glooms   995
Of evening, and the moanings of the wind.

   And in those days she made a little song,
And called her song 'The Song of Love and Death,'
And sang it: sweetly could she make and sing.   999

   'Sweet is true love though given in vain, in vain;

------

989 ...saying 'Peace to thee   BM-2
989 (C)   73

990 ...sister' whom...calm;   BM-2
990 ...sister' whom...   L-II
990 (C)   59

992 ...friends fair voice   V

993 Approaching, thro' ...darkness call'd;...   BM-2
993 (C)   L-II

994 ...her and...   BM-2
994 (C)   L-II

997 (No par. indent.) ...song   BM-2
997 ...song   L-II
997 (C)   59

998   her   love
   ...call'd t̸h̸e̸ song 'the song of l̸i̸f̸e̸ & ...   Tn-39
998 ...and Death,   59
998 (C)   62

1000 ...l̸o̸v̸e̸ h̸o̸w̸e̸v̸e̸r̸ g̸i̸v̸e̸n̸ i̸n̸ v̸a̸i̸n̸   Tn-39
1000 (Par.) "Sweet...   BM-2
1000 (C)   70

And sweet is death who puts an end to pain:
I know not which is sweeter, no, not I.

   'Love, art thou sweet? then bitter death must be:
Love, thou art bitter; sweet is death to me.
O Love, if death be sweeter, let me die.   1005

   'Sweet love, that seems not made to fade away,
Sweet death, that seems to make us loveless clay,
I know not which is sweeter, no, not I.

1001 ...~~death that closes human pain~~   Tn-39

1003 (Par.) ~~If love be sweet how bitter~~...   Tn-39
1003 (Par.) Love...   BM-2
1003 (Par.) "Love...   "/ (I)   L-II
1003 (Par.) "Love...   F
1003 (C)   73

1004 If love be bitter, sweet...   Tn-39

1005 And if he call too sweetly
      And love is very bitter: let...   Tn-39

1006 (Par.) "Sweet...   BM-2
1006 (C)   70

1009   follow
      (Par.) Fain would I   love ~~& live~~, if...   Tn-39
1009 (Par.) I...   BM-2
1009 (Par.) "I...   "/ (I)   L-II
1009 (Par.) "I...   F
1009 (C)   70

Alt. after 1009
      But since I cannot sweet is death to me.
      Ah death & love too bitter; let me die   Tn-39

1010 Yet must I follow...   Tn-39
1010 ...death who...   BM-2
1010 (C)   L-II

'I fain would follow love, if that could be;
I needs must follow death, who calls for me;   1010
Call and I follow, I follow! let me die.'

   High with the last line scaled her voice, and this,
All in a fiery dawning wild with wind
That shook her tower, the brothers heard, and thought
With shuddering, 'Hark the Phantom of the house   1015
That ever shrieks before a death,' and called
The father, and all three in hurry and fear

1011	...follow - let...die."	BM-2
1011	...die."	F
1011	(C)	70
1012	...this	BM-2
1012	(C)	L-II
1013	in fiery dawning wild	
	All ~~on~~ a ~~stormy~~ ~~morning~~ ~~red~~ with wind	Tn-39
1014	her	
	...shook ~~the~~ tower...heard ~~her~~ ~~sing~~; & said	Tn-39
1014	...heard and said	BM-2
1014	thought	I MS
	...heard, and ~~said~~	L-II
1014	(C)	F
1015	With	
	~~In~~ ~~whispers~~	
	~~And~~ shuddering...	Tn-39
1015	...shuddering 'Hark...	BM-2
1015	(C)	73
1016	&	
	...death' ~~they~~ call'd	Tn-39
1016	...death' and...	BM-2
1016	(C)	L-II
1017	...father and...	BM-2
1017	(C)	L-II

Ran to her, and lo! the blood-red light of dawn
Flared on her face, she shrilling, 'Let me die!'

As when we dwell upon a word we know,   1020
Repeating, till the word we know so well
Becomes a wonder, and we know not why,
So dwelt the father on her face, and thought
'Is this Elaine?' till back the maiden fell,
Then gave a languid hand to each, and lay,   1025
Speaking a still good-morrow with her eyes.

1018 Ran to her, bloodred	
~~Enter'd~~ & lo! the ~~red and stormy~~ light...	Tn-39
1018 ...bloodred	BM-2
1018 (C)	73
1019 ...shrilling 'Let...	BM-2
1019 (C)	73
1020 ...know	BM-2
1020 (C)	73
1021 In reading or repeating...	Tn-39
1022 ~~We know not why~~ becomes a wonder ~~to us~~ & we	Tn-39
1022 ...wonder and...	BM-2
1022 (C)	73
1023 ...face and...	BM-2
1023 (C)	73
1024 ...Elaine? & back...	Tn-39
1024 ...Elaine?' and back...fell	BM-2
1024 till	I MS
...Elaine?' ~~and~~ back...	L-II
1024 (C)	F
1025 ...lay	BM-2
1025 (C)	L-II
1027 Sweet brothers, while I lay last night awake	
The pleasant holy days wherein ye took	V
1027 ..said 'Sweet...	BM-2
1027 (C)	73

At last she said, 'Sweet brothers, yesternight
I seemed a curious little maid again,
As happy as when we dwelt among the woods,
And when ye used to take me with the flood   1030
Up the great river in the boatman's boat.
Only ye would not pass beyond the cape
That has the poplar on it: there ye fixt
Your limit, oft returning with the tide.
And yet I cried because ye would not pass   1035

1028 & row me then a little maid
      were delightful to me   V
1028 ...again   BM-2
1028 (C)   L-II

1029-1030 A̸s̸ h̸a̸p̸p̸y̸ a̸s̸ w̸h̸e̸n̸ y̸e̸ t̸o̸o̸k̸ m̸e̸ w̸i̸t̸h̸ t̸h̸e̸
                              f̸l̸o̸o̸d̸   Tn-39

1030 ...when you used...   F
1030 (C)   69

1031 ...river: merrily went the boat   Tn-39
1031 ...river: merrily went the boat   BM-2
1031 ...river: merrily went the boat.   L-II
1031 (C)   F

1032 Only ye never past the little cape   V
1032 Only you would...   F
1032 (C)   69

1033 ...there you fixt   Tn-39
1033 ...there you fixt   BM-2
1033 (C)   69

1034 The limit...   V

1035 Tho oft I cried...   V
1035 And yet I
     I̸ o̸f̸t̸e̸n̸ cried:..   Tn-39
1035 ...because you would...   F
1035 (C)   69

LANCELOT AND ELAINE

Beyond it, and far up the shining flood
Until we found the palace of the King.
And yet ye would not; but this night I dreamed
That I was all alone upon the flood,
And then I said, "Now shall I have my will:"   1040
And there I woke, but still the wish remained.
So let me hence that I may pass at last
Beyond the poplar and far up the flood,
Until I find the palace of the King.
There will I enter in among them all,   1045
And no man there will dare to mock at me;

1036-37 Go on & see the palace of the King.   V

1036 ...it and...   BM-2
1036 (C)   L-II

1037 ...the king.   BM-2
1037 (C)   73

1038 And so last night I dreamed I was (alone ?)   V
1038 ...yet you would...   F
1038 (C)   <u>69</u>

1039 There in the boat & to myself I said   V

1040 Now will I have my wish: & there I woke   V
1040 ...said 'Now...will:'   BM-2
1040 ...said "Now...   59
1040 (C)   73

1041 And made resolve that I wd go alone   V

1042 ...I to may pass...   V

1043   far
     Beyond the poplar c̸a̸p̸e̸ & up the r̸e̸a̸c̸h̸ flood   V

1044 ...the king.   BM-2
1044 (C)   73

1045 ...enter in before them all   V

692

But there the fine Gawain will wonder at me,
And there the great Sir Lancelot muse at me;
Gawain, who bad a thousand farewells to me,
Lancelot, who coldly went, nor bad me one: 1050
And there the King will know me and my love,
And there the Queen herself will pity me,
And all the gentle court will welcome me,
And after my long voyage I shall rest!'

   'Peace,' said her father, 'O my child, ye seem   1055
Light-headed, for what force is yours to go

1046 And there is none will dare to laugh at me		V
1046 man mock		
And t̸h̸e̸r̸e̸ i̸s̸ n̸o̸n̸e̸ no o̸n̸e̸ there...to l̸a̸u̸g̸h̸		
at...		Tn-39
1046 ...me,		BM-2
1046 (C)		L-II

1047 And there the Prince Gawain will look at me	V

1048 And the great Sir Lancelot gaze upon me	V
1048 ...at me,	BM-2
1048 (C)	L-II

1049 Gawain who...	BM-2
1049 (C)	L-II

1050 ...went nor...one.	BM-2
1050 ...went nor...	L-II
1050 (C)	73

1051 there himself will hear me speak	
And t̸h̸e̸ K̸i̸n̸g̸ &̸ court will welcome me	
all the gentle	V

1055 (Par.) 'Peace' said her father 'O my child!	
ye seem	BM-2
1055 (Par.) 'Peace' said her father 'O my child,	
you seem	F
1055 ...child, you seem	59
1055 (C)	<u>69</u>

1056 ...to go,	BM-2
1056 (C)	73

So far, being sick? and wherefore would ye look
On this proud fellow again, who scorns us all?'

   Then the rough Torre began to heave and move,
And bluster into stormy sobs and say,   1060
'I never loved him: an I meet with him,
I care not howsoever great he be,
Then will I strike at him and strike him down,
Give me good fortune, I will strike him dead,

1057 So far, being	
~~Béìng~~ ~~sò~~ sick? ...	Tn-39
1057 ...would you look	F
1057 (C)	<u>69</u>
1059 Then suddenly the rough Sir Torre began	V
1059 heave &	
...began to move ~~himself~~	Tn-39
1060 To make a sobbing tumult by the bed.	V
1060 stormy	
...into ~~wrathful~~ sobs...	Tn-39
1060 ...say.	BM-2
1060 ...say	67
1060 (C)	73
1061 I never loved him	
Alt. after 1061 I hated him at first - fine fair & false	
the greatest	
Too fine for me - a great knight [so]	
they say	V
1062 I care not howsoever great a knight	V
1062 ...he be	BM-2
1062 (C)	L-II
Alt after 1062 But if I meet him [an anywhere	V
1063 down,	
...him ~~dead~~	Tn-39
1063 ...down,	BM-2
1063 (C)	73

For this discomfort he hath done the house.'   1065

    To whom the gentle sister made reply,
'Fret not yourself, dear brother, nor be wroth,
Seeing it is no more Sir Lancelot's fault
Not to love me, than it is mine to love
Him of all men who seems to me the highest.'   1070

    'Highest?' the father answered, echoing 'highest?'
(He meant to break the passion in her) 'nay,

1064	God give me fortune!] I will strike at him	V
1064	...dead	BM-2
1064	(C)	L-II
1065	I care not how	
	For this discomfort he has done...	V
1066	(Par.) To which the...reply	BM-2
1066	(Par.) To which the...	59
1066	(C)	73
1068	Seeing it is no more the fault of Sir Lancelot's	
	Because fault	V

1070 (Par.) 𝘛𝘰 𝘵𝘩𝘪𝘴 𝘩𝘦𝘳 𝘧𝘢𝘵𝘩𝘦𝘳 𝘢𝘯𝘴𝘸𝘦𝘳'𝘥 𝘲𝘶𝘪𝘤𝘬𝘭𝘺 'highest?'
                     echo'd
   Her father caught the word & 𝘢𝘯𝘴𝘸𝘦𝘳'𝘥 'highest?

			Tn-39
1070	...highest'		BM-2
1070	. .highest.'	☉/ (I)	L-II
1070	(C)		F
1071	Then said the Lord of Astolat Highest nay		V
1071	(No par. indent.) Her father caught the word and		
	echo'd, 'highest?'		BM-2
1071	(Par.) 'Highest?' the Baron answer'd, echoing/		
	'highest?' (1st, I)		L-II
1071	...the Father...		F
1071	(C)		73
1072	...'nay		BM-2
1072	(C)		L-II

Daughter, I know not what you call the highest;
But this I know, for all the people know it,
He loves the Queen, and in an open shame: 1075
And she returns his love in open shame;
If this be high, what is it to be low?'

   Then spake the lily maid of Astolat:
'Sweet father, all too faint and sick am I
For anger: these are slanders: never yet   1080
Was noble man but made ignoble talk.
He makes no friend who never made a foe.
But now it is my glory to have loved
One peerless,without stain: so let me pass,
My father, howsoe'er I seem to you,   1085

1073 at	
...not whom ye call...	V
1073 ...what ye call...	Tn-39
1073 ...what ye call...highest,	BM-2
1073 ...what ye call...	L-II
1073 (C)	F
1074 But this I know & this $t̸h̸e̸$ is known to all -	V
1074 ...know for...it	BM-2
1074 (C)	L-II
1075-76 He loved the Queen & she returns his love	
Why need I speak it is an open shame.	V
1075 & in	
...Queen, $i̸t̸$ $i̸s̸$ an...	Tn-39
1076 his love in	
...returns $i̸t̸$ $i̸s̸$ $a̸n̸$ open...	Tn-39
1076 ...shame.	BM-2
1076 ...shame:	62
1076 (C)	75
1078 Softly the daughter answer'd Speak not this	V
1078 ...Astolat	BM-2
1078 ...Astolat;	L-II
1078 (C)	73
1079 Sweet father $I̸$ $a̸m̸$ all too sick & faint am I	V

696

Not all unhappy, having loved God's best
And greatest, though my love had no return:
Yet, seeing you desire your child to live,
Thanks, but you work against your own desire;
For if I could believe the things you say   1090
I should but die the sooner; wherefore cease,
Sweet father, and bid call the ghostly man

1080   know   aim   is (blot)
    For anger & I see your ~~strife~~ to link
    And (blot)
    My passion - these are slanders ~~of the court~~
                                    never yet   V

1083 But now
    It is my glory to have loved ~~a knight~~   V

1084 One
    Peerless without a stain~~less~~ so let me pass   V
1084 ...stain; so...   BM-2
1084 (C)   L-II

1086 ...having ~~worthily~~ loved the best   V

1088   seeing   your child to live
    And ~~thanks~~ for ~~truly if~~ you desire ~~my life~~   V
1088 Yet
    ~~And~~, seeing...   Tn-39
1088 ...live   BM-2
1088 (C)   L-II

1089 Thanks ~~to live~~ but you work...   V

1092 ff Sweet father, let me shrive me clean & die.
        Hither &   & bid call a ghostly man
        Doubtless - and I have heard it - he hath fought
        In the Queen's guard as he would ~~in mine~~ have
                        done
        Doubtless in mine (when we had no return?)   V

1092   the
    ...call ~~a~~ ghostly...   Tn-39

697

Hither, and let me shrive me clean, and die.'

   So when the ghostly man had come and gone,
She with a face, bright as for sin forgiven,   1095
Besought Lavaine to write as she devised
A letter, word for word; and when he asked
'Is it for Lancelot, is it for my dear lord?
Then will I bear it gladly;' she replied,
'For Lancelot and the Queen and all the world,   1100
But I myself must bear it.' Then he wrote
The letter she devised; which being writ
And folded, 'O sweet father, tender and true,
Deny me not,' she said--'ye never yet
Denied my fancies--this, however strange,   1105
My latest: lay the letter in my hand
A little ere I die, and close the hand
Upon it; I shall guard it even in death.
And when the heat is gone from out my heart,

1094 ...the H̸ø̸l̸y̸ ghostly...	Tn-39
1098 ...Lancelot,' is...lord	BM-2
1098 (C)	L-II
1099 ...gladly' she replied.	BM-2
1099 (C)	L-II
1101 ...it;' then he...	BM-2
1101 ...it:' then he...	L-II
1101 (C)	F
1104 ...said - 'you never...	Tn-39
1104 ...said - 'you never...	BM-2
1104 ...said - you never...	59
1104 ...said - 'you never...	62
1104 (C)	<u>69</u>
1106 the	
...lay t̸h̸i̸s̸ letter...	Tn-39
1116 ...black,	BM-2
1116 ...black/. ⊙ (I)	L-II
1116 (C)	F

Then take the little bed on which I died   1110
For Lancelot's love, and deck it like the Queen's
For richness, and me also like the Queen
In all I have of rich, and lay me on it.
And let there be prepared a chariot-bier
To take me to the river, and a barge   1115
Be ready on the river, clothed in black.
I go in state to court, to meet the Queen.
There surely I shall speak for mine own self,
And none of you can speak for me so well.
And therefore let our dumb old man alone   1120
Go with me, he can steer and row, and he
Will guide me to that palace, to the doors.'

    She ceased: her father promised; whereupon
She grew so cheerful that they deemed her death
Was rather in the fantasy than the blood.   1125
But ten slow mornings past, and on the eleventh

1117 ~~And this way will~~ I...   Tn-39
1117 ...Queen   BM-2
1117 ...Queen~~/~~ .   ⊙ (I)   L-II
1117 (C)   F

1118 ...self   BM-2
1118 (C)   L-II

1120 So let our deaf & dumb...   Tn-39
1120 So let our deaf and dumb old man alone   BM-2
1120 (C)   F

1122 ...guide to...   Tn-39
1122   me
   ...guide to ...   BM-2
1122 (C)   L-II

1123   ceased
   (Par.) she ~~said~~: her...   Tn-39
   ~~seem'd~~   ~~hoped~~
1124 She grew so...they deem'd her...   Tn-39

1125   the   ye
   ...in ~~her~~ fantasy than ~~indeed her~~ blood.   Tn-39

Her father laid the letter in her hand,
And closed the hand upon it, and she died.
So that day there was dole in Astolat.

But when the next sun brake from underground,   1130
Then, those two brethren slowly with bent brows
Accompanying, the sad chariot-bier
Past like a shadow through the field, that shone
Full-summer, to that stream whereon the barge,
Palled all its length in blackest samite, lay.   1135
There sat the lifelong creature of the house,
Loyal, the dumb old servitor, on deck,
Winking his eyes, and twisted all his face.
So those two brethren from the chariot took
And on the black decks laid her in her bed,   1140
Set in her hand a lily, o'er her hung
The silken case with braided blazonings,

1130 ...underground   BM-2
1130 (C)   59

1131 So, those two bretheren with bent heads   V

1132 ...the dark chariot-bier   V

1133 ...thro' the ɣ⃥a⃥n⃥d⃥ field that...   V
1133 ...the fields that:..   BM-2
1133 (C)   L-II

1134 Full summer, ...   BM-2
1134 (C)   L-II

1139 Then those...   V

1146 ...rose the deaf old...   Tn-39
1146 ...rose the deaf old...dead   BM-2
1146 ...dead.   L-II
1146 (C)   73

1147 Steer'd by the deaf went...   Tn-39
1147 Steer'd by the deaf went...   BM-2
1147 Steer'd by the dumb went...   L-II
1147 ...dumb went...   F
1147 Steer'd by the dumb went...   59
1147 (C)   73

And kissed her quiet brows, and saying to her
'Sister, farewell for ever,' and again
'Farewell, sweet sister,' parted all in tears.   1145
Then rose the dumb old servitor, and the dead,
Oared by the dumb, went upward with the flood--
In her right hand the lily, in her left
The letter--all her bright hair streaming down--
And all the coverlid was cloth of gold   1150
Drawn to her waist, and she herself in white
All but her face, and that clear-featured face
Was lovely, for she did not seem as dead,
But fast asleep, and lay as though she smiled.

That day Sir Lancelot at the palace craved   1155
Audience of Guinevere, to give at last
The price of half a realm, his costly gift,
Hard-won and hardly won with bruise and blow,
With deaths of others, and almost his own,
The nine-years-fought-for diamonds: for he saw   1160
One of her house, and sent him to the Queen
Bearing his wish, whereto the Queen agreed
With such and so unmoved a majesty
She might have seemed her statue, but that he,
Low-drooping till he wellnigh kissed her feet   1165
For loyal awe, saw with a sidelong eye

1153 ...dead		BM-2
1153 (C)		73
1155 ...palace, craved		BM-2
1155 ...palace⁄ craved	(I)	L-II
1155 (C)		F
1157 H̷i̷s̷ c̷o̷s̷t̷l̷y̷ g̷i̷f̷t̷ the price...		Tn-39
1158 ...hardly-won...blow		BM-2
1158 ...hardly⁄won...	(I)	L-II
1158 (C)		F
1159 With		
T̷h̷e̷ deaths...		Tn-39
1166 saw		
...awe, b̷e̷h̷e̷l̷d̷ with...		Tn-39

LANCELOT AND ELAINE

The shadow of some piece of pointed lace,
In the Queen's shadow, vibrate on the walls,
And parted, laughing in his courtly heart.

All in an oriel on the summer side,   1170
Vine-clad, of Arthur's palace toward the stream,
They met, and Lancelot kneeling uttered, 'Queen,
Lady, my liege, in whom I have my joy,
Take, what I had not won except for you,
These jewels, and make me happy, making them   1175
An armlet for the roundest arm on earth,
Or necklace for a neck to which the swan's
Is tawnier than her cygnet's: these are words:
Your beauty is your beauty, and I sin
In speaking, yet O grant my worship of it   1180
Words, as we grant grief tears. Such sin in words

1167   ~~piec~~
       ...shadow of a piece...   Tn-39
1167 ...of a piece...lace   BM-2
1167 ...of a piece...lace,   ,/ (I)   L-II
1167 ...of a piece...   F
1167 (C)   73

1170-1172 That day Sir Lancelot & the stately Queen
          Met, for an audience ~~by~~ asked by Lancelot,
          All in an oriel on the summer side,
          Vine clad, of Arthur's palace toward the
                    stream.   V

1172 ...Lancelot first bespake her '(1 ?), Queen,   Tn-39
1172 ...Lancelot first bespake her, 'Queen,   BM-2
1172 (C)   L-II

1174 Take what...you   BM-2
1174 (C)   59

1175   them
     ...making ~~these~~   Tn-39

1178 ...cygnet's : these...   BM-2
1178 (C)   L-II

702

Perchance, we both can pardon: but, my Queen,
I hear of rumours flying through your court.
Our bond, as not the bond of man and wife,
Should have in it an absoluter trust   1185
To make up that defect: let rumours be:
When did not rumours fly? these, as I trust
That you trust me in your own nobleness,
I may not well believe that you believe.'

    While thus he spoke, half turned away, the
                         Queen   1190
Brake from the vast oriel-embowering vine
Leaf after leaf, and tore, and cast them off,
Till all the place whereon she stood was green;
Then, when he ceased, in one cold passive hand
Received at once and laid aside the gems   1195

1179 ...beauty and...		BM-2
1179 ...beauty, and...	,/ (I)	L-II
1179 (C)		F

1186 ...defect. let...	BM-2
1186 (C)	L-II

1191   em
    ...the vast &x̸ Oriel - bowering vine   Tn-39

1192 ...them o̸f̸f̸ down	Tn-39
1192 ...cast them down	BM-2
1192 off,	I MS
...cast them d̸o̸w̸n̸	L-II
1192 (C)	F

1193 ...green:		BM-2
1193 ...green;	;/ (I)	L-II
1193 (C)		F

1194 Then   he ceased   one cold passive
    A̸n̸d̸ when h̸i̸s̸ v̸o̸i̸c̸e̸ w̸a̸s̸ s̸i̸l̸e̸n̸t̸, in h̸e̸r̸ hand   Tn-39
1194 Then when...   BM-2
1194 (C)   F

1195   at once
    Received & c̸o̸l̸d̸l̸y̸ laid...   Tn-39

There on a table near her, and replied:

'It may be, I am quicker of belief
Than you believe me, Lancelot of the Lake.
Our bond is not the bond of man and wife.
This good is in it, whatsoe'er of ill,   1200
It can be broken easier. I for you
This many a year have done despite and wrong
To one whom ever in my heart of hearts
I did acknowledge nobler. What are these?
Diamonds for me! they had been thrice their worth   1205
Being your gift, had you not lost your own.
To loyal hearts the value of all gifts
Must vary as the giver's. Not for me!

1196 ...her & return'd.		Tn-39
1196 ...and return'd.		BM-2
1196 ...and replied.		L-II
1196 ...and replied;		73
1196 (C)		75

1197   quicker
    ...am éásiér of...   Tn-39

1200 That good...whatsoever ill   V

1201 It can be broken with more ease. farewell: V

1202 Have I for you, my lord, so many years   V

1203 Done wrong to him whom in my heart of hearts   V

1204 It still acknowledge nobler? fare you well.
     Diamonds   V

1205 they had been thrice their worth   V

1207 But to true souls the value of the gifts   V
1207 To loyal   value of all
     Búť ťó ťrúé hearts the wórťh óf ány giftś   Tn-39

1208 ...giver's: not...   BM-2
1208 (C)   L-II

704

For her! for your new fancy. Only this
Grant me, I pray you: have your joys apart.   1210
I doubt not that however changed, you keep
So much of what is graceful: and myself
Would shun to break those bounds of courtesy

1209 Give them to your new fancy, noble knight
    You   V
1209 Give them to your new fancy, noble knight
    You truest lover of a sinful man   V
1209-1210 Give them to your new fancy, only this
    I pray you, grant me: have your joys
        apart   Tn-39
1209-1210 For your new fancy, only grant me this
    I pray you: have your new delights
        apart   Tn-39
1209-1210 For your new fancy: but I know of you
    Keep her apart away: it is not for her health
    Not mine, not yours, however brave you be/
    To bring her hither. Have your joys/apart.
                       Tn-39

1210 ff grant/me/ I pray you
    I pray you, grant me: have your joys apart/
    It was not for her health/, not mine, not yours/
    To bring her hither. I/ that who knew you once/
    Doubt not that &   Tn-39
1209 ...fancy: only...   BM-2
1209 (C)   L-II

1210 ...apart: BM-2
1210 (C)   L-II

1211 I trust
    I doubt/not
    I trust that howsoever changed...   Tn-39
1211 I trust that howsoever changed, ...   BM-2
1211 (C)   L-II

1212 So much
    Some touch of what is graceful: so for me/and...
                         Tn-39

1213 Wd shun to
    I must not break...   Tn-39

In which as Arthur's Queen I move and rule:
So cannot speak my mind. An end to this!   1215
A strange one! yet I take it with Amen.
So pray you, add my diamonds to her pearls;
Deck her with these; tell her, she shines me down:
An armlet for an arm to which the Queen's
Is haggard, or a necklace for a neck   1220
O as much fairer--as a faith once fair
Was richer than these diamonds--hers not mine--
Nay, by the mother of our Lord himself,
Or hers or mine, mine now to work my will--
She shall not have them.'

1214 ...& ƙḝíǥń rule   Tn-39
1214 ...Arthur's queen I...   F
1214 (C)   73

Sketch C 1215
    I cannot speak my mind. an end to this
    O me. But I had not lookd for such an end
    But since it comes I like it. let it be.
    Nay   V

1215 ...mind: an...this.   BM-2
1215 (C)   L-II

Alt. after 1215 ƮƴÞé ƫḥáƫ Í ṣ́ćáƴćé ḥáḋ ĺóόƙƴḋ ƒόƴ ṣ́ύćḥ
                       áń ćńḋ   Tn-39

1216 A strange one, yet
        Ḃύƫ ṣ́íńćé íƫ ćόḿé/ I...   Tn-39
1216 ...one, yet...   BM-2
1216 (C)   L-II

1217 I pray you add my diamonds to her pearls   V

1218 ff Deck her with these tell her she ẅíĺĺ shines me
                            down
            Nay by
            The much experienc'd
            Then must you needs disparage me now Queen (?)
            She laughs your praise of ruder innocence   V
1218 You let her wear them, let her shine me down   V
1218 ...down.   BM-2
1218 (C)   L-II

706

Saying which she seized,   1225
And, through the casement standing wide for heat,
Flung them, and down they flashed, and smote the
                    stream.
Then from the smitten surface flashed, as it were,
Diamonds to meet them, and they past away.
Then while Sir Lancelot leant, in half disdain   1230
At love, life, all things, on the window ledge,

1219 O as much fairer - as your faith was there -
      If I go on I shall (dispare ?) my duty. (1 ?)   V

1221 O as much fairer as a faith once fair
      ~~O~~ ~~as~~ ~~much~~ ~~whiter~~ ~~/~~ ~~to~~ ~~they~~ ~~are~~ ~~hers~~ ~~not~~
                        ~~mine~~ ~~/~~   Tn-39
1221 ...fairer as...   BM-2
1221 ...fairer - as...   -/ (I)   L-II
1221 (C)   F

1224 Nay, by the mother of our Lord Himself   V

Sketch 1224 ~~hers~~ ~~they~~ ~~may~~ ~~be~~   Tn-39

1225 She shall not either.
               Saying this she siezed   V

1226 And thro' the open casement flung the gems   V
1226 And thro' ...heat   BM-2
1226 (C)   L-II

1227 Down flashd the diamonds till they smote
                        the stream   V

1228 And from...   V

1230   Sir Lancelot
     ...while ~~he~~ leant, in half disgust ~~at~~ ~~love~~   Tn-39
1230 ...leant, in half disgust   BM-2
1230 (C)   73

1231 At love
     ~~And~~ life, ~~&~~ all...   Tn-39

Close underneath his eyes, and right across
Where these had fallen, slowly past the barge
Whereon the lily maid of Astolat
Lay smiling, like a star in blackest night.   1235

   But the wild Queen, who saw not, burst away
To weep and wail in secret; and the barge,
On to the palace-doorway sliding, paused.
There two stood armed, and kept the door; to whom,
All up the marble stair, tier over tier,   1240
Were added mouths that gaped, and eyes that asked
'What is it?' but the oarsman's haggard face,
As hard and still as is the face that men

1232 ...eyes and...	BM-2
1232 (C)	L-II
1233 ...fallen slowly...	BM-2
1233 (C)	L-II
1236 (No par. indent.)	BM-2
1236 (C)	L-II
1239 ...to these	Tn-39
1239 ...door; to these,	BM-2
1239 (C)	L-II
1242 ...face	BM-2
1242 (C)	59
1244 ...their fancy out of broken...	Tn-39
1244 ...their fancy out of broken...	BM-2
1244 (C)	L-II
1245 ...them and...said	BM-2
1245 ...them and...	L-II
1245 (C)	59
1246 ...e̶n̶c̶h̶a̶n̶t̶e̶d̶,̶ ̶I̶o̶ ̶h̶e̶ ̶c̶a̶n̶n̶o̶t̶ ̶s̶p̶e̶a̶k̶,̶	Tn-39
1246 ...she	BM-2
1246 (C)	L-II

Sketch C. 1247
   And she, how fast she sleeps! what is it? truth

Shape to their fancy's eye from broken rocks
On some cliff-side, appalled them, and they said,   1245
'He is enchanted, cannot speak--and she,
Look how she sleeps--the Fairy Queen, so fair!
Yea, but how pale! what are they? flesh and blood?
Or come to take the King to Fairyland?
For some do hold our Arthur cannot die,   1250
But that he passes into Fairyland.'

Sketch C. 1247 (continued)
    Or glamour? fairies come for fairyland
    To fetch the king to Avalon   Tn-28

1248 Yea, but   flesh & blood?
    A̶n̶d̶ y̶e̶t̶ how...they? h̶u̶m̶a̶n̶? n̶a̶y̶!   Tn-39

1249 Or
    T̶h̶e̶y̶ come...   Tn-39
1249 ...the king to fairy land?   BM-2
1249 ...to fairy land?   59
1249 ...to fairyland?   73
1249 (C)   84

1250   do   our Arthur
    For some t̶h̶e̶r̶e̶ b̶e̶ t̶h̶a̶t̶ hold h̶e̶ cannot die,   Tn-39

1251   that he passes
    But g̶o̶e̶s̶ t̶o̶ A̶v̶a̶l̶o̶n̶, into fairy land.'   Tn-39
1251 ...into fairy land.'   BM-2
1251 ...into fairyland.'   73
1251 (C)   84

Alt. after 1251
    'A̶n̶d̶ w̶h̶a̶t̶ i̶s̶ A̶v̶a̶l̶o̶n̶? A̶v̶a̶l̶o̶n̶ i̶s̶ a̶n̶ i̶s̶l̶e̶
    A̶l̶l̶ m̶a̶d̶e̶ o̶f̶ a̶p̶p̶l̶e̶ b̶l̶o̶s̶s̶o̶m̶ i̶n̶ t̶h̶e̶ w̶e̶s̶t̶,
    A̶n̶d̶ a̶l̶l̶ t̶h̶e̶ w̶i̶n̶d̶s̶ a̶r̶e̶ f̶r̶a̶g̶r̶a̶n̶t̶, & t̶h̶e̶ w̶a̶v̶e̶s̶
    A̶b̶o̶u̶t̶ i̶t̶/&/t̶h̶e̶ f̶a̶i̶r̶i̶e̶s̶ l̶i̶v̶e̶ u̶p̶o̶n̶ i̶t̶!
    A̶n̶d̶ t̶h̶e̶r̶e̶ a̶r̶e̶ t̶h̶o̶s̶e̶ h̶a̶v̶e̶ s̶e̶e̶n̶ i̶t̶ f̶a̶r̶ a̶w̶a̶y̶
    S̶h̶i̶n̶e̶ l̶i̶k̶e̶ a̶ r̶o̶s̶e̶ u̶p̶o̶n̶ t̶h̶e̶ s̶u̶m̶m̶e̶r̶ s̶e̶a̶,
    A̶n̶d̶ t̶h̶i̶t̶h̶e̶r̶ g̶o̶e̶s̶ t̶h̶e̶ K̶i̶n̶g̶, & t̶h̶e̶n̶c̶e̶ r̶e̶t̶u̶r̶n̶s̶
    [̶F̶o̶r̶ s̶o̶ t̶h̶e̶y̶ s̶a̶y̶ t̶h̶a̶t̶ M̶e̶r̶l̶i̶n̶ s̶a̶i̶d̶]̶/t̶o̶ r̶u̶l̶e̶
    H̶e̶r̶e̶a̶f̶t̶e̶r̶, f̶o̶r̶ s̶o̶m̶e̶ h̶o̶l̶d̶ t̶h̶a̶t̶ M̶e̶r̶l̶i̶n̶ h̶e̶l̶d̶,
    I̶ k̶n̶o̶w̶ t̶h̶e̶ m̶a̶n̶, t̶h̶a̶t̶ A̶r̶t̶h̶u̶r̶ c̶a̶n̶n̶o̶t̶ d̶i̶e̶.'   Tn-39

LANCELOT AND ELAINE

While thus they babbled of the King, the King
Came girt with knights: then turned the tongueless
                      man
From the half-face to the full eye, and rose
And pointed to the damsel, and the doors.   1255
So Arthur bad the meek Sir Percivale
And pure Sir Galahad to uplift the maid;
And reverently they bore her into hall.
Then came the fine Gawain and wondered at her,
And Lancelot later came and mused at her,   1260
And last the Queen herself, and pitied her:
But Arthur spied the letter in her hand,
Stoopt, took, brake seal, and read it; this was all:

1252 ...the king, the king	BM-2
1252 (C)	59
1253 Come girt...	BM-2
1253 (C)	L-II
1260 2 1	
And later Lancelot came...	Tn-39
1261 ...herself and...	BM-2
1261 (C)	73
1263 ...all.	BM-2
1263 (C)	73
1264 (No par. indent.) ...the lake,	BM-2
1264 ...the lake,	L-II
1264 (C)	59
1265 sometime fair	
I ~~whom~~ ~~men~~ ~~called~~ the Maid of Astolat	V
1265 I sometime...Astolat	BM-2
1265 (C)	L-II
1266 Come, for ye ~~not~~ ~~taking~~ ~~leave~~ ~~of~~ ~~me~~ left me...	V
1266 ...for ye left...	BM-2
1266 (C)	F
1267 Thither to take my ~~latest~~ ~~leave~~ of you.	
last farewell	V

'Most noble lord, Sir Lancelot of the Lake,
I, sometime called the maid of Astolat,   1265
Come, for you left me taking no farewell,
Hither, to take my last farewell of you.
I loved you, and my love had no return,
And therefore my true love has been my death.
And therefore to our Lady Guinevere,   1270
And to all other ladies, I make moan:
Pray for my soul, and yield me burial.
Pray for my soul thou too, Sir Lancelot,
As thou art a knight peerless.'

                              Thus he read;
And ever in the reading, lords and dames   1275
Wept, looking often from his face who read

1268 I loved you, & you answerd not my love had
                         no return
     ~~I~~ ~~loved~~ ~~&~~ ~~my~~ love has been my death   V

1270 ...our lady Guinevere,   BM-2
1270 (C)   73

1271 And therefore my true
     And ~~I~~ therefore to all ladies make my moan   V
1271 ...moan.   BM-2
1271 (C)   92

1272 ...soul & give me...   V

Alt. after 1272
     ~~I~~ ~~take~~ ~~my~~ ~~God~~ ~~to~~ ~~witness~~ ~~that~~ ~~I~~ ~~died~~
     ~~A~~ ~~maiden~~ ~~clean~~ ~~in~~ ~~heart~~ ~~&~~ ~~deed~~   V

1274 ~~this~~ ~~was~~ ~~all~~
     this he read;   V
1274 ...read,   BM-2
1274 (C)   73

1275   ever
     And   in the reading ~~of~~ ~~it~~ lords & Dames   V
1275 ...reading, Lords and Dames   BM-2
1275 (C)   59

1276 ...for ye left...   Tn-39

To hers which lay so silent, and at times,
So touched were they, half-thinking that her lips,
Who had devised the letter, moved again.

    Then freely spoke Sir Lancelot to them all: 1280
'My lord liege Arthur, and all ye that hear,
Know that for this most gentle maiden's death
Right heavy am I; for good she was and true,
But loved me with a love beyond all love
In women, whomsoever I have known.   1285

1278   se   her
    ...were they, halfthinking that the lips   V
1278 ...lips   BM-2
1278 (C)   L-II

1279 Who w̶h̶ had...   V

1280 (No par. indent.) ...all   BM-2
1280 ...all   L-II
1280 ...all;   59
1280 (C)   73

1281 'My lord King Arthur, & all his ladies leal,   V
1281 My lord liege K̶ Arthur & all ye that year
    G̶r̶e̶a̶t̶ ̶l̶i̶e̶g̶e̶ ̶m̶y̶ ̶l̶i̶e̶g̶e̶ ̶l̶a̶d̶i̶e̶s̶ ̶&̶ ̶a̶l̶l̶ ̶g̶o̶o̶d̶
                    k̶n̶i̶g̶h̶t̶s̶   Tn-39
1281 ...hear   BM-2
1281 ...hear,   ,/ (I)   L-II
1281 (C)   F

Alt. after 1281 And all true bretheren of the Table
                  Round   V

1283 I am right-heavy. Good she was & fair   V

1285   whomsoever
    In whatsoever woman I have known.   V

1286 But to be loved will make no love in men   V
1286   makes not to love again
    But to be loved i̶s̶/̶t̶h̶a̶t̶/̶a̶/̶c̶a̶u̶s̶e̶/̶t̶o̶/̶l̶o̶v̶e̶/̶   Tn-39
1286 But to be...again.   BM-2
1286 (C)   L-II

```
Yet to be loved makes not to love again;
Not at my years, however it hold in youth.
I swear by truth and knighthood that I gave
No cause, not willingly, for such a love:
To this I call my friends in testimony,          1290
Her brethren, and her father, who himself
Besought me to be plain and blunt, and use,
To break her passion, some discourtesy
Against my nature: what I could, I did.
I left her and I bad her no farewell;            1295
Though had I dreamt the damsel would have died,
```

1287 Not at my time - however...	V
1288 I swear by Him that made me that I gave	V
1288 ~~truth~~ &	
...by ~~whitest~~ knighthood that...	Tn-39
1290 For this I (blot) appeal to my good friends	V
1290 ...call in testimony my friends,	Tn-39
1291 ...father who ...	BM-2
1291 (C)	L-II
1292 Besought me to be harsh & rough , & use	V
1292 & blunt ~~with her~~	
...plain & ~~rough~~ & use	Tn-39
1292 ...use	BM-2
1292 (C)	59
1293 To blunt her passion some discourtesy	V
1293 break	
To ~~blunt~~ her...	Tn-39
1293 ...passion some...	BM-2
1293 (C)	59
1295 ...I bid her no farewell.	BM-2
1295 bad	I MS
...I ~~bid~~ her no farewell.	L-II
1295 ...farewell.	F
1295 (C)	73
1296 But had I dreamt the maiden wd have died	V
1296 Tho'	
~~But~~ had...	Tn-39

713

I might have put my wits to some rough use,
And helped her from herself.'

                        Then said the Queen
(Sea was her wrath, yet working after storm)
'Ye might at least have done her so much grace,   1300
Fair lord, as would have helped her from her death.'
He raised his head, their eyes met and hers fell,
He adding,

1297 I would have put my wit   V
1297   rough
    ...some ~~sharp~~ use,   Tn-39

1298 ...Queen.   BM-2
1298 (C)   F

1299 [Her wrath was sea yet...   Tn-39
1299 [Her wrath was sea yet...   BM-2
1299 (C)   L-II

1300 You might...   V
1300 'You might...   F
1300 (C)   69

1301 ...lord, as to have help'd...   V
1301   would
    ...as ~~might~~ have...   Tn-39

1302 And Lancelot raised his head & lookd upon her
     And in that interchange of eyes hers fell   V

Sketch 1302 ~~[Var/]y And Lancelot raised his head &~~
              ~~lookyd upon her~~
            ~~And in that interchange of eyes hers~~
                    ~~fell~~   Tn-39

1303 He added this.
                    She wd...   V

1304-1305 Save that I took her for my wedded wife
          I shall not wed. then she needs wd be
          My slave or (servant ?) vassal thro' the
                    world.   V

'Queen, she would not be content
Save that I wedded her, which could not be.
Then might she follow me through the world, she
asked;   1305
It could not be. I told her that her love
Was but the flash of youth, would darken down
To rise hereafter in a stiller flame
Toward one more worthy of her--then would I,
More specially were he, she wedded, poor,   1310
Estate them with large land and territory
In mine own realm beyond the narrow seas,
To keep them in all joyance: more than this

1305 ...me as page or thrall?   Tn-39
1305 ...me as page or thrall?   BM-2
1305 ...ask'd.   L-II
1305 (C)   59

1306 Wh could...   Tn-39
1306 Which could...   BM-2
1306 (C)   L-II

1307 Was but a flash of youth to darken down pass
                        & die   V

1308 But And burn hereafter in a stiller flame   V

1309 To one who might be worthier. & I made   V
1309   then would I
     ...her ₰ I m̷a̷d̷e̷   Tn-39
1309 ...would I   BM-2
1309 (C)   L-II

1310 This proffer, that I would, when this should be,
     For I was much beholden to her love
     More specially were he, she wed with, poor   V
1310 T̷h̷i̷s̷ p̷r̷o̷f̷f̷e̷r̷/ i̷f̷ s̷h̷e̷ w̷e̷d̷d̷e̷d̷/ t̷h̷a̷t̷ I w̷o̷u̷l̷d̷   Tn-39

1311 Endow them with broad lands & territory,   V

1312 ...seas   BM-2
1312 (C)   L-II

1313   joyance
     ...all p̷l̷e̷n̷t̷y̷: more...   V

I could not; this she would not, and she died.'

   He pausing, Arthur answered, 'O my knight,   1315
It will be to thy worship, as my knight,
And mine, as head of all our Table Round,
To see that she be buried worshipfully.'

1314 ...not and...	BM-2
1314 (C)	L-II

1315 He spake & there was silence: then the **K**ing	V
1315 (Par.) He paused, & after silence, the King	
said	Tn-39
1315 (Par.) He paused, and after silence, the king	
said	BM-2
1315 ing, Arthur answer'd 'O my knight	I MS
(Par.) He pausḙḍ/ ḁṅḍ ḁf̶t̶ḙr̶ s̶i̶l̶ḙn̶c̶ḙ/ t̶h̶ḙ k̶i̶n̶g	
s̶ḁi̶ḍ/	L-II
1315 ...answer'd 'O my knight	F
1315 (C)	59

1316 ...to your worship...	V
1316 ...to your worship as our knight	Tn-39
1316 ...to your worship as our knight	BM-2
1316 my	I MS
...to your worship, as o̶u̶r̶ knight,	L-II
1316 ...to your worship...	F
1316 (C)	<u>69</u>

1317 ...all the Table...	V
1317 And ours as head of all the Table...	Tn-39
1317 And ours as head of all the Table Round	BM-2
1317 mine our	I MS
And o̶u̶r̶s̶, as head of all t̶h̶ḙ Table Round,	L-II
1317 (C)	F

1318 ...worshipfully.	BM-2
1318 (C)	L-II

1319-1321 Was costliest to the c̶o̶s̶t̶l̶i̶ḙs̶t̶ shrine wh then	
Then on the morrow, Lancelot at their head,	
Moved all the knighthood of the Table	
Round,	V

So toward that shrine which then in all the realm
Was richest, Arthur leading, slowly went   1320
The marshalled Order of their Table Round,
And Lancelot sad beyond his wont, to see
The maiden buried, not as one unknown,
Nor meanly, but with gorgeous obsequies,
And mass, and rolling music, like a queen.   1325
And when the knights had laid her comely head

1319   at
        (Par.) Then slowly toward thé shrine which in
                        the realm
                    ŧħáŧ ħóúŕ   Tn-39
1319 (Par.) Then slowly toward that shrine which in
                        the realm   BM-2
1319 (C)   L-II

1320   richest
        Was ćóśŧĺíéśŧ, with King Arthur at their
                        head,   Tn-39
1320 Was richest, with King Arthur at their head,   BM-2
1320 (C)   L-II

1321 Moved all the knighthood of the Table Round,   Tn-39
1321 Moved all the knighthood of the Table Round,   BM-2
1321   their   I MS
        The marshall'd order of ħíś Table Round,   L-II
1321 ...marshall'd order of...   F
1321 (C)   73

1322 He stern & sad beyond his wont, to see   V

1323 ...unknown   BM-2
1323 ...unknown,   ,/ (I)   L-II
1323 (C)   F

1325 ...music like a Queen.   BM-2
1325 ...a Queen.   L-II
1325 (C)   73

1326   laid
        ...had śééń her...   Tn-39

717

Low in the dust of half-forgotten kings,
Then Arthur spake among them, 'Let her tomb
Be costly, and her image thereupon,
And let the shield of Lancelot at her feet   1330
Be carven, and her lily in her hand.
And let the story of her dolorous voyage
For all true hearts be blazoned on her tomb
In letters gold and azure!' which was wrought
Thereafter; but when now the lords and dames   1335

1327 Low in
    M̸i̸x̸x̸ w̸i̸t̸h̸ the dust...   Tn-39

1328 ...them 'let...   BM-2
1328 (C)   59

1329 ff Her feet upon
    Upon her right the shield of Lancelot
    And in her hand the lily
    And we have the story of her life
    Blazed on her tomb for all true hearts to be
    In likeness, gold & azure   V

1329   costly
    Be s̸u̸m̸p̸t̸u̸o̸u̸s̸, & ...   Tn-39
1329 ...thereupon.   BM-2
1329 (C)   84

1331 ...hand   BM-2
1331 (C)   L-II

1332   let
    And b̸e̸ the...   Tn-39

1333 Be   upon her tomb
    Blazed on her tomb for all true hearts t̸o̸ b̸e̸ Tn-39
1333 Be blazed for all true hearts upon her tomb   BM-2
1333 (C)   L-II

1334 ...letters, gold...   BM-2
1334 (C)   L-II

And people, from the high door streaming, brake
Disorderly, as homeward each, the Queen,
Who marked Sir Lancelot where he moved apart,
Drew near, and sighed in passing, 'Lancelot,
Forgive me; mine was jealousy in love.'   1340
He answered with his eyes upon the ground,
'That is love's curse; pass on, my Queen, forgiven.'
But Arthur, who beheld his cloudy brows,
Approached him, and with full affection said,

1337 ...Queen	BM-2
1337 (C)	L-II

1338 And as Sir Lancelot frcm the burial came	
Guinevere stood beside the path & said	V
1338 ...Lancelot moving all apart	Tn-39
1338 ...Lancelot moving all apart	BM-2
1338 (C)	L-II

1339 ...near & at her penitent whisper - love	Tn-39
1339 Drew near and at her penitent whisper 'love	BM-2
1339 ...passing, 'Lancelot, / (I)	L-II
1339 ...passing, 'Lancelot,	F
1339 (C)	73

1340 Forgive me: mine was jealousy of love	V
1340 ...love'	BM-2
1340 (C)	L-II

1341 And He...	V
1341 ...ground	BM-2
1341 (C)	L-II

1342 ...pass on you are forgiven	V
1342 my Queen,	
...on/ ￥￠ ￡ forgiven.'	Tn-39
1342 ...on my...	BM-2
1342 (C)	L-II

1343 ...Arthur who...brows	BM-2
1343 (C)	73

'Lancelot, my Lancelot, thou in whom I have   1345
Most joy and most affiance, for I know
What thou hast been in battle by my side,
And many a time have watched thee at the tilt
Strike down the lusty and long practised knight,
And let the younger and unskilled go by   1350
To win his honour and to make his name,
And loved thy courtesies and thee, a man

1344   Drew near him & with full affection
                        flung
Alt. after 1344 One arm about his neck & said to
                        him   V
1344   ...affection flung
Alt. after 1344 One arm about his neck & spake &
                        said.   Tn-39
1344   Drew near him and with full affec-
                        tion flung
Alt. after 1344 One arm about his neck and spake
                        and said.   BM-2
1344   Drew near him, and with full af-
                        fection flung   (, I)
Alt. after 1344 One arm about his neck, and spake
                        and said.   (, I.)   L-II
1344   ...affection flung
Alt. after 1344 One arm about his neck, and spake
                        and said.   F
1344   (C)   73
Alt. after 1344 (C)   73

1345 (Par.) My Lancelot my dear friend in whom I have V

Sketch 1346 ff
        Most love & most affiance would to heaven -
        Because the people say wild things of thee
        Wh for my sake & thine I not believe
        My fault perchance to dream the best of men.
        While the world howls the worst - but wd to God V
1346 Most love &...   Tn-39
1346 most love &...   H-119a
1346 Most love and...   BM-2
1346 (C)   73

LANCELOT AND ELAINE

Made to be loved; but now I would to God,
Seeing the homeless trouble in thine eyes,
Thou couldst have loved this maiden, shaped, it
                                    seems,   1355
By God for thee alone, and from her face,

1348   many a time
       And øḟṭéⁿ ḥáṿé Í watch'd thee at the tilt   H-114a
1348 ...at the joust   Tn-39
1348 ...thee at the joust   BM-2
1348   tilt   I MS
       ...thee at the ĵøú́ṣ́ṭ́   L-II
1348 (C)   F

1349 ...long-practised knight   BM-2
1349 ...long-practised knight,   (,I)   L-II
1349 ...long-practised...   F
1349 (C)   78

1353 Made to be loved; & therefore thee I sent   H-114a
1353 ...loved; - but...   F
1353 (C)   67

Alt. after 1353
       Long years ago, to bring me home my bride
                            an (2 ?) to her
       Thee as my best: but now, I wd to Heaven -
       Unknown to thee
       Because the people say wild things of thee -
       My fault, perhaps, to dream the best of men
       When the world howls the worst - but wd to God
                                                      H-114a
Alt. for 1354 For the wild people say wild things
                            of thee   Tn-39
Alt. for 1354 For the wild people say wild things
                            of thee,   BM-2
Alt. for 1354 (C)   73

1356   ...this damsel - from her face
       (3 ?) by God's own hand for thee - & from (1 ?)   V
1356 By God only for thee, & from her face,   H-114a

721

If one may judge the living by the dead,
Delicately pure and marvellously **fair**,
Who might have brought thee, now a lonely man
Wifeless and heirless, noble issue, sons   1360
Born to the glory of thy name and fame,

1359-1360   given
            Who might have ~~brought~~ thee noble issue,
                          sons   V

1359 ...thee now...   BM-2
1359 (C)   L-II

1360   heirless
        Wifeless & ~~childless~~, noble...   Tn-39

1362 ...of the lake.'   BM-2
1362 (C)   59

1363 ff And Lancelot answer'd 'She was beautiful
         Most tender & I knew it; tho-methinks
         How beautiful I never knew till now: V

1363   Fair
        ...Lancelot ~~pure~~ she..   Tn-39
1363 ...Lancelot 'Fair...my king,   BM-2
1363 (C)   59

1364 Pure,   ~~would~~ ever
        ~~And stainless~~ as ye wish...   Tn-39
1364 ...as ye ever...   BM-2
1364 (C)   F

1365   fairness   n eye
        ...her ~~pureness~~ were to want a ~~heart~~   Tn-39

1366   pureness   heart -
        ...her ~~fairness~~ were to want a~~n~~ ~~eye~~   Tn-39

1367 Yea to be loved: but love will not be bound.   V
1367 Yea, worth all love, if what is worthiest love
                                                             Tn-39
1367 Yea, worth all love, if what is worthiest love BM-2
1367 (C)   L-II

722

My knight, the great Sir Lancelot of the Lake.'

    Then answered Lancelot, 'Fair she was, my King,
Pure, as you ever wish your knights to be.
To doubt her fairness were to want an eye,   1365
To doubt her pureness were .to want a heart--
Yea, to be loved, if what is worthy love
Could bind him, but free love will not be bound.'

    'Free love, so bound, were freest,' said the King.
'Let love be free; free love is for the best: 1370

1368   bind
     Could ~~hold~~ him best
     ~~One to be loved~~, but love...   Tn-39
1368 ...him best, but love will...   BM-2
1368 (C)   L-II

1369 ff That is no marvel, Lancelot, said the King.
        Right well know I that love will not be bound.
        My marvel is that such a love as this
        Coming in such a beauty has no power,
        My friend, to bind thee, being, as I think,
        (1375 same)   V
1369 ff (Par.) 'That is no marvel, Lancelot' said the
                    King
        'We know that love will not be bound, but still
        ~~I seem~~ Amazed I seem
        ~~My wonder grows~~ that love so pure as this
        Coming in such a beauty, had no power,
        My friend, to bind thee, being, as I think,
                           Tn-39

1369-1371 'That is no marvel, Lancelot,' said the king
           'We know that love will not be bound, but
                       still   BM-2

1369 (Par. symbol I) ...the king.   · (I)   L-II
1369 ...the king.   F
1369 (C)   59

1370 'Let...   '/ (I)   L-II
1370 (C)   F

And, after heaven, on our dull side of death,
What should be best, if not so pure a love
Clothed in so pure a loveliness? yet thee
She failed to bind, though being, as I think,
Unbound as yet, and gentle, as I know.'   1375

   And Lancelot answered nothing, but he went,
And at the inrunning of a little brook

1371 (C)	L-II
1372 Amazed I seem that love so pure as this	BM-2
1372 (C)	L-II
1373 Coming in such a beauty, had no power,	BM-2
1373 (C)	L-II
1374 My friend, to bind thee, being, as I think,	BM-2
1374 (C)	L-II
1376 ...went	BM-2
1376 (C)	59
1378 ...cove and...	BM-2
1378 ...cove, and... ,/ (I)	L-II
1378 (C)	F
1379 The bull-rush way & sure lifted...	V
1380 ...barge she came in moving...	V
1380 ...barge she came in moving...	Tn-39
1380 (Same)	BM-2
1380 that brought her	I MS
...barge s̸h̸e̸ c̸a̸m̸e̸ i̸n̸ moving...	L-II
1380 (C)	F

Draft 1382-1416 (Cancelled)
    'This damsel, doubtless, loved me with a love
    Far purer & more tender than the Queen's.
    Her love is mixt with pride & selfregard
    Latterly with respect to her good name.
    Why did the King dwell on my name to me?
    My own name shames me seeming a reproach,

LANCELOT AND ELAINE

Sat by the river in a cove, and watched
The high reed wave, and lifted up his eyes
And saw the barge that brought her moving down,   1380
Far-off, a blot upon the stream, and said
Low in himself, 'Ah simple heart and sweet,
Ye loved me, damsel, surely with a love

Draft 1382-1416 (Cancelled)
        Lancelot, whom the Lady of the Lake
        Stole from his mother - as the   story runs:
        She chanted snatches of mysterious song
        Heard on the winding waters, eve & morn
        She kiss'd me, saying, thou art fair, my child,
        As a king's son, & often in her arms
        She bare me pacing on the dusky mere.
        Would she had drownd me there. I needs must break
        These bonds that so disgrace me: not without
        She wills it, would I, if she will'd it? nay,
        Who knows? but if I would not, then may God,
        I pray him, send a sudden angel down,
        To sieze me by the hair, & bear me far
        And fling me deep in that forgotten mere
        Among the tumbled fragments of the hills'   Tn-39

1382 ...himself 'Ah...sweet   BM-2
1382 ...himself 'Ah...   L-II
1382 (C)   73

1383 (Par.) This damsel, doubtless, loved me with
                        a love   V
1383   p̶u̶r̶e̶ purer
p̶a̶m̶s̶e̶l̶, ye loved me surely with a   love   Tn-39
1383 ...me surely with a purer love   Tn-39
1383 ...me surely with a purer love   BM-2
1383 (C)   L-II

1383 You loved...   F
1383 (C)   69

1384 ff Far purer & more tender than the Queen's
        Her love is mixt with pride & self regard.
        (1 ?) with respect to her good name.   V

725

Far tenderer than my Queen's. Pray for thy soul?
Ay, that will I. Farewell too—now at last--   1385
Farewell, fair lily. "Jealousy in love?"
Not rather dead love's harsh heir, jealous pride?
Queen, if I grant the jealousy as of love,
May not your crescent fear for name and fame
Speak, as it waxes, of a love that wanes?   1390
Why did the King dwell on my name to me?
Mine own name shames me, seeming a reproach,

1384 And tenderer   my
     ~~Far purer & more tender~~ than ~~the~~ Queen's -   Tn-39
1384 And tenderer...   Tn-39
1384 And tenderer...   BM-2
1384 (C)   L-II

Draft 1385-1388 (Cancelled)
     Love mixt with pride, wrath, jealousy out of place
     But I forbear her ever for her love
     As if I grant her jealousy as of love   Tn-39

1385 Ay that will I: farewell...   BM-2
1385 (C)   L-II

1388 ...grant your jealousy...   Tn-39
1388 ...grant your jealousy...   BM-2
1388   the   I MS
     ...grant ~~your~~ jealousy...   L-II
1388 (C)   F

1389 May not this crescent fear for her good name   Tn-39
1389 May not this crescent fear for your good name Tn-39
1389 May not this crescent fear for your good name BM-2
1389 (C)   L-II

1390 ...waxes of...   BM-2
1390 (C)   L-II

1391 Why did the King (suggest ?) my name to me?   V
1391 ...the king dwell...   BM-2
1391 (C)   59

726

LANCELOT AND ELAINE

Lancelot, whom the Lady of the Lake
Caught from his mother's arms--the wondrous one
Who passes through the vision of the night--   1395
She chanted snatches of mysterious hymns
Heard on the winding waters, eve and morn
She kissed me saying, "Thou art fair, my child,
As a king's son," and often in her arms
She bare me, pacing on the dusky mere.   1400
Would she had drowned me in it, where'er it be!
For what am I? what profits me my name

1393 ...the lake   BM-2
1393 (C)   67

1394 Took from...   V
1394-1395 Stole from his mother - as the story
                                   runs -   Tn-39
1394-1395 Stole from his mother - as the story
                                   runs -   BM-2
1394-1395 (C)   73

1396 ...mysterious song   Tn-39
1396 ...mysterious song   BM-2
1396 (C)   73

1398 ...saying thou...   BM-2
1398 (C)   73

1399 ...son, and...   BM-2
1399 (C)   73

Alt. before 1401 (Cancelled)
                But these are dreams.
        Yet somewhere I remember the waste gleam
        On some deep water, whence I came, but now
        I have dream'd a dream wh seem'd as deep as truth
        And that will drown my soul.   Tn-39

1401 ...drown'd me there. I needs must break   V
1401 ...drownd me, whatsoeer she were,
        In that waste water wheresoeer it be.   Tn-39

727

Of greatest knight? I fought for it, and have it:
Pleasure to have it, none; to lose it, pain;
Now grown a part of me: but what use in it?   1405
To make men worse by making my sin known?
Or sin seem less, the sinner seeming great?
Alas for Arthur's greatest knight, a man
Not after Arthur's heart! I needs must break
These bonds that so defame me: not without   1410
She wills it: would I, if she willed it? nay,
Who knows? but if I would not, then may God,
I pray him, send a sudden Angel down
To seize me by the hair and bear me far,
And fling me deep in that forgotten mere,   1415
Among the tumbled fragments of the hills.'

    So groaned Sir Lancelot in remorseful pain,
Not knowing he should die a holy man.

1403 ...it, and bare it   BM-2
1403 (C)   L-II

Alt. after 1403
    And sin has made it nothing: the great name
    Makes the sin known; yea makes the sin seem
                    less;   Tn-39

1405   what use is such a my great name
        Part of myself: it seems to blaze my crime,   V
1405 Grown part of me: what use in such a name?   Tn-39

Alt. after 1406 Because the sinner had the name of
                        great   Tn-39

1407   sinless
        Or make sin The sinner sinning great.'   V

1409 ...heart! but I must...   Tn-39
1409 ...heart! but I must break   BM-2
1409 (C)   L-II

1410 The bonds that so disgrace me. not without   V

1414 ...far   BM-2
1414 (C)   L-II

1415 ...mere		BM-2
1415 ...mere,	,/ (I)	L-II
1415 (C)		F

REJECTED PASSAGES

The shackles of an old love shackled him
And honour rooted in dishonour kept
Faith where it was   V

       the true air of heaven
Find way to thy false blood   V

Why sd I leave such thoughts
Who being earthly loved an earthly man
As long as breath is in me I must love
And while my love is with me must I mourn.   V

The Holy Grail

Now when Sir Percivale had come back from the Quest
of the Holy Grail, he would have no more to do with tilt
& tournament but entered into a monastery & presently
after died.

But ere this one of the holy fathers who was his
chief friend in the monastery, would often ask him about
this Quest of the Grail, & how it all came about, & one
day Sir Percivale told him all he could remember.

O brother, this Holy Grail, is the cup out of which
our blessed Lord drank at the last supper. Joseph of
Arimathea brought it to Glastonbury & it healed many of
their diseases & wrought faith in their hearts: but the
times grew so wicked that it was caught up to heaven &
disappeared.

O brother, I had a sister a nun in the nunnery at
Camelot. No holier being ever wore the pavement with

731

her knee. Shut out as she was from the world, the
noise of an adulterous race beat thro' the gratings of
her cell, & she prayd & fasted the more.

Now her confessor, a holy Father, a hundred winters
old, told her this legend of the Holy Grail, which had
been handed down from the times of our Lord, by six or
seven old men, each a hundred winters old. If the Holy
Grail [he said] should reappear there might yet be hope
for the world. O Father she said would it appear to
me if I pray'd & fasted? & he answered 'Yea, daughter,
who knows but it might, if thy heart be as pure as snow.
& she prayd & fasted till the sun shone thro' her & the
wind blew thro' her.

Then on a day she sent to me to speak with her: &
I went to the nunnery, & behold her eyes were wonderful
in the light of her holiness & she told me that she had
seen the holy vessel. In the dead night, she had been
waked by a strain of sweet music, & there came in a long
beam of light, brighter than any sunbeam & down this
beam slowly past the Holy Grail & the white walls of her
cell were dyed in rose-colour, & the Grail past & the
beam, & the rose colour slowly faded away. Lo now, my
brother, she said, fast thou also & pray & tell thy

brother knights to fast & pray that peradventure the
holy thing may come to you also, & the world be healed
of it wickedness.

And I went away & spake of all this to my brother
knights & many among us pray'd & fasted. Now there was
a young man among us, Galahad, whom Arthur had knighted,
& there never was so young a man knighted before - some
said he was a son of Lancelot, some that he was begotten by enchantment - but when I spake with him of the
Grail, his eyes look'd so like my sister's that I could
have thought he was her brother. And there stood a seat
in our great Hall which Merlin had fashiond long ago before he past away; & it was carved with strange figures
& in & out the figures there were letters in a tongue no
man could read; & Merlin called the seat The Siege Perilous for he said no man can sit there but shall lose
himself & Galahad said If I lose myself I shall save myself.

And it chanced one night when the banquet was spread
in the Hall that Galahad would sit in the chair of Merlin.

And immediately there was cracking & riving & rending
of the rafters, & there entered in a beam seven times

733

more clear than day, & in the midst of the light the
Holy Grail past thro' the Hall, but it was hidden in a
luminous cloud & every man looked at his neighbour &
behold his face was glorious, & we stared at one another
like dumb men.

Then I arose among the knights & bound myself by a
strong vow that because I had not seen the Holy Grail
when it past I would go forth to the end of the world
till I found it. And Galahad & most of the Knights
sware with me: & even Gawain swore.

Then said the monk to Sir Percivale

And what said Arthur? did he allow your vows?

And Percivale answer'd

The king was not there albeit he had willed to be
there: he was sacking a bandit-hold over the hills.
howbeit he saw something of the marvel, for as he returned from the sacking, having slain the robbers, when
the land was darkening he looked up & he cried aloud Behold the roofs of our great Hall are roll'd in thunder-
smoke: pray heaven they be not smitten by the thunder-
bolt: for the roofs of the Hall seemd to smoke & the
Hall was dear to him seeing it is the costliest in the
world.

THE HOLY GRAIL

O brother had you known our mighty hall
Which Merlin built for Arthur long ago.
For four great zones of Sculpture, set betwixt
With many a mystic symbol, gird the Hall
And in the lowest beasts are slaying men.
And in the second men are slaying beasts
And in the third are warriors perfect men
And in the fourth are men with growing wings
And on the top a statue in the mould
Of Arthur, made by Merlin with a crown
And peakd wings pointed to the Northern Star.

& the statue faces the East & the crown & the wings are

golden & shine far over the land at sunrise.

Then the great King & his company rode swiftly up to

the Hall. And the King rode into the hall & I looked up

& saw the golden dragon blaze on his head.

And he spoke to me O Percivale [for there was tumult

among us] what is this.

And I told him what had chanced & his face darkened

& he said had I been here ye would not sware & he said O

Percivale didst thou see the Grail

Nay Lord I said I heard the sound & I saw the light

but the Grail was covered with a cloud. And the King

spoke again & asked us knight by knight whether any had

seen the holy Grail

And they answer'd & said Nay Lord for the Grail was

hidden & therefore we have taken our vows. And Galahad

cried out in a shrill voice

735

THE HOLY GRAIL

       But I Sir Arthur saw the Holy Grail
       I saw The Holy Grail & heard a cry
       O Galahad & O Galahad follow me!

Ah Gawain, Gawain said the King. Is this vision for

thee? but now O Percivale thou & the holy nun, thy sis-

ter, have broken up the fair order of my Table Round

which I founded for pure life, & the redressing of human

wrong. For many among you have taken this vow, who will

never see this vision, & many among you will follow wan-

dering fires & be lost in the quagmire, & this same

goodly company of knights will never meet again in my

hall.

       Wherefore my heart is sad unto death: but since I

may not disallow the vows ye have taken, lo now, let us

come together in the morning for one last tilt & tourney

of gracious pastime that I may see you once more all

together & rejoice in your prowess & the order which I

have made.

       Then we met together in the morning & I & Sir Galahad

overthrew most of the knights for the strength of the

Vision was in us.

       And when this was over the king & the Queen & many

ladies rode with us to the gates, & the women wept & the

men, & rich & poor wept, & the King could scarce speak

for weeping & the Queen shrieked & wailed & said It is
for our sins this has come upon us.

Then we parted & went each his own way: & I was glad
at heart, & I thought of my prowess in my lists & how I
had beaten down various knights, & the sun never seemed
so bright, nor the sky so blue, nor the earth so green,
& I felt that I should come upon the Holy Grail.

Then after awhile my mind was darkened & every evil
word I had spoken,& every evil thought I had thought, &
every evil deed I had done stood round about me like
fiends & cried aloud The Holy Grail is not for thee.
And I lifted up my eyes & I was in a land of sand &
thorns, & I was athirst even unto swooning & I said
'This quest is not for thee!

And I thought my thirst would have slain me: when
behold as I rode on I saw lawns of deep grass, & a running brook which made a sound among the stones, & great
appletrees with golden apples on either side of the
brook & among the lawns. and I said I will rest here:
I am not worthy of the quest. And I began to drink of
the brook & to eat of the golden apples, & while I was
eating, it all fell away into dust, & I was again among
the sand & the thorns.

737

THE HOLY GRAIL

And again I rode on & suddenly I was aware of a fair
woman, & she sat by the door of a house: & the house
was fair & pleasant to look upon, & the eyes of the
woman were kind & innocent & her ways were gracious &
she opened out her arms to me, as tho' she would say
rest here & I went up & touchd her & lo she fell into
dust & the house became a ruined shed & in it there was
a dead babe, & I was again among the sand & the thorns.

And again I rode foreward & there fell a yellow
gleam over the world, & it past over the plough'd field
& the plowman left his plough & fell down before it &
the milkmaid left milking her kine & fell down before it
& I thought it was the rising sun but the Sun had risen
& I turned & behold a giant with a jewelld helmet & in
golden armour & his horse in golden armour studded with
jewels. & he seemed the Lord of all the world he was so
huge & I thought he would slain me & I made ready to do
battle with him & behold he opened his arms wide to embrace me & I touchd him & he fell into dust, & I was
among the sand & the thorns

And again I rode onward & far off behold there was a
city on the top of a great hill: & the towers & pinnacles ~~thereof~~ were unbelieavable for the height thereof,

for they pierced thro' the clouds of heaven. And as I
drew near I saw a great company before the gates of the
city & they cried out to me as I clomb the hill Come up
Sir Percivale welcome thou greatest knight among men.
but when I came to the top there was no man there & I
went into the city & it was waste & desolate & there was
only one man in it of an exceeding old age & I spake to
him where is that great company that cried out t̸o̸ m̸e̸
upon me. and he had scarce any voice to answer but he
said Whence art thou & who art thou & even while he was
speaking he fell into dust & disappeared & I cried out
Lo if I find The Holy Grail itself & touch it it also
will crumble to dust

Then I went down into valley on the other side of the
hill & the valley was as low as the hill was high & at
the bottom was a little chapel & a hermitage & a hermit
& when I had told him all that chanced to me he answered
& said

O Son thou hast not true humility
The highest virtue, mother of them all,
For when the Lord of all things made himself
Naked of Godhead for his mortal change
Take thou my robe O Lord she said tis pure
And all her form shone forth in sudden light
So that the angels were amazed & she
Follow'd him down & like a flying star
Led on the grayheaded wisdom of the East

739

But her thou hast not known: for what is this
Thou thoughtest of thy prowess & thy sins
Thou has not lost thyself to save thyself.
As Galahad. And Sir Galahad as he spak

Rode up to the chapel: & when I lookd on the bright

faced boy knight his eye had power upon me, & I believed

w̶h̶a̶t̶ as he believed & my fear left me. And the Holy man

took away my burning thirst, & at the sacring of the

mass, & I saw but the blessed elements but he said

I saw the fiery face as of a child
That smote itself into the bread & went

And we left our horses with the hermit for there was a

mountain before us which none could climb but man. And

as we clomb the mountain I told Sir Galahad all that I

had told the hermit & he said Care not thou for thou

shall see the Grail even tho far away & I go to be

crowned King in the Spiritual City. And when we came to

the top of the mountain there brake on us a thunder & a

lightening so that I never saw the like of it; & as we

went down again, the lightning was so fierce it struck

here & there to the left & to the right, & the old

trunks & stems of trees that were dead brake into fire;

& at the bottom of the mountain there was a foul & black

swamp, and by the lightning I saw that in it there w̶e̶r̶e̶

lay the bones of men. And there were seven piers built

740

across the marsh & seven light bridges from pier to

pier. & ever one of the bridges was railed in with

roses. A̶n̶d̶ s̶a̶i̶ And at the end of the piers was a boat

and beyond it the Great Sea

    And Galahad ran along them bridge by bridge
    And every bridge as soon as he had past
    Sprang into fire & vanished

& he leapt into the boat & I was alone for I could not

follow and the boat went with an exceeding swiftness &

thrice over him the Heavens opened & blazed with thunder

like the shoutings of all the sons of God. And when

first they opened I beheld him far out on the Great Sea

& over his head was the holy Vessel clothed in white

samite or a luminous cloud. & when they blazed I beheld

him very far away & over him the holy vessel redder than

any rose whereby I knew that the veil had been with-

drawn from it: & when the Heavens opened & blazed the

third time I saw him no bigger than the point over an i

& far away behind him in the clear s̶p̶o̶t̶ o̶f̶ sky I saw the

gates of the Spiritual City no larger than a pearl &

over it a tiny bloodred spark, & dwelt there & I knew it

it was the Holy Grail. Then the Heavens came down as

tho they would drown the world & I saw no more & I was

glad at heart & I went back to the Hermitage & took my

741

charger & so rode back to the Court of the King, & I
had been from him a twelvemonth & a day.

And there sat the King in his hall which Merlin & all
his knights were before him, they that had not gone out
on the Holy Quest, & they had gone; & of these not ten
had returned, but among these were Sir Gawain & Sir
Lancelot

Then spake the King to Sir Gawain O Gawain was this
quest for thee?

Nay, Lord, said Sir Gawain, & I spake with a holy man
& he told me: this quest is not for thee, & I was weary
of the quest but I chanced upon merry maidens & the
twelvemonth & a day were pleasant to me.

And the King bow'd his head nor answered him but
turnd to me & s̸p̸a̸k̸e̸ ask'd me O Percivale, pure knight &
true, what hath chanced to thee?

And I told him all that chanced & the King bow'd his
head toward me, but answered me not & spake to Sir Lancelot

Thou also, Sir Lancelot, in whom I have most love &
most affiance hast thou seen the holy vision.

And Sir Lancelot dropt his head upon his breast, &
his colour wanned upon his face & till after a while he

spake not, & then he groaned & said

O King, my friend - happier are those that welter in
their Sin & are covered like the swine with the mud of
the sinner: but my sin was of so strange a kind that
all that was noble in me, and all that was knightly ~~is~~
grew to it & twined about it till the wholesome flower
& the poisonous flower were each as either & could not
be rent asunder. And I therefore took my vow with the
rest, that peradventure, if I might see & touch the Holy
Vessel, they would be rent asunder. And I went forth &
did spake with a holy man & he told me that save I could
rend them asunder my Quest was in vain: & I sware to
him to do according to all that he willed: & I past
forth from him & in striving to rend them asunder I fell
into my madness as of old: & my madness drave me into
waste fields where I was beaten down by mean knights, who
should have fallen before the whiff of my sword & the
shadow of my lance: & I came to the naked sea-shore, &
the land was flat & barren & nothing grew on the banks
of the Sea but a little coarse grass but a blast blew
along the sea & the shore.

    & heap'd in mounds & ridges all the sea
    Drove like a cataract & all the sand

THE HOLY GRAIL

Swept like a river & the cloudy sun
Was shaken with the motion & the sound

& there was a little boat tossing, brimful of seafoam,

anchored with chain; & I said to myself in my madness I

will embark & wash away my sin in the great sea

Seven days I drove along the dreary deeps
And with me drove the moon & all the stars
And the wind fell & on the seventh day
I heard the shingle grinding in the surge
                                  & behold
A castle like a rock upon a rock
With mighty portals open to the sea
And steps that met the breaker. There was none
Stood near it but a lion on each side
That kept the entry & the moon was full.

And from the boat I leapt & up the stairs
Those two great beasts rose upward like a man
Each gripped a shoulder & I stood between
And when I would stricken them came a voice
Doubt not, go forward if thou doubt the beasts
Will tear thee piecemeal; & with violence
It smote the sword out of my hand & went.
And up into the sounding hall I past
But nothing in the sounding hall I saw
No bench nor table, painting on the wall
Nor shield of knight only the rounded moon
Thro' the tall oriel on the rolling sea.
But always in the quiet house I heard
Clear as a lark, high oer me as a lark
A sweet voice singing in the topmost tower
To the eastward: up I clomb a thousand steps
With pain: as in a dream I seem'd to climb
For ever: last I reach'd a little door
A light was in the crannies & I heard
Then in my madness I essay'd the door

& it yielded, & there came out a light 7 times more

clear & therewithal a heat wh blasted my eyesight so

744

that I swooned away: but thro' the light & the heat

methought I saw the Holy Grail all pall'd in crimson

samite & around

Great Angels, awful shapes & wings & eyes

And but for my madness & my swooning & my sin I sd

know that I saw what I saw: yet what I saw was covered,

& I count himself as having fail'd in the Quest.

And the King said. O Lancelot thou hast erred with

thy tongue. Never could all that was noble in a man &

all that was cling round his one sin whatsoever it be,

but there was left a remnant of Knighthood & of noble-

ness, that grew apart. See thou to that.

And said I not well that few of those who went out to

the Holy Quest wd return: that most of you would follow

wandering fires & be lost in the quagmire, & that ever

after I should have to look at a barren board & a lean

order. and not ten among you have returned & of those

to whom the Vision came, he, my greatest Knight, holds

himself as having failed to see it: & another has seen

it afar off, & he will pass away into the Silent life &

be lost to me, & another has had the vision face & has

past away, & left his place empty here, however other-

where they may crown him.

THE HOLY GRAIL

And some among you said that if the King
            he w
Had seen the sight ~~I should~~ have sworn the vow
Not easily, seeing that the ~~appointed~~ King must guard
Must guard the realm & is   hind
That wh he rules I am but as the husbandman
To whom a space of land is given to plough
Who may not wander from the allotted field
Before his work be done.: & ~~after that~~ but,
                          being done,
Let visions of the night or of the day
Come as they will: & many a time they come
   this earth
Until I tread on seems not earth,
This light that smites mine eyelid is not light
This air that strikes my forehead is not air
But vision: ye have seen what ye have seen.

(The following prose and verse sketches were added
later.)

Then Ambrosius askd him again. O brother for in our

old books I find many such marvels & ~~like~~ miracles like

unto these - only I find not this Holy Grail; & when I

have read til my eyes are dazed & my head swims, & when

our holy offices have been accomplish'd, then I go forth

into our little thorpe & stand in the market, & have joy

in the chaffering & chattering of the men & the women, &

I gossip with them about all things, delighting myself

yea even with their hens & their eggs. O brother, didst

not thou also find men & women in thy quest, or ~~did~~

phantoms only

   O brother, said Percivale, to me so bound by vow as I

was women & men are but as phantoms. why wilt thou

shame me. to make me confess to thee that I falterd in

my quest & my vow. f̸o̸r̸ t̸h̸e̸ v̸i̸s̸i̸o̸n̸ h̸a̸d̸ n̸o̸t̸ c̸o̸m̸e̸ t̸o̸ m̸e̸, &

for I had lain many nights in the thicket, as I h̸a̸d̸ was

lean & meagre & the Vision had not come: & happened one

night that I drew near a goodly town with a great dwell-

ing in midst of it, & I went into it & I was disarmed by

fair maidens & when I came into the banquet hall, behold

the Princess of the Castle, was the one & that one only

which had ever made my heart leap. For I was a slender

page in her father's hall & she a slender damsel & my

heart went after with longing. But we never had kissed

kiss or claspt hand. & lo I had found her again & one

had wedded her & s̸he was dead & she had all his posses-

sions and I dwelt there & she gave me banquet each rich-

er than before, for her longing was to me; & one day

when I sat under the castle in an orchard she came to-

ward me & embraced me & call'd me the greatest of all

the Knights & gave herself with all her wealth to me, &

I rememberd Arthur's words & the Quest faded in my heart.

And her people came to us & said we have heard of thee,

do thou wed our lady, & rule oer us & be as Arthur in

the land. But one night I arose for I remember'd the

vow I had sworn, & past from her but I waild & wept & I

hated myself & the Holy Quest to which I had sworn.

> I walking in her orchard underneath
> The castle walls, she came upon there
> Lo now I came upon her once again
> And one had wedded her & he was dead
> And all his wealth & land & state was hers.
>
> And calling me the greatest of all knights
> Embraced me & so kiss'd me the first time
> And gave herself and all her wealth to me
> And I remember'd Arthurs warning to us
> That most of us would follow wandring fires
> And the Quest faded in my heart. Anon
> The heads of all her people came to me
> Rejoicing
> And there I dwelt & every day she ~~she~~ made
> A banquet richer than the day before,
> For all her longing after many years
> Was toward me, as before.
>
> Wed thou with her, & rule thou over us
> And show

(Prose and verse sketches for the tale of Sir Bors.)

Yea said Percivale for as I rode back thro' a wood

that was half stript of the leaf I beheld before me whom

afar I knew for Sir Bors for I knew him by the breadth

of shoulder & I rode up to him & we fell at talk & after

I had told him all I had seen & besought him also to

speak to me of his Quest the colour came into his visage

& the water to his eye & after a while he spake to me.

I went forth with the rest & wandring thru field &

forest Sir Lancelot dash'd across me on his great black

748

charger & I feard me that he had fallen into madness wh
had come on him before & made him the talk of the court
& I cried out to him to say Ridest thou thus madly after
so Holy Quest as ours? & he stayd not for a moment but
cried on withhold me not: there is a lion in the way &
he galloped on to the Great Sea & I lost him. & I rode
on softly for did I (4 ?) about the Quest, for I thought
if it will come it will come & I & the Quest are in the
hands of God. but about my brother was I troubled for
how should he ever come upon the Vision being as he was

And I rode on even until I came upon the Paynims of
the West, our blood & our folk, to whom the message had
not come but they yet dwelt in Pagan darkness & made
their circles of stone & struck up a straight stone &
fell before it, & call'd it God & knew no God but the
Sun. & when they saw a knight of the new faith & from
As court they mockd & told me that I followd a wandring
fire - believing in the words of Arthur - but our God is
an

By whom the blood beats, & the blossom blows
And the sea rolls & everything is done

& it would (1 ?) be well for this Britains hold the Xt
were put down & the Sunworship set up again

749

THE HOLY GRAIL

Siezed me & beat me & bound me & cast me down chamber
          wickerwork
(1 ?) told (1 ?) of Arthur's wain & in a moment (1 ?)
               across
The sevn cold stars in colour like a hand
Before a burning taper past the Grail

a young damsel.

                    & thro the cleft
I saw the torn sky & the flying rack   H-38

750

THE HOLY GRAIL

From noiseful arms, and acts of prowess done
In tournament or tilt, Sir Percivale,
Whom Arthur and his knighthood called The Pure,
Had passed into the silent life of prayer
Praise, fast, and alms; and leaving for the cowl   5
The helmet in an abbey far away
From Camelot, there, and not long after, died.

And one, a fellow-monk among the rest
Ambrosius,   loved him much beyond the rest,
And honoured him, and wrought into his heart   10
A way by love that wakened love within,
To answer that which came: and as they sat
Beneath a world-old yew-tree, darkening half
The cloisters, on a gustful April morn
That puffed the swaying branches into smoke   15
Above them, ere the summer when he died,
The monk Ambrosius questioned Percivale:

'O brother, I have seen this yew-tree smoke,
Spring after spring, for half a hundred years:
For never have I known the world without,   20
Nor ever strayed beyond the pale: but thee,
When first thou camest--such a courtesy

Draft 10-12
       A way By love that waken'd love within
       To answer that which came:
       And wrought a way into his heart by love
       That waked a counter-love: & as they sat   H-38

13 Beneath an world-old...   H-38

17 The good Ambrosius...   H-38
17 ...Percivale.   A-2104
17 (C)   L-HGI

19 ...spring for...   A-2104
19 (C)   L-HGI

21 ...-but you   H-38

22 When first you came - so much of courtesy   H-38

751

Spake through the limbs and in the voice--I knew
For one of those who eat in Arthur's hall;
For good ye are and bad, and like to coins,   25
Some true, some light, but every one of you
Stamped with the image of the King; and now
Tell me, what drove thee from the Table Round,
My brother? was it earthly passion crost?'

    'Nay,' said the knight; 'for no such passion mine. 30
But the sweet vision of the Holy Grail
Drove me from all vainglories, rivalries,
And earthly heats that spring and sparkle out
Among us in the jousts, while women watch
Who wins, who falls; and waste the spiritual
                      strength   35
Within us, better offered up to Heaven.'

---

23 Spake thro' your limbs & in your voice, I knew   H-38

24 As one...   H-38
24 For
   A̸s̸ one...   Tn-29
24   eat   I MS
   ...who s̸a̸t̸ in...   B-VI
24 (C)   H-HGP

25 For you are good & bad: & s̸o̸m̸e̸ like to coins   H-38
25   e
   ...good y̸o̸u̸ are...   Tn-29

27 ...the king; ...   A-2104
27 (C)   L-HGI

28 ...drove you from...   H-38
28 ...what drave thee...   Tn-29

30   c̸r̸o̸s̸t̸
   ...passion mine.   Tn-29
30 ...mine,.   (. I MS)   B-VI
30 (C)   L-HGI

32 Drave me...   Tn-29

33 ...heats that often sparkle out   H-38

752

THE HOLY GRAIL

To whom the monk: 'The Holy Grail!--I trust
We are green in Heaven's eyes; but here too much
We moulder--as to things without I mean--
Yet one of your own knights, a guest of ours,   40
Told us of this in our refectory,
But spake with such a sadness and so low
We heard not half of what he said. What is it?
The phantom of a cup that comes and goes?'

'Nay, monk! what phantom?' answered Percivale.   45
'The cup, the cup itself, from which our Lord
Drank at the last sad supper with his own.
This, from the blessed land of Aromat--
After the day of darkness, when the dead
Went wandering o'er Moriah--the good saint   50

Arimathaean Joseph, journeying brought
To Glastonbury, where the winter thorn
Blossoms at Christmas, mindful of our Lord.
And there awhile it bode; and if a man
Could touch or see it, he was healed at once,   55
By faith, of all his ills. But then the times
Grew to such evil that the holy cup
Was caught away to Heaven, and disappeared.'

    To whom the monk: 'From our old books I know
That Joseph came of old to Glastonbury,   60
And there the heathen Prince, Arviragus,
Gave him an isle of marsh whereon to build;
And there he built with wattles from the marsh
A little lonely church in days of yore,
For so they say, these books of ours, but seem   65

54-57
    And there awhile it dwelt, & heal'd all ills
    And wrought much faith; but presently the time
    Became so evil, that the Holy cup   H-38

56 ...ills; but...   A-2104
56 (C)   L-HGI

57 ...thy Holy cup   A-2104
57 (C)   L-HGI

58 ...Heaven, and...   ,/ (I)   B-VI
58 (C)   H-HGP

59 Then said the monk...   H-38
59 ...Monk, 'From...   A-2104
59 (C)   L-HGI

61 ...heathen King, Arviragus   H-38

64 ...in years of yore.   H-38
64   days
   ...in y̸e̸a̸r̸s̸ of yore   Tn-29

67 But who hath seen this holy Grail to-day?   H-38

68 A woman said t̸h̸e̸ Sir Percivale a nun   H-38

Mute of this miracle, far as I have read.
But who first saw the holy thing today?'

   'A woman,' answered Percivale, 'a nun,
And one no further off in blood from me
Than sister; and if ever holy maid   70
With knees of adoration wore the stone,
A holy maid; though never maiden glowed,
But that was in her earlier maidenhood,
With such a fervent flame of human love,
Which being rudely blunted, glanced and shot   75
Only to holy things; to prayer and praise
She gave herself, to fast and alms. And yet,
Nun as she was, the scandal of the Court,
Sin against Arthur and the Table Round,
And the strange sound of an adulterous race,   80

---

72 A holy maiden: never maiden glow'd,   H-38

73 ...her dawn of maidenhood,   H-38

75 ...blunted glanced...   A-2104
75 (C)   L-HGI

Sketch 76-81
    Only toward holy things: she gave herself
    My sister up to praise & alms & prayer
    And never saintlier being wore the stone
    With knees of adoration - yet, indeed,
    Nun as she was, the strange sin of the court
    Sin, & the noise of an adulterous race
    Right thro' the iron grating of her cell   H-38

76 O
    Ĭnly to holy things: to...   I MS
                              B-VI
76 ...things: to...   H-HGP
76 (C)   L-HGI

77 ...alms; and...   A-2104
77 (C)   L-HGI

80 ...race   A-2104
80 (C)   L-HGI

THE HOLY GRAIL

Across the iron grating of her cell
Beat, and she prayed and fasted all the more.

    'And he to whom she told her sins, or what
Her all but utter whiteness held for sin,
A man wellnigh a hundred winters old,   85
Spake often with her of the Holy Grail,
A legend handed down through five or six,
And each of these a hundred winters old,
From our Lord's time. And when King Arthur made
His Table Round, and all men's hearts became   90
Clean for a season, surely he had thought
That now the Holy Grail would come again;
But sin broke out. Ah, Christ, that it would come,
And heal the world of all their wickedness!

---

83 ...whom the maiden ever told	H-38
83 (Par.) And...	A-2104
83 (C)	L-HGI
84 All that her utter...	H-38
85 A H̸ø̸l̸y̸ man...	H-38
85 ...well-nigh...	A-2104
85 (C)	73
87 ...handed thro'...	H-38
89 ...time: and...	A-2104
89 (C)	L-HGI
90 ...& all men's hearts were pure	H-38
90 T	I MS
His T̸able round, ...	B-VI
90 His Table round, ...	H-HGP
90 (C)	L-HGI
91 But for a season...	H-38
92 ...Grail will come...	H-38
93 ...sin brake out...	Tn-29

"O Father!" asked the maiden, "might it come   95
To me by prayer and fasting?" "Nay," said he,
"I know not, for thy heart is pure as snow."
And so she prayed and fasted, till the sun
Shone, and the wind blew, through her, and I thought
She might have risen and floated when I saw her.   100

   'For on a day she sent to speak with me.
And when she came to speak, behold her eyes
Beyond my knowing of them, beautiful,
Beyond all knowing of them, wonderful,
Beautiful in the light of holiness.   105
And "O my brother Percivale," she said,
"Sweet brother, I have seen the Holy Grail:
For, waked at dead of night, I heard a sound

---

95 Sweet Father...	H-38
95 'O father!' asked the maiden, 'might...	A-2104
95 'O father!' asked the maiden, 'might...	S-925
95 (C)	L-HGI
96 ...fasting?' 'Nay,' said...	A-2104
96 (C)	L-HGI
97 Who knoweth for thy thoughts are pure as snow.	H-38
97 'I know...snow.'	A-2104
97 (C)	L-HGI
99 ...her till I thought	H-38
101 (Par.) For...	A-2104
101 (C)	L-HGI
105 Wonderful in a light...	H-38
106 And 'O my brother, Percivale,' she said,	A-2104
106 ...brother, Percivale," ...	L-HGI
106 (C)	73
107 'Sweet...	A-2104
107 (C)	L-HGI
108 For waked...night I heard...	A-2104
108 (C)	L-HGI

THE HOLY GRAIL

As of silver horn from o'er the hills
Blown, and I thought, 'It is not Arthur's use   110
To hunt by moonlight;' and the slender sound
As from a distance beyond distance grew
Coming upon me--O never harp nor horn,
Nor aught we blow with breath, or touch with hand,
Was like that music as it came; and then   115
Streamed through my cell a cold and silver beam,
And down the long beam stole the Holy Grail,
Rose-red with beatings in it, as if alive,
Till all the white walls of my cell were dyed
With rosy colours leaping on the wall;   120

---

110 ...thought, it is...   ,/ (I)   B-VI
110 ...thought, it is...   H-HGP
110 (C)   L-HGI

111 ...& the sweet thin sound   H-38
111 ...moonlight, and...   A-2104
111 ...moonlight'; and...   L-HGI
111 (C)   70

113 ...me & never horn nor harp   H-38

115 ...music. On a sudden, stream'd   H-38
115 ...and then¢¢   B-VI
115 (C)   H-HGP

116 Athwart my cell...   H-38

117 ...down the cold beam   H-38

118 ...in it as if it lived   H-38

119 ...cell were bathed   H-38

125 ...brother;, fast...   ,/ (I)   B-VI
125 (C)   H-HGP

128 ...heal'd.'   A-2104
128 (C)   L-HGI

And then the music faded, and the Grail
Past, and the beam decayed, and from the walls
The rosy quiverings died into the night.
So now the Holy Thing is here again
Among us, brother, fast thou too and pray,   125
And tell thy brother knights to fast and pray,
That so perchance the vision may be seen
By thee and those, and all the world be healed."

  'Then leaving the pale nun, I spake of this
To all men; and myself fasted and prayed   130
Always, and many among us many a week
Fasted and prayed even to the uttermost,
Expectant of the wonder that would be.

  'And one there was among us, ever moved
Among us in white armour, Galahad.   135

---

129 ...nun, I told the knights   H-38
129 (Par.) Then...   A-2104
129 (C)   L-HGI

130 The vision & myself...   H-38

133   e
    ...of th~~at~~ wonder...   Tn-29

134-142
    And one there was among us, Galahad -
    Some said he was a son of Lancelot - some,
·   Begotten by enchantment - how it was
    I know not - but the king had knighted him
    And never yet was any man so young
    Knighted of Arthur, & when I spake of this
    His eyes became her eyes so like ~~to them~~ her eyes,
    Methought he seem'd her brother more than I.   H-38

134   ever moved
    ...us, ~~Galahad~~   Tn-29
134 (Par.) And...   A-2104
134 (C)   L-HGI

Alt. after 134
    ~~Some said he was a son Lancelot, some~~   Tn-29

759

THE HOLY GRAIL

"God make thee good as thou art beautiful,"
Said Arthur, when he dubbed him knight; and none,
In so young youth, was ever made a knight
Till Galahad; and this Galahad, when he heard
My sister's vision, filled me with amaze;   140
His eyes became so like her own, they seemed
Hers, and himself her brother more than I.

  'Sister or brother none had he; but some
Called him a son of Lancelot, and some said
Begotten by enchantment--chatterers they,   145
Like birds of passage piping up and down,

---

136 'God...beautiful,'   A-2104
136 (C)   L-HGI

137   dubb'd
     ...he m̸a̸d̸e̸ him...   Tn-29

138 In y̸o̸u̸t̸h̸ so...   Tn-29

143 (Par.) Sister...   A-2104
143 (C)   L-HGI

144   & some
     ...Lancelot, o̸t̸h̸e̸r̸s̸ said,   Tn-29

145 ... - chatterers, they,   A-2104
145 (C)   L-HGI

146   piping   I MS
     ...passage p̸i̸p̸i̸n̸g̸ up and down,   ,/ (I)   B-VI
146 (C)   H-HGP;L-HGII

Sketch 149-155
     T̸h̸e̸n̸ m̸y̸ s̸w̸e̸e̸t̸ s̸i̸s̸t̸e̸r̸ s̸h̸o̸r̸e̸ h̸e̸r̸ h̸o̸l̸y̸ h̸a̸i̸r̸
     T̸o̸ m̸a̸k̸e̸ a̸ s̸t̸r̸a̸n̸g̸e̸ s̸w̸o̸r̸d̸-̸b̸e̸l̸t̸ &̸ p̸l̸a̸i̸t̸e̸d̸ i̸t̸
     W̸i̸t̸h̸ g̸o̸l̸d̸ &̸ s̸i̸l̸v̸e̸r̸ t̸h̸r̸e̸a̸d̸/ &̸ w̸o̸r̸e̸ t̸h̸e̸r̸e̸i̸n̸
     T̸h̸e̸ g̸o̸l̸d̸e̸n̸ v̸e̸s̸s̸e̸l̸ i̸n̸ a̸ s̸i̸l̸v̸e̸r̸ b̸e̸a̸m̸   H-38

149 (Par.) And then the holy maiden...   H-38
149 (Par.) But...maiden shore...   A-2104
149 ...maiden shore...   L-HGI
149 (C)   73

760

That gape for flies--we know not whence they come;
For when was Lancelot wanderingly lewd?

  'But she, the wan sweet maiden, shore away
Clean from her forehead all that wealth of hair   150
Which made a silken mat-work for her feet;
And out of this she plaited broad and long
A strong sword-belt, and wove with silver thread
And crimson in the belt a strange device,
A crimson grail within a silver beam;   155
And saw the bright boy-knight, and bound it on him,
Saying, "My knight, my love, my knight of heaven,

---

150 ...all the length of hair   H-38

151 That made a silken matting for...   H-38

153 ..., and woven with...   A-2104
153   v   I MS
   ..., and wo~~v~~e with...   B-VI
153 (C)   H-HGP;L-HGII

154 And golden in...   H-38;Tn-29;A-2104
154   crimson   I MS
   And ~~golden~~ in...   B-VIII
154 (C)   L-HGII

155 A golden grail...   H-38;Tn-29;A-2104
155   crimson   I MS
   A ~~golden~~ Grail...   L-HGI
155 (C)   L-HGII

156 ...him   A-2104
156 (C)   L-HGI

157 Saying my love, my knight of heaven   H-38
157   my
   ...love, ~~the~~ knight...   Tn-29
157 Saying, 'My ... heaven.   A-2104
157 Saying, 'My...   L-HGI
157 (C)   <u>69</u>

O thou, my love, whose love is one with mine,
I, maiden, round thee, maiden, bind my belt.
Go forth, for thou shalt see what I have seen,   160
And break through all, till one will crown thee king
Far in the spiritual city:" and as she spake
She sent the deathless passion in her eyes
Through him, and made him hers, and laid her mind
On him, and he believed in her belief.   165

   'Then came a year of miracle: O brother,
In our great hall there stood a vacant chair,
Fashioned by Merlin ere he past away,

---

160 ~~And/Know/that~~	shalt	
Go forth, for thou ~~will~~ see...		Tn-29
161	till	
...a, ~~&~~ one...		Tn-29
162	& as she spake	
...city: ~~& now farewell~~		Tn-29
162 ...city:' and...		A-2104
162 (C)		69
166 (Par.) Then...		A-2104
166 (C)		L-HGI
169 ...figures, in & out		H-38
169 n		I MS
And carve~~d~~ with...		B-VI
169 (C)		H-HGP
172 ...'The Siege perilous,'		A-2104
172 (C)		L-HGI
173 ...; 'for there,' he...		A-2104
173 (C)		L-HGI
174 cd sd		
...man ~~can~~ sit but he ~~shall~~ lose...		Tn-29
174 'No...himself:'		A-2104
174 (C)		L-HGI

And carven with strange figures; and in and out
The figures, like a serpent, ran a scroll   170
Of letters in a tongue no man could read.
And Merlin called it "The Siege perilous,"
Perilous for good and ill; "for there," he said,
"No man could sit but he should lose himself:"
And once by misadvertence Merlin sat   175
In his own chair, and so was lost; but he,
Galahad, when he heard of Merlin's doom,
Cried, "If I lose myself, I save myself!"

    'Then on a summer night it came to pass,
While the great banquet lay along the hall,   180
That Galahad would sit down in Merlin's chair.

   'And all at once, as there we sat, we heard

---

175 And he by misadvertance once had sat   H-38
175   Merlin once
   And H̸ḙ by misadvertance ø̸ṅ̸ḉ̸ḙ H̸ḁ̸ḏ sat   Tn-29
175 And Merlin once by misadvertance sat   A-2104
175   Merlin   I MS
   And M̸ḙ̸ṙ̸ḽ̸ḭ̸ṅ once by misadvertance sat   B-VIII
175 (C)   L-HGII

176 In this wierd chair & he was ḽø̸s̸ṫ wholly lost. H-38

177 But Galahad when he heard our Seer was lost   H-38

178 Said if I...   H-38
178 Cried, 'If I lose myself I save myself!'   A-2104
178 ...myself I...   L-HGI
178 (C)   74

179 ...summer eve it...   H-38
179 (Par.) Then...   A-2104
179 (C)   L-HGI

182   as there we sat
   (Par.) And all at once among the roofs ḇ̸ḙ̸ẙ̸ø̸ṅ̸
               we heard   H-38
182 (Par.) And...   A-2104
182 (C)   L-HGI

763

THE HOLY GRAIL

A cracking and a riving of the roofs,
And rending, and a blast, and overhead
Thunder, and in the thunder was a cry.   185
And in the blast there smote along the hall
A beam of light seven times more clear than day:
And down the long beam stole the Holy Grail
All over covered with a luminous cloud,
And none might see who bare it, and it past.   190
But every knight beheld his fellow's face
As in a glory, and all the knights arose,
And staring each at other like dumb men
Stood, till I found a voice and sware a vow.

  'I sware a vow before them all, that I,   195

---

183   cracking
        A ~~recking~~ & a riving ~~of the roots~~ of the roofs   H-38

186   And
        Then entered in the middle of the blast there
                                smote   H-38

191   knight
        ...every ~~man~~ beheld...   Tn-29

192 All in a glory
        ~~glorious~~ & all...   H-38
192 ...arose,   ,/ (I)   B-VI
192 (C)   H-HGP

195 (Par.) I...   A-2104
195 (C)   L-HGI

196 ...seen the Holy Grail   H-38

197 Would ~~wander~~ ride thro' all in quest of it   H-38

199 ...saw. & Galahad...   H-38
199 ...vow.   A-2104
199 (C)   L-HGI

200   cousin
        ...Lancelot's ~~brother~~, sware,   Tn-29

Because I had not seen the Grail, would ride
A twelvemonth and a day in quest of it,
Until I found and saw it, as the nun
My sister saw it; and Galahad sware the vow,
And good Sir Bors, our Lancelot's cousin, sware,   200
And Lancelot sware, and many among the knights,
And Gawain sware, and louder than the rest.'

    Then spake the monk Ambrosius, asking him,
'What said the King? Did Arthur take the vow?'

    'Nay, for my lord,' said Percivale, 'the King,   205
Was not in hall: for early that same day,
Scaped through a cavern from a bandit hold,
An   outraged maiden sprang into the hall
Crying on help: for all her shining hair
Was smeared with earth, and either milky arm   210

---

202 ...rest.	A-2104
202 (C)	L-HGI
203 ...him	A-2104
203 (C)	L-HGI
204 Did Arthur take the vow? what said the king?	H-38
204 ...the king? Did...	A-2104
204 (C)	L-HGI
205 (Par.) To whom Sir Percivale replied The King	H-38
205 (Par.) Nay, for my lord [said Percivale] the king	A-2104
205 ...my lord, said...'the king '/ (I)	L-HGI
205 (C)	69
206 ...in Hall: for...	A-2104
206 (C)	L-HGI
207 Scaped from a bandit hold beyond the hills	H-38
207 '/ Scaped...	B-VI
207 (C)	L-HGI
210 ...earth, & both her milky arms	H-38
210 earth	
...with c̶l̶a̶y̶, & ...	Tn-29

Red-rent with hooks of bramble, and all she wore
Torn as a sail that leaves the rope is torn
In tempest: so the King arose and went
To smoke the scandalous hive of those wild bees
That made such honey in his realm. Howbeit   215
Some little of this marvel he too saw,
Returning o'er the plain that then began
To darken under Camelot; whence the King
Looked up, calling aloud, "Lo, there! the roofs
Of our great hall are rolled in thunder-smoke!   220
Pray Heaven, they be not smitten by the bolt."
For dear to Arthur was that hall of ours,
As having there so oft with all his knights
Feasted, and as the stateliest under heaven.

---

211 Scratch'd red with...   H-38

212 ...sail, that leaves the rope, is...   A-2104
212 (C)   L-HGI

213 ...tempest: then the king   H-38
213 ...the king...   A-2104
213 (C)   69

214 To burn the scandalous home of...   H-38

215 ...realm: howbeit   A-2104
215 (C)   L-HGI

216 He saw some little of this wonder too he too
                                  saw   H-38

Sketch 217 ff
     'Lo yonder, O Sir Arthur, how the roofs
     Of our great Hall are roll'd in the thundersmoke'
          Then glanced the King ~~from~~ up from the
                                  darkening plain
     To where the sacred mount of Camelot
     Tower beyond tower, spire after spire arose
     By garden, grove, & rushing stream to where
     His palace crown'd the hill, & therebeside
     The many-pinnacled minster & the Hall   H-38

'O brother, had you known our mighty hall,   225
Which Merlin built for Arthur long ago!
For all the sacred mount of Camelot,
And all the dim rich city, roof by roof,
Tower after tower, spire beyond spire,
By grove, and garden-lawn, and rushing brook,   230
Climbs to the mighty hall that Merlin built.
And four great zones of sculpture, set betwixt
With many a mystic symbol, gird the hall:
And in the lowest beasts are slaying men,
And in the second men are slaying beasts,   235
And on the third are warriors, perfect men,

---

218 ...Camelot; for the king	H-38
218 ...the king	A-2104
218 (C)	69
219 Glanced up, & call'd aloud 'Lo there the	
roofs	H-38
219 ...aloud, 'Lo...	A-2104
219 (C)	L-HGI
219 ...aloud, "Lo there!	69
219 (C)	73
220 ...great Hall are rolled in...	A-2104
220 (C)	L-HGI
221 ...bolt.'	A-2104
221 (C)	L-HGI
222 ...hall of H̶i̶s̶ ours	H-38
224 ...as the costliest under...	H-38;Tn-29
224 ...the costliest under...	A-2104
224 (C)	69
225 (Par.) O brother, ...	A-2104
225 (C)	L-HGI
229 Tower beyond tower, spire after spire	H-38
229 after beyond	
Tower/b̶e̶y̶o̶n̶d̶ tower, spire a̶f̶t̶e̶r̶ spire,	Tn-29

And on the fourth are men with growing wings,
And over all one statue in the mould
Of Arthur, made by Merlin, with a crown,
And peaked wings pointed to the Northern Star.   240
And eastward fronts the statue, and the crown
And both the wings are made of gold, and flame
At sunrise till the people in far fields,
Wasted so often by the heathen hordes,
Behold it, crying, "We have still a King."   245

    'And, brother, had you known our hall within,
Broader and higher than any in all the lands!
Where twelve great windows blazon Arthur's wars,
And all the light that falls upon the board
Streams through the twelve great battles of our
                  King.   250
Nay, one there is, and at the eastern end,

---

241 And eastward fronts
    The statue ~~faces~~ ~~eastward~~, & ...   Tn-29

242 ...gold and...   A-2104
242 (C)   H-HGP

244 So often wasted by...   H-38

245 ...have yet a king.   H-38
245   still
    ...have ~~yet~~ a King,'   Tn-29
245 ...crying, 'We...a king.'   A-2104
245 (C)   73

246 (Par.) O brother...   H-38
246 (Par.) And...   A-2104
246 (C)   L-HGI

247 ...than any in any land.   H-38

248 And twelve high windows...   H-38

250 ...our king.   A-2104
250 (C)   H-HGP

251   there is   & at the
    Nay - one at the eastern end ~~is~~ ~~dim~~ ~~with/here~~ H-38

Wealthy with wandering lines of mount and mere,
Where Arthur finds the brand Excalibur.
And also one to the west, and counter to it,
And blank: and who shall blazon it? when and
                     how?--   255
O there, perchance, when all our wars are done,
The brand Excalibur will be cast away.

  'So to this hall full quickly rode the King,
In horror lest the work by Merlin wrought,
Dreamlike, should on the sudden vanish, wrapt   260
In unremorseful folds of rolling fire.
And in he rode, and up I glanced, and saw
The golden dragon sparkling over all:
And many of those who burnt the hold, their arms
Hacked, and their foreheads grimed with smoke,
                and seared,   265

252-253   That shows
      ~~And mount - the finding of Excalibur~~   H-38

253 ...brand, Excalibur.   A-2104
253 (C)   73

254-255 And one is blank & counter to it & who
        Shall blazon that? O brother, & with what. H-38

255 ...how? -   -/ (I)   B-VI
255 (C)   H-HGP

256   re   I MS
     O then, perchance, ...   B-VI
256 (C)   H-HGP

257 Perhaps Excalibur will be thrown away.   H-38

258 (Par.) So...the king,   A-2104
258 (C)   L-HGI

259 ...wrought   A-2104
259 (C)   L-HGI

264 ...burnt the bandit-hold   H-38

THE HOLY GRAIL

Followed, and in among bright faces, ours,
Full of the vision, prest: and then the King
Spake to me, being nearest, "Percivale,"
(Because the hall was all in tumult--some
Vowing, and some protesting), "what is this?"   270

    'O brother, when I told him what had chanced,
My sister's vision, and the rest, his face
Darkened, as I have seen it more than once,
When some brave deed seemed to be done in vain,
Darken; and "Woe is me, my knights," he cried,   275

265-267
    Their armour hack'd, their foreheads grimed & sear'd
    Pale with the sweat & labour of the day
    Follow'd, & in among us prest, who stood
    Brightfaced, & full of vision & the king   H-38

266 ..., ours   A-2104
266 (C)   L-HGI

268 ...nearest, 'Percivale,   A-2104
268 (C)   L-HGI

269 [For all the hall was fill'd with tumult, some   H-38
269 ...the Hall...   A-2104
269 (C)   L-HGI

270 ...protesting], 'what is this?'   A-2104
270 ...protesting], 'what is this?   H-HGP
270 (C)   L-HGI

271 (Par.) O brother,...   A-2104
271 (C)   L-HGI

274   brave
    ...some great deed...   H-38

275 Darken, & O my knights, my knights he s̸a̸i̸d̸
                        cried   H-38
275 ...and 'Woe...knights,' he...   A-2104
275 (C)   L-HGI

770

"Had I been here, ye had not sworn the vow."
Bold was mine answer, "Had thyself been here,
My King, thou wouldst have sworn." "Yea, yea,"
                    said he,
"Art thou so bold and hast not seen the Grail?"

'"Nay, lord, I heard the sound, I saw the light,   280
But since I did not see the Holy Thing,
I sware a vow to follow it till I saw."

'Then when he asked us, knight by knight, if any

276	'Had...vow.'	A-2104
276	(C)	L-HGI
Alt. 277	N̸a̸y̸,̸ L̸o̸r̸d̸,̸ I̸ a̸n̸s̸w̸e̸r̸'̸d̸,̸ ...	H-38
277	...answer, 'Had...	A-2104
277	(C)	L-HGI
278	it. Yea said he	
	...sworn a̸m̸o̸n̸g̸ t̸h̸e̸ r̸e̸s̸t̸	H-38
278	...sworn.' 'Yea, yea,' said...	A-2104
278	(C)	L-HGI
279	'Art...the grail?'	A-2104
279	(C)	L-HGI
280	T̸h̸e̸n̸	
	(Par.) Nay, Lord...	Tn-29
280	(Par.) Nay, Lord...	A-2104
280	(Par.) '" Nay, Lord...	69
280	(C)	73
282	...sware my vow...	Tn-29
282	...saw.	A-2104
282	(C)	L-HGI
283	And when	
	(Par.) W̸h̸e̸r̸e̸a̸t̸ he...	H-38
283	(Par.) Then...	A-2104
283	(C)	L-HGI

Had seen it, all their answers were as one:
"Nay, lord, and therefore have we sworn our vows."   285

'"Lo now," said Arthur, "have ye seen a cloud?
What go ye into the wilderness to see?"

'Then Galahad on the sudden, and in a voice
Shrilling along the hall to Arthur, called,
"But I, Sir Arthur, saw the Holy Grail,   290
I saw the Holy Grail and heard a cry--
'O Galahad, and O Galahad, follow me.'"

'"Ah, Galahad, Galahad," said the King, "for such

---

284 ...one,		A-2104
284 (C)		L-HGI
285 'Nay, Lord, and...vows.'		A-2104
285 "Nay, Lord, and...		L-HGI
285 (C)		73
286 (Par.) 'Lo now,' said Arthur, 'have...		A-2104
286 (Par.) 'Lo, now,' said Arthur, 'have...		H-HGP
286 (C)		L-HGI
287 ...see?'		A-2104
287 (C)		L-HGI
288-289		
Galahad on the sudden & in a voice		
But with a shrill voice Galahad called aloud		
That shrill'd along the hall to Arthur cried		H-38
288 Then		
(Par.) B̸u̸t̸ Galahad...		Tn-29
288 (Par.) Then...		A-2104
288 (C)		<u>69</u>
290 'But...		A-2104
290 (C)		L-HGI
292 O Galahad...me.'		A-2104
292 O Galahad...me."		L-HGI
292 (C)		69

As thou art is the vision, not for these.
Thy holy nun and thou have seen a sign--   295
Holier is none, my Percivale, than she--
A sign to maim this Order which I made.
But ye, that follow but the leader's bell"
(Brother, the King was hard upon his knights)
"Taliessin is our fullest throat of song,   300
And one hath sung and all the dumb will sing.
Lancelot is Lancelot, and hath overborne
Five knights at once, and every younger knight,

---

293 (Par.) 'Ah, ...Galahad,' said the King, 'for
                              such   A-2104
293 (C)   L-HGI

294 ...not for him   H-38

Alt. for 295 Gawain, nor for him: thou & the holy
                              nun,   H-38

295 ...a sign;   A-2104
295 (C)   L-HGI

297 Will maim this noble order...   H-38

Alt. after 297 For rightful strength redressing
                              human wrong.   H-38

298 But you, that...   Tn-29
298 But you, that...bell'   A-2104
298 But you, that...   L-HGI
298 (C)   73

299 ..., the king was...   A-2104
299 (C)   L-HGI

300 'Taliessin...   A-2104
300 (C)   L-HGI

Alt. preceding 302 A L̸i̸g̸h̸t̸ sound, a luminous cloud, a
                              holy nun   H-38

303 ...& every knight new-made   H-38

Unproven, holds himself as Lancelot,
Till overborne by one, he learns--and ye,   305
What are ye? Galahads?--no, nor Percivales"
(For thus it pleased the King to range me close
After Sir Galahad); "nay," said he, "but men
With strength and will to right the wronged, of power
To lay the sudden heads of violence flat,   310
Knights that in twelve great battles splashed and dyed
The strong White Horse in his own heathen blood--
But one hath seen, and all the blind will see.
Go, since your vows are sacred, being made:
Yet--for ye know the cries of all my realm   315

---

304 Unproven counts himself...   H-38

305   he learns: ~~his way~~ but ye
     Till overthrown by one: ~~& one hath seen~~   H-38

306   ?   I MS
     ...Galahads ~~≠~~ no, nor Percivales'   B-VI
306 ...Galahads? no, nor Percivales'   H-HGP
306 (C)   L-HGI

308 ...nay ~~but men~~ said...   Tn-29
308 ...; 'nay,' said he, 'but...   A-2104
308 (C)   L-HGI

309 With strength &
     ~~But men with~~ wills to...   Tn-29

314-316 Yet, for I may not disallow your vows
         Go therefore: but how often, O my knights, H-38

314   since
     Go, ~~for~~ your...   Tn-29
314 ...made -   A-2104
314 (C)   L-HGI

315 Yet, for...realm,   A-2104
315 Yet, for...realm~~/~~   H-HGP
315 (C)   L-HGI

THE HOLY GRAIL

Pass through this hall—how often, O my knights,
Your places being vacant at my side,
This chance of noble deeds will come and go
Unchallenged, while ye follow wandering fires
Lost in the quagmire! Many of you, yea most,   320
Return no more: ye think I show myself
Too dark a prophet: come now, let us meet
The morrow morn once more in full field
Of gracious pastime, that once more the King,

---

316 ...hall, how...   A-2104
316 (C)   L-HGI

317 ...vacant in our hall   H-38

318 The chance...   H-38;Tn-29
318   is   I MS
    Thé chance...   B-VI
318 (C)   H-HGP

319 ...while you wandering fires   H-38
319 ...while you follow...   Tn-29;A-2104
319 (C)   73

320 ...quagmire: many...   A-2104
320 ...quagmire? Many...   L-HGI
320 (C)   73

321 ...more: yet wherefore show myself   H-38

322 So dark...   H-38

323   in
    Once more the morrow morning f́ór one t́íĺt́ full
                         field   H-38

324   before
    ...that ónçé ḿóŕé the king ḿáý v́íéẃ   H-38
324 ...the king,   A-2104
324 (C)   L-HGI

775

Before ye leave him for this Quest, may count   325
The yet-unbroken strength of all his knights,
Rejoicing in that Order which he made."

    'So when the sun broke next from under ground,
All the great table of our Arthur closed
And clashed in such a tourney and so full,   330
So many lances broken--never yet
Had Camelot seen the like, since Arthur came;
And I myself and Galahad, for a strength
Was in us from the vision, overthrew
So many knights that all the people cried,   335
And almost burst the barriers in their heat,
Shouting, "Sir Galahad and Sir Percivale!"

---

325 ~~May see you all~~ Ye leave him for this doubtful
                          quest may count   H-38
325 Before you leave...this quest, ...   A-2104
325 Before you leave...   L-HGI
325 (C)   73

326   knights
...his ~~speaks~~,   Tn-29

327 ...that order...made.'   A-2104
327 (C)   L-HGI

328 (Par.) So...   A-2104
328 (C)   L-HGI

329 The whole round table of King Arthur closd   H-38

330   tourney
...such a ~~conflict~~ & ...   Tn-29

331 ...lances splinter'd - ...   H-38

332 Since Arthur ruled, had Camelot seen the like   H-38
332 ...came.   A-2104
332 (C)   69

333 ...for the strength   H-38

'But when the next day brake from under ground--
O brother, had you known our Camelot,
Built by old kings, age after age, so old   340
The King himself had fears that it would fall,
So strange, and rich, and dim; for where the roofs
Tottered toward each other in the sky,
Met foreheads all along the street of those
Who watched us pass; and lower, and where the long   345
Rich galleries, lady-laden, weighed the necks
Of dragons clinging to the crazy walls,
Thicker than drops from thunder, showers of flowers

---

334 ...the vision overbore   H-38

335 Most of the knights, till all the people cried H-38
335 So many   that
    M̷o̷s̷t̷ o̷f̷ t̷h̷e̷ knights t̷i̷l̷l̷ all...   Tn-29

337 Shouting 'Sir...Percivale!'   A-2104
337 Shouting "Sir...   L-HGI
337 (C)   73

338 (Par.) But...   A-2104
338 (C)   L-HGI

341 The king...   A-2104
341 (C)   L-HGI

342 So rich, so strange & dim - for where the roofs H-38

344 ...along the narrow street   H-38

345 Of those who gazed, & lower...   H-38

348 Thicker than rain in thunder, showers...   H-38
348   drops
    ...than r̷a̷i̷n̷ from...   Tn-29
348 ...thunder showers...   A-2104
348 ...thunder, showers...   (, MS)   H-HGP
348 (C)   L-HGI

777

Fell as we past; and men and boys astride
On wyvern, lion, dragon, griffin, swan,   350
At all the corners, named us each by name,
Calling "God speed!" but in the ways below
The knights and ladies wept, and rich and poor
Wept, and the King himself could hardly speak
For grief, and all in middle street the Queen,   355
Who rode by Lancelot, wailed and shrieked aloud,
"This madness has come on us for our sins."
So to the Gate of the three Queens we came,
Where Arthur's wars are rendered mystically,
And thence departed every one his way.   360

---

349 Fell on us as we past & boys & men   H-38
349 Fell, as...   A-2104
349 (C)   L-HGI

350 Horsed upon wyvern...   H-38

351 ...corners, naming each by name,   H-38

352 Bade us God speed but in the street below   H-38
352 ...in the street below   Tn-29
352 Calling 'God speed!' but in the street below A-2104
352 ...in the street below   L-HGI
352 (C)   73

353 The ladies & the knights wept & the rich   H-38

354 Wept & the poor: the king could hardly speak H-38
354 ...the king...   A-2104
354 (C)   L-HGI

355 For weeping & the Queen in the mid street   H-38
355 For sorrow & in the middle...   Tn-29
355 For sorrow, and in the middle street the
                            queen,   A-2104
355   grief   P MS
         For s̸o̸r̸r̸o̸w̸, and in the middle street the
                            Queen,   B-VIII
355 For grief, and in the middle street the
                            Queen,   L-HGII
355 (C)   73

778

'And I was lifted up in heart, and thought
Of all my late-shown prowess in the lists,
How my strong lance had beaten down the knights,
So many and famous names; and never yet
Had heaven appeared so blue, nor earth so green,   365
For all my blood danced in me, and I knew
That I should light upon the Holy Grail.

'Thereafter, the dark warning of our King,
That most of us would follow wandering fires,
Came like a driving gloom across my mind.   370
Then every evil word I had spoken once,

---

356 Riding with Lancelot waild...	H-38
357 ...madness comes upon us...	H-38
357 'This...sins.'	A-2104
357 (C)	L-HGI
358 And then we reach'd the madly-sculptured gate	H-38
358 And then we reach'd the wierdly-sculptured gate,	Tn-29;A-2104
358 (C)	73
359 ...wars were render'd...	H-38;Tn-29; A-2104
359 (C)	73
361 (Par.) And...	A-2104
361 (C)	L-HGI
363 And how my lance...	H-38
367 ...should come upon...	H-38
368 Thereafter t̸h̸a̸t̸ the...	H-38
368 (Par.) Thereafter...our king,	A-2104
368 (C)	L-HGI
371 Then every evil word I had spoken once, that once I spoke	H-38

And every evil thought I had thought of old,
And every evil deed I ever did,
Awoke and cried, "This Quest is not for thee."
And lifting up mine eyes, I found myself   375
Alone, and in a land of sand and thorns,
And I was thirsty even unto death;
And I, too , cried, "This Quest is not for thee."

'And on I rode, and when I thought my thirst
Would slay me, saw deep lawns, and then a brook,   380
With one sharp rapid, where the crisping white
Played ever back upon the sloping wave,
And took both ear and eye; and o'er the brook
Were apple-trees, and apples by the brook
Fallen, and on the lawns. "I will rest here,"   385
I said, "I am not worthy of the Quest;"
But even while I drank the brook, and ate
The goodly apples, all these things at once
Fell into dust, and I was left alone,
And thirsting, in a land of sand and thorns.   390

---

374 Stood up & cried...	H-38
374 ...cried, 'This quest is...thee.'	A-2104
374 (C)	L-HGI
375 ...up mine I found...	H-38
378 ...cried, 'This quest is...thee.'	A-2104
378 (C)	L-HGI
379 (Par.) And...	A-2104
379 (C)	L-HGI
380 ...lawns, and a clear brook	H-38
381 That f̸e̸l̸l̸ glanced in rapids where the crisping white	H-38
385 ...will rest there	H-38
385 ...lawns, 'I...here,'	A-2104
385 (C)	L-HGI
386 I said, 'I am...the quest;'	A-2104
386 (C)	L-HGI

'And then behold a woman at a door
Spinning; and fair the house whereby she sat,
And kind the woman's eyes and innocent,
And all her bearing gracious; and she rose
Opening her arms to meet me, as who should say,   395
"Rest here;" but when I touched her, lo! she, too,
Fell into dust and nothing, and the house
Became no better than a broken shed,
And in it a dead babe; and also this
Fell into dust, and I was left alone.   400

'And on I rode, and greater was my thirst.
Then flashed a yellow gleam across the world,
And where it smote the plowshare in the field,
The plowman left his plowing, and fell down
Before it; where it glittered on her pail,   405
The milkmaid left her milking, and fell down
Before it, and I knew not why, but thought
"The sun is rising," though the sun had risen.

---

387 And while I drank the brook & scarce began   H-38

388 To taste the goodly apples all these things   H-38

391 (Par.) And...   A-2104
391 (C)   L-HGI

392 Spinning, and...sat;   A-2104
392 (C)   L-HGI

396 'Rest here,' but...   A-2104
396 (C)   L-HGI

401 (Par.) And on I rode and...   A-2104
401 (C)   L-HGI

407 ...why; but...   A-2104
407 (C)   L-HGI

408 The sun was rising but...   H-38
408   tho'
     ...rising' b̸u̸t̸ the sun...   Tn-29
408 'The sun is rising,' ...   A-2104
408 (C)   L-HGI

Then was I ware of one that on me moved
In golden armour with a crown of gold   410
About a casque all jewels; and his horse
In golden armour jewelled everywhere:
And on the splendour came, flashing me blind;
And seemed to me the Lord of all the world,
Being so huge. But when I thought he meant   415
To crush me, moving on me, lo! he, too,
Opened his arms to embrace me as he came,
And up I went and touched him, and he, too,
Fell into dust, and I was left alone
And wearying in a land of sand and thorns.   420

411	Upon a casque	H-38
411	a	
	About h̶i̶s̶ casque...	Tn-29
414	Who seem'd...	H-38
415	...huge: but...	A-2104
415	(C)	L-HGI
418	up	(P MS, not Tenn.)
	And u̶p̶ I went and...	S-925
420	And wearied in...	H-38;Tn-29;A-2104
420	wearying	P MS
	And w̶e̶a̶r̶i̶e̶d̶ in...	B-VIII
420	(C)	L-HGII
421	Then on I rode &...	H-38
421	(Par.) And on I rode & ...	Tn-29
421	(Par.) And on I rode and...	A-2104
421	(Par.) And I...	L-HGI
421	(C)	69
422	And high at top a city...	H-38
424	There stood a crowd before the gates & they	H-38

THE HOLY GRAIL

'And I rode on and found a mighty hill,
And on the top, a city walled: the spires
Pricked with incredible pinnacles into heaven.
And by the gateway stirred a crowd; and these
Cried to me climbing, "Welcome, Percivale!   425
Thou mightiest and thou purest among men!"
And glad was I and clomb, but found at top
No man, nor any voice.   And thence I past
Far through a ruinous city, and I saw
That man had once dwelt there; but there I found   430
Only one man of an exceeding age.
"Where is that goodly company," said I,
"That so cried out upon me?" and he had
Scarce any voice to answer, and yet gasped,

425	...climbing, 'Welcome...	A-2104
425	(C)	L-HGI
426	...men!'	A-2104
426	(C)	L-HGI
428	...voice; and...	A-2104
428	(C)	L-HGI
429	Into a ruinous...	H-38
430	...had dwelt there once; & there I found	H-38
431	But one old man of an exceeding eld,	H-38
432	'Where...company,' said...	A-2104
432	(C)	L-HGI
433	...cried upon...	Tn-29
433	out	I MS
	'That so cried upon me?' and...	B-VI
433	(C)	L-HGI
434	He had	
	Scarce any voice for answer [yet] he gasp'd	H-38
434	...gasp'd	A-2104
434	(C)	73

783

```
"Whence and what art thou?" and even as he spoke    435
Fell into dust, and disappeared, and I
Was left alone once more, and cried in grief,
"Lo, if I find the Holy Grail itself
And touch it, it will crumble into dust."

    'And thence I dropt into a lowly vale,          440
Low as the hill was high, and where the vale
Was lowest, found a chapel, and thereby
A holy hermit in a hermitage,
To whom I told my phantoms, and he said:

    '"O son, thou hast not true humility,           445
The highest virtue, mother of them all;
```

435 ...as he gasp'd		H-38
435 ...he spake		Tn-29
435 'Whence..thou?' and...		A-2104
435 (C)		L-HGI
436 disappeared		
Fell into dust & I was left alone		H-38
437 & in my grief I cried		H-38
438 'Lo...		A-2104
438 (C)		L-HGI
439 ...dust.'		A-2104
439 (C)		L-HGI
440 And thence I past into...		H-38
440 (Par.) And...		A-2104
440 (C)		L-HGI
442 ...chapel and...		A-2104
442 (C)		73
445 (Par.) 'O son, ...		A-2104
445 (C)		L-HGI
446 ...all,;	;/ (I)	B-VI
446 (C)		H-HGP

THE HOLY GRAIL

For when the Lord of all things made Himself
Naked of glory for His mortal change,
'Take thou my robe,' she said, 'for all is thine,'
And all her form shone forth with sudden light   450
So that the angels were amazed, and she
Followed Him down, and like a flying star
Led on the gray-haired wisdom of the east;
But her thou hast not known: for what is this
Thou thoughtest of thy prowess and thy sins?   455
Thou hast not lost thyself to save thyself
As Galahad." When the hermit made an end,
In silver armour suddenly Galahad shone
Before us, and against the chapel door
Laid lance, and entered, and we knelt in prayer.   460
And there the hermit slaked my burning thirst,
And at the sacring of the mass I saw
The holy elements alone; but he,
"Saw ye no more? I, Galahad, saw the Grail,

---

452 Follow'd him down...   A-2104
452 (C)   73

457   As
   ...Galahad.' W̶h̶e̶n̶ the hermit...   Tn-29
457 As Galahad. As the...   A-2104
457 As Galahad.' As...   S-925;H-HGP
457   When   I MS
   As Galahad." A̶s̶ the...   B-VIII
457 (C)   L-HGII

461 ...thirst;   A-2104
461 ...thirst   L-HGII
461 (C)   73

463 The blessed elements...   H-38
463 ...he -   -/ (I)   B-VI
463 ...he -   H-HGP
463 ...he: L-HGI
463 (C)   73

464 ...more, he cried, I saw the grail   H-38
464 'Saw...   A-2104
464 (C)   L-HGI

THE HOLY GRAIL

The Holy Grail, descend upon the shrine: 465
I saw the fiery face as of a child
That smote itself into the bread, and went;
And hither am I come; and never yet
Hath what thy sister taught me first to see,
This Holy Thing, failed from my side, nor come   470
Covered, but moving with me night and day,
Fainter by day, but always in the night
Blood-red, and sliding down the blackened marsh
Blood-red, and on the naked mountain top
Blood-red, and in the sleeping mere below   475
Blood-red. And in the strength of this I rode,
Shattering all evil customs everywhere,
And past through Pagan realms, and made them mine,
And clashed with Pagan hordes, and bore them down,
And broke through all, and in the strength of this   480

---

465 ...Grail descend...   A-2104
465 (C)   L-HGI

467 ...went,;   ;/ (I)   B-VI
467 (C)   H-HGP

469 Hath this great vision which thy sister first   H-38

470 Taught me to see, fail'd from my side, nor ever H-38
470 This holy thing, fail'd...   A-2104
470 (C)   L-HGI

471 Come veil'd, but moving...   H-38

474 Or on the naked mountain far indeed   H-38

476 Blood red: and...rode   A-2104
476 (C)   L-HGI

477 ...customs in all lands,   H-38

479 ...Pagan hosts & bore...   H-38

481 ...victor: but...   A-2104
481 (C)   L-HGI

786

THE HOLY GRAIL

Come victor. But my time is hard at hand,
And hence I go; and one will crown me king
Far in the spiritual city; and come thou, too,
For thou shalt see the vision when I go."

'While thus he spake, his eye, dwelling on mine,   485
Drew me, with power upon me, till I grew
One with him, to believe as he believed.
Then, when the day began to wane, we went.

'There rose a hill that none but man could climb,
Scarred with a hundred wintry water-courses--   490
Storm at the top, and when we gained it, storm
Round us and death; for every moment glanced

---

483 ...city: come with me   H-38

484 ...I go.'   A-2104
484 (C)   L-HGI

485 (Par.) While...   A-2104
485 (C)   L-HGI

487 ...him, & believed...   H-38

488 ...began to fade we...   H-38
488 Then, when...wane we...   ,/ (I)   B-VI
488 ...wane we...   H-HGP
488 (C)   L-HGI

489 There rose a ~~mountain wh~~ hill wh...   H-38
489 (Par.) Then rose...   Tn-29
489   re   I MS
    (Par.) The~~n~~ rose...   B-VI
489 (Par.) There rose...   H-HGP
489 (C)   L-HGI

490 Scarr'd with ten thousand wintry...   H-38
490 ...watercourses -   A-2104
490 (C)   84

492 ...for every minute glanced   H-38

787

His silver arms and gloomed: so quick and thick
The lightnings here and there to left and right
Struck, till the dry old trunks about us, dead,   495
Yea, rotten with a hundred years of death,
Sprang into fire: and at the base we found
On either hand, as far as eye could see,
A great black swamp and of an evil smell,
Part black, part whitened with the bones of men,   500
Not to be crost, save that some ancient king
Had built a way, where, linked with many a bridge,
A thousand piers ran into the great Sea.
And Galahad fled along them bridge by bridge,
And every bridge as quickly as he crost   505
Sprang into fire and vanished, though I yearned
To follow; and thrice above him all the heavens
Opened and blazed with thunder such as seemed
Shoutings of all the sons of God: and first
At once I saw him far on the great Sea,   510
In silver-shining armour starry-clear;

---

495 Struck, that the...   H-38

503 ...the Great Sea.   A-2104
503 (C)   69

505 ...as he past   H-38

506 ...vanish'd; & the heavens   (omits 507)   H-38

510   by the flashes
    ...him out on the Great Sea   H-38
510 ...the great sea,   A-2104
510 (C)   69

512 ...the holy vessel hung   A-2104
512 (C)   75

514 ...the boat   A-2104
514 (C)   73

519 ...creature clothed with wings.   H-38

```
And o'er his head the Holy Vessel hung
Clothed in white samite or a luminous cloud.
And with exceeding swiftness ran the boat,
If boat it were--I saw not whence it came.              515
And when the heavens opened and blazed again
Roaring, I saw him like a silver star--
And had he set the sail, or had the boat
Become a living creature clad with wings?
And o'er his head the Holy Vessel hung                  520
Redder than any rose, a joy to me,
For now I knew the veil had been withdrawn.
Then in a moment when they blazed again
Opening, I saw the least of little stars
Down on the waste, and straight beyond the star        525
I saw the spiritual city and all her spires
And gateways in a glory like one pearl--
No larger, though the goal of all the saints--
Strike from the sea; and from the star there shot
A rose-red sparkle to the city, and there              530
Dwelt, and I knew it was the Holy Grail,
Which never eyes on earth again shall see.
```

```
520 ...the holy vessel hung                           A-2104
520 (C)                                                   73

521 ...rose, rejoicing me                               H-38

522 For thence I...                                     H-38
522    now
       For t̸h̸e̸n̸c̸e̸ I...                                  Tn-29

523 Then in...                                          H-38

526 ...city with all...                                 H-38
526        and
       ...city w̸i̸t̸h̸ all...                              Tn-29

527 ...pearl,                                          A-2104
527 (C)                                                 L-HGI

528 ...goal of all mankind                              H-38
```

Then fell the floods of heaven drowning the deep.
And how my feet recrost the deathful ridge
No memory in me lives; but that I touched   535
The chapel-doors at dawn I know; and thence
Taking my war-horse from the holy man,
Glad that no phantom vext me more, returned
To whence I came, the gate of Arthur's wars.'

'O brother,' asked Ambrosius,--'for in sooth   540
These ancient books--and they would win thee--teem,
Only I find not there this Holy Grail,
With miracles and marvels like to these,
Not all unlike; which oftentime I read,
Who read but on my breviary with ease,   545
Till my head swims; and then go forth and pass
Down to the little thorpe that lies so close,
And almost plastered like a martin's nest
To these old walls--and mingle with our folk;

-----

533 Then down the heavens plunged drown'ding the
                              world   H-38
533 ...drowning the world.   Tn-29
533   deep   I MS
    ...drowning the ~~world~~.   B-VI
533 (C)   L-HGI

534 So that I scarcely
    But ~~gladly~~ I recross'd the ridge; & there   H-38
534   ~~&et~~
    ~~And/what good angel helpt me cross/the ridge~~   Tn-29

535-536   ~~chapel   I know not~~
    ~~Back to the hermit cave who knows? but there~~   Tn-29

536 ...dawn, I...   A-2104
536 (C)   L-HGI

538 Glad for no...   H-38

539   Arthur's wars
    ...came the ~~wierd~~ gate of ~~the wars~~   Tn-29
539 ...wars.   A-2104
539 (C)   L-HGI

And knowing every honest face of theirs   550
As well as ever shepherd knew his sheep,
And every homely secret in their hearts,
Delight myself with gossip and old wives,
And ills and aches, and teethings, lyings-in,
And mirthful sayings, children of the place,   555
That have no meaning half a league away:
Or lulling random squabbles when they rise,
Chafferings and chatterings at the market-cross,
Rejoice, small man, in this small world of mine,
Yea, even in their hens and in their eggs--   560
O brother, saving this Sir Galahad,
Came ye on none but phantoms in your quest,
No man, no woman?'

                  Then Sir Percivale:
'All men, to one so bound by such a vow,

540	...Ambrosius, 'for...	A-2104
540	(C)	L-HGI
550	...theirs,	A-2104
550	(C)	73
554	...lyings in,	A-2104
554	(C)	L-HGI
560	...eggs:	A-2104
560	(C)	L-HGII
561	...Galahad	A-2104
561	(C)	73
563	And Percivale	HM-1323
563	(Indent.) Then, Sir...	A-2104
563	(C)	73
564	To one so bound by such a vow all men	HM-1323
564	one	
	...to ḿé so...	Tn-29
564	...men to...vow	A-2104
564	(C)	L-HGI

And women were as phantoms. O, my brother,   565
Why wilt thou shame me to confess to thee
How far I faltered from my quest and vow?
For after I had lain so many nights,
A bedmate of the snail and eft and snake,
In grass and burdock, I was changed to wan   570
And meagre, and the vision had not come;
And then I chanced upon a goodly town
With one great dwelling in the middle of it;
Thither I made, and there was I disarmed
By maidens each as fair as any flower: 575
But when they led me into hall, behold,
The Princess of that castle was the one,
Brother, and that one only, who had ever

---

565 ...women are as...   HM-1323

566 ...confess ~~to thee~~ how much   HM-1323
566   to thee
           ~~how far~~
...confess ~~to thee~~   Tn-29

567 I falter'd in my quest & in my vow.   HM-1323
567 ...quest & ~~from my~~ vow?   Tn-29

568 For I had lain for more than fifty nights   HM-1323
568 ...nights   A-2104
568 (C)   73

569 A bedmate of snail & eft, & snake, in grass   HM-1323

570 Hemlock, & burdock...   HM-1323

571 ...come   A-2104
571 ...come,   L-HGI
571 (C)   <u>69</u>

572   goodly
      ...upon a glittering town   HM-1323

574 Whither I...   A-2104
574 Thither   P MS
      ~~Whither~~ I...   B-VIII
574 (C)   L-HGII

Made my heart leap; for when I moved of old
A slender page about her father's hall, 580
And she a slender maiden, all my heart
Went after her with longing: yet we twain
Had never kissed a kiss, or vowed a vow.
And now I came upon her once again,
And one had wedded her, and he was dead, 585
And all his land and wealth and state were hers.
And while I tarried, every day she set
A banquet richer than the day before
By me; for all her longing and her will
Was toward me as of old; till one fair morn, 590

---

576 ..., behold   A-2104
576 (C)   73

578 ...only that had...   H-38

579 ...for I had been of old   H-38

580 ...page within her...   H-38

581 ...slender damsel & my...   H-38

582   after
    Went ~~toward~~ her...   HM-1323

583 Had never kiss'd or claspt a hand   H-38
583 ...kiss, or claspt a hand.   HM-1323

584 Lo now...   HM-1323

586   & state
    ...land & all his wealth were hers.   HM-1323
586 ...land & ~~all his~~/wealth...   Tn-29

587 And there I tarried; & each day she served HM-1323

589 Smiling, for all...   HM-1323

590 ...me as before; & on a morn   HM-1323
590   of old
    ...as ~~before~~; till...   Tn-29

I walking to and fro beside a stream
That flashed across her orchard underneath
Her castle-walls, she stole upon my walk,
And calling me the greatest of all knights,
Embraced me, and so kissed me the first time,   595
And gave herself and all her wealth to me.
Then I remembered Arthur's warning word,
That most of us would follow wandering fires,
And the Quest faded in my heart.   Anon,
The heads of all her people drew to me,   600
With supplication both of knees and tongue:
"We have heard of thee: thou art our greatest knight,
Our Lady says it, and we well believe:

591-2 I walking in her orchard underneath   HM-1232;Tn-29

593 The castlewall...   HM-1323
593 The castle-walls, ...   Tn-29

597 ...warning given   HM-1323

599 ...the quest...   A-2104
599 (C)   L-HGI

601 With adoration both of ~~tongue~~ knees & tongue.
                                                         HM-1323
601 ...tongue.   A-2104
601 (C)   H-HGP

602 ...art the greatest...   H-38
602 'We...knight: A-2104
602 (C)   L-HGI

605 ...land.'   A-2104
605 (C)   L-HGI

606 And there I staid, & one black night my vow   HM-1323

Sketch 606-609
        O me my brother, - but one night I rose
        Remembering And parted from her tho' I wept & waild
        Hating myself, hating my life, & evn
        The Holy Quest to which my life had come   H-38

Wed thou our Lady, and rule over us,
And thou shalt be as Arthur in our land."   605
O me, my brother! but one night my vow
Burnt me within, so that I rose and fled,
But waild and wept, and hated mine own self,
And even the Holy Quest, and all but her;
Then after I was joined with Galahad   610
Cared not for her, nor anything upon earth.'

Then said the monk, 'Poor men, when yule is cold,
Must be content to sit by little fires.
And this am I, so that ye care for me
Ever so little; yea, and blest be Heaven   615
That brought thee here to this poor house of ours
Where all the brethren are so hard, to warm
My cold heart with a friend: but O the pity
To find thine own first love once more--to hold,
Hold her a wealthy bride within thine arms,   620

---

609 ...her,;	;/ (I)	B-VI	
609 (C)		L-HGI	
612 cold			
...is h̸a̸r̸d̸,		Tn-29	
612 ...the Monk, 'Poor...		A-2104	
612 (C)		L-HGI	
615 ...be heaven		A-2104	
615 (C)		L-HGI	
616 thee of ours,			
...brought y̸o̸u̸ here...house t̸o̸ w̸a̸r̸m̸		Tn-29	
616 ...of ours,		A-2104	
616 (C)		73	
618 cold			
My p̸o̸o̸r̸ heart...		Tn-29	
619 thine			
...find y̸o̸u̸r̸ own...		Tn-29	
620 thine			
...within y̸o̸u̸r̸ arms,		Tn-29	

Or all but hold, and then--cast her aside,
Foregoing all her sweetness, like a weed.
For we that want the warmth of double life,
We that are plagued with dreams of something sweet
Beyond all sweetness in a life so rich,--   625
Ah, blessed Lord, I speak too earthlywise,
Seeing I never strayed beyond the cell,
But live like an old badger in his earth,
With earth about him everywhere, despite
All fast and penance. Saw ye none beside,   630
None of your knights?'

                                  'Yea so,' said Percivale:

---

624 ...are vext with...   Tn-29

631 ...Percivale,;   ;/ (I)   B-VI
631 ...Percivale;   H-HGP
631 (C)   L-HGI

632   my
    ...night, t̸h̸e̸ pathway...   Tn-29

633 I saw the plume of good Sir Bors   HM-1323
633   pelican on   our
    The l̸i̸o̸n̸ u̸p̸o̸n̸ the casque of g̸o̸o̸d̸ Sir Bors   Tn-29

634   o   moon/   I MS
    ...rising mo̸r̸n: B-VI
634 (C)   L-HGI

635 ...spurr'd and...   A-2104
635 (C)   73

636 ...ask'd   A-2104
636 (C)   L-HGI

637 'Where...him - Lancelot?' 'Once,'   A-2104
637 ...Lancelot?" "Once,"   L-HGI
637 (C)   73

638 ...Bors, 'he...   A-2104
638 (C)   L-HGI

'One night my pathway swerving east, I saw
The pelican on the casque of our Sir Bors
All in the middle of the rising moon:
And toward him spurred, and hailed him, and he me,   635
And each made joy of either; then he asked,
"Where is he? hast thou seen him--Lancelot?--Once,"
Said good Sir Bors, "he dashed across me--mad,
And maddening what he rode: and when I cried,
'Ridest thou then so hotly on a quest   640
So holy,' Lancelot shouted, 'Stay me not!
I have been the sluggard, and I ride apace,
For now there is a lion in the way.'
So vanished."

                        'Then Sir Bors had ridden on
Softly, and sorrowing for our Lancelot,   645
Because his former madness, once the talk

---

640 ...thou thus so...   HM-1323

641 ...holy? but he shouted...   HM-1323
641 So holy?' Lancelot shouted 'Stay...   A-2104
641 ...holy?' Lancelot...   L-HGI
641 (C)   73

642 ...sluggard and...   A-2104
642 (C)   L-HGI

Alt. after 643
    So vanish'd toward the sea: & on I past
    Softly & sorrowing for our Lancelot
    How sd the Holy thing appear to him
    Being as he was?   HM-1323

644 So vanish'd. (Par. Indent.) Then...   A-2104
644 (C)   L-HGI

645 Softly and...Lancelot.   A-2104
645 (C)   L-HGI

646   once the talk
    ...madness w̸h̸i̸c̸h̸ h̸a̸d̸ b̸e̸e̸n̸   Tn-29

And scandal of our table, had returned;
For Lancelot's kith and kin so worship him
That ill to him is ill to them; to Bors
Beyond the rest: he well had been content   650
Not to have seen, so Lancelot might have seen,
The Holy Cup of healing; and, indeed,
Being so clouded with his grief and love,
Small heart was his after the Holy Quest:
If God would send the vision, well: if not,   655
The Quest and he were in the hands of Heaven.

   'And then, with small adventure met, Sir Bors
Rode to the lonest tract of all the realm,

---

647 And scandal of   had
   ~~The talk of all~~ our table, ~~was~~ return'd   Tn-29

648   adore   so
   ...kin ~~so worship~~ him   Tn-29
648   so worship him   I MS
   ...kin ~~adore him so~~   B-VI
648 (C)   L-HGI

652 The holy cup of...   A-2104
652 (C)   L-HGI

654 ...the holy quest: A-2104
654 (C)   L-HGI

657 (Par.) And...   A-2104
657 (C)   L-HGI

658 Down to the last tongue-tip of Lyoness rode,   Tn-29;
                                                       A-2104
658 Rode to the lonest tract ~~part~~ of all the realm, I MS
   ~~Down to the last tongue-tip of Lyoness rode~~   B-VIII
658 (C)   L-HGII

(In HM-1323 - the sketch for the Tale of Sir Bors is
written in the first person, and was intended as the
knight's own narrative, told to King Arthur.)

Alt. before 660   riding on
   Far to the west I found a people there   HM-1323

And found a people there among their crags,
Our race and blood, a remnant that were left   660
Paynim amid their circles, and the stones
They pitch up straight to heaven: and their wise men
Were strong in that old magic which can trace
The wandering of the stars, and scoffed at him
And this high Quest as at a simple thing: 665
Told him he followed--almost Arthur's words--
A mocking fire: "what other fire than he,
Whereby the blood beats, and the blossom blows,
And the sea rolls, and all the world is warmed?"

---

660 ...that are left   HM-1323

661 Paynim, among their...   HM-1323

Sketch 663-667
    Hearing the quest I came on mock'd & jeer'd
    And told me wellnigh, Arthur, in thine own words
    I did but follow a flying fire.   HM-1323

664   scoff'd
   ... & m̸o̸c̸k̸'d̸ at...   Tn-29
664 ...him,   A-2104
664 (C)   L-HGI

665 ...high quest as...   A-2104
665 (C)   L-HGI

Alt. for 666-669
    Till our fair father Xt sd pass away
    And their diviner worship be restored.   HM-1323

Sketch for another Druid argument C. 669)
    King Arthur & his knighthood were a dream   HM-1323

667   mocking
   A f̸l̸y̸i̸n̸g̸ fire...   Tn-29
667 ...fire: what other...   A-2104
667 (C)   L-HGII

669 ...warm'd?   A-2104
669 (C)   L-HGII

And when his answer chafed them, the rough crowd,   670
Hearing he had a difference with their priests,
Seized him, and bound and plunged him into a cell
Of great piled stones; and lying bounden there
In darkness through innumerable hours
He heard the hollow-ringing heavens sweep   675
Over him till by miracle--what else?--
Heavy as it was, a great stone slipt and fell,
Such as no wind could move: and through the gap
Glimmered the streaming scud: then came a night
Still as the day was loud; and through the gap   680
The seven clear stars of Arthur's Table Round--

---

675 I heard...heavens blow   HM-1323
675 ...heavens roll   Tn-29
675   sweep   I MS
   ...the hollow-ringing heavens r̸ø̸l̸l̸   B-VI
675 (C)   L-HGI

676-677
     Oer me, till a great stone slipt & fell [by
                         miracle so I deem'd]
     Heavy as it was, a great stone slipt & fell HM-1323

676 Over him, till...else?   A-2104
676 Over him, till...   L-HGI
676 (C)   78

678-679 And the torn rack appeard & streaming
                         scud   HM-1323

681 ...Table round -   A-2104
681 (C)   L-HGI

Sketch 682-683   because they roll
     For, brother, so one night, we named the stars,
     Thro' such a round in heaven,
     Ø̸n̸é̸ g̸á̸ù̸d̸ý̸ ǹ̸i̸g̸h̸t̸ ẁ̸h̸é̸ǹ̸ ẁ̸é̸ ẁ̸é̸r̸é̸ m̸é̸r̸r̸ý̸ ẁ̸i̸t̸h̸ ẁ̸i̸ǹ̸é̸   Tn-29

682 For, brother, so one night, we named the stars,
                                               A-2104
682 (C)   H-HGP

For, brother, so one night, because they roll
Through such a round in heaven, we named the stars,
Rejoicing in ourselves and in our King--
And these, like bright eyes of familiar friends,   685
In on him shone: "And then to me, to me,"
Said good Sir Bors, "beyond all hopes of mine,
Who scarce had prayed or asked it for myself--
Across the seven clear stars--O grace to me--
In colour like the fingers of a hand   690
Before a burning taper, the sweet Grail
Glided and past, and close upon it pealed
A sharp quick thunder." Afterwards, a maid,
Who kept our holy faith among her kin
In secret, entering, loosed and let him go.'   695

---

683 Thro' such a round in heaven, because they
                              roll   A-2104
683 (C)   H-HGP
683 ...stars.   L-HGI
683 (C)   L-HGII

684 ...our king -   A-2104
684 (C)   73

685 ...these like...friends   A-2104
685 (C)   L-HGI

686 ...shone, 'and...me,'   A-2104
686 ...shone, 'And...me,'   L-HGII
686 ...shone, "And...   69
686 (C)   73

687 ... Bors, 'beyond...   A-2104
687 (C)   69

693 ...thunder: afterwards a maid   A-2104
693 ...thunder.' Afterwards a maid,   L-HGII
693 (C)   73

695 ..., entering loosed...   A-2104
695 (C)   L-HGI

THE HOLY GRAIL

      To whom the monk: 'And I remember now
That pelican on the casque: Sir Bors it was
Who spake so low and sadly at our board;
And mighty reverent at our grace was he:
A square-set man and honest; and his eyes,   700
An out-door sign of all the warmth within,
Smiled with his lips--a smile beneath a cloud,
But heaven had meant it for a sunny one:
Ay, ay, Sir Bors, who else?   But when ye reached
The city, found ye all your knights returned,   705
Or was there sooth in Arthur's prophecy,
Tell me, and what said each, and what the King?'

----

696 (Par.) Then spake the monk...   Tn-29
696 (No par. indent.; indent symbol in I MS) To
                 whom the monk, 'And...   B-VI
696 ...Monk, 'And...   H-HGP
696 (C)   L-HGI

697   pelican
    That ~~lion~~ on...   Tn-29

701 An out-door...   -/ (I)   B-VI
701 (C)   H-HGP

704 ...~~Bors, but, brother, when~~...   Tn-29
704 ...else? but...   A-2104
704 (C)   L-HGI

705 ...~~ye/there your knights return'd,~~   Tn-29
705 ...~~city,/brother, how were all things there?~~   Tn-29

Alt. for 706
    ~~And had the number of your knights return'd,~~   Tn-29

707 ...~~and how each spake, & how the King?~~   Tn-29
707 ...~~& what they said, & what the King?~~   Tn-29
707 ...the king?'   A-2104
707 (C)   L-HGI

708-712
    (Par.) ~~Then Percivale 'O brother when we~~
                     ~~reach'd~~   Tn-29

802

Then answered Percivale: 'And that can I,
Brother, and truly; since the living words
Of so great men as Lancelot and our King   710
Pass not from door to door and out again,
But sit within the house. O, when we reached
The city, our horses stumbling as they trode
On heaps of ruin, hornless unicorns,
Cracked basilisks, and splintered cockatrices,   715
And shattered talbots, which had left the stones
Raw, that they fell from, brought us to the hall.

'And there sat Arthur on the daïs-throne,

708-710
    Yea said the knight for I can tell thee all
    Seeing the winged words of men so great   Tn-29

708 ...Percivale, 'And...   A-2104
708 (C)   L-HGI

710 ...our king   A-2104
710 (C)   L-HGI

712 ...O, when...   ,/ (I)   B-VI
712 (C)   H-HGP

713 There my good warhorse, stumbling as he trode   H-38

714 All up the narrow st of C
    On headless dragons up the narrow street, hornless
                          unicorns   H-38
714   heaps of ruin
    On h̶e̶a̶d̶l̶e̶s̶s̶ d̶r̶a̶g̶o̶n̶s̶, hornless...   Tn-29

717 Raw, where they...brought us to the hall.   H-38

718 (Par.) A̶n̶d̶ there sat King Arthur...   H-38
718   And there
   (Par.) T̶h̶e̶r̶e̶ sat K̶i̶n̶g̶ Arthur...   Tn-29
718 (Par.) And...   A-2104
718 (C)   L-HGI

And those that had gone out upon the Quest,
Wasted and worn, and but a tithe of them,   720
And those that had not, stood before the King,
Who, when he saw me, rose, and bad me hail,
Saying, "A welfare in thine eye reproves
Our fear of some disastrous chance for thee
On hill, or plain, at sea, or flooding ford.   725
So fierce a gale made havoc here of late
Among the strange devices of our kings;
Yea, shook this newer, stronger hall of ours,
And from the statue Merlin moulded for us
Half-wrenched a golden wing; but now--the Quest,   730
This vision--hast thou seen the Holy Cup,

719	ose	
	And th~~ey~~ that...	Tn-29
719	...Quest, -	A-2104
719	(C)	L-HGI
720	...tithe of these,	H-38
720	...them -	A-2104
720	...them;	L-HGI
720	(C)	L-HGII
721	And they, that...	H-38
721	those	
	And ~~they~~, that...	Tn-29
721	...the king.	A-2104
721	...the King.	L-HGI
721	(C)	73
722	Who rising when he saw me, bad...	H-38
723	Saying 'a gladness in...	H-38
723	A welfare	
	Saying '~~The~~ ~~gladness~~ in...	Tn-29
728	Yea, even shook this newer, stronger hall	H-38
728	Yea, ~~even~~ shook...	Tn-29
730	...: but, now, my knight	H-38
730	...- the quest,	A-2104
730	(C)	73

That Joseph brought of old to Glastonbury?"

'So when I told him all thyself hast heard,
Ambrosius, and my fresh but fixt resolve
To pass away into the quiet life,   735
He answered not, but, sharply turning, asked
Of Gawain, "Gawain, was this Quest for thee?"

'"Nay, lord," said Gawain, "not for such as I.
Therefore I communed with a saintly man,
Who made me sure the Quest was not for me;   740
For I was much awearied of the Quest:
But found a silk pavilion in a field,
And merry maidens in it; and then this gale
Tore my pavilion from the tenting-pin,

---

731 ...the holy cup,   A-2104
731 (C)   L-HGI

732 That
     Ẅḧị¢ḧ Joseph...   Tn-29

735 ...the silent life   H-38

736 ...ask'd,   A-2104
736 (C)   L-HGI

737 ..., 'Gawain, ...this quest...thee?'   A-2104
737 (C)   L-HGI

738 (Par.) 'Nay, lord,' said Gawain, 'not...
                                  (''' I)   B-VI
738 (C)   L-HGI

740 ...the quest...me.   A-2104
740 ...me.   L-HGI
740 (C)   L-HGII

741 For I much awearied of...   Tn-29
741   was   I MS
    For I much awearied of the quest.   B-VI
741 ...Quest,   L-HGI
741 (C)   L-HGII

THE HOLY GRAIL

And blew my merry maidens all about   745
With all discomfort; yea, and but for this,
My twelvemonth and a day were pleasant to me."

      'He ceased; and Arthur turned to whom at first
He saw not, for Sir Bors, on entering, pushed
Athwart the throng to Lancelot, caught his hand,   750
Held it, and there, half-hidden by him, stood,
Until the King espied him, saying to him,
"Hail, Bors! if ever loyal man and true
Could see it, thou hast seen the Grail;" and Bors,

---

745 ...blew my maidens...   H-38

746 In strange discomfort - yea & save for this   H-38

747 ...to me.   A-2104
747 (C)   L-HGI

748 (Par.) He ceased; & Arthur turn'd to good
                          Sir Bors   H-38
748   ~~him~~ whom at first
    ...turn'd to ~~good/Sir/Bors~~   Tn-29
748 (Par.) He...   A-2104
748 (C)   L-HGI

749   push'd
    ...entering ~~press'd~~   Tn-29

750   caught his hand,
    Across the...Lancelot & ~~there stood~~   Tn-29

751 ~~Half-hidden by him till the King espied~~   Tn-29

752 ...King perceived him...   Tn-29
752 ...the king...him   A-2104
752 (C)   L-HGI

753 Say '~~Sir Bors~~, if ever honest man & true   H-38
753 Hail Bors   loyal
    ~~saying~~ if ever ~~honest~~ man...   Tn-29
753 'Hail,...   '/ (I)   B-VI
753 (C)   L-HGI

806

"Ask me not, for I may not speak of it: 755
I saw it;" and the tears were in his eyes.

   'Then there remained but Lancelot, for the rest
Spake but of sundry perils in the storm;
Perhaps, like him of Cana in Holy Writ,
Our Arthur kept his best until the last;   760
"Thou, too, my Lancelot," asked the King, "my friend,
Our mightiest, hath this Quest availed for thee?"

   '"Our mightiest!" answered Lancelot, with a groan;

754	...thou hast seen it: then Sir Bors	H-38
754	...the Grail,' and...	A-2104
754	(C)	L-HGI
755	'Ask...it,	A-2104
755	...it,	L-HGI
755	(C)	69
756	I saw it: & his eye was fill'd with tears.	H-38
756	...it:' and...	A-2104
756	...it:" and...	L-HGI
756	(C)	75
757	(Par.) Then...	A-2104
757	(C)	L-HGI
758	Spake but of storm & hard adventure	H-38;Tn-29
758	...storm,;	;/ (I) B-VI
758	(C)	H-HGP
760	...the last.;	;/ (I) B-VI
760	(C)	H-HGP
761	'Thou...Lancelot,' ask'd the king, 'my...	A-2104
761	(C)	L-HGI
762	...this quest...thee?'	A-2104
762	(C)	L-HGI
763	(Par.) 'Our mightiest!' answer'd...groan,	A-2104
763	(C)	L-HGI

807

"O King!"--and when he paused, methought I spied   765
A dying fire of madness in his eyes--
"O King, my friend, if friend of thine I be,
Happier are those that welter in their sin,
Swine in the mud, that cannot see for slime,
Slime of the ditch: but in me lived a sin
So strange, of such a kind, that all of pure,   770
Noble, and knightly in me twined and clung
Round that one sin, until the wholesome flower
And poisonous grew together, each as each,
Not to be plucked asunder; and when thy knights
Sware, I sware with them only in the hope   775
That could I touch or see the Holy Grail
They might be plucked asunder. Then I spake

---

764 'O king!' and...   A-2104
764 (C)   L-HGI

765 ...eyes,   A-2104
765 (C)   L-HGI

766-767
    'O king' said Lancelot 'for this friend of thine
    What can avail?' & all his colour wann'd   H-38

766 'O king, ...   A-2104
766 (C)   L-HGI

769 Mud of the ditch...   H-38
769 ...ditch - but...   A-2104
769 (C)   L-HGI

777 ...asunder: then...   A-2104
777 (C)   L-HGI

778 ...most holy man who t̸o̸l̸d̸ m̸e̸/wept...   H-38
778   saint
    ...holy m̸a̸n̸ who...   Tn-29
778 ...saint who...said   A-2104
778 (C)   L-HGI

779 ...asunder, all   ,/ (I)   B-VI
779 (C)   H-HGP

808

To one most holy saint, who wept and said,
That save they could be plucked asunder, all
My quest were but in vain; to whom I vowed   780
That I would work according as he willed.
And forth I went, and while I yearned and strove
To tear the twain asunder in my heart,
My madness came upon me as of old,
And whipt me into waste fields far away;   785
There was I beaten down by little men,
Mean knights, to whom the moving of my sword
And shadow of my spear had been enow
To scare them from me once; and then I came
All in my folly to the naked shore,   790

---

782   yearn'd &
     ...while I ~~daily~~ strove   H-38

783 ...asunder ~~if I might~~ in my heart,   H-38

784 ...of old   A-2104
784 (C)   L-HGII

785   whipt
    And drove me...   H-38
785 ...away,   A-2104
785 Stet ~~dash'd~~   ~~tore~~   I MS
    And ~~whipt~~ me into ~~waste~~ fields far
                         away,;   ;/ (I)   B-VIII
785 (C)   L-HGII

787 ...the (1 ?) of my sword   H-38
787 ...the ventage of...   Tn-29
787   e   I MS
    ...to whom the vántage of my sword   B-VI
787 ...to whom the ventage of my sword   H-HGP
787   ~~drawing~~ moving   (I, P MS)
    ...to whom the ~~ventage~~ of my sword   B-VIII
787 (C)   L-HGII

790 ...shore,   ,/ (I)   B-VI
790 (C)   H-HGP

809

Wide flats, where nothing but coarse grasses grew;
But such a blast, my King, began to blow,
So loud a blast along the shore and sea,
Ye could not hear the waters for the blast,
Though heapt in mounds and ridges all the sea   795
Drove like a cataract, and all the sand
Swept like a river, and the clouded heavens
Were shaken with the motion and the sound.
And blackening in the sea-foam swayed a boat,
Half-swallowed in it, anchored with a chain;   800
And in my madness to myself I said,
'I will embark and I will lose myself,
And in the great sea wash away my sin.'

791	Waste flats...		Tn-29
791	...flats, where...grew,	,/ (1st,I)	B-VI
791	...grew,		H-HGP
791	~~Seat~~ Wide	(I, P MS)	
	/~~Waste~~ flats, where...grew,		B-VIII
791	(C)		L-HGII
792	..., my king,...		A-2104
792	(C)		L-HGI
793	...blast blow down the shore...		H-38
794	You cd not hear the ocean for the blast,		H-38
795	...ridges/ all...		B-VI
795	(C)		S-925
797	...river, & the cloudy sun		H-38
798	Was shaken...		H-38
799	...boat		A-2104
799	(C)		L-HGI
800	Half swallowd in it		
	Brimful of seafoam, anchor'd...		H-38
802	I will...		A-2104
802	(C)		L-HGI

I burst the chain, I sprang into the boat.
Seven days I drove along the dreary deep,   805
And with me drove the moon and all the stars;
And the wind fell, and on the seventh night
I heard the shingle grinding in the surge,
And felt the boat shock earth, and looking up,
Behold, the enchanted towers of Carbonek,   810
A castle like a rock upon a rock,
With chasm-like portals open to the sea,
And steps that met the breaker! there was none
Stood near it but a lion on each side
That kept the entry, and the moon was full.   815
Then from the boat I leapt, and up the stairs.
There drew my sword. With sudden-flaring manes
Those two great beasts rose upright like a man,
Each gript a shoulder, and I stood between;

---

803 ...sin.		A-2104
803 (C)		L-HGI
809 And felt the shock & looking up, behold		H-38
809 ...up,	(, I)	B-VI
809 (C)		H-HGP
810 Behold̸, the...Carbonek.	,/ (I)	B-VI
810 Beheld the ...Carbonek.		A-2104
810 ...Carbonek.		H-HGP
810 (C)		L-HGII
813 ...breaker: there...		A-2104
813 (C)		L-HGI I
814 ...side,		A-2104
814 (C)		L-HGI
817 And drew...		H-38
818 right		
...rose upward like		H-38
819 ...between,,;	(; I)	B-VI
819 (C)		H-HGP

And, when I would have smitten them, heard a voice,   820
'Doubt not, go forward; if thou doubt, the beasts
Will tear thee piecemeal.' Then with violence
The sword was dashed from out my hand, and fell.
And up into the sounding hall I past;
But nothing in the sounding hall I saw,   825
No bench nor table, painting on the wall
Or shield of knight; only the rounded moon
Through the tall oriel on the rolling sea.
But always in the quiet house I heard,
Clear as a lark, high o'er me as a lark,   830
A sweet voice singing in the topmost tower
To the eastward: up I climbed a thousand steps
With pain: as in a dream I seemed to climb
For ever: at the last I reached a door,
A light was in the crannies, and I heard,   835

---

820 ...have stricken them...   H-38;Tn-29
820   smitten   I MS
   ...have ~~stricken~~ them...   B-VI
820 (C)   H-HGP

821 Doubt...   A-2104
821 (C)   L-HGI

822 ...piecemeal & with...   H-38
822   then
   ...piecemeal; & with...   Tn-29
822 ...piecemeal; then...   A-2104
822 (C)   L-HGI

823 ...hand, and...   (, I)   B-VI
823 (C)   H-HGP

824 ...hall I went,   H-38
824 ...past,   (, I)   B-VI
824 ...past,   H-HGP
824 (C)   L-HGI

826 ...the wall,   A-2104
826 (C)   L-HGI

'Glory and joy and honour to our Lord
And to the Holy Vessel of the Grail.'
Then in my madness I essayed the door;
It gave; and through a stormy glare, a heat
As from a seventimes-heated furnace, I,   840
Blasted and burnt, and blinded as I was
With such a fierceness that I swooned away--
O, yet methought I saw the Holy Grail,
All palled in crimson samite, and around
Great angels, awful shapes, and wings and eyes.   845
And but for all my madness and my sin,
And then my swooning, I had sworn I saw
That which I saw; but what I saw was veiled
And covered; and this Quest was not for me."

'So speaking, and here ceasing, Lancelot left   850

---

835 ...heard		A-2104
835 (C)		L-HGI
836 ...joy & blessing to...		H-38
838 ...door,;	;/ (I)	B-VI
838 (C)		H-HGP
839 ...gave,; and...	;/ (I)	B-VI
839 (C)		H-HGP
842 So fiercely that at once I swoon'd away -		H-38
842 With such a fierceness that		
S̸o̸ f̸i̸e̸r̸c̸e̸l̸y̸ t̸h̸a̸t̸ a̸t̸ o̸n̸c̸e̸ I...		Tn-29
842 ...away -	-/ (I)	B-VI
842 (C)		H-HGP
847 ...swooning I c̸d̸ s̸w̸d̸ had...		H-38
849 ...this quest...me.		A-2104
849 ...this quest...		L-HGI
849 (C)		73
850 (Par.) So...		A-2104
850 (C)		L-HGI

The hall long silent, till Sir Gawain--nay,
Brother, I need not tell thee foolish words,--
A reckless and irreverent knight was he,
Now boldened by the silence of his King,--
Well, I will tell thee: "O King, my liege," he said, 855
"Hath Gawain failed in any quest of thine?
When have I stinted stroke in foughten field?
But as for thine, my good friend Percivale,
Thy holy nun and thou have driven men mad,
Yea, made our mightiest madder than our least.   860
But by mine eyes and by mine ears I swear,

---

851 A hall long silent, till Sir Gawain - ~~brother~~
                                        my   H-38

852 ~~Why so I vex/thee with~~   foolish words
    Brother, I need not tell thee what he said -   H-38
852 ...words: -   -/ (I)   B-VI
852 ...words: -   H-HGP
852 (C)   L-HGI

854 ...silence o~~f~~ his king. -   -/ (I)   B-VI
854 ...his king. -   H-HGP
854 (C)   L-HGI

855-858 Well, I will tell thee O Percivale he
                                     said   H-38

855 ...thee: 'O king, my liege,'...   A-2104
855 ..."O king, my...   L-HGI
855 (C)   73

856 'Hath...   A-2104
856 (C)   L-HGI

858-859 Thou & thy holy nun...   H-38

858 ...thine, O ~~Percivale~~, my...   Tn-29
858 ...friend, Percivale,   A-2104
858 (C)   73

860 ...our greatest madder...   H-38

861 ...ears I vow,   H-38

I will be deafer than the blue-eyed cat,
And thrice as blind as any noonday owl,
To holy virgins in their ecstasies,
Henceforward."

        '"Deafer," said the blameless King,   865
"Gawain, and blinder unto holy things
Hope not to make thyself by idle vows,
Being too blind to have desire to see.
But if indeed there came a sign from heaven,
Blessed are Bors, Lancelot and Percivale,   870

862-863
    I will be blinder than a noonday owl,
    And deafer than a blue-eyed cat, will I   H-38
862-863
       deafer   the blue-eyed cat
    I will be b̸l̸i̸n̸d̸e̸r̸ than a̸ n̸o̸o̸n̸d̸a̸y̸ o̸w̸l̸,
    thrice as blind as any noonday owl,
    A̸n̸d̸/d̸e̸a̸f̸e̸r̸ t̸h̸a̸n̸ a̸ b̸l̸u̸e̸-̸e̸y̸e̸d̸ c̸a̸t̸,̸ w̸i̸l̸l̸ I̸/   Tn-29

863   rice   I MS
    And th̸i̸n̸e̸ as...   A-2104
863 (C)   S-925

865 Henceforward.' (Par.) 'Deafer,' said the blame-
                              less king,   A-2104
865 (C)   L-HGI

Sketch 865-867
        Deafer unto such as these,
    G̸a̸w̸a̸i̸n̸,̸ &̸ b̸l̸i̸n̸d̸e̸r̸ s̸a̸i̸d̸ t̸h̸e̸ b̸l̸a̸m̸e̸l̸e̸s̸s̸ K̸i̸n̸g̸
    Thou cans't make thyself by idle vows   H-38

866 ...unto such as these   Tn-29
866   holy things   I MS
    'Gawain, and blinder unto s̸u̸c̸h̸ a̸s̸ t̸h̸e̸s̸e̸ A-2104;B-VI
866 'Gawain, and blinder unto holy things   S-925
866 (C)   L-HGI

870 Blessed be ye, Lancelot & Percivale,   H-38

For these have seen according to their sight.
For every fiery prophet in old times,
And all the sacred madness of the bard,
When God made music through them, could but speak
His music by the framework and the chord;   875
And as ye saw it ye have spoken truth.

     '"Nay--but thou errest, Lancelot: never yet
Could all of true and noble in knight and man
Twine round one sin, whatever it might be,
With such a closeness, but apart there grew,   880
Save that he were the swine thou spakest of,
Some root of knighthood and pure nobleness;
Whereto see thou, that it may bear its flower.

---

871 For ye have...to your sight		H-38
872 ...prophet in the past,		H-38
872 And all the fiery prophets of old times		H-38
874 ...cd but give		H-38
875 His music thro the chordage & the wood		H-38
875 woodwork & the chord		
His music thro the chordage & the f̶r̶a̶m̶e̶		H-38
875 ...by the woodwork &...		Tn-29
875 ...by the woodwork and the chord,; ;/ (I)		B-VI
875 ...by the woodwork and...		H-HGP
875 framework		I MS
...by the w̶o̶o̶d̶w̶o̶r̶k̶ and the chord,	L-HGI;B-VIII	
875 (C)		L-HGII
877 (Par.) Nay - ...		A-2104
877 (C)		L-HGI
880 ...closeness, but there grew apart		H-38
882 ...knighthood & of nobleness		H-38
884 And s̶a̶i̶d̶ spake...		H-38
884 (Par.) And...		A-2104
884 (C)		L-HGI

'"And spake I not too truly, O my knights?
Was I too dark a prophet when I said   885
To those who went upon the Holy Quest,
That most of them would follow wandering fires,
Lost in the quagmire?--lost to me and gone,
And left me gazing at a barren board,
And a lean Order--scarce returned a tithe--   890
And out of those to whom the vision came
My greatest hardly will believe he saw;
Another hath beheld it afar off,
And leaving human wrongs to right themselves,
Cares but to pass into the silent life.   895
And one hath had the vision face to face,
And now his chair desires him here in vain,
However they may crown him otherwhere.

'"And some among you held, that if the King
Had seen the sight he would have sworn the vow: 900

886	To those that went...	H-38
886	...Quest	A-2104
886	(C)	L-HGI
888	...quagmire - lost...	A-2104
888	(C)	L-HGI
890	...lean order - ...	A-2104
890	...Order - ~~S~~carce	-/ (I)	L-HGI
890	(C)		L-HGII
892	My greatest scarcely will...	H-38
894	therefore	
	And ~~he~~ ~~will~~ leave to fight with human wrongs	H-38
895	And pass away into...	H-38
897	...desires here...	H-38
899	...you said that if...	H-38
899	(Par.) And ...held, that if the king	(, I)	B-VI
899	(C)		L-HGI
900	...he wd sworn the vow:	H-38

817

Not easily, seeing that the King must guard
That which he rules, and is but as the hind
To whom a space of land is given to plow.
Who may not wander from the allotted field
Before his work be done; but, being done,   905
Let visions of the night or of the day

901	...the king...	A-2104
901	(C)	L-HGI
903	To whom is a space of land is given to plough	H-38
903	...plough,	A-2104
903	(C)	84
904	...field,	A-2104
904	(C)	73
908	But that this earth he treads on is not earth,	H-38
908	...he treads on...	Tn-29;A-2104
908	walks	P MS
	...he t̸r̸e̸a̸d̸s̸ on...	B-VIII
908	(C)	L-HGII
909	...his eyelid is...	H-38
909	eyelid	
	...his f̸o̸r̸e̸h̸e̸a̸d̸ is...	Tn-29
909	...his eyelid is...	A-2104
909	eyeball	I MS
	...his e̸y̸e̸l̸i̸d̸ is...	B-VIII
909	(C)	L-HGII

Come, as they will; and many a time they come,
Until this earth he walks on seems not earth,
This light that strikes his eyeball is not light,
This air that smites his forehead is not air   910
But vision--yea, his very hand and foot--
In moments when he feels he cannot die,
And knows himself no vision to himself,
Nor the high God a vision, nor that One
Who rose again: ye have seen what ye have seen."   915

    'So spake the King: I knew not all he meant.'

911	...very hands and feet -	Tn-29;A-2104
911	hand and foot	I MS
	...very ~~hands and feet~~ -	B-VIII
911	(C)	L-HGII

914	...nor the X st	H-38
914	...that one	A-2104
914	(C)	69

| 915 | ...seen. | A-2104 |
| 915 | (C) | L-HGI |

916	...I know not what he meant	H-38
916	(Par.) So spake the king: ...meant.	A-2104
916	(Par.) "So spake the king: ...meant.'	L-HGI
916	...the king...	69
916	(C)	73

Pelleas and Ettarre

King Arthur made new knights to fill the gap
Left by the Holy Quest; and as he sat
In hall at old Caerleon, the high doors
Were softly sundered, and through these a youth,
Pelleas, and the sweet smell of the fields   5
Past, and the sunshine came along with him.

'Make me thy knight, because I know, Sir King,
All that belongs to knighthood, and I love.'
Such was his cry: for having heard the King
Had let proclaim a tournament--the prize   10
A golden circlet and a knightly sword,
Full fain had Pelleas for his lady won
The golden circlet, for himself the sword:

1   King
   (Par.) A̸n̸d̸ Arthur...   T-P

3 At hall...   T-P

8 ...I love'   A-2104
8 ...I love,'   L-HGI
8 (C)   73

9 ...cry; for...   A-2104
9 (C)   84

And there were those who knew him near the King,
And promised for him: and Arthur made him knight.   15

    And this new knight, Sir Pelleas of the isles--
But lately come to his inheritance,
And lord of many a barren isle was he--
Riding at noon, a day or twain before,
Across the forest called of Dean, to find   20
Caerleon and the King, had felt the sun
Beat like a strong knight on his helm, and reeled
Almost to falling from his horse; but saw
Near him a mound of even-sloping side,
Whereon a hundred stately beeches grew,   25
And here and there great hollies under them;
But for a mile all round was open space,
And fern and heath: and slowly Pelleas drew
To that dim day, then binding his good horse
To a tree, cast himself down; and as he lay   30
At random looking over the brown earth
Through that green-glooming twilight of the grove,
It seemed to Pelleas that the fern without
Burnt as a living fire of emeralds,

14	...the king	A-2104
14	...the King	L-HGI
14	(C)	73
16	...the isles,	A-2104
16	(C)	L-HGI
17	come	
	...lately s̸t̸e̸p̸t̸ to...	T-P
21	...the king...	A-2104
21	(C)	L-HGI
23	from his horse; but saw	
	...falling - t̸h̸e̸n̸ b̸e̸h̸e̸l̸d̸ a̸ m̸o̸u̸n̸d̸	T-P
24	...side	A-2104
24	(C)	69
26	...them.	A-2104
26	(C)	73

So that his eyes were dazzled looking at it.   35
Then o'er it crost the dimness of a cloud
Floating, and once the shadow of a bird
Flying, and then a fawn; and his eyes closed.
And since he loved all maidens, but no maid
In special, half-awake he whispered, 'Where?   40
O where? I love thee, though I know thee not.
For fair thou art and pure as Guinevere,
And I will make thee with my spear and sword
As famous--O my Queen, my Guinevere,
For I will be thine Arthur when we meet.'   45

   Suddenly wakened with a sound of talk
And laughter at the limit of the wood,
And glancing through the hoary boles, he saw,
Strange as to some old prophet might have seemed
A vision hovering on a sea of fire,   50
Damsels in divers colours like the cloud
Of sunset and sunrise, and all of them
On horses, and the horses richly trapt
Breast-high in that bright line of bracken stood:

40	whisper'd	
	...he m̸u̸r̸m̸u̸r̸'d 'where?	T-P
40	...whisper'd 'where?	A-2104
40	(C)	L-HGI
42	2 3 1	
	For thou art fair & pure...	T-P
44	Queen, my	
	...O my p̸e̸r̸f̸e̸c̸t̸ Guinevere	T-P
50	A hovering	
	S̸t̸r̸a̸n̸g̸e̸ a̸s̸ a̸ vision on...	T-P
52	all	
	...sunrise, & e̸a̸c̸h̸ of them	T-P
53	...trapt, (, I)	A-2104
53	(C)	L-HGI
54	...bracken/ stood:	A-2104
54	(C)	S-925

823

And all the damsels talked confusedly,   55
And one was pointing this way, and one that,
Because the way was lost.

                    And Pelleas rose,
And loosed his horse, and led him to the light.
There she that seemed the chief among them said,
'In happy time behold our pilot-star!   60
Youth, we are damsels-errant, and we ride,
Armed as ye see, to tilt against the knights
There at Caerleon, but have lost our way:
To right? to left? straight forward? back again?
Which? tell us quickly.'

                     Pelleas gazing thought,   65

59	...them, said	A-2104
59	(C)	L-HGI
60	...time appears our...	T-P
60	...time appears our pilot-star.	A-2104
60	behold	I MS
	...time *appears* our pilot-star.	L-HGI; B-VII1
60	(C)	L-HGII
65	(Par. break) And Pelleas gazing thought	A-2104
65	(Par. break) And Pelleas gazing thought,	L-HGI
65	(C)	86
67	bloom	
	..., & her *face*	T-P
Alt. after 68	Perfect her bosom, small her girdle-stead	T-P
Alt. after 68	Perfect her bosom, small her girdle-stead	A-2104;S-925
Alt. after 68	(C)	L-HGI
69	...limbs, mature in womanhood, (1st, I)	A-2104
69	...limbs mature in womanhood,	S-925
69	...womanhood,	L-HGI
69	(C)	73

PELLEAS AND ETTARRE

'Is Guinevere herself so beautiful?'
For large her violet eyes looked, and her bloom
A rosy dawn kindled in stainless heavens,
And round her limbs, mature in womanhood;
And slender was her hand and small her shape;   70
And but for those large eyes, the haunts of scorn,
She might have seemed a toy to trifle with,
And pass and care no more. But while he gazed
The beauty of her flesh abashed the boy,
As though it were the beauty of her soul: 75
For as the base man, judging of the good,
Puts his own baseness in him by default
Of will and nature, so did Pelleas lend
All the young beauty of his own soul to hers,
Believing her; and when she spake to him,   80

Alt. after 69 And slenderer miracles of hand & foot
               Never had woman: & herself was small,   T-P
Alt. after 69 And slenderer miracles of hand and foot
               Never had woman: and herself was small,
                                        A-2104;S-925
Alt. after 69 (C)   L-HGI

70 (Omitted A-2104; S-925; but written in I MS in A.)
70 ...shape,   L-HGI
70 (C)   76

72   well
   S̸h̸é might have seem'd...   T-P
72 She m   I MS
   M̸ight w̸é̸l̸l̸ have...with   A-2104
72 Might well have...with   S-925
72 (C)   L-HGI

73 For such as love the game: but as he gazed   T-P
73   dared   while   I MS
   For such as l̸ó̸v̸é the game: but á̸s̸ he gazed   A-2104
73 For such as love the game: but as he gazed   S-925
73 (C)   L-HGI

80 ...her, and...   A-2104
80 (C)   L-HGI

825

Stammered, and could not make her a reply.
For out of the waste islands had he come,
Where saving his own sisters he had known
Scarce any but the women of his isles,
Rough wives, that laughed and screamed against the
                          gulls,   85
Makers of nets, and living from the sea.

    Then with a slow smile turned the lady round
And looked upon her people; and as when
A stone is flung into some sleeping tarn,
The circle widens till it lip the marge,   90
Spread the slow smile through all her company.
Three knights were thereamong; and they too smiled,
Scorning him; for the lady was Ettarre,
And she was a great lady in her land.

    Again she said, 'O wild and of the woods,   95
Knowest thou not the fashion of our speech?
Or have the Heavens but given thee a fair face,
Lacking a tongue?'

                     'O damsel,' answered he,

89	...tarn	A-2104
89	(C)	S-925
91	Stet. T ~~spread~~	I MS
	~~spread~~ ~~the~~ slow smile thro all her company.	B-VIII
92	...were there among; and...smiled	A-2104
92	(C)	S-925
94	...her own land.	T-P
94	...her own land.	A-2104
94	(C)	L-HGI
95	O	
	...said '~~he~~ ~~is~~ wild & ...	T-P
95	...woods.	A-2104
95	(C)	S-925
102	...the king?"	A-2104
102	(C)	L-HGI

'I woke from dreams; and coming out of gloom
Was dazzled by the sudden light, and crave   100
Pardon: but will ye to Caerleon?   I
Go likewise: shall I lead you to the King?'

   'Lead then,' she said; and through the woods they
                       went.
And while they rode, the meaning in his eyes,
His tenderness of manner, and chaste awe,   105
His broken utterances and bashfulness,
Were all a burthen to her, and in her heart
She muttered, 'I have lighted on a fool,
Raw, yet so stale!' But since her mind was bent
On hearing, after trumpet blown, her name   110
And title, 'Queen of Beauty,' in the lists
Cried--and beholding him so strong, she thought
That peradventure he will fight for me,
And win the circlet: therefore flattered him,
Being so gracious, that he wellnigh deemed   115
His wish by hers was echoed; and her knights
And all her damsels too were gracious to him,
For she was a great lady.

                 And when they reached
Caerleon, ere they past to lodging, she,
Taking his hand, 'O the strong hand,' she said,   120
'See! look at mine! but wilt thou fight for me,
And win me this fine circlet, Pelleas,

---

103 (No par.) 'Lead then' she said, and thro the woods
                       they went,   (1st, I) A-2104
103 (No par.) 'Lead then' she said, and thro the woods
                       they went,   S-925
103 (C)   L-HGI

106 ...bashfulness,   ,/ (I)   A-2104
106 (C)   S-925

109 ...stale!' but since...   A-2104
109 (C)   S-925

114   therefore
  ...circlet: s̸o̸ s̸h̸e̸ flatter'd...   T-P

That I may love thee?'

         Then his helpless heart
Leapt, and he cried, 'Ay! wilt thou if I win?'
'Ay, that will I,' she answered, and she laughed,   125
And straitly nipt the hand, and flung it from her;
Then glanced askew at those three knights of hers,
Till all her ladies laughed along with her.

 'O happy world,' thought Pelleas, 'all, meseems,
Are happy; I the happiest of them all.'   130
Nor slept that night for pleasure in his blood,
And green wood-ways, and eyes among the leaves;
Then being on the morrow knighted, sware
To love one only. And as he came away,
The men who met him rounded on their heels   135
And wondered after him, because his face
Shone like the countenance of a priest of old
Against the flame about a sacrifice
Kindled by fire from heaven: so glad was he.

 Then Arthur made vast banquets, and strange
          knights   140
From the four winds came in: and each one sat,

---

123 Then his
  H̸i̸s̸ g̸r̸e̸a̸t̸ helpless...   T-P

124   Ay!
  ...cried 'A̸n̸d̸ wilt...   T-P
124 ...cried 'Ay!   A-2104
124 (C)   73

126 ...her.   A-2104
126 (C)   L-HGI

131 ...blood: A-2104
131 (C)   L-HGI

132 (Omitted)   A-2104
132 And greenwood ways,...   L-HGI
132   wood-ways
  And green̸w̸o̸o̸d̸ w̸a̸y̸s̸, and...   B-VIII
132 (C)   L-HGII

Though served with choice from air, land, stream, and
                sea,
Oft in mid-banquet measuring with his eyes
His neighbour's make and might: and Pelleas looked
Noble among the noble, for he dreamed   145
His lady loved him, and he knew himself
Loved of the King: and him his new-made knight
Worshipt, whose lightest whisper moved him more
Than all the ranged reasons of the world.

Then blushed and brake the morning of the jousts, 150
And this was called 'The Tournament of Youth:'
For Arthur, loving his young knight, withheld
His older and his mightier from the lists,
That Pelleas might obtain his lady's love,
According to her promise, and remain   155
Lord of the tourney. And Arthur had the jousts
Down in the flat field by the shore of Usk
Holden: the gilded parapets were crowned
With faces, and the great tower filled with eyes
Up to the summit, and the trumpets blew.   160

---

134 ...only; and as...   A-2104
134 (C)   L-HGI

145-146   for he dream'd
     His lady loved him, & he knew himself
     Noble among the noble, & knew himself   T-P

150 (Par.) At length the morning of the tourney
                     came: T-P
150 (Par.) At length the morning of the tourney
                     came: A-2104;S-925
150 (C)   L-HGI

151 ...Youth.'   A-2104
151 (C)   L-HGI

156 ...tourney; and...   A-2104
156 (C)   L-HGI

PELLEAS AND ETTARRE

There all day long Sir Pelleas kept the field
With honour: so by that strong hand of his
The sword and golden circlet were achieved.

Then rang the shout his lady loved: the heat
Of pride and glory fired her face; her eye   165
Sparkled; she caught the circlet from his lance,
And there before the people crowned herself:
So for the last time she was gracious to him.

Prose Draft c. 160
eyes to the summit & every day Sir Pelleas beat down so
many knights that he achieved the golden circlet.
Then he brought it to the lady Ettarde & the flush
came over her face for pride & glory & she crowned
herself with it, & her eyes sparkled & she was gracious
                                   to
him for the last time.
(Par.) And afterward she returned to her castle with her
damsels & her men at arms: & Pelleas followed her &
she said to her damsels Keep him away from me
all you may for he is flat & fulsome to me, & like
milk & water after spiced meats.
Would rather we had some rough old knight to ride along
with us who knew the worldly way & could beguile
us on our journey with tales of the court. And her
damsels did as she bad them with all manner of
devices so that he came not to speech with her: & she
entered into her castle & bad shut the gates of the
castle in his face, & he was left in the open field.
And he thought to himself These be the hard ways of
ladies to those who love them: & she doeth this
to prove me worthy of her & I will show myself a
true knight & faithful. And he abode there
making moan to himself & no one came out to him
& when the night came he withdrew to a priory a
league away & there lodged & every day he stood
before the castle & no one opened to him.
And he vexed & plagued her with his persistance till
her scorn of him turned into hate: & she sent out three
of her knights to drive him from the walls & if ye slay
him she said I care not but Sir Pelleas overthrew
all the knights & they went back into the castle.   T-S

830

```
    Then at Caerleon for a space--her look
Bright for all others, cloudier on her knight--        170
Lingered Ettarre:  and seeing Pelleas droop,
Said Guinevere, 'We marvel at thee much,
O damsel, wearing this unsunny face
To him who won thee glory!'  And she said,
'Had ye not held your Lancelot in your bower,         175
My Queen, he had not won.'  Whereat the Queen,
As one whose foot is bitten by an ant,
Glanced down upon her, turned and went her way.
```

---

164 ...loved; the heat   A-2104
164 (C)   L-HGI

165 ...face: her...   A-2104
165 (C)   L-HGI

166   caught
     ...she ~~took~~ the circlet...   T-P

169 ...space, her ~~eye look glance~~ look   T-P
169 (No par.) ...space, her look   A-2104
169 ...space, her look   S-925
169 (C)   L-HGI

170 ...knight,   A-2104
170 (C)   L-HGI

172 Said Guinevere ~~said spake~~
     ~~The good Queen~~ we marvel at...   T-P

sketch 173ff ~~turn~~
     ~~Damsel, why wear ye this unsunny face~~
     ~~On him/who won you glory? & she said~~
     ~~Had ye not held your Lancelot in your bower~~
     ~~He had not won it, & the Queen~~
     ~~As one whose foot is bitten by an ant~~
     ~~Glanced down at her, so turn'd & went her way~~   T-P

174 ...glory!' and...   A-2104
174 (C)   L-HGI

```
     But after, when her damsels, and herself,
And those three knights all set their faces home,      180
Sir Pelleas followed.  She that saw him cried,
'Damsels--and yet I should be shamed to say it--
I cannot bide Sir Baby.  Keep him back
Among yourselves.  Would rather that we had
Some rough old knight who knew the worldly way,        185
Albeit grizzlier than a bear, to ride
And jest with:  take him to you, keep him off,
And pamper him with papmeat, if ye will,
Old milky fables of the wolf and sheep,
Such as the wholesome mothers tell their boys.         190
Nay, should ye try him with a merry one
To find his mettle, good:  and if he fly us,
```

```
179 (Par.) But after this her damsels, & herself,      T-P
179 (Par.) But after this her damsels, and her-
                                         self,          A-2104
179 (C)                                                L-HGI

180 ...home.                                           A-2104
180 (C)                                                L-HGI

181 ...cried                                           A-2104
181 (C)                                                L-HGI

182 'Damsels, - and...                                 A-2104
182 (C)                                                L-HGI

Alt. after 182 ~~But howsoever much beholden to him~~   T-P

186 Albeit
    ~~They he were~~ grizzlier...                       T-P

187 ...you, keep him from me                           T-P
187 ...keep him from me                                A-2104
187 (C)                                                L-HGI

189          milky
    Old ~~loops~~ fables...                             T-P

Alt. after 189 ~~And tales that have/a moral thing &~~
               ~~tag/~~                                 T-P
```

Small matter! let him.' This her damsels heard,
And mindful of her small and cruel hand,
They, closing round him through the journey home, 195
Acted her hest, and always from her side
Restrained him with all manner of device,
So that he could not come to speech with her.
And when she gained her castle, upsprang the bridge,
Down rang the grate of iron through the groove, 200
And he was left alone in open field.

 'These be the ways of ladies,' Pelleas thought,
'To those who love them, trials of our faith.
Yea, let her prove me to the uttermost,
For loyal to the uttermost am I.' 205
So made his moan; and, darkness falling, sought
A priory not far off, there lodged, but rose

---

191 merry		
...with a w̷a̷n̷t̷o̷n̷ one		T-P
193 ...heard,	(, I)	A-2104
193 (C)		L-HGI
194 (Omitted) (T-P; A-2104; S-925.)		
194 (Written I MS into)		A-2104
194 (C)		L-HGI
195 And closing round him...		T-P
195 They		I MS
A̷n̷d̷ closing...home		A-2104
195 And closing...home		S-925
195 (C)		L-HGI
199 ...castle upsprang...		A-2104
199 (C)		L-HGI
202 ...thought		A-2104
202 (C)		L-HGI
203 To...		A-2104
203 (C)		L-HGI
205 ...am I."		A-2104
205 (C)		L-HGI

With morning every day, and, moist or dry,
Full-armed upon his charger all day long
Sat by the walls, and no one opened to him.   210

    And this persistence turned her scorn to wrath.
Then calling her three knights, she charged them,
                'Out!
And drive him from the walls.' And out they came,
But Pelleas overthrew them as they dashed
Against him one by one; and these returned,   215
But still he kept his watch beneath the wall.

    Thereon her wrath became a hate; and once,
A week beyond, while walking on the walls
With her three knights, she pointed downward, 'Look,
He haunts me--I cannot breathe--besieges me;   220

---

208 ...and moist or dry   A-2104
208 (C)   L-HGI

212 ...them 'Out!   A-2104
212 (C)   L-HGI

213 ...walls, 'and...   A-2104
213 (C)   L-HGI

215 ...& they return'd: T-P
215 ...and they return'd: A-2104
215 ...and they return'd.   L-HGI
215 (C)   69

216 And still...   T-P
216 And still...   A-2104
216 (C)   69

219 ...downward 'look   A-2104
219 (C)   L-HGI

Alt. after 221 A̸n̸d̸ r̸i̸c̸h̸ &̸ f̸u̸l̸l̸ s̸h̸a̸l̸l̸ b̸e̸ y̸o̸u̸r̸ g̸u̸e̸r̸d̸o̸n̸
               d̸o̸w̸n̸,   T-P

222 ...from the walls,'...   T-P
222 ...from the walls,' and down...   A-2104
222 (C)   L-HGI

Down! strike him! put my hate into your strokes,
And drive him from my walls.' And down they went,
And Pelleas overthrew them one by one;
And from the tower above him cried Ettarre,
'Bind him, and bring him in.'

                 He heard her voice;   225
Then let the strong hand, which had overthrown
Her minion-knights, by those he overthrew
Be bounden straight, and so they brought him in.

   Then when he came before Ettarre, the sight
Of her rich beauty made him at one glance   230
More bondsman in his heart than in his bonds.
Yet with good cheer he spake, 'Behold me, Lady,
A prisoner, and the vassal of thy will;
And if thou keep me in thy donjon here,
Content am I so that I see thy face   235
But once a day: for I have sworn my vows,
And thou hast given thy promise, and I know

---

223 ...one,		A-2104
223 (C)		L-HGI
224 And from the wall above...		T-P
224 And from the wall above...Ettarre $\neq$,	(, I)	A-2104
224 And from the wall above...		S-925
224 (C)		L-HGI
232 ...spake, 'behold me...		A-2104
232 (C)		L-HGI
233 ...will.		A-2104
233 (C)		L-HGI
234 me		
And so ye keep in your donjon here		T-P
234 And so ye keep me in your donjon here		A-2104
234 (C)		L-HGI
235 I am content if I may see your face		T-P
235 I am content if I may see your face		A-2104
235 (C)		L-HGI
237 ...hast ~~promised~~ given...		T-P

835

That all these pains are trials of my faith,
And that thyself, when thou hast seen me strained
And sifted to the utmost, wilt at length   240
Yield me thy love and know me for thy knight.'

   Then she began to rail so bitterly,
With all her damsels, he was stricken mute;
But when she mocked his vows and the great King,
Lighted on words: 'For pity of thine own self,   245
Peace, Lady, peace: is he not thine and mine?'
'Thou fool,' she said, 'I never heard his voice
But longed to break away. Unbind him now,
And thrust him out of doors; for save he be
Fool to the midmost marrow of his bones,   250

Sketch 239-241 And that thyself/ when I have proven
                                 my love
              Wilt yield   thyself/ & know me for thy
                          knight   T-P

239 ...thyself when...   A-2104
239 (C)   75

243 And all the damsels, ...   T-P
243 And all the damsels, ...mute.   A-2104
243 And all the damsels, ...   L-HGI
243 With   her
     And all the damsels, ...   B-VIII
243 (C)   L-HGII

244 ...great king,   A-2104
244 (C)   L-HGI

245 He found his tongue. 'For pity of your own
                    self,   T-P
245 He found his tongue. 'For pity of your own
                    self,   A-2104
245   thine
   ...pity of your own self,   B-VIII
245 (C)   L-HGII

He will return no more.' And those, her three,
Laughed, and unbound, and thrust him from the gate.

And after this, a week beyond, again
She called them, saying, 'There he watches yet,
There like a dog before his master's door!   255
Kicked, he returns: do ye not hate him, ye?
Ye know yourselves: how can ye bide at peace,
Affronted with his fulsome innocence?
Are ye but creatures of the board and bed,
No men to strike? Fall on him all at once,   260
And if ye slay him I reck not: if ye fail,
Give ye the slave mine order to be bound,
Bind him as heretofore, and bring him in:
It may be ye shall slay him in his bonds.'

---

246   peace   he not
     Sweet lady, s̷i̷l̷e̷n̷c̷e̷: h̷e̷ is thine & mine?'   T-P
246 Sweet lady, peace: is...   A-2104
246 (C)   L-HGI

247   his voice
     ...heard h̷i̷m̷ s̷p̷e̷a̷k̷   T-P
247 ...fool' she said 'I...   A-2104
247 (C)   L-HGI

251 ...more;' and...   A-2104
251 (C)   L-HGI

252 ...him out of door.   T-P
252 ...him out of door.   A-2104
252 (C)   L-HGI

254 ...saying 'There...   A-2104
254 (C)   L-HGI

255 ...door: A-2104
255 (C)   L-HGI

260 ...strike? fall on...   A-2104
260 (C)   L-HGI

She spake; and at her will they couched their
                            spears,   265
Three against one: and Gawain passing by,
Bound upon solitary adventure, saw
Low down beneath the shadow of those towers
A villainy, three to one: and through his heart
The fire of honour and all noble deeds   270
Flashed, and he called, 'I strike upon thy side--
The caitiffs!' 'Nay,' said Pelleas, 'but forbear;
He needs no aid who doth his lady's will.'

So Gawain, looking at the villainy done,

265	down they came &	
	(Par.) She spake; & couch'd their spears,	T-P
265	at her will they	I MS
	...and d̶o̶w̶n̶ t̶h̶e̶y̶ c̶a̶m̶e̶ and...	A-2104
265	...and down they came and...	S-925
265	(C)	L-HGI

| 267 | upon a̶ solitary   saw | |
| | Bound o̶n̶ adventure, glancing at the walls | T-P |

| 268 | Low down   ose | |
| | B̶e̶h̶e̶l̶d̶ beneath the shadow of thei̶r̶ towers | T-P |

269	s heart	
	...one: & in hi̶m̶ w̶o̶k̶e̶	T-P
269	thro'	I MS
	...and i̶n̶ his heart	A-2104
269	...and in his heart	S-295
269	(C)	L-HGI

270	all	
	...honour & o̶f̶ noble...	T-P
270	...deeds,	A-2104
270	(C)	L-HGI

271	Burnt &	
	A̶n̶d̶ he call'd o̶u̶t̶ 'I...	T-P
271	Flash'd	I MS
	B̶u̶r̶n̶t̶ and he call'd 'I strike...	A-2104
271	Burnt, and he call'd 'I strike...	S-925
271	(C)	L-HGI

PELLEAS AND ETTARRE

Forbore, but in his heat and eagerness   275
Trembled and quivered, as the dog, withheld
A moment from the vermin that he sees
Before him, shivers, ere he springs and kills.

    And Pelleas overthrew them, one to three;
And they rose up, and bound, and brought him in.   280
Then first her anger, leaving Pelleas, burned
Full on her knights in many an evil name
Of craven, weakling, and thrice-beaten hound:
'Yet, take him, ye that scarce are fit to touch,

---

272 ...forbear   A-2104
272 (C)   L-HGI

273 He needs   who doth his
    No aid ø̸f̸ t̸h̸i̸n̸e̸ I̸ d̸ø̸ m̸y̸ lady's will.   T-P

274 ...done   A-2104
274 (C)   L-HGI

275 ...eagerness,   A-2104
275 (C)   L-HGI

277 ...vermin, that...   A-2104
277 (C)   L-HGI

280 And up they rose, & bound...   T-P
280   up   I MS
    And u̸p̸ they rose, and bound...   A-2104
280 And up they rose, and bound...   S-925
280 (C)   L-HGI

281 ...Pelleas, flash'd   T-P
281   burn'd   I MS
    ...Pelleas, f̸l̸a̸s̸h̸'̸d̸   A-2104
281 ...Pelleas, flash'd   S-925
281 (C)   L-HGI

283 ...hound -   A-2104
283 (C)   L-HGI

284 Yet, ...   A-2104
284 (C)   S-925

Far less to bind, your victor, and thrust him out,   285
And let who will release him from his bonds.
And if he comes again'--there she brake short;
And Pelleas answered, 'Lady, for indeed
I loved you and I deemed you beautiful,
I cannot brook to see your beauty marred   290
Through evil spite: and if ye love me not,
I cannot bear to dream you so forsworn:
I had liefer ye were worthy of my love,
Than to be loved again of you--farewell;
And though ye kill my hope, not yet my love,   295
Vex not yourself: ye will not see me more.'

   While thus he spake, she gazed upon the man
Of princely bearing, though in bonds, and thought,
'Why have I pushed him from me? this man loves,

---

286 ...bonds		A-2104
286 (C)		L-HGI
287 ...short,		A-2104
287 (C)		L-HGI
289 ...beautiful -		A-2104
289 ...beautiful ⁄ ,	,/ (I)	L-HGII
289 (C)		69
291 evil spite		
By p̶a̶s̶s̶i̶o̶n̶ t̶h̶u̶s̶ - & if...		T-P
291 By evil spite - and...		A-2104
291 Thro' evil spite - and...		L-HGI
291 Thro' evil spite ⁄: and...	:/ (I)	L-HGII
291 (C)		69
292 ...forsworn -		A-2104
292 ...forsworn ⁄ :	:/ (I)	L-HGII
292 (C)		69
293 liefer		
I had r̶a̶t̶h̶e̶r̶ ye...		T-P
298 ...thought		A-2104
298 (C)		L-HGI

840

If love there be: yet him I loved not. Why?   300
I deemed him fool? yea, so? or that in him
A something--was it nobler than myself?--
Seemed my reproach? He is not of my kind.
He could not love me, did he know me well.
Nay, let him go--and quickly.' And her knights   305
Laughed not, but thrust him bounden out of door.

   Forth sprang Gawain, and loosed him from his bonds,
And flung them o'er the walls; and afterward,
Shaking his hands, as from a lazar's rag,
'Faith of my body,' he said, 'and art thou not--   310
Yea thou art he, whom late our Arthur made
Knight of his table; yea and he that won
The circlet? wherefore hast thou so defamed

---

299 ...loves –	A-2104
299 (C)	L-HGI
300 ...be – yet	A-2104
300 (C)	69
302 ...than myself,	A-2104
302 ...than myself?	L-HGI
302 (C)	L-HGII

Alt. after 303 T̸o̸o̸ c̸l̸o̸s̸e̸ a̸ f̸o̸l̸l̸o̸w̸e̸r̸ o̸f̸ t̸h̸e̸ K̸i̸n̸g̸ f̸o̸r̸
                              m̸e̸   T-P

305 ...quickly,' and...	A-2104
305 (C)	L-HGI
307 (Par.) A̸n̸d̸ Forth sprang...	T-P
308 ...and afterwards	A-2104
308 (C)	L-HGI
310 ...body' he said 'and...	A-2104
310 (C)	L-HGI
311 ...he whom...	A-2104
311 ...art – he whom...	L-HGI
311 (C)	L-HGII

Thy brotherhood in me and all the rest,
As let these caitiffs on thee work their will?'   315

    And Pelleas answered, 'O, their wills are hers
For whom I won the circlet; and mine, hers,
Thus to be bounden, so to see her face,
Marred though it be with spite and mockery now,
Other than when I found her in the woods;   320
And though she hath me bounden but in spite,
And all to flout me, when they bring me in,
Let me be bounden, I shall see her face;
Else must I die through mine unhappiness.'

    And Gawain answered kindly though in scorn,   325

---

313 The circlet; wherefore...   A-2104
313 (C)   L-HGI

316   are
  ...wills ~~were~~ hers   T-P

317   & mine hers
  ...the circlet; ~~therefore mine she that dwells~~   T-P
317 ...and mine, hers,   (,, I)   A-2104
317 (C)   L-HGI

Alt. after 317 ~~Here in her castle / & my will is~~
                 ~~hers/~~   T-P

320 ...woods -   A-2104
320 (C)   L-HGI

323 ...bounden - I ...face;   ; (I)   A-2104
323 ...bounden - I...   S-925
323 (C)   L-HGI

326 ...me, if...   A-2104
326 (C)   L-HGI

327 ...me, if...   A-2104
327 (C)   L-HGI

PELLEAS AND ETTARRE

'Why, let my lady bind me if she will,
And let my lady beat me if she will:
But an she send her delegate to thrall
These fighting hands of mine--Christ kill me then
But I will slice him handless by the wrist,   330
And let my lady sear the stump for him,
Howl as he may. But hold me for your friend:
Come, ye know nothing: here I pledge my troth,
Yea, by the honour of the Table Round,
I will be leal to thee and work thy work,   335
And tame thy jailing princess to thine hand.
Lend me thine horse and arms, and I will say
That I have slain thee. She will let me in
To hear the manner of thy fight and fall;

---

328   an
         But ~~if~~ she...   T-P

330 ...the wrist   A-2104
330 (C)   L-HGI

332 Howl as he may   but
    ~~Come/ye know nothing~~: hold me for your friend: T-P
332 ...may: but...   A-2104
332 (C)   L-HGI

Alt. after 332 ~~I pledge thee here my knightly plight &~~
                         ~~troth~~   T-P

334 ...Round   A-2104
334 ...Round,   ,/ (I)   L-HGII
334 (C)   69

336 ...thy gaoling princess...   A-2104
336 (C)   L-HGI

337 ...arms and...   A-2104
337 (C)   L-HGI

339 ...fall,   A-2104
339 (C)   L-HGII

843

Then, when I come within her counsels, then　　　340
From prime to vespers will I chant thy praise
As prowest knight and truest lover, more
Than any have sung thee living, till she long
To have thee back in lusty life again,
Not to be bound, save by white bonds and warm,　　345
Dearer than freedom.　Wherefore now thy horse
And armour:　let me go:　be comforted:
Give me three days to melt her fancy, and hope
The third night hence will bring thee news of gold.'

　　　Then Pelleas　lent his horse and all his arms,　　350

---

340 And when...counsels, ~~trust~~ then　　　　　　　　　T-P
340 And when I...　　　　　　　　　　　　　　　　　　A-2104
340 Then　　　　　　　　　　　　　　　　　(I MS another)
　　　~~And~~ when I...　　　　　　　　　　　　　　　　B-VIII
340 Then when I...　　　　　　　　　　　　　　　　　L-HGII
340 (C)　　　　　　　　　　　　　　　　　　　　　　　69

341　　　　chant
　　　...I ~~sing~~ thy...　　　　　　　　　　　　　　　T-P

342 As prowess knight...　　　　　　　　　　　　　　A-2104
342 (C)　　　　　　　　　　　　　　　　　　　　　L-HGI

344 ...again　　　　　　　　　　　　　　　　　　　A-2104
344 (C)　　　　　　　　　　　　　　　　　　　　　L-HGI

345 Not to be bound~~en~~ save by ~~binding arms~~ white...　T-P
345 ...bound save...warm　　　　　　　　　　　　　A-2104
345 ...bound save...　　　　　　　　　　　　　　　L-HGI
345 (C)　　　　　　　　　　　　　　　　　　　　L-HGII

346 Dearer than freedom:　wherefore now
　　　~~And claspings each of either/~~ ~~so~~ thy horse　　T-P
346 ...freedom:　wherefore...　　　　　　　　　　　A-2104
346 (C)　　　　　　　　　　　　　　　　　　　　L-HGI

350　　　　　all his
　　　...horse & arms, & ~~look~~　　　　　　　　　　　T-P

Saving the goodly sword, his prize, and took
Gawain's, and said, 'Betray me not, but help--
Art thou not he whom men call light-of-love?'

'Ay,' said Gawain, 'for women be so light.'
Then bounded forward to the castle walls,   355
And raised a bugle hanging from his neck,
And winded it, and that so musically
That all the old echoes hidden in the wall
Rang out like hollow woods at hunting-tide.

Up ran a score of damsels to the tower;   360
'Avaunt,' they cried, 'our lady loves thee not.'
But Gawain lifting up his vizor said,
'Gawain am I, Gawain of Arthur's court,
And I have slain this Pelleas whom ye hate:

---

352 ...said 'Betray me not but help		A-2104
352 ...said 'Betray...		L-HGI
352 ...said 'Betray...help ≠ !	! (I)	L-HGI I
352 ...said "Betray...		69
352 (C)		70
354 (Par.) 'Ay' said Gawain 'for...		A-2104
354 (C)		L-HGI
355 ...walls		A-2104
355 (C)		L-HGI
359 ...huntingtide.		A-2104
359 (C)		84
360 ...to the wall		T-P
360 ...to the wall		A-2104
360 (C)		L-HGI
361 'Avaunt' they cried 'our lady loves thee not'		A-2104
361 (C)		L-HGI
362 ...said		A-2104
362 (C)		L-HGI
364 ...whom ye l̶o̶a̶t̶h̶e̶ hate		T-P

Behold his horse and armour. Open gates,   365
And I will make you merry.'

                        And down they ran,
Her damsels, crying to their lady, 'Lo!
Pelleas is dead--he told us--he that hath
His horse and armour: will ye let him in?
He slew him! Gawain, Gawain of the court,   370
Sir Gawain--there he waits below the wall,
Blowing his bugle as who should say him nay.'

   And so, leave given, straight on through open door
Rode Gawain, whom she greeted courteously.

Alt. after 364
    And I will make you merry when I come in./
   (Par.) Then ran the damsels crying to Ettarre
   Pelleas is dead / Pelleas is dead,/who spoiled
   thy gates: wilt thou let him in, the man
   who slew him? there he waits below/the wall
   Blowing his bugle & as who as may/./   T-P

365   armour
   ...horse & harness. Open gate,   T-P
365 ...Open gate,   A-2104
365 (C)   73

367 ...lady 'Lo!   A-2104
367 (C)   L-HGI

369   armour
   ...horse & harness: will...   T-P

370 He
   Who slew him? there he waits below the wall,
   Blowing his bugle as who shall/say/me nay/
      Gawain, Gawain of the court,   T-P

373   And so,   on
   (Par.) The leave was given, & straight
                thro'...   T-P

374 ...Gawain whom...   A-2104
374 (C)   L-HGI

'Dead, is it so?' she asked. 'Ay, ay,' said he,   375
'And oft in dying cried upon your name.'
'Pity on him,' she answered, 'a good knight,
But never let me bide one hour at peace.'
'Ay,' thought Gawain, 'and you be fair enow:
But I to your dead man have given my troth,   380
That whom ye loathe, him will I make you love.'

    So those three days, aimless about the land,
Lost in a doubt, Pelleas wandering
Waited, until the third night brought a moon
With promise of large light on woods and ways.   385

    Hot was the night and silent; but a sound

---

375 ...ask'd, 'Ay, ay' said he   A-2104
375 (C)   L-HGI

377 ...him' she answer'd 'a good...   A-2104
377 (C)   L-HGI

379 ...'and ye be...   T-P
379 'Ay' thought Gawain 'and ye be...   A-2104
379 ... 'and ye be...   L-HGI
379 (C)   73

381 ...loathe him...   A-2104
381 (C)   73

382 So for three days, aimless...   A-S

383 Lost in himself, Pelleas, wandering   A-S

386 (Par.) The night was close: he could not rest,
                        but rode   A-2104
386 (Par.) The night was hot: he could not rest,
                        but rode   L-HGI
386 (Par.) The night was hot; he could not sleep:
                        a lay   HM-1324
386 (Par.) The night was hot: he cd not sleep:
                        sound
              a n̸o̸i̸s̸e̸   HM-19494
386 (C)   73

Of Gawain ever coming, and this lay--
Which Pelleas had heard sung before the Queen,
And seen her sadden listening--vext his heart,
And marred his rest--'A worm within the rose.'   390

    'A rose, but one, none other rose had I,
A rose, one rose, and this was wondrous fair,
One rose, a rose that gladdened earth and sky,
One rose, my rose, that sweetened all mine air--
I cared not for the thorns; the thorns were there.   395

    'One rose, a rose to gather by and by,
One rose, a rose, to gather and to wear,

387-403 (Omitted from A-2104 to 73)

387 Call'd by the Bards 'a worm within the rose' -
                                              HM-1324
387 Of Gawain ever coming, and this lay,
    ~~Call'd by the Bards 'a worm within the~~
                 ~~rose'~~   HM-19494

389   sadden listening
    ...her ~~move to weeping~~, vext his ears   HM-1324
389 ...his ear~~s~~   HM-19494

392 ...and that was...   HM-1324;HM-19494

395 He laughs who loves it - tho' the thorns be there
    ~~I cared not for the thorns, / the thorns were there~~
Note to 395 This makes the song more perfect as a song -
                          but
            the old reading has more pathos & will, I
                          think,
            be retained. - A.T.   (I MS)   HM-19494

396 ...rose, one rose...   HM-1324

397 ...rose, one rose...   HM-1324;HM-19494

Sketch 401-3 (Par.) This lay so shook him that he rose
                        & rode   HM-1324

848

No rose but one--what other rose had I?
One rose, my rose; a rose that will not die,--
He dies who loves it,--if the worm be there.'   400

    This tender rhyme, and evermore the doubt,
'Why lingers Gawain with his golden news?'
So shook him that he could not rest, but rode
Ere midnight to her walls, and bound his horse
Hard by the gates. Wide open were the gates,   405
And no watch kept; and in through these he past,
And heard but his own steps, and his own heart
Beating, for nothing moved but his own self,
And his own shadow. Then he crost the court,
And spied not any light in hall or bower,   410
But saw the postern portal also wide

---

401   &
    This tender lay, ~~with~~, evermore, the doubt
    ~~This lay so shook him that he rose and rode~~ HM-19494

403 And Pelleas would abide no more, but rode   A-S
403   night was close: he cd not rest -
    (Par.) The~~n~~ ~~Pelleas would abide no more~~, but
                        rode   T-P
403 So stirr'd him...   HM-19494

405 Beside the gates: the gates were wide agape   A-S
405 ...gates: wide...   A-2104
405 (C)   L-HGI

406 ...kept: & thro' the court he crost the gates
                               he went   A-S

409 ...shadow: thro' the court he crost   A-S
409 ...shadow: then...   A-2104
409 (C)   L-HGI

410 (Omitted A-S; T-P; A-2104)
410 (Added C)   73

411 And saw the postern portal gaping wide.   A-S
411 And saw...   T-P
411 And saw...   A-2104
411 (C)   73

Yawning; and up a slope of garden, all
Of roses white and red, and brambles mixt
And overgrowing them, went on, and found,
Here too, all hushed below the mellow moon,   415
Save that one rivulet from a tiny cave
Came lightening downward, and so spilt itself
Among the roses, and was lost again.

Then was he ware of three pavilions reared
Above the bushes, gilden-peakt: in one,   420
Red after revel, droned her lurdane knights
Slumbering, and their three squires across their feet:
In one, their malice on the placid lip
Frozen by sweet sleep, four of her damsels lay:

---

412 Yawning, and...   A-2104
412 (C)   L-HGI

413 ...red, & wild ones mixt   T-P
413 ...red, and wild ones mixt   A-2104
413 (C)   73

414 ...them, past on, ...   T-P
414 ...them, past one, and found   A-2104
414 (C)   L-HGI

415 There too all...   A-2104
415 (C)   L-HGI

419   white
    ...that ~~three~~ pavilions rose   T-P
419 (Par.) Then was he ware that white pavilions
                        rose,   (, I)   A-2104
419 (C)   73

420 Three
    ~~white~~ from the bushes, ...   T-P
420 Three from the bushes, gilden - peakt: in
                        one,   A-2104
420 (C)   73

429 Then, as a coward...   A-S

430 ...proven, or dog   A-S

850

And in the third, the circlet of the jousts   425
Bound on her brow, were Gawain and Ettarre.

   Back, as a hand that pushes through the leaf
To find a nest and feels a snake, he drew:
Back, as a coward slinks from what he fears
To cope with, or a traitor proven, or hound   430
Beaten, did Pelleas in an utter shame
Creep with his shadow through the court again,
Fingering at his sword-handle until he stood
There on the castle-bridge once more, and thought,
'I will go back, and slay them where they lie.'   435

   And so went back, and seeing them yet in sleep
Said, 'Ye, that so dishallow the holy sleep,
Your sleep is death,' and drew the sword, and thought,

---

431 Beaten, Sir Pelleas...   A-S
431   did
    Beaten, S̸i̸r̸ Pelleas...   T-P

432 Stole thro' the vacant castle court again   A-S
432 Creep
    C̸r̸e̸p̸t̸ with...   T-P

433 ...handle, till he stood   A-S

434 Once more upon the castle-bridge, & thought   A-S
434 ...thought   A-2104
434 (C)   L-HGI

436 ...back and...   A-2104
436 (C)   73

437 Groan'd 'Ye...   A-S
437 Said 'Ye...   A-2104
437 (C)   L-HGI

Alt. after 437 Now wd I slay you, only that the king
              Hath sworn me to his brotherhood'!
                   & then   A-S

438 ...death' and drew the sword and thought   A-2104
438 (C)   L-HGI

851

'What! slay a sleeping knight? the King hath bound
And sworn me to this brotherhood;' again,   440
'Alas that ever a knight should be so false.'
Then turned, and so returned, and groaning laid
The naked sword arthwart their naked throats,
There left it, and them sleeping; and she lay,
The circlet of the tourney round her brows,   445
And the sword of the tourney across her throat.

　　And forth he past, and mounting on his horse
Stared at her towers that, larger than themselves
In their own darkness, thronged into the moon.
Then crushed the saddle with his thighs, and
　　　　　　　　　　　　clenched   450

---

439 ...the king...   A-2104
439 (C)   L-HGI

440 ...brotherhood again,   ,/ (I)   A-2104
440 (C)   L-HGI

442 And turn'd & then returnd - & stoop'd & laid   A-S

443 ...sword across their...   A-S

444 ...sleeping - Lo she lay   A-S

445 ...tourney about her brows,   A-S
445 ...tourney about her brow,   T-P
445 ...tourney about her brow,   A-2104
445   round   brows   I MS
    ...tourney ⱥ⌀⌀ᵾⱦ her brow,   B-VIII
445 (C)   L-HGII

447 (Par.) He past & loosed his horse & leaping on
                           it   A-S

448 Glanced at her...   A-S

449 ...darkness, crowded to the moon   A-S

450 ...thighs and...   A-2104
450 (C)   L-HGI

PELLEAS AND ETTARRE

His hands, and maddened with himself and moaned:

'Would they have risen against me in their blood
At the last day? I might have answered them
Even before high God. O towers so strong,
Huge, solid, would that even while I gaze   455
The crack of earthquake shivering to your base
Split you, and Hell burst up your harlot roofs
Bellowing, and charred you through and through within,
Black as the harlot's heart--hollow as a skull!

---

451 His hands & ᴍ̶ᴏ̶ᴀ̶ɴ̶'d̶ & madden'd with himself &
                          moan'd   T-P
451 ...hands and...moan'd.   A-2104
451 (C)   L-HGI

452 (Par.) Would these have...   A-S

454 ...towers, that stand   A-S
454 ...strong   A-2104
454 (C)   L-HGI

455 So strong & solid, wd that as I gaze   A-S
455 So solid, would...   T-P
455 So solid, would...   A-2104
455 Huge,   I MS
    s̶o̶ solid, would...   B-VIII
455 (C)   L-HGII

457 Split
    R̶e̶n̶t̶ you...   T-P

458 Bellowing, & made you thro & thro within   A-S
458 ...within   A-2104
458 (C)   L-HGI

459 Black as the harlot's heart! so might ye stand
    Here thro' all time as hollow as a skull -   A-S;T-P
459 ...skull ≠ !   (! I)   A-2104
459 (C)   S-925

853

PELLEAS AND ETTARRE

Let the fierce east scream through your eyelet-
                holes,   460
And whirl the dust of harlots round and round
In dung and nettles! hiss, snake--I saw him there--
Let the fox bark, let the wolf yell. Who yells
Here in the still sweet summer night, but I--
I, the poor Pelleas whom she called her fool?   465
Fool, beast--he, she, or I? myself most fool;
Beast too, as lacking human wit--disgraced,

----

460 ...eyelet-holes,   (, I)   A-2104
460 (C)   S-925

461   whoredom
   ...dust of harlots round...   T-P
461 ...dust of whoredom round...   A-2104
461 (C)   L-HGI

462 & alt. after 462 ...snake! & let the churl
    Tending his goats, stung with old Nature's sting
    Chalk his true filth upon your rotting stones! A-S
462 & alt. after 462   helpless
    In dung & nettles - hiss, snake - & let the churls
    stung with the sting of his own/rams & goats
    Chalk nature's filth upon your rotting stones - T-P
462 & alt after 462 In dung and nettles - hiss, snake -
                and helpless churl
    Scrawl   I MS
    Chalk nature's filth upon your rotting stones-A-2104
462 & alt. after 462 In dung and nettles - hiss, snake -
                and helpless churl
    Scrawl nature's filth upon your rotting stones -
                               S-925
462 In dung and nettles - hiss, snake - I saw him
               there -   L-HGI
462 In dung and nettles ≠ ! hiss, snake ≠ ! I...
                    !! (I)   L-HGII
462 (C)   69

464 ...the sweet still summer...   A-S

465 ...fool -   A-2104
465 (C)   L-HGI

```
Dishonoured all for trial of true love--
Love?--we be all alike:  only the King
Hath made us fools and liars.  O noble vows!          470
O great and sane and simple race of brutes
That own no lust because they have no law!
For why should I have loved her to my shame?
I loathe her, as I loved her to my shame.
```

```
466  Fool?  beast?  he, she or I?  myself most fool  - A-S
466  Fool, beast - he she or I?  myself most fool; A-2104
466  (C)                                              L-HGI

467  ...-disgraced                                    A-2104
467  (C)                                              L-HGI

469  True love, true lust.  We are all of us alike.
                            The King                   A-S
469   love?           be
     T̸r̸u̸e̸ L̸u̸s̸t̸ - we a̸r̸e̸/all...                      T-P
469  ...the king                                       A-2104
469  (C)                                               73

470  ...liars binding us                               A-S
470           O noble vows!
     ...liars b̸i̸n̸d̸i̸n̸g̸ u̸s̸ h̸i̸s̸ k̸n̸i̸g̸h̸t̸s̸               T-P

Alt. after 470  By such vain vows as cannot sunder
                             men                       A-S
Alt. after 470  B̸y̸ v̸o̸w̸s̸ t̸o̸o̸ v̸a̸i̸n̸ e̸v̸e̸r̸ t̸o̸ s̸u̸n̸d̸e̸r̸ u̸s̸   T-P

471  From that great, sane & simple race of brutes    A-S
471  O              &
     F̸r̸o̸m̸ t̸h̸e̸ great sane & simple race of brutes     T-P

472  That have no lust...                              A-S
472        own
     That h̸a̸v̸e̸ no...                                   T-P

474  I loved her as I hate her to my shame.           A-S
474    loathe           loved
     I l̸o̸v̸e̸d̸ her, as I h̸a̸t̸e̸ her...                    T-P
```

I never loved her, I but lusted for her--   475
Away--'
        He dashed the rowel into his horse,
And bounded forth and vanished through the night.

    Then she, that felt the cold touch on her throat,
Awakening knew the sword, and turned herself
To Gawain: 'Liar, for thou hast not slain   480
This Pelleas! here he stood, and might have slain
Me and thyself.' And he that tells the tale

Alt. before 475   no purity,
        Honour in men, virtue in women - & I   A-S
475 Who thought I loved her have but lusted for
                              her -   A-S

476 Away -'   '/ (I)   A-2104
476 (C)   S-925

478   the   touch   on
    ...felt cold ~~íŕóń áćŕóśś~~ her throat   T-P
478 ...she, that...throat,   (,, I)   A-2104
478 (C)   S-925

479 Awakening
    ~~Áẇóḱé~~ & knew...   T-P
479 ...sword, and...   (, I)   A-2104
479 (C)   S-925

480 ...Gawain, 'Liar...   A-2104
480 (C)   L-HGI

481   stood
    ...he ~~ẇáś~~ & might...   T-P
481 This Pelleas - ! here he stood and... (! I) A-2104
481 ...stood and...   S-925
481 (C)   73

482 ...thyself;' and...   A-2104
482 (C)   L-HGI

Sketch 483 ff ~~says that her heart veer'd toward Pelleas~~
              ~~As the one only lover in this world~~
              ~~And therefore/noblest Knight, & that her~~
                          ~~life~~   T-P

Says that her ever-veering fancy turned
To Pelleas, as the one true knight on earth,
And only lover; and through her love her life   485
Wasted and pined, desiring him in vain.

   But he by wild and way, for half the night,
And over hard and soft, striking the sod
From out the soft, the spark from off the hard,
Rode till the star above the wakening sun,   490
Beside that tower where Percivale was cowled,
Glanced from the rosy forehead of the dawn.
For so the words were flashed into his heart
He knew not whence or wherefore: 'O sweet star,
Pure on the virgin forehead of the dawn!'   495

------

484 ...earth,   (, I)   A-2104
484 (C)   S-925

485 ...lover,; and...   ;/ (I)   A-2104
485 (C)   S-925

487   wild   way
    ...by w̸a̸s̸t̸e̸ & w̸e̸a̸l̸d̸ for...   T-P
487 ...way, for...night,   (,, I)   A-2104
487 (C)   S-925

488 s̸o̸ o̸n̸ b̸y̸ h̸a̸r̸d̸ & s̸o̸f̸t̸, striking...   T-P

491 Beside
    C̸l̸o̸s̸e̸ b̸y̸ that...   T-P

Prose draft C. 493 ff.
& the words came into his head he knew not whence or
why O pure star
Bright on the virgin forehead of the dawn
                    only
& then he would have wept but his eyes were d̸r̸y̸ hard &
dry as the bed of the fountain in midsummer: & in he
went & cast himself on a pallet & dreamed that the
                    (devil?)
in the form of Gawain had lit the world on fire & the
star fell into the flame.   T-S

495 ...dawn.'   A-2104
495 (C)   73

And there he would have wept, but felt his eyes
Harder and drier than a fountain bed
In summer: thither came the village girls
And lingered talking, and they come no more
Till the sweet heavens have filled it from the
                      heights   500
Again with living waters in the change
Of seasons: hard his eyes; harder his heart
Seemed; but so weary were his limbs, that he,
Gasping, 'Of Arthur's hall am I, but here,
Here let me rest and die,' cast himself down,   505
And gulfed his griefs in inmost sleep; so lay,
Till shaken by a dream, that Gawain fired

---

496 but that his eyes	A-S
496 ...wept but...	A-2104
496 (C)	L-HGI
497 Were hard & drier than...	A-S
498 In middle summer: there the village maidens came	A-S
499 And lingerd talking but they Whither the village maidens come no more	A-S
500 ...it ø*n*¢¢ from...	A-S
503 were Seem'd; *t*ø *h*i*m*s*e*l*f but *a*l*l so weary his limbs, that he,	T-P
504 *H*¢ *d*i*d *b*u*t gasping, 'Of...	T-P
505 cast ...die,' *f*l*u*n*g himself...	T-P
506 griefs inmost ...his *h*e*a*r*t in *a *d*e*e*p sleep...	T-P
506 so ...sleep; *a*n*d lay,	A-2104
506 (C)	S-925
507 ...by *a*n *o*l*d (?) dream...	T-P

858

PELLEAS AND ETTARRE

The hall of Merlin, and the morning star
Reeled in the smoke, brake into flame, and fell.

He woke, and being ware of some one nigh,   510
Sent hands upon him, as to tear him, crying,
'False, and I held thee pure as Guinevere.'

But Percivale stood near him and replied,
'Am I but false as Guinevere is pure?
Or art thou mazed with dreams? or being one   515
Of our free-spoken Table hast not heard
That Lancelot'--there he checked himself and paused.

---

509 R   brake into flame,
     R̸eel'd in the smoke, & c̸a̸u̸g̸h̸t̸ t̸h̸e̸ f̸l̸a̸m̸e̸ & fell.   T-P

511   upon
     ...hands o̸n̸ him, as i̸f̸ to tear...   T-P
511 ...,crying   A-2104
511 (C)   73

512   pure
     ...thee t̸r̸u̸e̸ as...   T-P

513 ...replied   A-2104
513 (C)   L-HGI

514   pure
     ...is t̸r̸u̸e̸.   T-P
514 ...pure.?   (? I)   A-2104
514 (C)   S-925

sketch 516 ff ...Table hast forgotten
                at Lancelot - there he check'd himself
                    & paus'd
          T̸h̸e̸i̸r̸/b̸a̸b̸b̸l̸i̸n̸g̸s̸ o̸f̸ o̸u̸r̸ L̸a̸n̸c̸e̸l̸o̸t̸ & o̸u̸r̸
                    Q̸u̸e̸e̸n̸?̸y̸   T-P

516 ...Table hast forgotten   A-2104
516 (C)   L-HGI

517   re   I MS
     ...Lancelot' - the̸n̸ he...   A-2104
517 (C)   S-925

859

```
    Then fared it with Sir Pelleas as with one
Who gets a wound in battle, and the sword
That made it plunges through the wound again,        520
And pricks it deeper:  and he shrank and wailed,
'Is the Queen false?' and Percivale was mute.
'Have any of our Round Table held their vows?'
And Percivale made answer not a word.
'Is the King true?' 'The King!' said Percivale.      525
'Why then let men couple at once with wolves.
What! art thou mad?'
```

---

519 ...battle, and...   (, I)   A-2104
519 (C)   S-925

520 ...again,   (, I)   A-2104
520 (C)   S-925

521   wail'd
    ...shrank & ~~ask'd~~   T-P
521 ...wail'd.   A-2104
521 (C)   L-HGI

523   any of   their   ?
    'Have our Round Table kept ~~the~~ vows ~~they sware?~~ T-P
523   they sware? I MS
    'Have ~~any~~ ~~of~~ our Round Table kept the~~ir~~ vows?' A-2104
523 'Have our Round Table kept the vows they sware?'
                                                         S-925
523   any of   held their vows?   P MS
    'Have our Round Table ~~kept~~ ~~the~~ ~~vows/they~~
                          ~~sware?~~   B-VIII
523 (C)   L-HGII

525 'Is the king true?' 'The king' said Percivale.
                                 ⊙ (I)   A-2104
525 'Is the king true?'   'The king' said Percivale. S-925
525 (C)   73

Alt. for 527 to 528 ~~But Pelleas leapt leaping up~~
    ~~call'd for his horse/ then/springing to the~~
                          ~~saddle~~   T-P

860

                        But Pelleas, leaping up,
Ran through the doors and vaulted on his horse
And fled: small pity upon his horse had he,
Or on himself, or any, and when he met   530
A cripple, one that held a hand for alms--
Hunched as he was, and like an old dwarf-elm
That turns its back on the salt blast, the boy
Paused not, but overrode him, shouting, 'False,
And false with Gawain!' and so left him bruised   535
And battered, and fled on, and hill and wood
Went ever streaming by him till the gloom,
That follows on the turning of the world,

------

527 ...Pelleas leaping up   A-2104
527 (C)   L-HGI

529 ...he,   ,/ (I)   A-2104
529 (C)   S-925

531 A cripple - , one...alms ⧸   (, I)   A-2104
531 A cripple; one...   S-925
531 (C)   L-HGI

534 ...him clamouring   T-S
534 Paused not but..., shouting 'False,   A-2104
534   s̸h̸o̸u̸t̸i̸n̸g̸ ȳf̸a̸l̸s̸e̸ stet   P MS
    Paused not but overrode him, w̸i̸t̸h̸ a̸ s̸h̸o̸u̸t̸, B-VIII
534 Paused not but..., shouting 'False,   69
534 (C)   73

535 False, false with...   T-S;T-P
535 False, false with Gawain,' and...   A-2104
535 A̸n̸d̸   P MS
    'False, false with...   B-VIII
535 (C)   69

536 And battered on the path; &   T-S
536   & hill & wood
to And batter'd, & fled on, ṳn̸till the gloom
537 Went ever streeming by him   T-P

537 ...gloom   (, I)   A-2104
537 (C)   S-925

        861

Darkened the common path: he twitched the reins,
And made his beast that better knew it, swerve   540
Now off it and now on; but when he saw
High up in heaven the hall that Merlin built,
Blackening against the dead-green stripes of even,
'Black nest of rats,' he groaned, 'ye build too high.'

    Not long thereafter from the city gates   545
Issued Sir Lancelot riding airily,
Warm with a gracious parting from the Queen,
Peace at his heart, and gazing at a star
And marvelling what it was: on whom the boy,

---

539 Drown'd them in night; but when he raised his
                          eyes   T-S

541 to 542 And saw far off
          ~~But when he saw~~ the hall that Merlin
                          built   T-S

543 ...of Even,   A-2104
543 (C)   L-HGI

544 Groan'd saying O thou sewer
                  he groand   too
    Black nest of rats ~~why do~~ ye build so high?   T-S

547   ~~from~~   ~~with~~   stet
    Warm ~~with~~ a gracious parting ~~from~~ the Queen,   T-P

550 ...seeded meadow grass   A-2104
550 ...seeded meadow-grass   L-HGII
550 (C)   84

551 ..., saying - 'What...   A-2104
551 (C)   L-HGI

553 'I have no name' he...   T-P
553 'I have no name' he shouted 'a...   A-2104
553 'I have no name,' he shouted, 'a scourge
                          am I,   L-HGI
553 (C)   92

```
Across the silent seeded meadow-grass                    550
Borne, clashed:  and Lancelot, saying, 'What name
                      hast thou
That ridest here so blindly and so hard?'
'No name, no name,' he shouted, 'a scourge am I
To lash the treasons of the Table Round.'
'Yea, but thy name?' 'I have many names,' he cried:  555
'I am wrath and shame and hate and evil fame,
And like a poisonous wind I pass to blast
And blaze the crime of Lancelot and the Queen.'
'First over me,' said Lancelot, 'shalt thou pass.'
'Fight therefore,' yelled the youth, and either
                      knight                          560
Drew back a space, and when they closed, at once
```

```
555 ...name.' 'I...names' he cried                A-2104
555 ...names' he cried                             L-HGI
555 ...names' he...                                   69

556 I am shame & scorn & hate, & all report          T-S

558 To blaze the sin of...                           T-S

559 First over my dead body shalt thou pass          T-S
559           me,' said Lancelot, 'overthrown
    'First over m̸y̸ d̸e̸a̸d̸ b̸o̸d̸y̸ s̸h̸a̸l̸t̸ t̸h̸o̸u̸ g̸o̸/      T-P
559 'First over me,' said Lancelot, 'overthrown    A-2104
559 (C)                                            L-HGI

560 Said Lancelot 'fight then' shriek'd the other,
                              & each                  T-S
560 Thou passest
    S̸a̸i̸d̸ L̸a̸n̸c̸e̸l̸o̸t̸ 'fight then' yell'd the other &
                              each                    T-P
560 Thou passest.' 'Fight then' yell'd the other
                              and each             A-2104
560 ..., yell'd that other, and each knight        L-HGI
560 ... yell'd the other, and...                      69
560 (C)                                               86

561 ...space, and...closed, at...        (,, I)    A-2104
561 (C)                                            S-925
```

863

PELLEAS AND ETTARRE

The weary steed of Pelleas floundering flung
His rider, who called out from the dark field,
'Thou art false as Hell: slay me: I have no sword.'
Then Lancelot, 'Yea, between thy lips--and sharp;   565
But here will I disedge it by thy death.'
'Slay then,'he shrieked, 'my will is to be slain,'
And Lancelot, with his heel upon the fallen,
Rolling his eyes, a moment stood, then spake:
'Rise, weakling; I am Lancelot, say thy say.'   570

----

562 ...floundering spilt   T-S;T-P
562 ...floundering spilt   A-2104
562   flung   P MS
    ...floundering s̸p̸i̸l̸t̸   B-VIII
562 (C)   L-HGII

563 to 564 ...out Thou art false as hell
            Slay me: I have no sword   T-S

563 ...rider, who...field   (, I)   A-2104
563 ...field   S-925
563 (C)   L-HGI

565   & sharp
    ...lips - ̸a̸ ̸s̸w̸o̸r̸d̸   T-P
565 ...sharp,   A-2104
565 (C)   L-HGI

566   But   will I
    S̸h̸a̸r̸p̸ ≠ b̸u̸t̸ I here disedge it...   T-P

567 'Slay then' he shriek'd 'my ...slain.'   A-2104
567 ...slain.'   L-HGI
567 (C)   84

568-569 And rolling his eyes Lancelot stood then
                     spake   T-S

569   2   1
    A moment stood, rolling his eyes, then spake   T-P
569 ...spake;   ; (I)   A-2104
569 ...spake;   S-925
569 (C)   L-HGI

864

And Lancelot slowly rode his warhorse back
To Camelot, and Sir Pelleas in brief while
Caught his unbroken limbs from the dark field,
And followed to the city. It chanced that both
Brake into hall together, worn and pale.   575
There with her knights and dames was Guinevere.
Full wonderingly she gazed on Lancelot
So soon returned, and then on Pelleas, him
Who had not greeted her, but cast himself
Down on a bench, hard-breathing. 'Have ye fought?'   580
She asked of Lancelot. 'Ay, my Queen,' he said.
'And thou hast overthrown him?' 'Ay, my Queen.'
Then she, turning to Pelleas, 'O young knight,

---

570 ...weakling, I...Lancelot, say...   A-2104
570 ...weakling, - I ... Lancelot, say...   L-HGI
570 (C)   L-HGII

571 ...war-horse...   A-2104
571 (C)   73

575 ...into Hall...   A-2104
575 (C)   L-HGI

577 Full
    A̶n̶d̶ wonderingly...   T-P

578 ...on Pelleas,   T-P
578 ...on Pelleas,   A-2104
578 (C)   L-HGI

579 ...her, but...   (, I)   A-2104
579 (C)   S-925

580 Down on
    U̶p̶o̶n̶ a bench...   T-P
580 ...bench hardbreathing...   A-2104
580 (C)   L-HGI

581 ...Lancelot, 'Ay, my queen' he said.   A-2104
581 (C)   L-HGI

582 ...my queen.'   A-2104
582 (C)   L-HGI

Hath the great heart of knighthood in thee failed
So far thou canst not bide, unfrowardly,   585
A fall from <u>him</u>?' Then, for he answered not,
'Or hast thou other griefs? If I, the Queen,
May help them, loose thy tongue, and let me know.'
But Pelleas lifted up an eye so fierce
She quailed; and he, hissing 'I have no sword,'   590
Sprang from the door into the dark. The Queen
Looked hard upon her lover, he on her;

---

583 ...Pelleas 'O...   A-2104
583 (C)   L-HGI

585 to 586   unfrowardly,
            ...not bide a̶ f̶a̶l̶l̶ f̶r̶o̶m̶ h̶i̶m̶
            A fall from him? then
            U̶n̶f̶r̶o̶w̶a̶r̶d̶l̶y̶ - &̶ since he spake not, ask'd,T-P

586 A fall from him?' then, since he spake not,
                          ask'd,   A-2104
586   answer'd not,   P MS
        A fall from him?' Then, for he s̶p̶a̶k̶e̶ n̶o̶
                          w̶o̶r̶d̶/   B-VIII
586 A fall from him?' Then, for he answer'd not, L-HGII
586 ...from him?' ...   69
586 (C)   86

587 ...griefs? if I, ...   A-2104
587 (C)   L-HGI

And each foresaw the dolorous day to be:
And all talk died, as in a grove all song
Beneath the shadow of some bird of prey;   595
Then a long silence came upon the hall,
And Modred thought, 'The time is hard at hand.'

589	lifted	
	...Pelleas l̸i̸g̸h̸t̸e̸d̸ up	A-2104
589 (C)		S-925
590	...sword'	A-2104
590 (C)		L-HGII
592	...her.	A-2104
592 (C)		L-HGI

594-595 (Omitted)(A-2104; L-HGI)   A-2104
594-595 And all talk died, as in a grove all sunny   I MS
        Beneath   P MS
        U̸n̸d̸e̸r̸ the shadow of some bird of prey,   I MS
                                                      B-VIII
594 (C)   L-HGII
595 ...prey,;   ; (I)   L-HGII
595 ...prey,   69
595 (C)   73

597 ...thought 'the...   A-2104
597 (C)   L-HGI

The Last Tournament

Sir Dagonet, the king's fool, stood before the hall of Arthur. & the wind was blowing & the leaves flying in the wood below.

[And below him there past into the wood Sir Lamorack & his head was down, & his heart darkened for he had heard that Queen Millicent was dead.]

And ~~the dwarf skipt~~

And below him riding three abreast there past into the wood Sir Gawain Sir Modred & Sir Gahins: & the face of Gawain was red as tho' with wine; & the face of Modred was white but he had bitten his thin lips till they were bloody: & so they past away.

And about an hour after there rode into the wood Sir Lamorack & his head was down & his heart darkend for his old love Queen Bellicent was dead.

And the dwarf skipt upon the steps before the hall &

869

out of the hall came Tristram & cried to him.

O fool why skippest thou?
And the dwarf pointed to the wood & said
'They are gone to keep the vows of the King'
And Tristram said who are gone.

And he answer'd The Sons of the Queen: for Lancelot

has kept the vows of the King, & Lamorack has kept the

vows of the King & thou also: for ye have all lain by

Queens,

So that no King knoweth this own son   H-40

THE LAST TOURNAMENT

Dagonet, the fool, whom Gawain in his mood
Had made mock-knight of Arthur's Table Round,
At Camelot, high above the yellowing woods,
Danced like a withered leaf before the hall.
And toward him from the hall, with harp in hand,   5
And from the crown thereof a carcanet
Of ruby swaying to and fro, the prize
Of Tristram in the jousts of yesterday,
Came Tristram, saying, 'Why skip ye so, Sir Fool?'

      For Arthur and Sir Lancelot riding once   10
Far down beneath a winding wall of rock
Heard a child wail. A stump of oak half-dead,
From roots like some black coil of carven snakes,
Clutched at the crag, and started through mid air
Bearing an eagle's nest: and through the tree   15
Rushed ever a rainy wind, and through the wind
Pierced ever a child's cry: and crag and tree
Scaling, Sir Lancelot from the perilous nest,
This ruby necklace thrice around her neck,
And all unscarred from beak or talon, brought   20
A maiden babe; which Arthur pitying took,
Then gave it to his Queen to rear: the Queen
But coldly acquiescing, in her white arms
Received, and after loved it tenderly,
And named it Nestling; so forgot herself   25
A moment, and her cares; till that young life
Being smitten in mid heaven with mortal cold
Past from her; and in time the carcanet
Vext her with plaintive memories of the child:
So she, delivering it to Arthur, said,   30
'Take thou the jewels of this dead innocence,
And make them, an thou wilt, a tourney-prize.'

---

1 ...his moods		B-III
1 ...his mood~~s~~		A-2101;T-LTP
1 (C)		72
4 ...the Hall.		A-2101
4 ...the ~~H~~all.	h/ (MS)	T-LTP
4 (C)		72
13 ...snakes		A-2101
13 (C)		75

THE LAST TOURNAMENT

To whom the King, 'Peace to thine eagle-borne
Dead nestling, and this honour after death,
Following thy will! but, O my Queen, I muse   35
Why ye not wear on arm, or neck, or zone
Those diamonds that I rescued from the tarn,
And Lancelot won, methought, for thee to wear.'

    'Would rather you had let them fall,' she cried,
'Plunge and be lost--ill-fated as they were,   40
A bitterness to me!--ye look amazed,
Not knowing they were lost as soon as given--
Slid from my hands, when I was leaning out
Above the river--that unhappy child
Past in her barge: but rosier luck will go   45
With these rich jewels, seeing that they came
Not from the skeleton of a brother-slayer,
But the sweet body of a maiden babe.
Perchance--who knows?--the purest of thy knights
May win them for the purest of my maids.'   50

    She ended, and the cry of a great jousts
With trumpet-blowings ran on all the ways
From Camelot in among the faded fields
To furthest towers; and everywhere the knights
Armed for the day of glory before the King.   55

---

36   or neck, or zone
    ...arm, ǿ̶t̶ ǿ̶ǻ̶t̶/̶ ǿ̶t̶ t̶ǿ̶ǿ̶ǿ̶ǻ̶   B-III

Alt. after 36 T̶h̶ǿ̶ ǵ̶ǿ̶t̶ǻ̶ǿ̶ǿ̶/̶ ǿ̶t̶ t̶h̶ǿ̶ t̶h̶t̶ǿ̶ǻ̶t̶/̶ t̶ǿ̶ ǵ̶t̶ǻ̶ǿ̶ǿ̶
                              t̶h̶ǿ̶ǿ̶/̶ t̶h̶ǿ̶ǿ̶ǿ̶   B-III

37 Those
    F̶ǻ̶ǿ̶t̶ diamonds...   B-III

39 ...rather ye had...   B-III;A-2101
39 (C)   73

49 Perchance - who knows?
    Å̶ǿ̶ǻ̶ ǿ̶ǿ̶ǿ̶t̶ ǿ̶t̶ ẁ̶ǿ̶t̶ǿ̶ the purest...   B-III

50 Should win...   B-III

872

THE LAST TOURNAMENT

But on the hither side of that loud morn
Into the hall staggered, his visage ribbed
From ear to ear with dogwhip-weals, his nose
Bridge-broken, one eye out, and one hand off,
And one with shattered fingers dangling lame,   60
A churl, to whom indignantly the King,

'My churl, for whom Christ died, what evil beast
Hath drawn his claws athwart thy face? or fiend?
Man was it who marred heaven's image in thee thus?'

Then, sputtering through the hedge of splintered
                              teeth,   65
Yet strangers to the tongue, and with blunt stump
Pitch-blackened sawing the air, said the maimed churl,

'He took them and he drave them to his tower--
Some hold he was a table-knight of thine--
A hundred goodly ones--the Red Knight, he--   70
Lord, I was tending swine, and the Red Knight
Brake in upon me and drave them to his tower;
And when I called upon thy name as one
That doest right by gentle and by churl,
Maimed me and mauled, and would outright have slain, 75

---

60 ...with shattered fingers...   '/ (I)   A-2101
60 (C)   T-LTP

62 (Par.) 'My...   '/ (I)   A-2101
62 (C)   T-LTP

64 ...who marred heaven's...   '/ (P)   A-2101
64 (C)   L-LTP

65 ...teeth   72
65 (C)   73

67 the maimed churl,   '/ (I)   A-2101
67 (C)   T-LTP

69   hold   was
   Some say he were a table-knight...   B-III

Save that he sware me to a message, saying,
"Tell thou the King and all his liars, that I
Have founded my Round Table in the North,
And whatsoever his own knights have sworn
My knights have sworn the counter to it--and say   80
My tower is full of harlots, like his court,
But mine are worthier, seeing they profess
To be none other than themselves--and say
My knights are all adulterers like his own,
But mine are truer, seeing they profess   85
To be none other; and say his hour is come,
The heathen are upon him, his long lance
Broken, and his Excalibur a straw."'

    Then Arthur turned to Kay the seneschal,
'Take thou my churl, and tend him curiously   90
Like a king's heir, till all his hurts be whole.
The heathen--but that ever-climbing wave,
Hurled back again so often in empty foam,
Hath lain for years at rest--and renegades,
Thieves, bandits, leavings of confusion, whom   95
The wholesome realm is purged of otherwhere,
Friends, through your manhood and your fealty,--now
Make their last head like Satan in the North.   .

---

76   sware me to a message thus
  Save that he s̶e̶n̶t̶ m̶e̶ m̶e̶ o̶n̶ a̶ m̶e̶s̶s̶a̶g̶e̶ s̶a̶y̶i̶n̶g̶   B-III
76 ...saying -   A-2101
76 (C)   T-LTP

Alt. after 80
  M̶y̶/̶k̶n̶i̶g̶h̶t̶s̶ a̶r̶e̶ a̶l̶l̶ a̶d̶u̶l̶t̶e̶r̶e̶r̶s̶ l̶i̶k̶e̶ h̶i̶s̶ o̶w̶n̶/̶
  B̶u̶t̶ m̶i̶n̶e̶ a̶r̶e̶ t̶r̶u̶e̶r̶ s̶e̶e̶i̶n̶g̶ t̶h̶e̶y̶ p̶r̶o̶f̶e̶s̶s̶   B-III

93   again   empty foam
  Hurl'd back so often in t̶h̶u̶n̶d̶e̶r̶ f̶r̶o̶m̶ o̶u̶r̶ c̶l̶i̶f̶f̶s̶/B-III

96 ...of otherwhere, -   A-2101
96 (C)   73

97   & your fealty,
  ...your f̶e̶a̶l̶t̶y̶ & manhood, now   B-III

874

My younger knights, new-made, in whom your flower
Waits to be solid fruit of golden deeds,   100
Move with me toward their quelling, which achieved,
The loneliest ways are safe from shore to shore.
But thou, Sir Lancelot, sitting in my place
Enchaired tomorrow, arbitrate the field;
For wherefore shouldst thou care to mingle with it,   105
Only to yield my Queen her own again?
Speak, Lancelot, thou art silent: is it well?'

    Thereto Sir Lancelot answered, 'It is well:
Yet better if the King abide, and leave
The leading of his younger knights to me.   110
Else, for the King has willed it, it is well.'

    Then Arthur rose and Lancelot followed him,
And while they stood without the doors, the King
Turned to him saying, 'Is it then so well?
Or mine the blame that oft I seem as he   115
Of whom was written, "A sound is in his ears"?
The foot that loiters, bidden go,--the glance
That only seems half-loyal to command,--

Sketch 108-114   'd
    (Par.) Thereto Sir Lancelot answering 'it is well'
    The King replied 'And is it then so well?   B-III

109 ...abide & ~~yield~~ leave   B-III

Alt. after 113
  ~~glanced for a moment northward, & then turnd~~
  ~~To Lancelot saying Yis it then so well~~   B-III

116 Of whom
    ~~Whereof~~ was...   B-III
116 ...written, "a sound is in his ears" -   A-2101
116 ...ears" -   72
116 (C)   73

118   only
    That ~~oft but~~ seems...   B-III
118 ...half-loyal...   -/ (I)   A-2101
118 (C)   T-LTP

875

A manner somewhat fallen from reverence--
Or have I dreamed the bearing of our knights   120
Tells of a manhood ever less and lower?
Or whence the fear lest this my realm, upreared,
By noble deeds at one with noble vows,
From flat confusion and brute violences,
Reel back into the beast, and be no more?'   125

    He spoke, and taking all his younger knights,
Down the slope city rode, and sharply turned
North by the gate. In her high bower the Queen,
Working a tapestry, lifted up her head,
Watched her lord pass, and knew not that she sighed. 130
Then ran across her memory the strange rhyme
Of bygone Merlin, 'Where is he who knows?
From the great deep to the great deep he goes.'

    But when the morning of a tournament,
By these in earnest those in mockery called   135
The Tournament of the Dead Innocence,

---

119   manner
    A ~~bearing~~ somewhat...   B-III

120   bearing
    ...dream'd the ~~manners~~ of...   B-III

121 Less manful & less gentle than when of old
        swept
    We ~~drave~~ the heathen from the Roman wall?   B-III

124   ences,
    ...brute viol~~ence~~,   B-III

126 (Par.) He spake & ...   B-III

132 ...Merlin, "Where...   A-2101
132 ...Merlin, "'Where...   (' MS)   T-LTP
132 (C)   72

133 ...goes."   A-2101
133 ...goes."'   (' MS)   T-LTP
133 (C)   72

Brake with a wet wind blowing, Lancelot,
Round whose sick head all night, like birds of prey,
The words of Arthur flying shrieked, arose,
And down a streetway hung with folds of pure   140
White samite, and by fountains running wine,
Where children sat in white with cups of gold,
Moved to the lists, and there, with slow sad steps
Ascending, filled his double-dragoned chair.

    He glanced and saw the stately galleries,   145
Dame, damsel, each through worship of their Queen
White-robed in honour of the stainless child,
And some with scattered jewels, like a bank
Of maiden snow mingled with sparks of fire.
He looked but once, and vailed his eyes again.   150

    The sudden trumpet sounded as in a dream
To ears but half-awaked, then one low roll
Of Autumn thunder, and the jousts began:
And ever the wind blew, and yellowing leaf
And gloom and gleam, and shower and shorn plume   155
Went down it. Sighing weariedly, as one
Who sits and gazes on a faded fire,
When all the goodlier guests are past away,

First draft, Alt. after 139
    M̶o̶v̶e̶d̶ ̶t̶o̶ ̶t̶h̶e̶ ̶l̶i̶s̶t̶s̶/̶ ̶&̶ ̶t̶h̶e̶r̶e̶ ̶w̶i̶t̶h̶ ̶s̶l̶o̶w̶ ̶s̶a̶d̶ ̶s̶t̶e̶p̶s̶
    A̶s̶c̶e̶n̶d̶i̶n̶g̶/̶ ̶f̶i̶l̶l̶'̶d̶/̶h̶i̶s̶ ̶d̶o̶u̶b̶l̶e̶-̶d̶r̶a̶g̶o̶n̶'̶d̶ ̶c̶h̶a̶i̶r̶/̶   B-III

Second draft, 140   folds of
    And p̶a̶s̶s̶i̶n̶g̶ down a streetway hung with pure   B-III

First draft, 142
    W̶h̶e̶r̶e̶ ̶l̶i̶t̶t̶l̶e̶ ̶d̶a̶m̶s̶e̶l̶s̶ ̶s̶a̶t̶ ̶w̶i̶t̶h̶ ̶c̶u̶p̶s̶ ̶o̶f̶ ̶g̶o̶l̶d̶   B-III

148 ...like a s̶l̶o̶p̶e̶ bank   B-III

Alt. before 151
    There as he fill'd the double-dragon'd throne, HM-1323

152 To one but...   HM-1323

156   sighing   ed
    ...it; w̶h̶i̶l̶e̶ a̶s̶ wearily as one   B-III

Sat their great umpire, looking o'er the lists.
He saw the laws that ruled the tournament   160
Broken, but spake not; once, a knight cast down
Before his throne of arbitration cursed
The dead babe and the follies of the King;
And once the laces of a helmet cracked,
And showed him, like a vermin in its hole,   165
Modred, a narrow face: anon he heard
The voice that billowed round the barriers roar
An ocean-sounding welcome to one knight,
But newly-entered, taller than the rest,
And armoured all in forest green, whereon   170
There tript a hundred tiny silver deer,

159-161, sketch
    And Lancelot groan'd in spirit when he saw
    The laws wh that day ruled the tourney field
    Violated twice or thrice a knight...   HM-1323

161 Broken, but spake not; then
    V̶i̶o̶l̶a̶t̶e̶d̶ t̶w̶i̶c̶e̶ o̶r̶ t̶h̶r̶i̶c̶e̶: a knight cast down B-III

Alt. after 163
    And three were there who thrice had hurld themselves
    Against the strong Sir Lamorack as in rage
    Whom thrice the strong Sir Lamorack overthrew
            HM-1323;present but cancelled, B-III

164 Where on the laces of a helmet burst   HM-1323
164 And once
    W̶h̶e̶r̶e̶o̶n̶ the laces of a helmet burst,   B-III

165 A̶n̶d̶ revealing like a...   HM-1323

166 T̶h̶e̶ n̶a̶r̶r̶o̶w̶ f̶a̶c̶e̶ o̶f̶ Modred...   HM-1323

Alt. from 166
    Modred, a narrow face; &̶ s̶o̶m̶e̶ y̶o̶u̶n̶g̶ k̶n̶i̶g̶h̶t̶
    [̶S̶o̶ l̶i̶k̶e̶ a̶ y̶o̶u̶n̶g̶n̶e̶s̶t̶e̶r̶ l̶o̶s̶t̶ a̶b̶o̶u̶t̶ t̶h̶e̶ c̶o̶u̶r̶t̶
    T̶h̶e̶ n̶a̶m̶e̶ o̶f̶ B̶e̶l̶l̶i̶c̶e̶n̶t̶ a̶n̶d̶ L̶a̶m̶o̶r̶a̶c̶k̶]̶ I̶ s̶a̶i̶d̶
    L̶o̶o̶k̶ w̶h̶e̶t̶h̶e̶r̶ h̶e̶ h̶a̶v̶e̶/n̶o̶t̶ t̶u̶m̶b̶l̶e̶d̶ h̶i̶s̶ o̶w̶n̶ s̶o̶n̶
    T̶h̶e̶ h̶a̶p̶p̶y̶ s̶i̶r̶e̶; Anon, S̶i̶r̶ L̶a̶n̶c̶e̶l̶o̶t̶ he heard B-III

THE LAST TOURNAMENT

And wearing but a holly-spray for crest,
With ever-scattering berries, and on shield
A spear, a harp, a bugle--Tristram--late
From overseas in Brittany returned,   175
And marriage with a princess of that realm,
Isolt the White--Sir Tristram of the Woods--
Whom Lancelot knew, had held sometime with pain
His own against him, and now yearned to shake
The burthen off his heart in one full shock   180
With Tristram even to death: his strong hands gript
And dinted the gilt dragons right and left,
Until he groaned for wrath--so many of those,

---

167 The throng that surged around...   HM-1323
167   voice   billow'd round
     The ~~fall~~ that ~~surged~~ ~~around~~/the barriers roar   B-III

171   tiny
     ...hundred ~~little~~ silver...   B-III

173 ...berries, & on his shield   HM-1323
173   ~~the~~
     ..., & on shield   B-III

174   harp
     A spear, a ~~lance~~, a bugle - Tristram whom   HM-1323
174 ...-Tristram - ~~whom~~ late   B-III

178 Sir Lancelot knew - had often held, with
                              pain   HM-1323
178 Whom
     ~~Sir~~ Lancelot...   B-III

180   his heart
     His burthening memories off ~~him~~ in ~~full~~ shock HM-1323

181 With Tristram to the death: his strong hands
                            crush'd   HM-1323
181   i
     ...hands gr~~a~~pt   B-III

183 ~~Until~~ ~~he~~ ~~groan'd~~ ~~again/~~ ~~beholding~~ ~~some~~   HM-1323
183 ...wrath, beholding some,   B-III

879

That ware their ladies' colours on the casque,
Drew from before Sir Tristram to the bounds,   185
And there with gibes and flickering mockeries
Stood, while he muttered, 'Craven crests! O shame!
What faith have these in whom they sware to love?
The glory of our Round Table is no more.'

   So Tristram won, and Lancelot gave, the gems,   190
Not speaking other word than 'Hast thou won?
Art thou the purest, brother? See, the hand
Wherewith thou takest this, is red!' to whom
Tristram, half plagued by Lancelot's languorous mood,
Made answer, 'Ay, but wherefore toss me this   195
Like a dry bone cast to some hungry hound?

---

184 ...on their casque   HM-1323

185 Draw from...   HM-1323
185 Draw from...   B-III

186-187
   And there remain, O craven crests, O shame, HM-1323

187 Stand, while...   B-III
187 ...O shame   72
187 (C)   73

First draft, 192 ff
   ..., brother,' Tristram said see the hand
Why do ye hand me this like a dry bone
From but a brave test to a hungry hound.
Let be thy fall Queen's fantasy. Strength of heart
And might of limb, but mainly use & skill
Are winners in this pastime of our King.
And then with lower accent O chief knight,
Right hand of Arthur in the battle-field,
Great brother, thou not I have made the world,
Be happy in thy fall Queen as I in mine -
Sweet damsels, each,- to him who worships you each
Sole Queen of beauty & of love, behold,
This day my Queen of beauty is not here.'
     of these were mute,
Then most were silent but some angel'd, one
Muttering /all courtesy is dead/ & one
/the glory of our round table is no more./   B-III

880

Let be thy fair Queen's fantasy. Strength of heart
And might of limb, but mainly use and skill,
Are winners in this pastime of our King.
My hand--belike the lance hath dript upon it--   200
No blood of mine, I trow; but O chief knight,
Right arm of Arthur in the battlefield,
Great brother, thou nor I have made the world;
Be happy in thy fair Queen as I in mine.'

    And Tristram round the gallery made his horse   205
Caracole; then bowed his homage, bluntly saying,
'Fair damsels, each to him who worships each
Sole Queen of Beauty and of love, behold
This day my Queen of Beauty is not here.'
And most of these were mute, some angered, one   210
Murmuring, 'All courtesy is dead,' and one,
'The glory of our Round Table is no more.'

    Then fell thick rain, plume droopt and mantle clung,
And pettish cries awoke, and the wan day
Went glooming down in wet and weariness: 215
But under her black brows a swarthy one

---

194   plagued by
        ...half-~~next~~ ~~at~~ Lancelot's   B-III

195   toss me
        ...wherefore ~~hand~~ ~~ye~~ this   B-III

196   cast
        ...love ~~lost~~ to...   B-III

207   Fair
        (Par.) ~~Dame/~~ damsels, ...   B-III

211 Murmuring 'All...   A-2101
211 (C)   T-LTP

213 ...droopt~~/~~ and...   A-2101
213 (C)   T-LTP

216 ...swarthy dame   B-III
216   one   I MS
        ...swarthy ~~dame~~   A-2101
216 (C)   T-LTP

Laughed shrilly, crying, 'Praise the patient saints,
Our one white day of Innocence hath past,
Though somewhat draggled at the skirt. So be it.
The snowdrop only, flowering through the year,   220
Would make the world as blank as Winter-tide.
Come--let us gladden their sad eyes, our Queen's
And Lancelot's, at this night's solemnity
With all the kindlier colours of the field.'

  So dame and damsel glittered at the feast   225
Variously gay: for he that tells the tale
Likened them, saying, as when an hour of cold
Falls on the mountain in midsummer snows,
And all the purple slopes of mountain flowers
Pass under white, till the warm hour returns   230
With veer of wind, and all are flowers again;
So dame and damsel cast the simple white,
And glowing in all colours, the live grass,
Rose-campion, bluebell, kingcup, poppy, glanced

---

217   shrilly crying   patient
    Laught. s̸a̸y̸i̸n̸g̸ m̸e̸r̸r̸i̸l̸y̸ 'Praise t̸o̸ a̸l̸l̸ the
                            Saints,   B-III
217 ...crying 'Praise...   A-2101
217 (C)   T-LTP

220   r̸i̸d̸g̸e̸   'd̸ ing a̸l̸l̸ thro
    The snow drop (blot) only floweri̸n̸g̸ t̸h̸r̸u̸ the
                        year/̸   B-III

First draft, 221
    T̸h̸e̸ w̸o̸r̸l̸d̸ w̸e̸r̸e̸
    W̸o̸u̸l̸d̸ m̸a̸k̸e̸ i̸t̸ n̸i̸g̸h̸ a̸s̸ b̸l̸a̸n̸k̸ a̸s̸ w̸i̸n̸t̸e̸r̸t̸i̸d̸e̸   B-III

221 ...as wintertide.   A-2101
221 ...as wintertide.   W/-/ (MS)   T-LTP
221 ...as winter-tide.   72
221 (C)   73

222 ...us comfort their eyes, our Queen   B-III
222   gladden   P MS
    ...us c̸o̸m̸f̸o̸r̸t̸ their...   A-2101;T-LTP
222 (C)   72

882

About the revels, and with mirth so loud   235
Beyond all use, that, half-amazed, the Queen,
And wroth at Tristram and the lawless jousts,
Brake up their sports, then slowly to her bower
Parted, and in her bosom pain was lord.

And little Dagonet on the morrow morn,   240
High over all the yellowing Autumn-tide,
Danced like a withered leaf before the hall.
Then Tristram saying, 'Why skip ye so, Sir Fool?'
Wheeled round on either heel, Dagonet replied,
'Belike for lack of wiser company;   245
Or being fool, and seeing too much wit
Makes the world rotten, why, belike I skip
To know myself the wisest knight of all.'
'Ay, fool,' said Tristram, 'but 'tis eating dry
To dance without a catch, a roundelay   250
To dance to.' Then he twangled on his harp,
And while he twangled little Dagonet stood
Quiet as any water-sodden log
Stayed in the wandering warble of a brook;
But when the twangling ended, skipt again;   255
And being asked, 'Why skipt ye not, Sir Fool?'
Made answer, 'I had liefer twenty years
Skip to the broken music of my brains

---

223 And Lancelot, at...		B-III
227 ...saying, as...	,/ (I)	A-2101
227 (C)		72
230 ...white, & the warm...		B-III
243 ...Fool?	'/ (I)	A-2101
243 (C)		T-LTP
252 ...stood		A-2101
252 ...stood,		T-LTP
252 (C)		84
256 Then being...		B-III;A-2101
256 (C)		73

Than any broken music thou canst make.
Then Tristram, waiting for the quip to come,   260
'Good now, what music have I broken, fool?'
And little Dagonet, skipping, 'Arthur, the King's;
For when thou playest that air with Queen Isolt,
Thou makest broken music with thy bride,
Her daintier namesake down in Brittany--   265
And so thou breakest Arthur's music too.'
'Save for that broken music in thy brains,
Sir Fool,' said Tristram, 'I would break thy head.
Fool, I came late, the heathen wars were o'er,
The life had flown, we sware but by the shell--   270
I am but a fool to reason with a fool--
Come, thou art crabbed and sour: but lean me down,
Sir Dagonet, one of thy long asses' ears,
And harken if my music be not true.

'"Free love--free field--we love but while we may: 275
The woods are hushed, their music is no more:
The leaf is dead, the yearning past away:
New leaf, new life--the days of frost are o'er:
New life, new love, to suit the newer day:

---

259 ...music ye can make.'   B-III;A-2101
259 (C)   73

262 ...the king's;   A-2101
262 (C)   73

265   daintier
      Her p̶r̶e̶t̶t̶i̶e̶r̶ namesake...   B-III

Alt. after 268
      Fool, art thou (1 ?)? There be many here
      W̶h̶o̶ k̶n̶e̶w̶ t̶h̶e̶e̶ m̶e̶r̶r̶y̶ [l̶o̶o̶s̶e̶] e̶n̶o̶w̶ b̶e̶f̶o̶r̶e̶/I c̶a̶m̶e̶ /̶
                                                            B-III

269 Fool, I came b̶u̶t̶ late, s̶o̶w̶/d̶ b̶u̶t̶ a̶s̶ o̶t̶h̶e̶r̶s̶ s̶o̶w̶/d̶ /̶
                           the heathen...   B-III

270   we
      ...flown, I̶ sware...   B-III

884

New loves are sweet as those that went before: 280
Free love--free field--we love but while we may."

   'Ye might have moved slow-measure to my tune,
Not stood stockstill. I made it in the woods,
And heard it ring as true as tested gold.'

   But Dagonet with one foot poised in his hand,   285
'Friend, did ye mark that fountain yesterday
Made to run wine?--but this had run itself
All out like a long life to a sour end--
And them that round it sat with golden cups
To hand the wine to whosoever came--   290
The twelve small damosels white as Innocence,
In honour of poor Innocence the babe,
Who left the gems which Innocence the Queen
Lent to the King, and Innocence the King
Gave for a prize--and one of those white slips   295
Handed her cup and piped, the pretty one,
"Drink, drink, Sir Fool," and thereupon I drank,
Spat--pish--the cup was gold, the draught was mud.'

-----

275 (Par.) "Free...			A-2101
275 (Par.) '"Free...		' (MS)	T-LTP
275 (C)			72
279 ...love to...			A-2101
279 (C)			72
281 ...love, - free...			A-2101
281 ...love/ - free...			T-LTP
281 (C)			72
284 And found it...			B-III
290 ...whomsoever...		(I)	A-2101
290 (C)			T-LTP
291 The small			
Twelve ~~little~~ damoselles...			B-III
295 ...prize - ~~1 part~~ & one...			B-III

     And Tristram, 'Was it muddier than thy gibes?
Is all the laughter gone dead out of thee?--   300
Not marking how the knighthood mock thee, fool--
"Fear God: honour the King--his one true knight--
Sole follower of the vows"--for here be they
Who knew thee swine enow before I came,
Smuttier than blasted grain: but when the King   305
Had made thee fool, thy vanity so shot up
It frighted all free fool from out thy heart;
Which left thee less than fool, and less than swine,
A naked aught--yet swine I hold thee still,
For I have flung thee pearls and find thee swine.'   310

     And little Dagonet mincing with his feet,
'Knight, an ye fling those rubies round my neck
In lieu of hers, I'll hold thou hast some touch
Of music, since I care not for thy pearls.
Swine? I have wallowed, I have washed--the world   315
Is flesh and shadow--I have had my day.
The dirty nurse, Experience, in her kind
Hath fouled me--an I wallowed, then I washed--
I have had my day and my philosophies--

299	was it	
	...Tristram '~~yet no~~ muddier...	B-III
299	...~~skilly a li/ty fool~~	B-III
300	Is	
	~~With~~ all...	B-III
301	marking	
	Not ~~knowing~~ how...	B-III
302	...the king - ...	A-2101
302	(C)	73
312	...my cap	B-III
316	all	
	Is ~~but~~ a shadow...	B-III
317	...experience, in ~~some sort~~, her kind	B-III

And thank the Lord I am King Arthur's fool.   320
Swine, say ye? swine, goats, asses, rams and geese
Trooped round a Paynim harper once, who thrummed
On such a wire as musically as thou
Some such fine song--but never a king's fool.'

    And Tristram, 'Then were swine, goats, asses,
                   geese   325
The wiser fools, seeing thy Paynim bard
Had such a mastery of his mystery
That he could harp his wife up out of hell.'

    Then Dagonet, turning on the ball of his foot,
'And whither harp'st thou thine? down! and
                      thyself   330
Down! and two more: a helpful harper thou,
That harpest downward! Dost thou know the star
We call the harp of Arthur up in heaven?'

    And Tristram, 'Ay, Sir Fool, for when our King
Was victor wellnigh day by day, the knights,   335
Glorying in each new glory, set his name

---

318   an I   then
    ...me - I̸ h̸a̸v̸e̸ wallow'd, I̸ h̸a̸v̸e̸ wash'd -   B-III

324   song
    ...fine a̸l̸l̸ - but...   B-III

328 ...of Hell.'   A-2101
328 ...of H̸ell.'   h/ (MS)   T-LTP
328 (C)   72

330   whither   ?   self
    'And t̸h̸i̸t̸h̸e̸r̸ harpest thou thine: down & thy o̸w̸n̸
                 s̸e̸l̸f̸   B-III

331   helpful
    ...more: a g̸o̸o̸d̸l̸y̸ harper...   B-III

332 at
    Tho̸u̸ harpest...   B-III

High on all hills, and in the signs of heaven.'

  And Dagonet answered, 'Ay, and when the land
Was freed, and the Queen false, ye set yourself
To babble about him, all to show your wit--   340
And whether he were King by courtesy,
Or King by right--and so went harping down
The black king's highway, got so far, and grew
So witty that ye played at ducks and drakes
With Arthur's vows on the great lake of fire.   345
Tuwhoo! do ye see it? do ye see the star?'

  'Nay, fool,' said Tristram, 'not in open day.'
And Dagonet, 'Nay, nor will: I see it and hear.
It makes a silent music up in heaven,
And I, and Arthur and the angels hear,   350
And then we skip.' 'Lo, fool,' he said, 'ye talk
Fool's treason: is the King thy brother fool?'
Then little Dagonet clapt his hands and shrilled,
'Ay, ay, my brother fool, the king of fools!
Conceits himself as God that he can make   355
Figs out of thistles, silk from bristles, milk
From burning spurge, honey from hornet-combs,
And men from beasts--Long live the king of fools!'

337	all		
	High on ~~the~~ hills...		B-III
341	...were king by...		A-2101
341	(C)		73
342	Or king by...		A-2101
342	(C)		73
348	Nay,		
	...Dagonet, '~~No~~, nor...		B-III
352	...the king thy...		A-2101
352	...the ~~King~~ thy...	K/ (MS)	T-LTP
352	(C)		72
353	ll'd		
	...& shri~~ekⁱd~~		B-III
353	...shrill'd,	,/ (I)	A-2101
353	(C)		73

888

And down the city Dagonet danced away;
But through the slowly-mellowing avenues   360
And solitary passes of the wood
Rode Tristram toward Lyonnesse and the west.
Before him fled the face of Queen Isolt
With ruby-circled neck, but evermore
Past, as a rustle or twitter in the wood   365
Made dull his inner, keen his outer eye
For all that walked, or crept, or perched, or flew.
Anon the face, as, when a gust hath blown,
Unruffling waters re-collect the shape
Of one that in them sees himself, returned;   370
But at the slot or fewmets of a deer,
Or even a fallen feather, vanished again.

So on for all that day from lawn to lawn
Through many a league-long bower he rode. At length
A lodge of intertwisted beechen-boughs   375
Furze-crammed, and bracken-rooft, the which himself
Built for a summer day with Queen Isolt
Against a shower, dark in the golden grove
Appearing, sent his fancy back to where
She lived a moon in that low lodge with him: 380

_____

359 ...away.   A-2101
359 (C)   73

360 But
    A̸n̸d̸ thro'...   B-III

364 With
    A̸n̸d̸ ruby-circled...   B-III

367   3   2   1
    For all that perch'd, or crept, or walk'd or
                         flew.   B-III

Alt. after 367
    S̸o̸ m̸a̸n̸y̸ a̸/b̸o̸w̸e̸r̸'̸d̸ l̸e̸a̸g̸u̸e̸ h̸e̸ r̸o̸d̸e̸. /A̸t̸ l̸e̸n̸g̸t̸h̸
    B̸e̸f̸o̸r̸e̸ t̸h̸e̸ c̸l̸o̸s̸i̸n̸g̸ e̸y̸e̸l̸i̸d̸ o̸f̸ t̸h̸e̸ w̸e̸s̸t̸   B-III

380   a moon
    ...lived a̸l̸o̸n̸e̸ in that...   B-III

889

Till Mark her lord had past, the Cornish King,
With six or seven, when Tristram was away,
And snatched her thence; yet dreading worse than shame
Her warrior Tristram, spake not any word,
But bode his hour, devising wretchedness.   385

    And now that desert lodge to Tristram lookt
So sweet, that halting, in he past, and sank
Down on a drift of foliage random-blown;
But could not rest for musing how to smoothe
And sleek his marriage over to the Queen.   390
Perchance in lone Tintagil far from all
The tonguesters of the court she had not heard.
But then what folly had sent him overseas
After she left him lonely here? a name?
Was it the name of one in Brittany,   395
Isolt, the daughter of the King? 'Isolt
Of the white hands' they called her: the sweet name
Allured him first, and then the maid herself,
Who served him well with those white hands of hers,
And loved him well, until himself had thought   400

---

381 Till   had past
    ~~And~~ Mark her lord the ~~craven~~ Cornish King,   B-III
381 ...Cornish king,   A-2101
381 (C)   84

382 With six or seven, when Tristram was away,
    ~~Whom no man loved, not even his own dogs,~~   B-III

383 And snatch'd her thence, yet
    ~~Took her again, but~~ dreading worse than shame   B-III

386   So
    (Par.) ~~And so~~ now...   B-III

393 But then
    How, for what...   B-III

394   here   a
    ...lonely ~~there~~? ~~the~~ name?   B-III

395 Was it the name
    ~~Had he not heard~~ of one...   B-III

He loved her also, wedded easily,
But left her all as easily, and returned.
The black-blue Irish hair and Irish eyes
Had drawn him home--what marvel? then he laid
His brows upon the drifted leaf and dreamed.   405

    He seemed to pace the strand of Brittany
Between Isolt of Britain and his bride,
And showed them both the ruby-chain, and both
Began to struggle for it, till his Queen
Graspt it so hard, that all her hand was red.   410
Then cried the Breton, 'Look, her hand is red!
These be no rubies, this is frozen blood,
And melts within her hand--her hand is hot
With ill desires, but this I gave thee, look,
Is all as cool and white as any flower.'   415
Followed a rush of eagle's wings, and then
A whimpering of the spirit of the child,

First draft, 398 ff
        T̶h̶e̶ ̶n̶a̶m̶e̶ ̶a̶t̶ ̶f̶i̶r̶s̶t̶ ̶a̶l̶l̶u̶r̶e̶d̶ ̶h̶i̶m̶/̶ ̶t̶h̶e̶n̶ ̶t̶h̶e̶n̶ ̶t̶h̶e̶ ̶m̶a̶i̶d̶
                                w̶h̶o̶m̶/̶
        T̶h̶e̶ ̶m̶a̶ ̶s̶h̶e̶ ̶l̶o̶v̶e̶d̶/̶h̶i̶m̶/̶m̶u̶c̶h̶/̶ ̶&̶ ̶f̶o̶r̶ ̶s̶o̶m̶e̶/̶w̶h̶i̶l̶e̶/̶ ̶h̶e̶
                             t̶h̶o̶u̶g̶h̶t̶
        H̶e̶ ̶l̶o̶v̶e̶d̶ ̶a̶s̶ ̶w̶e̶l̶l̶/̶ ̶&̶ ̶w̶e̶d̶d̶e̶d̶ ̶e̶a̶s̶i̶l̶y̶
        A̶n̶d̶ ̶l̶e̶f̶t̶ ̶h̶e̶r̶ ̶a̶l̶l̶ ̶a̶s̶ ̶e̶a̶s̶i̶l̶y̶ ̶&̶ ̶r̶e̶t̶u̶r̶n̶/̶d̶   B-III

400   until   thought
        ...well, t̶i̶l̶l̶ himself had d̶r̶e̶a̶m̶/̶d̶   B-III

401   w̶e̶l̶l̶ also
        ...her a̶l̶s̶o̶/̶h̶a̶d̶ wedded,   B-III

408 ...ruby-chain, & each   B-III

411   the Breton
        ...cried h̶e̶r̶ ̶f̶i̶n̶a̶l̶ look,   B-III

416 Follow'd
        T̶h̶e̶n̶ ̶c̶a̶m̶e̶ a rush...   B-III

417 A
    The whimpering...   B-III

891

Because the twain had spoiled her carcanet.

He dreamed; but Arthur with a hundred spears
Rode far, till o'er the illimitable reed,   420
And many a glancing plash and sallowy isle,
The wide-winged sunset of the misty marsh
Glared on a huge machicolated tower
That stood with open doors, whereout was rolled
A roar of riot, as from men secure   425
Amid their marshes, ruffians at their ease
Among their harlot-brides, and evil song.
'Lo there,' said one of Arthur's youth, for there,
High on a grim dead tree before the tower,
A goodly brother of the Table Round   430
Swung by the neck: and on the boughs a shield
Showing a shower of blood in a field noir,

---

419   He dream'd; but   with
    (Par.) S̸o̸ t̸o̸d̸e̸ K̸i̸n̸g̸ Arthur ⱥ a hundred spears   B-III

420 Rode far,
    F̸a̸r̸ o̸n̸, till o'er...   B-III

421   plash
    ...glancing m̸e̸r̸e̸ & ...   B-III

425 ...riot, b̸a̸n̸d̸i̸t̸s̸/a̸l̸l̸/s̸e̸c̸u̸r̸e̸ as from men secure B-III

428 ...Arthur's knights, for...   B-III

429 ...a great dead...   B-III

430 ...of The Table Round   A-2101
430 ...of T̸he Table Round   t/ (MS)   T-LTP
430 (C)   72

431   boughs   I MS
    ...the b̸o̸w̸s̸ a shield   A-2101
431 (C)   T-LTP

436 ...back: alone he...   A-2101
436 (C)   72

892

And therebeside a horn, inflamed the knights
At that dishonour done the gilded spur,
Till each would clash the shield, and blow the horn.   435
But Arthur waved them back. Alone he rode.
Then at the dry harsh roar of the great horn,
That sent the face of all the marsh aloft
An ever upward-rushing storm and cloud
Of shriek and plume, the Red Knight heard, and all,   440
Even to tipmost lance and topmost helm,
In blood-red armour sallying, howled to the King,

    'The teeth of Hell flay bare and gnash thee flat!--
Lo! art thou not that eunuch-hearted King
Who fain had clipt free manhood from the world--   445
The woman-worshipper? Yea, God's curse, and I!
Slain was the brother of my paramour

---

442   sallying
     ...armour *issuing*, howl'd...   B-III

443 ...thee flat!   72
443 (C)   73

First draft, alt. after 443
    Thou blating ass/ that hast a/mind to swing
    The fellow acorn of thy carrion therey
    Thou art like the eunch-hearted milky King
    That fain wd wreck free manhood in the world
    And overshines all with hypocrisy
    He is woman-worshipper/ so am I/   B-III

444 Lo!
    For art thou not that eunuch-hearted *fool* King, **B-III**

Alt. after 444
    Who got himself made witest/ while he strove
    To slime the world with his hypocrisy?   B-III

Variation on 446
    The -
    Thou/art a woman-worshipper? *So am I* yea, & I
                         myself   B-III

By a knight of thine, and I that heard her whine
And snivel, being eunuch-hearted too,
Sware by the scorpion-worm that twists in hell,   450
And stings itself to everlasting death,
To hang whatever knight of thine I fought
And tumbled. Art thou King?--Look to thy life!'

He ended: Arthur knew the voice; the face
Wellnigh was helmet-hidden, and the name   455
Went wandering somewhere darkling in his mind.
And Arthur deigned not use of word or sword,
But let the drunkard, as he stretched from horse
To strike him, overbalancing his bulk,
Down from the causeway heavily to the swamp   460
Fall, as the crest of some slow-arching wave,
Heard in dead night along that table-shore,
Drops flat, and after the great waters break
Whitening for half a league, and thin themselves,
Far over sands marbled with moon and cloud,   465
From less and less to nothing; thus he fell
Head-heavy; then the knights, who watched him, roared

---

448 ...her ~~wail~~ whine   B-III

453   King?   wife
   ...thou ~~he~~?' look to thy ~~l/f/e~~.   B-III
453 ...thy life!   72
453 (C)   73

459 ..., overbalancing ~~himself~~ his bulk,   B-III

460   to   swamp
   ...heavily ~~on~~ the ~~marsh~~   B-III

462   table-shore
   ...that ~~level shore~~   B-III

463 Drops
    ~~Falls~~ flat...   B-III

464   ~~sounding~~   ~~slowly their~~
    Stet ~~Whitening for half a league~~ & spin them-
                              selves ~~away~~   B-III

465 ...over sand marbled...   B-III

894

And shouted and leapt down upon the fallen;
There trampled out his face from being known,
And sank his head in mire, and slimed themselves: 470
Nor heard the King for their own cries, but sprang
Through open doors, and swording right and left
Men, women, on their sodden faces, hurled
The tables over and the wines, and slew
Till all the rafters rang with woman-yells,   475
And all the pavement streamed with massacre:
Then, echoing yell with yell, they fired the tower,
Which half that autumn night, like the live North,
Red-pulsing up through Alioth and Alcor,
Made all above it, and a hundred meres   480
About it, as the water Moab saw
Come round by the East, and out beyond them flushed
The long low dune, and lazy-plunging sea.

So all the ways were safe from shore to shore,
But in the heart of Arthur pain was lord.   485

Then, out of Tristram waking, the red dream

---

467   while
      Head-heavy, & the knights...   B-III
467 Head-heavy, while the knights...   A-2101
467 (C)   73

472   swording
      ...doors, & swirling left...   B-III

475 Till   woman-yells
    While all the rafters rang with women's/yells/ B-III

477 Then, yell with yell echoing, they...   B-III;A-2101
477 (C)   86

481 Around it, ...   B-III

486 But out of/   ing the red dream
    Meanwhile sir Tristram/awakening/ with a shout B-III
486 (Par.) Then, out...   ,/ (I)   A-2101
486 (C)   T-LTP

Fled with a shout, and that low lodge returned,
Mid-forest, and the wind among the boughs.
He whistled his good warhorse left to graze
Among the forest greens, vaulted upon him,   490
And rode beneath an ever-showering leaf,
Till one lone woman, weeping near a cross,
Stayed him. 'Why weep ye?' 'Lord,' she said, 'my man
Hath left me or is dead;' whereon he thought--
'What, if she hate me now? I would not this.   495
What, if she love me still? I would not that.
I know not what I would'--but said to her,
'Yet weep not thou, lest, if thy mate return,
He find thy favour changed and love thee not'--
Then pressing day by day through Lyonnesse   500
Last in a roky hollow, belling, heard
The hounds of Mark, and felt the goodly hounds
Yelp at his heart, but turning, past and gained
Tintagil, half in sea, and high on land,
A crown of towers.

---

487 Fled	& the low lodge return'd	
F̸o̸r̸ with a shout t̸h̸e̸ r̸e̸d̸ d̸r̸e̸a̸m̸ p̸a̸s̸t̸ a̸w̸a̸y̸,		B-III
487 ...return'd,	,/ (I)	A-2101
487 (C)		T-LTP

489 He whistled his good
$\quad$ W̸h̸i̸s̸t̸l̸l̸y̸d̸ t̸o̸ h̸i̸s̸ g̸o̸o̸d̸l̸y̸ warhorse...   B-III

490 ...upon i̸t̸ him,   B-III

492 ...near a w̸a̸l̸l̸ cross,   B-III

Alt. after 492
$\quad$ A̸n̸d̸ m̸i̸n̸d̸l̸e̸s̸s̸/o̸f̸ t̸h̸e̸ v̸e̸s̸s̸e̸l̸ a̸t̸ h̸e̸r̸ s̸i̸d̸e̸/   B-III

493 Stay'd him, 'Why...		A-2101
493 Stay'd him, . 'Why...	(. MS)	T-LTP
493 (C)		72

495 'What; an she $\qquad$ I would not this
$\quad$ 'P̸e̸r̸c̸h̸a̸n̸c̸e̸/ s̸h̸e̸ hates̸ me now? d̸o̸ I̸ w̸i̸s̸h̸ h̸e̸r̸
$\qquad\qquad\qquad$ h̸a̸t̸e̸?   B-III
495 'What, an she...   A-2101
495 (C)   73

896

                              Down in a casement sat,   505
A low sea-sunset glorying round her hair
And glossy-throated grace, Isolt the Queen.
And when she heard the feet of Tristram grind
The spiring stone that scaled about her tower,
Flushed, started, met him at the doors, and there   510
Belted his body with her white embrace,
Crying aloud, 'Not Mark--not Mark, my soul!
The footstep fluttered me at first: not he:
Catlike through his own castle steals my Mark,
But warrior-wise thou stridest through his halls   515
Who hates thee, as I him--even to the death.
My soul, I felt my hatred for my Mark
Quicken within me, and knew that thou wert nigh.'

---

496 What, an she love
    P̷e̷r̷c̷h̷a̷n̷c̷e̷ s̷h̷e̷ l̷o̷v̷e̷s̷ me still?   I would not
                          that.   B-III
496 What, an she...   A-2101
496 (C)   73

497 ...would.' then said...   B-III
497 ...to her, -   A-2101
497 ...to her, ⁄   T-LTP
497 (C)   72

504 T̷i̷n̷t̷a̷g̷i̷l̷/ T̷h̷e̷r̷e̷ b̷e̷f̷o̷r̷e̷ a̷ c̷a̷s̷e̷m̷e̷n̷t̷ s̷a̷t̷e̷   B-III

511 ...embrace   A-2101
511 (C)   73

512 ...aloud 'Not...   A-2101
512 ...aloud, 'Not...   ,/ (MS)   T-LTP
512 (C)   72

515 But   -wise thou
    T̷h̷o̷u̷ l̷i̷k̷e̷ a̷ warrior stridest...   B-III

516   ev'n
    ...thee e̷v̷/n̷ as I h̷a̷t̷e̷/him - to the death.   B-III

518   f̷e̷l̷t̷ knew
    ...me, & k̷n̷e̷w̷ that...   B-III

To whom Sir Tristram smiling, 'I am here.
Let be thy Mark, seeing he is not thine.'   520

   And drawing somewhat backward she replied,
'Can he be wronged who is not even his own,
But save for dread of thee had beaten me,
Scratched, bitten, blinded, marred me somehow--
                 Mark?
What rights are his that dare not strike for them?   525
Not lift a hand--not, though he found me thus!
But harken! have ye met him? hence he went
Today for three days hunting--as he said--
And so returns belike within an hour.
Mark's way, my soul!--but eat not thou with Mark,   530
Because he hates thee even more than fears;
Nor drink: and when thou passest any wood
Close vizor, lest an arrow from the bush
Should leave me all alone with Mark and hell.

---

522   he
    Can ~~Mark~~ be...   B-III

524   Mark!
    ...me somehow - ~~I know his eyes~~   B-III

525   are his
    ...rights ~~hath~~ he that...   B-III

526 Not lift a hand - not tho' he found me thus.
    ~~Not tho he found me thus / here in thine arms?~~ B-III

530 ...with him,   B-III
530   Mark   P MS
    ...with ~~him~~   A-2101
530 (C)   T-LTP

532   any
    ...passest ~~throy the~~ wood   B-III

535 ...for Mark,   A-2101
535 (C)   73

My God, the measure of my hate for Mark   535
Is as the measure of my love for thee.'

   So, plucked one way by hate and one by love,
Drained of her force, again she sat, and spake
To Tristram, as he knelt before her, saying,
'O hunter, and O blower of the horn,   540
Harper, and thou hast been a rover too,
For, ere I mated with my shambling king,
Ye twain had fallen out about the bride
Of one--his name is out of me--the prize,
If prize she were--(what marvel--she could see)--   545
Thine, friend; and ever since my craven seeks
To wreck thee villainously: but, O Sir Knight,
What dame or damsel have ye kneeled to last?'

   And Tristram, 'Last to my Queen Paramount,
Here now to my Queen Paramount of love   550
And loveliness--ay, lovelier than when first
Her light feet fell on our rough Lyonnesse,

---

542   mated
    ...I ¢ǿúṕĺéd with...   B-III

545 If so she were - what marvel - she could see -   B-III

546   &
    ...friend; but ever...   B-III

547   wreck
    To ṡĺáý thee...   B-III

550 ...love⁄   A-2101
550 (C)   T-LTP

Alt. for 551
    And lovelier now than even when at first she
                       sat   B-III

551 ...loveliness⁄ - ay, ...   -⁄ (P)   A-2101
551 (C)   T-LTP

Sailing from Ireland.'

Softly laughed Isolt;
'Flatter me not, for hath not our great Queen
My dole of beauty trebled?' and he said,   555
'Her beauty is her beauty, and thine thine,
And thine is more to me--soft, gracious, kind--
Save when thy Mark is kindled on thy lips
Most gracious; but she, haughty, even to him,
Lancelot; for I have seen him wan enow   560
To make one doubt if ever the great Queen
Have yielded him her love.'

To whom Isolt,
'Ah then, false hunter and false harper, thou
Who brakest through the scruple of my bond,
Calling me thy white hind, and saying to me   565
That Guinevere had sinned against the highest,
And I--misyoked with such a want of man--
That I could hardly sin against the lowest.'

He answered, 'O my soul, be comforted!
If this be sweet, to sin in leading-strings,   570

---

553 Softly
    S̷w̷e̷e̷t̷l̷y̷ laugh'd...   B-III
553 ...Isolt,   A-2101
553 (C)   73

554 And when she ask'd him Is not our great
                                  Queen   B-III
554 ...not, for is not...   B-III

555 Three times as beautiful as I am? he said   B-III
555 ...said   A-2101
555 (C)   T-LTP

564 ...my s̷h̷a̷m̷e̷ bond   B-III

568   hardly
    ...I cd s̷c̷a̷r̷c̷e̷l̷y̷ sin...   B-III

570 ...leading - strings,   -/ (P)   A-2101
570 (C)   T-LTP

900

If here be comfort, and if ours be sin,
Crowned warrant had we for the crowning sin
That made us happy: but how ye greet me--fear
And fault and doubt--no word of that fond tale--
Thy deep heart-yearnings, thy sweet memories   575
Of Tristram in that year he was away.'

    And, saddening on the sudden, spake Isolt,
'I had forgotten all in my strong joy
To see thee--yearnings?--ay! for, hour by hour,
Here in the never-ended afternoon,   580
O sweeter than all memories of thee,
Deeper than any yearnings after thee
Seemed those far-rolling, westward-smiling seas,
Watched from this tower. Isolt of Britain dashed
Before Isolt of Brittany on the strand,   585
Would that have chilled her bride-kiss? Wedded her?
Fought in her father's battles? wounded there?
The King was all fulfilled with gratefulness,
And she, my namesake of the hands, that healed
Thy hurt and heart with unguent and caress--   590
Well--can I wish her any huger wrong
Than having known thee? her too hast thou left

---

574 And fault &
   F̷a̷u̷l̷t̷/̷f̷i̷n̷d̷i̷n̷g̷ doubt̷s̷ - no...   B-III

575 Thy deep heart-yearnings
   I̷ l̷o̷o̷k̷t̷ f̷o̷r̷ a̷l̷l̷ thy [d̷e̷e̷p̷] sweet memories   B-III

577   And
   (Par.) B̷u̷t̷ suddenly...   B-III

First draft, 578 ff
   W̷e̷d̷d̷e̷d̷y̷ /̷I̷ h̷a̷d̷ f̷o̷r̷g̷o̷t̷t̷e̷n̷ i̷t̷ i̷n̷ t̷h̷i̷s̷ j̷o̷y̷
   T̷o̷ s̷e̷e̷ t̷h̷e̷e̷/̷ /̷L̷o̷n̷g̷i̷n̷g̷s̷ ⁒ a̷y̷ f̷o̷r̷ s̷w̷e̷e̷t̷e̷r̷ s̷e̷e̷m̷/̷d̷
   D̷e̷e̷p̷e̷r̷ t̷h̷a̷n̷ a̷n̷y̷ m̷e̷m̷o̷r̷i̷e̷s̷ o̷f̷ t̷h̷e̷e̷
   T̷h̷e̷ d̷e̷e̷p̷ f̷a̷r̷/̷r̷o̷l̷l̷i̷n̷g̷ w̷e̷s̷t̷w̷a̷r̷d̷/̷s̷m̷i̷l̷i̷n̷g̷ s̷e̷a̷s̷   B-III

579 ...for, m̷a̷n̷y̷ a̷n̷ hour by hour,   B-III

Alt. after 585
   While thou wert pacing with her, arm on waist, B-III

587 ...father's wars? wast wounded...   B-III

To pine and waste in those sweet memories.
O were I not my Mark's, by whom all men
Are noble, I should hate thee more than love.'   595

    And Tristram, fondling her light hands, replied,
'Grace, Queen, for being loved: she loved me well.
Did I love her? the name at least I loved.
Isolt?--I fought his battles, for Isolt!
The night was dark; the true star set. Isolt!   600
The name was ruler of the dark--Isolt?
Care not for her! patient, and prayerful, meek,
Pale-blooded, she will yield herself to God.'

    And Isolt answered, 'Yea, and why not I?
Mine is the larger need, who am not meek,   605
Pale-blooded, prayerful. Let me tell thee now.
Here one black, mute midsummer night I sat,
Lonely, but musing on thee, wondering where,
Murmuring a light song I had heard thee sing,
And once or twice I spake thy name aloud.   610
Then flashed a levin-brand; and near me stood,
In fuming sulphur blue and green, a fiend--

---

595   noble
    Are s̸e̸r̸a̸p̸h̸s̸ I sd...   B-III

597 I̸ d̸o̸ c̸o̸n̸f̸e̸s̸s̸: /s̸h̸e̸ l̸o̸v̸e̸d̸ m̸e̸ u̸t̸t̸e̸r̸l̸y̸:   B-III

First draft 599 ff
    And sweet, ye know, there be so many rungs
    Between the lowest in the scale of love,
    And this whereon we stand & breathe the heaven.
    Seem'd there
    T̸h̸e̸r̸e̸/s̸e̸e̸m̸s̸ a treachery of the body too?
    Not all a treachery of the heart. Isolt
    Isolt - the name was ruler of the night -
        hair is
    H̸e̸r̸ e̸y̸e̸s̸ a̸r̸e/b̸r̸o̸w̸n̸ & h̸l̸/z̸y̸ h̸e̸r̸ e̸y̸e̸s̸
    B̸l̸a̸c̸k̸ w̸a̸s̸ h̸e̸r̸ h̸a̸i̸r̸ b̸y̸ n̸i̸g̸h̸t̸; b̸l̸u̸e̸ w̸e̸r̸e̸ h̸e̸r̸ e̸y̸e̸s̸
    The sacred darkness ever made her thee.   B-III

602 And care not...   B-III

606   thee
    ...tell m̸e̸ now.   B-III

        902

THE LAST TOURNAMENT

Mark's way to steal behind one in the dark--
For there was Mark: "He has wedded her," he said,
Not said, but hissed it: then this crown of towers   615
So shook to such a roar of all the sky,
That here in utter dark I swooned away,
And woke again in utter dark, and cried,
"I will flee hence and give myself to God"--
And thou wert lying in thy new leman's arms.'   620

    Then Tristram, ever dallying with her hand,
'May God be with thee, sweet, when old and gray,
And past desire!' a saying that angered her.
'"May God be with thee, sweet, when thou art old,
And sweet no more to me!" I need Him now.   625
For when had Lancelot uttered aught so gross
Even to the swineherd's malkin in the mast?
The greater man, the greater courtesy.
Far other was the Tristram, Arthur's knight!

---

608   musing on thee, ~~musing on thee~~, wondering where
         Lonely, but ~~wondering at thy whereabouts~~,   B-III

609 ~~And~~ murmuring...   B-III

612 In   blue & green, a fiend -
    ~~A fiend in~~ fuming sulpher ~~green & blue~~   B-III

621   ever dallying with her hand
    (Par.) Then Tristram ~~making~~ slide ~~her marriage~~
                         ~~ring~~   B-III

Alt. after 621
    ~~Beyond the slender joint & back again~~   B-III

622   & gray
    ...when ~~thou art~~ old   B-III

628   greater
    The ~~nobler~~ man, ...   B-III

629 (Omitted)   A-2101
629 (C)   73

903

But thou, through ever harrying thy wild beasts-- 630
Save that to touch a harp, tilt with a lance
Becomes thee well--art grown wild beast thyself.
How darest thou, if lover, push me even
In fancy from thy side, and set me far
In the gray distance, half a life away, 635
Her to be loved no more? Unsay it, unswear!
Flatter me rather, seeing me so weak,
Broken with Mark and hate and solitude,
Thy marriage and mine own, that I should suck
Lies like sweet wines: lie to me: I believe. 640
·Will ye not lie? not swear, as there ye kneel,
And solemnly as when ye sware to him,
The man of men, our King--My God, the power
Was once in vows when men believed the King!
They lied not then, who sware, and through their
                              vows 645

----

637   me
     ..., seeing ~~I am~~ so...   B-III

639   ~~drink~~ suck
     ...I should ~~smell but~~   B-III

640 Lies like sweet wines
     ~~Flatteries as flowers~~:   lie.   B-III

643   the ~~force~~
     ...God, ~~what~~ power   B-III

644   men believed the King!
     ...in ~~knightly~~ vows when ~~knights were knights~~ B-III

645 They lied not then who sware,
     ~~And meant the things they sware~~ & thro'...   B-III

646   made
     ...prevailing ~~freed~~ his...   B-III

647 ...love ev'n...   B-III

648 Gray-hair'd, and...   ,/ (I)   A-2101
648 (C)   T-LTP

The King prevailing made his realm:--I say,
Swear to me thou wilt love me even when old,
Gray-haired, and past desire, and in despair.'

    Then Tristram, pacing moodily up and down,
'Vows! did you keep the vow you made to Mark   650
More than I mine? Lied, say ye? Nay, but learnt,
The vow that binds too strictly snaps itself--
My knighthood taught me this--ay, being snapt--
We run more counter to the soul thereof
Than had we never sworn. I swear no more.   655
I swore to the great King, and am forsworn.
For once--even to the height--I honoured him.
"Man, is he man at all?" methought, when first
I rode from our rough Lyonnesse, and beheld
That victor of the Pagan throned in hall--   660
His hair, a sun that rayed from off a brow
Like hillsnow high in heaven, the steel-blue eyes,

First draft, 649 ff
    (Par.) Then Tristram rose & pacing to & fro
    Answered her. 'couldst thou hold thy vow to Mark?
    A more or less than woman might have done it
    Not thou that art but woman? I am no liar.   B-III

650 ...did ye keep the vow ye made...   B-III;A-2101
650 (C)   73

651   say ye?
          Lied, h̸a̸v̸e̸ I̸? nay, but learnt̸,
    ...mine? t̸h̸a̸t̸ y̸e̸ s̸o̸ c̸a̸l̸l̸ m̸e̸/l̸i̸a̸r̸?   B-III

653   ing   ay
    My knighth̸o̸o̸d̸ taught me this - &̸, being apt, - B-III

654   thereof
    ...the soul o̸f̸ i̸t̸   B-III

Alt. after 655 N̸o̸ ⨯ n̸o̸t̸ t̸o̸ t̸h̸e̸e̸ w̸h̸o̸m̸ y̸e̸t̸ I̸ s̸w̸e̸a̸r̸
                   I̸ l̸o̸v̸e̸l̸   B-III

657 For
    A̸n̸d̸ once...   B-III

The golden beard that clothed his lips with light--
Morevoer, that weird legend of his birth,
With Merlin's mystic babble about his end   665
Amazed me; then, his foot was on a stool
Shaped as a dragon; he seemed to me no man,
But Michael trampling Satan; so I sware,
Being amazed: but this went by--The vows!
O ay--the wholesome madness of an hour--   670
They served their use, their time; for every knight
Believed himself a greater than himself,
And every follower eyed him as a God;
Till he, being lifted up beyond himself,
Did mightier deeds than elsewise he had done,   675
And so the realm was made; but then their vows--
First mainly through that sullying of our Queen--
Began to gall the knighthood, asking whence
Had Arthur right to bind them to himself?
Dropt down from heaven? washed up from out the
                              deep?   680
They failed to trace him through the flesh and blood
Of our old kings: whence then? a doubtful lord
To bind them by inviolable vows,
Which flesh and blood perforce would violate:
For feel this arm of mine--the tide within   685
Red with free chase and heather-scented air,
Pulsing full man; can Arthur make me pure
As any maiden child? lock up my tongue
From uttering freely what I freely hear?

---

665   ̷t̷a̷l̷k̷
      ...babble about...   B-III

669 ...by - the vows!   A-2101
669 (C)   72

690 ...one? The great world...   B-III;A-2101
690 (C)   72

691 Stet ̷v̷o̷w̷s̷/ ̷I̷ ̷a̷m̷
         ̷A̷n̷d̷ worldling...   B-III

693 Woo̷g̷s his...   A-2101
693 (C)   T-LTP

Bind me to one? The wide world laughs at it.   690
And worldling of the world am I, and know
The ptarmigan that whitens ere his hour
Woos his own end; we are not angels here
Nor shall be: vows--I am woodman of the woods,
And hear the garnet-headed yaffingale   695
Mock them: my soul, we love but while we may;
And therefore is my love so large for thee,
Seeing it is not bounded save by love.'

    Here ending, he moved toward her, and she said,
'Good: an I turned away my love for thee   700
To some one thrice as courteous as thyself--
For courtesy wins woman all as well
As valour may, but he that closes both
Is perfect, he is Lancelot--taller indeed,
Rosier and comelier, thou--but say I loved   705
This knightliest of all knights, and cast thee back
Thine own small saw, "We love but while we may,"
Well then, what answer?'

               He that while she spake,
Mindful of what he brought to adorn her with,
The jewels, had let one finger lightly touch   710
The warm white apple of her throat, replied,
'Press this a little closer, sweet, until--
Come, I am hungered and half-angered--meat,
Wine, wine--and I will love thee to the death,
And out beyond into the dream to come.'   715

---

696 ...may;	;/ (I)	A-2101
696 (C)		T-LTP
700 an		
'Good: ~~If~~ I...		B-III
705 Rosier, and...		72
705 (C)		73
708 Well then, what answer?		
~~What answer hast thou?~~		B-III
709 Mindful of		
~~Remembering~~ what...		B-III

So then, when both were brought to full accord,
She rose, and set before him all he willed;
And after these had comforted the blood
With meats and wines, and satiated their hearts--
Now talking of their woodland paradise,   720
The deer, the dews, the fern, the founts, the lawns;
Now mocking at the much ungainliness,
And craven shifts, and long crane legs of Mark--
Then Tristram laughing caught the harp, and sang:

'Ay, ay, O ay--the winds that bend the brier!   725
A star in heaven, a star within the mere!
Ay, ay, O ay--a star was my desire,
And one was far apart, and one was near:
Ay, ay, O ay--the winds that bow the grass!

---

716   were brought to full accord
   ...both ~~at last accorded well,~~   B-III

717   all
   ...him ~~what~~ he...   B-III

722   mocking
   Now ~~laughing~~ at...   B-III

724   laught & took the harp,
   Then Tristram ~~harped, all caution lost,~~ &
                     sang   B-III
724 ...harp, and...   ,/ (I)   A-2101
724 (C)   T-LTP

725   bend
   ...winds that ~~shake~~ the brier!   B-III

729 ...grass~~,~~   ! (I)   A-2101
729 (C)   T-LTP

Alt. after 731
   Ay ay O ay - a star was my desire -   B-III

734 And   ruby   S
   ~~Then Tristram~~ swung the carcanet & ~~she~~ cried   B-III

And one was water and one star was fire,   730
And one will ever shine and one will pass.
Ay, ay O ay--the winds that move the mere.'

   Then in the light's last glimmer Tristram showed
And swung the ruby carcanet. She cried
'The collar of some Order, which our King   735
Hath newly founded, all for thee, my soul,
For thee, to yield thee grace beyond thy peers.'

   'Not so, my Queen,' he said, 'but the red fruit
Grown on a magic oak-tree in mid-heaven,
And won by Tristram as a tourney-prize,   740
And hither brought by Tristram for his last
Love-offering and peace-offering unto thee.'

   He spoke, he turned, then, flinging round her neck,
Claspt it, and cried 'Thine Order, O my Queen!'
But, while he bowed to kiss the jewelled throat,   745
Out of the dark, just as the lips had touched,
Behind him rose a shadow and a shriek--

------

735 ...some ǿrder, which...   O/ (I)   A-2101
735 (C)   T-LTP

739 ...mid-heaven,   (, I)   A-2101
739 (C)   T-LTP

743   He   turn'd
     (Par.) So said he rose & flinging...   B-III
743   then   I MS
     (Par.) He rose, he turn'd, ánd flinging round
                         her neck   (, I)   A-2101
743 (Par.) He rose, he turn'd, then,...   T-LTP
743 (C)   84

744 Claspt it; but while he bow'd himself to lay   B-III
744   & cried 'Thine Order, O my Queen!   I MS
    Claspt it, b̷u̷t̷ ̷w̷h̷i̷l̷e̷ ̷h̷e̷ ̷b̷o̷w̷'̷d̷ ̷h̷i̷m̷s̷e̷l̷f̷ ̷t̷o̷ ̷l̷a̷y̷   A-2101
744 (C)   72

745 Warm kisses in the hollow of her throat,   B-III
745 But, while he bow'd to kiss the jewel'd throat, I MS
    W̷a̷r̷m̷ ̷k̷i̷s̷s̷e̷s̷ ̷i̷n̷ ̷t̷h̷e̷ ̷h̷o̷l̷l̷o̷w̷ ̷o̷f̷ ̷h̷e̷r̷ ̷t̷h̷r̷o̷a̷t̷/̷   A-2101
745 (C)   72

THE LAST TOURNAMENT

'Mark's way,' said Mark, and clove him through the
                              brain.

    That night came Arthur home, and while he climbed,
All in a death-dumb autumn-dripping gloom,   750
The stairway to the hall, and looked and saw
The great Queen's bower was dark,--about his feet
A voice clung sobbing till he questioned it,
'What art thou?' and the voice about his feet
Sent up an answer, sobbing, 'I am thy fool,   755
And I shall never make thee smile again.'

---

749   A̸s̸ - let   I MS
   ..., and w̸h̸i̸l̸e̸ he...   A-2101
749 (C)   T-LTP

750   death--
   All in a dumb And dead Autumn - dripping...   B-III

753   question'd it
   ...till he a̸s̸k̸d̸ t̸h̸e̸/v̸o̸i̸c̸e̸   B-III

756   smile
   ...thee m̸e̸r̸r̸y̸ again.'   B-III

THE LAST TOURNAMENT

Variants in "The Last Tournament"
Published in The Contemporary Review, Vol. XIX, pp. 1-22.

1 ...his moods	pg. 1
4 ...the Hall.	1
13 ...snakes	1
39 ...rather ye had...	2
76 ..., saying –	3
96 ...of otherwhere, –	4
116 ...written, "a sound is in his ears" –	4
132 ...Merlin, "Where...	5
133 ...goes."	5
211 Murmuring 'All...	7
216 ...a swarthy dame	7
217 ..., crying 'Praise...	7
221 ...as wintertide.	7
222 ...us comfort their...	7
227 ...them, saying as when...	7
252 ...stood,	8
254 Then being...	8
259 ...music ye can make.'	8
262 ...the king's;	8
275 (Par.) "Free...	9
279 ...love to...	9
281 Free love, — free...	9
290 ...to whomsoever came –	9
302 ...: honour the king - his...	9
328 ...of Hell.'	10
341 ...were king by...	11
342 Or king by...	11
352 ...the king thy...	11
359 ...danced away.	11
381 ...the Cornish king,	12
389 ...to smooth	12
430 ...of The Table Round	13
436 ...back: alone...	13
467 Head-heavy, while the knights, ...	14
477 Then, yell with yell echoing, they...	14
486 (Par.) Then out...	15
493 ...him, 'Why...	15
495 'What, an she...	15
496 What, an she...	15
497 ...to her, –	15
511 ...embrace	15
512 ...aloud 'Not...	15

Guinevere

Queen Guinevere had fled the court, and sat
There in the holy house at Almesbury
Weeping, none with her save a little maid,
A novice: one low light betwixt them burned
Blurred by the creeping mist, for all abroad,   5
Beneath a moon unseen albeit at full,
The white mist, like a face-cloth to the face,
Clung to the dead earth, and the land was still.

    For hither had she fled, her cause of flight
Sir Modred; he that like a subtle beast   10

---

5 ...abroad   BM-2
5 (C)   F

6 ...full   BM-2
6 (C)   F

7 ...mist like..face   BM-2
7 (C)   59

9   had she fled, her cause of flight
  ...hither o̸n̸ t̸h̸e̸s̸e̸ g̸r̸o̸u̸n̸d̸s̸ h̸a̸d̸ f̸l̸e̸d̸ t̸h̸e̸ Q̸u̸e̸e̸n̸,̸   Tn-39

10   he the
    Sir Modred; nearest to the king, h̸i̸s̸ h̸e̸i̸r̸   Tn-39
10 ...he the nearest to the King,   BM-2
10 (C)   <u>69</u>

GUINEVERE

Lay couchant with his eyes upon the throne,
Ready to spring, waiting a chance: for this
He chilled the popular praises of the King
With silent smiles of slow disparagement;
And tampered with the Lords of the White Horse,   15
Heathen, the brood by Hengist left; and sought
To make disruption in the Table Round
Of Arthur, and to splinter it into feuds
Serving his traitorous end; and all his aims
Were sharpened by strong hate for Lancelot.   20

    For thus it chanced one morn when all the court,
Green-suited, but with plumes that mocked the may,
Had been, their wont, a-maying and returned,
That Modred still in green, all ear and eye,
Climbed to the high top of the garden-wall   25
To spy some secret scandal if he might,
And saw the Queen who sat betwixt her best
Enid, and lissome Vivien, of her court

Alt. after 10 **His**
            And nephew, ever like a subtle beast Tn-39
Alt. after 10 His nephew, ever like a subtle beast BM-2
Alt. after 10 (C)   69

12 ...chance; for this,   BM-2
12 ...this,   F
12 (C)   67

21 ...court   BM-2
21 (C)   59

22 Green-suited but...   BM-2
22 (C)   F

28 Enid, & Viviane the wiliest   Tn-39
28 Enid, and Vivian the wiliest   BM-2
28 (C)   F

29 And worst of all her court; & more...   Tn-39
29 And worst of all her court, and...   BM-2
29 (C)   F

914

The wiliest and the worst; and more than this
He saw not, for Sir Lancelot passing by   30
Spied where he couched, and as the gardener's hand
Picks from the colewort a green caterpillar,
So from the high wall and the flowering grove
Of grasses Lancelot plucked him by the heel,
And cast him as a worm upon the way;   35
But when he knew the Prince though marred with dust,
He, reverencing king's blood in a bad man,
Made such excuses as he might, and these
Full knightly without scorn; for in those days
No knight of Arthur's noblest dealt in scorn;   40
But, if a man were halt or hunched, in him
By those whom God had made full-limbed and tall,
Scorn was allowed as part of his defect,
And he was answered softly by the King
And all his Table. So Sir Lancelot holp   .   45

---

30   saw
        He ~~spied~~ not...   Tn-39

31 Spied
   ~~saw~~ where...   Tn-39

33 ...flowering groves   H-36

34 Of grapes Lancelot...   BM-2
34 (C)   F

35 ...worm ~~besid~~ upon...   H-36

36 But
   ~~And~~ when...   Tn-39

37 He reverencing King's blood...man   BM-2
37 He reverencing King's blood...   F
37 (C)   59

40 ...scorn   BM-2
40 (C)   F

41 But if...   BM-2
41 (C)   F

To raise the Prince, who rising twice or thrice
Full sharply smote his knees, and smiled, and went:
But, ever after, the small violence done
Rankled in him and ruffled all his heart,
As the sharp wind that ruffles all day long   50
A little bitter pool about a stone
On the bare coast.   But when Sir Lancelot told
This matter to the Queen, at first she laughed
Lightly, to think of Modred's dusty fall,
Then shuddered, as the village wife who cries   55
'I shudder, some one steps across my grave;'
Then laughed again, but faintlier, for indeed
She half-foresaw that he, the subtle beast,
Would track her guilt until he found, and hers

---

46 ...Prince who rising, twice...		BM-2
46 (C)		62
47 ...knees and smiled and...		BM-2
47 (C)		F
48 But ever after the...		BM-2
48 (C)		F
51 ...little litter pool...		BM-2
51 (C)		F
53 ...Queen at...		BM-2
53 (C)		F
54 dusty		
...Modred's fall & t̸h̸e̸n̸		Tn-39
54 Lightly to...fall		BM-2
54 (C)		F
55 Then		
Shudder'd, as m̸i̸g̸h̸t̸ the village...		Tn-39
56 ...grave'		BM-2
56 (C)		F
57 ...again but...		BM-2
57 (C)		F

```
Would be for evermore a name of scorn.              60
Henceforward rarely could she front in hall,
Or elsewhere, Modred's narrow foxy face,
Heart-hiding smile, and gray persistent eye:
Henceforward too, the Powers that tend the soul,
To help it from the death that cannot die,          65
And save it even in extremes, began
To vex and plague her.  Many a time for hours,
Beside the placid breathings of the King,
In the dead night, grim faces came and went
Before her, or a vague spiritual fear--             70
Like to some doubtful noise of creaking doors,
Heard by the watcher in a haunted house,
That keeps the rust of murder on the walls--
Held her awake:  or if she slept, she dreamed
```

58	...he the...beast	BM-2
58	(C)	F
61	...in Hall	BM-2
61	...in Hall,	F
61	(C)	73
62	...elsewhere Modred's...	BM-2
62	(C)	F
63	...smile and...	BM-2
63	(C)	F
64	...too the...soul	BM-2
64	(C)	F
65	...die	BM-2
65	(C)	F
71	...doors	BM-2
71	(C)	59
72	...house	BM-2
72	(C)	59
74	...awake; or...	BM-2
74	(C)	F

```
An awful dream; for then she seemed to stand        75
On some vast plain before a setting sun,
And from the sun there swiftly made at her
A ghastly something, and its shadow flew
Before it, till it touched her, and she turned--
When lo! her own, that broadening from her feet,    80
And blackening, swallowed all the land, and in it
Far cities burnt, and with a cry she woke.
And all this trouble did not pass but grew;
Till even the clear face of the guileless King,
And trustful courtesies of household life,          85
Became her bane; and at the last she said,
'O Lancelot, get thee hence to thine own land,
For if thou tarry we shall meet again,
And if we meet again, some evil chance
Will make the smouldering scandal break and blaze   90
```

79 ...it till...		BM-2
79 (C)		F
83 ...grew,		BM-2
83 (C)		F
86 ...said		BM-2
86 (C)		59
87 ...Lancelot get...		BM-2
87 (C)		F
89 ...again some		BM-2
89 (C)		F
91 ...people and...King.		BM-2
91 (C)		F
92 And Lancelot promised, but he did not go,		Tn-39
92 And Lancelot promised, but he did not go,		BM-2
92 (C)		F
93 ...said		BM-2
93 (C)		59

Before the people, and our lord the King.'
And Lancelot ever promised, but remained,
And still they met and met. Again she said,
'O Lancelot, if thou love me get thee hence.'
And then they were agreed upon a night   95
(When the good King should not be there) to meet
And part for ever. Vivien, lurking, heard.
She told Sir Modred. Passion-pale they met
And greeted. Hands in hands, and eye to eye,
Low on the border of her couch they sat   100
Stammering and staring. It was their last hour,
A madness of farewells. And Modred brought
His creatures to the basement of the tower
For testimony; and crying with full voice
'Traitor, come out, ye are trapt at last,' aroused   105
Lancelot, who rushing outward lionlike
Leapt on him, and hurled him headlong, and he fell

---

94 ...Lancelot if...hence'   BM-2
94 (C)   F

97-98 And part for ever. Passion-pale they met   Tn-39
97-98 And part for ever. Passion-pale they met   BM-2
97-98 (C)   92

99 ...eye ȯn to eye,   Tn-39
99 ...greeted: hands...   BM-2
99 (C)   92

101 ...staring: it...   BM-2
101 (C)   92

102 ...farewells: and...   BM-2
102 (C)   F

105 'Come out, thou traitor, trapt...   Tn-39
105 'Come out, thou traitor, trapt at last'
                                aroused   BM-2
105 ...last' aroused   F
105 (C)   59

107 ...him and...   BM-2
107 (C)   F

Stunned, and his creatures took and bare him off,
And all was still: then she, 'The end is come,
And I am shamed for ever;' and he said,   110
'Mine be the shame; mine was the sin: but rise,
And fly to my strong castle overseas:
There will I hide thee, till my life shall end,
There hold thee with my life against the world.'
She answered, 'Lancelot, wilt thou hold me so?   115
Nay, friend, for we have taken our farewells.
Would God that thou couldst hide me from myself!
Mine is the shame, for I was wife, and thou

---

108 ...off	BM-2
108 (C)	73
109 ...she 'the...come	BM-2
109 ...she, 'the...come	59
109 (C)	73
110 ...ever' and he said	BM-2
110 ...said	59
110 (C)	73

Sketch 111-114
*Nay shame be mine, for I betray'd thee, sweet
liege-lady, but rise now, & let us fly
To my strong castle overseas, for there,
Love, will I hold thee against all the world.'* Tn-39

112 ...castle-overseas:	BM-2
112 (C)	F
113 till my life shall end,	
...I hold thee, *own liege lady mine*	Tn-39
114 ...world:'	BM-2
114 (C)	59
115 wilt thou hold me so?	
...'Lancelot, *flower of courtesy*,	Tn-39
115 ...answer'd 'Lancelot...	BM-2
115 (C)	73

Unwedded: yet rise now, and let us fly,
For I will draw me into sanctuary,   120
And bide my doom.' So Lancelot got her horse,
Set her thereon, and mounted on his own,
And then they rode to the divided way,
There kissed, and parted weeping: for he past,
Love-loyal to the least wish of the Queen,   125
Back to his land; but she to Almesbury

---

116 Nay friend, for we have taken our farewells.
    W̶h̶o̶ t̶a̶k̶e̶s̶t̶ a̶l̶l̶ t̶h̶e̶ s̶h̶a̶m̶e̶ t̶o̶ t̶h̶i̶n̶e̶ o̶w̶n̶ p̶a̶r̶t̶,̶   Tn-39
116 Nay friend...   BM-2
116 (C)   73

117 ...God, that...myself,   BM-2
117 ...God, that...   F
117 (C)   73

118 Mine is the shame
    T̶h̶e̶ s̶h̶a̶m̶e̶ i̶s̶ m̶i̶n̶e̶,̶ for...   Tn-39

119 Unwedded: w̶e̶/h̶a̶v̶e̶ t̶a̶k̶e̶n̶ o̶u̶r̶ f̶a̶r̶e̶w̶e̶l̶l̶,̶
                 yet rise now &
    T̶h̶e̶r̶e̶ m̶u̶s̶t̶ b̶e̶ s̶i̶n̶ n̶o̶ l̶o̶n̶g̶e̶r̶ let us fly   Tn-39
119 ...now and...fly   BM-2
119 (C)   F

120 For   draw
    B̶u̶t̶ I will/h̶i̶e̶ me...   Tn-39
120 ...sanctuary   BM-2
120 (C)   59

122 ...thereon and...   BM-2
122 (C)   59

123   then
    And s̶o̶ they...   Tn-39

125 Love-loyal   the
    O̶b̶e̶d̶i̶e̶n̶t̶ to the..of h̶i̶s̶ Queen,   Tn-39

Fled all night long by glimmering waste and weald,
And heard the Spirits of the waste and weald
Moan as she fled, or thought she heard them moan:
And in herself she moaned 'Too late, too late!'   130
Till in the cold wind that foreruns the morn,
A blot in heaven, the Raven, flying high,
Croaked, and she thought, 'He spies a field of death;
For now the Heathen of the Northern Sea,
Lured by the crimes and frailties of the court,   135
Begin to slay the folk, and spoil the land.'

    And when she came to Almesbury she spake
There to the nuns, and said, 'Mine enemies

Alt. before 127
        So fled the sad Queen thro' the moony night
        In which no moon appeared, but one vast place
        Of all the Heavens, moon white from verge to verge.
127 So fled the Queen by glimmering waste & weald   H-36

129 ...fled or...moan.   BM-2
129 (C)   F

130 ...moan'd 'too...   BM-2
130 (C)   73

131 Till in the cold wind that foreruns the dawn   H-36

132 High over the gray holt the Raven flew   H-36

133 Croaking & saw far-off a field of Death.   H-36
133 ...thought 'he..death   BM-2
133 ...thought 'he...   F
133 (C)   73

136 Began to slay the folk & waste the land.   H-36
136 ...folk and...   BM-2
136 (C)   F

138 ...nuns and said 'mine...   BM-2
138 ...said, 'mine...   F
138 (C)   73

922

Pursue me, but, O peaceful Sisterhood,
Receive, and yield me sanctuary, nor ask   140
Her name to whom ye yield it, till her time
To tell you:' and her beauty, grace and power,
Wrought as a charm upon them, and they spared
To ask it.
       So the stately Queen abode
For many a week, unknown, among the nuns;   145
Nor with them mixed, nor told her name, nor sought,
Wrapt in her grief, for housel or for shrift,
But communed only with the little maid,
Who pleased her with a babbling heedlessness
Which often lured her from herself; but now,   150
This night, a rumour wildly blown about
Came, that Sir Modred had usurped the realm,
And leagued him with the heathen, while the King

---

140 Receive and...	BM-2
140 (C)	F
141 ...name, to...	BM-2
141 (C)	73
142 ...you' and... beauty grace and power	BM-2
142 ...you' and...	F
142 (C)	67
143 Wrought like a charm...	Tn-39
143 Wrought like a charm...them and...	BM-2
143 (C)	F
145 ...nuns	BM-2
145 (C)	F
148 ...maid	BM-2
148 (C)	59
150 ...often kept her...	Tn-29
150 ...often kept her...now	BM-2
150 (C)	F
152 ...realm	BM-2
152 (C)	F

Was waging war on Lancelot: then she thought,
'With what a hate the people and the King   155
Must hate me,' and bowed down upon her hands
Silent, until the little maid, who brooked
No silence, brake it, uttering 'Late! so late!
What hour, I wonder, now?' and when she drew
No answer, by and by began to hum   160
An air the nuns had taught her; 'Late, so late!'
Which when she heard, the Queen looked up, and said,
'O maiden, if indeed ye list to sing,
Sing, and unbind my heart that I may weep.'
Whereat full willingly sang the little maid.   165

        'Late, late, so late! and dark the night and chill!
Late, late, so late! but we can enter still.

---

154 ...thought	BM-2
154 (C)	F
156 ...me' and...	BM-2
156 (C)	59
157 ...maid who...	BM-2
157 (C)	F
158 ...uttering 'late!...	BM-2
158 (C)	73
161 ...her 'late so late'	BM-2
161 ...her 'late so...	F
161 ...her; 'late...	59
161 (C)	73
162 ...heard the...up and said	BM-2
162 (C)	F
163 ...indeed thou list...	Tn-39
163 ...indeed thou list...	BM-2
163 ...indeed you list...	F
163 (C)	69
164 ...weep'	BM-2
164 (C)	F

Too late, too late! ye cannot enter now.

'No light had we: for that we do repent;
And learning this, the bridegroom will relent.   170
Too late, too late! ye cannot enter now.

'No light: so late! and dark and chill the night!
O let us in, that we may find the light!
Too late, too late: ye cannot enter now.

'Have we not heard the bridegroom is so sweet?   175
O let us in, though late, to kiss his feet!

---

166 ...late: & all so dark & chill	Tn-39
166 (Par.) "Late...and all so dark and chill	BM-2
166 (Par.) "Late...	F
166 (C)	70
169 (Par.) No..repent	BM-2
169 (Par.) "No...	F
169 (C)	70
170 ...this the...	BM-2
170 (C)	F
171 No no too late!...	Tn-39
171 No no too late! ye...	BM-2
171 (C)	F
172 No light no light & starless is the night	Y-IV;Tn-39
172 (No Par. indent.) "No light: so late: and starless is the night	BM-2
172 (Par.) "No...	F
172 (C)	70
174 No light? too late...	Tn-39
174 No light? too...	BM-2
174 (C)	F
175 (Par.) Have...	BM-2
175 (Par.) "Have...	F
175 (C)	70

GUINEVERE

No, no, too late! ye cannot enter now.'

So sang the novice, while full passionately,
Her head upon her hands, remembering.
Her thought when first she came, wept the sad
                              Queen.   180
Then said the little novice prattling to her,

   'O pray you, noble lady, weep no more;

---

177 Too late, too late!...   Tn-39
177 Too late, too late! ...now."   BM-2
177 ...now."   F
177 (C)   70

181 ...her.   BM-2
181 (C)   73

182 O Lady, pray you, grieve not overmuch;   H-32;H-36
182 (Par.) O pray...   BM-2
182 (C)   F

183   my
    But let ~~the~~ words of one so small, ~~As I~~   H-36

184 ~~One~~ who   knows but
    ~~And~~ knowing nothing, ~~only~~ to obey,   H-36
184 ...nothing, knows...   BM-2
184 (C)   F

Alt. before 186
    ~~Be solace for your griefs are not the sign~~ (?)
    ~~Of evil done + right sure/an/I/of/that~~
    ~~Dear/Lady/ not the~~   H-36

186 Comfort your sorrows, ~~on~~ for they do not flow H-36

187 ...that   BM-2
187 (C)   F

189 But I wd have you weigh your griefs with his H-32;
                                                      H-36
189 ...King's   BM-1
189 (C)   F

926

But let my words, the words of one so small,
Who knowing nothing knows but to obey,
And if I do not there is penance given--   185
Comfort your sorrows; for they do not flow
From evil done; right sure am I of that,
Who see your tender grace and stateliness.
But weigh your sorrows with our lord the King's,
And weighing find them less; for gone is he   190
To wage grim war against Sir Lancelot there,
Round that strong castle where he holds the Queen;
And Modred whom he left in charge of all,
The traitor--Ah sweet lady, the King's grief

---

190 Our Lord the king's & weighing feel them less
    For he is gone, they rumour, overseas   H-36
190 Our lord the king's, & weighing find them less.
    For gone is he, they rumour, overseas   H-32

191 ...there   BM-2
191 (C)   F

192 In his strong castle, where he holds the
                                    Queen: H-36
192 ...strong Castle where...   BM-2
192 (C)   59

193 ff
    And Modred his own nephew whom he left
    In charge of all, the regent due, has leagued
    With the wild Lords of the white Horse, & man all
    The rebel subject of the king, & seeks
    To reave his uncle of his life & crown.
    Whose
    His grief for wife & realm & his own self
    Must
    To treble ours. for me, I thank the saints
    I am not great: H-36
193 ff
    And Modred, his own nephew, whom he left
    In charge of all the regent here has leagued
    With the wild lords of the White Horse & seeks
    To reave his uncle of his life & crown.
    Must not his grief for kingdom & for Queen
    And this foul blot upon his Table Round
    Be, lady, thrice as great as any of ours.   H-32

927

For his own self, and his own Queen, and realm,   195
Must needs be thrice as great as any of ours.
For me, I thank the saints, I am not great.
For if there ever come a grief to me
I cry my cry in silence, and have done.
None knows it, and my tears have brought me good: 200
But even were the griefs of little ones
As great as those of great ones, yet this grief
Is added to the griefs the great must bear,
That howsoever much they may desire
Silence, they cannot weep behind a cloud: 205
As even here they talk at Almesbury
About the good King and his wicked Queen,
And were I such a King with such a Queen,
Well might I wish to veil her wickedness,

---

195 ...self and...Queen and realm		BM-2
195 (C)		F
199 ...silence and...done		BM-2
199 ...done:		F
199 (C)		75
200 ...it and...		BM-2
200 (C)		F
201 ...griefs of private ones		H-36;H-32
203 ...griefs ~~they have to bear~~ of public men		H-36
203 ...griefs of public men		H-32
205 ...cloud;		BM-2
205 (C)		F
206 As even now they...		H-36;H-32
207 ...& the wicked Queen		H-36;H-32
207 ...good king and...wicked queen,		BM-2
207 (C)		59

GUINEVERE

But were I such a King, it could not be.'   210

   Then to her own sad heart muttered the Queen,
'Will the child kill me with her innocent talk?'
But openly she answered, 'Must not I,
If this false traitor have displaced his lord,
Grieve with the common grief of all the realm?'   215

   'Yea,' said the maid, 'this is all woman's grief,
That she is woman, whose disloyal life
Hath wrought confusion in the Table Round
Which good King Arthur founded, years ago,
With signs and miracles and wonders, there   220
At Camelot, ere the coming of the Queen.'

---

208 ...a king with...a queen   BM-2
208 ...a king with...a queen,   F
208 (C)   59

209 I'd desire to hide her wickedness   H-36

210 ...a king it...not be.   BM-2
210 ...a king, it...   F
210 (C)   59

211 ...the Queen.   BM-2
211 (C)   73

213 But openly she spoke & said to her   H-32
213 .. answer'd 'must...   BM-2
213 (C)   73

216 (Par.) 'Yea' said the maid 'this...grief   BM-2
216 (Par.) 'Yea' said the maid 'this...   F
216 (C)   59

220 ...wonders there   BM-2
220 (C)   F

221 ...the Queen'   BM-2
221 (C)   F

929

GUINEVERE

    Then thought the Queen within herself again,
'Will the child kill me with her foolish prate?'
But openly she spake and said to her,
'O little maid, shut in by nunnery walls,   225
What canst thou know of Kings and Tables Round,
Or what of signs and wonders, but the signs
And simple miracles of thy nunnery?'

    To whom the little novice garrulously,
'Yea, but I know: the land was full of signs   230
And wonders ere the coming of the Queen.
So said my father, and himself was knight

---

222 ...again	BM-2
222 ...again;	59
222 (C)	73
223 ...prate?	BM-2
223 (C)	62
224 ...her.	BM-2
224 ...her;	F
224 (C)	73
225 ...shut in with nunnery...	H-32
225 ...maid shut...walls	BM-2
225 ...maid shut...	F
225 (C)	59
226 ...Round	BM-2
226 (C)	F

229 ff
    (Par.) And answer made the novice prattling to her
    'Yea but I know. my father knew the king
    And loved him & himself was Arthur's knight
    And at the founding of the Table round
    Whereto he rode from Lyoness, & he said
    That in those days the land was full of signs
    And as he rode an hour or maybe twain
    After the sunset down the coast he heard
    Strange cries & sounds, & passing turn'd & there
                                                           H-32

930

Of the great Table--at the founding of it;
And rode thereto from Lyonnesse, and he said
That as he rode, an hour or maybe twain   235
After the sunset, down the coast, he heard
Strange music, and he paused, and turning--there,
All down the lonely coast of Lyonnesse,
Each with a beacon-star upon his head,
And with a wild sea-light about his feet,   240
He saw them--headland after headland flame
Far on into the rich heart of the west:
And in the light the white mermaiden swam,

---

229 ...garrulously.   BM-2
229 (C)   73

233 ...of it   BM-2
233 (C)   F

237 ...paused and...   BM-2
237 (C)   73

Sketch 238 ff
    we rode along the shores of Lyoness
    an Far into the dark heart of the West
    Flamed headland after headland
    And strong manbreasted things stood from the sea
    And sent a wild seavoice along the hills
    A band of tiny dancers hand in hand
    Swung round the lighted lantern of the hall: H-31

238 We rode along the coasts of Layoness   H-31

239 Each with a fiery beacon on his head   H-31
239 ...upon its head   H-32

240 ...about its feet   H-32

241 [I saw them] headland after headland flamed   H-31

242 Far on into the dark heart of the west.   H-31

Alt. for 243 High i̸n̸ oer the world sea light the
                        seamen cried   H-31

And strong man-breasted things stood from the sea,
And sent a deep sea-voice through all the land,   245
To which the little elves of chasm and cleft
Made answer, sounding like a distant horn.
So said my father--yea, and furthermore,
Next morning, while he past the dim-lit woods,
Himself beheld three spirits mad with joy   250
Come dashing down on a tall wayside flower,
That shook beneath them, as the thistle shakes
When three gray linnets wrangle for the seed:
And still at evenings on before his horse

---

244 And strong man-breasted things stood from the sea	H-31
244 ...sea	BM-2
244 (C)	F
245 And sent a great sea voice across the land	H-31
247 Gave answer...	H-31
248-249 So said my father & he spake the truth. And then next morning in the twilight woods	H-32
248 ...yea and furthermore	BM-2
248 (C)	F
249 ...morning riding thro' the dim-lit...	Tn-39
249 Next morning riding thro' the dim-lit woods	BM-2
249 (C)	F

Sketch 250 ff
    I saw myself three spirits mad of delighted
    Come dashing down ~~of~~ on a hill of wayside flower
    That shook beneath them as the thistle shakes
    When three gray linnets wrangle for the seed.
    And when I reachd to catch them they (2 ?)   H-31

251 ...flower	BM-2
251 (C)	F
252 ...them as...	BM-2
252 (C)	F

The flickering fairy-cycle wheeled and broke   255
Flying, and linked again, and wheeled and broke
Flying, for all the land was full of life.
And when at last he came to Camelot,
A wreath of airy dancers hand-in-hand
Swung round the lighted lantern of the hall;   260
And in the hall itself was such a feast
As never man had dreamed; for every knight
Had whatsoever meat he longed for served
By hands unseen; and even as he said
Down in the cellars merry bloated things   265

---

253 ...seed.   BM-2
253 (C)   F

255 ...fairy-circle wheel'd...   Tn-39

256 ...again and...   BM-2
256 (C)   F

257 Flying for all the land was full of life   H-31

258 And when we gained the summit of the mount   H-31
258 And when we clomb the mount of Camelot   H-31
258 ...Camelot   BM-2
258 (C)   F

Alt after 258   slope
          All down the smooth ʂíḋé of the dewy
                         mount   H-31

Sketch 259 ff
     The flickering fairy circle wheel'd & broke
     The city was all dark but full of crowd
               crowd
     Fóṛ áĺl the people gather'd in the street to watch
          wreath
     A ḃáṅḋ of airy dancers hand in hand
     Swing round that lighted lantern of the hall.
     Nay - I here hear - I am not frequent there   H-31

259 ...hand in hand   BM-2
259 (C)   F

933

Shouldered the spigot, **straddling** on the butts
While the wine ran: so glad were spirits and men
Before the coming of the sinful Queen.'

    Then spake the Queen and somewhat bitterly,
'Were they so glad? ill prophets were they all,   270
Spirits and men: could none of them foresee,
Not even thy wise father with his signs
And wonders, what has fallen upon the realm?'

    To whom the novice garrulously again,
'Yea, one, a bard; of whom my father said,   275

---

266 ...spigot straddling...		BM-2
266 (C)		F
267 ...ram; so...		BM-2
267 (C)		F
269 But openly she spake and said to her		H-32
269 ...bitterly.		BM-2
269 (C)		73
272-273 This trouble that has fallen upon the		
realm		H-32
273 ...wonders what...		BM-2
273 (C)		59
274 And she made answer garrulously again.		H-32
274 ...again.		BM-2
274 (C)		73
275 Yea, yea, a bard. but I forget his name.		
Not Taliessin: but my father said,		H-32
275 ...bard, of...		BM-2
275 (C)		59
276 ...warsong...		BM-2
276 (C)		59
280 Had chanted...		H-32
280 ...mountain-tops		BM-2
280 (C)		F

934

Full many a noble war-song had he sung,
Even in the presence of an enemy's fleet,
Between the steep cliff and the coming wave;
And many a mystic lay of life and death
Had chanted on the smoky mountain-tops,   280
When round him bent the spirits of the hills
With all their dewy hair blown back like flame:
So said my father--and that night the bard
Sang Arthur's glorious wars, and sang the King
As wellnigh more than man, and railed at those   285
Who called him the false son of Gorloïs:
For there was no man knew from whence he came;
But after tempest, when the long wave broke
All down the thundering shores of Bude and Bos,
There came a day as still as heaven, and then   290

---

281 ...him came the spirits...	H-32;Tn-39
281 ...him came the spirits...	BM-2
281 (C)	F
282 With dewy hair blown back like cyclamen,	H-32
282 With dewy hair blown back like cyclamen:	Tn-39
282 With dewy hair blown back like cyclamen:	BM-2
282 (C)	F
283 ...night he sang	H-32;Tn-39
283 ...father - and that night he sang	BM-2
283 (C)	F
284 Of Arthur glorious wars & him the king	H-32
284 Of Arthur's...	Tn-29
284 Of Arthur's glorious wars and sang the king	BM-2
284 ...the king	F
284 (C)	59
285 ...man and...	BM-2
285 (C)	F
285 ...well-nigh...	59
285 (C)	73
289 ...the thundering coast of	H-32

935

GUINEVERE

They found a naked child upon the sands
Of dark Tintagil by the Cornish sea;
And that was Arthur; and they fostered him
Till he by miracle was approven King:
And that his grave should be a mystery   295
From all men, like his birth; and could he find
A woman in her womanhood as great
As he was in his manhood, then, he sang,
The twain together well might change the world.
But even in the middle of his song   300
He faltered, and his hand fell from the harp,
And pale he turned, and reeled, and would have fallen,
But that they stayed him up; nor would he tell
His vision; but what doubt that he foresaw
This evil work of Lancelot and the Queen?'   305

    Then thought the Queen, 'Lo! they have set her on,
Our simple-seeming Abbess and her nuns,

---

291 ...upon the shore	H-32
292 Of wild T. ...	H-32
292 Of wild Dundagil by...	Tn-39
292 Of wild Dundazil by the...	BM-2
292 Of wild Dundagil by...	59
292 (C)	<u>69</u>
293 ...Arthur, and...	BM-2
293 (C)	F
294 ...approven king:	BM-2
294 (C)	73
301 ...falter'd and...harp	BM-2
301 (C)	F
302 ...turn'd and reel'd and...fall'n	BM-2
302 (C)	F
306 ...Queen 'lo! ...on	BM-2
306 ...Queen 'lo! ...	59
306 (C)	73

To play upon me,' and bowed her head nor spake.
Whereat the novice crying, with clasped hands,
Shame on her own garrulity garrulously,   310
Said the good nuns would check her gadding tongue
Full often, 'and, sweet lady, if I seem
To vex an ear too sad to listen to me,
Unmannerly, with prattling and the tales
Which my good father told me, check me too   315
Nor let me shame my father's memory, one
Of noblest manners, though himself would say
Sir Lancelot had the noblest; and he died,
Killed in a tilt, come next, five summers back,
And left me; but of others who remain,   320
And of the two first-famed for courtesy--
And pray you check me if I ask amiss--
But pray you, which had noblest, while you moved
Among them, Lancelot or our lord the King?'

   Then the pale Queen looked up and answered her,   325
'Sir Lancelot, as became a noble knight,
Was gracious to all ladies, and the same

---

307 ...nuns   BM-2
307 (C)   59

308 ...me' and...   BM-2
308 (C)   59

310 ...garrulously   BM-2
310 (C)   F

312 ...'and sweet lady if...   BM-2
312 ...often 'and, ...   F
312 (C)   59

315 ...too: F
315 (C)   75

325 ...her.   BM-2
325 (C)   73

327 ...ladies and...   BM-2
327 (C)   F

In open battle or the tilting-field
Forbore his own advantage, and the King
In open battle or the tilting-field   330
Forbore his own advantage, and these two
Were the most nobly-mannered men of all;
For manners are not idle, but the fruit
Of loyal nature, and of noble mind.'

    'Yea,' said the maid, 'be manners such fair
                        fruit?   335
Then Lancelot's needs must be a thousand-fold
Less noble, being, as all rumour runs,
The most disloyal friend in all the world.'

    To which a mournful answer made the Queen:
'O closed about by narrowing nunnery-walls,   340
What knowest thou of the world, and all its lights
And shadows, all the wealth and all the woe?
If ever Lancelot, that most noble knight,
Were for one hour less noble than himself,
Pray for him that he scape the doom of fire,   345

332	men t͟h͟e͟m͟	
	...most noble-manner'd of all;	Tn-39
332	...most noble-mannered...	BM-2
332	(C)	F
334	loyal	
	Of m͟o͟r͟a͟l͟ nature...	Tn-39
334	...nature and...	BM-2
334	(C)	F
335	(Par.) 'Yea' said the maid 'be...	BM-2
335	(C)	59
339	...Queen	BM-2
339	...Queen.	F
339	(C)	73
340	...nunnery-walls	BM-2
340	(C)	F
341	...world and...	BM-2
341	(C)	F

And weep for her who drew him to his doom.'

    'Yea,' said the little novice, I pray for both;
But I should all as soon believe that his,
Sir Lancelot's, were as noble as the King's,
As I could think, sweet lady, yours would be   350
Such as they are, were you the sinful Queen.'

    So she, like many another babbler, hurt
Whom she would soothe, and harmed where she would
                    heal;
For here a sudden flush of wrathful heat
Fired all the pale face of the Queen, who cried,   355
'Such as thou art be never maiden more
For ever! thou their tool, set on to plague
And play upon, and harry me, petty spy
And traitress.' When that storm of anger brake
From Guinevere, aghast the maiden rose,   360
White as her veil, and stood before the Queen
As tremulously as foam upon the beach
Stands in a wind, ready to break and fly,
And when the Queen had added 'Get thee hence,'

---

342 ...the woe.		BM-2
342 (C)		F
346 ...her, who...		F
346 (C)		73
347 (Par.) 'Yea' said...novice 'I...		BM-2
347 (C)		59
355 ...cried		BM-2
355 (C)		59
358 ...upon and...		BM-2
358 (C)		F
360 ...rose		BM-2
360 (C)		F
364 ...added 'get...hence'		BM-2
364 (C)		73

Fled frighted. Then that other left alone   365
Sighed, and began to gather heart again,
Saying in herself, 'The simple, fearful child
Meant nothing, but my own too-fearful guilt,
Simpler than any child, betrays itself.
But help me, heaven, for surely I repent.   370
For what is true repentance but in thought--
Nor even in inmost thought to think again
The sins that made the past so pleasant to us:
And I have sworn never to see him more,
To see him more.'

                And even in saying this,   375
Her memory from old habit of the mind
Went slipping back upon the golden days
In which she saw him first, when Lancelot came,
Reputed the best knight and goodliest man,

365-366 Fled frighted. Then the Queen took heart
                & thought   H-73a

366 Sig'd and...   BM-2
366 (C)   F

367 It is my guilt. The simple fearful maid   H-73a
367 ...herself 'the...   BM-2
367 (C)   73

368 Meant nothing. Guilt is simple too to find H-73a
368 ...guilt   BM-2
368 (C)   73

Alt. after 368
    So much in craft. Would I had never seen
    The noblest & the truest knight of all   H-73a

370 To me the truest. But I repent   H-73a

371 And what is true repentence & remorse   H-73a

372 Save not   H-73a

373-374 The sin that made our past so sweet. I
                 vow   H-73a

Ambassador, to lead her to his lord   380
Arthur, and led her forth, and far ahead
Of his and her retinue moving, they,
Rapt in sweet talk or lively, all on love
And sport and tilts and pleasure, (for the time
Was maytime, and as yet no sin was dreamed,)   385
Rode under groves that looked a paradise
Of blossom, over sheets of hyacinth
That seemed the heavens upbreaking through the earth,
And on from hill to hill, and every day
Beheld at noon in some delicious dale   390
The silk pavilions of King Arthur raised
For brief repast or afternoon repose
By couriers gone before; and on again,

---

375 Never to see him more & saying this   H-73a
375 ...this   BM-2
375 (C)   59

377 Went slipping backward to the happy days   H-73a

378 ...first when home he came   H-73a

379 Reputed the first knight in all the world,   H-73a

380 Ambassador, to lead her to the king.   H-73a
380   lead
    ...to b̸r̸i̸n̸g̸ her...   Tn-39

384 & the time   H-73a
384 ...pleasure 'for...   BM-2
384 (C)   59

385 Was maytime & no sin as yet was dream'd   H-73a

Alt. after 385 But she was free to talk with him &
                        rode   H-73a

389 From flowering hill to hill & every day   H-73a

393 ...couriers sent before; & ...   H-73a
393 ...again   BM-2
393 (C)   F

941

Till yet once more ere set of sun they saw
The Dragon of the great Pendragonship,   395
That crowned the state pavilion of the King,
Blaze by the rushing brook or silent well.

But when the Queen immersed in such a trance,
And moving through the past unconsciously,
Came to that point where first she saw the King   400
Ride toward her from the city, sighed to find
Her journey done, glanced at him, thought him cold,
High, self-contained, and passionless, not like him,
'Not like my Lancelot'--while she brooded thus
And grew half-guilty in her thoughts again,   405
There rode an armed warrior to the doors.
A murmuring whisper through the nunnery ran,
Then on a sudden a cry, 'The King.' She sat
Stiff-stricken, listening; but when armed feet

---

394 Till once again ere...   H-73a

395 ...Pendragonship   BM-2
395 (C)   F

396 ...King   BM-2
396 (C)   F

398 And while she sat immersed in such a trance   H-36

400 ...point when first...   Tn-39
400 ...point when first...   BM-2
400 ...point, when first...   F
400 ...point, where first...   <u>69</u>
400 (C)   70

405 And almost guilty in her thoughts again   H-36

407 A whispering murmur in the nunnery woke,   TN-39
407 A whispering murmur in the nunnery woke,   BM-2
407 (C)   F

408 Then rose a cry the King the King. She sat   H-36
408 ...cry 'the King.'...   BM-2
408 (C)   73

409 ...armed steps   H-36

Through the long gallery from the outer doors   410
Rang coming, prone from off her seat she fell,
And grovelled with her face against the floor:
There with her milkwhite arms and shadowy hair
She made her face a darkness from the King:
And in the darkness heard his armed feet   415
Pause by her; then came silence, then a voice,
Monotonous and hollow like a Ghost's
Denouncing judgment, but though changed, the King's:

'Liest thou here so low, the child of one
I honoured, happy, dead before thy shame?   420
Well is it that no child is born of thee.
The children born of thee are sword and fire,
Red ruin, and the breaking up of laws,
The craft of kindred and the Godless hosts
Of heathen swarming o'er the Northern Sea;   425

---

410 ...outer door   H-36

416   then came
    ...her; silence f̶o̶l̶l̶o̶w̶'̶d̶, then...   Tn-39
416 ...a voice   BM-2
416 (C)   59

418 ...changed the King's.   BM-2
418 (C)   73

419 Liest thou so low, my wife, the child of one   H-36

420 I honour'd, who is dead before thy shame?   H-36
420 ...shame.   BM-2
420 (C)   F

421 ...that no babe is born...   H-36

422 ...fire   BM-2
422 (C)   F

425 ...Northern sea.   BM-2
425 ...Northern Sea.   59
425 (C)   73

943

Whom I, while yet Sir Lancelot, my right arm,
The mightiest of my knights, abode with me,
Have everywhere about this land of Christ
In twelve great battles ruining overthrown.
And knowest thou now from whence I come--from him,   430
From waging bitter war with him: and he,
That did not shun to smite me in worse way,
Had yet that grace of courtesy in him left,
He spared to lift his hand against the King
Who made him knight: but many a knight was slain;   435
And many more, and all his kith and kin
Clave to him, and abode in his own land.
And many more when Modred raised revolt,
Forgetful of their troth and fealty, clave
To Modred, and a remnant stays with me.   440

---

426 ...I while...Lancelot my...   BM-2
426 ...Lancelot my...   F
426 (C)   59

427 ...knights abode...   BM-2
427 (C)   F

431 I come from waging war with him; & he,   H-36
431 ...him; and...   BM-2
431 (C)   F

435 ...slain   BM-2
435 (C)   F

436 ...more and...   BM-2
436 (C)   F

437 ...him and...land   BM-2
437 (C)   F

442   for whom I live
    True men, who love me still & s̶h̶a̶l̶l̶ n̶o̶t̶ l̶e̶t̶   H-36
442 ...live;   F
442 (C)   59

944

GUINEVERE

And of this remnant will I leave a part,
True men who love me still, for whom I live,
To guard thee in the wild hour coming on,
Lest but a hair of this low head be harmed.
Fear not: thou shalt be guarded till my death.   445
Howbeit I know, if ancient prophecies
Have erred not, that I march to meet my doom.
Thou hast not made my life so sweet to me,
That I the King should greatly care to live;
For thou hast spoilt the purpose of my life.   450
Bear with me for the last time while I show,
Even for thy sake, the sin which thou hast sinned.
For when the Roman left us, and their law
Relaxed its hold upon us, and the ways
Were filled with rapine, here and there a deed   455
Of prowess done redressed a random wrong.
But I was first of all the kings who drew
The knighthood-errant of this realm and all
The realms together under me, their Head,

---

443   hour
     ...wild d̸a̸y̸s̸ coming...   H-36

444 Lest but a   low
    A̸ s̸i̸m̸p̸l̸e̸ hair of t̸h̸i̸s̸ thy head be harm'd   H-36

446-447   by ancient prophecies
    Howbeit I know I march to meet my doom   H-36

449 ...the king should...live,   BM-2
449 ...the king should...   F
449 (C)   59

450 For thou spoilt...   H-36

458-459   island
    The knighthood-errant of this ancient realm
    And all the realms together, here under me   H-36

458   realm
    ...of this i̸s̸l̸e̸ & all   Tn-39

945

GUINEVERE

In that fair Order of my Table Round,   460
A glorious company, the flower of men,
To serve as model for the mighty world,
And be the fair beginning of a time.
I made them lay their hands in mine and swear
To reverence the King, as if he were   465
Their conscience, and their conscience as their King,
To break the heathen and uphold the Christ,
To ride abroad redressing human wrongs,
To speak no slander, no, nor listen to it,
To honour his own word as if his God's,   470
To lead sweet lives in purest chastity,
To love one maiden only, cleave to her,
And worship her by years of noble deeds,

Sketch c. 460
    It was the coming back of that fair day
    Wh chanc'd on Britain many a year before
    When the great King founded a noble round
    To serve as model of the mighty world   H-31

460 ...fair order of...   BM-2
460 (C)   73

462   for
    To serve as model of the mighty world -   H-36

464 And made them swear to vows of chastity -   H-36

465 To reverence the king as tho' he were   H-36

466 ...as the king   H-36
466 ...as the King,   Tn-39
466 ...as the King,   BM-2
466 (C)   F

467 (Omitted)   BM-2
467 (C)   F

468 ...human wrong -   H-36

470 (Omitted)   BM-2
470 (C)   73

Until they won her; for indeed I knew
Of no more subtle master under heaven   475
Than is the maiden passion for a maid,
Not only to keep down the base in man,
But teach high thought, and amiable words
And courtliness, and the desire of fame,
And love of truth, and all that makes a man.   480
And all this throve before I wedded thee,
Believing, "lo mine helpmate, one to feel
My purpose and rejoicing in my joy."
Then came thy shameful sin with Lancelot;
Then came the sin of Tristram and Isolt;   485

472	To love one maiden & to cleave to her,	H-36
472	...maiden & to cleave...	Tn-39
472	...maiden and to cleave...	BM-2
472	(C)	F
476	...a maid	BM-2
476	(C)	59
479	...of fame	BM-2
479	(C)	F
481	...throve until I...	H-36;Tn-39
481	...throve until I...	BM-2
481	...throve until I...thee!	F
481	(C)	73
482	Saying 'behold my helpmate, one to feel	H-36
482	Believing 'lo...	BM-2
482	Believing "lo...	59
482	(C)	70
483	...joy.'	BM-2
483	(C)	59
484	...Lancelot,	BM-2
484	(C)	F
485	...Isolt	BM-2
485	(C)	F

Then others, following these my mightiest knights,
And drawing foul ensample from fair names,
Sinned also, till the loathsome opposite
Of all my heart had destined did obtain,
And all through thee! so that this life of mine   490
I guard as God's high gift from scathe and wrong,
Not greatly care to lose; but rather think
How sad it were for Arthur, should he live,
To sit once more within his lonely hall,
And miss the wonted number of my knights,   495
And miss to hear high talk of noble deeds
As in the golden days before thy sin.
For which of us, who might be left, could speak
Of the pure heart, nor seem to glance at thee?
And in thy bowers of Camelot or of Usk   500
Thy shadow still would glide from room to room,
And I should evermore be vext with thee

---

487 ...names	BM-2
487 (C)	F
490 ...thee; so...	BM-2
490 (C)	F
491 ...wrong	BM-2
491 (C)	F
492 ...lose, but...	BM-2
492 (C)	F
493-494 Sad were it to sit within my empty Hall	H-36
494 his	
...within m̷y̷ lonely...	Tn-39
495 Without the wonted...	H-36
496 And hear high talk & of noble deeds	H-36
498 ...us who..left could...	BM-2
498 (C)	F
499 ...thee;	BM-2
499 (C)	F

GUINEVERE

In hanging robe or vacant ornament,
Or ghostly footfall echoing on the stair.
For think not, though thou wouldst not love thy
                    lord,   505
Thy lord has wholly lost his love for thee.
I am not made of so slight elements.
Yet must I leave thee, woman, to thy shame.
I hold that man the worst of public foes
Who either for his own or children's sake,   510
To save his blood from scandal, lets the wife
Whom he knows false, abide and rule the house:
For being through his cowardice allowed
Her station, taken everywhere for pure,
She like a new disease, unknown to men,   515
Creeps, no precaution used, among the crowd,

---

504 ...stair:	BM-2
504 (C)	59
505 For think not me	
Thou dost not love thy lord	H-36
505 ...thou didst not...	H-36
505 ...would'st lose thy lord,	BM-2
505 (C)	F
506 he	
That I have wholly lost all love for thee.	H-36
506 ...lost all love...	Tn-39
506 ...lost all love for thee:	BM-2
506 (C)	F
508 ..., woman to...	BM-2
508 (C)	59
510 ...sake	BM-2
510 (C)	F
513 For being thro' his love or cowardice	H-36
514 Taken for pure, allow'd her station, she	H-36
515 Creeps like a new disease, unknown to men	H-36
516 And no precaution used, among the crowd.	H-36

GUINEVERE

Makes wicked lightnings of her eyes, and saps
The fealty of our friends, and stirs the pulse
With devil's leaps, and poisons half the young.
Worst of the worst were that man he that reigns!   520
Better the King's waste hearth and aching heart
Than thou reseated in thy place of light,
The mockery of my people, and their bane.'

    He paused, and in the pause she crept an inch
Nearer, and laid her hands about his feet.   525

Alt. after 516 Or peering oer the shoulder of her
                              lord   H-36

518 The fealty of his friends...   H-36

Alt. after 518
    With madness & with beatings, shakes the calm
    Of married station, & poisons half the young.   H-36

520 Far worse were that man he who rules a realm   H-36
520   now
    Much worse were that he who rules a realm   H-36
520   of
    Worse than the worst...that rules.   Tn-39
520 ...that rules.   BM-2
520 (C)   F

521 ...the king's waste...   BM-2
521 (C)   59

522 ...light   BM-2
522 (C)   F

523 That thou...   H-36
523 ...people and...   BM-2
523 (C)   F

524 ...paused and...   BM-2
524 (C)   F

525 Nearer and...   BM-2
525 (C)   F

950

GUINEVERE

Far off a solitary trumpet blew.
Then waiting by the doors the warhorse neighed
As at a friend's voice, and he spake again:

    'Yet think not that I come to urge thy crimes,
I did not come to curse thee, Guinevere,   530
I, whose vast pity almost makes me die
To see thee, laying there thy golden head,
My pride in happier summers, at my feet.
The wrath which forced my thoughts on that fierce law,
The doom of treason and the flaming death,   535
(When first I learnt thee hidden here) is past.

---

526 ...blew,	BM-2
526 (C)	F
528 ...again.	BM-2
528 (C)	73
529-530 Think not I come to curse thee,	
Guinevere,	H-36
529-530 Yet think not that I come to curse	
thee now	H-36
529 ...crimes	H-36
529 (C)	F
531 I whose...	BM-2
531 (C)	F
532 ...thee laying...	BM-2
532 (C)	F
533 ...pride in happier years, down at my feet.	H-36
Alt. after 533 I do not come to curse thee, my	
lost wife,	H-36
534 ...law	BM-2
534 (C)	F
535 ...treason & the death of fire.	H-36

951

GUINEVERE

The pang--which while I weighed thy heart with one
Too wholly true to dream untruth in thee,
Made my tears burn--is also past--in part.
And all is past, the sin is sinned, and I,   540
Lo! I forgive thee, as Eternal God
Forgives: do thou for thine own soul the rest.
But how to take last leave of all I loved?
O golden hair, with which I used to play
Not knowing! O imperial-moulded form,   545
And beauty such as never woman wore,

537-539 The pang which when I weigh'd my love with
                    thee
          Made tears too salt, is likewise partly
                         past.   H-36
537-539 The grief that when at first I knew thee
                    false
          Made tears too salt has wholly past away   H-36

537 ...pang, which...   BM-2
537 (C)   F

538 ...untruth in thine,   H-36

539 ...burn, is also past in part.   BM-2
539 ...past, in...   F
539 (C)   73

540 ..., and I   BM-2
540 (C)   F

541   Eternal
    I do now forgive thee as Almighty holy God   H-36
541 ...God f̸o̸r̸g̸i̸v̸   Tn-39
541 ...thee as...   BM-2
541 (C)   F

542 Forgives - do thou the rest for thine own soul   H-36

543 But how to take last leave of what I am.   H-36

952

Until it came a kingdom's curse with thee--
I cannot touch thy lips, they are not mine,
But Lancelot's: nay, they never were the King's.
I cannot take thy hand; that too is flesh,   550
And in the flesh thou hast sinned; and mine own flesh,
Here looking down on thine polluted, cries
"I loathe thee:" yet not less, O Guinevere,
For I was ever virgin save for thee,
My love through flesh hath wrought into my life   555

Alt. after 543 What in this last hour can I say
                            to thee   H-36

546 ...as woman never wore,   H-36

548   touch
     I cannot K̶e̶e̶p̶ thy lips - they are not mine   H-36

549 But Lancelots - they never were the kings   H-36

Alt. after 549 Thou hast not been for one hour true
                            to me.   H-36

550 I will not take thy hand...   H-36

552   & mine own flesh
     Cries looking down on thy polluted form   H-36

553 'I loathe thee:' yet...   BM-2
553 (C)   59

554 ⌈For I was ever virgin save for thee,   H-36

Alt. after 554 Nor ever knew sweet love except
                            thro' thee]   H-36

555 ...wrought upon my life   H-36
555 My love for thee hath wrought unto my being   H-36
555   thro' flesh
     ...love f̶o̶r̶ t̶h̶e̶e̶ hath...   Tn-39

953

So far, that my doom is, I love thee still.
Let no man dream but that I love thee still.
Perchance, and so thou purify thy soul,
And so thou lean on our fair father Christ,
Hereafter in that world where all are pure   560
We two may meet before high God, and thou
Wilt spring to me, and claim me thine, and know
I am thine husband--not a smaller soul,
Nor Lancelot, nor another. Leave me that,

Alt. before 556 That is the meed of my pure maiden-
                              hood   H-36

556 I love thee still tho false. so let it be.   H-36
556 So that I must forbear I love thee still.   H-36
556 So far that I must say I love thee still.   H-36
556   nevertheless
    O my much-sinning wife, I love thee still.   H-36
556   my doom is,
    ...that I ḿúśt śáẏ, I...   Tn-39
556 ...for that...   BM-2
556 (C)   F

557 Let no man doubt the folly of the king
    Nor doubt that like a child he lovers her
                          still.   H-36
557 ...man doubt but...   H-36
557 ...still -   BM-2
557 (C)   F

558 ...soul   BM-2
558 (C)   F

560-562 Hereafter, so thou purify thy soul,
        To meet me in a nobler world than ours
                                    claim
        There wilt thou cleave to me & óẃń me
                              thine   H-36

561 ...God and...   BM-2
561 (C)   F

562 Wilt cleave to me...   H-36;Tn-39

954

```
I charge thee, my last hope.  Now must I hence.        565
Through the thick night I hear the trumpet blow:
They summon me their King to lead mine hosts
Far down to that great battle in the west,
Where I must strike against the man they call
My sister's son--no kin of mine, who leagues        570
With Lords of the White Horse, heathen, and knights,
Traitors--and strike him dead, and meet myself
```
_____

562 Wilt cleave to me and...thine and...   BM-2
562 (C)   F

564 ...Leave me this,   H-36
564 ...another: leave...   BM-2
564 (C)   F

565 ...hope: now...hence: BM-2
565 ...hence: F
565 (C)   59

566 ...the trumpets blow   H-36

567 ...their king to...   BM-2
567 (C)   59

569-571 Where I must strike against my sister's son
        Leagued with the Lords of the White Horse,
                        & meet   H-36
569-571 Where I must strike against my sister's son
        Leagued with the lords of the White Horse
                        and knights   Tn-39;BM-2
569 (C)   69
569 (C)   69
571 With lords of the White Horse, heathen, and
                        knights   69
571 With lords of the White Horse, heathen, and
                        knights -   70
571 (C)   73

572 Once mine, and strike...   Tn-39;BM-2
572 (C)   69

Death, or I know not what mysterious doom.
And thou remaining here wilt learn the event;
But hither shall I never come again,   575
Never lie by thy side; see thee no more--
Farewell!'   And while she grovelled at his feet,
She felt the King's breath wander o'er her neck,
And in the darkness o'er her fallen head,
Perceived the waving of his hands that blest.   580

    Then, listening till those armed steps were gone,
Rose the pale Queen, and in her anguish found
The casement: 'peradventure,' so she thought;

---

573 Death or...	BM-2
573 (C)	F
574 ...event	BM-2
574 ...event,	F
574 (C)	59
576 ...side, see...more,	BM-2
576 (C)	73
578 ...neck	BM-2
578 (C)	F

579-580   ~~móvéd whéré hér héad~~
    And ~~thóúght thát~~ in the darkness over her fallen
                                      head
    Perceived
    ~~Shé félt~~ the waving...   H-36

579 ...head	BM-2
579 And, in...	F
579 (C)	70

581-582 ...steps had gone
                pale
        Rose the ~~sád~~ Queen...   H-36

581 (Par.) Then listening...gone	BM-2
581 ...gone	F
581 (C)	59

'If I might see his face, and not be seen.'
And lo, he sat on horseback at the door!   585
And near him the sad nuns with each a light
Stood, and he gave them charge about the Queen,
To guard and foster her for evermore.
And while he spake to these his helm was lowered,
To which for crest the golden dragon clung   590
Of Britain; so she did not see the face,
Which then was as an angel's, but she saw,
Wet with the mists and smitten by the lights,
The Dragon of the great Pendragonship

---

582 ...Queen and...   BM-2
582 (C)   F

583 ...'peradventure' so she thought   BM-2
583 ...'peradventure' so...   59
583 (C)   73

584 ...face and...   BM-2
584 (C)   F

585 ...lo! he...door   BM-2
585 (C)   F

586 And round him...   H-36

587 ...Queen   BM-2
587 (C)   F

589 ...lower'd   BM-2
589 (C)   F

591 ...face   BM-2
591 (C)   F

592 ...saw   BM-2
592 (C)   F

593 ...lights   BM-2
593 (C)   F

594 The dragon of the dread Pendragon blaze   H-36
594 The dragon of...   BM-2
594 (C)   59

Blaze, making all the night a steam of fire.   595
And even then he turned; and more and more
The moony vapour rolling round the King,
Who seemed the phantom of a Giant in it,
Enwound him fold by fold, and made him gray
And grayer, till himself became as mist   600
Before her, moving ghostlike to his doom.

Then she stretched out her arms and cried aloud
'Oh Arthur!' there her voice brake suddenly,
Then--as a stream that spouting from a cliff
Fails in mid air, but gathering at the base   605
Re-makes itself, and flashes down the vale--
Went on in passionate utterance:

---

595 And seem to fill the night with steem of fire;   H-36
595 Blaze making...   BM-2
595 (C)   F

597 ...moony vapors rolling...   H-36

598 Who seem'd a Giant phantom in the mists   H-36

600 And grayer, till he faded all away   H-36

603 ...suddenly ~~off~~,   H-36
603 ...Arthur' there...   BM-2
603 (C)   59

604 Then
        ~~And~~ as a...   H-36
604 Then as...   BM-2
604 (C)   F

605 Wastes in mid air, but...   H-36
605 ...air but...   BM-2
605 (C)   59

606 Remakes itself and...   BM-2
606 (C)   59

607 Went on passionate...   H-36
607 ...utterance.   BM-2
607 (C)   73

```
                              'Gone--my lord!
Gone through my sin to slay and to be slain!
And he forgave me, and I could not speak.
Farewell?  I should have answered his farewell.        610
His mercy choked me.  Gone, my lord the King,
My own true lord! how dare I call him mine?
The shadow of another cleaves to me,
And makes me one pollution:  he, the King,
Called me polluted:  shall I kill myself?              615
What help in that?  I cannot kill my sin,
If soul be soul; nor can I kill my shame;
```

```
608          thro'
     Gone f̸o̸r̸ my sin...                                H-36
608 ...slain                                           BM-2
608 (C)                                                F


611 But that his mercy choked me & my shame.          H-36
611 ...the king                                        BM-2
611 ...the king,                                       F
611 (C)                                                59


612 My Lord!  how dare I call him Lord of mine         H-36


613 Not mine.  the shadow of another cling             H-36


614 About me.  I am polluted:  (taking him?)           H-36
614 I was polluted.  Shall I kill myself               H-36
614          one        ion
     ...me a̸l̸l̸ polluted:  he,...                       H-36
614 ...the king,                                        BM-2
614 (C)                                                59


616-617 What use in that?  I could not kill my
                           shame                        H-36
616-617  What help in that?  I could not kill
                           my shame.                    H-36


Alt. before 617
     And make all dark that I may
     And pass into the dark & know no more.            H-36


617 If soul be soul I cannot kill myself               H-36
617 ...shame                                           BM-2
617 (C)                                                F
```

959

```
No, nor by living can I live it down.
The days will grow to weeks, the weeks to months,
The months will add themselves and make the years,      620
The years will roll into the centuries,
And mine will ever be a name of scorn.
I must not dwell on that defeat of fame.
Let the world be; that is but of the world.
What else? what hope?  I think there was a hope,        625
Except he mocked me when he spake of hope;
His hope he called it; but he never mocks,
For mockery is the fume of little hearts.
And blessed be the King, who hath forgiven
My wickedness to him, and left me hope                   630
```

```
618 No no nor can I live it down                          H-36

619          grow to                    to
    ...will  ḿáḱé t́h́é weeks, the weeks t́h́é months       H-36

620                   to make
    ...themselves ińt́ó the years                         H-36
620 ...themselves to make...                             Tn-39
620 ...themselves to make the years                      BM-2
620 (C)                                                  F

624 I am but not & the world:  let the world be:         H-36
624 ...be:  that...world,                                BM-2
624 ...world.                                            F
624 (C)                                                  78

625               I think
    What hope?  There was a hope h́é ĺéf́t́ ẃít́h́ ḿé        H-36
625 What hope?  There was a hope he left with me         H-36

Alt. after 625                    live
    That in mine own heart I can down sin
    And be his mate hereafter up in heaven               H-36

626 Did he not mock me, when he spoke of hope            H-36
626 ...of hope -                                          BM-2
626 (C)                                                  F
```

That in mine own heart I can live down sin
And be his mate hereafter in the heavens
Before high God. Ah great and gentle lord,
Who wast, as is the conscience of a saint
Among his warring senses, to thy knights--   635
To whom my false voluptuous pride, that took
Full easily all impressions from below,
Would not look up, or half-despised the height
To which I would not or I could not climb--
I thought I could not breathe in that fine air   640
That pure severity of perfect light--
I yearned for warmth and colour which I found

---

627 His hope he call'd it - nay he never mocks   H-36

628 For mocking is the work of little souls   H-36
628 For mocking is the fume of little souls   H-36
628   hearts
     ...little ~~souls~~.   Tn-39

629 ...the king, who...   BM-2
629 (C)   59

630 There was (1 ?) hope he left with me   H-36
630 ...him and...   BM-2
630 (C)   F

631 That in mine own self I can live down sin   H-36

633 ...Ah great & noble king   H-36
633 ...lord   BM-2
633 (C)   F

Alt. after 635
     Did ye not see him? did he not pass by?
     Did not worship him that God in man
     I dared not as I dare not worship God
     You might (ink blot)   H-36

641 ...light.   BM-2
641 (C)   F

642 I wanted warmth...   Tn-39
642 I wanted warmth...   BM-2
642 (C)   86

961

In Lancelot--now I see thee what thou art,
Thou art the highest and most human too,
Not Lancelot, nor another. Is there none   645
Will tell the King I love him though so late?
Now--ere he goes to the great Battle? none:
Myself must tell him in that purer life,
But now it were too daring. Ah my God,
What might I not have made of thy fair world,   650
Had I but loved thy highest creature here?
It was my duty to have loved the highest:
It surely was my profit had I known:
It would have been my pleasure had I seen.

---

643 ...art	BM-2
643 (C)	F
644 ...too	BM-2
644 (C)	59
645 ...Lancelot nor...	BM-2
645 (C)	59
646 ...the king I...	BM-2
646 (C)	59
647 (Omitted)	BM-2
647 Before he goes to the great Battle? none:	
(I MS)	L-IV
647 Now - ere	I MS
B̸e̸f̸o̸r̸e̸ he goes...	F
647 (C)	51
651 ...here.	BM-2
651 (C)	F
653 ...I known	BM-2
653 (C)	F

Alt. before 655 Lo my dear lord I love now to tell   H-36

Alt. after 655 I did not see it before   H-36

We needs must love the highest when we see it,   655
Not Lancelot, nor another.'
                         Here her hand
Grasped, made her vail her eyes: she looked and saw
The novice, weeping, suppliant, and said to her,
'Yea, little maid, for am I not forgiven?'
Then glancing up beheld the holy nuns   660
All round her, weeping; and her heart was loosed
Within her, and she wept with these and said,

     'Ye know me then, that wicked one, who broke
The vast design and purpose of the King.
O shut me round with narrowing nunnery-walls,   665

656-657   Here the Queen
     Felt her hand siezed, & looking down beheld   Tn-39

656 ...Here the Queen   BM-2
656 ...hand,   F
656 (C)   59

657 Felt her hand siezed, and looking down beheld   BM-2

658 ..., suppliant and...her   BM-2
658 ...her   59
658 (C)   73

660 Thence looking up...   Tn-39
660 Hence looking up...   BM-2
660   glancing   I MS
     T̶h̶e̶n̶c̶e̶ ̶l̶o̶o̶k̶i̶n̶g̶ up...   F
660 (C)   59

662 ...said.   BM-2
662 (C)   73

663 I am the Queen, that wicked one, who broke   H-36

665 O let me if you do not shudder at me   H-36

Meek maidens, from the voices crying "shame."
I must not scorn myself: he loves me still.
Let no one dream but that he loves me still.
So let me, if you do not shudder at me,
Nor shun to call me sister, dwell with you;   670
Wear black and white, and be a nun like you,
Fast with your fasts, not feasting with your feasts;
Grieve with your griefs, not grieving at your joys,
But not rejoicing; mingle with your rites;
Pray and be prayed for; lie before your shrines;   675
Do each low office of your holy house;
Walk your dim cloister, and distribute dole

---

666 ...crying 'shame,'   BM-2
666 (C)   59

669 ...at me   BM-2
669 (C)   75

670 ...with you,   BM-2
670 ...you,;   ; (I)   F
670 (C)   59

671 ...you,;   ; (I)   F
671 ...you;   59
671 (C)   73

672 ...feasts,   BM-2
672 (C)   59

674 And
    Let me mingle with your sacred rites,   H-36
674 ...rejoicing - mingle with your rites -   BM-2
674 (C)   F

675   - & do you for me sacred shrines
    Pray for the dead & haunt your h̶o̶l̶y̶ r̶i̶t̶e̶s̶   H-36
675 ...for, lie...shrines,   BM-2
675 ...for, lie...shrines,;   (; I)   F
675 (C)   59

676 Do all each low office of your nunnery,   H-36
676 ...house,   BM-2
676 ...house,;   ; (I)   F
676 (C)   59

964

GUINEVERE

To poor sick people, richer in His eyes
Who ransomed us, and haler too than I;
And treat their loathsome hurts and heal mine own;   680
And so wear out in almsdeed and in prayer
The sombre close of that voluptuous day,
Which wrought the ruin of my lord the King.'

She said: they took her to themselves; and she
Still hoping, fearing 'is it yet too late?'   685
Dwelt with them, till in time their Abbess died.
Then she, for her good deeds and her pure life,

Alt. before 678 I must be now for   H-36

678   poor men
     To s̸i̸c̸k̸l̸y̸ s̸o̸u̸l̸s̸ more worthy than myself   H-36
678 ...in his eyes   BM-2
678 (C)   73

679 ...than I,   BM-2
679 ...than I,;   ;   (I)   F
679 (C)   59

680   hurts
     ...loathsome s̸o̸r̸e̸s̸ & heal...   Tn-39
680 ...own   BM-2
680 ...own;   (; I)   F
680 (C)   59

682 ...of my voluptuous day   H-36
682 ...day   BM-2
682 (C)   F

686   died,
     ...Abbess p̸a̸s̸t̸   Tn-39
686 ...died,   BM-2
686 (C)   59

Alt. after 686
     T̸o̸ w̸h̸e̸r̸e̸ b̸e̸y̸o̸n̸d̸ t̸h̸e̸s̸e̸ v̸o̸i̸c̸e̸s̸ t̸h̸e̸r̸e̸ i̸s̸ p̸e̸a̸c̸e̸   Tn-39

687 ...she for...   BM-2
687 (C)   F

965

GUINEVERE

And for the power of ministration in her,
And likewise for the high rank she had borne,
Was chosen Abbess, there, an Abbess, lived   690
For three brief years, and there, an Abbess, past
To where beyond these voices there is peace.

---

690 ...there as Abbess...   Tn-39
690 ..., there as Abbess lived   BM-2
690 (C)   F

691   past
   ...Abbess d̶i̶e̶d̶.   Tn-39
691 ...there an Abbess past   BM-2
691 (C)   F

REJECTED PASSAGES
                        Ah noble heart
Ah flower of kindness o̶f̶ & courtesy
To take the shame & horror to thyself
When I betrayed thee   H-36

Out of his pure heart & his blamelessness
W̶h̶ n̶ And tender vast affectionate desire
To make all human beings like himself
He founded at the limits of the west
A table round of all great hearts & true   H-31

The Passing of Arthur

That story which the bold Sir Bedivere,
First made and latest left of all the knights,
Told, when the man was no more than a voice
In the white winter of his age, to those
With whom he dwelt, new faces, other minds.   5

    For on their march to westward, Bedivere,
Who slowly paced among the slumbering host,
Heard in his tent the moanings of the King:

    'I found Him in the shining of the stars,
I marked Him in the flowering of His fields,   10
But in His ways with men I find Him not.
I waged His wars, and now I pass and die.
O me! for why is all around us here
As if some lesser god had made the world,
But had not force to shape it as he would,   15
Till the High God behold it from beyond,
And enter it, and make it beautiful?
Or else as if the world were wholly fair,
But that these eyes of men are dense and dim,
And have not power to see it as it is: 20
Perchance, because we see not to the close;--

---

1 (Par.) The tale that once the bold Sir Bedivere,   A-S

2 ...left of A̶l̶l̶h̶o̶l̶y̶s̶ all...   A-S

6-28 (Omitted)   A-2104
6-28 (Added)   73

967

For I, being simple, thought to work His will,
And have but stricken with the sword in vain;
And all whereon I leaned in wife and friend
Is traitor to my peace, and all my realm   25
Reels back into the beast, and is no more.
My God, thou hast forgotten me in my death:
Nay--God my Christ--I pass but shall not die.'

Then, ere that last weird battle in the west,
There came on Arthur sleeping, Gawain killed   30
In Lancelot's war, the ghost of Gawain blown
Along a wandering wind, and past his ear
Went shrilling, 'Hollow, hollow all delight!
Hail, King! tomorrow thou shalt pass away.

---

29 (Par.) Before that last wierd battle in the West	A-2104
29 (Par.) Before that last wierd battle in the west	L-HGI
29 (C)	73
33 ...shrilling 'hollow,...	A-2104
33 (C)	L-HGI
34 Hail, king!...	A-2104
34 (C)	73
38 ...onward like...	A-2104
38 (C)	L-HGI
42 Far in	I MS
F̶r̶o̶m̶ o̶u̶t̶ the...hills	A-2104
42 (C)	L-HGI

Farewell! there is an isle of rest for thee.　　　　　35
And I am blown along a wandering wind,
And hollow, hollow, hollow all delight.'
And fainter onward, like wild birds that change
Their season in the night and wail their way
From cloud to cloud, down the long wind the dream　　40
Shrilled; but in going mingled with dim cries
Far in the moonlit haze among the hills,
As of some lonely city sacked by night,
When all is lost, and wife and child with wail
Pass to new lords; and Arthur woke and called,　　　45
'Who spake? A dream. O light upon the wind,
Thine, Gawain, was the voice--are these dim cries
Thine? or doth all that haunts the waste and wild
Mourn, knowing it will go along with me?'

43　　　　　　lonely city sack'd by night,　　　　　　I MS
　　As of some ~~town in the dead hour of sleep~~　　A-2104
43 (C)　　　　　　　　　　　　　　　　　　　　L-HGI

Alt. after 43
　~~sack'd by strange foes! when all the brave are~~　　
　　　　　　　　　~~fall'n!~~　　　　　　　　　　A-2104
Alt. after 43 (C)　　　　　　　　　　　　　　L-HGI

45　　　　call'd　　　　　　　　　　　　　　　　P MS
　...and ~~moan'd~~　　　　　　　　　　　　　　A-2104
45 ...and call'd　　　　　　　　　　　　　　　S-925
45 (C)　　　　　　　　　　　　　　　　　　　L-HGI

46 ...wind　　　　　　　　　　　　　　　　　　A-2104
46 (C)　　　　　　　　　　　　　　　　　　　S-925

THE PASSING OF ARTHUR

This heard the bold Sir Bedivere and spake: 50

50-78 (Omitted)   A-2104

First sketch 50 ff
                This heard the bold Sir Bedivere & past
Within the tent & spake my Lord, the King
I find a feeble whiteness as of dawn
In the far East
Wilt thou not rise & follow to the West
And
That all the sooner we may turn again
And see the sunrise light the golden wings
That Merlin gave thine image on the hill.
                Then spake King Arthur
O thinkest thou we shall ever turn again
To light & sunrise in the golden East.
We follow night & sunset in the West
And those who love the King will die with me.
                And therewithal return'd on Bedivere
The burthen of a hymn himself had sung
He clash'd his arms together & he said
                King art thou in East & West
Strike for the King & die: let the King reign.   H-39

Second sketch 50 ff
                O Sir King shall one sin eat out the
                        memory of all
thy noble deeds. Remember Thou how many a time we
                        fought
the Godless heathen & conquerd. how often we drave
                        them
in the west & from the Roman wall & when Rome had
                        grown too
weak to drive the heathen but sent to us for her
                        tribute as of
old how we prevailed against her; & now thro' the
                        sin of
Lancelot Sir Modred hath brought in the heathen
                        again, &
some of their own knights & of the people whom
                        thou hast
made some against thee yet doubt not thou--and go
                        forth
& conquer as of old.   H-37

970

THE PASSING OF ARTHUR

'O me, my King, let pass whatever will,
Elves, and the harmless glamour of the field;
But in their stead thy name and glory cling
To all high places like a golden cloud
For ever: but as yet thou shalt not pass.   55
Light was Gawain in life, and light in death
Is Gawain, for the ghost is as the man;
And care not thou for dreams from him, but rise--
I hear the steps of Modred in the west,

Third sketch, lines 50-54
          And answer made the bold Sir Bedivere
     O me Sir King let elf & fairy pass
     But thy great name shall ever cleave & cling
     To all high places in this realm of thine. like
                    a golden cloud   H-37

(Three MS drafts exist for lines 50-64. Two are in A-S
one enclosed in B-VIII. These lines were first printed,
with variants, in L-HGI. All variants now follow, line
by line.)

51-2 ...King, let elf & fairy pass,   A-S

51 ..., my king,...   L-HGI
51 (C)   73

52 Elves, the harmless...   B-VIII

53 And in their stead...   A-S

55 ...thou shall not...   L-HGI
55 (C)   69

56 Gawain was light in life & light in death   A-S

57 ...for his ghost...   B-VIII

58 Care not for dreams but rise & let us hence,   A-S
58 ...dreams ø𝑓 from him...   B-VIII

59   steps
   ...the 𝑠ø𝑢𝑛𝑑 of Modred...   A-S

And with him many of thy people, and knights   60

---

60 And many of thy people with him move   A-S
60 ...people and...   L-HGI
60 (C)   69

61 And knights whom thou hast loved, but now far
                               worse   A-S
61 ...loved, but now far worse   A-S
61 ..., but baser now   B-VIII
61 ..., but baser now   L-HGI
61   grosser   I MS
    ..., but ~~baser~~ now   B-VIII
61 (C)   L-HGII

62 Than heathen who disclaim thee for their king.   A-S
62   scoff at their vows and thee
   Than heathen ~~who disclaim thee with thy lips~~ A-S
62 ...heathen, scoffing at...   B-VIII
62 ...heathen, scoffing at...   L-HGI
62   spitting   I MS
   ...heathen, ~~scoffing~~ at...   B-VIII
62 (C)   L-HGII

63 ...the king.   L-HGI
63 (C)   69

Sketch for 66 ff.
     O me this fight is far other than those wherein
we drove the heathen from the West or the Roman wall.
     I fight against my people & the knights whom
I have made And that is to me even as mine own death
     That sweet smile wh Guinevere & Lancelot
smiled in the Maywoods was cause of many deaths
     They say that I am no King: they ~~not~~ know
not nor do I myself whence I came.
                    is
     Theirs then the blame who fostered me, &
spake softly to me, & hold   (Continued)

972

THE PASSING OF ARTHUR

Once thine, whom thou hast loved, but grosser grown
Than heathen, spitting at their vows and thee.
Right well in heart they know thee for the King.
Arise, go forth and conquer as of old.'

Then spake King Arthur to Sir Bedivere: 65
'Far other is this battle in the west
Whereto we move, than when we strove in youth,
And brake the petty kings, and fought with Rome,

Sketch for 66 ff. continued

                                              me (1 ?)
                        nor ever let a foul word be spoken
            before me & (1 ?) me delicately, & showd me the
                                              fields
        & hills & said this is
            Thy realm for ever they told me that I was a
                                    king's son
            but that I sd not see my father on earth
            And I believed them & believe them still
            But arise & go if we can find a way
            For ever since I learnt the sin of Guinevere
                                    so dense a fog
            Had hidden the world
            Nevertheless arise & we will best these
                                    traitors (1 ?)   H-37

Sketch 66 ff
    (Par.) Far other is this fight from those of old
    Wherein we broke the heathen-like mine own death
                to me
    To fight against my people & the knights   H-37

(Lines 65-78 first printed L-HGI)

67 From those we fought when glorying in our youth   A-S
67   when
   ...than we fought in youth   A-S
67 ...youth   L-HGI
67 (C)   69

68 (Omitted)   L-HGI
68 (C)   73

973

THE PASSING OF ARTHUR

Or thrust the heathen from the Roman wall,
And shook him through the north. Ill doom is mine   70
To war against my people and my knights.
The king who fights his people fights himself.
And they my knights, who loved me once, the stroke
That strikes them dead is as my death to me.
Yet let us hence, and find or feel a way   75
Through this blind haze, which ever since I saw
One lying in the dust at Almesbury,
Hath folded in the passes of the world.'

    Then rose the King and moved his host by night,
And ever pushed Sir Modred, league by league,   80
Back to the sunset bound of Lyonnesse--

---

69 We push'd the heathen...	A-S
69 And thrust...	A-S
69 And thrust...	L-HGI
69 (C)	73

70-72 And shook them thro' the North. The king who
                    fights
        Against his people fights against himself.   A-S

71 To strive against...   A-S

73 ...knights - who...once - the...   L-HGI
73 (C)   L-HGII

75 ...hence and...   L-HGI
75 (C)   L-HGII

76 ...since I l̸e̸a̸r̸n̸d̸   A-S

Alt. after 76 T̸h̸a̸t̸ t̸h̸o̸s̸e̸ I̸ l̸o̸v̸e̸d̸ s̸o̸ f̸a̸i̸l̸e̸d̸ i̸n̸ l̸o̸v̸e̸ t̸o̸
                            m̸e̸   A-S

79 ...the king...night,   A-2104
79 ...the king...   L-HGI
79 (C)   69

81 ...Lyonesse.   A-2104
81 (C)   L-HGI

974

A land of old upheaven from the abyss
By fire, to sink into the abyss again;
Where fragments of forgotten peoples dwelt,
And the long mountains ended in a coast   85
Of ever-shifting sand, and far away
The phantom circle of a moaning sea.
There the pursuer could pursue no more,
And he that fled no further fly the King;
And there, that day when the great light of heaven   90
Burned at his lowest in the rolling year,
On the waste sand by the waste sea they closed.
Nor ever yet had Arthur fought a fight

82-84 (Omitted from proper sequence, appearing instead
          after 86 with 83 ending) ...again.   A-2104
82-84 (C) (In sequence)   L-HGI

85 There the long mountain ended...   A-2104
85 There ended the long mountain in a coast   S-925
85 ...mountain ended...   L-HGI
85 (C)   69

Alt. before 86 (Par.) King Arthur push'd Sir Modred
                         to the west,   A-S

86 On ever shifting...   A-S
86 Of ever shifting...   A-2104
86 (C)   L-HGI

89 And he that fled the King no further fly.   A-S
89 ...the king.   ☉   (☉ I)   A-2104
89 ...the king.   S-925
89 ...the king;   L-HGI
89 (C)   69

90 And that same day when the great light of
                         heaven   A-S

92 ...closed.   ☉   (☉ I)   A-2104
92 (C)   S-925

93 Never had Arthur foughten in s̸u̸c̸h̸ a fight   A-S

Like this last, dim, weird battle of the west.
A deathwhite mist slept over sand and sea: 95
Whereof the chill, to him who breathed it, drew
Down with his blood, till all his heart was cold
With formless fear; and even on Arthur fell
Confusion, since he saw not whom he fought.
For friend and foe were shadows in the mist,   100
And friend slew friend not knowing whom he slew;
And some had visions out of golden youth,
And some beheld the faces of old ghosts
Look in upon the battle; and in the mist
Was many a noble deed, many a base,   105
And chance and craft and strength in single fights,
And ever and anon with host to host

---

94 As like to this last wierd battle in the west.   A-S
94 ...the West.   A-2104
94 (C)   L-HGI

96 (Par.) And he who breathed i̸t̸s̸ the mist into
                         his blood   T-S

97 Was chill'd at heart with f̸o̸r̸m̸l̸e̸s̸s̸ doubt & form-
                         less fear   T-S
97 ...blood, till...   (, I)   A-2104
97 (C)   S-925

98 Of what sd come; & even on Arthur fell   T-S
98 ...fear, and...   A-2104
98 (C)   69

99 Confusion till he knew where he was,   T-S
99 Confusion, for he...fought,   A-2104
99 ...fought,   L-HGI
99 (C)   78

Alt. after 99
    Nor whence he was nor whether he were king
    And still the heathen shouted in the haze
    Proclaiming Modred lord of all the realm.   T-S

100 ...foe look'd shadows & so like   T-S
100 And friend...   A-2104
100 (C)   L-HGI

976

Shocks, and the splintering spear, the hard mail hewn,
Shield-breakings, and the clash of brands, the crash
Of battleaxes on shattered helms, and shrieks   110
After the Christ, of those who falling down
Looked up for heaven, and only saw the mist;
And shouts of heathen and the traitor knights ,
Oaths, insult, filth, and monstrous blasphemies,
Sweat, writhings, anguish, labouring of the lungs   115
In that close mist, and cryings for the light,
Moans of the dying, and voices of the dead.

    Last, as by some one deathbed after wail

---

101 For friend struck friend not seeing - so close &
                          thick   A-S
101 That friend...not seeing whom...   T-S

105 ff. Were noble deeds & base & chance & strength
                          & ever & anon
        Shocks & the splintering   T-S

108 Were splintering of rough spears & hard mail
                          hewn   A-S

110 ...on shatter'd casques, & cries   A-S

111 After the X t from those...   A-S
111 ...Christ, of...   (, I)   A-2104
111 (C)   S-925

112 ...up to Heaven...   A-S
112 ...heaven, and...   (, I)   A-2104
112 (C)   S-925

115 ...writhings, wounds & labouring...   A-S

116 In that thick host & callings for the light   A-S

117 ...dying and...   A-2104
117 (C)   69

118 (Par.) Last as...   A-2104
118 (C)   L-HGI

Of suffering, silence follows, or through death
Or deathlike swoon, thus over all that shore,   120
Save for some whisper of the seething seas,
A dead hush fell; but when the dolorous day
Grew drearier toward twilight falling, came
A bitter wind, clear from the North, and blew
The mist aside, and with that wind the tide   125
Rose, and the pale King glanced across the field
Of battle: but no man was moving there;
Nor any cry of Christian heard thereon,
Nor yet of heathen; only the wan wave
Brake in among dead faces, to and fro   130
Swaying the helpless hands, and up and down
Tumbling the hollow helmets of the fallen,
And shivered brands that once had fought with Rome,

---

119 ...suffering, silence...   ,/ (I)   A-2104
119 (C)   S-925

120 Or deathlike swooning, over all that shore   A-2104
120 (C)   L-HGI

121 (Omitted)   A-2104
121 (C)   L-HGI

122 But   at length
    Then all was silent & that dim day   T-S
122   dolorous   I MS
    ...when the d̶r̶e̶a̶r̶y̶ day   A-2104
122 (C)   S-925

123   yet
    Grew dimmer in the closing twilight, came   T-S

124   bitter
    There came a wind, clear...   T-S

126 Rose & King Arthur look'd across...   T-S
126 Rose and the pale king...   A-2104
126 ...pale king...   S-295
126 (C)   73

127 Of battle; but...there   A-2104
127 Of battle; but...   S-925
127 (C)   L-HGI

And rolling far along the gloomy shores
The voice of days of old and days to be.   135

    Then spake King Arthur to Sir Bedivere,
And whiter than the mist that all day long
Had held the field of battle was the King:

    'Hearest thou this great voice that shakes the
                    world,

---

128 ...of Xn on the sand	T-S
128 ...thereon	A-2104
128 (C)	69
129 Nor any heathen; only the gray wave	T-S
129 ...the waste wave	A-2109
129 wan	I MS
...the ~~waste~~ wave	L-HGI;B-VIII
129 (C)	L-HGII
130 ...among the faces of the dead	T-S
132 Tumbling	
~~Rolling~~ the hollow...	T-S
132 ...helmets, of...	A-2104
132 (C)	73
133 And broken brands that once had the world	T-S
133 And brands that once had fought with mighty	
Rome	T-S
133 spears	I MS
...shiver'd ~~brands~~ that...	A-2104
133 (C)	S-925
134 rolling gloomy	
And ~~sending~~ far along the ~~dreary~~ shores	T-S
136 ...Bedivere	A-2104
136 (C)	S-925
138 ...the king.	A-2104
138 (C)	L-HGI
139 ...world	A-2104
139 (C)	S-925

And wastes the narrow realm whereon we move,   140
And beats upon the faces of the dead,
My dead, as though they had not died for me?--
O Bedivere, for on my heart hath fallen
Confusion, till I know not what I am,
Nor whence I am, nor whether I be King.   145
Behold, I seem but King among the dead.'

    Then spake the bold Sir Bedivere: 'My King,
King everywhere! and so the dead have kings,
There also will I worship thee as King.
Yet still thy life is whole, and still I live   150
Who love thee; but who hates thee, he that brought
The heathen back among us, yonder stands,
Modred, unharmed, the traitor of thine house.'

---

142 ...for me -	A-2104
142 (C)	L-HGI
144 ...know not where I am	W-S
144 Confusion till I know not where I am,	A-2104
144 ...not where I am,	S-925
144 (C)	L-HGI
145 ...be king.	A-2104
145 (C)	73
146 Behold, I am but king...	W-S
146 Behold, I am but king among...	A-2104
146 ...but king...	L-HGI
146 (C)	73
147 ...Bedivere, 'My king,	A-2104
147 (C)	L-HGI
148 ...kings	A-2104
148 (C)	S-925
149 ...as king.	A-2104
149 (C)	73
150 ...whole and...	A-2104
150 (C)	L-HGI

THE PASSING OF ARTHUR

   Then spake the King: 'My house hath been my doom.
But call not thou this traitor of my house   155
Who hath but dwelt beneath one roof with me.
My house are rather they who sware my vows,
Yea, even while they brake them, owned me King.
And well for thee, saying in my dark hour,
When all the purport of my throne hath failed,   160
That quick or dead thou holdest me for King.

Sketch 154 ff. spake the King
   (Par.) Then ~~answerd Arthur groaning Woe is me~~
  ~~That/I who drave the heathen here so slept~~
  ~~To mine house~~ my house hath been my doom.   W-S

154 ...the king, 'My...   A-2104
154 (C)   L-HGII

(Lines 154-156 lined out in L-HGI and the following
substituted in I MS.)
   Then spake the King I have but slept who drave
   The Heathen hence: My house hath been my doom.
   But call not thou this traitor of my house
   Who ~~did~~ dwelt awhile beneath one roof with me L-HGI

157-159
   My house are rather they who sware my vows
   Yea, even while they break them, owned me king.
                        (,, I)
   And well for thee, saying in my dark hour,
                     (1st, I) A-2109
157-159   ~~kept~~ out   I MS
   My house are rather they who ~~sware~~ my vows,
   And none have kept the vows nor they nor those I MS
   Yea, even while they brake them own'd me king.
   Yet   I MS
 ~~And~~ well for thee, saying in my dark hour, L-HGI
157-159 (C-save) (158) ...me king.   L-HGII
158 (C)   73

161 ...for king.   A-2104
161 (C)   73

THE PASSING OF ARTHUR

King am I, whatsoever be their cry;
And one last act of kinghood shalt thou see
Yet, ere I pass.' And uttering this the King
Made at the man: then Modred smote his liege   165
Hard on that helm which many a heathen sword
Had beaten thin; while Arthur at one blow,
Striking the last stroke with Excalibur,
Slew him, and all but slain himself, he fell.

    So all day long the noise of battle rolled   170
Among the mountains by the winter sea;

─────────────
162 ...I whatsoever...cry.   A-2104
162 (C)   L-HGI

164 Yet ere I pass,;' and uttering this the king
                              ;/ (I)   A-2104
164 Yet ere I pass;' and uttering this the king   S-925
164 Yet ere...the king   L-HGI
164 ...the king   69
164 (C)   73

165 ...man; then...   A-2104
165 (C)   L-HGI

166 Hard on a helm, which...   A-2104
166 (C)   L-HGI

167 ...thin, while...blow   A-2104
167 (C)   L-HGI

168 ...Excalibur   A-2104
168 (C)   L-HGI

172 ...Arthur's table, man...   42
172 (C)   L-HGI

173 ...their Lord,   42
173 (C)   L-HGI

Alt. preceding 174
    After the battle where King Arthur lost
    The flowers   all   earth
    The honour (?) of the w̸o̸r̸l̸d̸, his knights, wh
                         made   Tn-17

982

THE PASSING OF ARTHUR

Until King Arthur's Table, man by man,
Had fallen in Lyonnesse about their lord,
King Arthur. Then, because his wound was deep,
The bold Sir Bedivere uplifted him,   175
And bore him to a chapel nigh the field,
A broken chancel with a broken cross,
That stood on a dark strait of barren land:
On one side lay the Ocean, and on one
Lay a great water, and the moon was full.   180

    Then spake King Arthur to Sir Bedivere:

———————————
Alt. preceding 174
      After that battle where King Arthur lost
      The flower of all the earth, his knights, which
                              made   Tn-17

174 'The table round,' because his wound was deep   Tn-17
174 THE TABLE ROUND, because his wound was deep   H-21
174 ...Arthur: then, because...   42
174 (C)   L-HGI

Alt. after 175 Sir Bedivere, the last of all his
                              knights   Tn-17
Alt. after 175 Sir Bedivere, the last of all his
                              knights,   42
Alt. after 175 (C)   L-HGI

176   nigh
    ...chapel f̷r̷o̷m̷ the field,   Tn-17

177   ncel
    ...broken chap̷e̷l̷ with   Tn-17

178 ...land.   42
178 (C)   L-HGI

(In A-2104, quotation marks from line 181-432 are the
reverse of the system otherwise used throughout the
volume; i.e. first quotations double, internal quotations single quotation marks. This is corrected in
L-HGI.)

181 (Par.) Then spoke King...   Tn-17

THE PASSING OF ARTHUR

'The sequel of today unsolders all
The goodliest fellowship of famous knights
Whereof this world holds record. Such a sleep
They sleep--the men I loved. I think that we   185
Shall never more, at any future time,
Delight our souls with talk of knightly deeds,
Walking about the gardens and the halls
Of Camelot, as in the days that were.
I perish by this people which I made,--   190
Though Merlin sware that I should come again
To rule once more; but, let what will be, be,
I am so deeply smitten through the helm
That without help I cannot last till morn.
Thou therefore take my brand Excalibur,   195
Which was my pride: for thou rememberest how

Alt. after 181
    'Well said old Merlin ere his time was come
    "Experience never closes all-in-all
    But there is always something to be learned
    Even in the gate of Death." 'So clear a dream -
    Which I neglected with my waking mind -
    Came yesternight - Sir Gawaine as he lived -
    Most like Sir Gawain in his eyes & hair -
    Bareheaded, circled with a gracious light
    Seven ladies like the seven rainy stars
    For whom he fought & whom he saved from shame
    Beautiful, tearful: & he spoke & said
    Go thou not forth tomorrow to the fight
    But I went forth & fought it & lie here.   Tn-17

182 The issue of this day unsolders quite   Tn-17

184 Whereof the world...   Tn-17

185   the men I loved
    They sleep - I̶ t̶h̶e that we, I think, s̶h̶a̶l̶l̶
                    n̶e̶v̶e̶r̶m̶o̶r̶e̶   Tn-17

186 ...shall nevermore, at...   42

188 Walking among the...   Tn-17

191 Though Merlin...   42

        984

THE PASSING OF ARTHUR

In those old days, one summer noon, an arm
Rose up from out the bosom of the lake,
Clothed in white samite, mystic, wonderful,
Holding the sword--and how I rowed across   200
And took it, and have worn it, like a king;
And, wheresoever I am sung or told
In aftertime, this also shall be known:
But now delay not: take Excalibur,
And fling him far into the middle mere: 205
Watch what thou seest, and lightly bring me word.'

    To him replied the bold Sir Bedivere:
'It is not meet, Sir King, to leave thee thus,
Aidless, alone, and smitten through the helm--
A little thing may harm a wounded man;   210

---

192 ...more - but let...	42
192 ...; but let...	L-HGI
192 (C)	73
195 brand	
...my s̷w̷o̷r̷d̷ Excalibur	Tn-17
197 In the old days, one summer noon, there came	Tn-17
197 In the old days one summer noon there rose	Hth
198 From forth the peaceful bosom...	Tn-17
198 An arm from out the bosom...	Hth
199 An arm, clothed in white samite, wonderful	Tn-17
201 ...king:	42
201 (C)	L-HGI
203 In after years, this...	Tn-17
209 ...the healm.	42
209 (C)	L-HGI
210 ...man.	42
210 (C)	L-HGI

Yet I thy hest will all perform at full,
Watch what I see, and lightly bring thee word.'

   So saying, from the ruined shrine he stept,
And in the moon athwart the place of tombs,
Where lay the mighty bones of ancient men,   215
Old knights, and over them the sea-wind sang
Shrill, chill, with flakes of foam. He, stepping down
By zigzag paths, and juts of pointed rock,
Came on the shining levels of the lake.

   There drew he forth the brand Excalibur,   220
And o'er him, drawing it, the winter moon,
Brightening the skirts of a long cloud, ran forth
And sparkled keen with frost against the hilt:
For all the haft twinkled with diamond sparks,
Myriads of topaz-lights, and jacinth-work   225
Of subtlest jewellery. He gazed so long

---

211 But yet thy hest will I perform at full   Tn-17

Sketch 213-219
   (Par.) So saying from the ancient shrine he stept
   Into the moonlight: thro' the place of tombs
   Where lay the mighty bones of ancient men,
   Heroes - & stepping down from rock to rock
   He reached the shining levels of the lake.   Tn-17

213 ...shrine he went   Tn-17
213 ...stept   A-2104
213 (C)   L-HGI

214 ...in the moonlight thro' the place...   Tn-17

216 Heroes & over...   Tn-17

217 Shrill, cold with...   Tn-17

218 Thro' zigzag...   Tn-17
218 By
    Thro' zigzag...   Tn-17

220 (Par.) Then drew...   Tn-17

221 And over him the frosty moon ran out   Tn-17

That both his eyes were dazzled as he stood,
This way and that dividing the swift mind,
In act to throw: but at the last it seemed
Better to leave Excalibur concealed   230
There in the many-knotted waterflags,
That whistled stiff and dry about the marge.
So strode he back slow to the wounded King.

      Then spake King Arthur to Sir Bedivere:
'Hast thou performed my mission which I gave?   235
What is it thou hast seen? or what hast heard?'

      And answer made the bold Sir Bedivere:
'I heard the ripple washing in the reeds,
And the wild water lapping on the crag.'

      To whom replied King Arthur, faint and pale: 240
'Thou hast betrayed thy nature and thy name,
Not rendering true answer, as beseemed

Alt. 222-226
      So keenly, that he marvelled, tho he bore
      A hard unbroken spirit in his breast:
      For all the heft twinkled with diamond-studs
      Or glowed with topaz-stone. He gazed so long   Tn-17

224 ...diamond-studs   Tn-17
224 ...diamond studs,   42
224 (C)   A-2104

227 ...he mused   Tn-17
227 ...dazzled, as...   42
227 (C)   L-HGI

229 ...throw & at...   Tn-17

231 Amongst the many...   Tn-17

233 ...wounded king.   42

234 (Par.) Then spoke King...   Tn-17

239 ...water wrapping on...   Tn-17

241-242 Thou hast not spoken truly as beseemed   Tn-17

Thy fealty, nor like a noble knight:
For surer sign had followed, either hand,
Or voice, or else a motion of the mere.   245
This is a shameful thing for men to lie.
Yet now, I charge thee, quickly go again,
As thou art lief and dear, and do the thing
I bade thee, watch, and lightly bring me word.'

    Then went Sir Bedivere the second time   250
Across the ridge, and paced beside the mere,
Counting the dewy pebbles, fixed in thought;
But when he saw the wonder of the hilt,
How curiously and strangely chased, he smote

Sketch after 243
    It is a shameful thing for man to lie
    For he betrays his nature & his Lord.
    But now, I charge thee, quickly/go again,
    As thou art lief & dear, & do the deed
    I bad thee, watch & lightly bring me word.   Tn-17

247 But now...   Tn-17
247 ...go again   42
247 (C)   L-HGI

250 ...Bedivere, a second...   Hth
250 ...time,   42

251-252 With eyes, counting the stones, fixt in
                                resolve   Tn-17

255 ...aloud.   42
255 (C)   L-HGI

256 (Par.) Ay me!   & should I cast...   Tn-17

260-261 This done what good should follow?   harm,
                                undone   Tn-17

261   Deep harm
   What harm, undone? There well to disobey,
   And yet in disobedience/lies/great//harm.   Tn-17
261 ...undone? deep...   42
261 (C)   L-HGI

988

His palms together, and he cried aloud: 255

    'And if indeed I cast the brand away,
Surely a precious thing, one worthy note,
Should thus be lost for ever from the earth,
Which might have pleased the eyes of many men.
What good should follow this, if this were done?   260
What harm, undone? Deep harm to disobey,
Seeing obedience is the bond of rule.
Were it well to obey then, if a king demand
An act unprofitable, against himself?
The King is sick, and knows not what he does.   265
What record, or what relic of my lord
Should be to aftertime, but empty breath
And rumours of a doubt? But were this kept,
Stored in some treasure-house of mighty kings,
Some one might show it at a joust of arms,   270
Saying, "King Arthur's sword, Excalibur,
Wrought by the lonely maiden of the Lake.
Nine years she wrought it, sitting in the deeps
Upon the hidden bases of the hills."

---

262 B̸e̸c̸a̸u̸s̸e̸ obedience...   Tn-17
262 Because obedience...   Hth

263   demand
    ...a King r̸e̸q̸u̸i̸r̸e̸   Tn-17

264   unprofitable
    ...act w̸h̸i̸c̸h̸ p̸r̸o̸f̸i̸t̸s̸ n̸o̸t̸, against...   Tn-17

Alt. after 264 A question to be answered without
                              fear.   Tn-17

268 ...doubt? Say, this were kept   Tn-17
268 ...doubt? but...   42
268 (C)   L-HGI

272 ...the prudent Lady of the Lake.   Tn-17

273 ...it in the silent deeps   Tn-17

274   hidden   hills
    And by the s̸e̸c̸r̸e̸t̸ bases of the r̸o̸c̸k̸s̸"   Tn-17

So might some old man speak in the aftertime   275
To all the people, winning reverence.
But now much honour and much fame were lost.'

    So spake he, clouded with his own conceit,
And hid Excalibur the second time,
And so strode back slow to the wounded King.   280

    Then spoke King Arthur, breathing heavily:
'What is it thou hast seen? or what hast heard?'

    And answer made the bold Sir Bedivere:
'I heard the water lapping on the crag,
And the long ripple washing in the reeds.'   285

    To whom replied King Arthur, much in wrath:
'Ah, miserable and unkind, untrue,
Unknightly, traitor-hearted! Woe is me!
Authority forgets a dying king,
Laid widowed of the power in his eye   290

---

278 (Par.) So spoke he...   Tn-17

281 ...Arthur drawing thicker breath   Tn-17

284 ...water wapping on...   Tn-17

286 ...Arthur red with scorn.   Tn-17
286 ...Arthur filled with scorn.   Tn-17

288 Unknightly, sordid-hearted. N̸o̸w̸ I̸ s̸e̸e̸ Woe
                                   is me!   Tn-17

289 Authority deserts a dying...   Tn-17

291 ...thou art.   42

292 ...knights   69
292 (C)   73

295 Either for lust...   Tn-17

297 Yet
    B̸u̸t̸ - for...   Tn-17

    990

That bowed the will. I see thee what thou art,
For thou, the latest-left of all my knights,
In whom should meet the offices of all,
Thou wouldst betray me for the precious hilt;
Either from lust of gold, or like a girl   295
Valuing the giddy pleasure of the eyes.
Yet, for a man may fail in duty twice,
And the third time may prosper, get thee hence:
But, if thou spare to fling Excalibur,
I will arise and slay thee with my hands.'   300

    Then quickly rose Sir Bedivere, and ran,
And, leaping down the ridges lightly, plunged
Among the bulrush beds, and clutched the sword,
And strongly wheeled and threw it. The great brand
Made lightnings in the splendour of the moon,   305
And flashing round and round, and whirled in an arch,
Shot like a streamer of the northern morn,
Seen where the moving isles of winter shock

---

299 ...thou fail to fling...   Tn-17

301 (Par.) Then lightly rose...   Tn-17

302 And springing goatlike down the ledges,
                                plunged   Tn-17

303 Amongst   clutcht
    I̶n̶t̶o̶ the withered sedge & t̶o̶o̶k̶ the sword   Tn-17
303 Among the bullrush-reeds and...   H-21
303 ...the bulrush-beds, and...   42
303 (C)   73

304 ...strongly wheeling threw...   Tn-17

Sketch 305-310
    Spun flashing round & round & whirled in an arch
                ed   flying noise
    S̶u̶n̶k̶, whizzing like a f̶l̶i̶g̶h̶t̶ of fiery stones
    Shot
    F̶l̶u̶n̶g̶ from the moon. So flasht Excalibur.   Tn-17

308 ...moving thrones of winter...   Hth

By night, with noises of the Northern Sea.
So flashed and fell the brand Excalibur: 310
But ere he dipt the surface, rose an arm
Clothed in white samite, mystic, wonderful,
And caught him by the hilt, and brandished him
Three times, and drew him under in the mere.
And lightly went the other to the King.   315

    Then spoke King Arthur, drawing thicker breath:
'Now see I by thine eyes that this is done.
Speak out: what is it thou hast heard, or seen?'

    And answer made the bold Sir Bedivere:
'Sir King, I closed mine eyelids, lest the gems   320
Should blind my purpose, for I never saw,
Nor shall see, here or elsewhere, till I die,
Not though I live three lives of mortal men,
So great a miracle as yonder hilt.
Then with both hands I flung him, wheeling him;   325
But when I looked again, behold an arm,
Clothed in white samite, mystic, wonderful,
That caught him by the hilt, and brandished him
Three times, and drew him under in the mere.'

    And answer made King Arthur, breathing hard: 330
'My end draws nigh; 'tis time that I were gone.
Make broad thy shoulders to receive my weight,

---

309 ...the northern sea.   42
309 (C)   73

315 So lightly...   Tn-17

316 Then spoke the wounded Arthur, faint & pale   Tn-17

318 What is it thou hast seen? or what hast
                              heard   Tn-17
318 ...seen!"   42

319 To whom replied the bold...   Tn-17

323 Not though I...   42

325 ...him,   42

And bear me to the margin; yet I fear
My wound hath taken cold, and I shall die.'

   So saying, from the pavement he half rose,   335
Slowly, with pain, reclining on his arm,
And looking wistfully with wide blue eyes
As in a picture. Him Sir Bedivere
Remorsefully regarded through his tears,
And would have spoken, but he found not words;   340
Then took with care, and kneeling on one knee,
O'er both his shoulders drew the languid hands,
And rising bore him through the place of tombs.

   But, as he walked, King Arthur panted hard,
Like one that feels a nightmare on his bed   345
When all the house is mute. So sighed the King,
Muttering and murmuring at his ear, 'Quick, quick!
I fear it is too late, and I shall die.'
But the other swiftly strode from ridge to ridge,
Clothed with his breath, and looking, as he walked, 350
Larger than human on the frozen hills.
He heard the deep behind him, and a cry
Before. His own thought drove him like a goad.

339-341 Gently received & kneeling on one knee   Tn-17

340 ...not words,   42
340 (C)   L-HGI

Sketch 344-358
    (Par.) But ever as he went King Arthur breathed
    Against his shoulder heavily like one
    That hath not full an hour left to live.
    So stept he carefully from ledge to ledge
    Wrapt in his breath, & shunning where the rock
    Looked brighter glazed with ice, made firm his foot
    On juts of slippery crag that rang like (tin ?)
    Sharp smitten with the dint of mailed heels   Tn-17

347 ...ear "Quick...   42
347 ...ear 'Quick...   L-HGI
347 (C)   73

```
Dry clashed his harness in the icy caves
And barren chasms, and all to left and right        355
The bare black cliff clanged round him, as he based
His feet on juts of slippery crag that rang
Sharp-smitten with the dint of armed heels--
And on a sudden, lo! the level lake,
And the long glories of the winter moon.            360

    Then saw they how there hove a dusky barge,
Dark as a funeral scarf from stem to stern,
Beneath them; and descending they were ware
That all the decks were dense with stately forms,
Black-stoled, black-hooded, like a dream--by these  365
Three Queens with crowns of gold:  and from them
                                    rose
A cry that shivered to the tingling stars,
And, as it were one voice, an agony
Of lamentation, like a wind that shrills
All night in a waste land, where no one comes,      370
Or hath come, since the making of the world.
```

```
355 ...all from left to right                        H-21

357 ...slippery crag crag that ran                   Hth

364 ...forms                                          42

366 ...gold - and...                                  42
366 (C)                                              L-HGI

368 ...it were a voice...                            H-21

369 ...wind, that...                                  42
369 (C)                                              L-HGI

372 (Par.) Then murmur'd Arthur "Get thee down
                               with speed            H-21
372 ...barge,"                                        42
372 ...barge;'                                       L-HGI
372 (C)                                               73
```

Then murmured Arthur, 'Place me in the barge.'
So to the barge they came. There those three Queens
Put forth their hands, and took the King, and wept.
But she, that rose the tallest of them all   375
And fairest, laid his head upon her lap,
And loosed the shattered casque, and chafed his hands,
And called him by his name, complaining loud,
And dropping bitter tears against a brow
Striped with dark blood: for all his face was white 380
And colourless, and like the withered moon
Smote by the fresh beam of the springing east;
And all his greaves and cuisses dashed with drops
Of onset; and the light and lustrous curls--
That made his forehead like a rising sun   385
High from the daïs-throne--were parched with dust;
Or, clotted into points and hanging loose,
Mixed with the knightly growth that fringed his lips.
So like a shattered column lay the King;

373-374 And those three Queens received him, weeping
                              wild   Tn-17
373 And place me in the barge.' and those three
                              Queens   H-21
373 And to the...   42
373 (C)   69

375   rose
   ...that was the...   Tn-17

379 ...against his brow   Tn-17
379 ...against his brow   42
379 (C)   73

385 Which made...   Tn-17
385 ...rising star   H-21

386 ...with dust,   42

388 ...the stubborn growth...   Tn-17

Not like that Arthur who, with lance in rest, 390
From spur to plume a star of tournament,
Shot through the lists at Camelot, and charged
Before the eyes of ladies and of kings.

    Then loudly cried the bold Sir Bedivere:
'Ah! my Lord Arthur, whither shall I go? 395
Where shall I hide my forehead and my eyes?
For now I see the true old times are dead,
When every morning brought a noble chance,
And every chance brought out a noble knight.
Such times have been not since the light that led 400
The holy Elders with the gift of myrrh.
But now the whole Round Table is dissolved
Which was an image of the mighty world,
And I, the last, go forth companionless,
And the days darken round me, and the years, 405
Among new men, strange faces, other minds.'

    And slowly answered Arthur from the barge:

Sketch 390 ff
    ~~Unlike that Arthur who with lance in rest~~
    ~~Rapidly galloping at Camelot~~
    Not
    ~~Un~~like that Arthur who, with lance in rest
    ~~From/spur/to plume a star of tournament,~~
    ~~Rapidly galloping at Camelot, charged~~
            & of Kings
    Before the eyes of ladies ~~thrice as fair~~
    ~~As those that win the love of modern men~~ Tn-17
Sketch 390 ff
    ~~Rapidly galloping in the list, went by~~
    From spur to plume a star of tournament
    Rapidly galloping at Camelot charged
            ? charged at Camelot Tn-17

392 Rapidly galloping at Camelot charged Hth

394 ...Bedivere, 42
394 (C) L-HGI

402 ...whole ROUND TABLE is... 42
402 (C) L-HGI

'The old order changeth, yielding place to new,
And God fulfils himself in many ways,
Lest one good custom should corrupt the world.   410
Comfort thyself: what comfort is in me?
I have lived my life, and that which I have done
May He within himself make pure! but thou,
If thou shouldst never see my face again,
Pray for my soul. More things are wrought by
                              prayer   415
Than this world dreams of. Wherefore, let thy voice
Rise like a fountain for me night and day.
For what are men better than sheep or goats
That nourish a blind life within the brain,
If, knowing God, they lift not hands of prayer   420
Both for themselves and those who call them friend?
For so the whole round earth is every way
Bound by gold chains about the feet of God.
But now farewell. I am going a long way
With these thou seest--if indeed I go   425
(For all my mind is clouded with a doubt)--

---

407   slowly
     (Par.) And clearly answered...   Tn-17

Alt. after 407 ~~Comfort thyself: what comfort is in
                    me?~~   Tn-17

413 ...but thou -   42

417 Rise ~~for me~~, as a fountain...   Tn-17
417 Rise, as a fountain...   Hth

Sketch 424-432
     ~~Farewell then! / I am going a long way
     To the island→valley of Avilion
     If/I/may heal me of my grievous wound~~   Tn-17

424 And now...   H-153a

425 ...I go -   42
425 (C)   L-HGI

426 ...doubt]   42
426 (C)   L-HGI

```
To the island-valley of Avilion;
Where falls not hail, or rain, or any snow,
Nor ever wind blows loudly; but it lies
Deep-meadowed, happy, fair with orchard lawns          430
And bowery hollows crowned with summer sea,
Where I will heal me of my grievous wound.'

   So said he, and the barge with oar and sail
Moved from the brink, like some full-breasted swan
That, fluting a wild carol ere her death,               435
Ruffles her pure cold plume, and takes the flood
With swarthy webs.  Long stood Sir Bedivere
Revolving many memories, till the hull
```

---

430 ...with orchard-lawns	42
430 (C)	73
432 There I may heal...	H-159a
435 That piping a wild...	Tn-17
436 ...cold plumes &...	Tn-17

Sketch c. 441 ff.
```
   At length he groan'd saying Are these dark Queens
   They that sd help King Arthur at his need?
   Then came a sound as of a shouting heard
   Far off when some fair city is one voice
   Around her king returning from his wars.
```
~~He/Heard &/moved about & slowly clomb~~

Then moved Sir Bedivere &	A-S
441-445 (Omitted)	A-2104
441-445 (Added)	73

```
446 (Par.) At length he groan'd and turning slowly
                    clomb                          A-2104
446 (Par.) At length he groan'd, and turning slowly
                    clomb                          S-925
446 (C)                                            73
```

998

Looked one black dot against the verge of dawn,
And on the mere the wailing died away.   440

    But when that moan had past for evermore,
The stillness of the dead world's winter dawn
Amazed him, and he groaned, 'The King is gone.'
And therewithal came on him the weird rhyme,
'From the great deep to the great deep he goes.'   445

    Whereat he slowly turned and slowly clomb
The last hard footstep of that iron crag;
Thence marked the black hull moving yet, and cried,
'He passes to be King among the dead,
And after healing of his grievous wound   450
He comes again; but--if he come no more--

---

447 ...crag;	(; I)	A-2104
447 ...crag,		S-925
447 (C)		L-HGI
448 Thence		MS
A̸n̸d̸ mark'd the black hull moving yet, and		
thought		A-2104
448 And mark'd the black hull moving yet, and		
thought		S-925
448 (C)		L-HGI
449 ...be king among...		A-2104
449 (C)		73
450 (Omitted)		A-2104
450 (C)		L-HGI
451 But comes again,' then turn'd once more and		
clomb		A-2104
451 But comes again,' then turn'd once more, and		
clomb		S-925
451 He comes again - but, if he come no more,		L-HGI
451 (C)		L-HGII

THE PASSING OF ARTHUR

O me, be yon dark Queens in yon black boat,
Who shrieked and wailed, the three whereat we gazed
On that high day, when, clothed with living light,
They stood before his throne in silence, friends   455
Of Arthur, who should help him at his need?'

    Then from the dawn it seemed there came, but faint
As from beyond the limit of the world,
Like the last echo born of a great cry,
Sounds, as if some fair city were one voice   460

_____

Sketch 452 ff   & then he spake & wept
        O me, my lord the King, be these dark Queens
               ye   at
        With whom h̷e̷ past the three where̷o̷n̷ we gazed
        On
        T̷h̷e̷n̷ that high day when clothed with living light
                       thy
        They stood beside h̷i̷s̷ throne in silence, friends
                       thee
        Of Arthur who sd help h̷i̷m̷ at his need?   A-S

(452-462 omitted from A-2104 and S-925.
Added in L-HGI.)

452 ...me, be...   ,/ (I)   L-HGI
452 (C)   L-HGII

454 ...day when, ...   L-HGI
454 (C)   69

Sketch 457 ff it seem'd
        And then   that, fainter than the last
        Of many echoes awaken'd by one cry
        Among the hollow hills, there came the sound
        Of some far people in their time of joy   A-S

1000

THE PASSING OF ARTHUR

Around a king returning from his wars.

    Thereat once more he moved about, and clomb
Even to the highest he could climb, and saw,
Straining his eyes beneath an arch of hand,
Or thought he saw, the speck that bare the King,   465
Down that long water opening on the deep
Somewhere far off, pass on and on, and go
From less to less and vanish into light.
And the new sun rose bringing the new year.

---

462 Whereat he moved about once more & clomb   A-S

465 Or thought he saw the speck that bare the
                                king   A-2104
465 Or thought he saw the speck that bare the
                                king,   S-925
465 ...the king,   L-HGI
465 (C)   73

466 ...opening out to sea   A-2104
466 (C)   L-HGI

467 ...and on and go   A-2104
467 (C)   S-925

469 And   rose   MS
    Then rose the new sun bringing the new year. A-2104
469 (C)   L-HGI

Alt. after 469
    And on the heart of Bedivere rushed a
    A thorne of Merlin, /Where is he who knows?
    From the great deep to the great deep he goes./
                                    A-2104
Alt. after 469 (C)   L-HGI

Epilogue—To the Queen

O loyal to the royal in thyself,
And loyal to thy land, as this to thee--
Bear witness, that rememberable day,
When, pale as yet, and fever-worn, the Prince
Who scarce had plucked his flickering life again   5
From halfway down the shadow of the grave,
Past with thee through thy people and their love,
And London rolled one tide of joy through all
Her trebled millions, and loud leagues of man
And welcome! witness, too, the silent cry,   10
The prayer of many a race and creed, and clime--
Thunderless lightnings striking under sea

Alt. 2 The stainless ruler of a loyal realm -   H-32

3 ...rememberable morn   H-32

4   ǿʈ šȼȼm̸ȳđ the goodly
  When fever-pale, as yet, ǿȕʈ ǥǿǿđl̸ȳ Prince,   H-32

7 ˉᴘast
  Ɍǿđȼ with...   H-32

8   šẅáʈm̸ȋn̸ǥ   one tide of
  And l̸ǿȳál London roll'd h̸ȼʈ joy thro' all   H-32

11 The prayer of
  Fʈǿm̸ many a šȕb̸jȼȼʈ people, creed...   H-32

1003

TO THE QUEEN

From sunset and sunrise of all thy realm,
And that true North, whereof we lately heard
A strain to shame us 'keep you to yourselves;   15
So loyal is too costly! friends--your love
Is but a burthen: loose the bond, and gò.'
Is this the tone of empire? here the faith
That made us rulers? this, indeed, her voice
And meaning, whom the roar of Hougoumont   20
Left mightiest of all peoples under heaven?
What shock has fooled her since, that she should
                    speak

---

13   2   1
     From sunrise & sunset of...   H-32

15 A strain that shamed us 'Keep ye to...   H-32

16 For here we sicken of your loyalty: H-32

17 Your love is as a burthen: get you gone!'   H-32

18   this our faith
     Are these the tones of Empire? this our trust   H-32

Sketch c. 18-19
                              ~~this our trust~~
     ~~In our strong selves/ hearts/ hands & the (faithy~~
                              ~~That~~
     ~~Wh rules & made us rulers?~~   H-32

19 That   did (1 ?) is
     ~~In Him who~~ made us rulers? this her voice   H-32

21 ...peoples in the West?   H-32

22   shock   s fool'd
     What ~~chance~~ hath ~~shock'd~~ her...   H-32

26 ~~We know/the voice/ we heard it when they peal'd~~
     There rang her voice when all thy city peal'd   H-32

27   crown
     ...to their ~~Queen~~   H-32

1004

TO THE QUEEN

So feebly? wealthier--wealthier--hour by hour!
The voice of Britain, or a sinking land,
Some third-rate isle half-lost among her seas?   25
There rang her voice, when the full city pealed
Thee and thy Prince! The loyal to their crown
Are loyal to their own far sons, who love
Our ocean-empire with her boundless homes
For ever-broadening England, and her throne   30
In our vast Orient, and one isle, one isle,
That knows not her own greatness: if she knows
And dreads it we are fallen.—But thou, my Queen,
Not for itself, but through thy living love
For one to whom I made it o'er his grave   35
Sacred, accept this old imperfect tale,

Draft 28-36

                            own fair sons, who love
        Are loyal to their E̷m̷p̷i̷r̷e̷/̷&̷/̷n̷o̷t̷/̷p̷a̷s̷t̷/̷/̷1̷/̷7̷y̷
                f̷a̷i̷r̷   h̷o̷l̷d̷i̷n̷g̷ b̷y̷   t̷h̷i̷n̷e̷
        T̷h̷e̷i̷r̷ o̷w̷n̷ s̷o̷n̷s̷ b̷a̷c̷k̷ f̷r̷o̷m̷ c̷l̷e̷a̷v̷i̷n̷g̷ t̷o̷ t̷h̷e̷ c̷r̷o̷w̷n̷
        This T̷h̷e̷i̷r̷ ancient Ocean empire, & her throne
        T̷h̷e̷ s̷t̷r̷e̷a̷m̷ h̷a̷s̷ b̷o̷r̷n̷e̷ m̷e̷ d̷o̷w̷n̷ b̷e̷y̷o̷n̷d̷ t̷h̷e̷ m̷a̷r̷k̷/̷
        In o̷f̷ our vast Orient, o̷f̷ o̷u̷r̷ all her boundless
                                        homes
        H̷a̷i̷l̷/̷ E̷m̷p̷r̷e̷s̷s̷ o̷f̷ o̷u̷r̷ E̷a̷s̷t̷/̷ o̷f̷ b̷o̷u̷n̷d̷l̷e̷s̷s̷ r̷e̷a̷l̷m̷s̷
        Swarming for ever-m̷i̷g̷h̷t̷i̷e̷r̷ Englands,
        B̷e̷y̷o̷n̷d̷ t̷h̷y̷ p̷e̷o̷p̷l̷e̷s̷ k̷n̷o̷w̷i̷n̷g̷/̷ & one isle
                        i̷t̷s̷ her   if she knows
        That knows not h̷e̷r̷ own greatness! h̷a̷i̷l̷ & T̷a̷k̷e̷,
                        m̷y̷ Q̷u̷e̷e̷n̷
        And dreads it, we are fall'n,
        Not f̷o̷r̷ t̷h̷e̷m̷s̷e̷l̷v̷e̷s̷/̷ b̷u̷t̷ t̷h̷r̷o̷' t̷h̷y̷ l̷o̷v̷e̷ f̷o̷r̷ o̷n̷e̷
        T̷h̷e̷ p̷r̷i̷n̷c̷e̷l̷y̷ m̷a̷n̷ w̷h̷o̷ l̷o̷v̷e̷d̷ t̷h̷e̷m̷
        T̷o̷ w̷h̷o̷m̷/̷ I̷ m̷a̷k̷e̷ t̷h̷e̷m̷ s̷a̷c̷r̷e̷d̷/̷ t̷h̷e̷s̷e̷ o̷l̷d̷ t̷a̷l̷e̷s̷/̷   H-32

Draft 34-36

                        T̷h̷e̷ f̷u̷l̷l̷ s̷t̷r̷e̷a̷m̷
        H̷a̷s̷ b̷o̷r̷n̷e̷ m̷e̷ d̷o̷w̷n̷ ⫻ n̷o̷t̷ f̷o̷r̷ t̷h̷e̷m̷s̷e̷l̷v̷e̷s̷/̷ m̷y̷ Q̷u̷e̷e̷n̷/̷
        B̷u̷t̷ t̷h̷r̷o̷' t̷h̷y̷ l̷i̷v̷i̷n̷g̷/̷l̷o̷v̷e̷ f̷o̷r̷ o̷n̷e̷ t̷o̷ w̷h̷o̷m̷
        I̷ m̷a̷d̷e̷ t̷h̷e̷m̷/̷ a̷f̷t̷e̷r̷ h̷e̷ w̷a̷s̷ s̷i̷l̷e̷n̷t̷ h̷e̷r̷e̷
        T̷o̷ w̷h̷o̷m̷/̷ b̷u̷t̷ a̷f̷t̷e̷r̷ h̷e̷ w̷a̷s̷ s̷i̷l̷e̷n̷t̷ h̷e̷r̷e̷/̷
        I̷ m̷a̷d̷e̷ t̷h̷e̷m̷ s̷a̷c̷r̷e̷d̷/̷ t̷h̷e̷s̷e̷ i̷m̷p̷e̷r̷f̷e̷c̷t̷ t̷a̷l̷e̷s̷/̷
        S̷a̷c̷r̷e̷d̷/̷ a̷c̷c̷e̷p̷t̷/̷t̷h̷e̷s̷e̷ o̷l̷d̷ i̷m̷p̷e̷r̷f̷e̷c̷t̷ t̷a̷l̷e̷s̷   H-32

                            (Drafts continue overleaf)

New-old, and shadowing Sense at war with Soul,
Ideal manhood closed in real man,
Rather than that gray king, whose name, a ghost,
Streams like a cloud, man-shaped, from mountain
                                    peak,   40
And cleaves to cairn and cromlech still; or him
Of Geoffrey's book, or him of Malleor's, one
Touched by the adulterous finger of a time
That hovered between war and wantonness,
And crownings and dethronements: take withal   45
Thy poet's blessing, and his trust that Heaven
Will blow the tempest in the distance back
From thine and ours: for some are scared, who mark,
Or wisely or unwisely, signs of storm,
Waverings of every vane with every wind,   50
And wordy trucklings to the transient hour,

Draft 33-36
                    but thou, my Queen,
        Not for itself, but thro' the living love,
        Thy living love for one true man, to whom
        I made it, after he was silent here,
        Sacred - accept this old half finished tale,   H-32

37 ...Soul   A-2111
37 (C)   99

38 (Omitted)   A-2111
38 (C)   99

39   p̸h̸a̸n̸t̸o̸m̸ a mist,
    ...name, a̸ m̸i̸s̸t̸   H-32

41   cleaves to cairn &   still;   or
    And c̸l̸i̸n̸g̸s̸ to cromlich m̸o̸u̸n̸t̸ &̸ c̸a̸i̸r̸n̸s̸; n̸o̸t̸
                              him   H-32

42   book,   or him   fabling o̸n̸e̸
    Of Geoffrey's a̸s̸ t̸h̸e̸ P̸r̸i̸n̸c̸e̸ of Malleor's (2 ?)
                              one   H-32

43 Touch'd by the adulterous finger of the times
   H̸a̸l̸f̸-̸t̸a̸i̸n̸t̸e̸d̸ b̸y̸ t̸h̸a̸t̸ o̸l̸d̸ a̸d̸u̸l̸t̸e̸r̸o̸u̸s̸ c̸o̸u̸r̸t̸   H-32

TO THE QUEEN

And fierce or careless looseners of the faith,
And Softness breeding scorn of simple life,
Or Cowardice, the child of lust for gold,
Or Labour, with a groan and not a voice,   55
Or Art with poisonous honey stolen from France,
And that which knows, but careful for itself,
And that which knows not, ruling that which knows
To its own harm: the goal of this great world
Lies beyond sight: yet--if our slowly-grown   60
And crowned Republic's crowning common-sense,
That saved her many times, not fail--their fears
Are morning shadows huger than the shapes
That cast them, not those gloomier which forego
The darkness of that battle in the West,   65
Where all of high and holy dies away.

_____

alt 45 Of our fine-featured Edward! take withal   H-32

46   trust
   ...& his ~~hopes~~ that...   H-32

47 Will May blow...   H-32

48   & ours
   From ~~thee~~ & thine for...   H-32

50   every
   ~~In~~ Waverings of ~~the~~ vane...   H-32

53   breeding
   ...softness & ~~the~~ scorn...   H-32

56   with
   ...Art, ~~a~~ poisonous...   H-32

59 ...harm. Yet--if our slowly-grown   H-32

alt. after 61 ~~That made her first & freest upon~~
                       ~~earth~~   H-32

62 That
   ~~And~~ saved ...   H-32

1007

DATE DUE